The International Encyclopedia of Dogs

The International Encyclopedia of
DOGS

Edited by Stanley Dangerfield and Elsworth Howell

with special contributions by
Maxwell Riddle

McGraw-Hill Book Company
New York - St. Louis - San Francisco

This book was designed and produced by
Rainbird Reference Books Limited
Marble Arch House, 44 Edgware Road, London W 2
and published in the United States and Canada by
McGraw-Hill Book Company, New York, St. Louis, San Francisco,
in association with Howell Book House Inc., New York

House editors: Tony Birks, Penelope Miller
Picture research: Frances Latty
Designer: George Sharp

The text was set in Monophoto Times New Roman and Univers by
Jolly & Barber Limited, Rugby, England.
The book was printed and bound by Dai Nippon Printing
Company Limited, Tokyo, Japan.

First U.S. printing 1971

ISBN 07-015296-9

Library of Congress Catalog
Card Number 70-161547

Contributors

Douglas and Carol Appleton
International show judges, dog breeders and kennel management experts

C. A. Binney
Secretary, The Kennel Club, England 1964–71

Dr Marca Burns
Geneticist

Dr Antonio Cabral
Veterinarian, dog breeder and President of the Portuguese Kennel Club

Dr A. Barone Forzano
Veterinarian and President of the Brazilian Kennel Club

G. N. Henderson, B.Sc., M.R.C.V.S.
Veterinarian and canine dietary consultant

John Hodgeman, M.R.C.V.S.
Veterinarian

John Holmes
International dog trainer for television and films

Robert M. James
International show judge of racing hounds

Maxwell Riddle
International all-breed show judge, author, journalist, breeder
and President of the Ravenna Kennel Club

Mary Roslin-Williams
Breeder of sporting dogs and field trial expert

R. H. Smythe, M.R.C.V.S.
Veterinarian and canine anatomy specialist

Catherine Sutton
Breeder and kennel management expert

Ivan Swedrup
Secretary, The Swedish Kennel Club

Hope Waters
Saluki breeder and coursing expert

Robert C. White, M.R.C.V.S.
Veterinarian

Major photographers contributing to this encyclopedia include:

C. M. Cooke, Anne Cumbers, Thomas Fall, William P. Gilbert,
Joan Ludwig, L. Hugh Newman, Jack Ritter, Anne Roslin-Williams,
Ianthe Ruthven, Evelyn Shafer, Morry Twomey
and Sally Anne Thompson

Editors' Foreword

This encyclopedia was conceived, right from the beginning, as an international work. In order to present the world of dogs to readers in many countries, contributors and artists were commissioned wherever possible from the appropriate country to write with authority on breeds, kennel clubs, shows and specialist subjects. Because so many dog breeds originated in Britain, editorial and illustrative activities have been co-ordinated in London, and to provide consistency, British spellings have been adopted for colours and technical terms. Similarly, where a breed is known by several names, its main entry has been placed under the British name – e.g. *King Charles Spaniel* – and cross-referenced under its alternative names – e.g. *English Toy Spaniel.*

As a work of reference, ease of use was given high priority in planning the encyclopedia, and a single alphabetical sequence for all entries was adopted. Thus, glossary items such as *Brindle* and *Brisket* are found in alphabetical order between the main entries on *Briard* and *Brittany Spaniel*, and a cross-reference to the latter is found under *Breton Spaniel*. In addition, where it is thought that the reader may gain information by cross-referring to other entries, SMALL CAPITALS are used within articles to indicate those entries which may be found useful. For example, in the article on Boston Terrier, the words BULL TERRIER and BULLDOG are so marked the first time they appear.

The colour illustrations have been divided into four sections for technical reasons, but Gun Dogs (Sporting Dogs), Hounds, Working Dogs and Terriers are each kept together within a single section, and all colour pictures are indicated alphabetically on page 7 and at the end of the breed article. Many of the dogs illustrated in colour and in black and white will be known to specialist readers, and many of them are Show Champions. While the abbreviation 'Ch.' is used for named dogs which are Champions, it was decided that for simplicity the further abbreviations for Show Champions, Field Champions, Dual Champions, etc., should be omitted. Neither dogs nor owners should feel neglected. Without the help and enthusiasm of all those who submitted photographs to the publishers, this book would not have been possible. Our only regret is that limited space prevented us from using them all.

Color Plates

Afghan Hound 178
Airedale Terrier 372
Alaskan Malamute 303
Alsatian 296
Australian Terrier 377

Basenji 190
Basset Hound 185
Beagle 185
Bedlington Terrier 376
Belgian Sheepdog 297
Belgian Tervuren 296
Bernese Mountain Dog 290
Bloodhound 184
Border Terrier 379
Borzoi 181
Boston Terrier 186
Bouvier des Flandres 291
Boxer 301
Briard 302
Brittany Spaniel 92
Bulldog 186
Bull Mastiff 301
Bull Terrier 369

Cairn Terrier 377
Cavalier King Charles Spaniel 380
Chesapeake Bay Retriever 82
Chihuahua 382
Chow Chow 188
Clumber Spaniel 89
Cocker Spaniel, American 90
Cocker Spaniel, English 91
Collie, Bearded 295
Collie, Border 292
Collie, Rough 294
Collie, Smooth 293
Curly-coated Retriever 84

Dachshund, Long-haired 192
Dachshund, Miniature Long-haired 192
Dachshund, Miniature Smooth 192
Dachshund, Smooth (dappled) 192
Dachshund, Wire-haired 192
Dalmatian 187
Dandie Dinmont Terrier 374
Deerhound, Scottish 179
Dobermann Pinscher 298

English Setter 87

English Springer Spaniel 89
English Toy Spaniel 380
English Toy Terrier 381

Finnish Spitz 191
Flat-coated Retriever 82
Foxhound, American 183
Foxhound, English 182, 183
French Bulldog 186

German Shepherd Dog 296
German Short-haired Pointer 85
German Wire-haired Pointer 85
Golden Retriever 82
Gordon Setter 87
Great Dane 299
Greyhound 182
Griffon Bruxellois 384
Groenendael 297

Harrier 182

Irish Setter 86
Irish Terrier 373
Irish Water Spaniel 84
Irish Wolfhound 180
Italian Greyhound 381

Jack Russell Terrier 374
Japanese Spaniel 384

Keeshond 191
Kelpie 293
Kerry Blue Terrier 373
King Charles Spaniel 380

Labrador Retriever 83
Lakeland Terrier 373
Lhasa Apso 189

Maltese 383
Manchester Terrier 372
Mastiff 300
Miniature Pinscher 381

Newfoundland 290
Norfolk Terrier 378
Norwegian Elkhound 191
Norwich Terrier 378

Old English Sheepdog 295
Otterhound 185

Papillon 384
Pekingese 189
Pointer 81
Pomeranian 382
Poodle, Miniature 95
Poodle, Standard 96
Poodle, Toy 95
Pug 384
Pyrenean Mountain Dog 290

Rhodesian Ridgeback 179
Rottweiler 298

Saint Bernard 300
Saluki 177
Samoyed 289
Schipperke 191
Schnauzer, Giant 94
Schnauzer, Miniature 93
Schnauzer, Standard 94
Scottish Terrier 375
Sealyham Terrier 375
Shetland Sheepdog 297
Shih Tzu 189
Siberian Husky 302
Silky Terrier 379
Skye Terrier 376
Smooth Fox Terrier 371
Soft-coated Wheaten Terrier 374
Staffordshire Bull Terrier 374
Sussex Spaniel 91

Tibetan Spaniel 188
Tibetan Terrier 187
Toy Fox Terrier 370

Vizsla 92

Weimaraner 92
Welsh Corgi, Cardigan 304
Welsh Corgi, Pembroke 304
Welsh Springer Spaniel 88
West Highland White Terrier 377
Whippet 181
Wire-haired Fox Terrier 370

Yorkshire Terrier 378

A

Aberdeen Terrier The original name for the breed now known as the SCOTTISH TERRIER was Aberdeen Terrier, so called because of its early association with that city. It was re-named by the Kennel Club in 1890 as it was thought that the description 'Aberdeen' was too local for a breed which was distributed throughout Scotland.

Right Aberdeen Terrier was the original local name for the Scottish Terrier.

Abnormalities, Hereditary see Hereditary Abnormalities.

Abortion This term is applied to the premature delivery of an immature puppy, or of the contents of the uterus of a pregnant bitch. Injuries, severe illness and shock can cause this, while in many cases the precise cause may not be determinable.

Some experts consider that hereditary influences may affect the ability of a bitch to maintain pregnancy.

Where a bitch repeatedly loses her puppies, it is inadvisable to continue attempting to breed with her.

Within the past few years, infectious abortion in dogs has been found in the western portions of the American Midwest, and in the Southwest. For the most part, the disease has been found in large kennels of BEAGLES used for trailing rabbits, or for field trials. But the disease has been found in isolated cases in at least two other breeds.

Scientists at the Cornell University Veterinary Virus Research Institute have now isolated a bacterium which they have named *Brucella canis*. It has been proved to be the cause of Brucellosis, or infectious abortion, in dogs. Moreover, they have now isolated this organism in 38 states. There is cause to believe that it may be spreading. It is not yet known whether this disease can infect man. But since, under certain conditions, the other strains of this bacterium can do so, care must be taken if this disease is suspected.

Young bitches approaching breeding age are susceptible, and they are highly so during pregnancy. Infected bitches usually abort 30 to 50 days after the beginning of pregnancy. Older, proven matrons, when infected, may fail to become pregnant. Males suffer severe inflammation of the seminal duct. Young males may experience defective growth of the testicles, and testicular atrophy may be complete.

Kennels which have a bitch which miscarries should take both the bitch and the dead whelps to a veterinary hospital immediately. Health authorities should be notified if this disease is suspected. These measures are important both to isolate the infection, if it exists, and to protect people who have come into contact with the animals involved.

Abscess This is a localized collection of pus which can occur within the body but is usually seen in, or under, the skin. A single abscess is usually the result of a puncture wound where infection is introduced. It develops rapidly (two to three days) and will either burst, or be reabsorbed. The area should be kept clean and frequently bathed with warm water to which can be added Epsom salts in the proportion of a tablespoonful to a pint of water. This helps to bring the abscess to a head. Once the abscess bursts, bathing should be continued to remove all pus, and repeated several times a day until healing is complete. If the abscess comes to a head, it should burst and then heal. If this does not happen, or if, after healing, a new abscess develops, a veterinarian should be consulted.

Multiple abscesses, where a number of these erupt in a group or in a line, are more serious and must have expert attention at once.

Accidents Accidents occur about as frequently in dogdom as within the human population. They include all those which can be imagined, and dozens which are beyond imagination. A gambolling dog jumps to its death from an apartment house roof. Another dies after swallowing two golf balls.

Some people are considered to be 'accident-prone'. There is little evidence to indicate this condition exists among dogs. But almost certainly accident-prone owners create potentially dangerous conditions for their dogs.

Right Accidents. This is the correct way to move an injured dog onto a stretcher.

One can categorize canine accidents quite as easily as those involving people. For example, dogs which roam often meet death or serious injury in traffic; and these accidents occur more frequently during the breeding season when dogs of both sexes are preoccupied with courtship.

Home accidents include the loss of a foot to a lawn-mower, scythe, or clippers. Dogs are frequently burned or killed by insecticides or other poisons. Dogs have been killed by being run over by their master's automobile, while sleeping in their own driveway. Many a dog has had a part of its tail trapped while trying to scoot through a slamming door.

Dogs used in field sports have fallen into uncovered and abandoned wells and drowned. It is not uncommon for one to get trapped in a wire fence, or to get a leg trapped in the fork of tree limbs. Another hazard for such dogs is the careless gun handler. Dogs have been killed by trains while hunting, and even by aircraft. Others out hunting have sunk into quick-sands or bogs. House dogs have died from eating sweaters, silk stockings, toys, marbles, and light bulbs. The habit of placing toys or presents under a Christmas tree makes a special hazard for the dog. House plants can kill dogs. Details of such plants are given under POISONS.

The kitchen stove is almost as great a hazard for the family dog as it is for babies. Pans of boiling liquids may be tipped upon the dog. In such cases, the hazard is greater for the toy dog, since a greater area of its body will be burned. Turning the handles of pans inward is a simple safety measure.

Toy dogs are susceptible to a special class of injuries because of their diminutive size. A leg may easily be broken under a man's foot. The sharp heel of a stumbling woman has pierced a dog's rib cage. But perhaps the most common injuries sustained by toy dogs are those resulting from jumping off beds and chairs.

See BANDAGING; RESPIRATION; TOURNIQUET; TRAFFIC ACCIDENTS.

Acetone This is present in urine during illnesses which affect the utilization of food within the body. In advanced cases the smell (which is similar to that of nail varnish remover) is detectable on the breath.

Acetone is produced in great amounts when the dog has diabetes, and when a dog is fed excessive fat and no carbohydrate.

Achondroplasia A condition of abnormal osteogenesis, or bone formation. It is, in fact, a form of dwarfing affecting the long bones of the limbs before birth. It is sometimes seen when large dogs are bred with small ones. BASSETS and DACHSHUNDS are sometimes called achondroplastic, but in these breeds, the abnormality has become a normality, as the breed standards insist on this type of leg.

Acid Milk The milk of the bitch is usually considered to be either neutral or slightly alkaline. But in recent years, examination has shown that it is more likely to be neutral to slightly acid than the reverse. The standard test is to use blue litmus paper.

When tested with blue litmus paper, normal bitch's milk should not change the colour of the paper, or should leave it only slightly pinkish. If, however, the paper turns a very 'angry' pink or red, then the milk is said to be acid. One can make a comparison test by putting a drop of milk on one end of the paper, and one of vinegar on the other. There will then be no doubt as to the colour truly acid milk will turn the paper.

Dangerously acid milk usually causes digestive disturbances in the puppies. They will lie apart from the mother, be bloated, feel cold to the touch, and they will utter plaintive cries. The mother will abandon them. The puppies are then likely to die from both constipation and starvation.

Acid milk is, of course, an indication of illness in the mother, and a veterinarian should be consulted at once. However, the acidity can usually be corrected without too many problems.

It is important to keep the puppies warm. They can be given two or three drops of milk of magnesia, and perhaps a few drops of water warmed to blood heat of

Left Accidents. Roaming dogs — especially those preoccupied with courtship during the mating season — often meet death or serious injury in traffic.

101–102°F. A gentle abdominal massage may help. The puppies should be fed a simulated bitch's milk until they can be returned to their mother.

See MILK, BITCH'S.

Affenpinscher The Affenpinscher is a charming and comic little dog of supposedly German origin which probably suffers from its difficult name. Terms such as Bulldog and Water Spaniel give some indication as to the work and the size of such dogs. But Affenpinscher means little to anyone not German, or who is not familiar with the breed. And even a German may be confused by the name.

One German dictionary translates the name Affenpinscher as PUG, but this definition is incorrect. In the German language, *affen* is a verb meaning 'to mock' or 'to hoax'. And the adjective *affenartig* means 'monkey-like'. *Affenschande* means a 'great shame'. And perhaps this word should be remembered, too, in connection with the Affenpinscher.

The Affenpinscher is sometimes called the 'monkey terrier'. It is a shame that Affenpinscher was not directly translated into other languages as Monkey Terrier, since 'Pinscher' is the German word for 'terrier'.

People who see the dog invariably remark that it looks like a monkey. This, it is said, is because it has a chin tuft on a prominent chin and a moustache. But monkeys do not have prominent chins. Few have chin tufts, and even fewer have any sign of a moustache. Yet Affenpinschers have an undeniably comic expression, and people everywhere tend to associate a comic look with a monkey.

The breed is said to be the ancestor, or progenitor, of the Brussels Griffon, or GRIFFON BRUXELLOIS. But there is little concrete evidence to support this view. The latter breed was well known by 1900 under its present name. There were then many guesses as to its ancestry, but no mention at that time of the Affenpinscher.

Right Affenpinscher. Ch. Aff-Kins Kleine Lorelei.

The two breeds do appear to be closely related. They may be parent and offspring, but it seems more likely that they are cousins coming down from now-unknown parentage. Paintings of the seventeenth century and earlier show dogs similar to both. But it is hard to believe that dogs in those days got the coat-care and grooming which does so much to give type to modern dogs.

The Affenpinscher began to be noticed in the world of the purebreds shortly before the Second World War. Its progress was held up by that war. Since then it has gradually improved in popularity. But it is still behind its cousin, or if you like, its descendant, the Brussels Griffon.

Essentials of the breed: The Affenpinscher is a toy dog which should not exceed 10¼ inches at the shoulder, and should weigh no more than 8 lb. Smaller dogs, if sound, are even more to be desired. The coat is of wiry texture, and usually black, although black with tan markings, red, grey and other mixtures are permitted.

The hair is relatively long and shaggy on the legs, and around the eyes, nose, and chin.

The head: round with a domed forehead. The ears are set high, and erect, and in America are clipped to a point. The eyes are round, rather large, black and luminous to the point of brilliance. The muzzle is short, but rather pointed. The lower jaw is slightly longer than the upper. This permits a slight undershot condition, although it is preferred that the teeth of the two jaws mesh.

The body: roughly square. That is, the length from the junction of neck and shoulders to the root of the tail equals the height at the withers, or shoulders. There is little top line slope. The chest is deep, and there is little tuck up at the loins.

The hind legs are almost straight, with virtually no bend at the stifle. They are set well under the body. The tail, which is set high, is docked short. The feet are round, small, compact, and are turned neither in nor out.

Afghan Hound The British Museum houses an Athenian pictorial fabric entitled 'Departure of Warriors', estimated to belong to the 6th century B.C. It shows a variety of GREYHOUND with a feathered tail which bears an unmistakable likeness to the Afghan Hound.

A papyrus found in Sinai and attributed to the period 3,000 B.C. refers frequently to a Cynocephalus, freely translated as 'a baboon- or monkey-faced hound'. Coupled with this, illustrations on contemporary tombs point again to an Afghan. Finally, a story persists that it was an Afghan which was taken into the Ark by Noah.

Readers are free to reject as much of this so-called 'evidence' as they feel inclined. However, it is certain that long-coated Greyhounds of Afghan type existed thousands of years ago in the Middle East. What we do not know is how they travelled a thousand miles across Arabia and Persia and finally became established in the inhospitable countryside of northern Afghanistan.

It is a mystery unlikely to be solved. What must be accepted is that when the first European explorers entered that country the Afghan was already there.

11

It was used for hunting wolves, gazelles and foxes. There were stories indicating that these dogs were 'highly prized by the local aristocrats' and very difficult for mere foreigners to obtain. Although this, like the story of the Ark, may be discounted, it is evident that the long sojourn in unusual countryside had, presumably by a process of selective breeding, modified the original Greyhound until it was more useful and presumably more valued.

One example of the changed appearance was the highly carried tail, with its distinctive ring at the end. This enabled watchers to know the exact whereabouts of the dog when it was working in thick and dense undergrowth. Then there were the high, wide-set hip bones, giving it the ability not merely to twist and turn on rocky hillsides but to leap almost like a monkey. Its thick, silky hair provides the warmth so necessary to enjoy life in winter conditions at high altitudes.

The first Afghan to reach Great Britain arrived in 1894. It had all of the qualities of the breed sufficient to arouse interest and enthusiasm. The Afghans which followed during the next ten years were not so interesting and may not all have been pure in origin.

Then came *Zardin*, imported by Captain Banff. Exhibited at the Kennel Club Show in Crystal Palace in 1907, he won sensationally. So much was written about him that he interested Queen Alexandra who requested that he be brought to Buckingham Palace for her examination.

The Afghan had arrived. It continued to arrive in the years which followed as more and more were imported. A Breed Club was formed and in 1926 they were given a separate register and Challenge Certificates by the English Kennel Club.

In that same year Afghans made their first appearance in the United States, but it has to be admitted that progress there was comparatively slow in the early days. Since then, however, they have gained friends all over the world and are now more popular than ever before in their history. Exchanges between Great Britain and the United States are by no means unusual. In the early days the dogs tended to move westward. However, as the American Afghan became increasingly stylish and smart there developed a tendency for British breeders to reverse the usual trend and import dogs from the United States. Parallel with this they became increasingly popular in other countries, principally in Sweden, Canada and Australia.

Their character is so clearly written in their expression that it hardly needs defining. At a glance one can see the Eastern inscrutability; the conviction that they are royalty; the certainty that they are above lesser breeds. They have dignity, aloofness, yet kindness. Most important, their once somewhat suspect temperaments have recently undergone a rapid and marked improvement.

Now these dogs, distinctive in so many ways, are refreshingly normal and doglike in character. Of course, if invited, they readily accept the luxury of the silken cushion. But given the opportunity, are equally at home in the hurly-burly of the outdoor chase.
See SPEED OF DOGS.

Essentials of the breed: Head: the skull is long, not too narrow, with a slight stop and long, punishing jaws; eyes preferably dark, golden not disbarred (although American standards fault light eyes); nearly triangular. Ears: set low, well back, close to head. Back: level, falling slightly away to the stern; hip bones prominent and wide; good, deep chest. Hindquarters: powerful, with great length between hip and hock. Feet, strong, large, profusely covered with hair. Tail, set low, raised high in action, with ring at the end. Coat, long and fine; silky topknot on head. Saddle from shoulder backwards where hair should be short. Hair on foreface, short. All colours acceptable. (AKC) Height: dogs 27 inches;

Afghan Hound.
Top left Ch. Coastwind Gazebo.
Top right (below) Detail from an early Indian manuscript.
Bottom Afghans have the speed to hunt gazelles.
Right Aristocratic ancestry and love of the silken cushion are still evident in the modern Afghan Hound. A head study of Baluch Safinaz Nour.

bitches 25 inches. Weight: dogs about 60 lb.; bitches about 50 lb.

See colour plate p. 178.

After-Birth This is a spongy organ which has nourished the puppy and is attached to the puppy by the umbilical cord. The after-birth, or placenta, is generally expelled from the bitch very soon after the puppy is born. It is essential that the bitch gets rid of each after-birth because if it is retained in the uterus it will cause a lot of trouble. Most bitches instinctively wish to eat the after-births and varied views are held on this subject. It is generally agreed that if a bitch wishes to devour some of this foetal envelope it is better to let her carry on. It is quite obviously a natural thing for her to do and further it is inadvisable to interfere with her any more than is absolutely necessary at such a time. However, the foetal membrane, although nourishing and containing a high vitamin level together with a considerable amount of hormone, is also extremely laxative. A small amount ingested can do no harm and will help the uterus to contract and induce the milk supply, but a large volume can only cause diarrhoea at a time when the fluid loss so induced could have been utilized to produce additional milk.

The after-birth is accompanied with clear fluid in which will be a mixture of blood and blood breakdown products, the latter usually being green in colour.

See WHELPING.

Age (Longevity) One of Medicine's cherished quips is 'If you want to live to be ninety, have parents who lived to be ninety'. This can be at least partially applied to dogs, for there appear to be definite inheritance factors governing longevity. These apply both to breeds, and to individuals within breeds.

A working rule is that the bigger the dog, the shorter its life span. Thus, while a few Irish Wolfhounds might live to what would be for them a great old age, eight to ten years would be a good age. But medium-sized dogs might average twelve to fourteen years. And toy dogs might live to be eighteen or twenty. The exceptionally small dogs, however, are relatively short lived.

It is not easy to authenticate record ages. Just as one hears of a man living in Mongolia who is 164 years old, so one hears of dogs living to be twenty-six or twenty-eight. Proving such records is sometimes impossible. Yet there is a record of three generations of Toy Poodles, all of whom were alive at over twenty, and all of whom had been registered by the American Kennel Club. The *Guinness Book of World Records* reports that a Labrador Retriever, *Adjutant*, was born 14 August 1936, and died 20 November 1963, aged 27. This is the only authenticated record for such a long life.

Quite apart from heredity, there are many other factors affecting lifespan. Modern, well-balanced diets have played a part. Modern sanitation has been as important in canine health as in human living. Preventive medicine has either eliminated canine disease scourges, or has reduced their severity.

In 1900, for example, most dogs lived upon inferior and defective diets. Dogs which survived distemper

often lived on in weakened health. Seven years was an average lifespan. The same dog today might live to be eleven or twelve.

It used to be said that one year of a dog's life equalled seven of a man's. Other comparisons have been made, but most can be reduced to absurdity. One, for example, was based upon reproduction. A dog might become a mother, or sire a litter, at one year of age. A girl might become a mother at 14; a boy a father at 15. But a child of six has become a mother. And a puppy at six months has become a father. On the other hand, reproductive delays have been just as extreme.

The better part of reason therefore might be to refuse to make comparisons. It is better to say that any dog which passes fifteen has beaten the canine average for small and medium-sized dogs. One which is ten or over has beaten the average for the giant breeds such as Great Dane.

Aged Dog, Care of the The lives of dogs have been extended by as much as a third to a half during the past fifty years. Among the reasons for this are better foods, the remarkable advances made in veterinary care, a standard of living which has made that care possible, and a reduction in parasitism, both external and internal.

The dog ages in much the same fashion as its owner. Its eyes weaken and cataracts may develop. It may suffer a loss of some, or all, of its hearing. There will be muscle

Above After-birth. It is natural after whelping for most bitches to eat the spongy organs which have nourished their puppies in the womb.

Right Airedale Terrier. Ch. Bengal Sabu.

the stress which a radical change in diet might cause.

Special diets are required for such diseases as diabetes mellitus and nephritis. A recent development is the geriatric food supplement. Such a supplement usually contains additional amino acids, such as lysine and methionine, and factors which aid in the digestion of proteins, carbohydrates, and other substances.

FLEAS seem to have a special affection for ageing dogs, so regular attention is required to eliminate them. The hair tends to thin out and to lose its gloss. The reduction in the thickness of the hair blanket means that the dog suffers a greater loss of body heat, and is at the same time less well insulated against the cold outside. A warm, draught-free bed is therefore important. Frequent brushing will help to keep the skin and hair in condition.

Airedale Terrier As with so many breeds the name describes the origin and habits of the dog. Airedale: a district in Yorkshire. Terrier: through the French *terre* from the Latin *terra*, meaning earth or ground. A dog coming from the Airedale district, used for going to earth, theoretically at least, after quarry such as fox or badger. It is necessary at once to query whether in fact it was ever used for this purpose. Surely it is too big to go to ground in the accepted fashion? True, with its strength, the Airedale could dig if time permitted. But would not most huntsmen prefer to use a dog of a size which enabled it to pursue its quarry below ground without special preparation? A dog, moreover, which would manoeuvre and fight in restricted confines?

But to doubt whether the Airedale was normally employed below ground is not to doubt that it is a true terrier. It is, in mind, in heart, and in behaviour. It exudes terrier temperament. In fact it has terrier character almost to excess. It is the King of Terriers, and knows it.

The Airedale is largely a descendant of the now extinct black-and-tan terrier, a dog to which much is owed also by the IRISH, WELSH and even FOX TERRIERS. Whereas with these others there was a deliberate emphasis on breeding to reduce or at least contain size, with the Airedale offshoot the emphasis was always increasing it. The object was a dog which would tackle an adult badger or an otter.

To this end it was even crossed with the OTTER HOUND. This certainly brought size and substance, even skill in water. But it also brought a rather heavy, sometimes unattractive, hound ear which is occasionally seen to this day.

This was a hundred years ago. Then the breed was called by various names including the Working, Waterside and Bingley Terrier. In 1879 the breed was officially classified at a dog show for the first time. Almost inevitably this was in Yorkshire, England; the district was Bingley and the organization the Airedale Agricultural Society. From then onwards the breed grew in popularity. Its smart appearance, gay spirits and sporting background took it to the top of the British popularity poll despite its great size.

Additionally a large number of dogs, many of the highest quality, were sent to the United States. They were top show dogs and they proved it by winning the highest honours.

weakness. The dog may tire easily, or become incontinent.

There may be a need for dental care, including treatment for the gum disease, pyorrhoea (see GUMS). Some aged dogs develop HEART DISEASES. Others suffer from nephritis (see KIDNEY DISEASES), cystitis, DIABETES MELLITUS, etc. Various types of cancer may occur (see TUMOURS, MALIGNANT). Decreasing activity, and a consequent lowering of the metabolic rate, cause an OBESITY problem in some dogs.

The ageing dog should be given a careful physical examination at least once every six months. This is best given by a veterinarian who has the dog's complete health record available to him. These enable him to know what particular disease or accident stresses have been placed upon the dog during its life.

Home care is recommended for all but the critically ill and major surgical cases. The dog will be happier and less worried about itself when in its home environment. The home routine, and the gentle and sympathetic care of the owner – particularly of a woman – are major care factors. Many veterinarians have noted the therapeutic benefits derived from the tender voice of a woman who is used to talking to her dog. See NURSING SICK DOGS.

Some NUTRITION authorities believe that the highest quality commercial dog foods may be better than special diets for the old dog. This is particularly true if the dog has been fed such foods in the past. It then will not suffer

Akita The Akita of Japan, or the *Akita-Inu*, is one of three breeds in the Japanese Islands which are roughly similar except in size. All resemble the CHOW CHOW of China. But they are short or medium-haired, and they do not have the blue tongue and mouth tissues of the Chow Chow. The Akita is the largest of these dogs. The average height is $25\frac{1}{2}$ to $27\frac{1}{2}$ inches at the shoulder. Males weigh 85 to 110 lb., and bitches 75 to 95 lb.

In Japan, the breed has been used for hunting bear and deer. In addition, it has been used for guard work, and it is considered by the Japanese to belong to the 'police dog' group. It takes its name from the province of Akita on Honshu Island.

American occupation troops became impressed by the size, intelligence, and guard-dog ability of the Akitas, and began to bring them back to the United States. As they became more numerous, the American Kennel Club granted the breed 'miscellaneous class' status, and a breed standard, based on that of Japan, was formulated. The breed is gradually spreading to other countries. Mexico has granted full registration status to the breed, and it is now recognized by the Federation Cynologique Internationale.

Essentials of the breed: The head: massive and broad, with a rather flat skull, free of wrinkles, and with a distinct stop. The muzzle is of moderate length, but it matches the skull in size and strength. The teeth meet in a level bite. The ears are short, with a wide base, and are erect. The eyes are dark, with tight fitting lids. Visible HAW is a fault.

The body is longer than the dog is tall, but it is powerfully made with deep, wide chest, and with little abdominal tuck-up. Legs and feet are strong with pasterns slightly sloping. The tail is carried over the back, often in a double curl. It may also be carried over the back but slightly to one side. If stretched out, the tail reaches to the hock. The coat is double, with the outer hair being slightly harsh. All colours are permitted. However, white should not exceed one-third of the total. It can appear as a blaze, though never extending onto the muzzle, on the chest as a white collar, and on the forelegs, hind paws, and tail tip.

Alaskan Malamute The Alaskan Malamute is one of a group of very similar Arctic sledge dogs which belong to the great SPITZ family of breeds. The sledge-dog breeds include the SAMOYED, SIBERIAN HUSKY, and ESKIMO. Other members of the family include the FINNISH SPITZ, the NORWEGIAN ELKHOUND, Norwegian Buhund, AKITA, CHOW CHOW, KEESHOND and POMERANIAN.

The Malamute, formerly spelled Mahlemut, is named after the Eskimo group which supposedly developed the breed. The Malamutes live along the shores of Kotzebue Sound which is roughly bisected by the Arctic Circle. Much of the area behind the shore lines is mountainous. The Malamutes lived in a hunting and fishing environment which therefore included mountains. The Alaskan Malamute is the largest of the sledge-dog breeds, and the one most fitted for hauling heavy loads over mountainous territory.

Left Airedale Terrier. A portrait of the King of the Terriers, famed for its smart appearance, gay spirits and sporting background.

Akita.
Top right Mexican Ch. Fukumoto's Ashibaya Kuma San-Dan.
Bottom right An early nineteenth-century Japanese woodcut with an Akita-type dog in the foreground.

Parallel with this, some were sent to Germany, a country which at that time was relatively disinterested in either sport or shows. Life was serious. Dogs had to work for a living, and they pulled small carts. Perhaps it was this which made Germany the first nation to realize the Airedale's working qualities. In a short time they used them as guard dogs, frontier dogs, police dogs, and the final irony, war dogs. Thus, the Airedale, an essentially British breed, flowered as a dog of war in service against the country which had produced it!

Wars over, nobody held this against the breed. Indeed the decline which it has since suffered was due to the fact that it is comparatively large for a shrinking world. There has been a recent revival in the Airedale's fortunes and the breed is once again becoming reasonably popular.

If Airedales have another practical drawback it is their coat. Though it is a most attractive feature, the harsh, tight, usually rich tan and jet-black covering is unfortunately not easy to keep in perfect trim. Left untended for too long, Airedales rapidly grow into woolly bears! Lovable still, but hardly glamorous.

The alternative is hard work, stripping out dead coat with finger and thumb. Regrettably the short cut of using clippers ruins both the texture and the colour of the coat. Many think the more tedious form of grooming is a small price to pay for ownership of a noble beast.

Essentials of the breed: Head: skull long and flat, not too broad, stop hardly visible. Jaws: deep, powerful, strong, showing strength of foreface. Lips: tight; nose black. Eyes: dark and keen. Ears: V-shaped with side carriage, topline folding level with skull. Mouth: strong and level. Neck: clean, muscular, and of moderate length. Shoulders: long, well laid back. Body: short, strong, and level. Ribs: well sprung, and chest deep but not broad, Hindquarters: long and muscular. Hocks should be well let down. Feet: small, round, compact. Tail: set high and carried gaily. Coat: hard, dense, and wiry. Colour: head and ears tan except dark markings on side of skull; Legs, tan; body, black or dark grizzle. (AKC) Height: dog 23 inches; bitches slightly less. See colour plate p. 372.

The term 'Malamute' may once have signified any very large Arctic sledge dog. There are references, for example, to 'giant Mackenzie River Malamutes', and the Mackenzie is in Western Canada, not Alaska.

Drivers often boasted that their dogs were pure-bred, tamed wolves, or were the result of tamed wolf-dog crosses. Most, or all, of such claims must have been pure fabrications. For the Malamutes were somehow transformed from savage wolves into gentle and affectionate pets. In 1832, three careful researchers and students of Arctic life – Leslie, Jameson, and Murray – wrote: '. . . the avidity with which the wolf devours these, his supposed tamed brothers, does not indicate so close an affinity.' The history of a dog called *Snowbird*, and called later, *Sandy*, and still later *Goldfang* (a dentist fitted him with a gold tooth) bears this out.

Two brothers, white trappers who used the names Black Luk and Black Beaver, shot a wolf just as it was killing a bitch dog. The dying dog crawled to a spot where two pups, not two weeks old, were found. One of these was Snowbird. He was white. His mother had been black with white markings. Snowbird was called a Malamute. In 1910, he led a dog team which hauled half a ton of freight 1100 miles over a mountainous winter trail. Two weeks after completing that haul, 'Iron Man' Johnson made him his lead dog in the first All Alaskan Sweepstakes. The Johnson team won, racing 408 miles in slightly more than 72 hours.

Whether or not wolves could even have been crossed into the Arctic dogs, other dog breeds certainly were. Edgerton R. Young, famed missionary-author of Eastern Canada, had used ST. BERNARDS as sledge dogs. *Blossom*, one of Alaska's most famous dogs, had St. Bernard blood.

It seems fair to conclude, therefore, that crosses with other breeds had little effect upon the Arctic dogs. They are a dominant Spitz type, and they are admirably fitted for Arctic work. Those cross-breeds which could survive the climate and the work were bred back to Arctic dogs, and the offspring were of Arctic-Spitz type.

One tends to think of the Malamute as being a sledge dog only. But Malamutes were also used as pack animals. One of the great dogs of Alaskan history was a Malamute named *Arctic*. There is a picture of Arctic in Caldwell's *Alaska Trail Dogs*. It was taken about 1904, and shows Judge H. H. Hildreth as he and Arctic were about to walk eighty miles to a mining site. Arctic appears to have been loaded with about 40 lb. of equipment. He weighed about 80 lb.

Pack dogs were used in summer when sledges could not be hauled. Packs were strapped under the belly. Pots and pans hung from the sides. Some dogs were reputedly able to carry 50 lb. up to twenty miles a day.

Alaskan Malamutes began to appear in numbers in the United States and the more temperate zones of Canada after World War II. They have proved their ability to stand the temperate climate, and even that of California where they are very popular. They are, however, kept primarily as pets. The breed is among the forty most popular in the United States with more than 3,000 being registered annually.

Essentials of the breed: Skull: broad and slightly rounded between medium-sized, erect ears, rounded at the tips. Eyes: usually brown. Muzzle is massive, narrowing only slightly at the nose. Body is strongly made and not short coupled, chest reaching to elbows, and top line sloping slightly to the stern. Legs: heavily boned and muscled. Feet: large, well knuckled up, with thick pads.

Colour: usually grey with intermediate shadings of black, with white underbodies. Only permitted solid colour is white. Dark cap or mask face markings are usual, and a white blaze is also common. Broken colours and uneven colour splotching on the body are not desired.

Coat is double with an outer coat of thick, coarse guard hairs, and a dense undercoat an inch to two inches long. Tail has a thick brush and should not be tightly curled, nor rest on the back. Tail is set along the line of the spine.

Desired size for males is 25 inches at the shoulder and 85 lb. weight; bitches, 23 inches and 75 lb. Malamutes range considerably, both above and below these figures.

See colour plate p. 303.

Alopecia see Moulting.

Alpine Mastiff 'Alpine Mastiff' was one of the early names for the breed we now know as the ST BERNARD. About 1815, the artist Edwin Landseer, then a boy, drew a picture of an Alpine Mastiff named *Lion*. Landseer's brother, Thomas, made an engraving from the picture. Four years later, Sir Edwin painted two of Lion's offspring as Alpine rescue dogs. It was he who created the conception of St. Bernards with small casks of rum or wine tied to their necks, but Landseer called the picture *Dogs of St. Gothard*. The Alpine Mastiff was related to the Old English MASTIFF, and may have been descended from the TIBETAN MASTIFF.

Alpine Spaniel The Alpine Spaniel may never have existed as a distinct breed. Some believe that the term once applied either to the ST. BERNARD, or to smaller dogs closely related to it. It was said to have resembled the modern CLUMBER SPANIEL.

Alsatian (German Shepherd Dog) The name Alsatian is often used for the breed which throughout a very large part of the world is known as the GERMAN SHEPHERD DOG.

The name Alsatian was chosen by those who introduced the breed to Britain at a time of anti-German feeling immediately after the First World War. It is still in common use in Britain and is also used in some parts of the British Commonwealth. The breed is dealt with fully under German Shepherd Dog.

American Cocker Spaniel Cocker Spaniel is actually the proper name for two distinct breeds. One is the COCKER SPANIEL (ENGLISH), and the other is the American Cocker. The English Cocker is the older of the two. In the United Kingdom and in most of the

Commonwealth countries, it is called simply, the Cocker Spaniel. In the United States, the American Cocker Spaniel is officially called the Cocker Spaniel. This could lead to confusion in the many areas of the world having both breeds, and so they distinguish them as the 'English' and the 'American'.

Spaniels may have originated in Spain (the name could be a corruption of 'Spanell' or 'Espagnol'). Small spaniels were used by the English for woodcock hunting, and so were called cocking, or cocker spaniels.

The modern Cocker Spaniel, both English and American, can be traced back to an English dog, Mr. Farrow's *Obo*, whelped in 1879. Four years later, the Cocker Spaniel was granted show classification in England, and in 1893, official breed status for stud book registrations.

Obo had a son, *Obo II* in 1880. He was sent to America. Obo II became the great foundation sire of the Cocker Spaniel in America, as his sire was becoming in England. Obo II had such a success in America that breed recognition was granted in 1883, and it was in this year that the American Spaniel Club was formed.

But the line of Obo II branched away from that of his sire. A gradual breed transformation took place. Cocker Spaniels weighing 28 to 35 lb. eventually were called English Cockers, while those under 28 lb. were considered American Cockers. In addition, the muzzle of the American dog was shortened and the skull shape was gradually altered. The skull became higher, more prominent, and more rounded in the supra-orbital process and in the frontal crest, that is, in the area above and behind the eyes.

The two varieties continued to be interbred, but by the early 1930s, the differences had become so great that total breed separation became necessary. Thereafter, the American dog was given sole possession – in America – of the name Cocker Spaniel. The American Spaniel Club continued to be the parent club of the breed. But in 1935, the English Cocker Spaniel Club of America was formed to support the parent breed, the English Cocker Spaniel.

Despite this separation, both breeds were permitted to compete against each other in field trials. For a time, field trials for the two breeds were popular, particularly along the Atlantic and Pacific Coasts. Trials for ENGLISH SPRINGER SPANIELS gave stakes for the Cockers, and vice versa. But the American Cockers began to drop out, to be followed by the English Cockers. Both breeds are still used to some extent in pheasant and woodcock shooting. But the great popularity of the American Cocker has been as a house pet and show dog.

After World War II the American Cocker became the most popular breed in the United States, and it reached a similar stature in Canada. The breed has since dropped from the leadership, but it remains as one of the more popular breeds. It is now well established in the South American countries. Some breeders in England have imported American Cockers despite the handicap of a long quarantine period.

At the height of the breed's popularity in the United States, the American Kennel Club agreed to split the breed into three varieties. They are the *Black, Any Solid Colour Other Than Black* (commonly called Ascob) but including Black and Tan, and *Parti-Colour*. The Canadian Kennel Club created a special category for the *Black and Tan*. At American dog shows, no Best of Breed award is made, except at breed speciality shows. Instead, the three Best of Variety winners enter the sporting group to compete with the other sporting dogs for higher honours. In Canada, the four Best of Variety winners compete for Best of Breed, and only the latter competes in the sporting group.

Alaskan Malamutes are outstanding pack and sledge dogs.
Top left Gripp of Yukon, the leader of a team of Malamutes seen here enjoying a respite in the snow with his driver, was the first champion Alaskan Malamute in the world.
Bottom left Tote-Ums Arctic Hawk.

Right American Cocker Spaniel. Ch. Burson's Blarney.

The change in skull shape has been accompanied by the appearance in some dogs of hydrocephaly, or water on the brain. Hydrocephaly is a condition in which an abnormal volume of cerebrospinal fluid collects within the skull, and from which it cannot escape. Accurate figures are not available, but it has been estimated that as many as 20 per cent of American Cockers have the abnormality to some degree. However, it does not appear to be so severe as to limit mentality.

American Cockers differ from the English breed in the inheritance of a gene for a very long and profuse coat. The official breed standard, as amended in December 1957, recognized this and suggested that the dog be not so excessively coated 'as to hide the Cocker Spaniel's true lines and movement or affect his appearance and function as a sporting dog.' It adds: 'Excessive coat or feathering shall be penalized.' However, American breeders and exhibitors generally ignore this. Thus, the dogs may be shown with body coat actually touching the ground.

The skull is clipped, though a tuft of hair may be left on the top. Eyebrows are left bushy. The top and sides of the neck are clipped, as are the back and sides down to mid-ribs. The remaining body and leg hair is left as long as possible. Hair on the feet is left unclipped, though the foot hair is shaped by trimming with scissors. Hair on the ears is clipped to about half way down, and lobe feathering is allowed to grow long.

Essentials of the breed: The standard calls for a well developed, rounded skull with pronounced eyebrows and stop, and with round, full eyes. The teeth mesh into a scissors bite. The ears are set no higher than eye level, and the leather reaches to the end of the muzzle. The body is square, with the height at the withers equalling the distance from the junction of withers and neck to the root of the tail. The ribs are well sprung, and this is accentuated by body hair. The tail is set on line with the spine. The hind legs are strongly angulated at the stifle joints. This gives the dog a sloping top line.

Much attention is paid to colour. Black dogs should not have a brown or liver sheen to the coat. A small amount of white on the throat and chest is permitted, though penalized. White on any other part of the body brings disqualification from the show ring. The same provisions apply to other solid colours, although lighter colouring of the feathers is permitted. Buff, honey, or golden colours are much in favour.

Black and Tans must have a solid jet black with definite tan markings, and with clearly defined lines between the two colours. The amount of tan is restricted to 10 per cent. It must consist of clear spots over each eye, on the sides of the muzzle, on the undersides of the ears, on all feet and legs, and under the tail.

Parti-Colours must have at least two definite colours clearly defined. A primary colour of more than ninety per cent, or a secondary colour limited to one spot, disqualifies. Roan patterns are rare in the American Cocker, and they compete with Parti-Colours.

An effort has been made to standardize size by height rather than by weight. The ideal height for males is 15 inches at the highest point of the withers, and 14 inches for bitches. A height greater than 15½ inches for males and 14½ inches for bitches disqualifies. See colour plate p. 90.

American Coonhounds Hunting the raccoon in America is one of the roughest and most testing of all sports involving wild game, dogs, and men. For this sport, six breeds of Coonhounds have been developed. The American Kennel Club recognizes only one of them, but the United Kennel Club, which began registering Coonhounds in 1900, registers all six. Annual registrations total more than 40,000.

Raccoons inhabit all of the American states, except for Hawaii and Alaska, and they also live within the forest belt of the Canadian provinces. The name comes from an Indian word, *arakun*. American and Canadian hunters seldom use the correct title, but simply call the animal a coon, and themselves coon hunters.

The raccoon is a nocturnal animal which spends its days in trees. It comes down at night to hunt for food. It likes to live in thick forested areas, in swamps, and near streams. It is a powerful swimmer and has been known to drown inexperienced dogs four times its size.

Below American Cocker Spaniel. Shorter in the muzzle, higher in the skull than the English Cocker.

Coon hunting is a night sport. While training in the woods may go on all the year, except for the breeding season, actual hunting is done in the fall and winter. It involves following the voice of a hound through woodlands, across streams, and through swamps in the dark of night, and often through rain and snow.

Coonhounds descend, for the most part, from FOXHOUNDS. It was the refusal of the American Kennel Club to register the dogs as Coonhounds which caused breeders to turn to the United Kennel Club for support. They felt that dogs which had been bred and trained for generations to trail nothing but raccoons should not have to be registered as Foxhounds.

The Black and Tan Coonhound was the first to be registered by the United Kennel Club. Unlike the others, it has BLOODHOUND background, and some of the Bloodhound champions in the period of 1900 to 1910 in the United States were actually Black and Tan Coonhounds, or had Coonhound blood. This was the one breed recognized by the American Kennel Club in 1945.

The other five breeds, in the order of their recognition by the UKC, are the Redbone, English Coonhound, Bluetick, Treeing Walker, and Plott. Each of the six breeds is governed by a UKC chartered club. In Canada, the Canadian Coonhound Association, which is also UKC chartered, governs all six breeds.

More than 500 night field trials are licensed annually. 'Casts' or 'heats' may last three to four hours with dogs, owners, and judges assembled in a strange forest. Owners must be able to identify the voices of their hounds as they 'open' on a cold or hot trail. Thus, the importance of the hound voice and the honesty of both dogs and owners is easily understood. Dogs are judged on points which include 'opening on the trail', 'treeing' the coon, and remaining there until owners and judges arrive. They lose points for a variety of misdeeds, including treeing an opossum instead of a coon.

The UKC also licenses daytime water races. In these, a coon is fastened upon a float in the river. The dogs are loosed from shore, and as they near the float, it is drawn to the far side. The coon is then led to a tree, which it climbs. Water races are nearly as popular as night trials. In addition, there are Coonhound bench shows. Often the same field trial meeting will include all three events.

Below Coonhounds. The last dog hurls itself after the raccoon float in this water race for Coonhounds.

There are also daytime events for so-called 'coon dogs'. The difference between a Coonhound and a coon dog is important. The latter can be a mongrel, or a dog of any breed which has been taught to follow a coon trail. The Coonhound is a pure-bred dog of a specific breed. These daytime coon chases are not licensed, and they are primarily gambling events upon which large sums are wagered, and rich money prizes are paid to the winners.

Essentials of the Breed: Coonhounds range in size between 22 and 26 inches. The Black and Tan, as registered by the American Kennel Club, shows more resemblance to the Bloodhound than do the lighter, faster, and shorter-eared UKC registered hounds. The other breeds resemble the American Foxhound, in being lighter and faster than the English Foxhound. They have remarkable strength and endurance. The importance of voice is clearly indicated in the breed standards, from which some examples follow.

Black and Tan: 'Open, deep, free, bugle bawl, not choppy.' *Bluetick:* 'A free tonguer on trail, with a medium bawl or bugle voice when striking or trailing, may change to a steady chop when running, with a steady, coarse chop at the tree.' *Treeing Walker:* 'Preferably a clear ringing bugle voice on a cold trail, changing to a chop or turkey mouth on a running trail. A deep, throaty, loud chop mouth at tree.'

American Field – Field Dog Stud Book

The American Field was founded in February 1874. It conducted its first formal field trial for pointing dogs in October of that year. Since that time, it has been the recognized organ for pointing dog trials in America. It publishes a weekly magazine, and operates the Field Dog Stud Book. The American Field compiled the first three volumes of canine registrations ever made in America. Its records became the first three volumes of the National American Kennel Club.

As years passed, the American Kennel Club came to dominate registrations and dog shows. Discontented sportsmen began to feel that field dogs and field trials were being ignored, even though field trials were very popular. The American Field then founded the Field Dog Stud Book in 1900. In 1969, it registered 28,699 dogs, all in hunting breeds, but principally POINTERS and ENGLISH SETTERS.

The American Field governs field trials under rules formulated by the Amateur Field Trial Clubs of America. More than 750 trials are given annually under the minimum rules of this group. They include about 2,600 stakes, usually Puppy, Derby, All-Age, Shooting Dog, and Championship. Some 52 championship stakes are given each year. Starters average 3,600 annually.

Pointers dominate the trials, with over 23,000 competitors compared to 7,600 English Setters. BRITTANY SPANIELS are third with some 2,300 starters, followed by 2,000 GERMAN SHORT-HAIRED POINTERS, 300 WEIMARANERS, and 700 in other breeds.

The American Field Magazine carries results of the trials, and even includes some held under American

American Coonhounds.
Above left A Treeing Walker. Ch. Merchant's Bawlie.
Left A coon dog makes hopeful leaps at the raccoon cage — the goal of an arranged daytime coon trial.

Kennel Club rules. It also publishes complete information on all registrations made in the Field Dog Stud Book.

American Foxhound see Foxhound, American.

American Kennel Club see Kennel Club, American.

American Society for the Prevention of Cruelty to Animals see Humane Societies.

American Veterinary Medical Association
The American Veterinary Medical Association was founded in 1863 in New York City. It performs the same functions for its members as do the American Medical Association and the Royal College of Veterinary Surgeons in Great Britain.

Through various councils, it studies the problems which confront veterinarians in the technical application of veterinary medicine. In so doing, it offers assistance to its members in countries other than the United States. It also provides professional liability and group life insurance for its members.

Membership is limited to qualified veterinarians who must be members of constituent, usually state, associations. The AVMA had 20,383 members in the United States and its territories as of Dec. 31, 1970; 593 in Canada, and 202 in other countries. Its Women's Auxiliary has 9,495 members. The Association publishes the Journal of the American Veterinary Medical Association twice monthly, and the Journal of Veterinary Research monthly.

American Water Spaniel As its name implies, the American Water Spaniel is one of a scant dozen breeds developed in America. And that is about all that is certain as to its origin. It was originally called simply the Brown Water Spaniel, or the American Brown Water Spaniel.

The breed appears to have been developed about 1880, and by 1900 its type had become fixed. It looks much like the IRISH WATER SPANIEL in miniature, though it lacks the characteristic 'rat tail' of the latter. Breeds which may have played a part in its development are the Irish Water Spaniel, POODLE, and the now extinct English Water Spaniel.

The area of principal development of the breed was along the great waterfowl flyway above the Mississippi River and some of its northern tributaries. A second area of development was along the Atlantic flyway. However, the dog was primarily developed for inland fowling. In Minnesota, for example, the land is dotted with small lakes, ponds, and what are known simply as 'pot holes'.

'Pot hole' or 'jump shooting' was popular. Often, the hunter would walk from pond to pond, and would crawl the last 50 yards. His dog had to crawl by his side. If ducks were flushed and shot, the dog had to retrieve them, whether on land or in the water.

The small American Water Spaniel became an ideal dog for this kind of work. Its colour blended into the fall landscape. Its size aided in preventing detection until hunter and dog were close to the shore of pot hole or pond.

The dog is used to hunt other types of upland game, of which the pheasant is the principal one. On pheasants, American Water Spaniels work within gun range, use wind scents to locate the game, and then flush for shot. The dogs are inherently good markers and retrievers.

A national breed club was founded for the American Water Spaniel in 1938. The American Kennel Club granted full stud book recognition in May 1940. The

Right American Water Spaniel. Ozark Prince Aaron.

breed ranks about seventy-fifth among the 116 breeds registered by the American Kennel Club. Some 300 are registered annually.

Essentials of the breed: The standard calls for males to be 15 to 18 inches at the shoulder with a weight of 28 to 45 lb. The colour is solid liver or dark chocolate, but a bit of white on the chest or feet is permitted. The head lacks the topknot of the Irish Water Spaniel, and the tail is well feathered in contrast to the 'rat tail' of the Irish dog. The coat: rather tightly curled, or with a wave effect. It is dense but not coarse. The lobular ears are set slightly above the line of the eye. The eyes should be dark in colour, and a yellow eye disqualifies.

Anaesthesia, Anaesthetic Anaesthesia (often spelled anesthesia) is an induced general or local insensibility to pain or other sensations. An anaesthetic is an agent which causes anaesthesia. While anaesthesia is usually induced by drugs, it may be caused by disease, or it may be induced by cold, and in human beings by hypnosis. See also ANALGESIA.

There are various means of using anaesthetics, and the veterinarian has a wide choice of drugs from which to select. Anaesthesia was first induced by inhalation, and the first true anaesthetics were nitrous oxide, ether, and chloroform. Although successful, all involved some danger.

Modern techniques, however, have increased the safety factors, so that the use of inhalation anaesthetic such as halothane, ether and chloroform are now widely used. One reason is the development of the intratracheal method of using the vapours. Delicate machines mix the vapours with oxygen and these are passed through an endotracheal tube. There is, however, a problem in administering this form of anaesthetic which usually depends upon a primary anaesthetic to immobilize the dog. This can be done by intravenous injection with short-acting drugs, such as methohexital and surital, which induce rapid anaesthesia. The endotracheal tube can then be inserted, and another anaesthetic used. Sodium pentothal and surital may also be used alone in certain cases. Halothane can be used to induce anaesthesia by those skilled in its use.

Many of the above drugs, including the barbiturates, ether, and avertin, may be introduced rectally. Still others may be applied locally by injection. Among common ones are procaine, hydrochloride, and their derivatives.

Some anaesthetics are used as 'blocks'. That is, they are used to block the nerve supply to a given area. Thus, there are caudal, sacral, and other blocks. In a spinal block, the drug is injected directly into the spinal fluid. In many countries the use of these drugs is restricted to a qualified person.

Curare and curare-type drugs are in no sense an anaesthetic. But they are often used when relaxation of muscles is required. In such cases, they are used in combination with true anaesthetics.

Analgesia Analgesia is the name given to the loss of the sensation of pain without the loss of consciousness. While the condition is usually induced by a drug, it can be caused by such a disease as syringomyelia. Drugs which cause loss of the pain sensation are called analgesics.

Analgesics can be used upon the skin, or they can be taken orally, depending upon the requirements. When used upon the skin, they cause loss of pain and, as a rule, some loss of temperature sensation. The sense of touch, however, may not be disturbed.

Some analgesics, such as ASPIRIN, relieve headaches in dogs, reduce the pain of ARTHRITIS, and may reduce fever. In such cases, the analgesic is given orally. However, aspirin can be irritant to the stomach and cause vomiting. Soluble aspirin is less likely to do this.

The treatment of arthritis has become extremely complex and it is advisable to take expert advice rather than to attempt to treat the condition by oneself.

Anal Irritation There are at least a dozen ailments which can cause anal irritation, and sometimes these may be combined to cause the dog great misery. But the major cause is blockage of the anal glands. These glands are situated on each side of the rectum into which they empty through two ducts situated one on each side of the anus and emptying into the rectum about three-sixteenths of an inch from the exterior. When dogs meet they raise their tails and extrude a slight amount of the material contained in the glands.

If occlusion occurs, the anal substance becomes foul smelling. The dog may experience such pain that it delays evacuation. It may strain without success. And it may rub the anal area along the floor causing further irritation.

In most cases, the owner can empty the glands without trouble. Lateral pressure of the anus, between the thumb and forefinger, will empty each gland. Irritation can be eased by applying warm water packs for a few minutes.

Blockage is more common among dogs which get no exercise, pampered dogs on poor diets, and older dogs. Once blockage has occurred, it tends to repeat itself. The owner, who is in doubt as to the method of clearing the glands, can get a veterinarian to demonstrate the technique. Thereafter the occlusions may be relieved at home.

Prostatitis – acute or chronic inflammation of the prostate gland – may become so painful that the dog delays defecation until impaction sets in, and the disease can also obstruct urine flow. Complications

Left Anal Irritation. For relief the dog may rub its anal area along the floor, but this only increases the discomfort.

Right Anatomy of the Dog.
Top The skeleton.
Bottom Points.

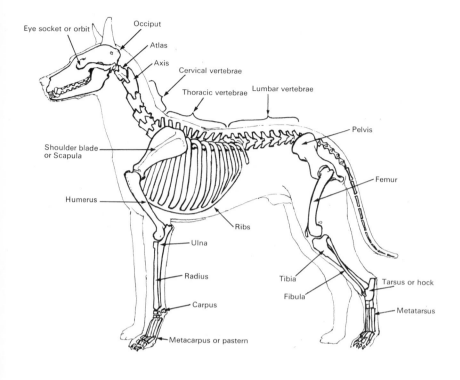

Eye socket or orbit
Occiput
Atlas
Axis
Cervical vertebrae
Thoracic vertebrae
Lumbar vertebrae
Pelvis
Shoulder blade or Scapula
Femur
Humerus
Ribs
Ulna
Radius
Tibia
Fibula
Tarsus or hock
Carpus
Metatarsus
Metacarpus or pastern

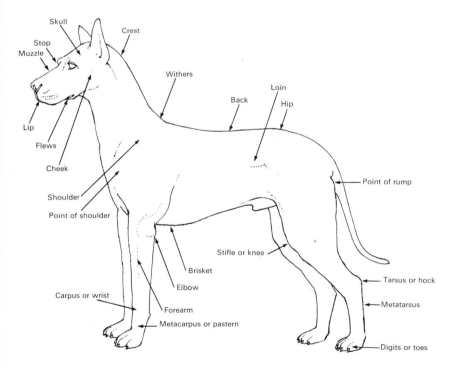

Skull
Crest
Stop
Muzzle
Withers
Loin
Back
Hip
Lip
Flews
Cheek
Point of rump
Shoulder
Point of shoulder
Stifle or knee
Brisket
Elbow
Tarsus or hock
Carpus or wrist
Metatarsus
Forearm
Metacarpus or pastern
Digits or toes

include bacterial infections, cystitis, and urethral diseases. Veterinary care is always necessary.

ABSCESSES, chronic DIARRHOEA, fistula, and proctitis – inflamed rectal wall – are other causes of anal irritation.

Anatomy of the Dog: The Skeleton In dogs, body shape varies in a manner common to no other species and the skeleton necessarily dictates the pattern. This is because few breeds, apart from the Greyhound family, Shepherd dogs and Spitz breeds, have retained their original shape, but have become re-shaped by selective breeding. In dogs of normal and abnormal shape the skeleton contains, with few minor exceptions, the same number of separate bones, but the relative proportions and relationships of individual bones may be very different.

There are seven cervical (neck) bones; thirteen dorsal vertebrae, each carrying a pair of ribs, the last pair being 'floating' ribs, not attached to the sternum (the chest bone) at their lower end. There are seven lumbar bones, a sacrum and pelvis followed by a variable number of tail bones, according to breed. Some varieties, such as the Old English Sheepdog, the Dobermann, Pembroke Corgi, Schipperke and Miniature Pinscher, have little or no tail. The shortness is often accentuated by surgical means soon after birth.

The spine of the dog is flexible throughout its length in the breeds which remain normal, but less so in the achondroplastic, or short-legged breeds, such as the Scottish Terriers, which are equipped with large heads and short limbs.

The back is relatively longer in the Greyhounds and Dachshunds although the number of vertebrae remains the same. The ribs exhibit some degree of difference among the various breeds in respect to their length, and in most breeds the ribs are expected to be well curved in their upper parts with rather more flattening as the first eight pairs of ribs approach the sternum. This well developed curvature ensures lung and heart room.

The bones of the limbs are indicated in the diagram on this page. The relative sizes of these bones vary considerably among breeds.

Above the hind limbs the pelvis is characteristic in that the ilium or top projection is flattened or spoon-shaped in its upper portion. In most breeds exhibition specimens have additional length of tibia and fibula (the lower hind leg bones) to ensure greater angulation of the limb. This has been achieved by selective breeding.

The male dog has a grooved bone in the penis giving cover to the membranous urethra.

No breed of animal shows so many variations in its skeleton as the domestic dog. Skulls show some remarkable differences in the relative proportions of their parts. In the *dolicocephalic* (long-headed) varieties, the jawbones are elongated so that the jaws are approximately equal in length to the cranial portion of the skull. This applies to collies, hounds and terriers, and the greyhound types. Such lengthy jaws carry a complete set of teeth with ease. In the upper jaw there are normally six incisor teeth, two canines or tusks, and on either side four premolars and two molar teeth.

In the lower jaw there are a similar number but with three pairs of molars instead of two (see DENTITION OF THE DOG).

In the short-faced (*brachycephalic*) breeds such as the Bulldog, Pekingese, Pug and Brussels Griffon, the jaws are shortened and the cranial portion of the skull is normal in length. Width of skull is afforded by increased curvature of the zygomatic arch (cheekbone) which provides protective cover for the eye and, behind it, a surface onto which the muscles of mastication may be attached.

In the short-headed dogs the lower jaw is often slightly longer than the upper, a condition called undershot. In some breeds there is only a moderate degree of jaw shortening. Such *mesocephalic* breeds include the Boxer, Bullmastiff and Cavalier King Charles Spaniel. Less marked shortening may be observed in the Shih Tsu. In some of the brachycephalic heads there is difficulty in accommodating a full set of teeth, though both Boxer and Bulldog sometimes carry additional incisors.

Ancestors of the Dog The evolution of the dog can be traced back through recent geological ages of the earth to the Eocene period of the Tertiary Epoch. But, as with the human being, there is still a missing link – the actual direct ancestor of the domestic dog. Until the geological past yields some concrete evidence, there can be only speculation as to who, or what, that ancestor was. The more distant past is, however, much more clear.

The dog's history begins with the creodonts. They were small flesh-eating mammals, members of the carnivora. Some animals, such as bears, are almost entirely plant-eaters. Yet both bears and dogs have a common ancestry amongst the creodonts, and we call both members of the great family of the carnivora.

The creodonts existed alongside the dinosaurs during the Cretaceous period which preceded the Tertiary era. They were mammals, and most of them were hardly bigger than mice. They had incisors with closed roots, and some other teeth which resembled those of the flesh-eating marsupials. Their brains were very small.

The end of the Cretaceous age has sometimes been called the period of the Great Death. There had been similar earlier ones, but nothing to equal this. It brought total extinction to the dinosaurs, large and small, and to many other families. It also destroyed multitudinous sea creatures such as ammonites, and others. Whilst climatic changes destroyed the dinosaurs, other species benefited, and the mammals increased, both in size and numbers.

All mammals have certain features in common. They give birth to live young which are fed milk from their mothers' breasts. They are warm-blooded, so that they have a superior ability to regulate their body temperature in spite of fluctuations in temperature about them. And they can maintain that body temperature within very narrow limits. They have body hair, flexible skin, both sebaceous and sweat glands, and complex lungs and hearts.

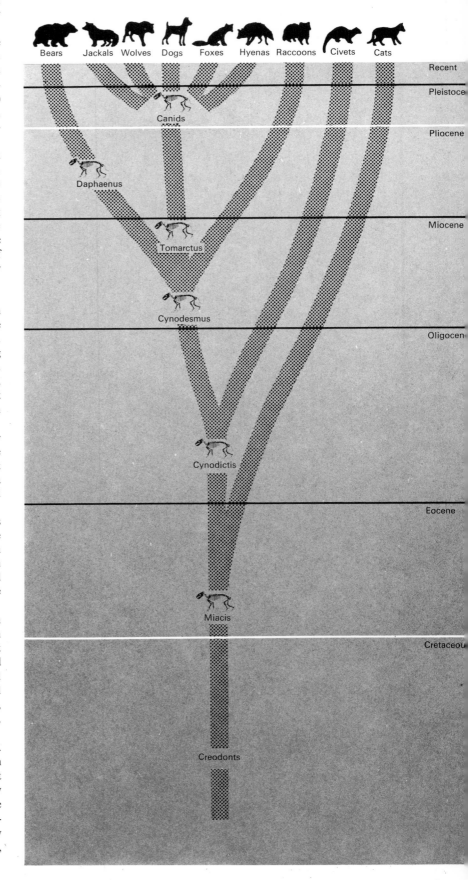

Different families of mammals have developed in different ways. It might help to understand the evolution of dogs, if we compare certain features of the flesh-eating dog to those of the herbivorous cow. The dog's jaw is relatively short and wide for powerful movements. The cow's is long and narrow, and is hinged for grinding, sideways movements as well as for opening and closing. The dog's lower incisors are sharp for piercing, holding, and tearing flesh. But those of the cow are blunt for cropping grasses.

The canine teeth of the dog are prominent for killing and dragging the animals which it will devour. In the cow, the upper canines are absent, and the lower ones resemble the incisors. The premolars and molars of the dog are blade-like for shearing. Those of the cow are long-crowned for the side motion we call cud chewing. Finally, in the dog, the articular condyle (or rounded bone end) of the lower jaw is far back and down. This permits the back teeth to engage first, so that the jaw movement creates a scissors effect.

Now the dog is a meat-eater, as is its prehistoric relative, the cat. Meat is digested in the stomach; grasses and cereals in the intestines. So the dog and cat have very large stomachs, containing a high content of hydrochloric acid. Their intestines are relatively short. But the cow has a compartmented stomach, and a relatively long and large intestine.

In the Eocene, some 40,000,000 years ago, one of the creodonts developed into a little animal now known as *Miacis*. The Miacidae were mink-sized, with long backs, short legs, extraordinarily long tails, and a slightly larger brain than most other creodonts.

Miacis may be considered the first of the true carnivora. Its legs were short and heavy, and it had five toes. It walked flat-footed, as does one of its descendants, the bear. It is believed that it was arboreal, a tree climber, and that it had at least partly retractile claws. But it is probable that it was also a den dweller.

The den dwellers inherit an instinct to keep their dens clean. Everyone who has had a litter of puppies knows that the mother cleans up after her puppies until they can walk. They then stagger out of their nests to relieve themselves. It is because of this ancient instinct that dogs can be housebroken. The dog might have inherited this instinct from an ancestor later than *Miacis*. But cats descend directly from *Miacis,* and they, too, have inherited the instinct. So it seems likely that *Miacis* also imprinted this instinct into the genetic pattern inherited by the dog.

Miacis also gave to its descendants some features which all carnivora still possess. These are separate anal and genital openings, a tail, feet with no less than four toes, compressed claws, and multiple mammary glands located in both pectoral and abdominal regions. *Miacis* also possessed specialized carnassial (or shearing) teeth.

Perhaps 20,000,000 years later, *Cynodictis* developed from *Miacis*. *Cynodictis* was still somewhat flat-footed. But its fifth toe, or thumb, was shortening into what would become the dew claw in modern dogs. And whereas the creodonts had separated toes, *Cynodictis* was developing shorter toes, connected with some degree of webbing, and being somewhat arched. *Cynodictis* was starting the evolution of the runner – the digitigrade animal which walks on its toes, as distinguished from the plantigrade creatures, such as the bear, which walk on their heels.

Cynodictis improved on the dentition of its ancient ancestors. It had forty-two teeth, made up of three incisors, one canine, four premolars, and two molars on each side of the upper jaw. The lower jaw had the same teeth, but added an extra molar on each side.

Both *Miacis* and *Cynodictis* have a direct descendant which closely resembles them. Because it has apparently changed so little in 40,000,000 years, it is called a 'living fossil'. It is the civet.

Modern dogs always sniff at the anal glands of visiting dogs. No one knows the exact reason for this. The glands give off a substance with a not too unpleasant odour. (If the gland gets clogged, then it must be cleaned by man, and the substance then has a horrible smell.) It is therefore of more than passing interest that the civet develops a strong, pleasant, aromatic substance in its anal glands. In Africa, civets are caught, put into stockades, and regularly 'milked' for this substance. It is the basis of most of the world's finest perfumes. One may assume, then, that *Miacis* and *Cynodictis* gave the modern dog a means of telling the condition of another dog's health by sniffing at the anal glands.

A descendant of *Cynodictis* was *Cynodesmus*. From one of *its* descendants, *Daphaenus*, the bears developed. And from another came the raccoons. *Cynodesmus* was still civet-like. But it continued the evolution of the runner. It was taller and had more dog-like feet. From another of its descendants, *Tomarctus*, came the great family of the Canids.

Tomarctus was very dog-like. It probably still lacked the advanced intelligence of the dog. But it may have imprinted the remarkable social instincts of the dog and wolf into all its descendants except the fox. One social relationship among both dogs and wolves is to hunt in packs, and to work in relays.

Biologists often speak of the great family called the Canoides. This is the living group which contains the Canidae (the dogs and their relatives), the Ursidae (or bears), and the Procyonidae (raccoons, coati-mundi, kinkajou, and cacomistle).

The Canidae are our main concern here. These include the wolves, domestic dogs, foxes, jackals, and some of their distant relatives. See CANINE; FALSE DOGS. The hyena was once considered to belong to the family, but is now generally excluded. Some would like, also, to exclude the fox. But foxes, wolves, and dogs have several common features which are absent in other Canoides: they have a caecum (appendix) and a duodeno-jejunal flexure in the intestines.

Chromosomal differences between foxes and dogs ensure that they are not interfertile, cannot be mated. The gestation period for the fox is about 50 days; that for the dog, 62 to 63 on average. The dog has a round eye pupil which, in bright light, closes to pinhead size. In the fox, the pupil is elliptical, and it closes into a vertical slit. The bony projection above the eyes of the

Left Ancestors of the dog. The dog's 'family tree' from its earliest known forebear, *Miacis*, to its modern relatives – an evolution spanning 40,000,000 years.

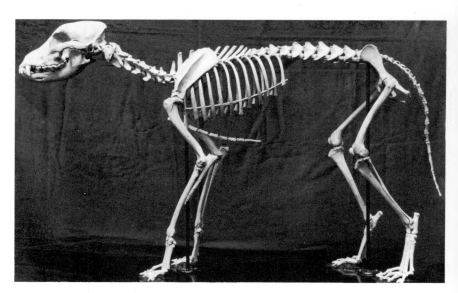

dog is enlarged and prominent. It is filled with air cells which might be called sinuses. These are absent in the fox, and the area is flattened. The foot pads of the fox are hairier than those of the dog. The tail or 'brush' of the fox is of extraordinary length, and is unmatched by that of any dog.

We come now to the question of the direct ancestor of the dog. Some have said that the dog is only a tamed wolf. Ivan Sanderson wrote that, if you skinned a dog, wolf, and coyote you would be hard put to it to distinguish one from the others. Other researchers have claimed that the dog is at least partly of jackal ancestry. Still others have claimed hyena descent.

Modern scientists have eliminated the hyena. For instance, hyena pups are born with their eyes open. They are able to stand and to walk within a few minutes. And an hour or two after birth they will attack viciously. Only a few scientists still claim any jackal ancestry for the dog.

Some have explained the astonishing plasticity of the dog's genetic inheritance by theorizing that the dog did not evolve from a single ancestor. They believe that many different parental stocks were involved. In this view, widely differing 'cousins' maintained cross breeding, so that the truly amazing breed differences in dogs are the result of genes from all these ancestral roots. Yet most modern dog breeds were created within the last 100 years.

The question of the wolf is more difficult to solve. Biologically, wolves and dogs *can* be cross-bred, and the offspring will be fertile. Wolf-dog crosses have been reported since early Greek times. It has been said that Eskimos mate their sledge dogs to wolves to give the dogs greater strength and size and that early explorers found their dogs leaving ship or camp to mate with wolves. Others reported that North American Indians tied bitches to trees outside village or camp areas, where they were then mated to wolves. In truth, the wolf would be more likely to kill the bitch.

Such reports are pure fabrications, either innocent or deliberate: they belong to the fox-dog stories, where a hunter will sometimes swear that he has witnessed a chase in which the pursued fox has stopped to mate with the pursuing dog.

Xenophon, the great Greek general and historian, wrote a treatise on hunting. For hare hunting, he said he preferred the fox breed. 'Those of the fox breed were so termed because they are bred from a dog and a fox, and through the length of time the natures of the two animals are completely amalgamated.' Xenophon also said he preferred dogs of the 'Indian breed' for hunting deer and wild boar. And Aristotle, one of history's most careful observers, described these Indian hounds. They were supposed to be a third generation cross between a tiger and a bitch. The bitch was tied to a tree. If the tiger proved amorous, he would mate with her. If not, he simply devoured her. Since the latter was the more common fate for the bitch, such Indian hounds were somewhat rare!

Foxes, tigers and dogs are not interfertile, and fox-dog and tiger-dog matings are simply impossible. For behavioural reasons, so are all wolf-dog matings,

except where the mating has been unnatural; as for example, where the wolf puppy has been raised with dog puppies since before its eyes opened.

But if such absurd stories have been told since Greek times, the mortal enmity between wolf and dog has also been known for an equally long time. Wolves and dogs invariably kill each other if they can. This is so even when the dog has never before come up against a wolf, and vice versa. See ALASKAN MALAMUTES.

There is, however, one simple and reasonable explanation for reports by otherwise reliable people of wolf-dog matings. Many dogs become feral. That is, they return to a wild state. They roam as predators, living upon such game as they can find and capture. Yet they tend to remain close to areas of human habitations. Such dogs would lurk about camps and could mate with camp bitches. Particularly in the Arctic, these dogs might be mistaken for wolves. Other people, not willing to miss fabricating a good story, would claim these feral dogs to be wolves.

Such feral dogs are still dogs. They are recognized as such by completely domestic dogs, and these receive the same recognition in return. This is so even when the two have had no previous experience of each other. When wolf and dog meet, mortal combat starts instantly, even though dog and wolf have never met before. Fighting to the death does not happen when domestic and feral dogs meet. There are many accounts of such meetings. If the dogs are antagonistic, the confrontation ends in submission, not death.

Feral dogs have quite often, and understandably, become sheep killers. Sheep dogs have been taught to guard their flocks. Feral dogs are often smaller and weaker than their fully domestic brothers, or they have inherited shyness. So when attacked by larger and more ferocious sheep dogs, they have rolled over on their backs, feet in the air. This is the universal dog sign of surrender. The guardian dogs would then allow the feral dogs to regain their feet and to run away. Huge trained dogs have often been used to hunt feral dogs. But always they have refused to kill them when the surrender sign was given. When wolf meets dog, however, the surrender sign is ignored.

Feral dogs can be returned to domesticity. And even when they cannot – if for example they are extremely man-shy dogs – their offspring, born in the wild, can become true domestic dogs. Wolf puppies can be captured and tamed to some degree. But their puppies will be completely wild, and must be tamed in turn.

Eskimo owners of dog teams along the northern shore of North America have been carefully questioned about introducing wolf blood into their dogs. They have denied making such crosses. The dogs may be chained for days on a frozen, snowless shore or on ice. They curl up and sleep while waiting to work. According to the Eskimos, wolves are too nervous to stand this, and simply waste their strength in pacing. How the Eskimos discovered this without making such crosses is not answered. What is certain is that the dogs are neither entire wolves nor part-wolf.

But, if the dog is not merely a tamed wolf, what then is its origin? No one knows. One possible guess is that its immediate ancestor was a small circumpolar wolf. This wolf, if it ever existed, is now extinct. If it was indeed the ancestor of the dog, then it could be said that wolves and dogs are not brothers but cousins.

Others believe that the ancestor of all the breeds of dogs was a small Pleistocene canid of Asia. It is suggested that it was a mutant, a much smaller animal than other canids of its time. Northern Asia is suggested as the place of its birth. The northern areas of that continent have not been searched for fossils to the extent that the other continents have been, and, many scientists believe that Asia still holds the keys to many anthropological problems.

There is also the theory of radiation. When people or animals radiated out from a cultural centre, they tended to remain static, to maintain their original culture. If one travels back towards the centre, he will find ever greater changes. For example, village dwelling people might well breed dogs selectively for size, herding, and guardian aptitudes. And they would be quick to take advantage of mutations which might be helpful. But those radiating out from the centre would be unable to do this. This theory would account for the successively larger dogs that came with the great western migrations of peoples during the bronze and iron ages. In later days, the giant 'Mollosian Dog' and the TIBETAN MASTIFF came out of Asia.

The dog can be no closer to the wolf than first cousin. Whatever its ancestor was, it did something which the wolf cannot do: it leaped across the mighty canyon that separates the wild and the domestic.
See DOMESTICATION OF THE DOG.

Angulation The angles formed at joints, such as formed by the upper and lower thighs, and the shoulder and upper arm. The bones meeting at the hock joint also produce angulation, or lack of it.

Ankylosis see Arthritis.

Antidotes see Poisons.

Antiseptics Such terms as antiseptic, disinfectant, asepsis, and germicide are widely misunderstood and consequently misused. Antiseptics are substances, usually but not always organic or inorganic compounds, which inhibit the growth of bacteria without necessarily killing them. A bactericide is one which does kill them, while a bacteriostat completely stops, or inhibits their growth or reproduction. Most antiseptics are basically protoplasmic poisons. As such, they must be effective against bacteria without killing or injuring live tissue.

Disinfectants are highly toxic substances used to kill bacteria, that is, to sterilize. They may be powerful concentrations of an antiseptic, or they may be completely different chemical compounds.

Before Lord Lister (1827–1912) surgeons tried to *destroy* infection in a wound. They believed that germs were either spontaneously generated in the incision, or that they were generated by oxygen in the air. They

Ancestors of the dog.
Top left A complete skeleton found at an Early Bronze Age site showing the anatomy of an early dog.
Middle left Some researchers have claimed that the dog is partly of jackal descent. Most likely, the jackal is only a cousin.
Bottom left 'The dog is only a tamed wolf'. Some wolves, like the timber wolf (p.394 top) look remarkably dog-like, but this maned wolf shows that the theory is at best over-simplified.

tried to destroy infection, decay, and putrefaction in the wound. But this was often impossible either because the substances used could not penetrate to the depths of the infection, or because they destroyed living tissue more disastrously than the bacteria were doing. Common vinegar had been the most successful wound or injury disinfectant for centuries. Its success was probably due to its effect upon coliform bacteria.

Coliform bacteria live in the intestines of men and animals. In earlier ages, when there were no sanitary sewage systems, and no purified water supplies, contamination by both human and animal excreta was common, and the coliforms invaded wounds. But they require an alkaline medium in which to reproduce. Vinegar contains around 5 per cent acetic acid, sufficient to set up an acid medium inhospitable to coliforms.

Vinegar is almost totally forgotten in modern veterinary practice. Yet coliform bacteria often, for example, invade the ears of dogs. A change in the amount of alkaline sometimes clears up these infections when other agents, including the antibiotics, fail.

The vinegar-coliform 'anti-relationship' demonstrates a problem with antiseptics. Some bacteria require an acid medium in which to live and reproduce. Some may be sensitive to one antiseptic but will not be affected by another. Antiseptics can work well in the laboratory but fail in the field because of the presence of blood, serum, or other organic material.

The discovery by Pasteur that pathogenic bacteria caused infection gave Lister the idea of placing an antiseptic barrier between an injury and the bacteria which might enter it. In 1865, he first used phenol – carbolic acid – after an amputation. In later experiments he reduced the strength of the phenol. Though he was using one of the poorest antiseptics, and one of the most damaging to living tissues, Lister revolutionized both medicine and sanitation.

The practice of antisepsis grew into asepsis. In aseptic surgery, an attempt is made to exclude harmful bacteria completely. Instruments and surgical gowns are sterilized. Even the air may be disinfected.

The chemotherapeutic products, such as penicillin and the sulfa drugs have shown remarkable success when applied to wounds as an antiseptic. However, they are not considered as such, because they are so commonly used systemically, by injection or orally.

In making a choice of antiseptics the veterinarian or kennel owner must consider many factors. These include the type of infection present, the rapidity of action, success against a wide variety of harmful bacteria, and the duration of that action. They must also consider any toxic properties the substance may have for living tissues.

Soaps and detergents are, in an important sense, antiseptics. While they do not have in themselves any bactericidal properties, they greatly reduce the numbers of bacteria on the skin.

Hexachlorophene, a bacteriostat, is added to some soaps. This is effective against many skin flora, including those causing human sweat odours, but it is ineffective against the coliforms.

Quickest acting of all the antiseptics are 70 per cent ethyl alcohol and 2 per cent iodine. Veterinarians may cleanse the hair and skin with alcohol before giving an injection. Or having shaved the area, they may paint the skin about an operation site with iodine. The latter is, however, harmful to living tissue, and so must be used with care. Some authorities recommend against its use in wounds, feeling that it does more harm to tissue than bacteria might. This problem, however, is not limited to iodine, since many antiseptics injure tissue or inhibit the healing process.

In the case of skin infections, veterinarians may paint the skin with an analine dye, such as gentian violet. In doing so, they are trying to create an alkaline skin surface which will be inhospitable to the growth of certain bacteria. This is the reverse of the vinegar use. The analine dyes have excellent penetrating power, but they are also slightly toxic and irritating.

Hydrogen peroxide liberates oxygen. But its effect is short lasting and is negated by the presence of organic material. It is therefore a poor antiseptic, though the bubbling action may help to cleanse wounds.

The hypochlorites have been used for many years as kennel and veterinary hospital disinfectants. These chemicals release a potent disinfectant, chlorine, but again they are quickly inactivated by organic material. Their use as either kennel antiseptics or disinfectants is therefore limited.

The acridine dyes, or flavines, are slow-acting and long-lasting. They are useful in wound infections, and are virtually non-toxic. These include diflavine, proflavine, and acriflavine. While used chiefly as an antiseptic, acriflavine is sometimes used in intravenous injection. Acriflavine hydrochloride, or acid acriflavine, is used for the same purposes. But because it is acid it is slightly irritating.

But perhaps the most powerful and useful of all kennel disinfectants is 'lye', commonly known as caustic soda or sodium hydroxide. It is a poison which must be handled with care. One of the most valuable uses of lye is as a destroyer of ROUNDWORM eggs. These are untouched by most disinfectants. Lye kills them quickly, as indeed it does all parasites and bacteria.

A disinfectant solution is made by dissolving two pounds of lye in ten gallons of cold water. Cold water is necessary to prevent excess boiling up of the liquid. Care must be taken not to get the solution in the eyes or on the skin, and not to breathe in lye dust.

At disinfectant strength, a lye solution is not harmful to bare wood floors, concrete, rubber, or cotton clothing. It will damage varnished floors and leather shoes. Rubber boots or rubber overshoes should be worn when working with it. In kennel disinfecting, operators should be careful to treat areas where infection and parasites breed. These are corners, cracks around posts, and the space under fence run-dividers.

After treatment with lye, the area should be left for one hour, then thoroughly washed out with water. It is then safe for the return of the dogs.

Chlorine is recognized as an extremely effective bactericide and is also effective against virus. The usual domestic bleaches can be used in their normal dilution. However, the action of chlorine is greatly reduced if dirt, or contamination of any sort is present. This means that it can only be used when a kennel has been thoroughly cleansed.

The action is rapid. The kennel can be thoroughly hosed out after half an hour, to remove the remains of the bleach. Two comments must be made here: firstly, chlorine reacts to aluminium so all aluminium bowls should be removed. Secondly, the fumes are strong and this disinfecting should be undertaken only when the kennel is unoccupied.

As antiseptics, the cresols, or cresylics, have not proved too successful. They are harmful to living tissue, and they are inactivated by organic materials. But they have been used as kennel disinfectants for many years. They are not an all-purpose disinfectant like lye, but when manufacturers' instructions are followed, they do an excellent job. They are safer to handle than lye.

Antiserum, Immune Serum Antiserums, or immune serums, deal with antigens and antibodies. In simple terms, an antigen is any substance which stimulates the production of antibodies when injected. An antibody is a substance which appears in the body fluids to protect against a specific disease. When antibodies are produced, the serum in the body renders the body immune, and the serum is called immune serum, or antiserum. In other words, the body has been immunized against specific bacteria, or viruses, and contains antibodies against the disease-causing agent concerned.

Another type of antiserum is known as an antitoxin. Antitoxins are immune therapeutic agents which protect against tetanus, diphtheria, and snake venoms. The production of tetanus antitoxin is a classic example which will serve to explain antiserums in general. Extremely small doses of tetanus toxin are injected into horses. Antigens carried by the toxin cause the formation of antibodies. The doses injected are gradually increased until the horse has produced huge quantities of antibodies, and is consequently immune to large doses of the toxin. Some blood is removed from the horse, and the serum with its antibodies is separated from the blood. It is then ready to neutralize the toxin of the tetanus bacteria.

Antiserums give powerful immediate protection. But the immunity thus conferred is of brief duration. An antiserum which is familiar to most dog breeders is one developed to prevent distemper. In some areas this antiserum is known as 'puppy shots'. These are given to puppies at two week intervals until the puppy is considered to be ready to receive more lasting protection. Such shots are often given to dogs when it is expected that they might be exposed to DISTEMPER, as for example, before their first dog show.

Appetite, Perverted see Coprophagy.

Apple-Headed This term is used to describe dogs with a high, domed skull. It is seen in some, but

Top right Apple-headed. The high, domed skull is a feature of the Chihuahua.

Bottom right Apron. Abundant hair on the chest which is characteristic of the Rough Collie.

not all, of the short-headed (*brachycephalic*) dogs, and particularly in some of the toy breeds. The CHIHUAHUA is an example. In apple-headed dogs, the bones forming the brain case, the neuro-cranial area of the skull, are strongly arched.

Apron The frill or longer hair on the underside of the neck and on the frontal section of the chest, seen characteristically on the Rough COLLIE.

Apso see Lhasa Apso.

Arab Greyhound see Saluki.

Arabian Gazelle Hound see Saluki.

Arthritis The main limb joints act as hinges. When such a joint is examined, it is seen to be far from simple in structure. The ends of the limb bones are faced with cartilage to give a smooth surface to the joint. These surfaces are enclosed by the joint 'capsule' which is lined with the synovial membrane. This membrane manufactures synovial fluid (synovia or joint oil) which lubricates the joint. The joint is bound together by the cord-like ligaments.

Arthritis is inflamation of a joint. One or more of the structures which make up the joint may be involved. When the condition is confined to the synovial membrane it is referred to as synovitis. In the dog, arthritis is usually the result of some injury such as a slip or fall. If a wound involves the joint capsule, the synovial fluid will escape and infection may follow to produce a septic arthritis.

Chronic arthritis is a serious problem. The joint may suffer considerable changes and its range of movement may be severely restricted. In extreme cases the bone is involved and the joint may become permanently fixed [ankylosis]. The veterinarian will employ X-rays to determine the extent of the condition. In some cases injections of corticosteriods into the joint and the surrounding tissues will produce some improvement.

The first symptom of arthritis is lameness. The joint is hot and swollen and the dog shows signs of pain when the part is handled. The immediate treatment of suspected arthritis is rest. The dog should be confined as much as possible and only allowed the minimum exercise. The veterinarian may bandage the part to give it support. Pain-relieving drugs and anti-inflammatory agents may also be prescribed.

A mild arthritis may resolve within a week but it is wise to restrict the dog's exercise for a few days longer to be certain that the recovery is complete.

Old dogs, particularly of the heavier breeds, may suffer from arthritis in more than one joint as the result of wear and tear. It is difficult to give relief in these cases, but if the dog is overweight, slimming will make it easier for it to move about.

Artificial Insemination Artificial insemination is the transfer of semen from the male to the female by the use of instruments.

There are several reasons for employing artificial insemination. Firstly, it can be used to consummate a mating which is difficult, or may be impossible, for some anatomical, physiological or psychological reason. Sometimes these reasons are such that it would be wiser to avoid the mating as the pups might inherit the defect, but when there is likely to be no detriment to the progeny, artificial insemination is justifiable. Secondly, artificial insemination can be used when natural mating is impossible for geographical reasons. For example, semen collected from a Beagle in England has been flown to the United States of America and used to inseminate a bitch on heat there. The result was a normal litter of pups.

Thirdly, artificial insemination might be used to increase the use of a particularly valuable sire. Dr Stephen Seager of the University of Oregon has been able to store dog semen for a year and then to produce healthy puppies. The method is to dilute the semen with a suitable buffer medium and then to freeze it. These developments have made the storage and transport of dog semen an everyday occurrence.

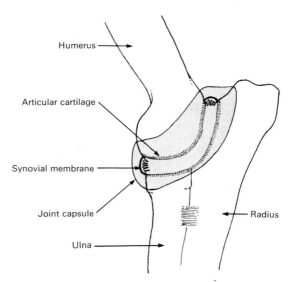

Left Arthritis. The inflammation of a joint often results from an injury, but for elderly dogs it is a hazard of old age.

Humerus

Articular cartilage

Synovial membrane

Joint capsule

Radius

Ulna

The actual procedure is carried out in two stages. The semen is first collected from the male using an artificial vagina. Not all dogs are prepared to co-operate in this performance, even when encouraged by the presence of a bitch on heat. If the semen can be collected successfully it can be examined prior to the insemination of the bitch. This examination is a valuable guide to the probable fertility of the male. The volume and density of the semen can be measured and a specimen can be examined microscopically. Under the microscope the mobility of the sample can be assessed and it is possible to examine individual spermatozoa for abnormalities. If the specimen is satisfactory the bitch can be inseminated, the semen being deposited into the cervix using a syringe and a long pipette.

The KENNEL CLUB of England is prepared to register the progeny of artificial insemination provided permission has been given beforehand. Permission would be given in cases where the veterinary surgeon has advised that artificial insemination is necessary or justifiable. An application for permission should be accompanied by a veterinary certificate. There is no point in going to the trouble and expense of artificial insemination unless the Kennel Club has already signified that it is prepared to register the pups.

The importation of dog semen into Britain is controlled by the Ministry of Agriculture, Fisheries and Food. In other countries, import licences are not required.

'The American Kennel Club accepts registration of a litter resulting from artificial insemination if the sire and dam are present during the artificial mating and if both the extraction and insemination are done by the same licensed veterinarian. It requires a certification of such breeding to be signed by the owners of the stud and dam and by the veterinarian.'

Artificial Respiration see Respiration.

Aspirin Aspirin is a common analgesic (see ANALGESIA). It is probably of all drugs the most widely used by human beings, who also use it indiscriminately upon their pets. Aspirin is acetylsalicylic acid, and as such, is a derivative of phenol. Phenol is highly toxic to cats, but less so to dogs.

Aspirin is used to relieve pain, such as that of ARTHRITIS. It is also used as an antipyretic, to lower fever. Repeated heavy dosages have been known to kill.

It can cause severe gastric irritation and even slight stomach haemorrhages. It should be used sparingly, and in small doses, and then only upon the advice of a veterinarian.

Asthma This is the name given to a deep cough which is 'triggered off' by the lungs, with a resulting difficulty in breathing.

True asthma is a nervous condition affecting the actual lungs and is often brought about by stress or allergy. There is some evidence that the condition may be hereditary in some breeds.

The name asthma is also applied to the cough which results from a heart condition that affects the circulation of blood to and from the lungs.

Naturally, all these conditions need veterinary treatment. Most will improve if treatment is begun at an early stage. It is essential to restrict exercise and helpful to use inhalants to ease the condition.

Australian Cattle Dog Australia has developed two superlative working dogs, the Australian Cattle Dog, and the Australian KELPIE. The former breed's history begins about 1840. The first working cattle dogs, now extinct, were known as Black Bobtails. They were big, clumsy, could not stand either heat or long trips, and in the words of one breed historian '. . . bit like an alligator and barked like a consumptive'.

There followed in 1840 crosses with another long since extinct breed, the Smithfield. The blood of the DINGO, the Kelpie, the Smooth COLLIE (probably blue merles), and of the DALMATIAN was introduced. The breed has been known as the Australian Heeler, the Blue Heeler, and the Queensland Heeler, but the official name is now the Australian Cattle Dog.

Despite such former names as Blue Heeler, many of the Australian Cattle Dogs are red speckled. And these reds are said to be more savage biters than the blues.

The dogs are required to round up, drive, and pen range cattle. These animals are wild and difficult to control, so the dog required to round them up, or to drive a 'mob', must be rugged, extremely agile, highly intelligent, and a strong biter. It must not, however, bite high enough on the hind legs to cripple the animal, or damage his meat or hide.

A dog customarily tests the kicking speed and ability of unfamiliar range animals by feinting. It then snaps or bites the heel of the leg bearing the animal's weight. If it bit the other leg, a lightning-fast and well-aimed kick could kill it. After the bite, the dog drops flat so as to be under the kick as the bull or steer frees its weight from that leg and lashes out.

Essentials of the breed: Australian Cattle Dogs are born either white or white with black speckles, regardless of later colour. They are about 18 inches at the shoulder and weigh between 33 and 40 lb. when mature.

Right Australian Cattle Dogs have to be hardy and intelligent at work to outwit the vicious steers they herd. They are also seen at shows.

The head forms a broad V; ears are pricked; the muzzle has a scissors bite. Eyes are dark, and white blemishes disqualify.

The chest is rounded and the loins powerful. The hind legs are well angulated with bow or cow hocks being serious faults. The coat is short. The tail reaches to the hocks, has a brush, and should not be carried forward of the root.

Colours are blue, blue mottled with or without black markings. The head is blue but can have black and tan markings. Tan markings on legs and feet and about the vent, and on the cheeks, follow the normal genetic patterns for most breeds of dogs.

Faults include dew claws on the hind legs, curly coat and lop ears after six months of age. Overshot or undershot jaws bring disqualification. A tan undercoat

is permitted provided it does not show through the blue outer colour.

In red speckles, the colour should be even, including the undercoat, which must not be white or cream. However, darker red markings on the body and head are permitted.

Australian Kelpie see Kelpie (Australian Collie).

Australian National Kennel Council see Kennel Council, Australian National.

Australian Terrier Australia is a country which might almost be said to specialize in producing strange animals. Examples which spring to mind are Kangaroos and Wallabies. Then there are Koala Bears. These are animated, cuddly toys devoid, it would appear, of ambition other than to eat leaves and sleep in the fork of a tree.

Australia also produced the talking budgerigar, estimated to be the most popular individual pet in the world today. The 'down under' country has however made another significant, if more orthodox, contribution to the world of pets in the shape of the Australian Terrier.

Admittedly this animal is not as bizarre as the Kangaroo, as quaint as the Koala or as popular as the Budgie. Neither for that matter is it as purely Australian.

The reality is that this national dog has a background wholly British. What the Australians claim is the curious combination of ancestors which produced a terrier markedly different from the others. Amongst other things it has the distinction of being the only true terrier widely and generally accepted by the world which did not originate in the British Isles.

Nobody knows quite what ingredients were used to produce this 'canine cocktail'. The men that first bred them had work in mind. They cared little about fancy points, and even less about pedigrees.

By the time the breed made its first public appearance at Sydney Royal Show in 1899, breeding had already been going on for more than 20 years. The beginnings were already misting over. Most would agree, however, that amongst other breeds used were CAIRNS, DANDIE DINMONTS, IRISH TERRIERS, SCOTTISH TERRIERS and almost certainly the diminutive YORKSHIRE TERRIER.

The result was a low-set, compact dog with abundant activity and agility. This latter characteristic soon ensured local popularity. A dog which can kill a rat or a rabbit in seconds was assured of a welcome in Australia. The welcome became even more enthusiastic when these little terriers took to killing snakes. This they sometimes do by leaping straight off the ground, turning in mid-air, landing behind the snake and seizing it by the neck.

Britain was slow to grant the 'Aussie' official recognition. A few appeared in 1906 but excited little interest.

In 1921 things improved when Lady Stradbroke, whose husband had been Governor of Victoria, imported some. By 1936 they were sufficiently established and numerous to warrant inclusion in the Kennel Club registers. The Duke of Gloucester gave the breed an international boost when he became attracted to it during his Australian tour as Governor General.

Recognition was even slower in the United States than in Britain. Indeed the Australian Terrier was completely ignored there until 1960. Since then however the scene has changed sharply. While not exactly booming, Australian Terriers are certainly becoming more popular and several importations have been made direct from Australia. The dog is now in the top sixty breeds in the United States.

Whether or not the breed will ever be really fashionable is debatable. In these days it is usually glamour which gains favour. The workmanlike qualities of a breed – and the Australian has an abundance of these – are all too frequently forgotten.

Essentials of the breed: Head long, skull flat with soft hair topknot. Long, powerful jaw, black nose. Eyes, small and dark. Ears small, set high, pricked or dropped towards the front. Teeth level. Neck comparatively long for size of dog with frill of hair. Legs straight, set well under body which is rather long but well ribbed up. Hindquarters strong with hocks slightly bent. Feet clean, small and with black toe-nails. Tail docked. Colour blue or silver grey body, with tan markings on legs and face, or clear sandy or red all over with soft topknot. Average weight 10 or 11 lb. (Britain) 12 to 14 lb. (America).
See colour plate p. 377.

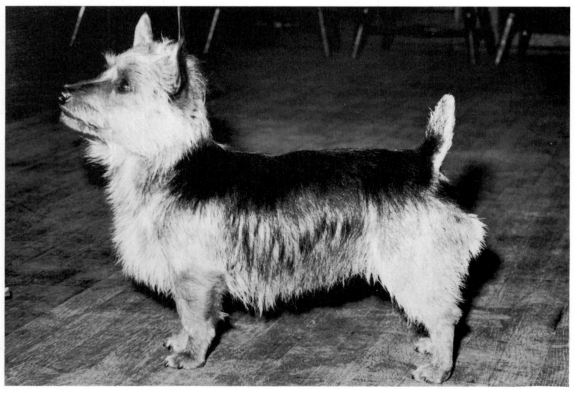

Australian Terrier. Australia specially produced this little Terrier for its ratting and rabbiting skills. It is noted for its stamina and agility.
Left Ch. Tinee Town Talewagger.

Right Dripshill Hans.

B

Babesiasis (Canine Piroplasmosis) see Protozoan Diseases.

Bad Breath The common causes of foul breath are tartar upon the teeth, pyorrhoea (pus under, in, or around the gums), loose and rotting teeth, and ulcerative stomatitis. In the last named disease, grey ulcers form on the insides of the cheeks and lips. They may be caused by rubbing against diseased teeth. Gingivitis – spongy gums from which blood oozes and where food particles decompose – may also cause bad breath.

Tartar may be the common very hard form, or it may be soft and slimy so that it makes a perfect medium for the growth of bacteria causing stench. In some cases a veterinarian can show the owner how to scale away tartar and from then on the owner can do the job at home. But in many cases it is essential that this dental care should be carried out under a general anaesthetic to be certain that the gums are not badly damaged, to prevent unnecessary pain, and to ensure a good 'finish'.

Ulcerative stomatitis is quickly cured by scaling away tartar, pulling loose teeth, filling dental cavities when they occur, and cauterizing the ulcers; but all these treatments are jobs for the veterinarian.

Foul breath may be caused by foreign bodies caught in the teeth or throat, by lung and stomach diseases, and by diseases of the nasal passages. In rare cases, the sinuses and nasal passages may be invaded by a worm known as *linguatula taenioides*. A symptom of nasal or sinus diseases, other than foul breath, is forced breathing through the mouth.

Since foul breath can be a symptom of very serious trouble, a thorough examination by a veterinarian is always indicated. If no disease can be found, but foul breath continues, chlorophyll tablets can be used. Such preparations as those used to destroy oestral odours and the smell from certain diseases, are available from veterinarians and sometimes from pet shops. However, it is better to cure the cause rather than treat the symptom.

Anal glands, if active, can also taint the body and produce an unpleasant mouth odour. A smell of acetone (similar to the smell of nail varnish remover) is an indication of a disturbance to the glucose control of the body and should be reported to the veterinarian immediately.

Badger Digging with Dogs The European badger (*Meles meles*) is widely distributed in Europe. It is a mammal of an average adult weight of 22 to 26 lb., although specimens of over 55 lb. have been recorded.

Badgers sometimes make their homes or 'sets' in a disused rabbit warren, leading to underground chambers. They settle mostly in woods or copses bordering pastureland, also on hills or mountain sides, quarries and cliffs but never in marshy ground.

Badger sports are not practised in the U.S.A. Badger-baiting with dogs was at one time widely practised in Europe but is today illegal. Digging with terriers, however, is legal and frequently occurs in parts of Britain. This is one of the most controversial of blood sports more especially as this mammal does considerable good and scant harm. However, the terriers that are used are specially bred, and must have great courage. The essence of the sport is the test of the terrier's courage when facing a much stronger, heavier and better armoured opponent.

The terrier, or terriers, are put into the entrance of the set to locate the badger. They then vocally indicate its whereabouts and hold it at bay while those present dig it out with shovels and kill it.

While badger digging has a great many opponents as a sport, it does have a large and enthusiastic following. Various types of terriers, including the smaller-sized pedigreed ones, are used and the type differs somewhat according to the various parts of the country. The main variety is the 'Hunt' or JACK RUSSELL TERRIER. It is important to note that terriers used to go underground must, when docked, have four inches of tail left on. This docking-length differs from that used on most of the Jack Russells that have become popular as companion dogs, where about one inch or less of tail is left on. The reason why this length of tail is essential is that the handler, when he wishes to withdraw his terrier from a set, has sufficient tail to grasp in order to pull the dog out. Manually withdrawing the terrier is often essential, as the holes are frequently too narrow for the dog to turn.

Below left Badger digging with dogs. Badger-digging terriers must have four inches of tail left undocked in case they need pulling out of a set's narrow entrance.

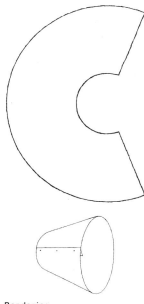

Baldness see Moulting.

Bandaging.
Above A circle of cardboard with an inner circle cut to fit the dog's neck and a side opening is the basis of an Elizabethan collar. The drawing shows how the ends of cardboard are attached by stapling or lacing to form a funnel shape around the dog's neck and head.
Above right The Elizabethan collar will prevent this dog from scratching its bandaged eye.

Bandaging.
Above Great care should be taken to ensure that a bandage is not too tight, or it may cause more damage than the wound it covers.

Bandaging For many reasons bandaging is best left to the veterinarians. Bandages are difficult to apply to a dog. If the wound to be bandaged is upon the leg, then both care and experience are required to prevent damage to the circulation. The person bandaging the dog could do it greater harm than might the untreated wound. Finally, since dogs do not understand bandages, and do not like them, they generally begin to tear them off immediately.

The veterinarian can apply the first bandage, and in so doing, can demonstrate to the owner how to apply future wound coverings. Yet most owners will lack the training and skill to place the bandages with even reasonable success. For home bandaging, at least three widths of bandage should be kept in the first aid kit. Adhesive tapes of varying widths and adhesive pads of several sizes should also be available.

Liquid adhesive is an unusual product which is very useful in dressing wounds on dogs. It can be used for covering body wounds but should not be applied to the wound itself unless under veterinary supervision. The procedure for using liquid adhesive on the body is as follows. The hair about the wound is clipped away. The wound is then covered with a gauze pad, or by several thicknesses of bandage. The edges are then glued to the skin with the liquid adhesive which dries rapidly.

Dogs with thin, upstanding ears are often attacked by flies which may bite or lay eggs in this area. Once blood has been drawn, all the flies in the neighbourhood appear to be alerted. They attack in droves, in spite of ointments and even repellents.

To bandage fly-bitten ears, the hair is clipped as short as possible. All eggs, maggots and dirt are removed. Bandage is folded over the ear tips, and is then glued to the skin. If the bandage is thick enough, the flies cannot reach the wound. Liquid adhesive is lifted as the hair grows. It then can be cut away without pain or discomfort to the dog.

There are several ways of preventing dogs from tearing off bandages. One is the use of an Elizabethan collar. This can be made quite simply out of stiff corrugated cardboard. A neck hole exactly the size of the dog's neck, but smaller than the head, is cut out. From the edge of the hole to the outer edge will be two to eight inches, depending upon the size of the dog. A cut from the outer edge to the hole allows the collar to be slipped on to the dog. A second piece of corrugated cardboard should then be stapled to the cut to hold it closed. A variation is illustrated.

The collar prevents the dog from turning its head and neck far enough to reach the injury and tearing away the bandage. While a dog is wearing such a collar, it may be necessary to help it to eat and to drink.

Still another type of collar can be made at home out of corrugated cardboard, heavy leather, or even from a strip of linoleum. This is simply a collar wide enough to cover the entire neck from the throat to the shoulder. This collar restricts turning movements of the head. It can also protect neck wounds from scratching with the hind legs.

Dog coats can sometimes be used to protect body wounds and bandages. In some cases, linoleum has been wrapped about the body and sewn to make a protective sheath.

It is quite difficult to bandage ears, except as noted, because a major problem is preventing the dog from constantly shaking its head. Such shaking further injures the wound, and may cause a haematoma, or blood blister under the skin. In such cases, a footless sock can be pulled over the head. Or, the veterinarian may bandage the ears to the head. If the Elizabethan collar is also used, the dog will be unable to scratch at the ear bandages.
See TOURNIQUET.

Bandog (obsolete). An ancient term for a dog tied by day and released by night. A term used for MASTIFFS and other guard dogs.

Banjara see Greyhound, Eastern.

Barrel Chested An overly rounded rib cage.

Barrenness see Infertility.

Basenji Most devotees claim for their breed that it is not merely unusual but unique. Those who say this about the Basenji can hardly be accused of exaggeration.

It has many unusual characteristics. The one most frequently mentioned is the Basenji's inability to bark. But to concentrate on this is to omit much else that is interesting. For example, although they cannot bark they are by no means mute. Some say they are too noisy, but those who love them most insist that their vocal efforts are midway between a chortle and a yodel. Despite this engaging description it has to be admitted that not everyone likes the way that they draw attention to themselves.

In contrast, almost everybody likes their cleanliness. They clean themselves all over, and when doing it they look and behave almost like a cat. This also applies to their method of inviting you to play. A front paw is drawn over the ears, over the nose and repeated until it has the desired effect.

Although Basenjis are comparatively new in the western world they have been known in central Africa for centuries. They were used by the natives for a variety of 'pot filling' chores. They are said to be capable of pointing, of retrieving, of driving game and of tracking wounded animals. However, none of this is new. Dogs somewhat similar to this were in use in Egypt thousands of years ago. The western world knew little of them until an English explorer brought two back from Africa in 1895.

CRUFT'S, then a dog show in its infancy, was more than prepared to welcome such newsworthy dogs. Two were entered and described as Congo Terriers. Although they aroused much interest, little was achieved because they both died of DISTEMPER before breeding.

In 1923, Lady Helen Nutting brought six more specimens to Britain and these also died of distemper. A further attempt made in 1937 was more successful. The dogs brought in then bred and with the help of later imports, established a strain which has since spread to several other countries.

The United States began to show interest at the same time as Britain. Mrs. Byron Rogers took two to New York in 1937 but, alas, they also died of distemper; proof, if it were needed, that dogs coming from countries where the disease is unknown are particularly vulnerable. However, two African-bred puppies reached Massachusetts in 1941 and survived. Others followed and in 1942 the Basenji Club of America was formed.

Having mentioned those early pioneers of the breed, it is reasonable to refer to Miss Veronica Tudor Williams, a present day fancier, who, with her tireless enthusiasm, built up her Congo strain and with it the breed, almost throughout the western world. She has made more than one journey into remote parts of Africa in search of animals suitable for breeding. She has brought them home despite the difficulties involved. One of these dogs was *Fula* whose name has become almost a legend already and who has imposed a stamp upon the breed in a way which is unlikely ever to be surpassed.

In these days of smaller houses, a medium-sized dog which needs a minimum of grooming has a lot to recommend it. When additionally it is sharply distinctive in appearance there is a strong possibility that it will edge ever forward in popularity. In the comparatively short time it has been known, it has made great progress. The probability is that the Basenji will make even more in the years to come.

Essentials of the breed: A lightly-built dog comparatively high on the leg. Skull: flat, of medium width, tapering towards nose. Fine, profuse wrinkles on forehead particularly when ears are pricked. Black nose desirable. Dark, almond-shaped eyes. Small, pointed, erect, hooded ears set well forward. Mouth: level.

Neck: crested and of good length. Shoulders: laid back. Bone: fine; body: short and level, well sprung, a definite waist. Feet: small and compact; tail: high set, curled tightly over spine and lying close to thigh. Coat: short, sleek, fine. Colour: pure bright red, pure black or black-and-tan or with white feet, chest and tail tips. White legs, white blaze, white collar optional. Height (AKC): dogs 17 inches; bitches 16 inches. See colour plate p. 190.

Basset Hound

'My hounds are bred out of the Spartan kind,
So flew'd, so sanded; and their heads are hung
With ears that sweep away the morning dew;
Crook-knee'd and dew-lapp'd, like Thessalian bulls.'

So wrote William Shakespeare in *A Midsummer Night's Dream*. Those who know the Basset can have little doubt that this was the breed he had in mind when he put the above words into the mouth of Theseus. If the reference to the long ears, the crooked front and the heavy dew-lap is not proof enough, read on of hounds:

'Slow in pursuit, but match'd in mouth like bells,
Each under each. A cry more tuneable
Was never holla'd to, nor cheer'd with horn.'

The music of a Basset is still exceptional. In the case of the pet Basset the so-called 'music' – in other words the bay or howl – is rarely, if ever, acceptable. However, the cry of a Basset pack in full flight is, in the opinion of connoisseurs, a most pleasing and tuneful performance.

Fortunately there is still plenty of opportunity to hear the cry of packs as several remain in existence in England and Ireland. There are also limited numbers in other European countries.

Bassets perform much the same function as BEAGLES; they pursue hares. There are those doubters who wonder if the ponderous Basset can keep up with the sprightly hare. In truth it is the human followers who drag back.

It is they who have little hope of keeping up with the Basset. Despite the apparent evidence to the contrary, these massive dogs move with startling agility.

Moreover, when their nose is on the trail they drive on regardless of the distance covered or the effort involved.

The Basset is interesting as it is one of the comparatively few universally known hunting hounds which is neither American nor British in origin. However, it flowered in Britain, having originally reached there from France and Belgium where it was used principally for trailing deer, hares and rabbits. Bassets were particularly adept at these tasks because despite being a mere 15 inches high, they had strength and bulk of 50 or more pounds. This made them particularly valuable when hunting in dense cover.

Lord Galway was the first to own these hounds in England when, in 1866 the Comte de Tournow sent him a pair, subsequently named *Basset* and *Balle*. A litter bred from these in 1872 was sold to Lord Onslow who further augmented his pack from one of the larger French breeders. His lordship finished with some fourteen or fifteen couples and from these hounds all that is best in the breed in Britain was descended. Their blood also courses through the veins of the majority of the other Bassets in the world.

Bassets have a peculiar style of hunting. Their scenting powers are extraordinary and are possibly equal to that of the BLOODHOUND. This is no mere coincidence. The Bloodhound also came from Normandy and it is a fact that the Basset's head is required to be remarkably similar to the Bloodhound's in appearance.

The Breed Standard calls for the same pronounced peak, insists that the head have heavy FLEWS and deeply sunken eyes; British requirements also demand a long, narrow head. All of this produces a dog remarkably solemn in appearance. A stolid, worthy, slightly mournful character, a caricature of a High Court judge.

Basenji.
Top left A Basenji will draw its paw over its ears and nose as an invitation to play. But this dog's hurt look comes from its profusely wrinkled forehead, a breed characteristic, not from refusals.
Bottom left Ch. Reveille Re-Up.

Right Basset Hound. Fredweil Charmar.

This appearance is wildly deceptive.' Prospective owners viewing solemn puppies must accept that, young or old, a Basset Hound will never have the sedentary habits of an elderly schoolmaster. Moreover one must accept that they are not ideal town dogs despite the fact that an ever-growing number are kept in cities throughout the world. This phenomenon is in part due to the popularity brought upon them by the use of the breed to advertize the brand of footwear called 'Hush Puppies'. The advertizers undoubtedly intended the dogs to sell the shoes. All the evidence is that the shoes are selling the dogs!

A mere home in the country is not sufficient. What Bassets need is ample exercise, that is, galloping over fields once or twice a week. Left to amuse themselves they develop a taste for wandering, and the countryside has ample opportunity to hear their remarkable voices.

The growth rate of this breed has been quite phenomenal. The indications are that this rise has not ended. Purists deplore the fact that numerous Bassets find their way into unsuitable homes which have not faced the fact that Bassets are large and hearty beasts.

It would be sad if this fact led later to a loss of goodwill. There is nothing wrong with the dog. Nothing except that it is frequently chosen by the wrong people.

Essentials of the breed: In general appearance a short-legged hound of considerable substance. Head: domed with prominent peak. Skull: of medium width, tapering slightly to the muzzle. Foreface: comparatively lean, moderate wrinkle and skin on head very loose; heavily flewed. Nose: black except in light-coloured hounds. Eyes: brown or hazel. Expression: calm and serious. Showing slight red haw. Ears: low set, very long, reaching at least to end of muzzle. Supple, fine and velvety mouth, a scissors bite. Shoulder-blades laid back, forelegs short, powerful; elbows turned neither in nor out. Knees: slightly crooked inwards. Knuckling over is a bad fault. There may be wrinkles of skin between knee and foot. Breast bone is prominent, back rather broad, level, withers and quarters approximately the same height, hindquarters muscular, hocks low to ground, feet massive, well padded, and forefeet either straight ahead or turned slightly out. Tail should be long, high set, tapering to tip, carried well up and curving gently over back. Coat: smooth, short and close. Colour: generally black, white and tan, or lemon and white but all recognized hound colours acceptable. Height (AKC): should not exceed 14 inches; over 15 inches disqualifies.
See colour plate p. 185.

Bat Ears Ears so-called because they resemble those of a bat, that is, erect, rather broad at the base, usually rounded in outline and facing directly forward.

The expression 'bat-eared' is used most commonly to describe the FRENCH BULLDOG and this is presumably because this feature shows the most marked distinction in head characteristics between the French and the English Bulldog. Other breeds also have bat ears of a type, for example the WELSH CORGIS, CHIHUAHUAS and, despite the fringes, even PAPILLONS.

Above Bat ears.

Left Basset Hound. The stolid, worthy, slightly mournful look of the Basset is wildly deceptive: it is energetic and joyous, especially on the trail.

Right Bathing a dog. A veterinary shampoo should always be used in preference to ordinary soap which is too harsh for a dog's sensitive skin.

Bathing a Dog While bathing is the most common method of keeping a dog clean, it is also the most inefficient. Some would go as far as to say that baths are totally unnecessary because a dog does not perspire through its skin.

While this is perhaps over-stating the case, it is a fact that regular brushing with the correct brush (see GROOMING) will keep a dog perfectly clean. There are, however, occasions when a bath is still necessary. One example would be medicated baths as prescribed or administered by a veterinarian. Since each of these would require different methods for different purposes there is no point in generalizing on them here.

Another instance would be when a dog has become particularly dirty through, for example, digging in the coal cellar or crawling under a car. Alternatively bathing may be necessary if the dog smells.

A veterinary shampoo should always be used, as many soaps manufactured for human beings are too harsh for the sensitive skin of a dog.

The dog should be stood in a sink, bath or suitable container and, before starting, the dog's ears should be plugged with cotton wool. The dog should then be rinsed all over with clean water, after which the shampoo should be rubbed in, starting from the head but taking particular care to keep the soap out of the eyes. Work down the dog's back and then down the legs to the feet. Afterwards, rinse thoroughly in clean, running water. Repeat the whole process and your dog is ready to be dried, something it will be only too pleased to organize for itself if given the opportunity.

The dog should then be taken or carried to a place where you do not mind having a shower bath, for it will certainly want to shake itself. Half the moisture will be disposed of in a matter of moments!

After this, dry thoroughly with a rough towel. If the weather is pleasant and mild, take the dog for a short walk on a lead, when body heat will dry off the remaining dampness. Before the dog is completely dry you should brush the coat carefully, and in the way you want it to grow.

they follow by the exquisiteness of their scent, and trace her footsteps through all her various windings with such exactness and perseverance that they afford most excellent diversion, and generally reward the hunter's toil with the death of the wearied fugitive. Their tones are soft and musical and add greatly to the pleasure of the chase.'

During that period, Beagles were often so small that they could be carried in the pockets of hunting coats. It was even reported that 10 to 12 couples of Beagles

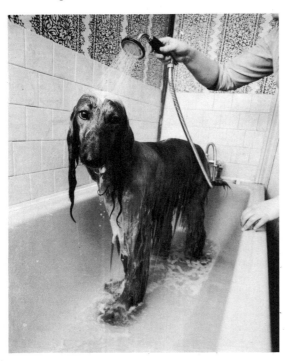

Bay The voice of a hound when on a fresh trail.

Beagle This dog was bred originally for use in tracking hare in the British Isles and in France, but it has achieved its greatest popularity in the United States and Canada where it is used for hunting the cottontail rabbit. More than 60,000 dogs a year are registered by the American Kennel Club.

There is considerable doubt as to the origin of the breed name. But it probably meant the 'smallest of the hounds'. In support of this belief, three roughly similar words are given, all of which meant 'small'. These are the Celtic, *beag*; the French, *beigh*; and the Old English, *begle*.

Perhaps the earliest use of the name occurs in the *Esquire Of Low Degree* published in 1475. It speaks of
"*With theyr beagles in that place*
And seven score raches at his rechase."
Raches was a name for a larger breed which is mentioned in Juliana Berners' *Boke of St. Albans*, a treatise on hunting and hawking which was published in 1486. By the time Thomas Bewick published his *General History Of Quadrupeds* in 1790, he could write that the Beagle is the smallest of the English dogs used for the chase, and it '... is only used in hunting the hare, although far inferior in point of speed to that animal,

could be carried in panniers, or saddle baskets, hanging from each side of the horse.

At various times in the history of the United States and Canada, the decline of upland game has led to an increased interest in the pursuit of the cottontail rabbit. At such times, the popularity of the Beagle has increased. In 1954, the Beagle led all other breeds in American Kennel Club registrations. Though now supplanted by three other breeds in total registrations, its popularity remains steady.

Beagles are sometimes used in packs, often with huntsmen on horseback. But for the most part, they are used singly, or in couples, by huntsmen on foot. Once started, the cottontail tends to travel in a large circle, so the huntsman is able to remain in roughly the same spot. He can then enjoy the music of the Beagle voice and can wait for the rabbit to come into view, or to go to cover. A change in the Beagle's voice usually advises him of the latter.

Oversize Beagles, as well as HARRIERS, are used in some tropical countries, such as Ceylon and Venezuela, for hunting jaguars and leopards where they are used in packs. The cornered leopard, surrounded by swiftly circling and feinting dogs, tends to lie down. The dogs keep it there until the hunters come up.

Beagles have become the most popular RESEARCH

Far left Bathing a dog. Regular grooming with the correct brush is more efficient than bathing for keeping a dog clean. But there are occasions when a bath seems proper: this Afghan is getting ready for Cruft's Show.

Beagle.
Above In the Middle Ages, Beagles were so small they could be carried in the pockets of hunting coats. Now there are two sizes: thirteen inches or under, and between thirteen and fifteen inches. This dog is thirteen inches tall.

Opposite top left A fifteen-inch Beagle. Ch. Kings Creek Triple Threat.
Opposite right Ch. Pinewood Crumpet.

DOGS for laboratory and medical research. This is because of their small size and uniformity in weight. Large colonies of genetically bred Beagles are now being produced in kennels and germ-free laboratories.

In the United States and Canada, Beagle field trials are very popular. Field events, sanctioned and licensed, constitute the largest single activity of the American Kennel Club, with some 3,000 annually. Beagle trials outnumber those for all other breeds combined. Trials may last four days or longer. As many as 250 dogs may

compete in a single event. Stakes are divided by sex and by size with those for dogs and bitches 13 inches or under at the shoulder and for dogs and bitches over 13 and not over 15 inches tall.

In the United States and Canada, Beagles are less fancied as show dogs, though they are always represented. In this respect, they are far more popular in their native islands. The same size varieties apply at bench shows as at field trials. Dogs as small as 10 inches at the shoulder have won championships. But as a rule, 13-inch Beagles tend to approach that height, and the large hounds will mostly measure 14 inches or over. In the United States, each Best of Variety winner competes in the hound group for higher honours. In England, and in many other countries, the two sizes must compete for Best of Breed, and only that winner enters the Group.

Essentials of the breed: The skull is fairly long and slightly domed at the occiput, with the cranium broad. The ears are set at about eye level and the rounded tips reach to the tip of the nose. The eyes are large, are set wide apart, and are hazel or brown in colour. The teeth meet in a scissors bite. The muzzle is clean, with no flews, and the neck is free of throatiness. Head faults include a Roman nose or a dish face.

The chest: deep, reaching to the elbows, and broad. The back: short and slightly arched over the loins. Long and sway backs are faults. The feet have close toes, well knuckled up, with deep, hard pads. The legs have sufficient bone to balance the sturdiness of the body. Flat feet, spreading toes, knuckling over at the knees, and out at elbows are faults. Stifle angulation is not excessive. The tail is set moderately high and is carried gaily, but never 'squirrel' fashion over the back. Colour can be 'any true hound colour'. However, there is a saying that: 'No good hound can be a bad colour.' In general, the Beagle looks like a miniature English FOXHOUND.

See colour plate p. 185.

Beard The thick, long hair of the underjaw in some breeds. It is usually brushed forward for shows.

Bearded Collie see Collie, Bearded.

Beauceron see Rare Breeds.

Beauty Spot This term is used in connection with Boston Terriers and Blenheim Spaniels in particular because they have a spot of coloured hair set in a white blaze on the skull between the ears.

Bedding Wood wool (fine wood shavings) is perhaps the best material for the kennel dog's bed. It is clean and hygienic and can be readily changed. Good wheaten straw, when available, is another very good form of bedding but, of course, it can harbour fleas and other insects. Pine or cedar shavings are used in some kennels but they tend to become hard and uncomfortable very quickly. Rugs and blankets are too expensive for general kennel use but are ideal for the home and toy kennels.

Whatever the form of bedding, it must be changed at least once a week, more often if two dogs or more share one bed. Beds should be made every day, wood wool, shavings and straw being shaken up, rugs and blankets unruffled and tidied. Foam rubber, two inches thick, and covered with waterproof material, makes a comfortable bed.

Dogs that are not given sufficient bedding are liable to have BED SORES. These can become infected and are painful to the dog. Whatever the bedding consists of, it must be deep enough to ensure that the bed is soft and so prevent pressure on bony parts of the dog's body. See BEDS.

Bedlington Terrier The Bedlington Terrier is an essentially British breed. It has been around for a long time. It probably originated in Northumberland, after which, as in so many 'histories' of dogs, intelligent guesswork and supposition must take the place of documented facts.

The earliest recorded Bedlington, not, it should be noted, then carrying this breed name, is said to be a dog called *Old Flint*, owned by Squire Trevelyan and whelped in 1782. His descendants are said to have been directly traceable until 1873.

From 1873 onwards life becomes easier for canine historians because the English Kennel Club was formed, and it collected and maintained accurate records.

Its first stud book contains the names of 30 Bedling-

tons. Almost inevitably, however, the majority of them were listed as pedigree 'not recorded', as 'unknown' or even as 'uncertain'! Only eleven of them had the names of their parents recorded and as these are usually *Scamp, Bess, Daisy, Rock* or others equally unidentifiable, there is no way of discovering whether or not they reach back to the original *Old Flint*.

During the uncharted years of the early nineteenth century these dogs were known as Rothbury Terriers largely because a well known dog of the breed, *Piper Allan* lived in this town.

In 1825 Mr. Joseph Ainsley, a mason, owner of a 'Young Piper' gave his dog the breed name of Bedlington Terrier. Once again there was a local or Northumbrian flavour, but the name stuck and became universal.

Opinions differ on whether the DANDIE DINMONT contributed in some way to the Bedlington or vice versa. Certainly the early specimens of both breeds had much in common.

As the breed became less used for its original task of going to ground in search of vermin and more in demand as a surface catcher of rabbits, its form and outline altered. The short legs were replaced by long ones, the robust and rugged frame by one more elegant and streamlined. Nobody has ever denied that the WHIPPET played some part in this transformation.

The combination of the gameness and endurance of the terrier and the fleetness of a racing hound made the dog invaluable for poachers. Even to this day some refer to the Bedlington as the 'Gypsy Dog'.

At the turn of the century, the breed took on a new role. It became the smart, drawing-room companion of the sophisticated. Surprisingly, in view of its working background, it produced gentle manners and a love of luxury.

At the same time the art of trimming, barbering, poodle faking – call it what you will – improved immeasurably; from being a rough and ready removal of surplus coat, it developed into an artistic shaping of the dog to enhance its already distinctive silhouette. The head became more pear-shaped, the brisket deeper, the hindquarters more powerful and sweeping. The coat is cut with scissors and although patience and time is necessary there is less skill demanded than in the preparation of most other terriers.

When moving, their action is light, springy, almost mincing in the slower paces. When galloping however their whole muscular bodies come into play; the spine almost jack-knifing, causing the hind legs to pass in front of the fores in the same way as GREYHOUNDS.

Bedlingtons have never been really popular, but there is little risk of their fading from the scene: Bedlington fanciers insist that once the breed has cast its spell on you there is no escape.

Not everybody would try very hard to escape the charms of a breed which so successfully combines the merits and virtues of terrier and hound, and couples with them a handy size and pleasing disposition.

Essentials of the breed: A graceful, muscular dog with pear-shaped head and distinctive mincing light action in slower paces. Head and skull, narrow. Jaw, long and

Bedlington Terriers have evolved from short-legged, robust-framed vermin catchers to graceful and streamlined rabbit hunters. But they have not lost their ratting skills.
Top left A modern Bedlington with the distinctive pear-shaped head and roached back. Ch. South Moors Dandie Desmo.
Bottom left Early Bedlingtons: Mr F. Armstrong's *Rosebud* and Mr A. Armstrong's *Nailor*.

Right Perrianne Petula.

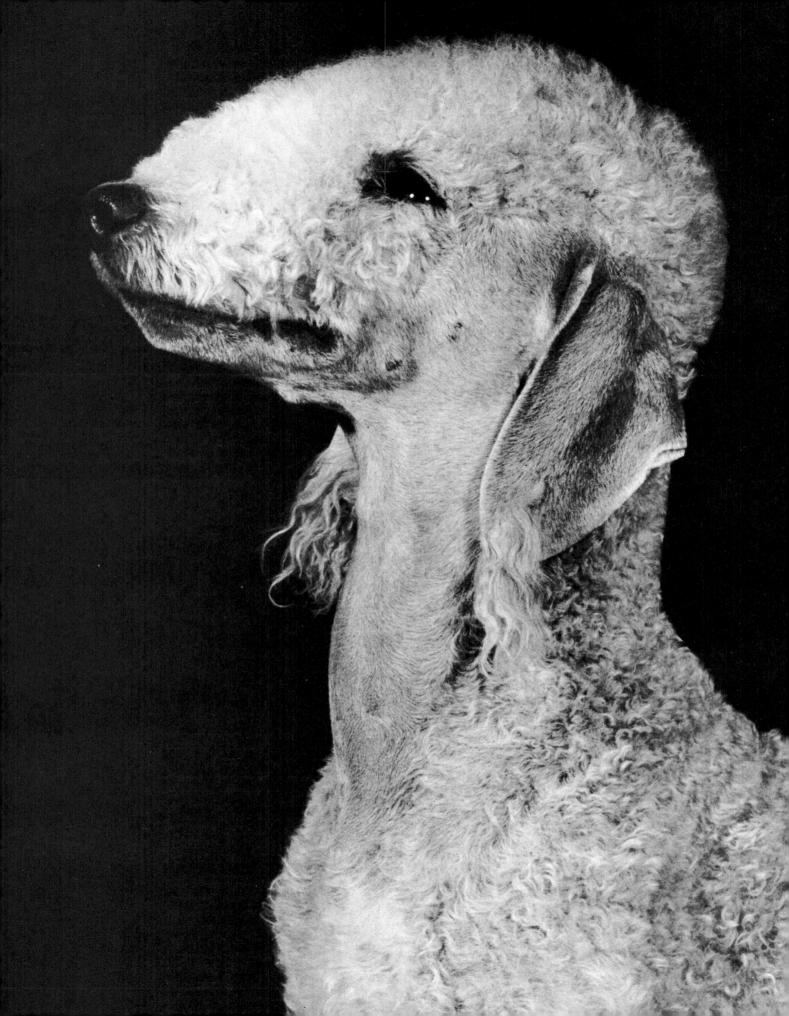

tapering. No stop. Nose: black for blues and tans, brown for livers and sandies. Eyes: small, bright, dark for blues and lighter for livers and sandies. Ears: filbert-shaped, low set, hanging flat to cheek. Mouth: level or pincer-jawed, neck long, tapering; no throatiness. Forelegs: straight, wider apart at the chest than at the feet. Body: muscular yet flexible, flat, ribbed deep through brisket. Back: roached and loin arched. Muscular, galloping quarters, fine and graceful. Hindquarters muscular, hind legs, because of the roached back and arched loin having the appearance of being longer than fores. Feet: long with ample pads. Tail: thick, tapering, gracefully curved, set on low. Coat: thick and linty, standing well out, not wiry, but with a tendency to twist, particularly on head. Colour: blue, blue and tan, liver or sandy. Height (AKC): dogs 16½ inches; bitches 15½ inches. Weight: 17 to 23 lb.
See colour plate p. 376.

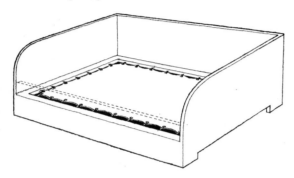

Beds All beds whether in the kennel or in the home should be raised off the floor to avoid draughts. Most kennel dogs are accommodated in raised benches, the size depending on the breed of the dog and the number expected to occupy it.

There are many different dog beds on the market for the dog who lives in the house. These vary from reasonably priced wicker baskets, boxes and canvas beds to the ultra smart expensive 'dog houses' fully carpeted and lined with silk.

Until a puppy has finished teething (around six months) which encourages chewing, a home-made bed is satisfactory. This can be built with three sides of wood and the bottom made of either wood or webbing. It should be raised off the floor by the addition of legs.

Puppies should be encouraged to feel at home even in temporary boxes or wire crates. Dogs in their wild state live in caves, and domestic dogs soon learn to accept a wooden box or wire crate as a safe sanctuary. Enclosed boxes may help in HOUSE TRAINING, as no dog or puppy likes to soil its bed.

Beds are a matter of what is best for the particular household and any well-mannered dog who has been sensibly brought up will fit in anywhere.

During the last year beds made of fibre glass have been developed. Originally these beds were not successful as the occupant chewed the edges, but it is now possible to buy fibre glass beds with aluminium welded onto the edges, which overcomes the problem. These beds are clean, and do not need extra rugs.
See BEDDING.

Bed Sores These are sores that develop when a dog lies on a hard surface, the weight of the animal damaging the skin. They are usually on the external aspects of the elbow, hock and stifle and are usually an indication that a soft bed, or blanket, should be supplied for the dog. They are especially common in the large and heavy breeds.

Bed sores will also develop on a dog that lies for long periods because of illness or age. In a case of this nature, the problem is one that the veterinarian must treat.

Beefy Unusually heavy muscular development of the hindquarters, as seen in some BULLDOGS.

Behaviour Patterns This is a term which modern psychologists prefer to use in place of such words as 'instinct'. Instinct has often been used to refer to a spontaneous action which we see, but do not understand, and the action is usually based upon a complex of forces. Instinct is sometimes defined as the taking of a proper action automatically, without premeditation, and without prior learning. It is inherited. Apparently instincts can be strengthened by selective breeding and they may be modified by other factors, both inherited and learned.

The puppy instinctively finds its way to its mother's nipple. If separated from the mother and the other pups, it will crawl slowly and indecisively, but in a circle, to try to regain the nest. Once back, it will crawl over and under other puppies in its effort to reach a nipple. If that particular breast is no longer producing an adequate milk supply, the puppy will try to displace another at one which is giving a richer quantity.

Later, the puppy will learn to lap. It can do this because its jaw and tongue are properly formed for lapping. Thus, this instinct is bound to body form, the nervous system, and also to the gene which orders it to operate. Yet it is not easy to say that the lapping is entirely due to instinct. The puppy sees its mother lapping. Or the owner pushes the puppy's nose into the milk. The puppy chokes, licks its lips, and then the instinct orders it to lap. Perhaps, then, learning also plays a part.

There are other factors which commonly confuse the observer. One is intelligence. Others are trainability, mental capacity or the ability to learn more and more, and attention focusing. The latter is sometimes inseparable from trainability. Dogs and children which will not pay attention learn very little, yet they may have a high degree of intelligence for, say, problem-solving.

Careful studies have indicated that there is little or no difference in the intelligence quotient of the various breeds of dogs when all modifying factors have been eliminated as nearly as is possible. But individuals have differed greatly. It is not definitely known whether intelligence is an inheritable trait. But certainly the capacity to learn and trainability are genetic traits. For example, certain breeds are, as a whole, difficult to train because few of them will give you their attention. Sometimes, their attention can be held for only a brief period.

Left Beds should be raised off the floor and be enclosed on at least three sides to avoid draughts. The sides on the bed illustrated would be 7½ inches deep on a bed 2 feet wide, and 10 inches deep on a 3-foot bed. The dotted line indicates the top of a front panel to hold in any extra bedding.

Some canine qualities appear to be pure instincts. There will be others which, for want of a better term, can be called hereditary aptitudes. And there will be still others which are so involved by other factors that only 'behaviour patterns' covers them.

We are able to house-break puppies because they inherit from their den dwelling ancestors the instinct to keep their beds clean. The first staggering, half crawling, steps of the puppy will take him to the edge of the nest where he will relieve himself. The cow, in contrast, is a range animal. It has no permanent bed and there is no necessity for it to keep its territory clean. So it cannot be house-broken by man, despite thousands of years of domestication. Few, if any, monkeys can be house-broken, despite their high order of intelligence. They simply lack this particular instinct.

Many dogs turn around two or three times before lying down. Some try to scratch up their rugs. They then try to sleep upon the pile which must be extremely uncomfortable. These dogs are often house dogs; they have been taken from their mothers at weaning; they have never seen a wolf or a feral dog make a bed. The wandering wolf, unable to find a den, hunts a tree whose roots are above ground. In the depression leaves will have blown. The wolf turns about two or three times, stirs up the leaves, then curls into the hollow. It is protected from the wind, and the leaves may hold part of the scent which might be carried down wind to a possible enemy.

When house dogs do this, they are performing an instinctive, but useless and unintelligent action. However, if these dogs were to be lost in a forest, the instinct would operate in a useful manner.

Certain breeds, such as the GERMAN SHEPHERD and the DOBERMANN PINSCHER, have extremely strong guardian instincts. They combine the instinct with aggressiveness, (the latter may be partly instinct, partly an aptitude, and partly training). We could call the combination a behaviour pattern. Since these breeds are of recent origin and are the result of crossing various earlier breeds to achieve certain goals, it is evident that the behaviour pattern has been inherited.

In sections on the ANCESTORS and DOMESTICATION of the dog, it has been pointed out that the dog and wolf are mortal enemies. This is almost certainly an inherited instinct. Their mutual instant reaction on first contact is to kill.

Similarly, thousands of outdoorsmen have been astonished at the instant reaction of their dogs to their first contact with a deer. The dogs may have been trained to trail only rabbits or foxes. Or they may be wind-scent hunters, such as the setters or spaniels. Yet at the sight of the startled deer, they give instant chase, leaving their frustrated owners shouting uselessly behind. This, too, must be an ancient, but strongly inherited, instinct.

Dogs hunt in one of three ways. Some, such as the GREYHOUND, hunt by sight. Some follow game trails, working out the trail by careful sniffing of scents. Still others – the setters and the spaniels – raise their noses and test the wind for scents borne by air currents from the bodies of the quarry. Most students believe that these are true instincts. They may be combined with other factors so that they become a behaviour complex. Training affects them. Thus, both the sight hunter and the wind-scent dog may learn to trail. Many a trained pheasant dog learns to trail and capture the crippled pheasant.

An example of how instinct will prevail over training can be shown in the following case. The dogs involved were an ENGLISH SPRINGER SPANIEL thoroughly trained as a wind-scent dog to locate and flush pheasants, and a WHIPPET. The latter is a sight hunter. His quarry is the rabbit or hare. The owner took the two dogs for a walk in a large, flat field of corn stubble. There was an inch or so of snow upon the ground. A rabbit was started about 10 yards in front of both dogs, and both gave chase.

When pressed, the rabbit made a sudden right angle change of course. The Whippet, unable to make the turn, fell into a somersault. But when it righted itself, it was facing in the direction of the rabbit, and it continued the chase. But the spaniel over-ran the turning point by 20 yards. It stopped, obviously puzzled, then began to run in circles. Finally it picked up the trail and began to follow it.

One can interpret the spaniel's actions in this way. Both dogs saw the rabbit, and both began to hunt by sight. But then, the wind-scent instinct took over in the spaniel, after he failed to see the rabbit turn.

As long ago as biblical times, observant people noted that 'a dog will return to its own vomit'. This, too, may be instinct. The dog must carry things in its mouth. But it must also use its teeth to defend itself. A bitch with puppies might have to hunt for an entire day to find food for herself and her brood. In case of danger, it might be unwilling to drop the food for fear that it would be stolen. The solution would be to swallow it. Later, after the threat had passed, the bitch would return to her puppies and regurgitate the food for them.

However, the urge to empty the stomach in times of great danger is itself instinctive, or at least it is a reaction of the autonomic nervous system. When preparing for flight or fight, the dog clears its stomach, and if there is time it may empty its bladder and bowels as well. If a fight develops and the dog is successful, it will then retrieve its meal.

Dogs have very different methods of fighting. These may be instincts which have developed along with body structure. For example, the BULLDOG grabs and hangs on. He may do this instinctively. But he has a short, *brachycephalic* skull and pushed back nose which makes it possible to hang on without interference with his breathing.

BULL TERRIERS, with their amazingly heavy jaws (all that bone before the eyes, as the breeders say), tend to crush and worry into deeper holds. They are intent upon crushing bones and destroying flesh. Here again, the jaw formation and the unusually well developed cheek muscles make this method both possible and successful.

Greyhounds are coursing dogs. They are fairly tall, but are lightly built and graceful. In the chase, they tend to slash with their jaws and teeth, so as to slow down and cripple the quarry. Here again an instinctive system of fighting is combined with body formation. In a dog fight, the Greyhound tends to dash in and out against his opponent, slashing with his own teeth while trying to avoid those of the other dog.

Some dogs, unless driven into a terrible rage, are poor fighters. They may nip and do little or no damage. Their nips may be a sort of token, given as an attempt to avoid a real battle. Other dogs appear to have an instinct to grab and back up. Finally, there are dogs which fight silently, while others roar and cry.

A modern analogy may indicate to some degree how

be driven over the causeways and into the huts of the primitive herders. Three types of dogs had to be eliminated: those that bit and held on; those which chopped their way into the flesh; and those which slashed and crippled. What was needed was a dog which would nip but not cause damage. The dog had to fight silently, since the roaring fighter might cause the flock or herd to stampede. Dogs are often said to be servile animals. But the shepherd's dog had to have a sufficiently domineering personality to drive the cattle, as well as the courage and size to fight predators.

In like manner, primitive men bred both sight and trailing hounds. They must have seen the necessity to breed selectively for the long-jawed Greyhounds and

these various types of dogs came to be developed. A lion tamer does not teach his lion a new trick. The lion cub was cage bred, as probably also were his parents. The lion tamer watches a litter of cubs. As they grow they play and engage in mock fights. Suddenly, the man sees a cub do something which he has seen no other cub do before. Perhaps later, the cub repeats this.

The trainer then works out a method of teaching the cub to repeat the action, or an adaptation of it, into what will become a trick. The trainer has not really taught the lion anything. He has only trained it to release an instinctive behaviour pattern at a given signal. The lion must perform upon command that action which it did naturally.

Our unknown predecessors recognized certain actions in their dogs, and they related them to necessity. After the domestication of sheep and cattle, primitive men needed a flock or herd guardian. They observed those dogs which had some degree of guardian instinct, plus a natural aggression. They selected these dogs, and they selectively bred them, to become shepherd dogs. But sheep have to be herded and cattle must be driven. At night, for example, they had to

Wolfhounds. And they must have fixed and improved slashing instincts. They noted that some dogs would pull a load. And so they developed the great sledge dogs of the Arctic. Dogs which, during a fight, grabbed and backed up, were altered in conformation so that they could enter burrows. They could then seize and back up, thereby dragging the quarry from the burrow.

Today, comparatively few dogs are selectively bred for their instincts, aptitudes, and learning capacities. Sporting and hound breeds are still bred for hunting and coursing. Greyhounds are bred for coursing and track racing. With the exception of the Border COLLIE, KELPIE, and AUSTRALIAN CATTLE DOG, the shepherd breeds are rarely used. The vast majority of purebred dogs are bred for conformation and for house pets. The ancient instincts and behavioural patterns have been diffused, so that they may appear in mongrels, or even in breeds not associated with those patterns. One can observe, for instance, the ancient urge to drive and herd in the thousands of dogs, mongrels and purebreds, which chase bicycles and autos, or which nip at the heels of running children.

Above Behaviour patterns. Whippets will slash with jaws and teeth as they run down a quarry, and continue to do so during a race.

Behaviour Patterns – Aberrant Abnormalities of behaviour have been classified into many types. Some specific examples have been given in other sections on BEHAVIOUR PATTERNS. Here we can classify other major types. There are those which are caused by disease; those due to bodily changes during old age; to traumatic experiences of puppies; to genetic factors; to environmental factors; sexual aberrations; frustration behaviour; spite reactions; and pica, or depraved appetite. An often seen abnormality is the male dog which has become feminized to the extent that other males are attracted to it, as they would be to a female in oestrus. In such cases, the cause can often be discovered as a testicular tumor in the sertoli cells.

Old age brings changes in many dogs. They may become crotchety, deaf, and blind. Many of them lose control of their kidneys to some extent. It often happens that a bitch, which has been spayed too young, will develop incontinence.

Sometimes, emotion shattering, or traumatic experiences, make a permanent imprint upon the dog. This can happen when a very young puppy is plumped down upon the veterinarian's examining table, and is then hurt. The dog may thereafter fear the veterinarian, his hospital, and even tables. Some dogs are so severely injured by traumatic experiences that, when similar circumstances seem imminent, the fight or flight reaction occurs. They may vomit, urinate, and empty the bowels. And they may react savagely by attacking. Long isolation during the socialization and adaptive periods causes what dog breeders commonly call 'kennel shyness'. Although the dog may adapt to some extent, recovery is never quite complete.

Right Behaviour patterns – aberrant. Psychological disturbance may be a cause of persistent barking. Or a noisy dog may simply be bored.

Shyness and fear-biting are often genetic factors. Some breeds are notably timid with people, but show no tendency to attack out of fear. The fear-biter, in sudden insane terror, attacks because it fears an attack. For example, a small mongrel dog was lying on its master's lap, sleeping, while the owner read the evening paper. The man turned the page. The dog awoke, and in sudden and unreasoned fear at the movement of the arm, bit its owner savagely. The dog had done this before. 'Always,' said the owner, 'the dog calmed down and seemed sorry for what he had done.'

The sort of timidity represented by fear-biting is usually inherited. The researcher Thorne showed that when a fear-biting Basset Hound was crossed with a Saluki of normal temperament the offspring inherited the fear-biting. In other crosses, a majority of the offspring were fear-biters.

Frustration always contributes to abnormal behaviour. For example, the tied dog is always more aggressive than one which has freedom. Many dogs appear to have more energy to use up than do others. Such dogs always suffer more from being tied. Perhaps at first, they lunge on the end of the chain just to get to people. But eventually, the lunging can include biting.

Dogs in runs try to amuse themselves in various ways. One is to run along the fence, barking at passers by, and barking even louder at passing dogs. They bark themselves into a frenzy, and often become biters.

It is supposed that dogs inherit the pack instincts of their wild ancestors. This may explain why a group of individually gentle puppies may combine to kill a child. Packs of roaming dogs are often responsible for killing flocks of sheep. Individually, these dogs might ignore sheep. But in a pack an ancient instinct takes over.

Frustrated dogs often suffer from boredom. They dig holes in the lawn, and they chew up everything except their toys. Occasionally, the chewing is due to spite, as will be shown later. Bored dogs often become compulsive eaters. An occasional one will chew and even swallow stones. This should not be confused with the typical puppy habit of investigating everything with its teeth; such a puppy is acting normally.

'Pica' is a technical term for a depraved appetite. The causes can be physical. Coprophagia – the eating of faeces – is sometimes caused by an endocrine disturbance, such as pancreatitis. It is believed also to be caused by an improper diet, especially one lacking in certain vitamins and minerals. HOOKWORM infestations are a common cause. Yet puppies investigate everything, and so it is natural for them to investigate stools, particularly if these are hard or are frozen. They may play with these because of boredom. The playing – and ingestion – can become a habit.

Thousands of dogs make life miserable for their owners by spite reactions. These dogs are invariably spoiled, over-indulged, and over-protected, except that an occasional dog may have a pathological fear of being left alone. Usually, the spite reactions occur when the dogs are left alone, or when there has been a change in household routine to which the dog objects. Its method of gaining revenge may be to howl until neighbours call the police. Or it may go into the master's bedroom and leave a stool in the middle of the bed. This seems to be a favourite method of revenge for such dogs.

Homosexuality has been noted among dogs. This may be the case when two dogs have been raised together since four or five weeks of age, and have had no opportunity for proper socializing with other dogs. Many such dogs will refuse to mate normally. A noted Irish Terrier champion had, what appeared to be, an undue modesty. He would refuse to mate in the presence of people, but would do so when certain that no person was watching.

Cannibalism is sometimes noted among bitches. The causes are not known. One bitch, which was known to do this, was watched carefully. She nursed her litter carefully, but was not allowed to be with the puppies at night. On the eighth night, she was left with them. In the morning, it was found that the entire litter had been devoured.

Peter Freuchen, the Arctic explorer, recorded the sad experience of a sledge dog which was forced to whelp while in harness with her mates. As each pup dropped, it was seized and eaten by one of the following dogs in the team. But as the last one was expelled, the bitch turned and devoured her own puppy. She then continued to pull with the team as before.

Behaviour Patterns in Puppies and Young Dogs

A puppy is born helpless, unable to stand, and with little if any ability to hear, and none to see. This is in direct contrast to the hyena pup, which can stand within an hour or so, can see and hear perfectly, and will attack viciously. The dog puppy will, nevertheless, react to certain stimuli: the puppy's brain is only partially developed; the motor cortex – the external grey layer of the brain – is the most advanced.

A number of reflexes which can be demonstrated in the newly-born puppy can also be shown to operate in the newly-born human infant. One is vocalization. Both cry when the need for attention is felt. Among the others are the crossed extensor and magnus reflexes. In the former, if you pinch one hind leg of the puppy, it will flex, but the other leg will stretch out, or extend. In the magnus, if the head is twisted to the right, then the limbs on that side will extend while those on the left side will flex.

An important reflex in the newly-born puppy concerns elimination. If the genital area of the puppy is gently massaged, urination and defecation take place. The bitch stimulates this by licking the parts. Dog breeders massage the area to prevent constipation in orphan puppies. This reflex disappears within the fourth week of life. It is somehow keyed to the puppy's increasing ability to walk and to leave the nest to relieve itself.

The ability to feel pain is very poor in the newly born puppy. Moreover, the nerves carrying pain sensations to the brain seem to tire very quickly, and even to cease to function. If the tail of a puppy is docked – cut off – at two to three days of age, the puppy may give a single cry. But then it will return to nursing or to sleep and will give no sign that it is experiencing any discomfort.

The so-called rooting reflex is present in the newly born puppy. It is this rooting reflex that pushes the

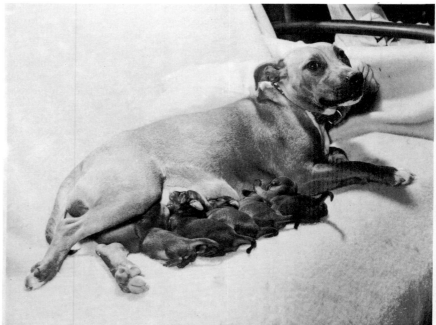

puppy to a nipple, and which will help it to burrow under other puppies in its quest. If a puppy is separated from its mates, and its head is gently touched, it will move forward. It can move for yards in this way, and will show astonishing endurance in doing so. This reflex disappears at about four weeks.

The newly-born puppy of even the long jawed breeds has a short muzzle. As the puppy nurses, it pushes into the breast in a regular rhythm. It has been suggested that this is done to push back the breast so that the puppy can breathe while sucking, but the full reasons for this are poorly understood. For example, it may be a method of stimulating milk production in the breast. This kneading of the breast ceases when the puppy is about four weeks of age.

Probably most puppies have their eyes open at 14 days of age. But their vision is still very poor for the retina does not become fully formed until sometime during the fourth week. At 14 days, puppies show no response to noise. But during the third week of life, the startle reflex begins to appear. At first, the noise will startle a sleeping puppy, while one which is awake will ignore the sound.

During the fourth week, the startle reflex to sound becomes pronounced. Both the ears and eyes are functional even though the section of the brain concerned with sight may not be complete before the seventh or eighth week. It is during this fourth week that the puppy begins to notice both its litter mates and people. Earlier it has shown little interest in its litter mates. Now it begins to see and recognize them. It tries to communicate. The first effort of the human baby to communicate is to smile. The puppy begins at the other end of the body. It wags its tail. At this stage the puppy also begins to practise growing up. It begins to growl and bark. It chews on the ears and legs of its litter mates. And it rolls and tumbles in mock fights. At this stage pain sensation is fully developed. If its mate bites too hard, the puppy howls.

Psychologists call this period in the life of a puppy the time of socialization. It is one of the two most critical in the psychological development of the puppy. The period begins at 21 to 24 days. For most puppies it may end at 35 days. But for some, it will continue as long as the 49th or 50th day of life. It shows interest in its litter mates, and it begins to investigate everything in sight. If one puppy investigates something, the others rush to help. Lack of colour in some breeds is sex-linked with deafness. But deafness is difficult to detect in puppies during the socialization period because they watch each other so carefully, and react so quickly as a group.

It is during the socialization period that the puppy makes his bond with man. An earlier relationship between the two is weak and, for the puppy, does not last. But if man and puppy associate during the period of 21 to 35 days, then a permanent dog-man bond will be fixed in the puppy. This bond, once strongly fixed, will never be entirely broken, regardless of the future experiences of the adult dog.

However, if a puppy is taken from its litter mates at, say 14 days of age, and then is raised without seeing

other dogs until the socialization period has passed, the puppy will be severely damaged psychologically. It may never recognize itself as a dog. Its territorial instinct will be abnormally strong. It will be extremely aggressive toward other dogs, male and female alike. It may be gentle with its human family while being a fear-biter and vicious towards strangers, or when in a strange environment.

Because this period of socialization is so vital to the mental health of the puppy, students of canine behaviour warn that puppies should not be taken from the litter before they are weaned. That is, they should remain in the nest until 42 to 49 days old. It is during the period of from 42 to 49 days of age that the second critical stage in the puppy's life begins.

Puppies must adapt to the world about them. Virtually all studies have shown that this adaptive stage comes between the sixth and twelfth weeks of life, although it may occasionally last until the fourteenth week. If, during this period, the puppy remains in a pen, it will adapt to pen life. Then when taken out, it will be shy and afraid. Although it may adapt, this adaptation will never be complete. For thousands of years, it has been the custom of experienced dog breeders to sell their puppies at six to seven weeks of age. Behavioural studies now show that this is the proper time to do so. The puppy then makes an easy and quick adjustment.

The instinct to seize a territory and to guard it, appears to be basic in virtually all living beings, including man, and it is strong in dogs. Both primitive and modern men have bred dogs selectively for it. It may be abnormally strong in dogs which were taken from the litter at four to five weeks of age.

Dogs seem to have an inherent understanding of territory; they are known to respect the rights of other dogs. Thus, if a dog enters territory claimed by another

Behaviour patterns in puppies and young dogs.
Top left New-born puppies are helpless, unable to stand, hear or see.
Middle left The 'rooting reflex' drives a puppy instinctively to its mother's nipple which it pushes back in a steady rhythm, maybe to ensure a regular breathing space while it nurses.
Bottom left The dam gently massages a tiny puppy's genital area with her tongue to help stimulate urination and defecation.

Above The period of socialization when puppies explore relationships with each other and with man is critical for a dog's psychological welfare.
Right When pups begin to grow up they practise barking and growling, and play at fighting.

dog, it does so rather timidly. The home dog, though perhaps both smaller and weaker, will drive out the intruder with a great show of courage and noise making. The intruder flees to neutral ground and the chaser is satisfied. But if it should enter the home territory of the chased dog, then the situation is reversed. The other dog becomes bold and aggressive, and drives off its former pursuer.

However, if during this adaptive stage, the puppy is taken to visit neighbourhood homes, including the children and dogs, then the territorial instinct seems to be weakened. The puppy adapts to the idea that the entire neighbourhood is its territory. It may permit, and even welcome, neighbourhood dogs into its home ground. But it may drive a strange dog out of the entire neighbourhood area.

During this period of adaptation, conditioned reflexes can be developed and 'fixed' in the puppy. For example, all owners want their dogs to come instantly when called, no matter what the dog is doing at the time. The following examples will indicate how this can be done.

A trainer of field dogs wishes to make his dogs come instantly when a whistle is blown. He has someone divert the attention of the puppies at the far end of the run. He does this at meal time. He then blows his whistle. The startled puppies see their master and rush to him. Meanwhile, he sets down the food pans. After a dozen repetitions, the puppies associate the whistle with the master rather than the food. So they become conditioned to respond instantly to the whistle signal to come.

Since a dog must use its jaws as hands, carrying and retrieving are basic instincts, although they are sometimes called inherited aptitudes. The latter term may be the more correct as both carrying and retrieving abilities appear to vary both by breed and in individual dogs. Professional trainers try to develop carrying and retrieving into useful acts. The trainer will not give severe formal training to puppies six to fourteen weeks old. But, as with coming when called, he may try to condition or fix the reflex action in the puppy during this adaptive stage. His problem will be this. Even though carrying and retrieving may be basic instincts or aptitudes, retrieving to the trainer's hand is not. The puppy may carry off the thrown object to a secluded spot where it can chew upon it at leisure. So the trainer puts a light cord upon the dog. He then draws the puppy to him, takes the retrieve from it, and rewards it with much petting and voice compliments. Two or three repetitions three times a day for a week will condition the puppy to retrieve to hand. Then, even if the lessons are not repeated for a year, the dog will always re-learn quickly.

Sexual drives become evident at about the fourth week of life. Puppies of both sexes mount each other and engage in typical pumping actions. This has been called sexual play, and it probably is common to all animals. The lamb, for instance, may try to mount its mother at three days of age. The mounting pattern starts first in the male. If bitches are spayed at twelve weeks, some of them may continue mounting the owner's leg

even when grown. Severe punishment will, of course, stop this.

The male begins to raise his leg to urinate at between five and ten months, depending both upon the breed, and the speed of development of the puppy. The act is not done as a learned response to seeing older dogs do it. Instead, it is controlled by a hormone. However, it is a well observed fact that female dogs may also raise a leg even when squatting to urinate.

Urinating is also a powerful sex stimulant. If given her freedom during œstrus, the female urinates in as wide an area as possible. It is her way of luring suitors. The male will urinate repeatedly during direct courtship. The urine of the female will contain traces of chemical odours which draw the male, and which may stimulate the release of powerful hormones into his own urine. But whether this actually is the case is not certainly known.

Urinating also serves as a means of communication. The dog approaches some landmark – a tree or stump, a post, or a fire hydrant, and releases a few drops of urine. He may then scratch with his back legs.

Another dog, reaching the spot, studies the odour left by the other dog. From this, he probably learns whether the first dog is friend or foe, whether it is sick or healthy, fed or hungry and, if a bitch, whether or not it is in oestrus (see OESTRUM). Bits of soil, carried to the area and left there during the scratching action of the hind legs, may also tell the second dog whence came the first, or give it other information, possibly even where it is going.

Urination is used by wolves and wild dogs to stake out a home territory. And it is often used to mark possession, or to identify or to locate it. Thus, a dog which is unable to eat all of its food, may then urinate in the food pan. A wolf, unable to eat all of its kill, may urinate on the remains as a warning to other wolves to stay away. Finally, many dogs will bury bones, then urinate on the spot so that they can relocate it easily. A Great Dane was thus observed to go daily to six buried bones. She would dig them up in turn, gnaw on them for a time, then rebury them, and would finish by urinating on the spot.

Belgian Malinois The Belgian Malinois is a variety of Belgian sheepdog which is known in its own country as the *Chien de Berger Belge Malinois*. It takes its name from the town of Mechlin, which is popularly called Malines. But it seems to have reached its greatest popularity in Central Belgium. Most authorities agree that it was standardized as a breed somewhat later than the Groenendael (BELGIAN SHEEPDOG) and BELGIAN TERVUREN. Others claim that the breed descends from Central European sheep and guard dogs.

In the period from 1912 to just before World War II, both herding and police dog trials were popular in Belgium. The Malinois distinguished itself in both types of trials. Despite this record, the Malinois has failed to achieve the popularity outside Belgium which has been granted to the Groenendael and the Tervuren. The Malinois resembles the GERMAN SHEPHERD in its general conformation, although it is smaller and more

Top right Belgian Sheepdog: the black, long-haired Groenendael has had exclusive right to this name since an American Kennel Club edict of 1959.

Bottom right Belgian Malinois. Ch. Lagardaire de la Mascotte Royale.

lightly made. It has been suggested that this resemblance is unfortunate, since it has caused the Malinois to be overshadowed by the world-wide popularity of the German dog. Those liking the size, substance, and heavier bone of the German Shepherd would tend to regard the Malinois as just a poor copy. They would then refuse to recognize the Malinois' undoubted qualities, such as agility, a great capacity for training, and an excellent temperament for guarding.

In the United States efforts were made to establish the breed. At first, the Malinois had to compete with the Groenendael and Tervuren under the general heading of Belgian Sheepdog. In 1959, the breeds were separated and the first two became the Belgian Sheepdog and the Belgian Tervuren respectively. However, there were so few Malinois in the country that full recognition was not given until 1965 when the American Kennel Club gave the breed full status and approved its standard. At present only a few dogs are registered annually, but the position may improve.

Essentials of the breed: The head of the Malinois is long, with the skull flat on top, and with a powerful muzzle. The muzzle, from tip of the nose to the stop is equal to the length of the skull from the stop to the occiput. The teeth should mesh into a scissors bite, although an even bite is permitted. The ears are triangular, and are carried erect.

The body resembles that of the German Shepherd in being slightly longer than it is tall. This is one of the major differences in conformation between the other Belgian breeds. The chest is deep, reaching to the elbow. There is also less slope from the withers to the rump than in the other Belgian breeds. The tail has a medium heavy brush. It reaches to the hock and is carried down when standing. In action it may be carried slightly above back level and tends to have a slight hook.

The coat is often called 'half a coat' in that it is not short enough to be called smooth, and not long enough to be called long. It is dense, and heavier about the neck and throat than on the body. There is a longer fringe on the back of the hind legs. Colour of the Malinois is tawny, flecked with black, or even slightly brindled. It is desirable that the head colour be as black as possible.

The Malinois is less heavily boned than the German Shepherd, and is somewhat straighter in pasterns. It lacks the radical angulation of the hind legs which is a feature of the German dog. The feet are rounded, strongly knuckled up, and deeply padded.

Belgian Sheepdog The modern history of all the varieties of the Belgian Sheepdog begins at the time when the need for sheep herding dogs in Belgium was declining. The European wolves had disappeared. Grazing lands were fenced. The coming of the railroads made long sheep drives to market unnecessary. But at the same time, dog shows were becoming popular.

In the past, breeders of sheepdogs had ignored type, and had usually bred for performance only. Now these breeders did not want their great dogs to disappear. Dog shows offered a chance to preserve the best types. The period was 1880 to 1890, and thereafter. At least six types had become more or less well established. Yet it proved difficult to get breeders first to agree on type, and then to breed for it.

In 1891, a Professor Reul gathered together a group of dogs which he studied for type. At the completion of his study, he recommended that dogs be bred for coat type and colour, as well as for conformation and herding ability. The Belgian Kennel Club did not at first agree to this. First recognition came from the Royal Society of St. Hubert, which recognized six varieties. In 1897, the Belgian Kennel Club decided to recognize three varieties for registration. One of these is the Groenendael or, as it is known in the United States, the Belgian Sheepdog. For the other varieties, see BELGIAN TERVUREN, and BELGIAN MALINOIS.

About 1880, M. Rose of the town of Groenendael had begun the breeding of black, long-haired sheepdogs. His black bitch, *Petite*, was born in 1885. Rose located a black male of similar type, named *Piccard D'Uccle*, bred by M. Bernaert. Rose bought Piccard and mated him with Petite. It was this mating which really begins the history of both the Belgian Sheepdog and the Belgian Tervuren.

The litter produced *Duc*, *Pitt*, *Baronne*, *Margot*, and *Bergere*. All figure in the pedigrees of modern Belgian Sheepdogs. Duc was a sensation as a show dog in 1898. As a result, many bitches were bred to him. Since M. Rose lived in the town of Groenendael, the long-coated black dogs became known as the Groenendael breed. The name has persisted, and is still used in many countries.

During World War I, these black Groenendaels, or Belgians, were trained for army service. For the most part they were used as messenger and Red Cross dogs. But some were used as guards, and as police dogs. Their reputation became so great that, after the war, any black German Shepherd was apt to be called a Belgian Sheepdog.

The Groenendaels became popular in France and The Netherlands. They were taken to the United States as early as 1907. At first, they did not prosper. But after World War I, their fame was so great that they gained a dominant position.

In 1959, the American Kennel Club granted to the Groenendael the exclusive use of the name, Belgian Sheepdog. At the same time, it granted separate breed status to the Belgian Tervuren, and the Belgian Malinois.

Though the Belgian Sheepdog has been bred almost entirely from pure black stock since the days of M. Rose, an occasional one shows an underlying sheen of liver or brown when seen in certain lights. Moreover, these blacks often show 'frost' about the muzzle when only two or three years of age. This causes those unfamiliar with the breed to believe that the dogs are old when, in fact, they are still quite young.

Since they are still basically sheepdogs, the Belgians show suspicion, but not fear, of strangers. The great rise to popularity of the German Shepherd causes many to think Belgian Sheepdogs to be black German Shepherds. Yet the two breeds differ sharply: the Belgian Sheepdogs are longer in coat, shorter in back, and lighter in bone than are the German Shepherds. This structure makes it possible to start and to stop

Below Belgian Sheepdog. When shepherding dwindled in Belgium, the popularity of this breed was saved and increased by shows.

suddenly, and to turn quickly. This agility is a valuable quality in a sheep-herding dog.

Essentials of the breed: The standard of the Belgian Sheepdog calls for a dog with proud head carriage and erect ears. Males should be 24 to 26 inches at the withers, and bitches 22 to 24 inches. The length, measured from the point of the breast bone to the point of the rump, should equal the height. Males under $22\frac{1}{2}$ or over $27\frac{1}{2}$ inches, and bitches under $20\frac{1}{2}$ or over $25\frac{1}{2}$ inches, must be disqualified from the show ring.

It is preferred that the dogs be totally black. But Belgians are permitted to have a small strip or patch on the forechest, between the pads of the feet, and on the tips of the hind toes. White on the tips of the front toes is a fault, but is allowed. Frosting on the chin and muzzle is common and is permitted. It may be white or grey.

The skull: flattened rather than rounded, and the muzzle moderately pointed, rather long, and not snipy. The length of the muzzle from the stop to the tip of the nose equals that of the skull from stop to occiput. The eyes are dark brown. Teeth form an even, or scissors, bite. The top line slopes slightly from withers to hip joints. The chest: deep, reaching to the elbow, and forming a gentle curve. The tail reaches the hock joint, and is carried high when at work, but without a hook. The feet are round, strongly knuckled up, and with deep pads. Disqualifications, besides height as mentioned, include viciousness, white except as mentioned above, hanging ears, and cropped or stump tail. See colour plate p. 297.

Belgian Tervuren Much of that which has been written about the BELGIAN SHEEPDOG, or Groenendael can be written about the Belgian Tervuren. In some countries, both breeds are shown in competition against each other as Belgian Sheepdogs. It is chiefly in the United States that the breeds have been separated, since 1959. At that time, there were only a few Tervurens in the country; but since then, the breed has prospered. Many of the best Tervurens have not been exported to the United States from Belgium, but from France and The Netherlands.

The history of the Belgian Tervuren is fairly well documented. M. F. Corbeel, of the town of Tervuren was a breeder of sheep dogs. He had a dog and a bitch, named *Tom* and *Poes*. Both were fawn-coloured, but with black tipped hair. Corbeel bred the two together, and from the resulting litter obtained a bitch named *Miss*. She was sold to a M. Danhieux who bred her to *Piccard D'Uccle*, the foundation sire of the Groenendaels, or Belgian Sheepdogs.

Piccard was a black. Yet he carried a factor for fawn. And as pointed out in the article on Belgian Sheepdogs, many of the blacks show a sheen of liver or brown under the black. The mating of Miss to Piccard D'Uccle produced a fawn with blackened tips, named *Milsart*. He was whelped before 1900. But he must have been a durable dog, for in 1907, he became the first Tervuren champion.

In most of the world, the Tervurens are less well known than are the black Belgian Sheepdogs. But since the two were given separate breed status in 1959, the Tervuren has made rapid progress in the United States.

Below Belgian Tervuren. Ambre de Château Blanc, Ch. Flair de Fauve Charbonne, and Ch. Kandice de Fauve Charbonne.

Rudy Robinson, an American pioneer importer of the blacks, imported the first registered Tervurens into the country in 1954.

Essentials of the breed: The standard for the Belgian Tervuren closely approximates to that of the Belgian Sheepdog. The major difference is in colour. In the Tervuren, it is a rich fawn to russet mahogany, with a black overlay. That is, the tip of each fawn hair should be blackened. On the chest, the colour is a mixture of black and grey. The face mask and ears are mostly black. The tail has a black tip. The under parts are a light beige. Some tendency to lose the blackened tip is seen on the bodies of some dogs. As with the Belgian Sheepdog, a bit of white is permitted on the chest. The tips of the toes may also be white.

The final colours often do not become set until the Tervurens are eighteen months old. Therefore, some allowance must be made for lighter coloured dogs under eighteen months. Dogs so black as to resemble the Belgians, and washed out colours, are to be penalized.

Disqualifications include males under 22½ and over 27½ inches at the shoulder, and bitches under 20½ or over 25½ inches. Other faults bringing disqualifications are hanging, hound ears, a cropped or stump tail, white markings other than those specified, and a pronounced undershot jaw.

See colour plate p. 296.

Belton A genetic factor which produces orange or blue belton mottling in ENGLISH SETTERS. It produces small spots of pigmented hair on the white background. In short-haired dogs the belton factor produces ticking, but in long-haired dogs, such as the English Setter, the colours are blurred. Liver and lemon may also produce belton colours.

Bernese Mountain Dog This breed is without doubt one of the most unfortunate in the world. For some reason which is difficult to explain, it has been virtually ignored by a large number of prominent dog breeding countries which can normally be guaranteed to welcome with open arms the unusual and the distinctive.

Until quite recently, fewer than fifty dogs were registered annually in the United States, and the dog was not included in the first hundred most popular breeds. In 1970, 103 were registered by the American Kennel Club.

In Britain, admitted to be an unusually strong market for dogs, the breed is virtually unknown. It is believed that two were imported some years ago and that another two arrived recently.

Since Britain and the United States each have strong spheres of influence, the result is that the Bernese is very much neglected in a score of Caribbean, Central and South American countries. Only continental Europe and Scandinavian countries have appreciated the value of this breed. The possibility is that in the near future this omission will be corrected.

In size and general outline the Bernese Mountain Dog is not unlike the GOLDEN RETRIEVER, and in movement

perhaps somewhat similar to the Scotch COLLIE. In coat texture it is rather like both of these breeds – perhaps at its best about mid-way between the two.

Colouring of the Bernese Mountain Dog, however, is sharply different from that of the Retriever. It is jet black but with rich tan markings. These markings are precisely placed, over each eye, on the cheeks and on the upper part of both fore and hind legs. And then for good measure there are huge symmetrical splashes of white: white feet, a white blaze on its head and a huge white star on its chest.

When you add to this striking appearance of cheerful good nature, robust constitution and a great aptitude for learning, it is easy to see that you have a potentially popular dog.

The legend is that the Roman Legions took them to Switzerland 2,000 years ago. With their armies strung out all over Europe supply lines and depots were important. These needed guarding. And the Romans realized the importance of dogs for this work. The depots in the Alps were a particular problem because of the severe climatic conditions. Only strong, hardy dogs would do. These dogs, which were originally like long-haired MASTIFFS, filled the bill.

Their descendants stayed on in Switzerland. They became acclimatized and took up other work for which they were equally well suited. They became DRAUGHT DOGS, and used to pull small carts, particularly for the weavers in the canton of Berne.

Slowly but surely, the more spectacular ST. BERNARD with its glamorous background and history began to push the Bernese from favour. By the beginning of this century, they were extremely rare. Those which did exist were frequently of poor quality.

Then a prominent Berne citizen took a hand. He searched all over the country, collected the best, and bred from them. He formed a breed club to popularize the breed, and helped to put the Bernese Mountain Dogs back on their feet again.

Now they are firmly established in Switzerland and are becoming better known in neighbouring countries. One day they may become well-known everywhere.

Essentials of the breed: A balanced active dog between 21 and 27 inches high according to sex. Head has definite stop, strong jaw, dark eyes, V-shaped ears close to head. Compact body and broad chest. Tail covered with long hair carried fairly low. Colour: jet black with deep tan markings on all four legs, spot above forelegs, on chest and over each eye, preferably with white feet, tail tip, star on chest and blaze on forehead.
See colour plate p. 290.

Bichon Frise The term 'bichon' has often been used to refer to a family of small, usually white, dogs to which the Belgian Bichon, the MALTESE, and the Teneriffe Dog belong. The latter has been introduced into the United States as the Bichon Frise. It is said to be a breed of quite old lineage. The Bichon Frise Club of America is now well established, and more than 1,000 of the breed have been registered with it. The breed has yet to be recognized by the American Kennel Club.

Bernese Mountain Dog.
Top left Ch. Florian von Goetschiacker.
Bottom left The breed has precise deep tan markings on the legs and chest and over each eye. White feet, tail tip, blaze and star on the chest complete the distinctive patterning.

Right Bichon Frise was the name given to the small, white Teneriffe Dog on its introduction to the United States.

Essentials of the breed: The standard calls for a dog between 8 and 12 inches at the shoulder, slightly longer than tall, pure white, or with cream, apricot, or grey on the ears, and occasionally on the body. The coat is double, with the outer hair profuse, silky, loosely curled, and in adults two inches or longer. A corkscrew tail and black hairs in the coat disqualify.

Bird Dog Member of a breed of dogs trained to hunt upland game birds – Pointers, Setters, Spaniels, etc.

Birth of Puppies With normal labour the first sign of a puppy to be born is the appearance of a water bag. This prepares the way for the puppy. Usually the bitch ruptures the water bag with her vigorous licking, then there is a sudden flow of water which the dam will lick up. Shortly after this the first puppy should arrive and if it has not done so by one hour, or one hour and a half at the latest, then professional help should be summoned. In most normal births the puppy should arrive head first. The delivery of the head requires the greatest effort on the part of the bitch. After the birth of the first puppy, others may reasonably be expected to follow at intervals of from fifteen minutes to three hours. In a small litter of say three or four, whelping could be completed within a couple of hours but with a large litter it could extend over a very much longer period. See WHELPING.

Biscuits Dog biscuits can be made of almost anything but usually consist of proteins, fats, and carbohydrates, plus such supplements as vitamins and minerals, made into a dough and then baked. They are usually baked at a high temperature so that the moisture content is 10 per cent or less. They are then very hard and will keep indefinitely, but the baking may destroy some of the vitamins.

Dog biscuits are marketed in various shapes, sizes, and even flavours. These are usually fed dry. Dogs enjoy them, since they satisfy the dog's love of chewing. They help to keep the gums healthy, aid somewhat in preventing tartar deposits and tooth discoloration, and aid in keeping the jaws strong.

A popular method of marketing dog biscuits is to bake them into huge cakes, then to grind them into coarse meal. In this form, they are designed to be fed by adding hot water. They then give off an appetizing aroma which is most pleasing to dogs.

Nutritionists warn that the high temperatures used in baking and drying dog biscuits may destroy some of the important amino acids – the building blocks of proteins – in the finished food. They therefore recommend that meat supplements be added to the ground biscuit. Dog biscuits are, however, rich in carbohydrates.
See NUTRITION.

Bite A term indicating the jaw formation and teeth positions in the dog.
See LEVEL BITE; SCISSORS BITE; UNDERSHOT; OVERSHOT; and PIG JAW.

Bites Dogs have strong jaws and bite hard. Their canine teeth penetrate deeply while the remaining teeth crush.

When a dog bites and the person or animal bitten does not move, damage to the tissues is relatively small. But when the person or animal pulls away – the instinctive reaction – the canine teeth are pulled through skin and muscles making deep tears. Apart from the physical injury caused by a bite, the wound is usually contaminated. All wounds should be carefully cleaned. A little bleeding is a 'blessing in disguise' as it flushes the wound and removes most contamination. Heavy bleeding should be stopped by using a bandage or TOURNIQUET.

When a human being is bitten, the area of a bite must be considered, together with the age of the person. Those under eighteen years of age are bitten more often in the face or neck than in other areas of the body. About ninety per cent of the bites received by children under ten are on the head or neck. Adults are most often bitten upon the legs or hands. Face and neck bites are more dangerous than body or leg bites. Should the wound become infected, the infection is closer to the brain. There is also a greater possibility of disfigurement.

In nations where RABIES is known to exist there is often a morbid fear that every dog bite makes a rabies case. For that reason many areas require that doctors, clinics, and hospitals report all dog-bite cases which they have treated. The police are then ordered to investigate. If the biting dog cannot be found, a series of anti-rabies inoculations is prescribed.

In many areas of the world, doctors routinely give tetanus antitoxin for any puncture wound. This is because the tetanus bacillus, clostridium tetani, can grow only in the absence of oxygen. It may find such a situation in a deep puncture wound.

The legal aspects of dog bites must also be considered. Under English Common Law, an owner is usually held to be responsible for the damage done by his dog. This has been interpreted by some courts to be an absolute liability. An extreme example has been to hold an owner liable even when his dog bites for cause, as in the case where the person bitten is a trespasser committing a wrongful act. Attempts by legislative bodies to soften

such interpretations have often been struck down by the courts.

Most courts hold that once a dog has bitten someone, whether for just cause or not, the dog has proven itself to be vicious. So, if the dog bites a second time, the owner can be held liable. It will be ruled that he has knowingly harboured a vicious dog. Growling, and threats of attack, have also been held by the courts to prove the vicious nature of the dog.

When a dog has been bitten by another dog the usual result is deep puncture wounds or tears. Again, the wounds should be cleaned and severe bleeding stopped.

It is usual for these bites to become infected so suitable antibiotic treatment should be given by a veterinarian. Because of the danger of infection, short tears in the skin are often not sutured to allow drainage. Obviously major tears and injuries must have surgical attention. See LEGAL STATUS OF THE DOG.

Black and Tan Miniature This is one of the many names under which a Miniature Manchester Terrier is known.

Since in England, its native home, it is now officially designated OLD ENGLISH TERRIER (BLACK AND TAN), it will be found under that heading.

Black Tongue see Gums; Heart Diseases.

Blanket Solid colour extending over the back and sides, and usually from the neck to a part of the tail, so as to create a blanket effect. A BEAGLE often exhibits this feature.

Below left Blanket of solid colour on a Beagle's back.
Below Blaze.

Blaze A white facial stripe, usually between the eyes.

Blenheim Spaniel see Cavalier King Charles Spaniel.

Bleu de Gascogne see Rare Breeds.

Blindness In dogs blindness can be caused by the ageing process, by injury or disease, or by hereditary factors which can affect the eyeball itself, the lens, the retina, or the optic nerve. In many cases, more than one of these parts will be affected at the same time. Diseases of the optic nerve and retina seldom, if ever, yield to treatment. Wounds, and the diseases which may cause later blindness, should be treated by the veterinarian as early as possible. It is wise, for example, to have careful examination of the eyes following distemper or neuritis.

Pannus and pterygium are inherited defects, with the latter often following the former. Pannus in dogs may be seen in almost any breed but it is most commonly met in GERMAN SHEPHERDS and BOXERS. In this affliction, a system of blood vessels grows over the cornea. In pterygium, the membrane grows over the eye, starting at the inner corner. It is characterized by connective tissue growing between the corneal epithelium and the stroma. The eyeball itself is enlarged by the process.

Everyone is familiar with cataracts. They are common among aged dogs. A gradual whitening of the lens occurs until opacity results. However, in many cases of cataract sufficient light may be let through to permit the dog to get about safely. Successful surgery is sometimes possible, but should only be attempted when sight in both eyes has been lost.

Glaucoma is a disease of the eyeball. The eyeball itself is enlarged. The pupil, if visible at all, is widely dilated, and yet there is little or no response to light. The cornea is hazy. The onset is often sudden. Primary glaucoma can often be treated successfully. Secondary glaucoma, so-called because it follows from other diseases or defects, results in blindness. Pain is always present.

The lens may sometimes become loose and displaced, a situation called lenticular luxation. While it may be caused by injury, a tendency towards it appears to be inherited by Wire-haired FOX TERRIERS and AMERICAN COCKER SPANIELS. Although the displaced lens interferes with vision, this is not entirely lost. Surgical removal of the lens is recommended. Lenticular luxation is a major cause of secondary glaucoma, and in such cases blindness does result.

There are three hereditary retina and optic nerve abnormalities which are of major concern to dog owners. The first, and least known of these, is congenital hemeralopia, or day blindness. Congenital is probably a poor term, since it means 'present at birth'. However, the trouble usually is evident by the time the puppies are eight weeks of age. The puppies are blind during daylight, but have normal vision at night. The abnormality seems limited almost entirely to ALASKAN MALAMUTES, and those dogs known as 'Alaskans'. It has been reported very occasionally, however, in POODLES. It is known to be caused by a RECESSIVE gene.

Congenital excavation of the optic nerve occurs chiefly in COLLIES. It is often possible to recognize the defect as soon as the eyes open, for the eyes are abnormally small in those puppies which are afflicted. Later, it will be noted that the blue eyes at birth do not give way to the normal brown, but always appear pale. The defect gets its name from a 'crater' in the optic nerve. Depending upon the size of this crater, loss of vision may be slight or total.

Progressive retinal atrophy is the best known and most widely distributed of the hereditary eye defects in dogs. It is seen most commonly in IRISH SETTERS, Poodles, LABRADOR RETRIEVERS, and Collies. The first recognizable symptom for the layman is night blindness.

As its name indicates, the defect gets worse until total blindness results. There is a gradual atrophy of the retinal light receptor cells, plus a progressive reduction in the size of the retinal blood vessels. Treatment is of no value. Prevention depends upon the rigid testing and culling of breeding stock. And this in turn depends upon the immediate reporting of the problem as soon as the defect appears within a breed.

Atrophy of the optic nerve may follow distemper and may result in blindness. Retinitis sometimes follows severe diseases. Though it may result in blindness, it does not always occur, and usable vision will remain. Choroidoretinitis is another such disease. Still another is papilledema, a swelling of the optic nerve. Papilledema has been reported in CHIHUAHUAS, where it has been associated with both choroidoretinitis and hydrocephalus ('water on the brain').
See EYE DISEASES.

Blinker A pointing dog which, upon locating, points the bird, then leaves, or which skirts the bird and moves on. A spaniel which, upon locating, fails to flush or does so only upon urging.

Bloat Bloat or gastric tympany is an acute, fatal disease of the large deep chested breeds such as the ST. BERNARD, IRISH WOLFHOUND, DEERHOUND, GREAT DANE, MASTIFF, IRISH SETTER and BOXER. Very rarely it may occur in a small breed like the DACHSHUND. Usually the affected dog is elderly. Fortunately bloat is an uncommon disease. It has been suggested that it runs in certain families within a breed.

The attack occurs an hour or so after a meal. The abdomen becomes rapidly distended as gas collects in the stomach. The dog suffers great discomfort and has difficulty in breathing. Unless surgical intervention is successful the condition will prove fatal within a few hours. No form of first aid is effective. Professional help should be sought as soon as a case of bloat is suspected.

The treatment of bloat is complicated by the fact that the stomach becomes twisted upon itself so that gas is trapped in the stomach and cannot escape naturally. As the twisting of the stomach appears to occur before the gas collects many authorities refer to the condition as torsion of the stomach rather than as gastric tympany or bloat. Because of the twisting of the stomach it is usually impossible for the veterinarian to relieve the condition by passing a stomach tube, and even if this procedure is effective an operation may still be necessary to correct the displacement of the stomach. Trocharization or puncturing of the stomach to allow the escape of the gas is usually the first stage in treatment. The cause of bloat is not properly understood. The modern hypothesis is that there is delayed emptying of the stomach following a normal meal. Certainly the nature of the meal appears to have little to do with the development of the disease, as most cases of bloat occur on a diet to which the dog is well accustomed. The size of the meal may have some bearing on the problem as most cases occur in dogs which only have one large meal each day. Possibly the condition could be prevented by feeding several small meals during the day rather than one large one.

Blocky Square headed. Head too heavy for the proper balance with the body.

Bloodhound The general appearance of this remarkable animal is described as follows in a paragraph of the official Breed Standard issued by most Kennel Clubs:

'The expression is noble and dignified, and characterized by solemnity, wisdom and power.'

Certainly its unique, even bizarre, appearance is no new and modern gimmick. Doctor Caius, writing in 1553 of the Bloodhound, described a somewhat similar dog to the one we know today. He went on to explain their name by saying: 'It is well known that they follow their prey, not only while alive but also after death, when thay have caught the scent of blood.' A quite different explanation for the name comes from another source – that the word 'blood' was merely meant to denote that this hound was a member of an aristocracy: many people still refer to pedigreed horses as 'blood' horses.

Even so, it is the fearsome reputation of the relentless tracker which has survived. The legend, with overtones of the pursuit of criminals through swamps, of escaping slaves, of fearsome baying, of saliva dripping from gaping jaws, has survived. Coupled with this, there is in some minds the thought that like the police-trained GERMAN SHEPHERD, the Bloodhound will seize its prey at the end of its traditional tracking task.

The facts are these. The Bloodhound has the keenest sense of smell of any known domestic animal. It has the necessary mentality to apply this keen sense of smell to its task. With Bloodhounds, however, tracking is the sole aim. They like doing it but they are not interested in the end product. Far from wanting to bite their quarry, they tend to lick his face and even congratulate him on laying an interesting trail.

There is an authenticated story of a hound from Kentucky called *Nick Carter*, which picked up a trail 105 hours old and helped in the arrest of a man who had burned down a chicken house. In October 1954 three hounds were set to the task of finding a man, his wife and 13-year-old son, who had disappeared in the heavily wooded region of Oregon. When the car which was to provide the clue was found, the family had already been lost for a whole week. Thus, the trail was seven days old when the hounds were set the task of finding the three people. They succeeded and it was no fault of theirs that they were too late because the people were already dead.

From the foregoing, it will be seen that the Bloodhound which is presumed to have come from continental Europe, has been more readily appreciated for its usefulness in the United States.

Perhaps there has been opportunity to use the dog naturally in the United States. In Europe it is more restricted to exercises and competitions. Fortunately,

however, these have a great following and the many trials held each year have at least ensured that the dog retains both its traditional appearance and its working qualities.

As with so many breeds its head is its most distinctive feature, being furnished with an abundance of loose skin. When the dog drops its head this falls into pendulous ridges and folds, especially over the forehead and sides of the face. Small wonder that Landseer, a somewhat sentimental animal artist, portrayed it as a judge complete with robes and attendant officials!

To those who know it well, however, the Bloodhound is quite a different dog. It is affectionate, very even tempered, sensitive, even shy.

Essentials of the breed: Head: narrow and long, tapering slightly from temple to muzzle. Equidistant from stop to tip of nose and occiput, which should be very pronounced. Abundant loose skin with deep flews and dewlap. Deep set eyes with heavy flews underneath. Ears: thin, soft, long and low. Forelegs: straight. Body: chest well let down with deep keel, loins slightly arched. Tail: long, tapering, set on high, carried scimitar fashion. Hocks should be well let down and set square. Colours: black and tan, liver and tan, and red. A small amount of white is permissible on chest, feet and tail tip. Average height: 24 inches – bitches; 26 inches – dogs. Weight: 80 to 100 lb. and 90 to 110 lb., respectively, the heavier being preferred.
See colour plate p. 184.

Blooding Practice of allowing young hounds to kill the quarry in an effort to increase their hunting desire. In American Foxhound hunting it is considered an unforgivable crime.

Bloom The perfect condition of a dog's coat.

Blue Merle Blue and grey mixed with black.

Boarding Kennels Boarding kennels are service facilities to house and care for dogs, and sometimes cats. They have become a necessity in modern times because so many dog owners now travel extensively and are not able to take their dogs along. No one may be at home to care for the dog, or dogs, and owners are unwilling to leave their pets with relatives or neighbours.

Veterinary hospitals are usually not satisfactory for boarding. They are built for the care of sick dogs. Few have outside runs suitable for healthy medium and large dogs. Dogs boarded at hospitals would thus have to spend most of their time in cages.

Most boarding kennels are located in the country to allow sufficient space around them so that the barking of the dogs will not disturb neighbours. Some kennels surround their entire facility with a high board, concrete, or stone fence. This fence guards against the escape of dogs, prevents contamination from outside, and acts as a sound barrier. Many such kennels offer free collection and delivery service. Others are located near airports, so that travellers can deliver and collect the dogs easily. Operators of boarding kennels require

proof of vaccination against DISTEMPER, HEPATITIS, and LEPTOSPIROSIS, within the past year. Bitches with young puppies are normally not accepted. Proof of worming of young dogs may also be required.

Many boarding kennels also offer a grooming service. Some make it a routine practice to bathe dogs on the day they are to return to their homes. The dogs are also checked for fleas.

Dog owners are strongly individualistic in their feeding procedures. To compensate for this, many boarding kennels will permit the owners to bring their own food, and will agree to feed the dogs on the schedules provided by the owner.

It is a common practice for owners to visit a number of kennels before deciding upon one which fits the situation desired. Some considerations involved are cleanliness of the kennels, whether or not the dog must share a run with another dog, closeness to the owner's home, and the apparent health of the dogs present at the time of the visit. Reservations must often be made well in advance.

Boarhound The 'boarhound' of Greek and Roman times was a large, powerful dog used to hunt wild boars. Its relationship to modern dogs is uncertain. The Greeks used a breed called Seres which probably came from Tibet. The Molossian Dog of Tibet may also have been used. The GREAT DANE has been erroneously called the GERMAN BOARHOUND.

Bobtail A dog born tailless, or one with the tail docked very short. Term often used for an OLD ENGLISH SHEEPDOG.

Body Temperature The body temperature of adult dogs varies from 101·5° to 101·6° Fahrenheit (38·61° to 38·66° Centigrade). This is true of all dogs, whether they are hairless, smooth coated, or heavily furred. In puppies, healthy temperature may range up to 101·8° (38·77° Centigrade). A temperature of 102° (38·88° Centigrade) is a slight fever. One of 105° (40·55° Centigrade) is extremely serious. One of 106° (41·1° Centigrade), often called hyperpyrexia, indicates that the dog is near collapse. Temperature must always be taken rectally, using a rectal THERMOMETER.

A sudden temperature rise in a previously healthy dog can indicate pneumonia or early distemper. Sun stroke can also cause such a rise. If the temperature rises in a dog recovering from an infection, it indicates resurgence of infection has begun. When it is necessary to bring down temperature quickly, veterinarians have a wide range of drugs which they can use. It is not true that a hot nose indicates fever. Dogs with high fever may have a cool nose, and dogs with no fever may have a warm one.

If a sick dog which has been having a fever has a sudden drop of temperature to 100° (37·77° Centigrade), the condition is serious. At 98° (36·66° Centigrade), the dog is near collapse. In dogs with severe wasting diseases, a temperature of 96° or 97° (35·55° or 36·11° Centigrade) indicates that death is near.

Dogs in SHOCK may have a temperature of 96° or 97°.

Bloodhound.
Top left Ch. Abingerwood Winged Pharaoh.
Bottom left Abingerwood Angus.

In such cases, it is necessary to bring the temperature up quickly. Whisky in warm water can be given. The dog can be wrapped in a blanket or a heating pad can be folded over it. These measures will help until a veterinarian can take over.

A bitch when whelping often has a subnormal temperature.

Bone A term used to describe the girth of the leg bones. Example: 'He has good bone'.

Bones as Food Bones have no food value. However, this is not to say that they are valueless. On the contrary, no dog's life is really complete without the occasional bone. The principal advantage is that they give dogs pleasure. A side benefit is that they aid digestion. More important still they keep the teeth and gums in good condition. Loose, spongy GUMS, leading ultimately to a form of pyorrhoea, are far less likely to occur if the teeth are given occasional hard work. This becomes of increasing importance now that more and more soft food is given to dogs. The teeth will only remain tight in their sockets and surrounded by hard, healthy gums if pressure is exerted on them. One way of achieving this is by feeding occasional large, hard, dry biscuits. Another is by giving bones, say, twice a week.

These must be chosen carefully. Although dogs can digest all bones through the acid in their stomachs, dispersion is slow and disposal inefficient. The tendency is for the remnants to remain in the bowel and rectum where they compact. Dogs who eat bones as distinct from gnawing them usually suffer from constipation. Their stools are hard and white.

Bones from chicken, game and even chops are not suitable, and can be dangerous. These small bones are brittle and when broken have sharp, jagged edges. If they become lodged in the throat or intestine the result can be fatal.

The best are huge shin bones from beef and a sawn marrow bone is excellent. The correct size naturally varies with the size of the dog but a good guide is that the bone should be as large as the dog can carry. Bones should be boiled for just a few minutes.

Boots see Coats and Boots.

Border Collie see Collie, Border.

Border Terrier When searching for adjectives to use in connection with the Border Terrier it would be a resourceful man who could avoid the obvious ones – 'honest', 'workmanlike', 'down to earth'.

Perhaps one should not even try to avoid them as they describe so well the character and instincts of this tough little dog which came originally from the slopes of the Cheviot Hills that form the Border country between Scotland and England.

Dogs somewhat similar to the modern Border Terrier have been used for centuries in these regions to hunt and destroy foxes. In a district where even lambs are prey to the attacks of the powerful hill foxes, men want a dog that is above all things game; it matters little if

they have not quite the elegance of some of the more fashionable members of the terrier group.

The preamble to the breed standard issued by the English Kennel Club sums up the dog admirably in a few words. It says: 'The Border Terrier is essentially a working terrier; it should be able to follow a horse and combine activity with gameness.' Almost without exception they fulfil these requirements, and it is frequently said that the breed has been spoiled less by the march of 'progress' than any other current breed of terrier.

One can imagine the mixed feelings of the hunting men who used this little dog when they first heard in 1920 that the breed was to be officially recognized by Britain's ruling body in the dog world. Shows have been known to over-beautify a breed at the expense of its working qualities. Would Mr. James Davidson, of Hyndlee, who wrote to an acquaintance in 1800 that he had bought 'twa red devils o' terriers that has hard wiry coats and would worry any damned thing that crepit' have been confident that popularity in fashion-

Above Bones as food. Although they have no nutritional value, bones are indispensable for keeping teeth and gums healthy, aiding digestion, and, of course, giving pleasure.
Left Border Terrier. Survival of the fittest may prove this tough, hard-working little terrier, which adapts remarkably well to suburban living, a popular breed of the future. Ch. Hawksbourn Beaver.

Right Borzoi. Ch. Mokhayl of Tam-Boer.

able shows in England would leave this, one of the smallest of all terriers, unspoiled?

Any such misgivings were unnecessary. Dogs that are bred right stay right, and even now that many Border Terrier fanciers have no intention of using the dogs in their original roles, they have kept to the same unwritten rules as the originators of the breed. Even though they breed for an entirely different market – most modern Borders are destined to be family pets and fireside companions – they stick to the same strict code. Temperament comes before appearance.

Having stressed the working background, it is perhaps necessary to make the point that Border Terriers have no instinct to fight with other dogs; just as they work happily together with their kind in foxes' earths, so they are equally content to mix in city streets without the fireworks so often produced by more excitable terriers.

Other ways in which they differ from some of their cousins are that they do not have to be stripped, and their tails are never docked. Equally distinctive is the head, which is required to resemble that of an otter, be moderately broad in skull, and have a short, strong muzzle.

As with all breeds in this modern age, however, their future is bound up with their suitability as suburban pets, and for the man who wants a terrier, the Border has many advantages. Clean, of handy size, adaptable, trouble free and intensely loyal, particularly gentle with children, the 'red devil' may well be a breed with a rosy future.

In Britain, their registration numbers have doubled in the last decade. In the United States, they still hang fire and they are one of the few breeds whose registrations dropped in 1970. They are not amongst the hundred most popular breeds.

Essentials of the breed: Head: like that of an otter, moderately broad in skull, with short strong muzzle; black nose preferable. Eyes: dark. Ears: small V-shaped, dropping forward close to cheek. Teeth: should have scissor-like grip but a level mouth is acceptable.

Forelegs: straight and not too heavy in bone. Body: deep, narrow and fairly long; ribs not over-sprung, capable of being spanned by both hands behind the shoulder. Feet: small with thick pads. Tail: moderately short, thick at base, then tapering, set high and carried gaily. Coat: harsh and dense with close undercoat. Colour: red, wheaten, grizzle and tan or blue and tan. Weight: dogs, between 13 and 15½ lb.; bitches, between 11½ and 14 lb.

See colour plate p. 379.

Borzoi The Borzoi came to the West from Russia. Indeed, until comparatively recently, it was known as the Russian Wolfhound, a title which, although descriptive, was possibly misleading.

First, it must be understood that this breed did not, and was not expected to attack and fight wolves unaided. It was used by the aristocracy of the Imperial Court of the Russian Empire for the traditional, almost ceremonial, hunting, or rather coursing, of the wolf. The whole affair was a glorious extravagance. Beauti-

fully and formally dressed aristocrats mounted on exquisite horses. Elaborate celebrations and hunt dinners. Well trained and liveried hunt servants. And the Borzois. Finely bred, carefully reared, immaculately prepared, restrained by colourful silken leashes. Style was everything; symmetry and elegance the essentials which would commend the dogs to the luxury loving noblemen who owned them.

In the field the wolf was beaten out of cover. Immediately a brace of Borzois was slipped after it. Aesthetic considerations demanded that the dogs be identical in colour and markings. More practically, they had to be matched in size and speed. One which outdistanced its partner and reached a wolf alone would have suffered severely for its keenness!

Their job was to seize the wolf by the neck and throw it. The huntsman then proved his valour by hurling himself from his horse and dispatching the wolf with a dagger.

After this bloodthirsty beginning it should be recorded that the breed is mild, benevolent and kind, well disposed not only to mankind, but to the remainder of the animal kingdom. To this should be added the fact that although it was Russia which produced the breed, it was almost certainly the Middle East which made the major contribution to the bloodlines.

All coursing dogs – that is running hounds – have points in common. Thus, the Borzoi, DEERHOUND, GREYHOUND, SALUKI, WHIPPET and IRISH WOLF-HOUND are somewhat similar in outline and probably spring from common stock.

The origin of the Borzoi dates back three hundred years to the time of a Russian Duke with a liking for fast hunting dogs. He imported a number of Arabian Greyhounds which were similar, if not identical, with the Saluki. They were fast. But their coats were no match for Arctic winters and they perished. More were then bought and immediately crossed with a native, long-legged COLLIE type which had a thick, heavy and wavy coat. The Borzoi had arrived.

For the next two centuries very few left Russia, principally because other than as a presentation gift, there was no way of obtaining them. In 1812 an English visitor to Russia described the breed in detail in a magazine article.

Thirty years later two were presented to Her Majesty Queen Victoria, a gift so appreciated that the Czar promptly made further presentations to the Royal Family.

English aristocracy took the breed to its heart. Early exhibitors of these crowd-drawing dogs at nineteenth century shows included the Duchess of Manchester, the Duke of Hamilton, King Edward VII, Queen Alexandra and the Duchess of Newcastle, who ultimately established one of the most important kennels of the breed ever known.

Concurrently with this, the breed reached America at first from England in 1889 and later when in 1903 Mr. Joseph B. Thomas started importing direct from Russia. Almost inevitably his source of supply was yet another member of the aristocracy; the Grand Duke Nicholas Romanoff.

Now their owners are more every-day. Even so, they are not a poor man's breed, needing plenty of space, adequate leisure time for grooming and a deep pocket to feed so huge an animal. A good male Borzoi stands 30 inches high at the shoulders!

The principal requirements of the breed may be summed up in five words. They are size, speed, strength, symmetry and style. Possibly the last is the most important in this age when the dogs can no longer be used for their original purpose. Unless they exude good breeding by their movement, their manners and their bearing, they are not typical Borzois.

Essentials of the breed: Head: long and lean measuring the same from inner corner of eye to both nose and occiput. Skull: domed and narrow, stop imperceptible. Nose: large and black. Eyes: dark, almond shape, set obliquely. Ears: small, fine, responsive. Neck: reasonably long and powerful. Very deep, narrow brisket with ample heart room. Back: arched from near shoulder. Muscled body. Loins: powerful, quarters wider than shoulders, and muscular hind legs. Tail: low set, feathered and carried low. Coat: long and silky, short on head, ears and front legs. Profuse frill on neck. Chest, hindquarters and tail profusely feathered. Height: 28 to 31 inches. Weight approximately 75 to 105 lb. Bitches smaller.
See colour plate p. 181.

Bossy Over-development of the shoulder muscles.

Boston Terrier The Boston Terrier is one of a dozen breeds and varieties of breeds which have been developed in the United States. It is one of the most popular breeds in the country, and has been listed among the 20 most popular in American Kennel Club registrations since 1920. It enjoys comparable popularity in Canada. And it has spread to the British Isles and to Australia and New Zealand despite quarantine restrictions so rigid as to discourage most exports.

The breed was apparently started by men who used dogs for pit fighting in the Boston area. They crossed BULLDOGS and BULL TERRIERS to improve fighting qualities. The Boston Terrier was developed from some of these crosses. The early progenitors would be named after the owner, and the name would change with the dog's ownership. For example, *Mulvaney's Jeb* would become *Sheahan's Jeb*, and later *Harbor's Jeb*.

The known history of the breed begins about 1870. A dog, supposedly imported from England but of uncertain ancestry, passed through several ownerships. In 1875, he went to Robert C. Hooper. Thereafter, he was known as *Hooper's Judge*. It is surmised that he was closer to Bulldog than to terrier type.

Hooper's Judge was bred to *Burnett's Gyp*. A son, *Well's Eph*, was bred with *Tobin's Kate*. That litter, whelped in 1877, produced *Barnard's Tom* and *Atkinson's Tobey*. Tom is generally considered to be the foundation pillar of the breed. But bitches sired by Tobey were the greatest producers of their time. Incestuous breeding to both dogs was practised.

Atkinson's Tobey and Barnard's Kate were entries in

Above Bossy.

Left Borzoi. A head study of Ch. Springett Copper Beech. The wolfhound of the Russian aristocracy is still not a poor man's breed: it needs large spaces, big meals and constant grooming.

the Massachusetts Kennel Club Show of 1878. Tobey was then ten months old. The dogs had to be entered as Bull Terriers. Since they were obviously not Bull Terriers, they could not win against such competition. Some four years later, the Boston club provided classes for them as 'Round-headed and bull terriers, any colour'.

In 1891, the Bostonians formed the American Bull Terrier Club. It petitioned the American Kennel Club for recognition of the breed. This was denied. The club then changed its name to Boston Terrier Club, and the breed was recognized as the Boston Terrier in 1893. The breed's origins, however, still cause confusion. Thousands of owners call their dogs 'Boston Bulls' or 'Toy Bulldogs'.

After 1920, Bostons became so popular that the breed might account for twenty to thirty per cent of the entries at a show. Speciality shows might have as many as 200 entries. But in more recent years, the breed has dropped to a steady level, and has had a higher ratio of excellent dogs. English and American show entries are now comparable, and dogs bred in England have become champions both in Canada and in the United States.

Boston Terriers are not easily bred. Virtually all of them must be delivered by a CAESAREAN OPERATION. Puppies with the desired head structure can seldom pass through the cervix of the uterus. Thus, to save the lives of both bitch and puppies, delivery by abdominal incision is performed. The expense of such surgery has tended to eliminate the breeding of unfit stock.

Essentials of the breed: Boston Terriers can be shown in one of three weight classes: Heavyweight, 20 lb. and not exceeding 25 lb.; Middleweight, 15 lb. and under 20 lb.; and Lightweight, under 15 lb. Though 25 lb. is the desired maximum for the breed, there is no disqualification for overweight.

Brindle and white is the preferred colour, though black and white is permitted. Preferred markings are white muzzle, even white blaze over the head, white collar, breast, and part or all of the forelegs, and below the hocks on the hind legs. Solid black, black and tan, liver and mouse colours disqualify. So do a DUDLEY NOSE, a docked tail, or any artificial means used to deceive the judge. (Exhibitors once painted the desired white markings on their dogs.)

The skull is square, flat on top, free of wrinkles, with a well defined stop. The muzzle is short, square, wide and deep, shorter in length than it is deep, and about one third the length of the skull. It should not be DOWN-FACED. The teeth meet in an even bite, or the jaws may be undershot to square the muzzle. The ears, carried erect, are either cropped or natural 'bat', and are set as near to the corners of the skull as possible.

The chest is deep and broad with ribs carried well back. The body is short, but not chunky. There is a slight slope from rump to set on of the tail. The tail is set on low, is either straight or screw, and is not longer than half the distance to the hock. Roach or sway backs, and a gay or gnarled tail, are faults.
See colour plate p. 186.

Bouvier des Flandres The Bouvier des Flandres is the only one of four varieties of Flemish drovers' dogs which has survived to become prominent on any but a local basis. The Bouvier has spread to many parts of Europe, and to the United States and Canada. Both of these nations now have sufficiently large reservoirs of excellent stock, so that they are able to export to other countries.

The breed has been known by other names, for example, *Chien de Vacher*. But its final name is *Bouvier*, meaning cowherd or ox driver, and *des Flandres*, meaning 'from the East and West provinces of Flanders' in Belgium. However, Flanders once comprised also the Dutch province of Zeeland, and even a part of France. Thus, the breed developed in an area somewhat larger than the present Belgian provinces.

A Belgian veterinarian, Dr. Keul, is credited with having worked tirelessly to promote the breed. But M. Poiret of Ghent is, so far as is known, the first person to exhibit Bouviers in a dog show. He entered *Nelly* and *Even* in a May international show. Authorities do not agree whether this first showing was in Ghent or Brussels. In any case, the dogs attracted immediate attention. Dog show enthusiasts began to scour Flanders for dogs of good type. Both the Société Royale St. Hubert, and the Club St. Hubert du Nord became interested. M. Fontaine, vice-president of the Club St. Hubert, drew up a standard. However, there were at one time, four different standards for the breed.

World War I almost destroyed the breed. But a Belgian Army veterinarian, Captain Darby, saved some stock. His great dog, *Ch. Nic de Sottegem*, was exhibited at the Antwerp show of 1920. Nic was both a show sensation and a great stud dog. He therefore became the virtual foundation sire of the breed.

The development of railroads, trucks, wire fences, and paved highways brought the usefulness of drovers' dogs to an end. Bouvier owners turned their interest to training the dogs for police, war dog, and home guardian purposes. In all these fields, the Bouviers have proved their worth.

Essentials of the breed: The standard for the breed calls for dogs 23½ to 27½ inches at the shoulder, with a minimum for bitches of 22¾ inches. The coat is double, with the outer one being rough and wiry. Colours range

Boston Terrier.
Top left Ch. Wenlyn Cheyenne of Brigwood.
Bottom left The correct head structure presents problems at birth, and most Boston Terrier puppies have to be delivered by Caesarean section.

Below Bouvier des Flandres. Ch. Naris du Posty, clipped as neat as a topiarist's paradise.

from fawn to black; pepper and salt; grey; and brindle. A white star on the chest is allowed. Chocolate brown with white spots is a fault.

The skull is slightly longer than the muzzle and flat on top. Brows are arched but the stop is shallow. Eyes are brown and nearly oval. Black eyes are permitted but not desirable. The muzzle is wide and deep, with dry, tight lips, and a scissors bite. Muzzle hair forms a beard. Ears are set high, and are cropped to form a triangle.

The body is approximately square, from ground to withers to root of tail. The tail is docked to about four inches. The chest is deep, and the rump is broad, and with little slope to the tail. Rear legs angulation is not excessive. The toes are arched with deep pads and black nails.

Breed faults include yellow, staring, or protruding eyes; brown, pink, or spotted noses; out at elbows; cow hocks; splayed feet; and soft or silky body coat. See colour plate p. 291.

Boxer A remarkable feature of this breed is the way in which it suddenly sprang to popularity some three decades ago. So rapid was this that looking back now, it is difficult to appreciate that Boxers were hardly known outside Germany thirty years ago.

Although the first specimens were taken to England early this century they made no progress. At the outbreak of the last war they were standing around seventy-fifth in the popularity poll. In the United States also, the general public hardly knew of Boxers before the war.

Now the position is so changed that the young could be excused for thinking that the Boxer had always been a part of the English-speaking world. The name does not sound foreign. And then there is its head; surely this dog is first cousin to that essentially British animal, the BULLDOG?

In fact the Boxer is a pure continental European. Only in countries which had to be vigilant at frontiers is it likely to have been evolved, for the Boxer was designed for a purpose.

In common with many European countries, Germany has had a permanent land frontier problem. Illegal entry, smuggling and similar activities are rampant. Because of this Germans have always been interested in what are loosely called 'police' dogs but could perhaps be better described as general-utility-security dogs.

They are variously required to guard, attack, and protect areas of land, scent strangers, search for such items as smuggled coffee and drugs, and other similar tasks. With this in mind, the Boxer was developed in Munich, Southern Germany. The period, as far as can be ascertained was during the closing decade of the last century.

Precise details of all of the contributing breeds are not known. Intelligent guesswork must be mixed with the few known facts to produce a credible whole. There must have been a mixture of various continental Pinschers, chosen principally for their muscular activity. One imagines the use of some member of the

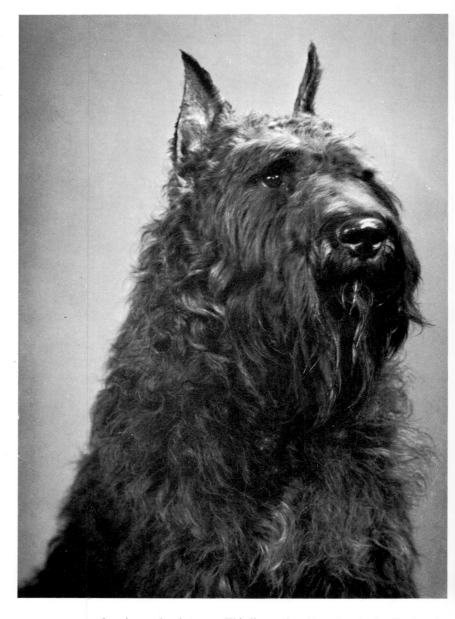

MASTIFF group for size and substance. Thirdly, and perhaps principally, the Bulldog must have been used; the aim being to produce a liberal dose of courage and tenacity.

The end product was a hardy and alert dog, strong, powerful, particularly active and yet still not a giant and certainly without a giant's ideas on bed and board.

Early in the twentieth century some Boxers reached Britain. Few noticed them. At the outbreak of the Second World War they were still virtually ignored. Immediately after the War however, the position changed dramatically. Returning Servicemen having seen them in Germany came back full of enthusiasm. Within a few brief years public enthusiasm took them straight up into the 'Top Ten'.

The pattern of breed popularity followed a similar course in the United States of America. Once established in those canine strongholds its spread over the world followed rapidly; from Britain to all corners of the

Above Bouvier des Flandres. Asgard Bravado.

Boxers' ears are usually cropped for exhibition in the United States and Germany.
Top right Ch. Barrage of Quality Hill.
Centre Ch. Salgray's Auntie Mame.
Bottom right Ch. Summerdale Defender.

Commonwealth; from the States to every corner of the 'Americas'.

Strangely enough, a similar story had been previously enacted by the GERMAN SHEPHERD or Alsatian. This also was a Germanic breed. It only blossomed in English-speaking countries after the close of the Second World War.

One thing which puzzles the layman is why there are such strong feelings against white boxers. It also puzzles the expert, although for different reasons!

The background story is simple. One of the early Bulldogs used in the building of this breed was to all intents and purposes white. From this it is easy to imagine that, the laws of heredity being what they are, a number of white or nearly white puppies would be born in the early days. It is also easy to see that those breeders would dislike white puppies because their colour would make them most unsuitable for frontier police work as they would be far too conspicuous. They therefore decided that white was not a permissible colour. To minimize the risk of breeding whites, they never used white parents. Many went further and destroyed white puppies at birth.

To this day the occasional white pup is born. Some are taken in as family pets. The owners are then surprised to find that they are not popular and are unacceptable at dog shows.

Clearly a pet white Boxer can be as charming a pet as one of any other colour. Equally clearly it cannot be considered typical any more than could a smooth-coated Poodle, a long-legged Dachshund, or a Whippet built on the lines of a Bull Terrier. Therefore, it cannot win prizes.

The breed's English-sounding name has a curious origin. Certain English words have become international. Football and Whisky are two. Box (that is, to fight) is another. So the breed took its name from the curious habit of starting to play, and even to fight, by striking with their front paws. They have proved remarkably docile and tractable despite their heritage and origin. Indeed as a pet for the family, which includes young and boisterous children, the breed is one of the best.

Essentials of the breed: A medium-sized dog, agile, active, but not racy. The head is most important. The muzzle, which should be deep and square, is one-third of total length of head. Stop is deep and tip of nose is higher than root. Eyes: dark. Ears: fairly small, thin, lying close to cheek. In certain countries, principally in the United States of America and Germany, ears are normally cropped for exhibition. Jaws: wide and strong, undershot. Chest: deep, body square in profile, and back short and muscular. Hindquarters: strong, muscular. Feet: small and tight. Tail: set on and carried high, docked short. Coat: short and smooth. Colours: fawn or brindle both with or without white markings. Black mask essential. Height 21 inches to 25 inches at shoulder.
See colour plate p. 301.

Bracco Italiano see Rare Breeds.

Brace A brace can be defined as any two dogs, but usually of the same breed. When competing in a special brace class at a dog show, preference is sometimes given to a mixed brace, that is, one of each sex where the match is fairly close for size, style, colour, type, etc., but where the difference between the sexes is subtly emphasized by masculinity and femininity in overall conformation and expression.

Brach A term formerly used for some breeds of hunting hounds. Now used for some pointing breeds, such as the BRACCO ITALIANO.

Brachycephalic Short headed. Dogs with 'pushed in' faces, such as Pugs, Bulldogs, etc.

Brazilian Fila see Fila Brasileiro.

Brazilian Tracker (Rastreador Brasileiro) This Brazilian breed, unlike others achieved by crossing different breeds, results from crossbreeding within the varieties of one breed, the American FOXHOUND. Other types used were the COONHOUNDS: the Blue-Tick, the Walkerhound, as well as the English Foxhound. Inevitably the Brazilian climate later influenced the breed's hide and hair.

The breed was created by the Brazilian hunter Oswalde Aranha Filho and is used particularly in the hunt of the South American jaguar. When in pursuit of a jaguar the Tracker can follow the cat's track for six or seven hours and surmount the most difficult obstacles, such as rivers, swamps, and woods without losing the scent.

Essentials of the breed: The head is flat and round with little stop. Eyes: yellow and metallic in appearance. The chest must be large and deep. Tail: sabre-like. The hair is short and rough to the touch.

Breaking The term 'breaking' has a number of meanings. One meaning is treated in HOUSE TRAINING. The term is commonly used to mean the field training of sporting dogs. In advertisements for trained dogs, one often sees the term 'broken', which simply means that the dog has been trained for hunting.

Yard or garden breaking is the term applied to basic obedience training which has been given for centuries to sporting dogs. The extent to which this training is applied depends upon the breed.

The major requirements for all of them are that they should walk at heel, to man or horse; that they come instantly when called; and that they sit, or lie, and remain in that position until told to move. Pack hounds must learn to heel to a man or to a horseman as a pack. Retrieving is normally a part of breaking for spaniels and retrievers, and the German pointing breeds. It may not be required for Pointers and setters, unless they are fully trained to become gun dogs. Retrievers are taught to 'take a line' to a blind retrieve, and to stop upon whistle command, and then to take directions from their owners, even though the owner may be 60 to 100 yards away.

Following are some basic steps in breaking. But the reader should also read the sections on GUN DOGS, TRAINING OF, and HOUSE TRAINING.

Puppies can be taught to come instantly when called by tying a light cord to the collar. When the puppy is called, the owner begins to pull it to him. Even though the puppy struggles not to come, the owner encourages it by voice, and rewards it with much petting. The lesson is repeated over and over, and under conditions in which the puppy will prefer to ignore the call – for example, when it is out of sight, in another room, or around the corner of the house, or when eating. Later, the puppy can also be taught to come on a whistle signal. It must never be scolded for disobeying, but must always be praised, even when you have to chase, capture, and drag the puppy to the spot from which you called or whistled.

Heeling and sitting can be taught in one lesson. The dog walks at your left side. If it pulls ahead, it is jerked back and the command 'heel' is given. If it walks too wide or far apart, it is drawn closer and the same command is given. Some dogs pull upon the leash until they choke. Carry a cane, stick, or umbrella. Tap the puppy on the nose and command 'heel', while drawing it back.

Brazilian Tracker. *Above left and right* This breed was created by a hunter to track South American jaguars, and resulted from cross breeding varieties of American Foxhound and Coonhound.

Left Brace. A pair of Finnish Spitz. The brace is matched to show the differences in character between the sexes.

The cane can then be used as a guide to keep the puppy from pulling ahead until it learns to stay at your side.

When you practise this off the leash, you must always be prepared to reach down and collar the puppy if it tries to bolt. Lessons should be about five minutes long, but can be repeated after fifteen minute rest and play periods.

When the dog is walking at heel, you stop, command 'sit' and simultaneously pull back on the collar while pushing the puppy's rear end down. Hold the puppy down with repeated commands to sit until the instant you start forward. Then command 'heel'.

If you are trying to educate a very young puppy, remember that the puppy's legs, shoulders, and hip assemblies are chiefly cartilage at the time of birth. Bone gradually replaces the cartilage. You must be careful not to injure the puppy during this period. In breaking, this danger should be over by the time the puppy is six months old.

A dog learns quickly to heel to a horse. A simple method is to tie a check cord to the dog's collar, and to tie the other end to the saddle horn. As the horse moves forward, you call 'heel' to the puppy. It may fear the horse and hold back. So you reassure it with your voice. You may need a pole of some sort by which you prevent the puppy from getting too close to the horse's heels. In this way, the pole is a guide which teaches the puppy to stay at a proper distance from the horse.

Every puppy likes to retrieve thrown articles. If the puppy is on a light check cord, then you can draw it to you. If you do not, the puppy may try to run off with the article. Although this lesson is a part of yard breaking, it is most easily taught along a narrow corridor so that the puppy has only one way to go. But play retrieving differs from formal work in which the puppy must obey.

Stylish retrieves result if the puppy is first taught to hold something in its mouth until told to give; is then taught to carry; and only later is taught to retrieve. The steps to follow are these.

Right Breech birth. A puppy presented tail first at the pelvic entrance can be gently manipulated to ease the birth.

The puppy sits at your left side. You say 'fetch', and with your left hand, you force its lips against the teeth so that it opens its mouth. You then get the dummy, which can be rolled up newspaper tied with cord or a rubber band. You force the puppy to hold the dummy until you say 'give'. Then you heap praise upon the dog.

Once the dog will hold the dummy until told to give, you put it on a leash. You continue to say 'fetch' and you lightly draw the dog forward. It will try to spit out the dummy, but you force it to hold it while you back up. You can do this by keeping one hand under the chin.

When it will always carry the object, you let it walk beside you repeating 'fetch' and praising the puppy. When you now try true retrieving, you may have to teach the dog to pick up the dummy. This you do by drawing its head to the floor, forcing the mouth open, and slipping the dummy in. Only a few lessons are needed.

The final step is to teach the dog to retrieve whatever it is ordered to. You can start with the wing of a pigeon, duck, or pheasant nailed to a block of wood. You follow with dead carcasses, and finally with fresh shot game.

'Taking a line' can also be taught in the yard. You place the dummy at one end. You sit the dog at your left side. You swing your left arm forward in the direction of the dummy (which the puppy can see) and then send it to retrieve.

You follow by hiding the dummy. Again, with the puppy sitting at your left side, you swing your arm forward to give the direction and then send the dog with the usual 'fetch' command.

If you have taught the puppy to sit upon a whistle signal, you can stop him when it is off line. Then you give directions with either arm. If the puppy doesn't go far enough out, you can stop him, and then, using a forward motion of your arm, command 'get back'.

Breath, Bad see Bad Breath.

Breech Birth This is caused by the puppy or whelp being wrongly presented at the entrance to the pelvis. Such an abnormality in presentation is one of the most common causes of whelping problems in the bitch. The normal position for a foetus in the pelvis is when the head is directed outwards. When the head has been brought to the exterior the remainder of the body will follow easily. If a puppy is reversed so that the tail and hind legs come first this does not usually present any great difficulties. It is, however, advisable in such cases to help the puppy along by easing and carefully pulling the hind legs as the dam strains. If this birth is delayed it can result in the puppy suffocating. If the puppy lies transversely across the womb this can be very difficult to manipulate and should be left to the expert skill of the veterinarian who may be able to make an extraction by the use of forceps. Where difficulty cannot be corrected, a CAESAREAN OPERATION is indicated.

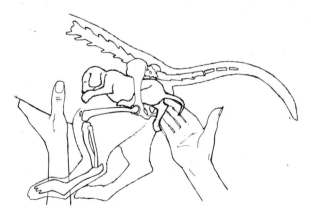

Breeching Colour of hair about the rear end of the dog.

Breed Club See Speciality Club.

Breeder A dog breeder is one who mates dogs for such purposes as improving the breed, selling the progeny for profit, competing with them at dog shows, field trials, and obedience contests. He may also mate dogs whose progeny will work as herding dogs, as leaders of the blind, or as animals for research.

From a legal standpoint, a breeder is the person who owns, or leases (preferably by an arrangement registered with a recognized canine organization), a bitch at the time she is mated.

Breed Histories So-called histories of the various breeds are quite frequently little more than legends. One difficulty in compiling authentic histories is that prior to 1873 no Kennel Club existed anywhere in the world. Thus before this date there were, with rare exceptions, no systems of either registration or record in existence.

Consequently few details referring to periods more than a century ago are verifiable. In rare cases commentators such as Samuel Pepys or Dr Caius left reliable written observations but even these, being unsupported by pictorial evidence, are not conclusive. The meaning of words, particularly of names, frequently changes over the years. Perhaps the most useful guides are found in paintings which include dogs.

To say that one must approach breed histories with caution is no reason to ignore them. They are therefore included in this volume because apart from being of great interest they are as near as we shall get to the truth.

Breeding The age at which a bitch is ready to be bred varies with the breed. Quite obviously the toy breeds are ready to be bred much sooner than their bigger sisters. Though nature prepares a bitch to conceive at her first season, most owners of the larger breeds wait until they are fully mature, and this can be anything up to two years. On the other hand, it is desirable to breed some of the toy breeds before the bones of the pelvis become too set and thus produce whelping difficulties. It is a great mistake to breed an immature animal and it is safe to say that a bitch that has its first season at six to eight months is quite unready to be bred, even in the toy breeds. See BROOD BITCH.

Bitches intended for motherhood should be kept in top class condition and not mated unless in this condition. Careful thought must always be given to the choice of the STUD DOG. It is not enough to assume that the neighbour's dog will suffice. Breeding is a fascinating adventure and deserves a certain amount of planning whether the bitch belongs to a breeder or just a pet owner.

The laws which govern heredity are under constant study nowadays and there is no longer any reason why breeding of livestock should be considered either a mystery or a lucky dip. Breeders are usually happy to advise the amateur on the use of a stud dog that will suit a particular bitch. If a bitch is weak in some particular point then one should look for strength in this point in the stud dog. A golden rule for beginners is never to mate two animals who appear to have the same fault.

Many faults are RECESSIVE. This means that any animal in which a fault appears must be carrying the gene for it in the duplex state. This in turn implies that the progeny of two such animals will probably show this particular fault. LINE BREEDING, that is, the pairing up of two related animals but not so closely

related as to entail INBREEDING, is a safe plan for amateurs to follow. An inbred bitch is, of course, more likely to transmit her qualities, be they good or bad, to her offspring, particularly if her mate is bred on similar lines. To inbreed closely, it is essential to have a good knowledge of the dogs in the pedigrees and to be aware of their faults and their virtues. Novices would not have this information so readily available to them and therefore it is much wiser for them to stick to line breeding. To establish type and eventually a strain of one's own, line breeding is essential and it is useless to decide on a dog that does not in any way tie up with the bitch's pedigree.

Inbreeding involves such relationships as mother to son, father to daughter, brother to sister combinations. Line breeding on the other hand involves mating related animals but not those which are very closely related. This method of breeding allows an owner to develop his, or her, own strain with its own special characteristics. To do this and to produce a winning strain needs great patience, study, experiment and at all times the ability to gain from the experience of every litter.

Breed Standards Sets of specifications compiled by Kennel Clubs, usually with the assistance of breed clubs, describing in detail the construction, form and coat of each of the different recognized breeds.

Breton Spaniel see Brittany Spaniel.

Briard The Briard appears to be a member of a very old race of sheepdogs which entered Europe with one or another of the Asian invaders who swept into Europe from late Roman times to the late Middle Ages. To this group belong the Hungarian KOMONDOR and KUVASZ, the Russian Owcharka, and perhaps the

Breed Histories.
Top left Hogarth's 'Pug' is included in the artist's self portrait of 1745. *Top* A Greyhound appears in a sixteenth century painting of Diana the Huntress. The Egyptian dog *above* dates from 4000 BC, and the dog under the crusader's feet *below* dates from the thirteenth century.

Above Briard. Leon Hubert.

Bearded COLLIE, OLD ENGLISH SHEEPDOG, and Hungarian PULI. While these breeds differ in many respects, they are all roughly similar both in conformation, and in the work which they have been bred to perform.

The French authority, Cornevin, called the Briard a cattle dog. But Abbé Rozier, writing in 1809, described two varieties of sheepdogs, the *Chien Berger de la Brie*, and the *Chien Berger de la Beauce*. The former was described as being long-haired, and the latter short-haired and of MASTIFF type. M. Paul Mégnin also described both breeds in 1889, and he was partly responsible for a thorough description of the two breeds in 1896. The Chien Berger de la Brie is the Briard. It seems to have undergone very little change since then.

A French sponsoring club, *Les Amis du Briard* (Friends of the Briard) was formed about 1900. Although a tentative standard was agreed upon at that time, no official standard was approved until 1925. This was altered in 1930.

The Briard distinguished itself as a French Army dog during World War I. Back packs were made for it, and it was used to carry ammunition, small machine gun parts, and other equipment, from the rear to the front lines. It was also used for Red Cross work. It was taught to locate the wounded, and it carried first aid supplies. Front line troops used the dogs for sentry duty to prevent surprise attack.

The Briard has made considerable progress in the United States and Canada. First U.S. registrations came in 1922, and the Briard Club of America was organized at about the same time. The present American breed standard became official in 1963.

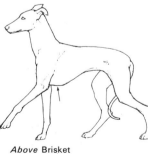

Above Brisket

Essentials of the breed: The Briard ranges from 23 to 27 inches at the shoulder, with bitches averaging 22 to $25\frac{1}{2}$ inches. Size below these limits brings disqualifica-

tion in the show ring. All solid colours, except white, are allowed, but dark colours are preferred. Usual colours are black, black with some white hairs, dark and light grey, tawny, and combinations of these colours, provided there are no marked spots, and the transition from one colour to another is gradual and symmetrical. Oddly, while white is not allowed, white dogs cannot be disqualified. However, white hair on the feet of other than white dogs does require disqualification.

The coat is long, slightly wavy, stiff, and strong. A curled coat disqualifies; so does short hair on the head, face, or feet. A white spot on the breast, and white nails are serious faults.

The head is large and long with the muzzle and the skull being of equal length, measured from the stop. The nose always is black, and spotted or light coloured noses disqualify as do spotted eyes. Teeth meet in an even bite. The hair on top of the skull, about the ears, and on the muzzle is heavy and long, although it should not veil the eyes. The ears are of moderate size, and are carried semi-erect. If cropped they are carried erect.

The chest is broad and deep, and the top line is straight to the rump, which slopes slightly. The hind legs are well angulated, but a slightly 'set under hock' is required. That is, the metatarsus, or heel, is not vertical as required for most breeds. Two DEW CLAWS are required on each hind leg. Absence of dew claws brings disqualification. Presence of only one prevents the dog from getting any award, but does not disqualify. The well-feathered tail forms a crook at the end, and reaches to the hock joint or lower. Absence of a tail, or a docked tail, disqualifies.
See colour plate p. 302.

Brindle A mixture of black hairs with those of a lighter colour, such as brown or grey.

Brisket The forepart of the body below the chest, between the forelegs.

Brittany Spaniel The Brittany Spaniel is the world's only pointing spaniel. The spaniels, pointers, and setters use wind-borne scents to locate their quarry. They are called 'bird dogs' because they are chiefly used to find feathered game. The spaniels are required to work within range of the hunter's gun, and to flush within that range. Pointers and setters have a wider range, are more lightly made and are faster, and they 'point' the sitting or hiding game, then attempt to keep it 'pinned' until the hunter can come up. It is to this latter group that the Brittany Spaniel belongs.

Spaniels, pointers, and setters may have originated in Spain. If so, they were taken first to France, and then to the British Isles. This term 'spaniel' could be a corruption of 'Espanol'. In the case of the Brittany, there may have been a return of ENGLISH SETTER blood from England. Brittany was, and is, a popular shooting territory for English sportsmen, who particularly enjoyed woodcock shooting there. Many took

along their English Setters, and it is theorized that these were crossed with the Breton, or Brittany.

Whether true or not, the Brittany Spaniel developed into a superb woodcock dog. It worked well in swampy areas, and its range was both wide enough and fast enough for huntsmen on foot. It was also successful at locating grouse, and would enter the cold water of ponds and streams to retrieve game, including water-fowl.

Brittany Spaniels were exhibited at the Paris dog show of 1900. Very shortly after, French shows had entries of 75 or more dogs. Official recognition of the breed came on February 8th, 1905 when M. de Pontavice's *Boy* was registered in the French stud book, the *Livre des Origines*. Until then, the dog had sometimes been known as the *Armorican*, or the *Armorique*. Thereafter, *Epagneul Breton*, or its English equivalent, Brittany Spaniel, became the correct name. A standard for the breed was prepared in 1907, but was altered in 1908.

The Brittany improved in type and uniformity during, and in spite of, World War I. Those owners who could afford to keep breeding stock, kept only the best, and they kept rigidly to type. By 1925, when some 100 Brittanies were exhibited at Rennes, the modern type had become completely set.

The Brittany has become one of the most popular of American hunting dogs. Its small size and short coat have helped to make it an excellent house dog. Its size also is excellent for car riding. It has adapted well to American hunting conditions, and has proved capable at pheasant hunting. But its history in America actually begins in Mexico. J. Pugibet, a Frenchman living in Vera Cruz, imported Brittany Spaniels for hunting in Yucatan. Another, Louis A. Thebaud, spent much time in Mexico hunting, although he lived in New Jersey. Thebaud also imported Brittany Spaniels. In addition, he set up a breeding programme with

Eudore Chevrier, the French Canadian, who lived in Winnipeg, Manitoba. Chevrier, imported, bred, and sold thousands of sporting dogs of various breeds, including Brittany Spaniels, to American sportsmen. Thebaud helped to found the Brittany Spaniel Club of North America. This was a casualty of World War II, but the American Brittany Club was founded in 1942.

Essentials of the breed: The Brittany Spaniel standard calls for a dog between 17½ and 20½ inches at the shoulder. Heights under or over disqualify. The dog is born tail-less, or the tail is docked to four inches or less. A tail substantially longer disqualifies. Preferred colours are dark orange and white or liver and white. Some ticking is allowed; so are roan patterns. Black in the coat, or a nose dark enough to appear black, disqualifies.

The coat is dense, flat, or wavy, but never curly or silky. Excessive feathering is to be penalized. The ears are shorter than those of other spaniels, and are set above eye level. The skull for a dog 19½ inches tall is about 4¼ inches long and 4⅜ inches wide. The muzzle is about two-thirds the length of the skull. A scissors bite is proper, and a dry lip, free of drooling, is required. Body length equals height, and the chest reaches to the elbow in depth. Stifles should be well bent. Leg bone: only moderate as is fitting for a fast moving dog. The toes should be deeply padded and well knuckled up. See colour plate p. 92.

Broken An unfortunate choice of word used to describe a dog which has been trained. Thus 'broken for the gun' means trained for the gun.

Broken Coat This is the old way of describing a harsh, short, wiry coat such as that found on Wire-Haired FOX TERRIERS. At one time the expression Broken-Haired Terrier was used to describe the sort of

Brittany Spaniel.
Above left Detail from a William Hogarth portrait showing a dog resembling a Brittany Spaniel in the role of a lady's companion. Although a sporting dog – it is the world's only pointing spaniel – it is still considered an excellent house dog.
Above Ch. Thorn Patche of Cedar Grove.

Above Broken-up face.

Above Broken coat

terriers which were the ancestors of some of the present day breeds. Varieties which could be said to have a 'broken coat' include AIREDALE, WELSH, LAKELAND, SCOTTISH and SEALYHAM Terriers.

Broken Colour A dog whose major colour is broken by white or another colour.

Broken-Up Face One with a receding, or pushed in nose, deep stop, undershot jaw, and wrinkles. Example: PEKINGESE.

Brood Bitch The breeding, or bloodlines, of a brood bitch is all important. Although not necessarily a show specimen, she should be free from any of the glaring faults of her breed. The same principles should apply as in the choice of a STUD DOG.

A bitch's faults may be transmitted to her offspring. They may not come out in the first generation but might appear in later generations. It is a fallacy to believe that because a good stud dog is used, all puppies will be good ones. The brood bitch should be as good as possible both in her breeding and in her looks. A chance-bred bitch is just as unreliable as a brood as a chance-bred dog is as a sire.

Health and temperament are important considerations in the brood bitch. A shy, nervous, highly-strung bitch must be avoided. In a brood bitch, a slightly longer loin, and width, are desirable. This will, of course, depend to some extent on the breed, but shallow bitches should generally be avoided for breeding.

Brood bitches should always be kept in good, hard condition. If they are allowed to become lethargic and fat they will not be fit for their function and in many cases will not come into season regularly.

The age at which a maiden bitch should be mated varies from breed to breed and also depends on the development of the bitch herself. See BREEDING. A brood bitch is generally at her best as a brood from about 18 months to five or six years. Generally she should not be bred more frequently than once a year, even less with the larger breeds. In deciding whether to mate a bitch at two successive seasons it is necessary to take into consideration the number of puppies she has reared from her previous litter. A big strong bitch of her breed that has only reared two or three puppies and has lost no condition may quite safely be bred from again at her next season. But a bitch that has reared satisfactorily a large litter should not be asked to produce for at least another year. A bitch that has been overworked as a brood cannot be expected to produce top class healthy puppies. She must be allowed sufficient time between litters to recover from the strain imposed upon her.

In the toy breeds it is not advisable to breed from very small bitches. In the toy breeds a larger bitch should be bred to a small dog. This should ensure that the puppies are small enough for normal whelping. Toy brood bitches, like their larger sisters, must be strong, fit and well. It is useless to use small weedy specimens as broods. One must also remember that a true toy is small because it carries the genes which produce smallness and not because it has been poorly reared and a weakling from birth.

Brown Mouth This is the name given to a condition of the gums which leads to brown discoloration and bad smell. It is usually associated with a general bacterial infection of the body and can be treated.

Brucellosis see Abortion.

Brush A bushy tail.

Brushes see Grooming.

Brussels Griffon see Griffon Bruxellois.

Bullbaiting The now-outlawed sport of using dogs, mainly BULLDOGS and BULL TERRIERS, to torment bulls.

Bulldog The Bulldog is essentially British, but it is probably not the most ancient of British breeds. In its present form, the Bulldog is comparatively modern. True, the breed has its roots far back in history but it is the spirit of the dog, the courage, determination and tenacity, rather than the outward appearance that have weathered the centuries.

The *Survey of Stamford* has one of the earliest references to the sport of bull-baiting and therefore to the dogs used in this pastime. It reads, 'William, Earl Warren, Lord of this town in the reign of King John (1209) standing upon the walls of his castle at Stamford, saw two bulls fighting in the castle meadow, till all of the butchers' dogs pursued one of the bulls, which was maddened by the noise and multitude, through the town. This so pleased the Earl that he gave the castle meadow to the butchers of the town on condition that they should find a "mad bull" on a day six weeks before Christmas for the continuance of that sport for ever.'

Inevitably in that less civilized age, the sport prospered, became fashionable and was patronized by both nobility and Royalty. With this popularity came the breeding of dogs most suited to the task, probably by the crossing of the Old English MASTIFF and the lighter and therefore more active local terriers.

The first mention of the Bulldog as a distinct breed occurs in a letter in 1631 by Prestwich Eaton from San Sebastian to George Wellingham of London, asking for a Mastiff and two good 'Bulldogs'. It is doubtful whether these animals would be recognizable members of their breed today as until a century ago they were built much more like the modern STAFFORD-SHIRE BULL TERRIER and lacked the pronounced strength of head and turn-up of under-jaw which are now considered essential.

Early breeders knew that a dog that had to fight a bull must be powerful in front, deep and strong chested, have a massive jaw and light hindquarters to defeat the bull's efforts to shake him off. The irony is that not until long after bull-baiting was made illegal in 1835 were dogs produced that were theoretically capable of fulfilling all the functions for which they were designed.

The next task was to breed dogs of the right type, but to eliminate the ferocity. This was so successful that today it is one of the most dependable, good-natured and amiable breeds. Bulldogs are now more popular than they once were, in both the USA and Great Britain. While opinions differ on whether they are objects of beauty or ugliness, few criticize their temperament, their love of human beings, their sense of fun, their comfortable, amiable way of life or their friendliness and devotion. These qualities, at least to Bulldog devotees, shine out through the slightly forbidding exterior form.

Before leaving this breed mention must be made of the extraordinary influence it has had on other breeds. Despite the fact that the BOXER is German, it owes much to the Bulldog. So does the FRENCH BULLDOG; also the national dog of the United States (the BOSTON TERRIER), the BULL TERRIER, and the BULLMASTIFF.

Essentials of the breed: The head is distinctive with wrinkles and deep indentations. The skull in front of the ears should be equal in circumference to the height at the shoulder. Between the ears, the skull should be flat. The jaws: broad and square, the lower projecting considerably in front of the upper and turning up. The large nose set back between the eyes which are wide apart; the ears; high on the head, small and thin. The stout and strong front legs are placed wide apart, the development of the forearms gives them a bowed outline but bone should be straight. Hind legs are longer than the front which gives the animal an awkward gait. The back: short and strong, very broad at shoulders and tapering at loins, making a roach back. Body pear-shaped, tucked up at belly. Stern is set on low, and carried downwards.

See colour plate p. 186.

Bullmastiff William Shakespeare (1564–1616) wrote: 'That island (England) breeds very valiant creatures; their mastiffs are of unmatchable courage.'
Christopher Smart (1722–1771) wrote:
> 'Well, of all dogs it stands confessed
> Your English Bulldogs are the best!'

Neither of these Poets mentioned the Bullmastiff. The breed did not exist in their time. The MASTIFF has lived in Britain for 2,000 years. The Romans sent the breed to Rome to fight in arenas against both wild beasts and men. Great size and courage made them formidable adversaries, but they were not really aggressive. Instinct fitted them better for the role of guard because they dislike attack and normally only used strength in defence.

A form of BULLDOG has existed in Britain since the thirteenth century. For six hundred years it baited bulls for the amusement of spectators in a rougher and coarser age. It did not have a heritage of guarding. Bulldogs had a fighting instinct; determination, courage and a willingness to suffer pain without flinching.

They found a new role in the latter part of the nine-

Bulldog.
Top left A Goya painting of dogs fighting a bull. The sport of bull-baiting, which developed Britain's national dog, was outlawed in 1835.
Middle left Two famous Bulldogs, *Rose* and *Crib*, painted by Abraham Cooper in the nineteenth century.
Bottom left Ch. Blockbuster Best Bitter.

Right Bullmastiff. Ch. Pixie's Imp of Cascade.

teenth century when poachers in England grew bolder, perhaps from need, making life increasingly difficult for the estate gamekeepers. Penalties became increasingly severe. The crime of stealing game was ever more vigorously punished. This made the position worse. Faced with the certainty of harsh sentences, poachers preferred to fight it out with the gamekeepers if surprised at night. It was better to shoot and escape. Gamekeepers ultimately came to fear not merely for their masters' game but for their own lives.

They retaliated by enlisting the aid of special dogs designed and created for a specific purpose: a cross between a Mastiff and a Bulldog which produced an animal with a combination of virtues.

The keepers wanted a dog faster, more agile and more aggressive than the Mastiff; less ferocious and bigger than the traditional Bulldog. An animal that would remain silent at the approach of the 'enemy'; that would attack only on command, throw down and hold but never savage or maul. And with the Bulldog and Mastiff cross they achieved it.

Little is recorded of their actual prowess in the field. Perhaps both sides were anxious to avoid publicity. Even so, rivalry grew up among keepers as to whose dog was the best. Contests and demon-strations took place, one of which inspired the following account in *The Field* of 20th August 1901:

'Mr. Burton of Thorneywood Kennels brought to the show one Night-dog (not for competition) and offered any person one pound, who could escape from it while securely muzzled. One of the spectators who had had experience with dogs volunteered and amused a large assembly of sportsmen and keepers who had gathered there. The man was given a long start and the muzzled dog slipped after him. The animal caught him immediately and knocked down his man with the first spring. The latter bravely tried to hold his own, but was floored every time he got on his feet, ultimately being kept to the ground until the owner of the dog released him. The man had three rounds with the powerful canine, but was beaten each time and was unable to escape.'

Ultimately a breed club was formed and in 1924 the Bullmastiff was recognized by the Kennel Club (England). By this time the improvement in them was enormous. The original dark brindle, popular for reasons of night camouflage, had given way to reds and fawns. Type was consistent. To ensure progress, the Kennel Club insisted that only dogs with at least three generations of pure-bred Bullmastiff behind them

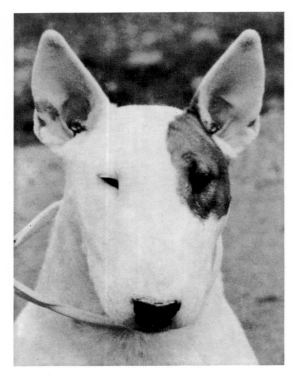

Bull Terrier. The one-time 'gladiator of the canine race' is now known as a boisterous but benevolent and loyal breed. *Above left and right* Ch. Abraxas Athenia.

could be registered. Crossing with either Bulldog or Mastiff had come to an end.

Seven years later the American Kennel Club also granted recognition and progress has been consistent since then. Breed registrations rise despite the dogs' great size and they have become more popular all over the world.

Essentials of the breed: A powerfully built symmetrical dog, strong but not cumbersome. Skull: large and square; in circumference the same as dog's height at shoulder. Muzzle: approximately quarter of total length of head. Dark or hazel eyes, ears V-shaped. Mouth: preferably level but undershot permissible. Chest: wide, deep and set down beneath forelegs. Shoulders: sloping and powerful. Body: short and straight. Hocks moderately bent, and feet well arched and not large. Tail set high, tapering and reaching to hocks. Coat: short and level. Any shade of brindle, fawn or red with dark muzzle. Small white chest marking permissible. Height: 24 inches to 27 inches. Weight: 90 to 110 lb., bitches; 110 to 130 lb., dogs. See colour plate p. 301.

Bull Terrier The Bull Terrier is sometimes called the gladiator of the canine race. From this it is easy to guess that it has a warlike background; it is also easy to guess that some part of the aura of the warrior still surrounds it, that some still think of the breed as aggressive and are afraid of Bull Terriers for their dogs and for themselves.

Like many ideas carried over from earlier times, the proposition is no longer valid. Dogs, like times, change. Development is both natural and inevitable, and the Bull Terrier, like most other breeds, has developed.

Even so, we cannot look at the Bull Terrier without

looking at its background, and this brings us to the abolition of bull-baiting in the early part of the nineteenth century – nearly 150 years ago.

The dogs used in this so-called 'sport' were BULL-DOGS, massive creatures of great strength and tenacity, often slow moving but always determined and courageous. But the mere passing of a bill forbidding a cruel and bloody pastime did not abolish the interest of the populace. Spectacles in a coarser and more brutal age were inevitably savage. Men liked to see one animal pitted against another in a fight to the death. Which means that when it was forbidden to set a dog against a bull, there was a quick change of plan. Dog was set against dog. The bloody battle remained but with the new twist it was inside the law.

It was soon realized that a different type of dog was needed – something with the inherent strength and will of the Bulldog but with a longer foreface; something more punishing and, even more important, faster and more agile.

So began the crossing of Bulldogs with terriers. It would, however, be quite wrong to suggest that anything approaching the modern version of the breed appeared in the early years of the crosses. Not until some considerable time had elapsed did any recognizable type become established, and then it was a type which was far more akin to what we know today as the STAFFORDSHIRE BULL TERRIER.

Dog fighting was in its turn abolished in 1835. It promptly went 'underground' and illegal contests flourished for some time afterwards. But by then, breeders had become interested in the dog for itself rather than for its fighting potential.

Yet another blow was to come to these fanciers. For half a century the dogs had had their ears cropped on the principle that if they did not have ears they could

Above Bull Terrier, Miniature. Topsy of Upend.

not be damaged in fights! In 1895, the Kennel Club (England) abolished the cropping of ears and the smart and typical head of the then existing Bull Terrier very soon vanished.

But breeders were determined. By a process of selection they soon produced dogs with small, neat and erect ears. These are the ears that are seen on the dogs of today.

Since the head is the most important and impressive feature of a Bull Terrier, it is worth examining in detail. Huge and powerful, it is shaped like an egg or a rugby or American football. There is no hollow or chiselling on the upper jaw. In this head is set a neat, black, almond-shaped eye. The non-terrier man sees this eye as glinting, hard and penetrating. The terrier fancier sees it as something almost soft in its jet black intensity.

Little trace of the breed's warlike background remains in its modern temperament. While still alert and lively, Bull Terriers are astonishingly benevolent in disposition and almost without exception the friend of man. Traditionally 'fond of children', it is an excellent friend, companion and *confidant* of a growing and boisterous boy.

One other surprising feature of this breed is the improvement in its relationship with other dogs. Look at a ringful of them at a Dog Show and you will be surprised; it is usually a ringful of waving tails!

Essentials of the breed: Head long, strong and deep; egg-shaped and completely filled and without hollows. Profile to curve gently down from skull to tip of black nose. Strong underjaw. Eyes: dark, triangular and well sunken. Ears: small, thin and capable of being held stiffly erect. Scissors bite. Arched muscular neck. Good round bone, sloping shoulders. Good spring of rib,

short strong back, underline curving gracefully upwards. Round compact feet. Tail: short, tapering, set on low and carried horizontally. Short harsh coat. Pure white (head markings permissible) or coloured, preferably brindle.

See colour plate p. 369.

Bull Terrier, Miniature This breed, or to be more correct, this variety of a breed, is only recognized in a few places outside Great Britain. It is a rarity in the United States and Canada. However, the Fédération Cynologique International, a body fairly generous with its recognition of rare and unusual breeds, accepts it, as does the English Kennel Club, which first granted the breed recognition in September 1943. The catalogue of CRUFT'S, lists the following information.

'The historical records reveal that "small Bull Terriers" existed in the early nineteenth century and the Miniature Bull Terrier has been evolved from this early small Bull Terrier and the old Toy Bull Terrier. There was considerable divergence in weight for some years and from 1900 to 1914 this was fixed at under 12 lb. Breeders, however, found it difficult to breed typical specimens of this size and many of them gave up breeding; by 1918 the breed was in danger of extinction. The weight was then raised to 18 lb. and better progress was made.'

Not all of the above statements are easily verified. For example, although these miniatures may 'have existed in the early nineteenth century', Stonehenge, a celebrated canine commentator of the day, did not even mention them in his all-embracing book *The Dog* (1859).

However, Rawdon Lee, a terrier specialist, in his *Modern Dogs* (1903) deals at length with the ever increasing tendency to breed larger and larger Bull Terriers. Indeed he expresses regret that a Mr. Shirley, a breeder of the time did not persevere with his small Bull Terriers.

The impression left by this chapter dealing with Bull Terriers' weight is that there were merely larger or smaller dogs of the same breed. The smaller ones were attractive, but it was the big ones which won in the show ring.

This gave rise to the practice of scheduling special classes for Bull Terriers under a certain weight, usually 16 lb. The intention was to remove the competition of the big dogs, thereby ensuring that some prize cards went to the owners of the little dogs to encourage them.

The only real encouragement these breeders ever had was the aforementioned official recognition of the Kennel Club and the publication of a breed standard in 1943. Even so, it has to be recorded that in Britain, their original home, they have failed to get into the top 100 breeds! Charm they have, but it appears to be little recognized.

Essentials of the breed: The standard is the same as for that of the Bull Terrier with the following exceptions: Height must not be more than 14 inches. Weight should not be more than 20 lb.

temporary soreness. Such burns, unless about the face or the soles of the feet, are rare in dogs. The dog's fur either prevents such burns, or prevents them from entering the second class.

The skin has a number of layers. A second degree burn is one which kills the outer layers of skin only, and which causes blisters which often break and weep. A third degree burn is one which destroys all layers of skin, and usually, underlying tissues as well.

First degree burns can be treated by the use of any burn remedy available for human use. For example, a sunburn ointment might be used, and is generally available in homes. If one is not available, the area can be bathed in a strong solution of tea. In fact, strong tea is an excellent first aid treatment even for third degree burns.

Second degree burns should be treated by a veterinarian. If one is not immediately available, strong tea can be used. In addition, hair likely to become impacted in the scab that will form should be clipped away.

Third degree burns present two problems. The first is to prevent shock, and the second is to prevent infection. In such burns, blood plasma leaves the blood and moves into the tissues beneath the burns. It then leaks out. If sufficient plasma is lost in this way, there is insufficient blood to return to the heart. The heart cannot maintain normal blood pressure. The dog then goes into SHOCK. In modern medicine, there is a rule that, if the patient cannot be treated for shock within two to three hours of the burns, then any shock treatment is useless. It is therefore of vital importance to get the dog to a veterinarian immediately.

He will not wait for shock to develop, but will give treatment, possibly infusions of plasma, whole blood, or a salt solution. He may also give glucose. And he will then try to prevent infection from developing in the killed areas of the flesh. A ten per cent tannic acid solution helps to start a scab which helps to prevent infection from outside. However, an infection may develop underneath the scab. The veterinarian will try to prevent this by using antibiotics, or by using a chemical, such as gentian violet, which discourages the development of certain bacteria.

Diet cannot be ignored in either second or third degree burn cases. The dog will require a high protein diet, and one easily digested. Vitamin supplements to about four or five times the normal dosage should be added, and the diet should be low in fat. Severely burned dogs seldom have much appetite. Consequently forced feeding is often necessary.

There is a third factor which must be faced by the owner of a badly burned dog. If a dog receives second degree burns over fifty per cent of its body, recovery is doubtful. Similarly, if it receives third degree burns over more than twenty per cent of its body, recovery is also doubtful. Moreover, healing is both a very slow and a painful process. Hair can never grow over the burned areas. Sedatives, even when administered lightly to ease pain, can cause death. And therefore, the owner must make a major decision. Will he permit the dog to live, perhaps only to die after months of agony, or will he give it merciful death without delay?

Left Burns and scalds. Boiling liquids accidentally spilled from cooking pots are a major source of burns and scalds.

Burns and Scalds Burns can be classified as external and internal. External burns to dogs can be caused by flames, hot water or other liquids, and occasionally from chemicals. A major source of such burns comes from boiling liquids accidentally spilled from cooking pots. Internal burns come from inhaling flames, hot smoke, and steam. Burning homes, piles of burning leaves from which the wind causes sudden bursts of flame, and broken steam pipes, are frequent causes.

Burns are classified in another way – first, second, and third degree. First degree burns are those which sear only the outer layer of skin, and cause only redness and

Colour plate Pointer. Ch. Waghorn Statesman.

(Continued on p. 97)

Top left Flat-Coated Retrievers. Left to right, Collyers Christina, Collyers Banda, Collyers Patch, Ch. Collyers Blakeholme Brewster and Ch. Asperula.

Middle left Golden Retriever. Ch. Sharland the Scot.

Bottom left Chesapeake Bay Retriever. Ryshott Welcome Yank.

Right Labrador Retrievers. Candlemas Simon of Keithray and Ch. Candlemas Rookwood Silver Moonlight.

Top left Irish Water Spaniel.
Ch. Jakes of Tarbay.

Bottom left Curly-Coated
Retriever. Banworth Victor Hugo.

Top right German Wire-Haired
Pointer. Ch. Rusty v. Schnellberg.

Bottom right German Short-
Haired Pointer. Ch. Happy
Hollow's Tricky Target.

Left Irish Setters. Ch. Wendover Caskey, Caskey's Cleoni and Orichalc Irvine.

Top right Gordon Setter. Ch. Torrance of Ellicott.

Bottom right English Setter. Yankee of Neighbours, groomed in English style.

Left Welsh Springer Spaniel. Ch. Deri Darrett of Linkhill.

Top right English Springer Spaniel. Ch. Teesview Titus.

Bottom right Clumber Spaniel. Ch. Fraston Anchorfield Bardolph.

pages 88–89

Left Cocker Spaniel, American. Ch. Be Gay's Tan Man.

Top right Cocker Spaniel, English. Bradpark Blondette.

Bottom right Sussex Spaniel. Ch. Chesara Chervil of Sedora.

pages 92–93

Top left Schnauzer, Standard.
Bond Pankow's Black Irishman.

Bottom left Schnauzer, Giant.
Ch. Camoli's Gemini of the East.

Top right Poodle, Miniature.
Ch. Stanlyn Cleopatra.

Bottom right Poodle, Toy, in
puppy clip.

(Continued from p. 80)

Top right Button ear.
Bottom right Butterfly nose.

Chemical burns usually result from splashing, in which case the coat may lessen the damage, or from walking in a strong acid or alkali substance. The dog licks its paws or fur, and then burns its tongue. The chemical will continue to act as long as it comes into contact with the flesh. As a rule, it can be sufficiently diluted to be harmless, or it can be washed away, simply by bathing in water. The veterinarian should be consulted as to further treatment.

Inhalation burns present a different problem. No direct treatment of the burned areas – usually the throat, trachea, and lungs – is possible. The veterinarian will administer antibiotics to prevent infection, and he may administer oxygen therapy.

Burr The inside of the ear. An irregular formation within the cup of the ear.

Butterfly Dog see Papillon.

Butterfly Nose A parti-coloured nose. Usually a black nose with pink spots.

Button Ear An ear folded forward, lying close to the head, and pointing towards the eye. The ear of the WHIPPET, GREYHOUND, or BORZOI when held back against the neck is described as 'buttoned back'.

Buying a Puppy Which is the best way to choose and buy a puppy? Perhaps the best way of answering this question is to look at three of the worst ways.

The first is for a man to take his wife and children round a dogs' home or pound. Soulful eyes gaze out. Reason promptly departs from all of the family. In a record short time they have acquired a pup. It may well be completely unsatisfactory in both size and temperament, but by then it is too late. Every pup is a super self-salesman. So accept that he who looks is lost!

Another bad system is to visit a fashionable shop in a fashionable part of town. Once again the pups will sell themselves and not until one is home will one wonder whether a ST. BERNARD is really preferable to a PEKINGESE. This method of buying is also expensive.

Finally, a man could adopt either course but without taking or consulting his family. He would make the same number of mistakes but he would be reminded of them more often! All of this implies that the best method is to discuss the proposition before taking action. Individual members of the family may want a GERMAN SHEPHERD, a YORKSHIRE TERRIER, an IRISH SETTER or a POODLE.

Then there are practical considerations: is the house big enough for a Shepherd? Will the little Yorkshire relish boisterous games? Is there time to exercise a Setter? Will Poodle grooming cost too much? The end result may be a compromise. For example, this family might finally decide a COCKER SPANIEL would be best.

Consider carefully because you can only really be happy with a dog that can be happy with you. He has no part in the choice. But he still has to live with you for perhaps a dozen years.

Consider space. A big dog is not likely to be happy in a small house. Remember also that big dogs have big and therefore expensive appetites. Hearty exercise-loving types do not go well with CHIHUAHUAS. Moreover, very few toy dogs really like high-spirited children. If time is short, beware of the long-coated breeds. AFGHANS, OLD ENGLISH SHEEPDOGS and Poodles look wonderful when in full bloom. But there is a lot of backstage grooming needed to keep them that way.

An evening's study should enable most people to produce a short list of possible breeds. Then the final choice belongs to the lady of the house. Despite the promises, she is the one who will have to feed, groom, exercise and live close to the dog.

At this point you know what breed you are looking for. Now you need to know where to look. Most Kennels specialize in breeds and therefore you can avoid the risk of being sidetracked by an appealing but unsuitable dog. If you do not know a Kennel, a Breed Club or Society will help by telling you of one, and Breed Society addresses can be obtained from the Kennel Club.

You are now ready to go out shopping and you have a much better chance than the 'impulse buyer' of becoming a successful dog owner.

Contrary to popular opinion, most dog BREEDERS are honest. But you should still take reasonable precautions when buying an animal which will fit closely into your life.

Colour plate Poodle, Standard. Ch. Springett Polar de la Fontaine, Springett Park Quite the Lady, and their seven-week-old family.

Not all litters bred from local pets by loving but comparatively inexperienced owners are well reared. Professionals and show Kennels cannot afford the luxury of second-rate propositions with the attendant criticism and loss of goodwill.

If money is no object take a veterinarian with you; otherwise, use a layman's common sense thereby avoiding serious mistakes. Shun pups with runny noses, runny eyes or diarrhoea. All indicate ill health, possibly serious. Spots on the stomach may foretell distemper. Sore or smelly ears, red or spongy gums are also danger signals.

Although you are not buying the Kennels have a look round. Then look at the bitch. If both appear clean, fresh and healthy, good management has probably ensured the puppy a bright start.

Unless you are buying a show dog, do not worry over so-called 'show points'. If you are buying a pet what you want are 'pet points'. For example, a good temperament matters much more than a long or short nose. A robust constitution is of greater interest than a well-placed tail.

Serious faults are aggression and timidity. The first is never present in a puppy and wise upbringing will prevent its development. Timidity shows very early. Avoid pups which cringe and shrink away. Also beware of those which hide under tables and cry in terror when lifted. Dogs should be friendly. So look for friendly and bold puppies. Take to your heart the one which takes you to his.

It is impossible to give a price on the cost of a puppy. This depends on a large number of factors of which the modern tendency towards inflation is but one. The quality of the animal is another. Additionally it is obvious that chic breeds in fashionable areas will inevitably cost far more than down-to-earth breeds in less prosperous districts.

Before you leave the kennels there are various things you should ask for. First you should always obtain a Pedigree Form, and if the puppy has been registered with a Kennel Club, a signed Transfer Form should be handed over to enable you to re-register the puppy in your own name. You should also check if it has been wormed or inoculated. Moreover you should request a diet sheet even though you may already have strong ideas on the best method of feeding dogs. It is important to avoid too many changes in routine at the same time. If the diet is to be changed you would be wise to leave things as they are until the dog has settled into the new household.

See CHOOSING A BREED.

Bye or Bye-dog An odd dog at a field trial for which there is no brace-mate.

Left Cairn Terrier. Fearless, jaunty but unaggressive, hard-working and strong — this shaggy little terrier is the ideal 'man's dog'. Thax Dixie Dan.

C

Caesarean Operation The Caesarean operation is so called because tradition has it that Julius Caesar was delivered in this way. In principle, the operation is very simple, the abdomen being opened and the pups removed from the uterus. The technique is far from simple for the aim of the operation is to end up with a live bitch and a litter of live pups. Great skill is required not only on the part of the surgeon, but also by the anaesthetist and the nurses.

The surgeon refers to the operation as a Caesarean section or Caesarean hysterotomy. The only call for the operation is in those cases where the bitch is unable to deliver the pups in the normal way. The most common reason is some disproportion between the size and shape of the pups and the bitch's pelvis. Certain breeds such as the BOSTON TERRIER and the SCOTTISH TERRIER have difficulties of this nature. There are unfortunate individual cases in all breeds where there is only one pup which grows to such an enormous size that it cannot possibly be delivered naturally. Sometimes there may be some obstruction to delivery, as in the case of a bitch which has been in a motor accident and suffered a fracture of the pelvis. Occasionally two pups get so wedged at delivery that they cannot be delivered by external manipulation.

Uterine inertia is another reason for a Caesarean operation. Either the bitch never really starts to whelp at all or else she becomes exhausted and stops trying. In either case injections may help, but more often surgery is required.

The veterinarian is the only one who can decide if and when a Caesarean operation is necessary. The breeder should accept his decision. The experienced breeder can tell if a whelping is progressing normally and knows when to call for professional assistance. The less experienced should remember the old rule: it is better to be safe than sorry, and call for help early rather than too late. If an operation should be necessary the veterinarian will ask if the bitch is required for further breeding. The reason for this question is that occasionally at the operation it is found that all the pups are dead, or the uterus is damaged or diseased. In this situation it may be better to remove the uterus *in toto*, thus converting the operation to a Caesarean hysterectomy.

A Caesarean operation is nearly always successful and does not tire the bitch nearly as much as a long, hard and fruitless labour. If this operation is performed in good time, that is before the bitch becomes too exhausted, she can be nursing her litter within three or four hours. If a bitch once has a Caesarean section it does not necessarily mean that the next time she mates she will not whelp naturally, and it does not affect her in any detrimental way. Several Caesareans can be performed on one bitch, although many experts consider that a bitch should not be allowed to have a further litter if she has had two Caesarean operations.

Right Caesarean operation. If for some reason pups cannot be delivered normally or by external manipulation, a veterinarian will cut open the bitch's abdomen and remove her pups from the uterus.

Cairn Terrier The early history of this breed, currently one of Britain's most popular terriers, was not documented at the time. The dog's background is shrouded in discreet anonymity. The reason for this is simply that the Cairn was a working breed owned by working breeders. The men of Scotland who used these dogs to keep down vermin got on with the job and left canine historians to fend for themselves.

However, this much can be said with certainty. The Cairn was in existence for many years, possibly centuries before it made its first appearance in the show ring in 1909. Seventy years before this, Martin's *History of the Dog* had given an excellent written description of the breed.

Until they came to dog shows, however, Cairns were little known outside the districts in which they lived and worked. These were the Western Highlands and some of the Islands off the west coast of Scotland, of which Skye is the best known. Perhaps in view of their association with this island, it was inevitable that they should become confused with the already firmly established SKYE TERRIER. There were even determined attempts to call the dogs 'Short Haired Skye Terriers'. This move was frustrated, not as one might have thought by the Cairn contingent, but by the Skye specialists! The ultimate choice of name was in any case far more apt because it was in the cairns, or piled heaps of stones and rocks of Scotland, that these hardy little dogs had first proved their value by their determined efforts to destroy all vermin including otters, foxes and even wild cats.

It is a widely held opinion that dog shows have spoiled, possibly ruined, a number of working terrier breeds. Fortunately, this is an accusation that has never been levelled against the Cairn because the emphasis throughout its show career has been in preserving not only its working qualities but its workmanlike appearance. Fancy barbering is frowned upon, although a little tidying up of the coat is acceptable. Too close a resemblance to the slightly overdone modern Scottish Terrier is also considered undesirable. The breed standard or 'blueprint' of the breed sums up its appearance succinctly by insisting that it must appear fearless, gay, hardy, shaggy and strong.

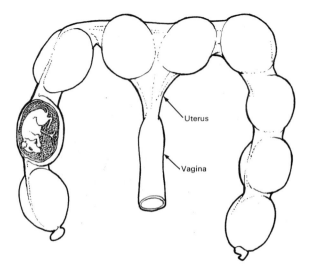

Uterus

Vagina

Probably what has taken this breed into the forefront of terriers is the fact that it combines all of the advantages of its race with none of the disadvantages. Terrier lovers like a dog that is cheeky and full of fire. But this is not to say that they like their dog involved in frequent fights. The Cairn while jaunty and game is not usually aggressive.

Many terrier lovers also like dogs with harsh, weatherproof coats. Not all however, like regular trips to the hairdresser. A Cairn needs the minimum of tidying up, and even that only when show-going. More important, it is the right size for this modern age, and so adaptable that it takes to either town or country life with equal facility. Standing under 10 inches high, weighing a mere 14 lb., it can be tucked under the arm in city traffic or let loose on a grouse moor. Its appetite for food is modest, for life unlimited! It gets on well with children, will learn to respect the family cat, perform tricks, obey instructions and still look like a terrier. In short, it is the ideal 'man's dog' and often irresistible to women.

Essentials of the Breed. Skull broad, with a decided indentation between the eyes; hair full on forehead. Muzzle: powerful. Very strong jaw, neither under- nor over-shot. Eyes: set wide apart; medium size; dark hazel. Shaggy eyebrows. Ears: small, pointed, erect, not too closely set. Neck: well set on, not short. Forequarters: sloping shoulder and a medium length of leg; good, but not too large bone. Forelegs should not be out at elbow. Legs: covered with hard hair. Body: compact, straight back, of medium length, well sprung deep ribs. Very strong hindquarters. Forefeet should be larger than hind, and slightly turned out. Pads: thick and strong. Tail: short, well furnished with hair but not feathery; carried gaily but should not turn down towards back. Coat must be double, with profuse hard outer coat. Undercoat: short, soft and close. Head should be well furnished.

Colour: red, sandy, grey, brindled or nearly black. Dark points such as ears and muzzle very typical. In America, any colour except white. Ideal weight: 14 lb. Height: 10 inches (dogs); 9½ inches (bitches). See colour plate p. 377.

Calcium see Nutrition.

Canadian Kennel Club see Kennel Club, Canadian.

Cancer see Tumours.

Canine From Canidae. The animals of the dog family, such as wolves, dingoes (feral), and dogs (domestic).

Canine Babesiasis see Jaundice.

Canine Piroplasmosis (Babesiasis) see Protozoan Diseases.

Canines The two upper and the two lower long, sharp corner teeth. Synonyms: fangs, tusks and (colloquially) tushes.

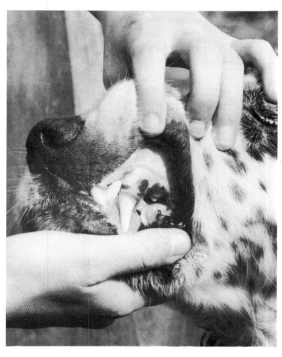

Top left Cairn Terrier. A small Cairn-like dog from Jan van Eyck's Arnolfini marriage portrait, painted 1434.

Middle left Canine. Wolves are wild members of the dog family.
Bottom left Canines: the lower and upper corner teeth.

Canine Typhus see Gums; Heart Diseases.

Canker see Ear Diseases.

Cannibalism In some wild animal species, the mother may kill her young. Some rodents, under certain circumstances of stress, will kill and devour their young. Such cannibalism is rare in dogs. When it does occur, it is usually considered that the bitch is insane in that particular respect. Cannibalism apparently occurred more frequently one hundred years ago than it has in the last several decades. This fact opens two possibilities other than insanity. One is that an hereditary factor has been lost in the modern dog. The second is that a severe dietary imbalance may have been the cause.

Occasionally, a case will be reported in which the dam has eviscerated some, or all, of her puppies. The cause is not known, but the problem is not considered to be true cannibalism.

Those bitches which entirely devour their puppies are considered to be incurable. A Gordon Setter, which was known to have devoured two previous litters, whelped a third time. She was watched closely until the puppies were four weeks old and the weaning process had begun. Yet the bitch devoured the entire litter during one night.

Cape Hunting Dog see False Dogs.

Cardigan Corgi see Welsh Corgi, Cardigan.

Care of the Sick Dog see Nursing Sick Dogs.

Carlin see Pug.

Castration Castration consists in the surgical removal of the testicles. It can be performed at any age. The younger the puppy, the simpler the operation. However, the castration of very young puppies has been blamed by some people for inability to control the bladder in later life. At one time it was considered that the dog became obese, and the fat was so placed upon the body that, even at a great distance, one instantly recognized the castrated dog. In fact this is now known to occur where the castrated dog is overfed. The food requirement of a neutered dog is less than that of an entire animal.

The veterinarian may advise castration for medical reasons. But the usual reasons for such surgery are to keep the dog from siring pups, and to keep him from chasing after neighbourhood bitches when in season, or when a dog becomes bad-tempered. Males which chase often become neighbourhood roamers. They become a nuisance, and their lives may be shortened, both because of dog fights, and the much greater danger of dying in traffic.

Copulation is not necessary for the health of the male dog. In fact, most dogs go through life without ever experiencing it. The castrated dog may chase after the bitches as he formerly did; however once the hormones produced by the testicles have disappeared from the bloodstream (after some months) the castrated dog usually becomes more docile and loses his sexual drive.

Many veterinarians suggest that castration be postponed until the dog is close to sexual maturity. And that, in the meantime, he be guarded from the chance to experience sex.

Cataracts see Blindness; Eye Diseases.

Cat-foot A compact rounded foot; one with short third digits.

Cattle Dog see Australian Cattle Dog.

Cavalier King Charles Spaniel It may seem a curious way to clarify an issue to start by confusing it! Nevertheless, to appreciate the story of the Cavalier one must first know the story of that similar breed which causes confusion in so many minds: the KING CHARLES SPANIEL.

Briefly, the King Charles, often for the sake of clarity referred to by the nickname of 'Charlie', has been known in Britain for over four centuries. It was a race of diminutive spaniels which were never used for sport. They were, and remain, pet dogs.

We know that the English King Charles II kept large numbers of them and was devoted to them, and that they took their name from him. In his company they adorn canvases and tapestries, all of which show that they were allowed free access at all times to Whitehall, Hampton Court and the other Royal Palaces.

We know that Samuel Pepys, the diarist, was sharply critical of this, writing: 'All I observed was the silliness of the King, playing with his dogs all the while and not minding his business'. Even this however did not stop the breed from becoming the established favourite with the aristocracy of the time.

Right Cavalier King Charles Spaniels show a strong resemblance to a much older type of dog, like the one shown sitting comfortably in this early eighteenth-century painting by Giuseppe Maria Crespi.

The spaniel heritage of these dogs is important. If we think of them almost as miniature Cockers we have some idea of their appearance. Around the middle of the nineteenth century, however, subtle changes took place in their appearance, probably because of the introduction of foreign blood. They became smaller, distinctly shorter in the muzzle and nose, and more rounded in the skull. In short, the breed lost some of its characteristically spaniel-like appearance and took on that of the Toy.

Important developments began about 1920. The fuse was lit by Mr. Eldridge, an American citizen living on Long Island who realized that the spaniels had strayed far from the originals painted so often by the great masters of the sixteenth and seventeenth centuries.

He offered additional first prizes of £25 ($60) at CRUFT's Dog Show for 'Blenheim Spaniels' of the old type which should have 'long faces, flat skulls, no inclination to be domed, no stop and a beauty spot in the centre of the forehead'.

If that was what he wanted, that is what he was going to get. British breeders starting from scratch reconstructed the original type in a remarkably short time. The Cavalier King Charles spaniel had arrived. The breeders, meantime, pocketed a great deal of Mr. Eldridge's cash, and one suspects that originally they were more interested in this aspect of the subject than of the purity in type.

The formation of a breed club followed soon afterwards in 1928. From then on, at least in Britain, their popularity increased until it passed that of the original King Charles Spaniel. In 1960 the Cavaliers received a further boost. Princess Margaret and the Earl of Snowdon took one into their home, and into the pages of the glossy magazines. They named him *Rowley*, an amusing reference to the Princess's ancestor whose nickname had been 'Old Rowley'.

Although only admitted to the Kennel Club (Britain) registers in 1944, they are already within striking distance of entering the twenty most popular breeds. In the United States they are still not recognized officially and, although the four varieties of English Toy Spaniel are fully recognized, the Cavalier is allowed to compete only in Miscellaneous Classes. One imagines that they will be promoted from this humble position in the fairly near future.

Essentials of the breed: Active, graceful, sporting in character and free in action. Head: almost flat between the ears, without dome. Stop: shallow; length from base of stop to tip about 1½ inches. Muzzle: tapered to point. Eyes: large, dark, spaced well apart. Ears: long and set high; mouth, level.

Shoulders not too straight. Legs: moderate bone. Body: short-coupled with spring of rib. Level back. Moderate chest. Feet: compact, cushioned and feathered. The length of tail in balance with body. Coat: long, silky and free from curl, with ample feathering. Colour: *Black and Tan* – black with bright tan markings above eyes, on cheeks, inside ears, on chest and legs and underside of tail; *Ruby* – whole-coloured rich red; *Blenheim* – rich chestnut markings on pearly white, evenly divided on head leaving room between the ears for the lozenge; *Tri-colour* (Prince Charles) – black and white with tan markings over the eyes, on cheeks, inside ears, inside legs and on underside of tail. Weight: 10 to 18 lb.

See colour plate p. 380.

Chaining Dogs Most authorities are agreed that chaining a dog out of doors, or to a small outside kennel is about the worst thing that can happen to it. Dogs cast in their future with man thousands of years ago. They want to be with people. And that means they are happiest when they are in the home.

Because of dog control laws (see LEGAL STATUS OF THE DOG), dogs can seldom be allowed to roam at large. And with modern automobile traffic such as it is, death or injury in the streets waits for most roaming dogs. So it may happen that dogs have to be chained outside,

Cavalier King Charles Spaniel.
Above left The enthusiasm of Mr Eldridge for the old-type 'Blenheim Spaniels' with their long faces, flat skulls, and absence of dome and stop, produced the breed known in Britain as Cavalier King Charles Spaniels.
Above Ch. Dickon of Littlebreach.

Right Chaining dogs outside for long periods is unwise as serious character faults may develop; but if a dog must be tied up, a lead attached to a wire strung between, say, a post and a tree is better than a fixed chain.

but this should be for short periods and not overnight.

When dogs are chained out for entire days, or permanently, they usually develop character faults. These are caused by frustration and boredom. The dog has no way to work off its energy, and boredom causes additional frustration.

Chained dogs often solve this by continuous barking. Many insult passers-by, canine and human, by barking and lunging at the end of the chain. Thousands of children who approach too closely, get severely scratched, as the dog lunges and stands on his hind legs, his front legs pawing the air. This lunging, barking, and scratching eventually turns to biting.

A wire run from home to the back of the garage, or to a tree, helps. The dog can then go to the far end of the run to relieve itself. But dogs seldom exercise for the love of exercise. Consequently, they are likely to use the run only to go to the far end to relieve themselves. Or they may rush up and down the length of the run to bark and growl at passing dogs or children. The result is the same as with the dog on a short chain, except that the dog on the wire run, has a greater opportunity to do damage.

Preferable to any form of chaining are fenced areas out of doors, and wood or wire crates indoors when a dog must be restricted or left without human attention and control at times.

Challenge Certificates In Great Britain and the majority of countries in the British Commonwealth, plus other countries like Argentina, the title of Champion is earned by winning three Challenge Certificates under three separate judges.

The judge in Britain must have permission from the Kennel Club to award Challenge Certificates, which are limited in number and linked with the number of dogs represented annually. Thus the most popular breed in Britain has thirty-eight sets of Challenge Certificates annually while some of the minor breeds have only five. When annual registrations are particularly restricted, no Challenge Certificates at all are available so that it is not possible to make a champion although the purity of the breed is still officially recognized. Some examples in Britain are the CHESA-PEAKE BAY RETRIEVER, and AFFENPINSCHER which are well-known in other countries but exist in England in such low numbers as to make an award of the title Champion meaningless.

A judge awarding Challenge Certificates can only do so to Best of Sex, and then only if he is clearly of the opinion that the dog is worthy of the title of Champion. A statement to this effect is signed on a card which is presented to the owner. If the judge is not clearly of this opinion the instructions are precise. He *must* withhold it and mark his judging book accordingly. While never popular with exhibitors, there are many judges whose integrity forces them to withhold the award on occasions.

Championship Points see Championships; Championships, American; Championships, British; Championships, Canadian; Federation Cynologique Internationale.

Championships The title of Champion is widely misunderstood by the layman. It is not a generalization denoting a good class of dog. Therefore loose statements such as, 'My dog has never been shown but is a championship dog', are manifestly incorrect.

Equally the title is not automatically awarded to substantial prize winners. It is, in every country in the world, a title competed for under precise rules and which is only gained by successful competition at a minimum of three or four different shows in special classes designated in advance as carrying eligibility towards the allocation of that title. Although all countries have broadly this same requirement, it has to be admitted that the difficulties encountered in pursuit of the title vary from one country to the next.

As with other administrative questions there are three main schools: the British, the American and the Federation Cynologique Internationale. Statistically it is most likely that a show dog will become a champion under F.C.I. rules. It is least likely under Kennel Club (Britain) rules. In other words, a lesser proportion of dogs shown under British rules become champions than under American rules, while American rules produce proportionally fewer champions than F.C.I. rules.

Even so, the implication that champions are common in the United States, and very common in continental

Europe is misleading. Commonness depends on which breed and where the dog comes from. To give a simple example of the system: Zambia, running under modified British rules might muster a dozen GERMAN SHEPHERDS at its dog shows. So it is easier to make a champion in Zambia than under F.C.I. rules in Germany where there may be over 500 German Shepherds competing.

Equally there are some specimens of numerically weak breeds in Britain who have titles they could never have won in the stronger competition of those breeds in the United States. These contradictions also happen in reverse and suggest that it is wise to avoid block comparisons.

See CHAMPIONSHIPS, AMERICAN; CHAMPIONSHIPS, BRITISH; CHAMPIONSHIPS, CANADIAN; FEDERATION CYNOLOGIQUE INTERNATIONALE.

Championships, American
Show, or conformation, championships in the United States are awarded on the basis of a points system. It requires 15 points to become a champion. But a dog must win at a minimum of two shows that have a rating of three points or better, and under different judges. One or more of the remaining points must be won under at least one other judge. A three points win is called a 'major', four points, a 'four point major'; and five, a 'five point major'.

The points system is based upon three factors, and the nation is divided into zones. The factors are the number of dogs in a given breed registered annually in the zone, the number of dogs of the breed which compete in the zone, and the number of shows given annually in the zone. Point ratings are revised regularly as the three factors fluctuate.

There are shows, at which, because of insufficient entries, no points can be won. The lowest point rating is one, and the highest is five. In some breeds, and in some zones, the point rating will vary between the sexes. Only the dogs winning in the Winners' class – Winners' Dog and Winners' Bitch – can win championship points. If points are uneven, then the dog getting Best of Winners is entitled to the higher point rating.

In computing points won at a show, absentees are not counted; neither can dogs be included which have been disqualified, dismissed for any reason, or from which all awards have been withheld. A judge may withhold the Winners' award, and therefore championship points, for lack of merit. If a dog, which competed in the regular classes and won Winners, then goes on to win the group or Best in Show, he or she is entitled to the highest rating given to any dog in the group, or in the show, as the case may be. In counting eligible dogs, champions cannot be included unless they competed in the Open class.

Examples of point ratings follow. The one requiring the fewest competitors is for the rarer breeds. With two dogs competing, one point is given; three yield two points; four give three; five give four; and six yield five. Sometimes, in these rare breeds, the sexes are combined. There is then only one Winners' Dog or Bitch, but the yield in championship points is greater.

Highest number of eligible competitors for points is

MEJOR DE EXPOSICION

Championships. Many countries are members of the Federation Cynologique Internationale and hold shows under its rules. *Above* Ch. Karellmar Arrow's Target wins Best in Show at Mexico City.

required in GERMAN SHEPHERD competition. In this breed, as in other popular breeds, the points ratio may vary between dogs and bitches. Here are examples, using German Shepherds. Required for one point in the East-North U.S. zone are seven dogs and bitches; for two, 18 dogs, 19 bitches; for three, 46 dogs, 56 bitches; and for five, 70 dogs and 80 bitches. In California, the ratings for the same breed are: for one point, seven dogs and bitches; for two, 24 dogs, 20 bitches; for three, 46, dogs, 40 bitches; for four, 55 dogs and 58 bitches; and for five points, 66 dogs, 64 bitches.
See FIELD TRIALS, AMERICAN.

Championships, British
The title of Champion under the British system is awarded to any dog which is awarded three CHALLENGE CERTIFICATES, usually abbreviated to C.C.'s, and there must be at least one open class in each sex in the breed for which they are offered.

The judge can award a C.C. to the best of sex provided that he is 'clearly of the opinion that the dog is worthy of the title of Champion'. He signs a statement to this effect in each instance. If he is not clearly of that opinion he *must* withhold the Challenge Certificate. This is not infrequently done and it has never, at least in Britain, been allowed to develop into an automatic award.

The major difference between this and other systems is that there is no special class for Champions only. They are entered in the open class. Thus aspiring champions must compete against not only other contenders but also against the already established.

Championships, Canadian
Canadian dog shows are very close to American shows in their mode of operation. Canadian dogs also win points in much the same manner as American dogs. But there are differences. A dog must earn ten or more championship points under at least three different judges. It must defeat at least one dog of its own breed, or it must place

THE AMERICAN KENNEL CLUB
CHAMPIONSHIP CERTIFICATE

This certifies that

GORDON SETTER

PINEPATCH LUCKY ACE OF SPADES   SA-502376

owned by   CHARLES F. ZIMMER

*having completed the requirements for a championship
on* SEPTEMBER 1, 1969 *has been officially recorded a*

CHAMPION

by The American Kennel Club.

Roy H. Celberg
Secretary

Above Championships, American. A typical challenge certificate. A dog exhibited at American shows must collect fifteen points under regulated conditions to become a champion.

in a group in which at least five breeds are competing. A major difference between Canadian and American events is that a dog must compete in all classes and groups for which it is eligible, or all awards made at that show are cancelled. Thus, if a dog wins Best of Breed, it must stay for group judging unless excused by a veterinarian.

Canada, like the United States, divides its nation into territories. Point ratings are worked out much as they are in the United States, but because there are both fewer dogs and fewer shows, the number of dogs required to make points is lower. As in the United States, the point requirements for GERMAN SHEPHERDS are highest. Two dogs make one point, seven make three, and fifteen make five in one zone. In rare breeds, a single entry can win one point, four make three points, and eight make five.

Championships, International see Federation Cynologique Internationale.

Check The point at which scent is lost, thus requiring the hound to 'check back' to find the trail.

Cherry Nose An off-coloured, pink nose. A disqualification in FOX TERRIERS.

Chesapeake Bay Retriever The history of the Chesapeake Bay Retriever begins in 1807 with the wrecking of an English brig off the coast of Maryland. Among those rescued were two puppies said to have been NEWFOUNDLANDS. Tradition says that one was a dingy red dog named *Sailor*, and the other a black bitch named *Canton*. Both dogs were apparently superior water dogs, and were mated with local retrievers of various types with some success.

In 1827, a 'Gentleman of Philadelphia' wrote in the *American Shooting Manual*: 'The Newfoundland breed makes the best water dogs, and will plunge into the most rapid stream, or break through ice in the coldest

weather, to bring out the ducks.' It is assumed, though there is no proof of this, that he was in fact writing of the offspring of the rescued Newfoundlands and local retrievers. If the Newfoundlands of that day were as large as the modern dog, it seems unlikely that they would have been taken on duck shoots. But their offspring from smaller retrievers could have been so used.

The local retrievers were probably a mixed lot. O. D. Foulks, who wrote for the *American Sportsman* after the Civil War of 1860–65, claimed the Newfoundlands were crossed with 'English water poodles'. He called the offspring 'Red Chester' or 'Brown Winchester' dogs. Another writer claimed that the crosses were made to yellow and tan Coonhounds. Foulks wrote a classic description of the work of the dogs, which could stand for the modern dogs as well, and is here quoted in part:

'He does not shiver like a setter, or raise and drop his fore-feet like a wet spaniel; the shaking he has given his coarse, oily coat, has freed it entirely from ice and water; he cannot be enticed into a kennel, but must sit out on the frozen shore, rain or shine, and watch as well as the gunner.

'If one of the fallen birds chance to be only crippled, he swims past dead ones, keeping the wounded in sight; when it dives, he swims to the spot and there continues turning round and round, now and then throwing himself high in the water, especially if the waves are heavy.' Foulks also wrote that the dogs could be directed by hand to ducks that they had not marked, or could not see.

Modern enthusiasts claim that the Chesapeake Bay has no equal in rough, heavy seas, and in very cold weather. Yet the breed's popularity has never matched its reputation. It has not become a popular breed with dog show enthusiasts because it is often considered a homely dog. Until recent times, Chesapeake Bay Retrievers were too individual to make good kennel dogs. In this respect, the modern dogs are much better, while breeders have managed to keep the qualities of courage and determination so outstanding in this breed.

Human population increases and pressures have cut down on water-fowling as a sport. But this has been more than matched by the extraordinary increase in the popularity of retriever field trials. In trials for all breeds of retrievers, the Chesapeakes have not shown up well. This is chiefly because of the speed and dash of the LABRADOR RETRIEVERS which perform spectacularly in trials. But the trials are not held under conditions which prove the qualities of the Chesapeake. Their slower, persistent, but more methodical work is at a disadvantage where the demand is for showmanship.

The American Chesapeake Bay Retriever Club was founded in 1918 at Albert Lea, Minn. The founders were men who took their dogs into the rugged lake areas of Manitoba and Minnesota, and who lived beneath the famed Mississippi flyway, one of the world's great migratory bird routes.

Essentials of the breed: The remarkable oily coat, mentioned by Foulks more than 100 years ago, is still a distinctive feature of the breed. The outer coat is rather harsh and, because of the oil, sheds water. The undercoat is so dense as to insulate the dog's body from the ice cold water. A curly coat is not permitted. The colour is dark brown to a faded tan or to a dead grass colour. The latter is considered the ideal camouflage for a duck dog. Black or liver colours disqualify, as does white on any part of the body, except the breast, belly, or spots on the feet. Tail feathers over 1¾ inches long also disqualify.

The skull is broad and rounded with a powerful muzzle of medium length. Small ears are set high, and hang loosely. The eyes are yellow. The body is of medium length with a deep, rounded barrel chest. The top line approaches hollowness rather than roach, with hindquarters as high or higher than the withers. Dewclaws on the hind legs disqualify. Weight: dogs 65 to 75 lb.; bitches 55 to 65 lb. Height: dogs 23 to 26 inches; bitches 21 to 24 inches.
See colour plate p. 82.

Chihuahua The Chihuahua is the world's smallest dog, ranging in weight from one to six pounds, but with two to four pounds being both average and desired. Besides its size, it is remarkable as the dog 'with the hole in its head'. This is the mollera, or fontanelle, an area in which the skull bones have failed to join. It can be seen in any newborn human baby. Not all Chihuahuas have the mollera. It appears to be chiefly restricted to this breed, although it has been noted in an occasional JAPANESE SPANIEL.

The Chihuahua is named after the Mexican state and city of that name. But so far as the breed's history is concerned, that is about all that can be said with certainty. Some claim it was brought to Mexico about 100 years ago by the Chinese, who were dwarfing dogs, as they were trees. Another claim for its origin is that it was a breed developed by the Aztecs or Toltecs, and descended from dogs brought in by the Spanish conquerors.

The *Conquistadores* were mostly ignorant of natural history. They saw hundreds of life forms which, however similar, were not known in Europe. The dog-like animals they called dogs. Among these were the coatimondi, raccoon, opossum, gopher and others. Some of the Conquistadors said that the dogs climbed trees; most said that the dogs were mute. True dogs do not climb trees, and no true dog is mute.

Other writers have said flatly that there were no true dogs in America when the Spaniards arrived, just as there were no horses, cows, pigs, sheep or goats. Figurines which pre-date the conquest are certainly dog-like yet there is insufficient detail to call them true dogs. The Aztecs were said to have buried their dogs with their masters. Yet one Mexican archaeologist, Dr. Isaac Ochoterena, has said that no true dog remains have ever been found in authentic Aztec graves.

The Aztecs were destroyed as a nation by the invaders. Their people were impoverished and made virtual slaves. It seems then, that if the Chihuahua existed at that time, it was saved and developed by the Spaniards and not the Indians. But in either case, why is there silence, between the Conquest and about 1875 or

Above Chesapeake Bay Retriever. Ch. Eastern Waters Brown Charger.

later, concerning one of the world's most remarkable dogs? The *pelon*, or HAIRLESS DOG is mentioned as inhabiting the Mexican-American border towns as early as 1848. Why not the Chihuahua?

Many of the early U.S. breeders believed that the Longcoat Chihuahua was the original Chihuahua dog, but it was the Smoothcoat that caught the public fancy. The first Chihuahua to be registered by the American Kennel Club was *Midget*, in 1904, 22 years after registration of the first Mexican Hairless. One of the early Longcoats became the first great foundation sire of the breed; his name was *Caranza*. Other Longcoats came from Brazil and Colombia. How they got there, no one knows. Some writers have suggested that the Smoothcoat is the true Mexican breed, and that the Longcoat is a result of mixing many toy breeds.

The reader is entitled to believe what he pleases about the origin of the Chihuahua. What cannot be denied is that the breed is today one of the most popular breeds. Chihuahuas now in Mexico descend from American stock.

Essentials of the breed: The Chihuahua has an 'apple domed' head, with or without the mollera. The large ears are carried erect or at a 45 degree angle when in repose. The nose is short and slightly pointed, and the teeth meet in a level bite.

The top line is level, chest rounded but not barrelled. The dog is slightly longer than tall, but short backed males are preferred. The tail is carried sickle, or in a loop that just touches the back. A furry tail is desirable. Only rarely is a bobtail or tail-less dog born. Such a

condition is not to be held against a good dog. But a cropped tail disqualifies, as do broken down or cropped ears. All colours are permitted. Smoothcoats have soft textured, close, glossy hair, although a slightly heavier coat with an undercoat is permitted.

The Longcoat is judged under the same standard as the Smoothcoat, except for coat. This should be soft, lie flat or be slightly waved, with a definite undercoat. The ears are heavily fringed, and there should be feathers on all legs, with 'pants' on the rear of the hind legs. The tail has a full plume. Too thin a coat, approaching bareness, disqualifies.
See colour plate p. 382.

China Eye A clear blue eye.

Chinese Crested Dog see Hairless Dogs.

Chinese Fighting Dog This is a canine which deserves an entry despite the fact that it is, as far as can be traced, not officially recognized by any of the major canine control councils. This dog, while admittedly not the most distinctive or bizarre, must surely count as one of the most unusual in the world.

At first glance, one wonders whether it is indeed a true dog. It weighs perhaps as much as a BULL TERRIER and is about the same size. Its form, however, is totally different. In build and outline it in some ways resembles a diminutive hippopotamus, or maybe a wild boar. The dog's drab gray-brown colour increases the similarity.

The head is distinctive in that the muzzle is blunt, a description which accurately applies to no other breed.

Additionally, and even more unusual, the canine teeth are curved like scimitars. The difficulty of freeing the jaws when once a hold has been established can be imagined.

Equally distinctive is the coat. This is short, bristly and unusually harsh. It is pig-like and unpleasant and uncomfortable for other canines to hold in their mouths.

The breed has been kept in China for centuries; the dogs fight for the profit of their gambling owners and for their own pleasure. Like primitive animals their interest is in violence; they need no urging to attack. Wherever they are and whatever they appear to be doing, they are in fact biding their time and silently waiting for the opportunity of attacking and vanquishing every other dog in sight, regardless of size.

After which it is necessary to record that they are invariably amiable and entirely friendly towards the human race. It is this friendship to man which finally persuades the doubter that they are in fact true dogs.

Chiselled Clean-cut in head, particularly beneath the eyes.
See LEAN HEAD.

Choice of Parents In dog breeding, it is normally the owner of the bitch who decides to which dog it will be mated. Choice is limited to dogs at public stud, or owned by, or made privately available to, the owner of the bitch. The criteria by which a STUD DOG is selected vary considerably, influenced by, among other things, the knowledge, objectives, discernment, affluence and freedom to travel, of the breeder.

Factors such as convenience ('the dog round the corner') and cheapness are not given weight by serious and experienced breeders, for whom the following are probably the most important considerations: (1) The stud dog's wins: in the show ring, working trials, or races as the case may be. This gives an indication of the quality of the dog, though it was a wise man who said 'Don't tell me what it's won. Tell me what it's beaten'. Success in competition inevitably depends on many environmental factors and cannot give an accurate estimate of the dog's merit, still less of its breeding value. However, an impressive array of awards to one or both parents certainly helps to sell the puppies, and this economic consideration may at times outweigh genetic ones. Puppies by a fashionable stud dog are likely to sell well, even if their dam was not particularly well suited to him.

(2) Individual faults and virtues: the breeder endeavours to assess the points of each potential sire and dam, and to make matings which appear to have a good chance of retaining or improving virtues while reducing or eliminating faults. There are differences of opinion as to how this should be done. For example, should a bitch too fine in skull be mated to a dog with a correct width of skull or to one which is too coarse?

(3) Progeny known to the breeder: most often these are only a small sample and tend to be the best, because they are usually seen at shows, or at other breeders' kennels. The pups sold off as pets or destroyed due to major faults are generally not known to the breeder trying to choose a stud dog. This gives the big kennels an advantage, since they keep their own stud dogs and have the opportunity to study large numbers of progeny.

(4) Pedigree: is considered of the utmost importance by some breeders and given scant attention by others. Some try to breed to certain lines and avoid others, or line breed to a particular ancestor, while others merely check whether the pedigrees of the prospective sire and dam are, in their opinion, suited to each other.

Can genetics offer any real help in this vital process of selecting mates? It must be appreciated that all scientific disciplines arise from the need to solve practical problems. They are therefore highly relevant. However, breeders who make their decisions on the basis of accurate observation and objective judgement unbiased by sentiment or jealousy of competitors, are certainly not being unscientific. The application of more sophisticated genetic techniques may be quite inappropriate, especially in small kennels run primarily as a hobby. The success of breeders over the years in creating and maintaining so many distinctive breeds is proof that practical skill and knowledge abound.

However, an understanding of the principles of genetics should enhance progress and add to the interest and pleasure of breeding. When certain problems arise, genetic knowledge is essential to their solution. This applies particularly to hereditary abnormalities. The establishment of a new or rare colour or pattern; breeding of natural prick-ears in a breed previously cropped to appear prick-eared; the saving of a breed reduced to such small numbers that it is in danger of extinction; these are all situations in which a knowledge of genetics may be invaluable. Turning, however, to the usual situations, it may be useful to comment further on the above four considerations usually taken into account in selecting a stud dog for an individual bitch.

(1a) Show or working trial wins obviously depend to a very large extent (though not exclusively) on non-genetic factors: the owner's skill in rearing and handling, the personal preferences of the judges, the standard of competition encountered, the opportunities available for competing, and many other factors. The bitch's owner must therefore try to make an estimate of the extent to which the dog's winning record reflects his real merit as a specimen of the breed. Wins in working competitions are more meaningful in that a dog must be good to win consistently; but his virtues may not be so much genetic ones as the result of clever training and handling, whilst possibly some dog of outstanding genetic merit may never achieve fame because it belongs to the wrong person.

(2a) It is here that the application of accurate genetic knowledge would be most effective. Many important features, such as coat colour, depend on major genes whose inheritance has been worked out by scientists, is well understood, and is very little affected by the normal variation in environmental factors. Other features are dependent on polygenic control (many genes acting on one trait) and the mating of extremes in these instances is very likely to produce puppies intermediate between sire and dam. If this is desired, it is most likely to be maintained by mating intermediate to intermediate. Where, on the other hand, the intermediate condition is produced by the heterozygous state of one gene pair, it is only the mating of extremes which will produce 100 per cent intermediates. In some dog breeds faulty coat types, either too profuse or too sparse, occur regularly among the offspring of correctly coated parents, which could possibly be due to the desired coat being dependent on heterozygosity, as in roan shorthorn cattle, discussed under MENDELISM.

(3a) Progeny tests are a valuable method of assessing an animal's breeding worth, but it can be misleading to judge an animal by a small, selected number of its offspring, especially if no attention is paid to what they may have derived from the other parent. Frequently a stud dog is condemned as 'throwing long backs' or 'siring oversized specimens' because he has been mated to a bitch prepotent for these faults. The dog which has sired winners from a large number of bitches, themselves from various strains, is rightly recognized as an outstanding sire, provided the bitches were not too much above average quality. Sometimes a famous dog's winning offspring are good because they resemble their champion dams, rather than their sire. A famous dog gets the opportunity to serve the best bitches in the breed, and he may be genetically no better than a less famous dog having fewer outstanding mates and opportunities. The percentage of top-quality puppies is the important thing, and this is difficult to assess under the ordinary conditions of dog breeding.

(4a) A dog's pedigree is a list of its ancestors, usually recording their names and perhaps registration or stud book numbers. Titles such as 'champion', are usually indicated. It is unusual for any further details to be given. A pure-bred dog is one all of whose ancestors for several generations were of the same breed. It is normally assumed that all 'pedigreed' dogs are pure-bred, but strictly speaking a pedigree need not be confined to dogs of one breed: a cross between a pedigreed Airedale and Greyhound could be described as a pedigreed dog. And most pedigrees contain so little information that a novice might well be impressed by such a pedigree!

In practice dog-breeders rely mainly on memory – their own or their friends' – to give meaning to the list of names. Faults and virtues of the animals in the pedigree are recalled, with occasional assistance from photographs and show reports. Information about the champions and other famous dogs is usually available, though not necessarily accurate. Most pedigrees however, contain names, particularly of bitches, about which little is known, but whose influence might be substantial.

It would obviously be desirable to have objective descriptions of every animal, but these would have to be filed at, for example, the Kennel Club or breed clubs, because no breeder could be expected to enter so much detail on pedigree forms. The compilation of pedigrees, especially for pets, is already a time-consuming and unrewarding chore.

Of all the genes possessed by any individual, half come from the mother and half from the father. Thus,

Above Choke chains. If correctly used, these collars are helpful in training all but the most sensitive dogs. The drawing illustrates how to begin making the loop which goes around the dog's neck.

the genetic contribution from an ancestor several generations back will be very small, though it may be important. A knowledge of the parents, grandparents and great-grandparents is quite sufficient, and effort may be concentrated on getting as much information as possible about them. This has the advantage that such relatively close ancestors may still be alive, or well remembered by breeders still available for discussion. If any further-back ancestor occurs several times, it may be important to know more about it. The same may apply in special cases such as when it is desired to revive a recessive coat-colour not seen for several generations, and the genes must be sought in known descendants of dogs and bitches far back in the pedigree. Otherwise there is seldom need to demand a five-generation pedigree from the breeder. Three generations is enough.
See GENES.

Choke Chains The term choke chain is an unfortunate one as this type of collar was never intended to choke a dog and, unless the dog is wrongly tied up with one, is unlikely ever to do so. It is widely used in training and, with the majority of dogs, can be a great asset. Not, as some people imagine, as a magic means of controlling a dog, but simply as an implement which helps the trainer to control the dog. Some sensitive dogs resent this type of collar and, with these, its use will hinder rather than help in training. An ordinary leather collar or modern double action slip collar is much better on such dogs.

A choke chain is simply a piece of chain with a ring on each end. To put it on, hold it by one ring in the right hand and allow the chain to hang vertically. Take the bottom ring in the left hand and turn it to a horizontal position. Now drop the middle part of the chain carefully through this ring so that it forms a loop.

Next take this loop in both hands with the two rings in the left hand. Stand facing the dog and slip the collar over his head. This means that, with the dog on the left side the choke chain can instantly be pulled up tight and, just as important, will drop back to the slack position immediately it is released. If it is put on the wrong way round it can be tightened just as quickly but is liable to 'jam' on top of the dog's neck. It therefore stays tight and defeats its purpose. It is the general practice amongst trainers to keep dogs on the left but, if there is any special reason for having the dog on the right, the above procedure can be reversed.

The choke chain should be long enough to enable it to be put over the dog's head easily but not so long that, when hanging loose round the neck, there is any risk of the dog putting his foot through it.
See COLLARS.

Choking Choking, or difficulty in swallowing, is called dysphagia. It is usually associated with the oesophagus. An exception would be the blockage of the pyloric end of the stomach. The pylorus is the circular opening from the stomach into the duodenum.

When dysphagia occurs suddenly, the cause is usually the swallowing of a foreign object which has become lodged in the gullet. Fish and fowl bones may cause choking. The stings of swallowed insects, such as honey bees, may bring sufficient swelling to close the gullet. Sometimes hysteria is a cause.

If dysphagia develops slowly, a growth of some sort may be the cause. If emaciation is present, then a malignancy is likely, and a veterinarian should be consulted. Many dogs develop a cough, or choking attack, when inflammation of the throat is present.
See ASTHMA.

Choosing a Breed In this electronic age, any competent computer could select a 'perfect' canine companion. Like a modern matrimonial agency it would first want to know your vital statistics: it would ask age, health, income, temperament, hobbies, number in family, house size, area of garden, attitude towards exercise, and so on. The more information it had the better. Once the machine had your measure, it could thumb through its list of available breeds and come up with a satisfactory answer in record time.

Since no canine compatibility computer service currently exists, the equally effective alternative when choosing a breed is common sense. It might be thought that everybody uses some of this when selecting an animal intended to share hearth and home for a decade. Unfortunately, it is not so. Merely as an example it is recorded that Britain's Royal Air Force has never yet had to buy a dog although it uses thousands of them to protect its air bases all over the world. All the GERMAN SHEPHERDS (Alsatians) it uses were 'presented' by people who forgot that the cuddly little puppy they bought would one day grow into a boisterous giant. No mistake is so obvious that it will not be made.

Self-examination is even more important than puppy examination. Hearty, exercise-loving types would obviously be unwise to choose a CHIHUAHUA or indeed any of the toy breeds. These dogs will take a modicum of exercise in their own way and at their own leisure. A walker up mountains and over plains is more likely to be happy with a setter, a BEAGLE, a BOXER, or even a DALMATIAN, which will do twenty miles then wag its tail and ask for more!

The owner of a small house and a small income should not have a GREAT DANE, a ST. BERNARD or a MASTIFF. These beasts are impressive in appearance, but they weigh up to twenty times as much as a Toy POODLE. Needless to say, they also take up around twenty times as much room and cost around twenty times as much to feed.

Poodles, OLD ENGLISH SHEEPDOGS and AFGHANS are eye-catching but time consuming. Grooming is a daily necessity and to be kept in full bloom a minimum of three hours a week should be set aside. If intended for the show ring this estimate can be doubled or trebled. By contrast, a WHIPPET or Smooth-haired Miniature DACHSHUND can be kept clean, fresh and smart with fifteen minutes' work per week.

Temperament and background are important. For example, FOX TERRIERS and garden lovers do not always see eye to eye. House-proud wives and wet gundogs are not an ideal combination. Neither, con-

trary to popular opinion, are one's ageing parents and boisterous young BASSET HOUNDS.

But there is an ideal breed for everyone. And it is necessary to take the trouble to find out which before buying a dog. The alternative is dissatisfaction, for both dog and owner. And it's not even the dog's fault. He just has to suffer for it!

This is how the choice of the perfect breed should be made: first list all the breeds each member of the family likes, including even those which are manifestly absurd; then all cross out those which are clearly unsuitable, which should leave at most three or four.

From this safe harbour you can afford the luxury of an emotional choice. Or you could even shut your eyes and point, as long as you then return to sanity before taking the next step, which consists of studying the entry in this book under the heading of BUYING A PUPPY.

Chop Short, sharp baying notes of a trailing hound. The voice of some COONHOUNDS.

Chops The jowls, or pendulous flesh of lips and jaws, particularly of the BULLDOG.

Chorea Chorea is called St. Vitus' Dance when it attacks human beings. The latter name derives from epidemics of dancing manias during the Middle Ages. Afflicted people visited the chapels of St. Vitus, believing they could be cured there. Today, in veterinary practice, chorea is called by such names as tic, flexor spasm, and hyperkinesia. It is characterized by the involuntary twitching of groups of muscles. Most often affected are those of the limbs, face, and jaws.

Although dogs sometimes howl when severely afflicted, pain is not believed to be present. The howling then is simply an involuntary action like a muscle twitching. The twitching may be slight or violent. When violent in the jaws, eating becomes difficult. In all cases where the twitching is violent, exhaustion tends to occur. In many cases, twitching stops during sleep, but in others it is so violent as to prevent sleep.

Chorea normally follows attacks of DISTEMPER or encephalitis. It may become evident just at the time the dog appears to have made a complete recovery. Though the twitching may be slight at first, it tends to get worse. Modern distemper prophylaxis has helped to reduce the incidence of the disease greatly. The disease is caused by viral invaders which damage the nerves of the cerebral cortex. Such damage cannot be repaired, but dogs can be given relief by the use of muscle relaxants, anti-spasmodic drugs, and sedatives. Vitamin therapy is also used.
See RABIES.

Chow Chow It is perhaps best to start this entry by disposing of an unpalatable fact. This is that in Cantonese the word 'chow' means food. It is widely accepted that this particular breed was produced by the Chinese as a delicacy for the table, that the Chow Chow was little more than an oriental canine broiler fowl.

Right Chow Chow. Ch. Eastward Liontamer of Elster.

Like many such stories it is a mixture of fact and fiction. Certainly at one time the Chinese did eat dogs. Perhaps in the more remote parts the practice is still continued, and certainly on formal feast days. It must also be admitted that a dog resembling the Chow is the natural and indigenous mongrel in many parts of China. From this it would follow that if any dog were at any time to be eaten it would be somewhat similar in type to this breed.

But to say this is not to accept that the Chow Chow which the Western world knows was ever bred for this purpose, because the modern Chow is essentially a Western creation. Many dogs in China do have a 'ruff' and curly tail but the perfection of coat, colour and form is something that owes nearly everything to Europe in general and England in particular.

In any case even the 'ruff' and curly tail when coupled with the prick ear and the straight hock merely remind us that the Chow is in fact a northern breed; a SPITZ, a dog from the Arctic Circle; and therefore one of the same family as the ELKHOUND, HUSKY, SAMOYED, KEESHOND and POMERANIAN.

Probably it sprang from a union of one or more of these breeds, coupled with one of the many heavy Eastern MASTIFFS. This, however, is to theorize; facts evade us because of the lack of documentation. The dog was produced for work to pull carts, sledges, etc. and was bred for its aptitude for this task.

Curiously enough, some Chows reached Britain as early as 1780. They were said to have the unique blue-black tongue. No other canine has this curious feature. They were also said to have a head somewhat similar to that we know now, and certainly to have had the typical scowling expression which has made them disliked, mis-trusted and indeed feared by a very large number of people ever since.

Below Chow Chow. A 'pride' of Chows. In spite of their fierce expressions and leonine ruffs, Chows are affectionate and entirely predictable towards their masters. Here are, left to right, Red Thai Silk, Clarissa Mai of Kyliang, and Rajah of Kyliang.

It perhaps needs to be said that a dog's facial expressions, when judged by human standards, are misleading. At its simplest, when a dog is pleased it does not smile, it wags its tail. If it shows its teeth in a grimace, once again it is not smiling, indeed it may be threatening to bite. Equally we must accept that a so-called scowl is no indication of temperament for the simple reason that a dog with aggressive intentions would raise its hackles rather than lower its brow.

Perhaps even less well deserved is the reputation this breed has for treachery. This word clearly implies a dog that turns on those who trust it; that bites without warning and when a bite is totally unexpected and undeserved. This is certainly not the case with Chows. It has to be accepted that they are well described as 'one man' dogs. They do not bestow their favours lightly on strangers. Consequently if any person forces his attention on this remote, aloof dog then he can expect trouble.

The Chow is, however, remarkably affectionate and entirely predictable towards those it likes and lives with. There is about it something of the inscrutability of the East and something of the deep-seated loyalties and strong family affection known to the Orient.

Although not really popular during this present century, there has never been any risk of it fading from the scene. Moreover, its distinctive outline is as well known as almost any other dog existing. Clearly this is in part due to its similarity to the lion. Indeed it is difficult to talk of the Chow without using the adjective leonine.

It has been said that the Chow will die for its master but not readily obey him; walk with him but not trot meekly to heel; honour him, but not fawn on his friends and relations. Most owners would ask little more of a dog.

Essentials of the breed: Active, compact, short-coupled and well balanced. Skull: flat and broad with little stop. Muzzle: broad from eyes to point. Nose: black, large wide. Dark, small eyes, preferably almond shaped. Ears: small, thick, slightly rounded, carried stiffly erect and wide apart, which gives the characteristic scowl. Teeth: strong and level. Tongue: blueish-black. Flews and roof of mouth: black. Gums: preferably black. Neck: strong and slightly arched. Forequarters: shoulders muscular, forelegs straight, and with good bone. Chest: broad and deep. Back: short, straight and strong. Powerful loins. Hindlegs: muscular, with hocks well let down and perfectly straight to produce typical stilted gait. Small cat-like feet. Tail: set high, carried over back. Coat: Abundant; outer coat coarse with woolly undercoat. Colour: whole-coloured black, red, blue, fawn, cream or white, frequently shaded but not in patches.
See colour plate p. 188.

Chromosomes This is the name given to tiny structures present within the nucleus of every normal cell. They carry the GENES which are usually considered to be arranged in single file along them, like vertebrae in a backbone. With the exception of certain repro-ductive cells, every cell in every normal dog contains thirty-nine pairs of chromosomes. This pairing of the chromosomes is very important. During ordinary cell division, such as during body growth or replacement of the coat, each chromosome doubles so that each 'daughter cell' receives the full complement of thirty-nine chromosome pairs. But at one special kind of cell division – during the production of sperm and ova – only *one* chromosome of each pair goes into each new cell, so that the sex-cells have only half the normal number. When fertilization takes place, each puppy receives thirty-nine chromosomes from its sire and thirty-nine from its dam, so that the full number, seventy-eight (thirty-nine pairs), is restored.

It is this separating and recombining of chromosomes which underlies the segregation and recombination of hereditary factors first described by Mendel (see MENDELISM). Genes situated on different chromosome pairs behave independently of each other, but those situated on homologous chromosomes (that is, chromosomes which can pair with each other) show behaviour called 'linkage' and 'crossing over'. Genes which are located at different sites along the length of one chromosome tend to remain together from one generation to the next, and are said to be 'linked'; they part only when the chromosome breaks, in the 'crossing over' process in which there is an exchange of material between homologous pairs. Although quite a large number of genes have been identified by their effects on dogs, none have yet been definitely shown to be linked, but this may be because very few experiments of the kind that would reveal linkage have ever been carried out on dogs.

Under the microscope it can be seen that the chromosomes of any pair closely resemble each other in length and shape, whilst differing from chromosomes belonging to other pairs. However, there is one special pair in which, in male dogs, the two chromosomes are not alike, one being much smaller than the other. The small one is called the 'Y-chromosome', and is never present in normal females. The larger chromosome is the 'X-chromosome', and in bitches, two X-chromosomes are present, instead of one X and one Y. These are the sex-chromosomes, and the genetic sex of every puppy is determined at the time of fertilization of the egg from which it develops. All puppies receive an X from the dam, but the sex-cells of the male are of two kinds, some carrying an X-chromosome, and some a Y. So if an ovum is fertilized by a Y-bearing sperm the puppy will be a dog, while an ovum fertilized by an X-bearing sperm will develop into a bitch. This is normal but, very occasionally, something goes wrong either during sex-cell formation or development of the embryo, which leads to a sexually abnormal individual, either an inter-sex (of uncertain sex) or, even more rarely, an animal which is functionally of one sex but genetically of the other.

For all ordinary purposes it may be taken that the sex of a puppy depends on whether it gets the X- or the Y-chromosome from its sire. Of course, every puppy also gets all the other chromosomes (called autosomes), 38 of them plus an X or Y from its sire, and 38 plus an X from its dam. Genes carried on the X-chromosome are the bearers of 'sex-linked' traits such as hemophilia (bleeding disease). Genes of this kind are recessive so if a bitch has the normal gene on one X and the abnormal one on the other, she will not herself suffer from hemophilia. However, about half her sons will get the X with the 'hemophilia gene'.

As the Y they receive has few genes, these puppies will develop hemophilia and die. Hemophiliac puppies practically never live long enough to breed, so it is the carrier bitches which are responsible for maintaining the disease.

Classes at Shows – American The regular classes at American dog shows – those which lead to championship points – are Puppy, Novice, Bred-by-Exhibitor, American-bred, and Open. At licensed, or championship shows, no dog under six months of age can enter. The Puppy class is for puppies six months or older on the opening day of the show, but not more than one year old on the opening day. Puppy classes may be divided into six-to-nine months dogs, and dogs nine-to-twelve months old.

The Novice class is for dogs which have not won more than three first ribbons in that class, nor one first in American-bred, Bred-by-Exhibitor, or Open, nor any championship points. The Bred-by-Exhibitor class must have dogs shown by their breeder-owners, or by a member of their families – husband, wife, father, mother, son, daughter, brother, or sister. Champions are barred. The American-bred class is for non-champions whelped in the United States from a mating made in the United States. The Open class shall be for any dog six months of age or over except in Member Speciality shows held only for American-bred dogs, in which case the Open class shall be only for American-bred dogs.

Class winners then compete for Winners Dog or Bitch. These two then compete in Best of Breed competition with the champions, and with dogs which have apparently completed championships but which have not had official confirmation of this. The winner of a non-regular class, the Veterans class, also competes for Best of Breed.

Other non-regular classes include Local in which the boundaries are set by the show committee, Stud Dog and Get, Brood Bitch and Offspring, and sometimes classes such as Bred in Puerto Rico, Hawaii, Alaska, or California. Brace and team classes may also be given.

Classes at Shows – British When dog shows first started one hundred years ago it was the practice to provide one class at a show for each breed, provided, of course, that there were sufficient dogs of the breed to justify a separate class. At the first show in Newcastle in 1859 there were two classes only, one for Pointers, and one for Setters, but as dog showing became more popular, show promoters found it necessary to provide a variety of classes for the most popular breeds and to charge a separate entry fee for each class in which a dog was entered. Until recently, when describing a dog show the canine press always quoted the number of class entries and never the number of dogs entered for

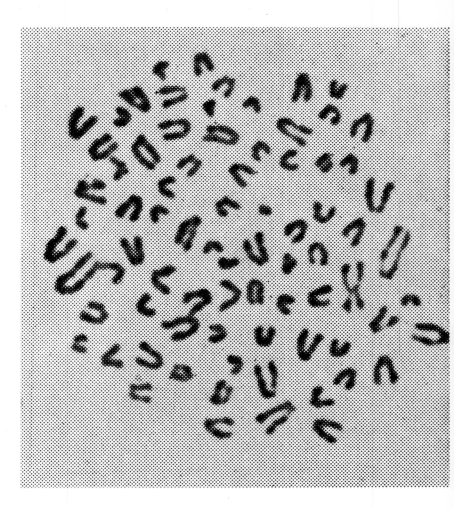

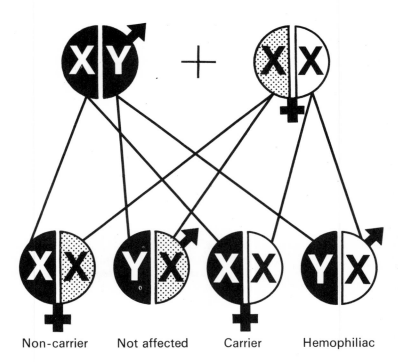

Non-carrier   Not affected   Carrier   Hemophiliac

the show. The number of class entries at a show indicated the amount of money received and a low entry could mean 'cancellation for lack of entries'.

Recognizing in the early days only the handicaps of very young and old dogs, separate classes were provided for puppies and veterans, but as the time went on dogs were classified by their previous wins and this system is still the basis of the Kennel Club show classification. The system of show classification is divided into two sections, firstly for Members' shows and secondly for Open shows. The latter includes Championship shows, which are officially described as Open shows at which CHALLENGE CERTIFICATES are offered.

A dog which has won a Challenge Certificate (or for that matter, the equivalent of a Challenge Certificate under the Rules of a Club recognized by the Kennel Club) is ineligible for entry at a Members' show and also for many classes at Open shows. First prizes of up to £1 in value are counted only when entering for a Members' show. First prizes of more than £1 count at Open and Championship shows to establish the rank of the dog. Otherwise the definitions of classes for Members' and Open shows are similar.

The following is a list of the range of classes currently available to Open and Championship show organizers in Britain. The full range is rarely used, because prize money would have to be paid in each class, possibly against small entries. In practice, numerically small breeds such as the JAPANESE SPANIEL, SKYE, etc., frequently have only two classes for each sex; well represented breeds such as ELKHOUNDS and GREAT DANES around six to eight per sex; and the really popular breeds, such as Alsatians (GERMAN SHEPHERDS) and POODLES, anything up to sixteen or even eighteen classes per sex.

PUPPY: For dogs of six and not exceeding twelve calendar months of age on the first day of the show.

JUNIOR: For dogs of six and not exceeding eighteen calendar months of age on the first day of the show.

MAIDEN: For dogs which have not won a Challenge Certificate or a First Prize of the value of £1 or more (Puppy and Special Puppy Classes excepted).

NOVICE: For dogs which have not won a Challenge Certificate or three or more First Prizes each of the value of £1 or more (Puppy and Special Puppy Classes excepted).

TYRO: For dogs which have not won a Challenge Certificate or five or more First Prizes each of the value of £1 or more (Puppy and Special Puppy Classes excepted).

DEBUTANT: For dogs which have not won a Challenge Certificate or a First Prize of the value of £2 or more (Puppy and Special Puppy Classes excepted).

UNDERGRADUATE: For dogs which have not won a Challenge Certificate or three or more First Prizes each of the value of £2 or more (Puppy and Special Puppy Classes excepted).

GRADUATE: For dogs which have not won a Challenge Certificate or four or more First Prizes each of the value of £2 or more, in Graduate, Post Graduate, Minor Limit, Mid Limit, Limit and Open Classes, whether restricted or not.

POST GRADUATE: For dogs which have not won a Challenge Certificate or five or more First Prizes each of the value of £2 or more, in Post Graduate, Minor Limit, Mid Limit, Limit and Open Classes whether restricted or not.

MINOR LIMIT: For dogs which have not won two Challenge Certificates or three or more First Prizes in all each of the value of £2 or more, in Minor Limit, Mid Limit, Limit and Open Classes, confined to the breed, whether restricted or not, at shows where Challenge Certificates were offered for the breed.

MID LIMIT: For dogs which have not won three Challenge Certificates or five or more First Prizes in all, each of the value of £2 or more, in Mid Limit, Limit and Open Classes, confined to the breed, whether restricted or not, at shows where Challenge Certificates were offered for the breed.

LIMIT: For dogs which have not won three Challenge Certificates under three different judges or seven or more First Prizes in all, each of the value of £2 or more, in Limit and Open Classes, confined to the breed, whether restricted or not, at shows where Challenge Certificates were offered for the breed.

OPEN: For all dogs of the breeds or varieties for which the class is provided, and eligible for entry at the Show.

VETERAN: For dogs of an age specified in the Schedule but not less than five years on the first day of the Show.

FIELD TRIAL: For dogs which have won prizes, Awards of Honour, Diplomas of Merit, or Certificates of Merit in actual competition at a Field Trial held under Kennel Club or Irish Kennel Club Field Trial Rules and Regulations.

It is evident from the table that as a successful dog matures it becomes ineligible for the lower classes and must be entered in more senior classes until it finally arrives at the Open class, but there is nothing to prevent an ambitious owner entering an inexperienced dog in the top class, for the classification system is based on a handicap principle. Exhibitors tend to enter in classes as low, and therefore as relatively easy, as they are permitted because of the prize money.

Generally speaking a novice dog can challenge a Champion, but the Champion cannot challenge the novice. Occasionally, classes are provided which require a dog to win certain awards in order to qualify for entry, and CRUFT'S SHOW has accepted this principle as a means of reducing an excessive number of entries. At Cruft's Show a dog must have won a Challenge Certificate or a first or second prize in a breed class at a Championship show during the previous year in order to qualify for entry. But the entries at some other British shows are now reaching such proportions that they too may well impose restrictions on their entries.

Chromosomes are located in the nucleus of animal cells and each normal cell in the dog contains thirty-nine pairs. Usually bunched closely together, they separate and can be seen under the microscope when the cell is about to divide. In the chromosomes from a newly divided cell *left* all seventy-eight chromosomes are visible. Amongst them is the special pair governing the sex of the dog. When the so-called Y chromosome (a very small one just right of centre) is present with the much larger X chromosome (lower right, shaped like an X) it indicates a male cell. In this instance the chromosomes are from a male Beagle.

Chromosomes. The female dog carries two X chromosomes. If one of these bears abnormal genes for a trait such as hemophilia (*left* white) they will be 'masked' by the normal genes on the other X chromosome (*left* dotted) and the bitch will appear normal but will be a carrier of the disease. She will pass one of the chromosomes to each of her offspring. Thus about half of her puppies will receive abnormal genes, and of these the females with a normal X chromosome from the father will be carriers of the disease and the males will develop hemophilia and die.

Classes at Shows – Canadian Regular official classes at Canadian shows are roughly the same as those at American shows. No dog under six months old can enter a licensed championship event. The classes are Junior and Senior Puppy, Novice, Canadian-bred, Bred-by-Exhibitor, and Open.

Canada specifies four varieties of AMERICAN COCKER SPANIELS: black, solid colour other than black, parti-colour, and black and tan. Classes divided by sex must be given for all four varieties, and also Winners Classes. English COCKER SPANIELS are divided into solid colour and parti-colour. The four Best of Variety winners in American Cockers compete for Best of Breed, along with any champions entered. In English Cockers, and in thirteen- and fifteen-inch BEAGLES, the Best of Winners in each variety compete with the champions.

Canadian shows also have competition for best Canadian-bred puppy in breed, best Canadian-bred in breed, and on to Best in Show awards for puppies and Canadian-bred older dogs.

Cleft Palate Cleft palate is a congenital abnormality which most frequently affects the short-nosed breeds of dog. One or more pups in a litter may be affected in varying degrees. If the pup's mouth is opened, the roof of the mouth can be inspected and the defect is obvious. The first sign of a cleft palate is very often the behaviour of the pup when feeding, as it is unable to suck properly. The defect may be so bad that the pup is unable to suck at all and will die of starvation unless it is humanely destroyed.

Small defects in the hard palate can sometimes be repaired surgically so the advice of the veterinarian should be sought.

Hare lip is a defect often found at the same time as cleft palate. The same arguments apply. Severely affected pups should not be allowed to live but minor defects may be subject to surgical repair.

Clipping Opinions vary on the advisability of clipping dogs. Many breeds are double coated. In warm weather, the undercoat is shed. The outer coat, made up of guard hairs, protects the dog from the sun, and from insect pests such as flies and mosquitoes. In tropical areas where mosquitoes are carriers of the heart worm, clipping adds to the danger of infection. Insect powders can be applied to the skin of the dog which has shed its undercoat about as easily as upon that of the clipped dog, and the powder may adhere longer.

Clipping and shaving may be done nowadays for aesthetic reasons, as in the case of POODLES. Terriers are sometimes clipped instead of being plucked or stripped. But professionals do not recommend this. If stripping is not done, shortening the coat with a comb guard razor is preferred.

When dogs are suffering from skin ailments, clipping and even shaving may be recommended in the affected and surrounding areas. Curative medicines are more easily applied and so are bandages when required. The skin can be more easily cleansed, and the danger of secondary infection is reduced.

Cloddy Low, heavy-set. Sometimes used to describe an awkward gait.

Close-Coupled Comparatively short from withers to hipbones, or withers to set on of tail.

Clumber Spaniel Guesses hazarded on the number of any particular breed currently existing in any particular country invariably end up with misleading answers. For example, registration figures over recent years suggest that some 500 Clumber Spaniels are living in Great Britain today. This makes them sound commonplace. But to get this figure into perspective, it must be appreciated that there is a total British canine population of five millions. This means that only one dog in 10,000 is a Clumber Spaniel! Put another way, as many people do not see 10,000 different dogs in a lifetime, the odds are that most Britons have never set eyes on a Clumber Spaniel. This is a pity.

Writing at the turn of the century a canine commentator said of the Clumber: 'He is one of the most useful and popular of the several varieties of Sporting Spaniel.

Top left Cleft palate is immediately evident on opening the mouth of an afflicted dog.
Bottom left Clipping. When a dog's face is being clipped, care should be taken to protect the eyes and ears.

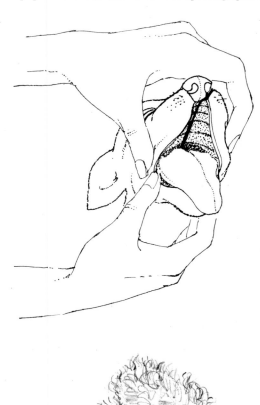

He is also one of the oldest. He is at once the most dignified and yet most docile. Most daring and yet most tractable.'

Save only that the description of the Clumber as 'daring' is a puzzle, most experts of today would agree with this early assessment. They would also agree with the many other flattering things that have been written about this highly unusual spaniel. The breed is quite unlike all the other varieties of spaniel. So different, in fact, that it is difficult to see anything other than a very indirect relationship.

First and foremost, Clumbers are massive. Not tall, but long-bodied with strong, heavy bone and a huge, square head with heavy beetling brows. Because of these heads, Clumbers were at one time thought to be descended from ALPINE SPANIELS and therefore related to ST. BERNARDS. They were also said to have reached England originally as a gift from the Duc de Noailles to the Duke of Newcastle at Clumber Park in 1875.

Both stories are unlikely. Much more probable is that these dogs were deliberately bred at Clumber using only dogs which existed there at the time. This would

clearly exclude the St. Bernard which had not then arrived.

Although it is easy to suggest many breeds which might have played a part, this is profitless, as nothing can be proved. Concentrating on fact, we know that deliberate efforts were made to breed heavyweight spaniels. The idea was to produce a gundog which made a more stately approach to shooting than some of the volatile types. In theory this was because the dense undergrowth in certain areas demanded it. Frequently, however, it was the increasing girth of the sportsmen which dictated the pace of the drive. In short, slow-moving men wanted dogs which flattered them by moving at their own speed.

After which one is almost reluctant to admit that Clumbers became Royal favourites. King Edward VII was particularly fond of them. Indeed he kept a large number, and his Sandringham bloodlines greatly influenced the breed. Its benefits are still felt today.

King George V also used them exclusively on the Royal Estates in Norfolk. The probability today, however, is that their future can only be assured by the

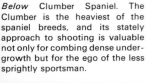
Below Clumber Spaniel. The Clumber is the heaviest of the spaniel breeds, and its stately approach to shooting is valuable not only for combing dense undergrowth but for the ego of the less sprightly sportsman.

Above Clumber Spaniels are scarce. These two-month-old puppies helping to swell the numbers are from a very good family: their parents — Anchorfield Eastway Bouncer and Old Holbans Anchorfield Flare — are both show champions.

support of show-going exhibitors and pet owners.

To this must be added a modest but certainly welcome interest in America, where there is plenty of open space and variety. Perhaps only here can sufficient work of the type to which the breed was accustomed be readily found.

Essentials of the breed: A heavy, massive but active dog with thoughtful expression. Head: large and square, of medium length, broad on top. Heavy brows with deep stop; heavy muzzle, well developed flews. Square nose. Eyes: dark amber, slightly sunk. Ears: large, vine-leaf shaped, and well coverd with straight hair, and hanging slightly forward. Mouth: level; neither over nor undershot. Neck: fairly long, thick and powerful; well feathered. Forequarters: shoulders strong, sloping. Chest: deep. Legs: short, straight, thick and strong. Body: long and heavy, near the ground, well-sprung ribs. Back: straight, broad and long. Hindquarters: very powerful. Loin: powerful. Hocks low, stifles well bent and set straight. Feet: large, round, and covered with hair. Tail: set low, well feathered and carried with back. Coat: abundant, close, silky and straight; well feathered legs. Colour: plain white, with lemon markings; orange permissible but not desirable; slight head markings and freckled muzzle with white body preferred.

Weight: Dogs about 55 to 70 lb. Bitches about 45 to 60 lb. In the United States, bitches 35 to 50 lb. See colour plate p. 89.

Clydesdale Terrier This breed, known variously during its existence as a SKYE TERRIER and a Paisley Terrier, is of interest principally because it demonstrates how dissension amongst breeders can not only cause damage within a breed, but even sow the seeds of its own extinction.

Captain W. Wilmer, writing in 1907 said: 'The Clydesdale or Paisley Terrier is the rarest, as he is the most beautiful of the terrier breeds.' James Garrow wrote in 1935 of it: 'There is no disputing the fact that it was the most beautiful of all this family of terriers.' The use of the past tense will be noticed. Between 1907 and 1935 the Clydesdale had bowed its way off the canine stage. Since no breed standard follows, a brief description might be helpful.

In general form and outline, including ear shape, placement and carriage, it was a prick-eared Skye. Its weight however was positively restricted to 18 lb. The big difference was its coat which, in the standard of points issued at the time, somewhat improbably accounted for 50 of the total 100 available. It was long, straight, very glossy and silky in texture. Moreover it had to be bright steel blue from back of head to root of tail, with head, legs and feet of bright, golden tan.

The regular Skye exhibitors hated it; first because it was originally shown in Skye classes; then because its coat was *required* to be silky. They had been destroying soft-coated Skyes for years and disliked this reminder that such a condition existed. They claimed that this fancy variety was not pure Skye, and that it was the result of crosses with a DANDIE DINMONT, a POODLE, a YORKSHIRE TERRIER. The latter is at least feasible.

Breeding of this type was virtually restricted to Glasgow, which is in the valley of the River Clyde and of which Paisley is a suburb.

By 1884 breeders were so irritated by the rebuffs of the Skye adherents that they broke away and formed the Clydesdale Terrier Club. More trouble followed. Many thought that the Paisley name should have been preserved. Others thought the dogs should have been called Glasgow Terriers or even Rutherglen (another suburb) Terriers. They showed their disapproval by withholding support from the new club.

By the turn of the century arguments still persisted although records show that there were a mere two or three exhibited in England! They still existed in fair numbers in Scotland. Even so there was only one Champion surviving in the breed. His name was *Ch. Ballochmyle Wee Wattie* and he was owned by Sir Claude Alexander, of Ballochmyle. The writing was on the wall. A breed allowed to sink so low has little chance of permanent recovery.

But perhaps the writing had appeared much earlier. It may have been the exaggerations of the animal rather than the bickering about its name which brought the breed to the end of the road.

Here is a contemporary record of one dog, *Blythswood Pearl,* considered to be the best Clydesdale Terrier ever exhibited. 'He was born in September 1891 and shown successfully for eleven years. He won forty first prizes including two at successive Cruft's. He had a beautiful coat which his owner, Mr. Erskine, spent three to four hours a day grooming. The coat measured $22\frac{1}{2}$ inches in length, $11\frac{1}{4}$ inches on either side.'

Coats and Boots Coats are often more of a luxury status symbol than a useful article of wearing apparel for the dog. Dogs have thick coats which serve as an insulation blanket to keep out cold. Eskimos sometimes use coats for their dogs when temperatures get to 25 degrees below Fahrenheit, and the wind blows. Under such conditions, the wind makes the temperature equivalent to 50 below, and then the flanks of the dogs may freeze. However, Eskimos usually do not travel under such conditions.

In urban areas where dogs are kept in the home, coats do have certain uses. They are a protection for sick dogs which must be taken out of doors, and for clipped dogs. They also keep the dog dry when it must be exercised in rain and snow. There are a dozen types of coats. Some are simply blankets which fit over the back and have tie straps at the belly. Others have two front leg holes, and still others four holes. Some have collars, and others even have attached caps. They are made from wool, vinyl, orlon, or combinations of these. Some, made of terry cloth, are designed for use after a bath. Both mink and ermine coats have been made for dogs.

Boots are used to protect sore feet, to keep the feet dry during bad weather, to protect the feet from prolonged contact with chemical snow melters, and to protect against hot pavements during extremely hot weather. Boots are also used in the Arctic when dogs must travel long distances over sharp ice crystals. As a rule, they are made of leather or vinyl, and are available in three or four sizes.

Cobby Short-bodied, compact, close-coupled.

C.O.C.A. (The Confederation Canina Americana) The Confederation Canina Americana is an amalgamation of National Kennel Clubs in South America. It was thought desirable because of the large area of that continent, and the rising interest in pedigree dogs.

Coats and Boots.
Top right One way to keep a well-groomed dog clean and tidy on the journey to the show is to dress it in a travelling suit.
Middle right Nature has fitted out most dogs with all the coat they need. However, sick or clipped dogs or dogs which are exposed to freezing conditions benefit from man-made covering.
Bottom right Cobby.

Additionally there was the surge of small canine societies which were crowding the official ones recognized by the FEDERATION CYNOLOGIQUE INTERNATIONALE. It followed the pattern of the 'Scandinavian Kennel Union' and was intended as an entity which would unify and defend the traditional clubs of each country.

During the 'Exposicao Internacional' of the 'Kennel Club do Chile', held in Vina del Mar, 19 February 1968, the delegates of the Kennel Clubs of Argentina, Chile, Colombia, Brazil and Peru founded the Confederation.

The rules seek continental unification of the Rules of the Dog Shows, Judges, Genealogic Registers, and Breeding. It also exchanges information on the buying and selling of dogs on an international basis and encourages international publicity on the desirable features of different breeds.

During its brief existence, C.O.C.A. has succeeded in unifying most of the Latin American Kennel Clubs affiliated to the F.C.I., creating harmony amongst them and has supported the appointments of the Kennel Club of Paraguay as an Associated Member of the F.C.I. It has also been successful in unifying national and international breed clubs.

The cost of maintaining C.O.C.A. is divided annually among the member countries which consist of the following, recognized by the F.C.I: Brazil, Mexico, Argentina, Venezuela, Colombia, Peru, Chile, Uruguay and Paraguay.

Coccidiosis see Protozoan Diseases.

Cocker Spaniel, American see American Cocker Spaniel.

Cocker Spaniel, English The Cocker Spaniel, known in some parts of the world as the English Cocker Spaniel, is one of the friendliest little dogs known to man. It is determined to love everybody and particularly insistent upon the promotion of its master to the realm of the gods.

It is and always has been a merry little dog; a busy-body who likes to have its nose in everything. A dog that could charm the hardest heart.

The Cocker Spaniel is, of course, only one, many claim the best one, of a large race of spaniels, all of which may have come originally from Spain. Early mention of this was provided by Dr. John Caius, writing in 1576, who said: 'The common sort of people call them by one general word, namely spaniells as though these dogs came originally and first of all out of Spain.' This does at least show that they were well established and known even then and the probability is that they had been in Britain, since the known close connection which existed between that country and Spain in Plantagenet times.

Spaniel, however, merely meant a dog from Spain. True, it meant one of the many breeds which we now refer to as gundogs or bird dogs. More particularly, it did describe the whole race of what we still call spaniels. What it did not do was decide between one type and another. And it was a matter of types rather than of varieties or breeds which existed in that time. We know that in the seventeenth century there were both large and small spaniels. There were also those with long or short bodies, the fast, racy type, and the slow, heavily-built animals. From this melting pot slowly emerged the various spaniels which we know today, such as the SUSSEX, the FIELD, the SPRINGER and the Cocker.

It is not certain how this latter acquired its name. Some say that it was because it was used to spring or 'cock' the game for the net and later the gun. Others that it was because of its special aptitude when being used on small game such as Woodcock. Either way it is a fact that this was the name by which it was widely recognized at the time that the Kennel Club (England) came into being in 1873. One of that body's first tasks, having established a Stud Book, was to encourage the formation of a breed standard for this attractive little dog.

From then on its popularity slowly increased until in 1935 it achieved the position of Great Britain's top dog. It held that position for 20 years. Even more important its popularity spread over a large part of the British Commonwealth and there are still a dozen countries in which it is one of the best-liked breeds. Particularly interesting is the fact that in Argentina it still remains top dog, surpassing in numbers even the GERMAN SHEPHERD DOG. This feat is particularly impressive in a South American country where a dog's guarding potentiality is considered of major importance.

One of the Cocker's most attractive features has always been its coat which is flat and silky in texture. It is enhanced by the feathering on the legs which should not be too profuse. These coats need remarkably little attention except for periodic grooming and occasional attention with scissors to clip the hair from between the toes. Surplus hair from the upper part of the ear can also be removed with the help of trimming scissors.

While the many attractive colours are dealt with in the abbreviated standard, it may be necessary to mention that in the past some red or golden cockers have had less satisfactory temperaments than the other colours. There is no apparent reason for this and it is not invariable. The tendency however, does exist.

Many consider that the Cocker is one of the most efficiently designed of all breeds. Every part of it is functional. For example its robust, compact body is deliberately small though powerfully built because of the necessity of forcing its way through thick undergrowth. Inevitably the shoulders must slope because otherwise it could not stand up to a hard day's galloping. Its neck must be strong and sufficiently long to enable it to lift game which is heavy in proportion to the dog's weight. Even the length of this neck is needed to clear a cumbersome load from the ground. Its jaw needs firmness. Its bone must be good and so must its feet.

Physical aptitude for work is therefore self-apparent. Even so, mention must be made of its gameness and courage, and its devotion and willingness. Additionally, there is its sense of fun and occasional irrepressible high spirits.

Is it these qualities which have made the Cocker

Right Cocker Spaniel, English. Ch. Scotswood Warlord.

Spaniel such a firm favourite in so many lands? In part the answer is *Yes*. Perhaps in greater part however it is its head that has done the trick. It is a beautiful head. And the eyes are even more beautiful: brown or hazel, liquid eyes; kind, sad yet wise eyes, guaranteed to make man feel as kindly disposed towards the dog as the dog already does towards man.

Essentials of the breed: Square muzzle and level jaw, with distinct stop. Adequate brain room. Nose: wide. Eyes: full, hazel or brown with a gentle, intelligent expression. Ears: set on low, not extending beyond nose. Neck: long, muscular, set on sloping shoulders. Chest: deep but not too round. Legs: well boned and straight. Body: compact, giving impression of concentrated power. Short back. Hindquarters: well rounded and muscular. Feet: firm, round and cat-like. Tail should be set low with carriage in a line with back, the lower the better, and not docked too short. Coat: flat and silky, with sufficient feather. Not too profuse and never curly. Colour: various, including black, red, blue roan, strawberry roan, black and white, and tricoloured. Weight: about 25 to 28 lb. Height (AKC): dogs 16 to 17 inches; bitches 15 to 16 inches. Weight: dogs 28 to 34 lb.; bitches 26 to 32 lb.
See colour plate p. 91.

Cod Liver Oil An important source of vitamin D which, in adequate amounts, prevents RICKETS.

Cold Nose It is a mistake to believe that a dog with a warm nose is unwell and sickening for a fever. The dog has sweat glands on the nose and if for some reason moisture is leaving the body or blood stream by other means, the nose will become warm and dry.

Most dogs have dry noses after a sleep but as soon as they get up and move around again the nose becomes moist and cold. Lack of drinking water can also cause the dog's nose to become dry.

Collar White markings around the neck.

Collars It is a wise policy to teach puppies from an early age to wear a collar. Eight weeks is not too young, if the collar is only worn each day for an hour or so. Getting a youngster accustomed to wearing a collar at this stage will save endless bother later. Dogs that have not been trained to wear collars until reaching maturity resent them and can prove very difficult.

As the puppy grows the collar must be adjusted and later replaced with a larger one. A collar should never be too tight and should not be left on for lengthy periods as this tends to mark the dog's neck and can even set up an irritation.

Collars should not be left on dogs in kennels. If the collar gets caught in the wire or some part of the kennel, it can have disastrous results. The dog gets agitated and worried in trying to release itself, twists itself round, pulls and tugs, and the collar tightens. Eventually the dog may choke itself.

An alternative to a collar is a harness but this is not recommended, first because it spoils the coat and next

Above Cocker Spaniel, English. One of the most efficiently-built of all breeds, the Cocker is also one of the most charming and is popular even in unlikely countries like the Argentine where it is a top dog. Ch. Crosbeian Cascade.

because it encourages some dogs' natural tendency to pull, which can throw out their shoulders and elbows. See CHOKE CHAINS.

Collie, Bearded The Bearded Collie, although shown extensively in Great Britain and various continental countries, particularly Scandinavia, has yet to appear in numbers in the United States. A breed club has however been formed there and doubtless in due course the Bearded Collie may be recognized by the American Kennel Club. It has been officially recognized in its homeland, Britain, only since 1944.

This is strange because a dog somewhat similar to it has a long history. One theory is that it is related to the KOMONDOR, and that hundreds of years ago it travelled north-west with the Magyar and Slavonic peoples into what is now Poland. There is a history of the Poles trading with other countries, one of these being Scotland, from the fourteenth century onwards. The Poles sent grain and in return received sheep. It is at least possible that they left some of their sheepdogs in Scotland. Perhaps even before that a Collie type was established there. A very early description which could have applied to the breed reads, somewhat unflatteringly, as follows: 'A big, rough, "tousy" looking tyke with a coat not unlike a doormat, the texture of the hair hard and fibry and the ears hanging close to the head.' The special reference to the ears must surely be to distinguish it from the rough and smooth COLLIES which have very neat prick ears with folded over tips.

It would seem that before the twentieth century, the

Above Collars. Round collars are better for long-haired breeds; flat ones for short-haired dogs.

Collie, Bearded.
Above left A detail from a nineteenth century painting by John F. Herring, a stage-coachman turned animal painter, of a hound and a Bearded Collie sitting on a hunting coat.
Above right Will o' Wisp of Willowmead.

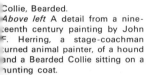

Bearded Collie was known as the Highland Collie. Its history is largely unrecorded because they were purely working dogs and not the glamorous pets of the fashionable set. Even so it is a reasonable supposition that the 'Beardie' was used more as drovers' or cattle dog than a sheepdog only. That is to say it accompanied the shepherd into the hills, drove his cattle or sheep in the required direction but probably did less intelligent rounding up than the pure Collie. This is not to discredit it: the OLD ENGLISH SHEEPDOG or 'Bobtail' performed the same task.

There is indeed some resemblance between the Beardie and the Bobtail. A picture in *The Sportsman's Cabinet* dated 1908 shows a dog perhaps midway between the two. It is not possible to deduce which one was the forerunner of the other. *The Book of the Dog* written in 1907 admits that the Beardie and the Bobtail are much alike, but points out that the Bearded Collie is a more racy animal with a head resembling that of a DANDIE DINMONT. However, it also reproduces photographs of Mr. J. Dalgliesh's *Ellwyn Garrie,* a winner of several first prizes at important shows and a most elegant animal, typical by today's standard, in the shape of Lord Arthur Cecil's *Ben.*

Despite the formation of a breed club in Edinburgh in 1912, the breed seemed to fade from the public gaze. A Mrs. Cameron Millar tried to revive interest but made the serious mistake of crossing all of those which she acquired with Bobtails.

In January 1944 a Mrs. Willison acquired a Beardie by accident and, understandably, she did not recognize it. She was in search of a Shetland Sheepdog, bred from working parents, but the farmer from whom it was ordered sent this chocolate-coloured replacement. By the time is was identified for what it was, the dog had become very much a friend of the family. The dog, at first *Jeannie,* later *Champion Jeannie of Bothkennar,* became famous as the forebear of every Bearded Collie winning prizes today.

Since the breed standard is particularly descriptive, no further word picture is required here except to state that in the opinion of many the suggestion that the head resembles a Dandie Dinmont is incorrect. Rather it is reminiscent of that other noble, elegant and essentially highland dog, the Scottish DEERHOUND.

Essentials of the breed: The general appearance is of an active dog with long, lean body, none of the stumpiness of the Bobtail, and an enquiring expression. Head: broad; fairly long foreface with moderate stop. Eyes: toning with coat colour, set rather widely apart, big and bright. Eyebrows: arched and forward. Ears: medium-sized, drooping, with longish hair. Neck: of fair length, muscular and slightly arched. Legs: straight with flexible pasterns, all covered by shaggy hair. The body must be fairly long, the back level, with flat ribs. Hindquarters: muscular thighs with well-bent stifles and hocks. Oval feet with well-padded toes.

The tail is set low, covered with abundant hair, carried low when dog is quiet but with an upward swirl when excited.

Coat, which must be double, is sparse on the bridge of the nose, slightly longer on the sides covering the lips, while behind this falls the beard with a moderate amount of hair under the chin. Colours: slate grey or reddish fawn, black, all shades of brown and sandy, with or without white markings.

The ideal height is dogs: 21–22 inches; bitches: 20–21 inches.

See colour plate p. 295.

Collie, Border The Border Collie is one of the world's finest sheepdogs. It has proven its ability in all areas of the world where sheep are raised in numbers. Moreover, it has been demonstrating its ability in sheep herding trials since 1873. Thus, it has shown its worth to millions of people who have never been in an area where dogs are required to 'work' sheep.

Herders and farmers the world over call it the 'old fashioned sheep dog', or the 'Farm Collie', or 'Working Collie'. This is to distinguish it from the immensely popular Collie of the home and show ring.

The Border Collie is bred for working ability, rather than for type. That is, only those dogs which have proven both their intelligence and their trainability are used for breeding. In most countries, they are registered in their own stud books, instead of those of the national bodies governing dog shows or other types of field trials.

Yet the dogs do conform reasonably well to type. They are black, grey, or blue merle, with white points; or black, white, and tan. Males are 18 inches at the shoulder and weigh up to 45 lb. Bitches are smaller. The skull is fairly broad, with moderate stop, and

the muzzle is slightly blunt. The ears are semi-prick. The body is slightly longer than tall. The tail is set on low, is carried low, but has a slight upward swirl. It is bushy. The coat is dense, fairly long, and has a thick undercoat.

Border Collies do not compete in the regular conformation classes at bench shows. But they do sometimes compete in obedience trials in Great Britain and America. In such trials, they are conspicuously successful.

See colour plate p. 292.

Above Collie, Bearded. Ch. Willowmead Barberry of Bothkennar.
Below Collie. Border. Two obedience champions: Dirk of Twistwood and Corranlea Twistwood.

Collie Nose see Eczema.

Collie, Rough Some call this dog the Scotch Collie, but the national tag is superfluous. All Collies hail from Scotland. They would not warrant the name if they did not. A century ago the sheep in Scotland, usually dark in colour, were called 'Colleys', from the Anglo-Saxon word *Col,* meaning black. The dogs that worked them, lacking a breed name and frequently being black themselves, were referred to simply as the Colley Dogs. It was only a short step to Collies.

Why not then just call them Collies? Why the adjective? The answer is that there are three varieties of Collie: the Smooth, which has a short coat like a GREYHOUND; the Bearded which has a hard, shaggy coat like a WOLFHOUND, and a distinctive beard; and the Rough, with its very attractive, dense coat, and the addition of mane and frill.

Few if any other dogs are as attractive, as beautiful or as graceful as the Rough Collies. They have one distinctive feature which, in perfection, makes them stand out from the crowd. It is their expressive ears. In repose they are thrown back; on the alert they are brought forward and carried semi-erect.

Ears which are quite erect are not satisfactory; they destroy the expression. They give to the head a foreign look, like the face of a GERMAN SHEPHERD DOG, a BULL TERRIER, or an ELKHOUND. Conversely, a Collie with heavy ears which fold over too firmly has the soulful and untypical look of a hound.

These may be considered unimportant details but a Collie's ears are useful as well as decorative. With them it can pick up the whistle, even the voice, of a shepherd a mile away. They are turned towards the master like a sounding board, and they are nearly as efficient. 'For what purpose?' it may be asked. What use indeed is the whole exquisite creation? Surely Collies can no longer perform their original task? It has to be admitted that few pure-bred Rough Collies now herd sheep; the Border Collie is more efficient.

As a breed, the sheepdog is among the oldest known. Doubtless prehistoric man first enlisted the aid of hunting dogs to help him catch food. But soon afterwards, when sophistication brought him to agricultural pursuits, he needed dogs to guard and control his flocks. Like all working sheepdogs, the Scottish variety had abundant and weatherproof coats. Like all their kind they were agile, supple and fleet-footed. They had excellent eyesight, and above all, a willingness for work, an uncanny perception of their master's wishes and an overwhelming desire to please.

These dogs were invaluable in the mountains of Scotland. The number of men needed to control flocks of sheep, to drive them to new pastures, and to collect them and shepherd them to market without the Collies, would have been such that all the profits would have been swallowed by the wage bill.

So the dogs worked for centuries but remained unknown until Queen Victoria made her first visit to Balmoral in 1860. There she saw some of these dogs and immediately fell in love with them. She bought some and installed them in the Royal Kennels at Windsor.

Almost inevitably with this spotlight on them they quickly became popular in Britain and the United States. With rich people on both side of the Atlantic bidding for the best specimens, prices soared until for the first time in history the sum of £1,000 ($2400) was paid for one particular dog. They also rapidly became more elegant, more chic and more sophisticated; more, in fact, like the dogs we know today and less like their humble if hard-working forebears.

It is rumoured that BORZOIS and GORDON SETTERS were used to smarten them up and this is at least possible. Crosses however have not been resorted to in recent years.

Essentials of the breed: An abundance of coat, mane, and frill, with sweetness of expression, combine to present an elegant picture. Skull: flat and moderately wide between ears, tapering towards the eyes. The muzzle continues in unbroken line towards the nose. Slight, perceptible stop. Nose: black. Eyes: medium size, set obliquely, almond-shaped, dark brown except in merles, when one eye or both blue-and-white or china. Ears: moderately wide at the base; small; when alert brought forward and semi-erect, with tips drooping slightly. Mouth: lower incisors fitting closely behind the uppers. Neck: muscular, powerful and somewhat arched. Sloped shoulders. Forelegs: straight and muscular with fair bone. Body: rather long, well-sprung ribs. Deep chest. Loins: slightly arched and powerful. Feet: oval, well padded; toes arched and close. Tail: moderately long, carried low when quiet, may be gaily carried when excited but not over back. Coat – outer: dense and harsh, inner: soft, furry and close.

Right Collie, Rough. The two outstanding features of this beautiful breed are its luxuriant coat and its expressive ears which, when alert, can pick up a whistle a mile away. Ch. Lovely Lady of Glenmist.

Mane and frill or APRON abundant. Hair on brush profuse. Colour and markings are immaterial in Britain, but U.S.A. demands sable and white, tri-coloured, blue merle or white. Weight and Size: dogs, 22 to 24 inches at the shoulders; bitches, 20 to 22 inches. Dogs 45 lb. to 65 lb.; bitches 40 lb. to 55 lb. Height (AKC): dogs 24 to 26 inches; bitches 22 to 24 inches. Weight: from 50 to 65 lb.
See colour plate p. 294.

Collie, Smooth To many, mention of a Collie means what the fancier knows as a Rough Collie. The layman is surprised to find that there is more than one Collie, and he is even more surprised to find that one type is smooth-coated. The dog is required by the original breed standard to be precisely similar to the Rough in every respect except coat.

It is impossible to trace the beginnings of the Smooth and the Rough Collies. There is, however, a woodcut accompanying some rather limited text by Sydenham Edwards in his *Cynographia Britannica* dated 1800. This shows two similar but separate varieties. The *Shepherd's Dogs*, which could be roughly described as a modern BORDER COLLIE, and *The Cur* (subtitled *The Drover's Dog*) which is at least reminiscent of a rough-and-ready Smooth Collie but with a short tail. The text mentions that some of these are born 'self tailed' which means whelped without a tail.

This certainly gives some support to the widely held theory that the Rough was the dog which controlled the sheep on the hillsides while the Smooths were drovers, taking the sheep through lanes and highways to market. This suggests that originally there were two different breeds. Bewick, in his *History of Quadrupeds* hints that the Smooth was a descendant of the BANDOG, which in turn descends from the MASTIFF.

It is more certain that while the principal home of the Rough was Scotland, the Smooth was most frequently encountered in Northumberland, northern England.

For nearly the whole of last century however, they have been identical in form, outline and size. Until 1870 it was usual for Roughs and Smooths to compete against each other in the same classes. During that year Doncaster Dog Show introduced the innovation of giving Smooth Collies separate classes. However, at the time of the first speciality or breed club show for Collies, held in 1885, the catalogue shows that some of the Smooths being exhibited came from the same litter as some of the Roughs.

While there is no risk of the Smooth fading from the scene, it has always been over-shadowed by its glamorous and hairy cousin. At present in Britain there are seventy Roughs registered for every Smooth. America is almost certainly even more in favour of the Rough.

There are however two straws in the wind which may well alter the proportion, though not the relative positions. First, there is the remarkable improvement in type of the Smooths now being shown in Britain. Many of them are good enough to hold their own in the show ring against all comers with or without the advantages of hair. Next, there is an equally remarkable improvement in temperament. More and more people primarily interested in obedience are realizing that a Smooth Collie is the answer to their problem.

Essentials of the breed: The Smooth variety of Collie is

Left Collie, Rough. A size comparison between a Shetland Sheepdog and its much larger cousin. Ch. Debonair of Glenmist (Collie), Ch. Gypsy Star of Glenmist (Sheltie).

Collie, Smooth.
Top right Ch. Cotsbelle Blue Caprice.
Bottom right The plate from Sydenham Edwards' *Cynographia Britannica* entitled 'The Shepherd's Dog and the Cur'.

judged by the same standard as the Rough variety except that the coat should be hard, dense, and smooth. See colour plate p. 293.

Colour Inheritance The colouring matter found in the coat, skin, and eyes (except the retina) of mammals, is a pigment called melanin. This is formed in special cells, the melanophores, from colourless substances. Melanin in dogs comes in one of three colours; black, chocolate-brown, or yellow. Black and chocolate are mutually exclusive in the individual; that is, a dog can either make black pigment or chocolate pigment, but not both. The difference extends to all melanin formed anywhere in the body, and depends on a single GENE pair, B and b.

The yellow colours appear to result from a further biochemical process which can effect both black and chocolate pigment, turning them yellow, though of slightly different shades. Most of the yellowing genes have little or no effect on skin and eye pigment, which remains either black or chocolate, while the hair pigment becomes yellow in part or all of the coat. There are several genes, independent of each other, which produce yellowing. The simplest is the e gene, which when both partners in the gene pair are the same (that is, ee), turns all the hair pigment yellow. It is seen typically in yellow Labradors and lemon-and-white (including orange-and-white) Pointers. In Labradors, most yellows are descended from blacks and have black pigment in the skin (nose, eye-rims, etc.), whereas most lemon Pointers are bred from liver-marked animals and have chocolate noses and eye-rims. There are other genes, the chinchilla series, which reduce the quantity of pigment particularly when it is yellow, and are responsible for various shades from palest cream to red.

Probably the same series causes the varying shades of tan on 'bi-colour' dogs (black-and-tans, liver-and-tans, blue-and-tans). In bi-colours the yellow pigment is restricted to a characteristic pattern on the feet, underline, chest, muzzle, inside the ears, and the distinctive 'thumb spots' over the eyes. The pattern is produced by the recessive a^t gene. Another recessive, a^s, yellows the pigment over a more extensive area, leaving a dark saddle as in hound-marked dogs like AIREDALES. The heterozygote (or mixed gene pair) $a^s a^t$ probably has an intermediate amount of tan, but dogs with Aa^s and Aa^t gene pairs have no tan or yellow markings. The bi-colour genes are quite unconnected with the ee (extension yellow) genes although their effects cannot be seen in an ee animal because it is yellow all over. Some breeders, of COCKER SPANIELS, for example, think that tan markings come from crossing blacks with goldens (or blue-roans with lemon-roans) but this is not correct.

Yet another form of yellow is called 'dominant yellow', although its DOMINANCE relationships are not clear. It is responsible for the golden sables, found in COLLIES, GERMAN SHEPHERD DOGS and red DACHSHUNDS. Latest information suggests that in most breeds it can act only on animals with a^s or a^t genes, being suppressed by A, but it can suppress black in German Shepherd Dogs.

Apart from the colour of the pigment granules, coat colour depends on their distribution in the hair. The *d* gene clumps the granules together, giving smoky shades of blue, blue-fawn etc. The 'agouti' gene seems to 'switch' pigment formation 'on' and 'off' as the individual hairs grow, so that they have lighter and darker bands, such as a black tip, a tan band, a black band, and a creamy root end. This gives the wolf-grey and pepper-and-salt colours, in which the undercoat is usually, but not always, paler than the outer coat.

White markings are mainly controlled by the series of multiple genes, for example S, s', s^p, s^w. The dominant gene permits the whole coat to be pigmented, the others in descending order allow more white markings, so that the $s^w s^w$ animal is white with a few coloured patches, often confined to the ears.

Other genes are responsible for such patterns as BRINDLE, black MASK, silver, and roaning of white areas. Particularly interesting is the gene which produces BLUE MERLE colouring; it is known as a semi-lethal gene. The gene M is dominant and in mixed gene pairs Mm causes dark and light patches on coloured coats, restricting yellow less than black or chocolate. Indeed it is possible that Harlequin GREAT DANES are Mm with no yellowing gene, or they may have 'modifying' genes controlling colour which help the M gene to give white between the black or blue patches. Mm dogs which also have an $a^t a^t$ pair are the familiar blue merles seen in Collies and SHETLAND SHEEPDOGS, and dappled DACHSHUNDS also have this formula. The action of the gene on yellow and on chocolate coats is less conspicuous, but of the same kind, producing darker blotches on a paler yellow or fawn background. It is not certain that it can affect *ee* yellow coat colour. The Mm animals are almost normal, although they often have WALL EYES, but when the gene is homozygous (both sides of the pair the same), MM, it makes the puppy blind and usually deaf, and the coat is white. Merle x merle and harlequin x harlequin matings should therefore be strictly avoided. If made, white puppies should be destroyed at birth to avoid suffering.

See CHROMOSOMES.

Communicable Diseases see Transmissible Diseases.

Concussion

One usually associates concussion with the brain, which is often the organ affected. But a blow or explosive blast may cause concussion of the labyrinth of the ear, causing deafness. Concussion of the spine is usually followed by severe functional disturbances.

Brain concussion must be distinguished from brain compression. Both cause a state of SHOCK. In *concussion* there is usually partial unconsciousness, but unless this is complete, the animal can be aroused. The pulse is feeble, breathing is shallow, and there may be involuntary passage of urine. The eye pupils will be equally dilated, and show poor response to light. There may be bleeding from the ears or into the eyes.

Golden dog eeSS   mated to   Black & White bitch EEs^Ps^P

all offspring Black

EeSs^P   mated together   EeSs^P

can throw pups of 4 colour types

Black : 9
1 EESS   2 EESs^P
2 EeSS   4 EeSs^P

Golden : 3
1 eeSS   2 eeSs^P

Black & White : 3
1 EEs^Ps^P   2 Ees^Ps^P

Lemon & White : 1
1 ees^Ps^P

Above Colour inheritance. The diagram shows colour possibilities for two generations of offspring from different-coloured parents.

When *compression* of the brain occurs, the dog cannot be aroused, for it is in a total coma. There will be unequal dilation of the eye pupils, and the breathing will be loud, as though the dog were snoring. Some areas of the body will be paralyzed.

Condition, Conditioning

Condition is a term which, to the ordinary dog owner and to his veterinarian, means a state of health: excellent, good, or bad, or good for the dog's age. To the show exhibitor, condition means 'show condition', well trimmed, clipped, and groomed.

A field dog, on the other hand, is in good condition when its muscles are hard, its foot pads toughened, and its endurance has been built to maximum.

A dog can be conditioned by walking, tied to a long leash. Toes and pads can be strengthened by walks on pavements, along a sandy beach, and by climbing hills. Field running, increasing in length each day, puts the field dog into condition. Care should be taken not to over-exercise the dog unless supplementary food – such as protein, carbohydrate and pure corn oil – is added to the diet.

GROOMING of show dogs is an integral part of conditioning for the show ring. Field dogs also need grooming, though of a different sort. They must be examined for burrs, dust in the eye pockets and thorns or other injuries. Dust should then be brushed out of the coat. Correct NUTRITION also plays an essential part in conditioning the dog, whether for shows, or for field work.

Confederation Canina Americana see C.O.C.A.

Conformation Either as the result of selective breeding or by indiscriminate breeding, dogs now exist in many shapes and sizes. However, there are special types of conformation fairly firmly established and the major ones are considered below.

The shape of modern dogs has undergone change as the result of conditions known as *acromegaly* and *achondroplasia*. Acromegaly is akin to gigantism. The body grows to a large size wrapped in far too much skin. This forms folds and wrinkles particularly on the head, sometimes with the addition of a DEWLAP. It is seen in the BLOODHOUND and the BASSET HOUND, and in even larger breeds such as the ST. BERNARD. Achondroplasia causes the head to become large with the legs very short and stunted, or deformed. It is evident in the SCOTTISH TERRIER.

Other factors which give rise to distinctive conformation are encountered in the *brachycephalic* (short-faced) breeds such as the BULLDOG, PUG and PEKINGESE. The skull is large in its cranial portion and rounded. The upper jaw is very short between STOP and nostril. The excess skin forms folds with wrinkles on the forehead and long ear leathers, to utilize some of the surplus skin. The brachycephalic breeds vary in size from that of the Bulldog to the GRIFFON BRUXELLOIS.

The *dolichocephalic* (long-headed) breeds may be tall like the GREYHOUND family, or small like the SHETLAND SHEEPDOG and the ITALIAN GREYHOUND.

Neck and shoulder development are discussed elsewhere, while length of back, set-on of tail and length of limb are all specified for each variety by breed standards.

One marked modern change resulting from selective breeding concerns length and angulation of the hind limb. Increased angulation of the hind limb as in the GERMAN SHEPHERD DOG has been obtained by a lengthening of the tibia (shin-bone), in the belief that a longer, angulated hind limb assists body propulsion.

Conjunctivitis see Eye Diseases.

Constipation A tendency to constipation may be inherited, although this is rare. A condition causing the partial closure of the rectal opening may lead to constipation. This condition may also result from lack of exercise, or from *atony* – the lack of contractive ability in the muscles governing defecation, often a condition of old age.

Constipation may result from diseases which cause a severe loss in the body's fluids, for example, repeated attacks of vomiting or diuresis (increased excretion of urine). An abnormally enlarged prostate gland is

sometimes a cause, when the feces are ribbon-like, and so are intestinal TUMOURS.

A rather common cause is the swallowing of large quantities of small bones. Dogs have been known to break up and swallow half a dozen or more pork chop bones which become impacted in the intestines.

The swallowing of foreign bodies which cause an obstruction in the small intestine may lead to a condition which resembles constipation. The dog will strain as though constipated because the lining of the rectum is swollen, but will have nothing to pass because of the obstruction.

Surgery is usually required to remove the foreign bodies, which may be marbles, bones or even large items such as golf balls.

A rather common cause in long-haired dogs which live out of doors, and are given little attention by their owners, is a blocked anal orifice. Fecal material sticks to the hair. This steadily builds up until the entire area of the orifice is blocked. During the build up of this material, severe pain is caused by the passage of stools which pull at the hairs. The dog then tends to delay evacuation as long as possible, and this further contributes to the problem.

Whenever the signs of constipation appear, such as severe straining, abnormally hard and dry stools, vomiting, and the presence of hard masses which can be felt through the abdominal wall, the dog should be taken to a veterinarian.

Coonhound, Black and Tan see American Coonhounds.

Coonhound Hunting see American Coonhounds.

Coonhounds, other varieties see American Coonhounds.

Coprophagy Physical causes of stool eating, or coprophagy, are a severe debility following illness, severe infestations of parasites, usually ancylostomiasis or HOOKWORMS, and vitamin deficiency. In all cases, the dog should be given a complete physical examination. Vitamin therapy is often recommended. An old remedy was the feeding of raw potato peelings.

Puppies may form the stool-eating habit both because of their interest in almost everything and their habit of chewing on things and playing with them. They will, for example play readily with a frozen stool, although they might ignore a fresh one. Puppies kept in runs are more likely to develop the habit than are house dogs. Keeping the runs clean is essential to prevent this. If sticks and branches are left in runs, puppies will carry these instead and chew on them. Feeding once a day, very early in the morning, permits early cleaning of the runs, since the dogs tend to defecate shortly after eating. But this, of course, cannot be applied to a puppy which requires a number of meals each day.

Scattering large, hard biscuits, or raw knuckle bones about, also helps. The puppy will prefer to play and to chew on these rather than a stool. An excellent corrective measure is to put the stool-eating dog on a twelve-

foot long light rope. When he is taken to the spot where he normally defecates, it is natural for him to examine the stools. He should then be given a severe jerk. A few such lessons may break the habit.

Corded – Cords Hair curled around central hairs to form hanging cords, as distinguished from mats. Seen in corded PULIS, and, rarely, in POODLES.

Corgi see Welsh Corgi, Cardigan; Welsh Corgi, Pembroke.

Cough Canine coughs result from a variety of causes. The type of cough may indicate the cause to the experienced listener. Thus, a short, dry cough often indicates pharyngitis. A loud, hard, dry cough, comes accompanied by violet paroxysms can indicate laryngitis. Dogs often return from boarding kennels with such a cough. They have simply barked themselves into a state of laryngitis.

Wheezy, laboured respiration and coughs may be signs of asthma or emphysema. Coughs often follow DISTEMPER and pneumonia. In acariasis, worms escape into the air sacs of the lungs, and are coughed into the throat, then swallowed. Nephritis, a KIDNEY DISEASE, is often accompanied by a mild bronchial type cough.

In recent years, an air-borne disease, probably caused by a virus, has plagued kennels, veterinary hospitals, and boarding kennels. It is highly contagious, but both mild and self limiting. Treatment for this, as with many coughs, consists in giving a mild expectorant with codeine and antihistamine, and sick dogs should be isolated. Antibiotics are sometimes given by a veterinarian to prevent secondary infections.

A deep cough occurring whenever the dog becomes excited, tired, or even enters a room of a different temperature, may indicate a heart condition.
See ASTHMA.

Couples This is a term used in the hunting world to denote a pair of hounds of the same breed. When a young hound goes into kennels from his PUPPY WALK he has to learn kennel discipline and routine. Here the huntsman calls on the older hounds to help him.

The youngster is coupled to an experienced hound who will recognize his master's words of command and, in obeying, will draw the puppy after him. In this way the puppy soon learns to associate the command with the action that follows. Puppies will be left coupled with an older hound until they can be completely trusted not to chase dogs, cats, poultry, sheep, etc.

Hounds in a hunting kennel are counted in couples, so 14 couple are 28 hounds, and $14\frac{1}{2}$ couple are 29 hounds.

Couplings The body between the WITHERS and the hip bones. A dog can be said to be long or short-coupled, depending on the distance between the withers and the hip joints. This should not be confused with a short or long back which is the distance between the withers and the set-on of the tail along the vertebrae.

Coursing (Other than Greyhounds) Coursing probably started in the Middle East at the time of King Solomon, said to be the owner of a SALUKI named *Girt in the Loins*.

The Bedouin of the desert still courses hounds, not as a sport but to catch food. Originally it was an upper-class sport and then, as now, Arab sheiks coursed gazelle with a pair of Salukis, assisted by trained falcons which harassed any gazelle singled out of the herd by the dogs.

Today, coursing in Britain is organized for GREYHOUNDS and several of the other sighting hound breeds. The DEERHOUND, Saluki and WHIPPET Clubs all hold meetings, and once a year the three clubs have a combined meeting in Norfolk. The Deerhound and Saluki Clubs also hold a three-day meeting in Scotland, coursing the blue Mountain hare over long and difficult courses lasting several minutes. At all meetings the rules of the National Coursing Club are observed.

Recently there have been attempts to abolish coursing in the United Kingdom by an act of Parliament. The outcome is not yet known but the activity may soon be outlawed as public opinion is heavily against the sport.

The following information is not always appreciated. Firstly, all hares are coursed on their own ground where they have lived at least six months. The transporting of boxed hares to a 'course' is forbidden. Usually only about one in four of the hares coursed is killed. The rest escape. Those caught have a quick death and most have no visible mark on them. The kill in coursing is not the main object, which is rather to test the merits of two hounds after a wild hare. When hares become too numerous, hare-shoots are organized to preserve farmers' crops. At a single large-scale shoot, four times as many hares are killed as in a whole year of coursing in Britain.

In Portugal, GREYHOUND COURSING flourishes, English officials frequently being invited to participate. In America organized coursing meetings called 'hunts' are held by recognized breed clubs. Hounds of different breeds are coursed against each other after the jack-

Left Corded. Hairs of the coat curled round central hairs produce the extraordinary effect shown here on a rare corded Poodle.

Top right Cow-hocked. Turned-in hocks are a fault and considered a major fault in some breeds.

Cruft's Show.
Middle right The first poster advertising a show that was to become world-famous as Cruft's.
Bottom right Medals commemorating Cruft's Shows.
Far right The portly figure of Charles Cruft, who started his career as a dog-biscuit seller and became the 'Barnum and Bailey' of the dog world.

rabbit. In California several breeds are coursed against each other and more than two hounds may be coursed at a time so that slipping is done by the owners under the direction of the 'hunt master'.

In the Great Plains, coyotes, killers of lambs and calves, proved too fast and tough for Foxhounds while Greyhounds had not enough striking power to kill. Greyhounds from the Kansas track were crossed with the larger sighthounds, thus producing a 'coursing hound' big and robust enough to stand up to farm life and truck riding. When a coyote is sighted, a truck carrying hound cages in the tail, with slots for them to peer through, is driven past it. As the coyote turns back to run in the opposite direction, the truck is halted, the cages opened and the released hounds attempt to overtake the coyote by an initial burst of speed. As often as not the coyote gets away.

There is a National Coursing Association of America which holds a week-long Spring Trial in Kansas each year.

Cow-Hocked When the hocks turn inwards, and the feet outwards.

Crabbing Gait in which the body moves forward at a slight angle instead of in a straight line. Side-winding.

Crank Tail Tail carried downwards, and twisted to resemble a crank.

Crest The arched portion of the neck; the opposite to a ewe neck.

Cropping Ears see Ear Cropping.

Cross-Bred A dog whose parents are of different breeds.

Crossing Over Setting one foot down in front of, and slightly to the right or left of, the other foot. Weaving. Plaiting.

Croup The rump.

Crown Highest point of the head.

Cruelty to Animals see Humane Societies.

Cruft's Show Charles Cruft was born in 1851, eight years before the first organized dog show was held in Britain. His father, a jeweller in Bloomsbury, London, intended him to follow in his footsteps, but when young Charles left school, he found a job as shop-boy with James Spratt who had brought back from America the new-fangled idea of 'dog biscuits'. Young Cruft graduated to traveller and, when he visited the Continent in 1879, he was invited to organize the dog section at the Paris Exhibition. In 1886 he organized the Allied Terrier Show at the Royal Aquarium, London, with spectacular success and he was astute enough to see a great future in dog shows. He made a long-term contract with the Agricultural Hall in

Islington, and in 1891 staged what was to become the world-famous Cruft's Dog Show. Queen Victoria and the Royal Family patronized his show and until the introduction of quarantine regulations in 1901 he had entries from as far afield as Russia and India. Londoners found the appeal of strange breeds of dog irresistible and Cruft's success firmly established him as the 'Barnum and Bailey' of the dog world.

Kennel Club rules no longer permit the promotion of dog shows for private profit, and when Charles Cruft died in 1938, the Kennel Club acquired the show from Mrs. Cruft and staged it with ever increasing success at Olympia, London at the beginning of February each year.

The popularity of the pedigreed dog in recent years and the growth of dog showing led to a crisis in the history of Cruft's Show in the late 1950's when the number of entries exceeded the facilities, floor space, benching, printing, and perhaps more importantly, the time available to the judges to make their decisions. The Kennel Club decided to restrict the number of entries. The first curtailment was in the entry of puppies, but this was not enough, and for the 1967 show the Committee announced that entries would be restricted to dogs which had won first, second or third prizes at Championship shows in 1966, but Champions would be given a 'season ticket' for life. For a time this sufficed but entries continued to grow and in 1971 were

Cruft's Show.
Above left Bergerie Knur became in 1969 the Supreme Champion of Crufts. He shares his glory and his coveted trophy with his owner.
Above Cruft's has always enjoyed royal patronage from the early days when Queen Victoria entered dogs for exhibition to a recent visit by her great-great-grand-daughter, Queen Elizabeth II.

further restricted to dogs which had won first and second prizes in the previous year or a Challenge Certificate at any time. It is probable that entries one day will be restricted to first prize winners only.

Cruft's show is an irresistible attraction for the British public and nearly 50,000 people visit the show each year. It has taken its place in the calendar of sporting events in Britain with the Boat Race, the Derby, the Cup Final and Wimbledon. Because of the number of overseas visitors the Kennel Club provides special facilities at the show for the issue of export pedigrees and veterinary certificates.

Cryptorchid The term cryptorchid is a combination of the two words *crypt,* meaning hidden; and *orchid,* meaning testicle. In exact terminology, it means that neither of the testicles has descended into the scrotum. If only one has descended, the proper term is uni-lateral cryptorchid or monorchid. If neither has, the condition is termed true cryptorchidism. Anorchism is a condition in which testicles are entirely absent.

Testicles which remain in the body do not function properly, although sex hormones may be produced and the dog may even be oversexed. BODY TEMPERA-TURE is at least one degree higher in the abdomen than that of the scrotum, and the sperm cannot survive. Testicles remaining in the body usually atrophy, and cancer can sometimes result. Surgical removal is therefore often recommended. If only one testicle descends, it will be functional.

Testicles may not descend because they are too large to pass through the inguinal canal, or the stem or stalk upon which they are hung may be too short to permit descent. An operation to anchor an undescended testicle in the scrotum is called cryptorchido-pexy. Injections of gonadotropic hormones have proved unsuccessful in bringing the testicles into the scrotum.

Cryptorchidism is considered to be hereditary. Many countries disqualify both monorchids and cryptorchids from the show ring. Dogs upon which

cryptorchidopexy has been performed are also disqualified. Judges are required to examine all male dogs. However, dogs competing in field trials are not so examined, and the condition, if it exists, is ignored. It is inadvisable to breed from a monorchid dog.

Culotte Longer hair on the back of the thighs.

Cur see Mongrel.

Curly-Coated Retriever The Curly-coated Retriever is one of, if not the oldest of all the Retriever breeds. Unfortunately, in every country in the world, it is among, if not *the* least popular of them.

To say that a breed like this is old, does not of course give it a thousand years of history. The word is used relatively. Until comparatively recently retrievers were unnecessary to the sportsman. The range of guns was so limited that game shot fell almost at the sportsman's feet. He could pick it up for himself.

Increased velocity however meant that many birds, often flying overhead at high speeds, fell a long way in front. The Pointers and Setters used at the time were not always very good at finding them and frequently poor at bringing them back. It was work in direct contradiction to all their instincts and training. So entered the age of specialization. Dogs were wanted not for the general tasks of working hedgerows, pointing and setting the game and then springing it for the gun, but for the pure task of finding and retrieving.

At this point some non-gundog breeds were pressed into service. The GOLDEN RETRIEVER for example, a dog whose ancestry has never been satisfactorily solved; the LABRADOR with its background of retrieving not birds but fishing nets. Even before this, however, the Curly-coated Retriever had appeared on the scene. It was before the days of stud books and its breeding can only be guessed at.

'Stonehenge' writing in *The Dog* in 1859 said: 'This variety is always a cross between the St. Johns Newfoundland and a water spaniel, which is generally Irish!' Despite the note of certainty, many have disagreed with him since evidence points to the probability that this breed was developed in the early part of the nineteenth century and that breeds employed in its manufacture were principally the St. Johns dog, mentioned above, a small variety of Newfoundland in many ways similar to early Labrador Retrievers, and the Old Water Dog or Water Spaniel.

The latter were in no way *Irish* Water Spaniels. They did not, for example, have a topknot of hair like the dog from Ireland. Neither, it should be noted, has the Curly-coated Retriever. Undoubtedly POODLE crosses were also made and while these may have improved the quality of retrieving, they could not have improved the coat texture.

The distinctive feature of the Curly Retriever's coat is that it consists of a mass of close, crisp curls from the peak of the forehead to the tip of the tail. The effect is of the finest astrakhan! And it can be either jet black or deep liver-coloured.

This dog's delight is swimming. It has made it invaluable as a retriever, particularly of duck in marshy country or where streams and rivers have to be crossed. One short shake of that virtually waterproof coat and in seconds it is almost dry.

The dog has always been liked by gamekeepers because of its general strength and robust constitution. They admired its independent spirit and often forgave it for being a shade unsociable with its fellow workers in the field. They also appreciated that it was an excellent family dog, being prepared on the one hand to romp with the children but at the same time to give a good account of itself if asked to deal with unwelcome strangers.

A club was formed to promote the breed in 1896. It prospered, and wins both on the bench and in the field brought Curly-coated Retrievers to what must now be considered their heyday, between the wars. Since then, they have done little more than mark time and certainly they have not kept pace with the general increase in pedigree dogs. There are nevertheless enough faithful fanciers around to ensure they do not fade away.

Essentials of the breed: The general appearance is of a strong, smart, upstanding dog showing activity, endurance and intelligence. The head is long, well-proportioned with jaws strong and long but not SNIPY. Nose: black or liver according to coat colour. Eyes: black or brown, large but not prominent. Ears: rather small, set on low, lying close to the head. Neck should be moderately long. Shoulders should be very deep, muscular and well laid back while hindquarters are strong and muscular with hocks low to ground. The body has well sprung ribs, deep brisket, fairly short loin. Round, compact feet with well-arched toes. Tail: moderately short, carried fairly straight and covered with curls, tapering towards the point. The coat should be a mass of small, crisp curls. Colours: black or liver. Weight (Britain): 70 to 80 lb. Height (Britain): approximately 25 to 27 inches.
See colour plate p. 84.

Cushion Thickness of the upper lips in Pekingese, Boxers, etc.

Right Curly-Coated Retriever. Ch. Runglis Banworth Sunset.

D

Dachshund The Dachshund has evolved into six varieties. There are now standard and miniature sizes in Long-hairs, Smooths and Wire-hairs. In some countries, like Great Britain, the six compete separately as six distinct breeds. In others, for instance the United States, the Miniatures must compete against the Standards for championship consideration and higher honours.

'Dachshund' means, in German, 'Badger dog'. A badger dog is one which 'goes to earth'. It is an 'earth dog', a terrier. But when Dachshunds were first introduced into England, 'hund' was translated as 'hound' and the Dachshund was placed in the hound group, and there he has remained despite nearly 100 years of arguments.

Perhaps the best guess as to the origin of the Dachshund is that the German Dachshund and the French Basset were once the same dog. Early reliable writers said that the two could not be told apart. 'Basset' once meant a 'low dog'. The taller dogs could not 'go to earth'. That is, they could not enter the lair of the badger or fox and drag him out. The smaller dogs could – and did, and this gradually brought a separation of the breeds.

Dachshunds came to English attention in 1839 with Queen Victoria's *Dashy*. The following year, when the Queen married Prince Albert of Saxe-Coburg-Gotha, the Prince Consort brought more Dachshunds from Germany. The breed soon became popular in England.

Dachshunds appeared at English dog shows as early as 1866; they were shown in the class for 'foreign sporting dogs'. The KENNEL CLUB granted them separate breed status at the Crystal Palace show in 1873. The English Dachshund Club was formed in 1881, and it was the first such club in the world. England can thus claim a major role in the breed's development and subsequent world-wide popularity. The Germans did not write an official standard for the breed until 1879, and the Berlin Teckelclub was not founded until 1888. Two years before, in England, *Ch. Maximus*, owned by H. A. Walker and bred by William Arkwright, had won the top award at the breed's first speciality show, defeating nearly 200 entries.

Dachshunds appeared in numbers in the United States and Canada about 1870. A Dr. Twadell of Philadelphia, Pa., imported them for 'rabbiting'. William Loeffler of Preston, Minn., began exhibiting his German imports in 1880. Fifteen years later, the Dachshund Club of America was formed.

Some have claimed that the Long-haired Dachshund is as old a variety as the Smooth. Others state that it evolved from Smooth crosses to the FIELD SPANIEL. Crosses to wire-haired terriers are said to have produced the Wire-haired Dachshund. Grayce Greenburg, the noted American historian of the breed, believes the Wire-haired Dachshund descends from wire-haired Bassets.

Dachshunds are traditionally among the most popular breeds, although in Britain these distinctive dogs are currently showing a slight lessening in popularity. In recent years the miniature breeds have been gaining adherents at the expense of the old favourites, the Standard Smooths. The Miniature Smooth Dachshund is at present the most popular of the six, but very marked is the increase in the registrations of Miniature Long-haired Dachshunds, now the second most numerous breed. Although registrations at the Kennel Club (England) show a small numerical decline, the total is still a large one and one dog in every twenty registered in Britain is a Dachshund.

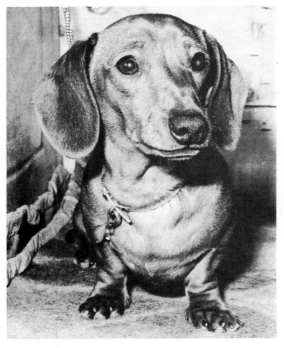

Dachshund.
Top left Miniature Wire-Haired Dachshund. Ch. Culdees Ulric. French Bassets and German Dachshunds are thought to have been originally the same breed.
Bottom left Miniature Smooth Dachshund. Selina Jane of Shalimar.

Top right Standard Smooth Dachshund. Ch. Herthwood's Mark of Rose Farm.
Middle right Standard Wire-Haired Dachshund. Ch. Silensus Scarlet.
Bottom right Standard Long-Haired Dachshund. Exeview Mari-Sana.

In America the Dachshund maintains its position and, with over 60,000 specimens registered each year by the American Kennel Club, the combined varieties vie with the BEAGLE for the third most popular breed in the States.

Essentials of the breed: Standard Dachshunds of all coats vary somewhat in size. Smooth-haired males should not exceed 25 lb. and bitches, 23 lb. Some countries recommend a slightly lighter Longhair and Wirehair. The head is long and evenly tapered, with a scissors bite, medium-sized dark eyes, ears of medium length, rounded and set high. An early deformity – crooked front legs – has been eliminated. The front legs are straight and true and fit close to the body. The neck is arched and the shoulders slope. The chest is deep, well carried back, and the breast bone is prominent. The top line is level with neither roach nor sway. The hind legs are well angulated. The tail tapers and should not be carried gaily.

Faults include undershot or overshot jaws, knuckling over, body hanging between the shoulders, poor top line, cow hocks, and 'glass' or wall eyes, except in grey or dappled dogs.

There are three colour groupings. The first is red (tan), and black – the so-called one colour dogs. Two-colour dogs include the popular black and tan, and chocolate, grey and white, each with rust-brown (tan) markings. A third colour class includes dapples (tiger) and stripes. The former is made up of clear brown or grey with dark irregular patches of darker grey, brown, red-yellow, or black. Striped dogs are brindle, being red or yellow with darker streakings.

Miniatures are what the name implies, but there are size variations in different countries. The German standard is based on chest circumference. Dwarf Dachshunds must not exceed 13·8 inches, and Rabbit Dachshunds, 11·8 inches at a year old. The United States and Canada limit Miniature Dachshunds to 'under nine pounds at twelve months'.

The English standard specifies a height of 7 to 8 inches for Smooth Miniatures, and a weight not to exceed 11 lb. The Long-haired Miniature also must not exceed 11 lb., and ideal for both Smooths and Long-haired is 7 to 9 lb. But a top limit of 12 lb. has been set for Miniature Wirehairs. Australia has a top weight of 11 lb. for all Miniatures.

See colour plates p. 192.

Dachshund, Long-haired, Long-haired Miniature, Smooth, Smooth Miniature, Wire-haired, Wire-haired Miniature see Dachshund.

Dalmatian The Dalmatian, as the name implies, comes from Dalmatia, on the Adriatic coast. Even so, it is a breed which flowered in Great Britain in those now far-away times when the English aristocracy was expected to indulge in bizarre eccentricities.

It is believed that specimens were brought back during the grand tours of Europe which were then a feature of the lives of upper-class Englishmen. They soon put the dog to work: it was to adorn their stately processions by horse and carriage. This the Dalmatian did by trotting with the entourage. Sometimes the dogs were content to station themselves underneath the rear axle. Occasionally however they were trained to precede the leading horse. Another refinement was for them to trot under the pole between the horses.

This ostentatious display however was merely the tip of the iceberg. In fact, the 'Dally' worked in many ways and always brought to its tasks the skill and intelligence gained by centuries of service to man in a variety of roles. It has been a dog of war, a sentinel, a draught dog and a shepherd. In the stables and fire stations of London it proved that it was no mere decorative mascot by destroying rats and other vermin. Almost inevitably, given its great capacity for exercise, it invariably turned out with the fire engine and raced with the horses through the streets.

It was during this time that it received one of its nick-names, the 'fire-house dog'. The breed was destined to be called by many affectionate alternatives to its correct title. For example, 'spotted Dick', the 'plum-pudding dog', and more recently, the 'Dally'.

Its appearance has ensured that it has frequently been used as a stage performer. Clowns have used it as an assistant for centuries past. Despite this, however, it would be unwise to lose sight of its sporting background.

Apart from the little extra substance, a requirement for an animal who had to work on hard roads during long and exacting journeys, its appearance is not vastly different from that of the POINTER, except for the spots. These are of course the most striking characteristics of the Dalmatian and show judges pay great attention to their shape, colour, density, and disposition. The essence of them is that they are spots and not intermingled blobs.

When the march of progress had taken all of its traditional tasks from it, many thought that the breed would join the ranks of those others which had dwindled as their roles diminished. But the Dalmatian took up a new role: that of family pet. And it brought to this all the flair to be expected from one who over the centuries has seen and survived many changes.

For about forty years – that is from 1920 to 1960 – it held its own in the world's popularity poll. It was a typically middle of the road performance.

This comfortable position might well have been maintained indefinitely had something not happened to prove the truth of the saying that 'some have greatness thrust upon them'. The something in question was a book written in Britain in 1956 by Dodie Smith entitled *101 Dalmatians*. Three years later that master of the animated cartoon, Walt Disney, made a film based on the book, which was distributed all over the world with instant success.

Almost immediately, the breed's popularity rose. For example, British registrations, which had been static at about 700 a year, shot up to double that number. Since then they have doubled again and are now around three thousand per annum. American Kennel Club registrations in the United States have shown a similar increase, and are now about 5,000 per annum.

All this means that the general public has belatedly discovered that Dalmatians not only look aristocratic but behave like gentlemen. Neat and clean, short-coated and sensible, their only drawbacks are a tendency to moult and an almost insatiable desire for exercise! When you have covered what you consider fully twice an adequate and reasonable distance, your Dalmatian will wave its tail, smile with those round and sparkling eyes, and demand 'When is the walk going to start?'

Essentials of the breed: A strong, active dog, symmetrical, free from coarseness and capable of endurance with fair speed. Head and skull: the head moderately long, the skull flat, broad between ears and showing slight stop. There should be no wrinkle. The muzzle long and powerful, lips clean. Eyes set well apart, medium size, round, bright, colour dependent on the markings. Ears set on rather high, moderate size, wide at base and tapering to rounded tip. Fine and thin in texture. Neck fairly long, arched but not throaty. Forequarters: clean muscular shoulders, forelegs straight, elbows close to the body. Body: Chest deep, capacious; ribs well-sprung; powerful back; strong, slightly arched loins. Hindquarters: hocks well let down. Forefeet round,

compact. Tail, strong at base and gradually tapering, not set on too low and carried with slight upward curve. Coat, short, hard, dense and glossy. Colour: the base must be pure white. In the black-spotted variety the deeper and richer the black spots the better. These dogs should have a black nose and dark (black or brown) eyes. In the liver-spotted variety, spots, nose and eye rims should be liver brown. Spots should be round, distinct and well defined, fairly large on body and smaller on the extremities such as head, face, ears, legs and tail. Weight around 55 lb. (dogs), 50 lb. (bitches). Size: 19 to 23 inches. The American Kennel Club disqualifies dogs or bitches over 24 inches. See colour plate p. 187.

Dam The female parent.

Dandie Dinmont When examining the background of this breed it is difficult to decide where legend ends and fact begins. The dogs are real enough; the name is a curious mixture.

A similar type of dog existed a couple of centuries ago on the Scottish Borders. It could have been an offshoot of the SCOTTISH TERRIER family, or, as some might insist, the CAIRN family, or the BORDER TERRIER family.

Most probably, these terriers were evolved parallel with and at the same time as the Dandie Dinmont. The latter may be related to the SKYE TERRIER, and, to those who point to the big difference in the ears, it should be said that until comparatively recently the majority of Skyes were of the drop-eared variety.

One of the earliest owners of the breed, or rather type, is said to be 'Piper' Allan of Northumberland. He kept about a dozen dogs. This same man is also credited with originating the BEDLINGTON TERRIER.

Allan's short-legged terriers intrigued the Duke of Northumberland. He coveted one called *Hitchem*. Having failed to buy it he offered Piper Allan a farm, rent free, in exchange. 'Nay my Lord,' came the reply, 'what would a Piper do wi' a farm?' Clearly we are close to the legend at this point. Piper's son is said to have carried on the terrier strain and to have bred a descendant of *Hitchem* which became *Old Pepper* (variations of this name occur later).

James Davidson, a border farmer of Lyndlea had a pack of short-legged, rough-haired terriers, and equally certainly, Sir Walter Scott knew both the farmer and his dogs. Even so he maintained that he had no particular person in mind when he created the character called Dandie Dinmont in his celebrated novel *Guy Mannering*. 'Dandie' was a border farmer who kept a pack of terriers. As Scott's novel became increasingly popular, interest sharpened in the type of terriers described. In the book the six dogs had the distinctive names of *Auld Pepper*, *Auld Mustard*, *Young Pepper*, *Young Mustard*, *Little Pepper*, and *Little Mustard*.

Scott wrote of them: 'They fear naething that ever cam wi' a hairy skin on't.'

At first those who owned similar dogs referred to them jokingly as 'Dandie Dinmont's terriers'. In time the possessive 's' was dropped and they became known in all seriousness as Dandie Dinmont Terriers.

137

In the Birmingham Show of 1867 the judge, Mr. M. Smith, threw all the Dandies out and refused to award any prizes on the grounds that they were nothing but a 'bunch of mongrels!' He subsequently wrote countless letters to *The Field* elaborating on this theme.

But this was long ago, and as with so many other breeds, the rough, unpolished prototype has received a great deal of attention since. Exactly which dogs were used is, as usual, shrouded in mystery, 'Stonehenge', a Victorian commentator on canine affairs, suggested OTTERHOUNDS. This is surely improbable. Much more likely is a Bedlington; if indeed Bedlington prototypes had not already been used to make the first Dandie Dinmonts. Probably the greatest improvement was achieved by selective breeding, with the objective of producing a terrier totally unlike any other. In place of the usual square-cut, sharply defined outline, the Dandie Dinmont has gently flowing curves, a domed skull, an arched back, a scimitar-like tail, and soft, silky hair on the skull. Even the colour is different. Officially it is described as 'pepper' or 'mustard'. In reality it is light to dark grey and reddish brown to pale fawn.

Essentials of the breed: Head strong and large, broad between ears, forehead well domed, covered with soft silky hair. Large, round, dark eyes. Ears: set low and hanging close to cheek, long and lightly feathered. Teeth: level on uppers, slightly overlapping. Chest: well let down inside short forelegs. Long flexible body with good ribs. Back: low at shoulders, arched over loin and dropping again to root of tail, which is 8 to 10 inches long, feathered and curved like a scimitar. Coat a mixture of hard and soft hair, either 'pepper' or 'mustard' coloured. Height 8 to 11 inches, weight around 18 lb., and in the U.S.A., up to 24 lb.
See colour plate p. 374

Dandruff Dandruff is a word derived from dander, the scales of hairy skin of any animal, including man. Dog dander may act as an allergen. Dandruff is the scales formed upon the skin in seborrhoea. Scurf is a term used for both dander and dandruff.

Seborrhoea is a derangement in the functions of the sebaceous glands, and *Seborrhoea sicca* is the most common form in dogs. The cause is not known, but there may be an increase in secretion, a decrease, or a change in quality of the secretion. Scales form tightly around hairs. As the hairs grow, the scales come loose.

Veterinary knowledge of dandruff and *Seborrhoea sicca* is similar to that in human medicine. Most authorities recommend vitamin therapy, usually Vitamins A, D, and B-6. Raw LIVER may be fed, or liver extract may be injected intramuscularly. Daily brushing with a stiff brush is also recommended. Linoleic acid may also be given in an effort to improve skin health. Certain medicinal shampoos are available to counteract this condition. Many of them contain selenium sulphide.

Danish Kennel Club see Kennel Club, Scandinavian Kennel Union.

Dappled Mottled markings of different colours, with no colour predominating.

Darwinism Evolutionary theory states that living organisms have developed and changed in the course of millions of years, the more complex being descended from simpler and less specialized ancestors. The directional trend of evolution is brought about by 'natural selection' and 'the survival of the fittest', so that those animals (or plants etc.) that are best adapted to their environment are the ones which tend to survive longest and to leave most offspring.

For dog breeders the important points are firstly that the breeder endeavours to substitute his own choice of parents (artificial selection for natural selection), and thus may preserve types which could not survive without human care and protection; secondly, that in consequence, breeders must be held responsible if, either carelessly or deliberately, they breed animals so abnormal that they suffer avoidable disabilities.

Despite our endeavours to protect domestic animals from adverse elements of their environment, some still die of disease, difficult whelpings, and other troubles attributable partly to genetic susceptibilities. Therefore the effects of natural selection, although reduced, are not eliminated.

Dandie Dinmont.
Above left A little-known and embryonic breed achieved fame and aroused interest when it was named after a character in Sir Walter Scott's novel *Guy Mannering.*
Above Ch. Shrimpney Sunstar.

Deadgrass A dull straw colour, as seen in CHESAPEAKE BAY RETRIEVERS. SEDGE.

Deafness Ageing dogs sometimes become partially, or even totally deaf, just like some of their masters. But total deafness is rare in dogs except when it is linked to lack of colour. Thus, in some breeds, as colour gives way to white, puppies may be born deaf. Examples are white BULL TERRIERS and DALMATIANS. Why breeding for white should produce deafness is not known, since there are white breeds in which deafness does not occur. Nor do veterinarians know why aged dogs lose their hearing.

Explosive blasts may cause deafness. Paralysis of the auditory nerve sometimes follows DISTEMPER. Growths sometimes fill the auditory canal so that deafness results. If the petrous bone of the skull is fractured, the ear on the affected side will be useless. External otitis (inflammation of the ear) and otorrhoea (when fluid leaks from the ear) cause temporary deafness. Many severe ear infections, which may result in partial deafness, are caused by over-zealous owners who create intense irritation while trying to treat the ears themselves. Temporary deafness may follow the use of certain drugs, such as quinine.

One of the commonest causes is that which is related to excessive wax production which completely blocks the ear. Removal of the wax, and plucking of hair from within the external auditory canal will often improve hearing.

Bad teeth can also affect the reception of sound. See EAR DISEASES.

Debarking Debarking is the surgical procedure by which the dog's vocal chords are removed in an attempt to render the dog mute. It is most commonly performed upon laboratory dogs which are being used for research. It is considered a necessity at hospitals having animal research facilities in areas where quiet must be maintained. Many medical schools do not debark their dogs where there is no necessity to prevent barking, and often the dogs are employed too quickly after arrival to make the surgery worthwhile.

Debarking is rarely permanent. Under the most careful surgery by skilled surgeons, the vocal chords still tend to regenerate. This can occur within two to four months; the dog's voice may then vary from a soft, muted bark to a strange, wild, and sometimes unpleasant tone. No psychological effect has been noted in debarked dogs. When the operation is properly performed under a general ANAESTHETIC, it is considered to be as safe as any other surgery.

In the normal home this operation is never considered. However, it sometimes happens that a noisy dog must be silenced to prevent annoyance to neighbours. Where no other course is available the operation is justified. It is relatively simple, but is not always guaranteed to render a dog mute.

Deerhound, Scottish

> Beneath the sculptured form
> which late you wore,
> Sleep soundly, Maida, at your
> Master's door.

So runs the inscription on the monument erected by Sir Walter Scott to his Deerhound. But this is not the only way in which the eminent author proved that he was a lover of the breed. Indeed today he would probably be called the Deerhound's P.R.O. For example, he wrote of Maida as 'the most perfect creature of heaven'. He also said of this hound: 'Maida, my great dog, had his portrait painted so often that he used to get up and walk away whenever he saw an artist take out his palette and brushes.'

This leads to another lover of the breed, Landseer, the artist who painted some remarkable pictures of these great hounds, capturing all the essentials of the breed: gentleness, strength, dignity and courage. He was once asked by Queen Victoria how he was able to brush into his pictures the individual character of dogs. He replied, 'By peeping into their hearts, Ma'am'.

This is a link to the third of the really prominent breed propagandists, Queen Victoria. As ever, when she associated her name with a breed it became very much better known and sought after.

One is not suggesting that they were new then. Indeed three hundred years before, Dr. Caius had written a brief essay on galloping hounds which included the following reference: 'Some are of a greater sorte, some are of a lesser; some are smoothe skynned and some curled, the bigger therefore are appointed to hunt the bigger beastes.' This was probably the first attempt to separate the countless varieties of running hounds. Since then the Deerhound has always been recognized as a distinct variety, though it has sometimes run under different names. It has been called Scotch Greyhound, and also called the Highland Greyhound.

Exactly when and how these dogs first reached Scotland is unknown. It is more than possible that they were brought to Great Britain by the Phoenician traders and that they then found their way north to the districts in which they could prove of the greatest value. It may also be that only after they became established in the comparatively inhospitable climate of Scotland that they developed their heavier, weather-resisting coat.

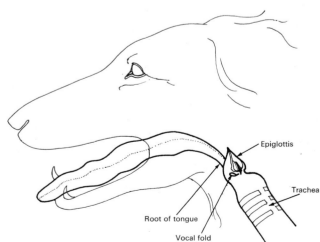

Below Debarking involves the removal of the vocal cords to try to silence a dog.

Epiglottis

Trachea

Root of tongue

Vocal fold

Deerhound, Scottish.
Left A portrait of Highland dogs –
including a Deerhound-type dog –
by the nineteenth-century animal
painter Landseer, who was often a
member of high-society deerstalk-
ing parties in Scotland.
Bottom left Dufault Flute of
Rotherwood.

Throughout their known history they have always been dogs with a both aristocratic and romantic background. Many were owned by Highland Chieftains and indeed there was a time when lesser ranks than Earls were forbidden to own them. During the 16th century deer-driving was a favourite amusement. However, inevitably the fire-arms of the eighteenth century, coupled with the increase in cultivated land and the collapse of the clan system after Culloden (1745), brought their previously favoured existence to an end.

They might have become extinct but for Mr. Duncan McNiel, later Lord Colonsay, who took a particular interest in the breed and during the period which later became known as the 'Colonsay revival' brought the Deerhound back to its former glory by systematic breeding for perfection.

However, even with the impetus later given to them by great figures of the Victorian age, there was little hope that they would ever become popular dogs. Today for example it is rare for either the American Kennel Club or the Kennel Club (England) to register more than a hundred during the course of a year. Perhaps this is desirable because comparatively few people have the space to house such a large dog or the opportunities to exercise it properly.

Even so, two world wars which destroyed so much, could not destroy the love of a few enthusiasts for a breed which makes one of the best companions a man could have. Judging by the crowd round the ringside at those dog shows where this breed is still featured it appears that the man in the street is still prepared to pay his respects to an ancient aristocrat, even if he does prefer a German Shepherd or fashionable Poodle for a pet.

Essentials of the breed: The head should be broad at the ears, the muzzle tapering towards the nose. It should be long, coated with moderately long hair, the nose black except in blue fawns where it is blue, and there should be a moustache of silky hair. Eyes dark, brown or hazel, moderately full. Ears set on high, folded in repose but raised when excited. A long neck with slight mane. Shoulders well sloped, forelegs straight, broad and flat. Body: general formation of a GREYHOUND, chest deep rather than broad but not too narrow or flat-sided. Loin: arched and drooping to the tail. A straight back is undesirable. Hindquarters: broad, powerful and drooping with wide set hips. Feet close and compact. Tail, thick at the root, tapering and reaching the ground. The hair on body, neck and quarters should be harsh and wiry with a slight fringe on fore and hind legs. Woolly coat is undesirable. Dark blue-grey is a preferred colour but there can also be darker and lighter greys, brindles, yellow and sandy red or red-fawn, especially with black points. White coloration apart from marks on chest and toes, is most undesirable. Weight should be from 85 to 105 lb. for dogs (to 110 lb. in America), and 65 to 80 lb. for bitches (to 95 lb. in America). General height: around 30 inches.
See colour plate p. 179.

Dentition of the Dog The teeth of the dog are basically those of the meat-eater. They are designed to bite, tear, cut, and grind. The normal dog has 42 teeth, with 20 in the upper jaw and 22 in the lower one. The six front teeth in the upper and lower jaws are called incisors – the biting teeth. Directly behind these are the canines, or tusks. Each jaw has two, with one on each side. These teeth serve several purposes. They seize and hold the prey, and they are used to tear off muscles and skin, and to tear out internal organs. The canines are deeply anchored into the jaw bone, so that they are difficult to remove.

The premolars and molars are used as cutters and crushers. The covering enamel is extremely hard. These teeth, combined with the immense jaw muscles, make it possible for dogs to crush bones.

The first teeth, called puppy or milk teeth, are lost during the growing period. Thus, the upper incisors are pushed out at about 14 weeks of age, as the permanent teeth erupt. The lower incisors are changed several weeks later, and the canines at about 18 weeks.

The period of tooth changing is a critical one in the life of the puppy. It is possible that it may develop a fever and may lose weight. The laying down of the tooth covering, or enamel, apparently requires an unusual amount of metabolic action. If, during this period, the dog is unfit, some of the essential enamel may not be deposited upon the teeth. For centuries, dog breeders have called the resultant pitting and discoloration 'distemper teeth'. However, any illness contracted during the eruption of the permanent teeth can cause the condition. The degree and location of the pitting may indicate to the veterinarian both the seriousness and the time of the puppy's illness.

In many breeds, the permanent teeth may not erupt through the sockets which held the milk teeth. Thus, the

elow right Dentition of the dog: here are twenty teeth in the pper jaw and twenty-two in the wer one. The last and largest of he upper premolars is called the arnassial tooth.

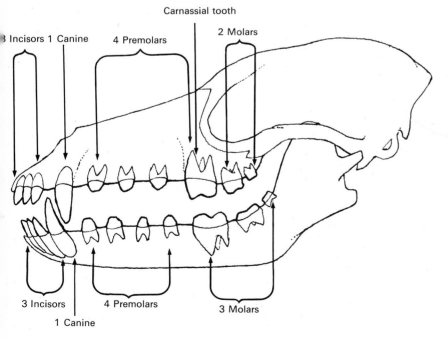

Carnassial tooth

3 Incisors 1 Canine   4 Premolars   2 Molars

3 Incisors   4 Premolars   3 Molars
    1 Canine

permanent teeth will not push out the milk teeth. A double row of teeth then results. The milk teeth then must be extracted.

The part of the tooth which is above the gum line is the crown. That between the crown and the root is the neck. The root is embedded in a socket. Some teeth have only one root, but others have several. Under the enamel is a softer substance, the dentine. This, in turn, covers the pulp which contains blood vessels and nerves. The covering of the roots and the interstices, or small openings of the crowns, are covered with cement.

Dogs seldom have dental caries, but often have tooth deterioration. Dog breeders frequently attribute the former to a diet which includes bones to be gnawed and hard dog biscuits to be crushed, but this is unproved. Deterioration of teeth may be due to poor dental formation where the teeth develop abnormally, or to the gross abnormality seen in the 'normal' mouth of some breeds where the breed standard has altered, through numerous generations, the shape of the jaw.

Depraved Appetite Dogs, particularly puppies, will sometimes swallow a variety of non-digestible articles. Dogs have died from swallowing marbles, golf balls, and Christmas tree bulbs which then became impacted in the intestines. Veterinarians have had to remove surgically such things as women's sweaters and nylons. In a classic case, a dog ate fourteen contraceptive pills, including the card and plastic dimples which contained them. His stomach was pumped and produced also a razor blade, a lipstick tube, and two rubber bands.

The causes for such actions are not certainly known, but they include curiosity in puppies and boredom in older dogs. It is inborn in all higher animals to take things apart. The dog does this with its jaws. In doing so he may swallow parts of the objects. A ravenous appetite, caused either by a physical or psychological defect, may also be a factor. The tearing apart of objects by a psychologically unbalanced dog may be the first step towards a depraved appetite.

An environment should be set up which will prevent most such actions. For example, dogs have died from eating the gravel or slag in their kennel runs. A paved surface would avoid this; or the dog might be muzzled when placed in the run for exercise. Knuckle bones, rawhide 'chew' sticks, or artificial indestructible bones can be given to the dog. If a dog shows signs of depraved appetite, a physical examination should be given by a veterinarian to determine whether or not the problem is caused by a physical defect or a dietary deficiency. See COPROPHAGY.

Derby A field trial stake for dogs usually between one and two years old.

Dew Claws These are to be found on the inner side of each forefoot corresponding with the human thumb in position. They sometimes occur on the hind feet but are seldom attached there by more than skin. In most breeds, dew claws must be removed, and this should be done a few days after birth. They should be cut off close to the limb with a pair of sharp scissors. Bleeding can be

quickly and effectively arrested by dabbing the wound with Permanganate of Potash. If this operation is left to a later stage when nerve and blood supplies to the dew claw are fully developed, it is much wiser to have it done under a local, or general ANAESTHESIA by a veterinarian.

The removal of dew claws gives a much cleaner and tidier line to the leg, and if left on they can often be the cause of trouble in later life. In certain breeds, however, dew claws are essential to the breed standard. The BRIARD, for example, must have dew claws on its hind legs.

If a dew claw becomes broken, the broken piece should be cut off as soon as possible with clippers. Bleeding can be stopped very quickly by applying dry cotton wool and a bandage.

Dewlap Loose, pendulous skin on the lower part of the neck, under the chin and throat. A marked characteristic of the BLOODHOUND.

Diabetes Insipidus (Water Diabetes) This is a condition in which the dog excretes large amounts of watery urine. The condition is caused by a malformation of the hypothalamus gland which fails to produce sufficient vasopressin – the anti-diuretic hormone.

Diabetes Mellitus (Sugar Diabetes) This is a condition where the sugar balance of the body is disturbed due to insufficient production of the hormone insulin. The condition develops when the insulin-producing cells in the pancreas are damaged. The actual cause of this damage is not always known although inflammation of the pancreas can initiate the condition, as can SHOCK.

The blood sugar level is raised and excessive amounts of sugar are excreted in the urine. There is an increased thirst and, without treatment, emaciation and collapse rapidly occur. The smell of ACETONE is sometimes detectable on the breath.

This condition is most commonly seen in dogs that are overweight, and in middle-aged or old dogs.

Diagnosis Diagnosis can be defined on two levels. The first is the ability of the dog owner to realize that his dog is ill, no matter how slightly. The other is the skill of the veterinarian, that of interpreting often confusing symptoms to reach an opinion as to the cause of the illness.

To practise his level of diagnosis, the dog owner needs to look at, and not through, his dog. He must notice unusual actions or situations immediately, and he must then determine whether these truly indicate illness.

The common symptoms of illness are a temperature higher or lower than normal, repeated vomiting, diarrhoea, constipation, lack of appetite, ravenous hunger, abnormal thirst, dullness of eyes, a harsh, dry coat, and distended abdomen, or any change from the normal.

Puppies which appear thin, or even emaciated, yet have pot bellies, can be suspected of having worms. If they have loose bowels, checks should be made by a

Above Dewlap.

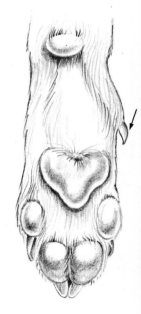

Below Dew claw.

veterinarian using a microscope, for both worms and coccidia or PARASITES.

Modern veterinarians use all the techniques of human medicine for diagnosis, but some have to be adapted as they are limited in many ways. They can only question the owner, not the patient. They cannot ask the patient to stop breathing for a few seconds while an X-ray picture is taken.

Biological service laboratories are available to undertake all biological tests – for instance, a blood sample can be tested for antibodies, leukemia, or blood parasites. Stethoscopes are used to study the heart and lungs. Blood and alimentary canal tracers are used. And studies are made under ANAESTHESIA. Yet in the end, the science of diagnosis depends upon training, experience, and often upon intuition.

Diaphragmatic Rupture see Hernia.

Diarrhoea Diarrhoea is a common symptom of gastrointestinal disease. As with human beings, it may be temporary and relatively mild. It is then normally described as 'loose bowels'. When diarrhoea is severe and chronic, it is often due to intestinal infection; infestations of worms, such as HOOKWORMS; or coccidia; or it may be caused by psychogenic factors. Arsenic, or similar poisons, may cause severe diarrhoea.

Recently, some scientists have made the startling suggestion that diarrhoea, or a tendency to it, may be inherited. The GERMAN SHEPHERD DOG seems to be afflicted more than any other breed, and five types of diarrhoea have now been isolated from sick dogs of this breed. A co-operative study is being conducted by

veterinarians at the University of Connecticut, along with researchers at the Yale University School of Medicine.

If diarrhoea lasts more than a day or so, it should be considered sufficiently serious for the owner to consult his veterinarian. The dog's physical condition will deteriorate rapidly, and he could become the victim of a fatal ailment. An immediate and complete physical examination by a veterinarian is required.

Digestion Digestion is the process by which material that is taken into the body is converted into a form that the body is able to utilize.

Proteins are broken down into their amino acids; carbohydrates into glucose and other monosaccharids; and fats into fatty acids and glycerol. In the dog, most absorption occurs in the small intestine. The surface of the wall of the intestine is covered with villi, minute hair-like projections. The intestinal wall appears to be smooth, but, greatly magnified looks like velvet. Amino acids, glucose, vitamins, minerals, salt, and water pass through the villi, and then are carried to the liver, and enter into the blood stream. Digested fats pass through the lymph channels, or lacteals, into the blood stream.

The digestive, or alimentary, tract begins with the lips, teeth, and tongue, and ends with the anus. The alimentary tracts of all mammals are basically the same as to parts, but differ radically in details because the animals have evolved differently, have differing ways of life, and therefore have differing requirements for sources of both life and energy.

Some comparisons between the dog, the horse, and man may be made; they indicate why people must not feed their dogs as they do themselves. The teeth of the dog are those of the carnivora. The dog tears flesh from the bone with his great corner teeth (tusks). He then turns his head and uses his sharpened molars to cut the meat into chunks small enough to swallow. Man's teeth are intermediate, with shorter tusks, and with more flattened molars, or cereal grinders. The teeth of the horse are those of the pure grazing animal – incisors for gathering and breaking off grasses, and molars for grinding grasses and cereals.

Below Digestion. The diagram shows the whole digestive tract.

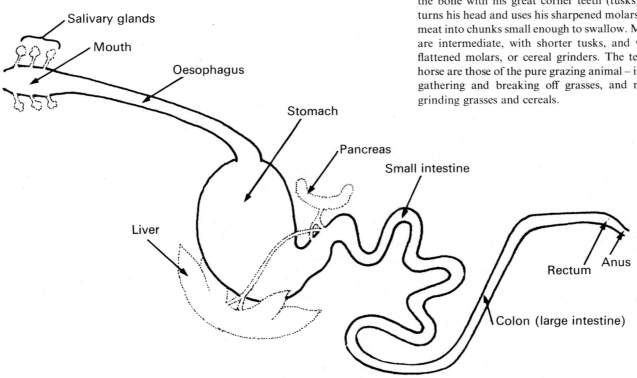

Salivary glands

Mouth

Oesophagus

Stomach

Pancreas

Small intestine

Liver

Rectum

Anus

Colon (large intestine)

The saliva of man and horse contains enzymes which break up starch granules, and to some extent, the fibrous walls of vegetables and grasses. The dog's saliva has little of this enzyme. If it is to be fed cereals, they must be ground and preferably cooked for it. The dog bolts its food since it has no need to mix it with saliva beyond the lubrication required to swallow it. And it has an expanding gullet, or oesophagus, to accommodate chunks four to five times the normal size of the gullet. Man and horse must grind and masticate their food to permit salivary amylase to work. But in addition, they must reduce the food in size to fit the gullet – the gullet of the horse is so small that horses have been known to choke upon a chunk of carrot.

Primary digestion of meat takes place in the stomach. That organ is therefore proportionately larger in the dog than in man or the horse. The dog's stomach may expand five or six times its empty size to accommodate astonishingly large meals. It has been estimated that the average dog's stomach may hold one and a fifth gallons, or about 60 per cent of the capacity of the entire digestive tract. A man's stomach will hold from 20 to 48 ounces. Because meat is digested in the stomach, it must remain there for long periods of time. But the horse, with the much smaller stomach for its size, will be passing grasses and hay through the stomach while still eating.

Cereals and fibrous foods are chiefly digested in the intestine. The average dog's small intestine will have a capacity of 1·7 quarts. In contrast, a man's small intestine will hold three quarts. That of the horse will hold 25 gallons or more. Even if we did not know it from observation, dentition and these figures would prove that the dog is basically a meat eater. It needs properly prepared cereals. The wild dog would get these in a sort of pre-digested form, by eating the guts of the grass-eaters which it has killed. If the dog is fed bulky vegetables, its small intestine will have difficulty handling them. Colonies of bacteria perform the final

digestive process in the large intestine of the horse, but not to the same extent in the dog or in man, in both of which the large intestine holds waste material until most of the water can be absorbed from it.

Actions of the lips, teeth, tongue, throat, and anus are considered to be controlled chiefly by voluntary nervous system actions or orders. But once swallowed, food proceeds by a delicately keyed rhythm known as peristaltic action. The automatic, or involuntary, nervous system controls peristalsis.

The stomach mixes gastric juice into the food. The gastric juice contains hydrochloric acid, which kills some bacteria. It also contains enzymes, which begin the digestive process, breaking up protein, coagulating milk, and digesting fats. When food has undergone gastric digestion, it is called chyme. As chyme leaves the stomach, it is mixed with bile from the liver, which changes it from an acid mixture to an alkaline one, and with pancreatic juice from the pancreas. The dog's liver is proportionately five to six times as large as that of man. Aside from its job of alkalinization of the chyme, bile aids in the emulsification, digestion, and absorption of fats. The pancreatic juice contains enzymes which help to digest starch, this being converted into malt sugar. The enzymes included are pancreatic amylase, steapsin, and trypsin. Steapsin breaks up fat into fatty acids and glycerol, and makes them ready for body use without further action. Some fatty acids combine with alkali to make soap, and the soap helps to emulsify other fats. By the time peristaltic action has moved the chyme to the ileocecal valve, both digestion and absorption have been mostly completed in the dog.

Several additional points may be mentioned, however. The enzyme rennin is present in the stomach of puppies, but is absent or almost entirely so, in the adult dog. Its function in the stomach of the puppy is both to coagulate milk and to slow its passage through the digestive tract. It is because of the absence of rennin in the adult dog that milk so often causes loose bowels. Its

Below Dingo. As the Dingo – the only true wild dog – is not, like the wolf, mortally antagonistic towards the domestic dog, the two species have interbred and there are few pure-bred Dingoes left.

Right Dish-faced. A Pointer.

absence permits the milk to pass into the intestine in an unprepared state. There it may be attacked by bacteria which cause putrefaction. The feces may then have a foul odour, as may gas which has been generated during the process. In some cases, too heavy a meat diet will also cause the production of gas with a foul odour. On the other hand, undigested cellulose may be attacked by bacteria which produce an intestinal gas which is odourless.

See also: NUTRITION; FEEDING.

Dingo The Dingo, or Warrigal, is the only true wild dog. Australia is the land of the marsupials – animals which carry their young in a pouch within which are the breasts. The Dingo was the only large non-marsupial mammal native to Australia in the eighteenth century.

As the marsupials are the precursors of the more normal mammals found in the rest of the world, and Australia must therefore have been cut off from other areas of the world for a very long time, it is believed that the Dingo was not originally native to Australia. Either the present race of aborigines, or an even earlier one, may have brought the Dingo.

It must at that time have been a domestic dog. But for reasons that cannot be known, it has returned to the wild state. Elsewhere we have pointed out the mortal enmity between dog and wolf. This enmity apparently does not exist between the domestic dog and the Dingo. Instead, each seems to recognize the other as a true dog. They treat each other as do the domestic and feral dogs of other lands. For this reason, the dogs of the white settlers have so interbred with Dingoes that purebred ones are now quite rare.

Dingo fossils have been reported with those of extinct Australian marsupials, such as the marsupial lion, and a creature which resembled the hippopotamus in size and structure. These creatures became extinct during a Pleistocene Ice Age, perhaps 50,000 years ago.

In the article ANCESTORS OF THE DOG, it was pointed out that it is now believed that the immediate ancestor of the dog was a small Pleistocene canid, perhaps of Asia. If, therefore, the Dingo is a living fossil from the Pleistocene epoch, then it must be very close to the ancestral dog. Indeed, cranial measurements of Dingo fossils, are close to those of the first dog remains found in Europe.

This creates a problem. It is not supposed that the

dog was domesticated until about 15,000 years ago. But if man brought the Dingo to Australia – how else could it have got there? – then the Dingo must have been domesticated at least 50,000 years ago.

The Dingo is intermediate in size between the wolf and jackal, with many being about 22 inches tall at the shoulder. It is generally yellowish-red to brown in colour, but many have white on the belly, tip of tail, and feet. Dingoes hunt singly or in pairs, and only rarely in packs.

Dish-Faced Dog with a concave nasal bone.

Disinfectant see Antiseptics.

Dislocation of Kneecap see Patella Luxation.

Distemper Canine distemper is a virus disease which afflicts dogs, wolves, foxes, ferrets, stoats, and mink. It does not infect human beings and it is quite different from the mis-named feline distemper. Cats, therefore, cannot get canine distemper, and dogs cannot get feline distemper. Canine distemper kills from fifty to eighty per cent of infected puppies. It may also kill older dogs who have no immunity or whose immunity level drops below the protective point.

The distemper virus belongs to a family of viruses called Myxovirus I. These include the viruses causing human measles and mumps. Myxoviruses are so-called because they are attracted to mucous (myxo) substances upon the walls of cells. The distemper virus looks not unlike a microscopic cucumber.

Viruses are parasites which invade and either kill cells or cause them to lose their identity as functioning units. Viruses appear unable to reproduce except within the cell. Since they have entered the cells before illness is detected, it is then impossible to kill them without killing the cells also. For this reason, the antibiotics have been useless except to prevent secondary invaders from attacking the dog.

Immunity to distemper is achieved by several methods. A dog which has recovered is immune for life. A bitch gives immune antibodies to her pups in the colostrum, the first milk from her mammary glands. The puppies will thereby gain what is usually called a passive immunity. This grows steadily weaker and has disappeared by the tenth to the twelfth week of the puppy's life.

Because distemper, like measles, is caused by a myxovirus, modified live measles virus vaccines are sometimes used to confer immunity on very young puppies. The measles vaccine probably does not itself confer the immunity, but it acts by entering the cells, which would be attacked by the distemper virus, and so stopping the virus attack. Various other types of 'shots' have been developed to protect puppies until the so-called permanent shots can be given safely. Since the virulence of the distemper virus may vary from area to area, veterinarians vary their methods accordingly.

It was once supposed that the live virus vaccines gave lifetime immunity. They apparently did in areas where dogs ran at large. But in those cases, the dog's immunity

level was kept at maximum because of constant exposure and challenge from ill dogs. Dogs kept confined, however, are not so exposed to live virus, and their immunity level drops. It is now recommended that dogs be given regular annual vaccinations against distemper. Distemper vaccine is often combined with other vaccines to protect against infectious canine HEPATITIS and LEPTOSPIROSIS.

The symptoms of distemper are so varied that it is difficult to diagnose the disease. They include listlessness, a temperature of 102 to 104°F, mucous discharge from the nose, or a discharge from the eye sockets, avoidance of light, and lack of appetite. In the case of unvaccinated puppies, the only practical procedure is to assume that the illness is distemper, and to rush the dog to the veterinary hospital.

Distemper can be treated in the early stages, but it is essential that supportive treatment is given. This may include antibiotics to destroy secondary invaders, vitamin therapy, appetite stimulants, etc. But these must always be under the supervision of a veterinarian.

Distemper Teeth Teeth discoloured, and often with pitted enamel, usually caused by disease such as DISTEMPER during the growth of permanent teeth.

Dobermann see Dobermann Pinscher.

Dobermann Pinscher The Dobermann Pinscher (spelled Doberman in the United States and Canada) is a deliberately manufactured breed whose origins are reasonably well known. Louis Dobermann of Apolda,

Thueringia, Germany, began experimental breeding to produce his dog between 1865 and 1870. By 1890, he had arrived at a type which at least partly suited him.

'Pinscher' means 'terrier.' And though the breed he developed was originally called Dobermann's Dogs, Louis Dobermann had the concept of a giant terrier. He wanted a dog with a terrier's agility, combined with the strength and guard dog aptitudes of some of the famed Thueringian shepherd dogs of the time. Otto Goeller, a later breeder, followed Dobermann's wishes and added Pinscher to the name.

The character of the early dogs can be understood from comments at the time. Philipp Gruenig, a noted judge and historian of the breed, quotes the Swiss pioneer breeder, Gottfried Liechti: 'They were certainly robust, had absolutely no fear – not of the devil himself – and it required a good deal of courage to own one.' Of *Alarich von Thueringen*, whelped in 1897, Gruenig himself wrote: 'He was known for his incredible sharpness and was correspondingly feared.' It is told of one dog exported to the United States that it was Best in Show three times before anyone dared to open its mouth. Then it was discovered that it had missing teeth – a serious breed fault.

Dobermann's basic stock seems to have been the black and tan ROTTWEILER, the old German Pinscher, and some of the famed Thueringian shepherd dogs of the period. Some of the early dogs were long-haired, and many were born tailless, a feature which disappeared with the introduction of the MANCHESTER TERRIER.

Manchester Terriers and GREYHOUNDS were used to

Dobermann Pinscher.
Left Achim Zeitgeist.

Right The Dobermann has ferocious reputation but its bree standard is specific in censurin vicious dogs. Many of the moder Dobermanns are intelligent, stab guard dogs and home companion Ch. Odin von Forell.

produce a less coarse body, a longer muzzle, and greater agility. At least one of the Greyhounds was a black bitch, described as 'ferocious'.

A group of local Apolda dogs, their relationship unknown, became the foundation dogs of the breed. These were *Lux, Landgraf, Rambo,* and Louis Dobermann's *Schnupp.* Schnupp was given the number one registration when the Dobermann Pinscher Club of Germany was organized in 1912. Horowitz, a noted authority of the time, described Schnupp and her pups as deplorable to look at and very ferocious. Lux and *Tilly I von Groenland* produced a litter of five great dogs in 1898, and this brought national attention to them.

Goswin Tischler founded his von Groenland Kennels in 1895. He named the kennel after Groenland (Greenland) Street in Apolda. His *Bosco* and *Caesi* produced the first champion, *Prinz Matzi von Groenland,* whelped 15 Aug. 1895. Philipp Gruenig describes him as having a coarse, heavy body, very long hair, and a light eye. Otto Goeller of Apolda founded his von Thueringen Kennels in 1901. Goeller, perhaps more than any other breeder, developed the modern type of Dobermann Pinscher. His *Hellegraf von Thueringen,* whelped 12 June 1904, is one of the patriarchs of the breed. He was, however, shorter in muzzle and heavier in head than are today's dogs. In 1910, *Bodo* and *Bob von Elfenfeld* were whelped. Both had the beautiful modern Dobermann head.

Dobermann Pinschers spread quickly to The Netherlands, Switzerland, and other European countries and, after World War I, to the United States and Canada. Their progress in England was less rapid, as usually happens in countries which prohibit ear cropping. However, the breed has gained great popularity in Australia. Meanwhile, its disposition has been changed so that it has become an intelligent, stable guard dog and home companion.

Essentials of the breed: The Dobermann Pinscher standard is the most specific of all breed standards in describing temperament: the present standard requires dismissal for shy or vicious dogs. A shy dog is described as one that refuses to stand for examination and shrinks away from the judge, if it fears approach from the rear, or if it shies at unusual noises. A vicious dog is specified as one which attacks or attempts to attack either the judge or its handler.

The standard calls for males averaging 27 inches at the withers, and bitches, $25\frac{1}{2}$ inches. Allowed colours are black, red, blue, and Isabella, or fawn. Black dogs have rust markings above the eyes, on the muzzle, throat, forechest, all four feet, and below the tail. A grey undercoat is permitted on the neck, and a white patch not larger than one half square inch on the breast.

The head is wedge-shaped, viewed from the front or in profile. A scissors bite. Four missing teeth, or undershot more than one-eighth inch or overshot more than three-sixteenths, disqualifies. The ears are normally cropped in the countries which permit this practice and are set on top of the skull. The top line slopes from withers to croup, and the chest reaches to the elbows. The legs and feet must be sound, the pasterns nearly

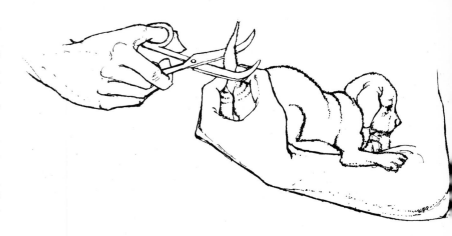

erect, the hind legs well angulated. The tail is docked at the second joint.
See colour plate p. 298.

Docking The shortening of the tail in breeds which are docked is usually done when the puppies are about three days old. This also applies to DEW CLAWS in the breeds that require these operations. Some breeders dock puppies' tails themselves but it is not recommended that a novice or an amateur attempt it. A puppy may die of SHOCK or excessive bleeding, and if the tail is not docked at the right spot it can look incorrect and often ugly when the puppy matures. While the operation is in progress the dam should be taken well away from the kennel so that she does not see her whelps and cannot hear any cries they may make.

In docking, the tail should be held just above the point where it is to be severed. The skin should be drawn well back towards the body. Then the scissors can cut through the cartilage and the skin will move forward again and cover the cut surface. Done properly, little or no bleeding will occur but if there is a tendency to bleed, the wound can be dabbed with permanganate of potash. When the dam returns to her puppies she will lick them so helping to heal the wound. The whelps feel little of this and when returned to the dam they will immediately forget all about it and very shortly will be seen contentedly sucking.

Dog Fights Dogs often make a great show of belligerence in defending their home territories. As a rule, an invading dog recognizes that it is a trespasser and flees to neutral ground. If the roles are reversed, again the trespassing dog will flee. Such behaviour, therefore, only occasionally results in a true fight. Even such shows of belligerence can be prevented if the owner of a puppy repeatedly takes it to meet other neighbourhood dogs, and allows these dogs to be brought on to the puppy's home ground.

Dogs separated by a fence may insult each other since they recognize that they can do so safely. Dogs which meet on leash may be aggressive towards each other because they also feel safe in doing so. Or, as has been suggested by some psychologists, they may feel it

Above Docking a puppy's tail needs a skilled hand, and should be done only under the supervision of a veterinarian.

necessary to 'defend' their masters, as they do their home territories. A gentle tug on the leash, a mild voice warning, or even a movement of a cane, may precipitate a fight. If the leashes are kept loose, and the dogs are allowed to stalk and smell, a fight is not likely to develop.

If the owners feel that a fight is probable, then stern measures are necessary. Both owners should give severe jerks on their leashes. The dogs can be tapped smartly on their noses. Sometimes simultaneous smacks across the rumps can end any ideas of a fight.

There are, however, 'killer' dogs which rush out and instantly attack passing dogs on leash. A permanent cure for this is to spray the dog with chemical mace, a spice derivative, which causes intense eye pain for a few minutes but does no permanent damage. An electric cattle prod, or one specifically designed to halt dog fights, will also stop the aggressor. This instrument is invaluable both in stopping kennel fights and in curing kennel dogs of fighting.

Interference by owners often causes dogs to fight harder. Many such fights would end quickly without damage to either dog if their owners let them fight it out. Moreover, the dogs might then make their own armistice so that later battles would not occur. Owners often get bitten when trying to separate dogs which are feinting and slashing. Pulling dogs apart may result in severely tearing the flesh of one or both dogs.

When a dog gets a 'death grip' on another, many suggestions are made for breaking it. These include

Below Dog fights. Unless one dog has a 'death grip' on another, it is unwise to interfere. To try to pull the dogs apart physically may only make matters worse for the weaker dog.

throwing a pail of water into the dog's face, spraying a water hose into his face, and pouring ammonia onto a broom and putting this under the dog's nose. But such solutions may not be possible because of the time or place of the fight.

Applying a lighted match or a burning cigarette to the male's testicles or the inner flank of the bitch is often suggested. There is one method which, however repulsive it may appear to be, will absolutely break the dog's hold: this is to put a finger sharply into the dog's rectum.

Dolichocephalic Long headed, like a GREYHOUND or BORZOI.

Domed Skull An evenly rounded topskull, as in the CHIHUAHUA.

Domestication of the Dog There are many problems concerning the domestication of the dog which have puzzled anthropologists for many years. It is agreed by all that the dog was the first domesticated animal. Beyond that, there is no agreement. Some of the problems are these: When was the dog domesticated? By whom? And why? Did man domesticate the dog, or did the dog do it itself? If the dog is not a domesticated wolf, then where are its fossil remains?

We have indicated in ANCESTORS OF THE DOG that the dog may be descended from a small mutant canid of the Pleistocene period, and that its probable birth place was Central or Northern Asia. If so, failure to find its fossil bones might be explained: most of Europe and North America have been thoroughly searched for fossils, but vast areas of Central and Northern Asia remain virgin territory for the students of the dog's past.

The true meaning of domestication is to cast one's lot with that of man. You can partially tame a lion. But it is not for that reason domestic; it cannot be fully trusted not to kill its master, or its master's dogs or chickens. It cannot be taught to herd sheep. And, it is well known that the rate of injuries to lion tamers is high. Moreover when two tamed circus lions, both born in captivity, are mated, the resulting cubs must still be tamed. And they are no more to be trusted than were their parents. The canary has been a cage bird for centuries – for hundreds of canary generations. Yet it is not a domestic bird. If it escapes into the wild, it will be difficult or impossible to catch. Nor is it likely to return to its home.

Yet certain animals have cast in their lots with man even when the latter wants no part of them. There is, for example, the rat. We trap rats. We poison them. Yet they still risk death by invading our homes and stores. They still travel the world with us on our ships. Rats are highly intelligent, and when permitted to be so, they become remarkably gentle and affectionate pets.

After the Spanish conquest of the New World, horses escaped into the wild. They remained wild for more than three centuries. Yet when captured, they were easily broken to saddle or harness, and slipped quickly back into complete domesticity. It can only have been because they carried in their genetic makeup a ready response to man and his training.

A complicating factor in the study of domestication is that all our domestic animals – and plants – were domesticated before recorded history began. Possible exceptions might be the turkey and the Australian shell parakeet or budgerigar. The turkey was at least partially domestic before the arrival of white settlers in America, and may still be not completely domesticated. The budgerigar 'may also have a natural urge towards domesticity. Both birds may be in an intermediate stage. But it is evident that no single species can become domesticated within the life span of a man, or even within several life spans. So we do not understand the process, nor how it began, nor even when.

Most probably, the domestication of the dog took place during a period of 13,000 to 15,000 years ago. However, the actual presence of fossils that clearly indicate a domestic dog in association with man does not extend back beyond 6000 B.C. Yet there are two indications that domestication may have occurred much earlier. The DINGO is a true dog. If it is true that Dingo fossils have been found in the Australian Pleistocene, beside those of giant marsupials, then the time of domestication may be no closer than 50,000 years ago. There is also a cave painting in Europe which shows a dog-like animal apparently hunting with

primitive men. The painting has been estimated to be 50,000 years old. If the date is correct, and if the animal is actually hunting with men, this would mean that the dog, a near dog, or the Pleistocene ancestor of the dog, had already been at least partially domesticated.

Let us consider now some of the theories given for the domestication of the dog.

Primitive man hunted for food. There were times when he feared to leave his camp, when giant predators waited for him on the forest edge. In his travels he perhaps killed a bitch wolf and noted that she was nursing pups. He may have taken the dead wolf home for food and the cubs as playthings for his children. Later the grown pups which he had tamed gladly joined him in the hunt. Since they were wolves, the love of the chase was genetically imprinted on their brains. They now recognized the man as master, companion and protector. But the smell of man upon them automatically made them enemies to their wolf relations. This forced them into domesticity.

A second theory is that man's garbage heaps tantalized the first true dogs. They lurked nearby, finding it easier to scavenge than to hunt for food. Man, on his part, encouraged them and made offers of friendship. Once the dogs had joined man, they performed a double service. They cleaned up the garbage, and they gave warning of danger by barking. This theory has been given added weight by a study of Stone Age peoples still living in New Guinea. It was observed that those tribes which had no dogs frequently had to move their villages. They had to do so both to escape the stench and the hordes of flies which bred in the garbage. But those tribes which had scavenging dogs to eat their garbage, had semi-permanent villages.

A third theory assumes that the dog was domesticated to serve as a beast of burden. That is, to pull a *travois* or sledge. Primitive man first learned to use his hands, and then began to make tools which were extensions of his hands – the bow and arrow and the spear. Later he turned to transportation, that is, he transferred the load from his back to that of an animal.

A travois consists of two trailing poles fastened into the dog's harness. They are held together by webbing upon which the load is lashed. Dogs may have pulled the travois in summer, as did the American Plains Indians of the last century, and a sledge upon winter snow. This theory gains some support from the finding of a sledge, dated at 6000 B.C., in deposits in Northern Europe. It is not known when the first migrants reached the Arctic. But they could not have survived without the possession of domestic dogs for transport.

A fourth theory claims that dogs may have been domesticated for food.

It is true that dogs have served as food in primitive societies. They were kept as a food reserve during periods of near starvation, and for food during religious ceremonies. Even in recent societies dogs have been eaten during times of starvation, as in the siege of Leningrad, during the Second World War. Lost and starving Eskimos have eaten their dogs, even though knowing that this last desperate act – the destruction of their transport – made their own deaths more certain.

Left Domestication of the dog. The dog cast in its lot with man maybe as long ago as 15,000 years. This prehistoric rock painting from Spain shows dog-like figures accompanying hunters on the trail.

Many scientists believe that all the domestic animals, including the dog, were first domesticated for purposes of divination. Until modern times, animals continued to be used for such purposes. Witchcraft has given place to modern medicine over most of the world, but it could be said that modern researchers still use animals widely for acquiring knowledge.

Whatever germ of truth there may be in these theories, they all come up against the fact that a wild animal is wild, and a domestic one, domestic. They are separated by a deep psychological canyon.

Professor William G. Haag of the Department of Anthropology, University of Kentucky, believes that the dog descends from an unknown mutant canid of the Pleistocene period. It is postulated that this canid was smaller than its ancestral stock, and this at a time when mammals generally were rapidly increasing in size. The smaller size would make life more difficult for this canid. It might also make it more fearful, and at the same time, more servile. An inherent servility might prepare it for domestication.

From this unknown canid may have come another mutant. At war with the wolves, and competing for the same food, this mutant might be forced to scavenge at the garbage heaps of men.

But domestication would not have come quickly. Over thousands of years, the dog must have studied man; must first have worked out some truce with him. The dog ate the garbage, barked warnings of danger, perhaps gradually slunk deeper into the camp to avoid that danger. The warmth of the fire would draw him closer. The dog must have recognized that both he and man had common enemies. Slowly over hundreds of generations, the dog came to realize man as its ally and guardian.

Adaptation must have been a slow and painful process; as other animals became domestic, the dog had to learn not to kill them, perhaps even to protect them. And it had to adjust to man's varying food habits. Finally, it had to adjust to living in all the areas of the world. That process of adaptation has not stopped. Today, some dogs have to learn to live on the fortieth floor of an apartment building, or to ride in space craft.

Dominant Gene, Dominance Genetic instructions or genes are always carried in pairs. In genetics, a dominant gene is that which is expressed, or noticeable, in the animal, the other member of the pair of genes being suppressed. Thus the animal shows only the effect of the dominant gene.

In a more general sense, when the genes have not been identified or the genetic situation is complex, a trait is said to be partially or completely dominant if it is conspicuous in the offspring of an animal showing the trait, mated to one which does not show it. For example, LABRADOR types may be said to be dominant in crosses with most other breeds, because such cross-breds usually resemble the Labrador parent more than the other breed. In this general sense, dominance and PREPOTENCY mean much the same thing.

In the science of animal behaviour, an animal to which one or more other animals are submissive is sometimes said to be the dominant animal. This behavioural dominance must not be confused with genetic dominance.
See RECESSIVE.

Downfaced Descriptive of a foreface which curves downwards from the stop to the tip of the nose, as in the BULL TERRIER.

Drag A trail prepared by drawing a bag of animal scent, often feces, over the ground. Used in draghound racing.

Draghounds, Draghound Racing see Hound Trials, Britain.

Draught Dogs Dogs were once used in Belgium, The Netherlands, and Switzerland for hauling the small carts of tradesmen. Their use declined with the arrival of modern means of transport. By 1967, the use of dogs for hauling had been abolished in Europe. Only in the Arctic are dogs still so used. The draught dogs of Europe were never of any specific breed, although dogs of many of the larger breeds were favoured for this purpose.

Draw The method of pairing dogs by drawing names from a container in advance of a field trial. The action of a terrier in entering a burrow and seizing and dragging the quarry out unaided.

Drever see Rare Breeds.

Drop Ear A folded ear.

Dropped Muscle Rupture of an inner loin or shoulder muscle, a hazard of GREYHOUND COURSING and racing.

Dropper Term for a cross-bred bird dog.

Drowning Drowning is a relatively rare occurrence in the dog population. Apparently-drowned dogs may sometimes be saved. If the dog can be lifted by its hind legs and swung, any water in the lungs will be forced out. The dog can then be placed upon its side and artificial respiration given. Pressure and release on the chest cavity should be at a rate of 25 to 35 times a minute for a large dog, and up to 50 for a small one. Mouth to mouth respiration is also possible. When this is used, the person must make certain that his mouth covers the nose of the dog, and that its mouth is closed. If breathing can be re-established, then supportive measures should be given under the direction of a veterinarian.

Dry Neck Term for a dog with taut neck skin.

Dual Champion A dog which has won both bench and field championships.

Dudley Nose Flesh coloured nose.

Dysplasia see Hip Dysplasia.

Below Draught dogs were used to pull light loads in Europe until comparatively recently.

E

Ear Cropping The practice of cropping the ears is permitted in many countries; in others, it is considered inhumane and is prohibited. However, it became a custom for a reason which was once considered partially humane. The ears of dogs are particularly vulnerable to injury during fights, either with other dogs, or against wild animals. Torn or punctured ears bleed profusely, and the dog is weakened accordingly. At one time, the ears of many hunting dogs were therefore cropped shortly after birth. For example, as late as 1940, some Salukis came from the Middle East with partially cropped ears. The ears of dogs destined for pit fighting were also cropped. Ear cropping today is done for purely aesthetic considerations.

In the United States there are some fourteen major breeds in which ear cropping is practised (in some of these breeds, however, the dogs can be shown either cropped or uncropped). The fourteen are the BOUVIER DES FLANDRES, BOXER, BRIARD, DOBERMANN PINSCHER, Giant, Standard, and Miniature SCHNAUZER, GREAT DANE, Standard and Toy MANCHESTER TERRIER, AFFENPINSCHER, GRIFFON BRUXELLOIS, MINIATURE PINSCHER, and BOSTON TERRIER.

Since ear cropping is now done for aesthetic reasons only, it is usually performed by specialists among veterinarians who are experts on some, or all, of these breeds. They then shape the cut to fit the present ideas of beauty, and the individual skull of the dog. These surgeons usually prefer to delay the operation until they can get a conception of the final shape of the skull and muzzle. They must then consider that the instrumentation developed for the operation has been designed for use on young puppies. Other veterinarians refuse to undertake this operation as they feel that an unnecessary operation should not be carried out.

Weight also is considered. For example, one specialist requires that Miniature Schnauzer puppies be ten to fourteen weeks old, with ten weeks being average. However, he will not crop a puppy of this breed which weighs less than six pounds. A Great Dane is considered too young to have its ears cropped at eight weeks, but the operation might be performed at ten weeks.

A further consideration is the length of time a puppy has been in its new home. When it leaves a kennel and enters its permanent home, the puppy necessarily suffers some shock and unsettling. It will require two to four weeks to make a complete adaptation. The veterinarian will then consider cropping its ears.

Ear cropping is done under a general anaesthetic, and the dog is also given one of the tranquilizing drugs. The effects of this will last about eight hours. Most surgeons perform the operation in the morning, sending the puppies home that evening. The ears are usually taped into protective racks and bandage, both to prevent pain and to train the ears into the desired position. In some cases, when the first cropping was poorly done, or when there is insufficient cartilage to

Above Ear cropping. Uncropped ears: some countries prohibit ear cropping as inhumane. Cropped ears: in countries where ear cropping is permitted, experts will wait until the final shape of the dog's head is evident before cropping the ears to suit the dog.

hold the ear erect, surgery must be repeated. In some cases, scarification along the edge of the cut is sufficient to hold the ear erect.

Ear Diseases Usual symptoms of ear trouble in dogs are carrying the head to one side, severe shaking of the head, and trying to put a foot into the ear.

Hematoma (blood blister) of the ear flap: Undue shaking of the head and scratching at the ear may lead to *hematoma* of the ear flap. The damage may be relatively minor resulting in slight swelling and thickening possibly affecting only part of the flap. If the damage is more severe the swelling may be very large and involve the whole of the flap. A small swelling will often resolve itself without treatment, but a large one will probably require a surgical operation. In any event the cause of the head shaking and ear scratching should be investigated.

Otitis externa (inflammation of the external ear): Dogs with pendant ear flaps and dogs with excessive hair in the external ear canal are particularly liable to suffer from *otitis externa*. An accumulation of wax in the ear often leads to disease.

Acute otitis externa is shown by the sudden onset of head shaking and ear scratching. The head is held on one side with the affected ear lowermost. Handling the ear causes pain. The cause may be draughts as in the case of the dog which hangs its head out of the car window, or the presence of a foreign body, usually a grass seed, or infestation with ear mites (otodex) contracted by contact with an infested cat, dog, or even grass. Veterinary help should be sought immediately *acute otitis externa* is suspected and no medicaments should be introduced into the external ear without professional advice.

Chronic otitis externa may follow the acute attack. The symptoms are similar but less marked. *Chronic otitis externa* often develops in neglected, dirty, hairy ears. Prolonged treatment may be necessary and it is inadvisable for the layman to attempt to deal with the condition.

Otorrhoea (canker) is the term used to describe ear disease complicated by a discharge. In many cases the discharge is profuse and offensive and the dog may show signs of general illness. Professional help is required as soon as symptoms are noticed.

Many cases of *otitis externa* can be prevented by plucking excess growth of hair from the external ear canal with the fingers. In the Miniature POODLE this should be done every time the dog is trimmed. If wax accumulates in the ear it may be removed by filling the ear canal with olive oil or medicinal liquid paraffin. Massage the ear to work the oil well down, then mop out the top of the ear with cotton wool or tissues but do not probe deep into the ear.

Otitis media (inflammation of the middle ear) may follow an attack of *otitis externa* if the infection penetrates the ear drum, or it may result from the spread of infection from the throat. In the latter case the infection may penetrate the ear drum and produce an *otitis externa* as well. The symptoms are similar to those in *otitis externa* but in addition the dog is obviously unwell, it walks in circles and shows signs of loss of balance. *Otitis media* is a frequent cause of deafness. As in cases of *otitis externa*, veterinary help is required.

Although the dog owner should leave the treatment of these diseases to a veterinarian, he can often help by preventing the trouble. The ailments are more common in long-haired, heavy- and pendulous-eared dogs than in other breeds. The owner can ensure better ventilation in the dog's ear by clipping the hair at the base of the ear flap, and even in some cases by taping the ears temporarily above the head.

Eastern Greyhound see Greyhound, Eastern.

Eclampsia see Nursing Mother.

Ectropion see Eye Diseases.

Eczema This is a common, but very little understood, skin problem in dogs. It may be considered as a dermatitis (inflammation of the skin), although not all dermatitis is an eczema. Eczema may be caused by a variety of irritants, but it is probably always accompanied by either a local or general predisposition to an attack. It may be temporary or chronic.

Among claimed causes are fungi (see FUNGUS ECZEMA), resulting in the so-called hot spots, fungitch, or summer eczema; allergic reactions to flea bites; overdosing with vitamins, or vitamin deficiency; lack of dietary fat, causing skin dryness and poor hair health; hormonal imbalance, including disorders of the sexual hormones in bitches; and photo-sensitivity (sensitivity to light), as in Collie nose (*eczema nasi*). Food allergies have been reported as a cause Protozoan allergies may appear with LEPTOSPIROSIS; bacterial allergies are associated with canine tuberculosis; and virus allergies often appear with, or follow, DISTEMPER.

Repeated bathing with deodorant soaps, such as those containing hexachlorophene, have been blamed as they have in human eczema cases. Kennel disinfectants containing chlorine have also been established as causes. Interdigital eczema appears between the toes of dogs, particularly of hunting dogs, and may extend up the insides of the legs.

Collie nose is the name of an abnormal reaction to sunlight. It is a disease chiefly found in COLLIES, SHETLAND SHEEPDOGS, and GERMAN SHEPHERDS. It is severe in summer but subsides in winter. Sun-screen materials help to reduce its severity.

'Summer itch', the eczema appearing around the root of the tail and along the spine over the rump, is probably the most common canine eczema. It causes intense itching, and the dog soon bites the area raw. Various fungicides have been developed to combat this. The now much maligned DDT, in a ten per cent solution, brings almost immediate relief in most cases. As a rule, this eczema begins in late summer and ends by the beginning of winter. However, it tends to come earlier and to last longer in susceptible dogs. Thus, any treatment must be regular, and should be begun in early spring before an attack starts.

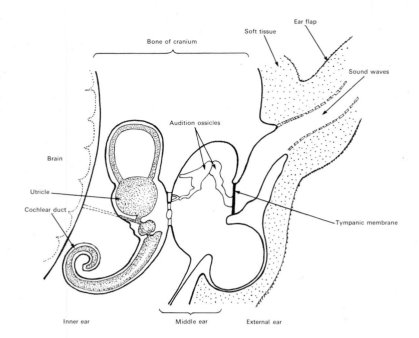

Dietary supplements, which aid in some types of eczema, have appeared in recent years. Many of these contain linolenic and linoleic acids which appear to work directly towards skin and hair health. Others may contain one or more of these acids, and such amino acids as cystine and methionine.

Because of the wide variety of causes, the dog owner should have his dog carefully examined by a veterinarian. The expert should be supplied with as much of the dog's past history as possible, both medical and ancestral.

Elephant Skin see Mange.

Elizabethan Collar see Bandaging.

Elkhound see Norwegian Elkhound.

English Foxhound see Foxhound, English.

English Setter The probability is that few, if any, breeds could earn a ninety-nine per cent vote on the score of beauty. People hold very different views on the aesthetic qualities of, for example, BULL TERRIERS, GRIFFONS, and CHOW CHOWS. Every rule has an exception, however, and surely on this point that exception would prove to be the English Setter.

The sportsman sees beauty in him because of his background and heritage. The artist because of his graceful lines. The engineer for his functional efficiency. The pet lover for the soulful look in those limpid eyes. And, if all else fails, there is always the character of the dog, symbolized by his gently waving tail, to persuade doubters that he is truly beautiful.

The English Setter's history is long. For example, as far back as 1485 a bond signed by a Mr. John Harris reveals that he covenanted 'to keep for six months a certain spaniel to set partridges, pheasants and other game in consideration of ten shillings of lawful English money'.

This gives a clue to the breed's name. The dog was a 'setting spaniel', later abbreviated to 'setter' and ultimately called English Setter to distinguish it from the many continental types which evolved over the same period. Its task was to 'set' the game, first for nets and much later for the gun.

The breed was neither so elegant, nor so fleet of foot in those far-off days. Indeed, the evolution to the animal we know today was brought about largely by Mr. Edward Laverack who in 1825 bought a brace called *Ponto* and *Moll*. They were from a pure and recognized line and with them a sustained and intense process of inbreeding was mounted.

The result was the development of a strain which for both beauty and ability swept all before it for fifty years. Wise animal men of the day were not surprised. They knew that, then as now, inbreeding does not introduce faults; it merely intensifies those which are there. Equally it intensifies virtues, and if these are present without faults, inbreeding is an excellent way to fix the virtues for ever in the breed.

Starting a little later than Edward Laverack, Mr. Purcell Llewellin became a major influence in the breed's history. The Llewellin dogs enjoyed even more sensational success. Indeed to this day we hear of 'Laverack' and 'Llewellin' setters with the implication that they were separate strains if not breeds. In fact, the records prove this assumption false. The latter dogs sprang from the former strain and they were merely a logical extension of a long-term breeding programme.

By this time the role of these dogs had changed considerably. Now they were employed on the moors of Britain, ranging far out in front of the guns and crossing ceaselessly to right and left. When they find the game they stop and 'point' in the traditional fashion, with nose held high, and one foreleg held from the ground as if to emphasize that they have 'frozen' in mid-flight. Then on the command of the sportsman they inch forward again, pressing slowly until the game loses its nerve and breaks for cover. What happens next is up to the man with the gun!

While shortage of open space has hurt the English Setter's popularity in Britain, this is the second most popular hunting dog in the bird dog group in the

Left Ear diseases . The anatomy of a dog's ear.

Below English Setter. Continental setters evolved over the same period as the English. Here are Louis XIV's shooting dogs *Bonne*, *Ponne* and *Nonne* painted by Alexandre-Francois Desportes.

U.S. and Canada. Smaller strains have been developed for hunting and field trials, and these are registered by the American Field. In America, the dogs must hold their point until after the huntsman has flushed the game.

Essentials of the breed: A medium-height dog of clean outline and elegant appearance. Head: long, reasonably lean. Muzzle: moderately deep and fairly square, with head equidistant before and behind the well defined stop. Eyes: bright, mild and dark hazel. Ears: moderately long, low set and hanging close to cheek. Neck: rather long, muscular, lean, slightly arched and not throaty. Oblique shoulders. Body: of moderate length with deep chest, well-sprung ribs. Hindquarters: muscular with long thigh from hip to hocks. Feet: close and compact. Tail: set on and carried in line with back, well feathered with soft, silky hair. Coat: long, silky and wavy with feathered forelegs and breeches. The American standard lists the following colours: black, white and tan (tricolour), black and white (blue BELTON), lemon and white (lemon belton), orange and white (orange belton), liver and white (liver belton), and solid white. Flecking is preferred to heavy patches. Weight: 55 to 65 lb. Height: from 24 to 27 inches according to sex. The American standard gives no recommendations for weight, and suggests a height of about 25 inches for dogs, about 24 inches for bitches. See colour plate p. 87.

English Springer Spaniel There are eight different varieties of spaniel. Of these, the Cockers are the most popular, the Field the most rare, the Irish Water the tallest and the Clumber the heaviest. This seems to leave little room for the English Springer to establish a record for itself. Yet it does so with ease.

It is the oldest, and best established, and almost certainly the tap root from which most of the other spaniels and indeed some other gundog varieties sprang. He is the daddy of them all.

Dr. Johannes Caius' treatise *Of Englishe Dogges,* written over 400 years ago, contains the first reference to the breed of spaniels. Dr. Caius wrote: 'The common sort of people call them by one general word, namely spaniells, as though these kind of dogges came originally and first of all out of Spaine. The most part of their skynnes are white, and if they be marked with any spottes, they are commonly red, and somewhat great therewithall, the heares not growing in such thickness but that the mixture of them may easely be perceaved. Othersome of them be reddishe and blackishe, but of that sorte there be but a very few.'

Thus at the beginning a spaniel was just a spaniel. There were no divisions. The large and the small, the fast and the slow were all lumped together as spaniels.

Slowly it emerged that they were of many different types, one of them being particularly dominant. This was the strong, robust, medium-sized dog which avoided all extremes. The dog which ultimately took its name from its work of 'springing' the birds originally for the nets, later for the guns: the Springer Spaniel.

Subsequently it became necessary to subdivide again. The other off-shoot was the Welsh variety, a smaller

English Setter.
Top left Ch. Guys 'n Dolls Shalimar Duke.
Bottom left Ch. Silbury Soames of Madavale.

Right English Springer Spaniel Ch. Hawkhill Derby Daydream.

dog with red markings on a white coat, described under WELSH SPRINGER SPANIEL.

There are three ways in which a breed can become firmly established: first by what is called show bench successes; next by outstanding qualities as a pet dog; and finally by its work in the field. The last way is the hardest. Characteristically, that is the way chosen by the English Springer.

It became the ideal gundog. Ideal because it is not a specialist but an all-rounder. The perfect animal for a shooting man who, by taste or necessity, uses only one dog. Maybe it is not quite as spectacular at finding game and then 'pointing' as the ENGLISH SETTER. Maybe it is not quite as energetic and forceful at searching dense undergrowth and hedgerows as the Cocker. Maybe it is not quite as stylish and polished in the retrieve of shot game as the LABRADOR.

But the English Springer does all three with equal willingness and more-than-average competence. The well balanced proportions of the dog, the strength, the trainability and sharp intelligence took this breed to the top in an increasing number of field trials.

This inevitably attracted attention and both exhibitors and pet owners began to take notice. Inevitably, too, it soon became accepted that the English Springer could easily have worked its way to the top through either of these other channels. In short, it was both a highly successful showdog and a very attractive family pet.

Only in 1902 were they sufficiently numerous to justify a separate register at the Kennel Club (England). In the United States official recognition did not come

for another 30 years. Since then progress has been consistent, if never startling.

True Springer fanciers would rather have it that way. As with all similar breeds the purist is always concerned lest popularity, with its attendant risk of a deterioration in type and temperament, comes too quickly. They probably worry without cause. This breed is too firmly rooted to suffer much even from the hazards of fashion.

Finally, brief mention of the tail. It should be docked, feathered, set low and carried level. This however is the official description. Unofficially the most important thing about the Springer's tail is the fact that it never stops wagging!

Essentials of the breed: The general appearance is of a symmetrical, compact, active and merry dog. Skull: rounded and of medium length with foreface in proportion. Medium-sized eyes, dark hazel in colour. Ears: lobular, set close to head and fairly long. Neck: strong and muscular. Forelegs: straight and with ample bone. Body strong, of medium length with deep chest, well sprung ribs, muscular loins with slight arch and broad, muscular thighs. Feet: should be tight, compact and rounded. Tail: feathered and set low. The weather-resisting coat should be close and straight. Any recognized land spaniel colour is acceptable but liver and white or black and white or either of those with tan markings preferred. Approximate height (U.K.): 20 inches. Weight: 50 lb. (U.S.A.) Height: dogs 20 inches; bitches 19 inches. Weight (20-inch dog): 49 to 55 lb. See colour plate p. 89.

English Toy Spaniel see Cavalier King Charles Spaniel; King Charles Spaniel.

English Toy Terrier (Black and Tan) There are many reasons, usually practical ones, why breeds fail to do much more than survive in this age of increasing interest in pedigree dogs. None of the usual reasons, such as unsuitability for small modern houses, can be applied to the English Toy Terrier. One therefore looks elsewhere for explanation, and comes up with the possibility that unpopularity may be owing to the constant and confusing changes of name with which this breed has been bedevilled during its four-hundred years of recorded history.

They started in England as Toy Manchester Terriers, progressed to Toy Black and Tans and then to Miniature Black and Tans. In 1962 they took over their present title in Britain which although too long for daily use, is at least descriptive.

In the United States they were Toy Black and Tans and are currently Toy Manchester Terriers, the name by which they were originally known in Britain. But whatever the name, the breed standard is much the same.

One of the most important things about these dogs is that they are small. They are also very game and spirited, pure terrier, and almost certainly long-established. Their history is however by no means well documented.

First known mention of them occurs in *Of Englishe Dogges* written by Dr. Caius in 1570, although he did not differentiate between the normal-sized Manchester and the miniature. Even so, it is to be presumed that bantam-weight offspring were occasionally produced by normal-sized parents.

By the middle of the nineteenth century, the indications are that they were by no means uncommon, and somewhat surprisingly they were used in the so-called 'sport' of killing rats in a pit. This is all the more remarkable when one realizes that their usual weight was around 6 lb.

Both before and after this date, rumours persisted of crosses to other breeds. Two which can almost certainly be discredited are the DACHSHUND and the WHIPPET because in their present form these breeds were unknown to Britain at that time. More likely, although undeniably unwise, was a cross to the KING CHARLES SPANIEL. One presumes that black and tans were used, and this might have served to establish colour. However, it totally destroyed type and took some time to breed out. A final suggestion is that ITALIAN GREYHOUNDS were used and this is more probable. While this would certainly introduce elegance and possibly smallness, it may also be responsible for the high stepping action and ROACH BACK which are still occasionally seen and regarded as faults. In those days, size was everything.

One big stumbling block for breeders over the years has been the insistence upon the precise black and tan

Above The English Springer is an ideal all-round gundog: it searches out game, 'points' and retrieves, and all with notable competence. Bricksclose Scilla, a field trials champion.

158

markings. For example, on a black head the muzzle should be tan but the nose black. Additionally there must be a tan spot on each cheek, and above each eye, while the throat and inside the ear are tan. Similar considerations apply to the body, posing in all a challenge to the breeder who seeks perfection and is endowed with endless patience.

Just why they are not more popular today is still hard to understand. They are certainly small enough for modern life and very undemanding on the subject of exercise. They have trouble-free coats and modest appetites. Despite their size they are quite hardy and certainly do not dislike damp and cold more than any of the other smooth-coated breeds.

But a feature of fashions in dogs is the insistence on new and preferably 'foreign' varieties. Only when a breed's very existence is threatened do people turn to it again with grandiose schemes of resuscitating the breed. Sometimes they leave this too late. There is too little to work on. Let us hope that this never happens to the charming and ancient little Black and Tan.

Above English Toy Terrier. Ch. Renreh Lorelei of Charmaron.

Essentials of the breed: Head should be long, narrow, slightly wedge-shaped with little cheek muzzle and tight-lipped jaws. Eyes: small, as near black as possible, oblique and not protruding. Ears: rather close together, moderately narrow at base with pointed tips, naturally erect. The neck should be reasonably long, slim and graceful. Chest: narrow between the legs, deep in the brisket. Body: moderately short with well-sprung ribs, back slightly arched at the loin and falling again at the rear. Forelegs: straight, well under the body. Feet: compact, well arched with black nails. Tail: moderately short, thick at the root, tapering to a point, not carried higher than the back or reaching below the hock. Coat must be smooth, short, close and glossy. Colour: jet black and rich mahogany tan, each clearly defined. A small tan spot over each eye, on each cheek, on each side of the chest above the front legs, each toe must be black pencil marked, but forelegs from knee down to be tan. White in any form is a serious fault. Weight: in America not exceeding 12 lb. In Britain the ideal is between 6 and 8 lb., with a shoulder height of between 10 and 12 inches.
See colour plate p. 381.

Enteritis Enteritis is an inflammation of the intestine which is frequently associated with or follows acute or chronic DIARRHOEA. It may itself be temporary or chronic, or it may attack only a small section of the small intestine, as for example, in regional or terminal ileitis. In the latter, *Proteus* or *Spirillum minutum* organisms have frequently been implicated as causes. Diagnosis and treatment by a veterinarian is required.

Entire This is a description of a male dog in which both testicles are seen to be present in the scrotum. Bitches which have not been spayed are also called 'entire'.

Entropion Entropion is an inversion of the eyelids which permits the lashes to brush against the cornea, thus causing intense irritation. In some breeds, such as

Chow Chows and Bulldogs, entropion is an extremely common defect. It may, however, be acquired following eye injuries, the improper healing of such injuries, or after long periods of excessive winking caused by other eye ailments. Entropion is sometimes confused with trichiasis, a condition which disqualifies in the Golden Retriever standard. Correction is by a surgical procedure called blepharoplasty.
See EYE DISEASES.

Epilepsy 'Epilepsy' comes from a Greek term meaning convulsion or seizure. So little has been known about canine epilepsy until quite recently that authorities often preferred to use the term 'epileptiform convulsions'. Today, thanks chiefly to the electro-encephalograph which plots the brain's electrical activity, it is known that many of the seizures of dogs closely parallel those of human beings.

Epilepsy has been described as a disorder of the central nervous system during which there are explosive nerve cell discharges. There are severe changes in the electrical activity of the brain cells, and the normal brain wave pattern is seriously disturbed.

When no cause can be determined, epilepsy is called idiopathic. *Grand mal* epilepsy is characterized by unconsciousness, tonic convulsion, dilated pupils, and spasms of all voluntary muscles. When the attack subsides, the animal usually falls into a deep sleep. There are hysterical forms in which the dog has no sense of what it is doing and during which, for example, it might snap and bite.

Puppies heavily infested with worms may have 'running fits' – a form of epilepsy. In very hot weather when dogs drink water excessively, without a corresponding intake of salt, and then pant heavily, an epileptic convulsion may occur. In America, electrical storms have been known to cause convulsions in dogs and in human beings.

Major causes of epilepsy in dogs have been listed by Dr. R. Barry Prynn of Ohio State University. Among them, he lists post distemper encephalitis, hydrocephalus, congenital defects, hereditary predisposition, brain damage through injury, inflammatory changes due to infectious diseases, tumours, and local biochemical changes. Factors which influence seizures include blood-glucose levels, blood-gas tensions, electrolytic composition of extra cellular fluid, endocrine changes, fatigue, nutritional deficiencies, and emotional stress.

There is evidence that epilepsy may be inherited. This has been shown to be so only in Poodles, American Cocker Spaniels, and Beagles. Since American Cockers are subject to hydrocephalus (water on the brain) in many cases, the two appear to be closely linked. Dr. Prynn, a Boxer breeder, believes that Boxers over five years of age are more prone to epilepsy than are ageing dogs in other breeds.

Apart from epileptiform convulsions which may disappear when parasitism, abnormal blood, or similar conditions are corrected, epilepsy is considered incurable. Anticonvulsant drugs bring relief in many instances, but even these offer little hope of help in

Left Eskimo dogs are among the great work dogs of the North, and the heroes of folk tales.

cases of diseases like cerebral neoplasia, hydrocephalus, toxoplasmosis, or when a progressive disease process becomes resistant to their effects. A major cause of failure of the anticonvulsant drugs is due not to the drugs themselves, but to the dog owners. They fail to follow the prescribed therapeutic regimen, or they give the drugs only intermittently. The missing of one single dose of the drug may bring on an attack. Sudden drug withdrawal may also key a seizure.

Drugs may be used singly or in combination. Dosages must be worked out for each individual dog. Several days of therapy are required to achieve effective tissue levels. Thus, the dog may have several seizures during the early days of treatment. But once the veterinarian has been able to work out both the drug or combination of drugs, and the correct dosages, it is sometimes possible to lower the dosages.

Eskimo The dog known simply as the Eskimo is a native of the Eastern Arctic, as far west as the MacKenzie River, in Greenland, Baffin Island, and Victoria Island. It is a draught animal and, one of the great work dogs of the North. It has failed to catch on as a show dog because of its intractable disposition, and because it has not adapted well to the temperate zone. It has also been unusually susceptible to DISTEMPER.

The stories of the ability of the Eskimo Dog are legion. MacMillan, the famed Arctic explorer, once drove a team in a continuous run of 100 miles in less than eighteen hours. The commander of the second Grinnell Expedition, Dr. Elisha Kent Kane, used a six dog team, which hauled a fully-loaded sledge about 750 miles in two weeks.

Such a sledge, when fully loaded, would normally weigh about 700 lb., according to a careful analysis made by the explorers. Normally a dog is not asked to draw more than 100 lb. So Kane's dogs were drawing more than a normal weight.

In recent years, Arctic dogs have been chained. In earlier times, they had to be tied by seal skin lines. To prevent them from chewing through these, their incisors or cutting teeth were broken. This meant that meat had to be cut, or if frozen, chopped into pieces which the dog could swallow whole. In *The Voyage of the Fox*, McClintock wrote that on one occasion he cut 65 lb. of seal meat into small pieces. His twenty-nine dogs devoured it all in forty-two seconds.

The Eskimo Dog is no longer recognized by the American Kennel Club, since years passed without a single registration application. The breed is still recognized by the Canadian Kennel Club.

Essentials of the breed: Eskimos come in all colours and markings. Males are 22 to 25 inches at the shoulder, and weigh 65 to 85 lb. Bitches are 20 to 30 inches tall, and weigh 50 to 70 lb. The outer guard coat is three to six inches long, but in some strains, hair length may surpass six inches. The undercoat is dense, and is from one to two inches long. The tail is carried curled over the back.

Estrus see Oestrum.

Euthanasia This is painless killing. Euthanasia can be administered to the individual dog in a number of ways. The preferred way, where possible, is to get the veterinarian to visit the home, so that the dog has no feeling of fear or desertion by its owner. An overdose of a barbiturate, such as phenobarbital sodium, is then injected. The dog simply closes its eyes, and only the slightest muscular shudders indicate the arrival of death. However, in some cases, excitement occurs which can be distressing to dog and owner. Many veterinarians prefer to carry out euthanasia at their consulting room, after the dog has been given a sedative at home to prevent distress.

The problem of euthanasia at animal shelters and homes has been extensively studied at the Dog's Home, Battersea, in England. Euthanasia of a large number of dogs can be painlessly and humanely carried out using electricity, carbon dioxide or carbon monoxide and the 'high altitude chamber' from which oxygen is withdrawn.

Ewe Neck Concave curve of the top neck line.

Exchanging In GREYHOUND COURSING, when the dogs of a brace alternatively move the hare from its course.

Exercise Dogs, no matter what breed, are naturally active animals and therefore require a good deal of exercise to keep them fit and happy.

Kennel dogs usually exercise themselves in runs or paddocks but even they appreciate being taken for a walk regularly. This is important, as road exercise on a lead is essential to harden the pads of the feet, strengthen the toes and keep nails short. See NAILS.

All dogs, even dogs of the same breed, have their own exercise requirements. Toy dogs need little more

exercise than that provided by running after their owner in the house.

It is a bad policy to over-do walks in the initial stages of a dog's life if you do not intend to keep up such a routine. The dog looks forward to getting out and expects it. If its exercise tends to get less and less it will become bored and there will be trouble ahead: a bored dog can learn destructive habits, simply to use up energy.

To keep in good health, a house dog really needs two good walks a day. If it has more than this it will still appreciate it but it is not necessary. Remember that on a country walk when the dog is off the lead it will cover two or three times the distance of its human companion.

Dogs bred for special purposes such as hunting or racing come into an entirely different category and need to cover long distances regularly.

If dogs get wet when being exercised they must be thoroughly dried before going back to their kennel or bed. Neglect in this respect can bring great discomfort and even rheumatism or pneumonia to the dog.

Export of Dogs Countries have been exchanging dogs for a long time. There is a record that the Romans appointed an officer in Britain to find dogs to send to Rome for use in the arenas.

As a nation, Britain has produced more breeds of dogs than any other country, and for a century dog breeders in all parts of the world have valued British stock. This interest in dogs caused travellers in many parts of the world to bring dogs back to Britain, and within a few years the breeds imported were themselves considered British and sought-after overseas.

The cult of pedigreed dogs has spread throughout the world and the export and interchange of dogs of quality from one country to another is now widespread.

In 1930 fewer than 50 dogs were exported each month from Britain. In 1950 the figure had risen to 100, and in 1970, 1,500 dogs were exported each month, nearly half of them to the United States.

The United States and Canada export dogs to South America, as do many of the European countries. British Commonwealth countries in the West Indies, Bermuda excepted, bar dogs from the United States and Canada. Bermuda imports from both countries but requires proof of vaccination against rabies. Australia bars North American dogs unless they first go through quarantine in England, and a further quarantine in Australia. Australia also bars the importation of GERMAN SHEPHERD DOGS (Alsatians) from any country.

After World War II, the Japanese became greatly interested in the breeding and showing of dogs as a sport. Previously, they had been interested in dogs purely as family pets, and for military or police purposes. During the latter half of the sixties Great Britain the United States and Canada all exported large numbers of dogs to Japan, but this traffic has now virtually ceased.

Eye Anatomy Some knowledge of the anatomy of the dog's eye and the surrounding structures is necessary for an understanding of the diseases of the eye. The diagrams show the most important features. The eye-

Below Eye anatomy. A cross section of the dog's eye.

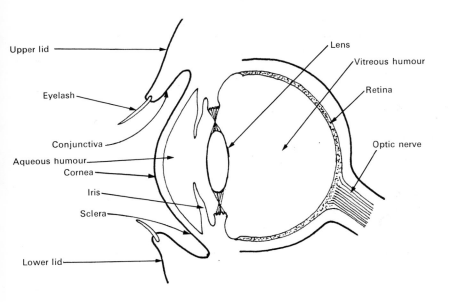

Upper lid

Eyelash

Conjunctiva

Aqueous humour

Cornea

Iris

Sclera

Lower lid

Lens

Vitreous humour

Retina

Optic nerve

ball is enclosed by the upper and lower eyelids. The inner surface of the eyelids is lined by a pink mucous membrane called the conjunctiva. At the inner canthus (or corner), a third eyelid is found inside the upper and lower lids. The third eyelid (*Membrana nictitans*) is more obvious in some breeds than in others. Whereas the upper and lower eyelids can be opened or closed at will, the third eyelid is not under the conscious control of the dog. If for reasons of disease or injury the eyeball sinks back or is drawn back in its socket, the third eyelid automatically comes over to provide added protection. When the eyeball comes forward again, the third eyelid is retracted, in fact, the eyeball actually pushes it out of the way. Harder's gland is found on the inner surface of the third eyelid.

The white part of the eyeball is the sclera. In most breeds it is a fault for the white of the eye to be shown, but it is there just the same. The inner part of the conjunctiva blends into the sclera. The front of the eyeball is called the cornea; this part is transparent. Through the cornea one can observe the iris which is usually pigmented. When the iris is not pigmented this produces a WALL EYE, which is a fault in most breeds, an exception being the merle COLLIE. The black hole in the iris is the pupil. In a bright light the iris constricts giving a pinpoint pupil, while in the dark, the iris dilates to show a large pupil and just a ring of pigmented iris.

The lens lies behind the iris; its function is to focus the light onto the retina at the back of the eye. The retina is sensitive to the light and passes the image to the brain via the optic nerve.

The eyeball is not empty. Between the cornea and the lens in what is known as the anterior chamber, there is a transparent watery liquid known as the aqueous humour. The main body of the eyeball is full of a jelly-like, transparent substance called the vitreous humour.

Eye Diseases The eyelids are subject to three main congenital defects. ENTROPION is an inturning of the eyelids. Both the upper and lower eyelids may be affected. The condition is serious as the eyelashes are brought into contact with the cornea and the constant irritation produces keratitis. Some breeds, such as the CHOW CHOW, are more likely to suffer from this defect than others.

Ectropion is a turning out of the lower eyelids to expose the conjunctiva. In some breeds, for example the BLOODHOUND and the ST. BERNARD, a certain degree of ectropion is accepted as being normal.

The third congenital defect of the eyelids concerns the lashes. There may be one or several ingrowing eyelashes (trichiasis) or sometimes even a double row (districhiasis). The PEKINGESE often suffers from this defect.

Entropion can be corrected by plastic surgery, but it is not always serious enough to require treatment. Ingrowing eyelashes can be removed by plucking or electrolysis.

The Harderian gland on the inner surface of the third eyelid may become diseased. In this case, the swelling is obvious and often the only treatment is surgical removal.

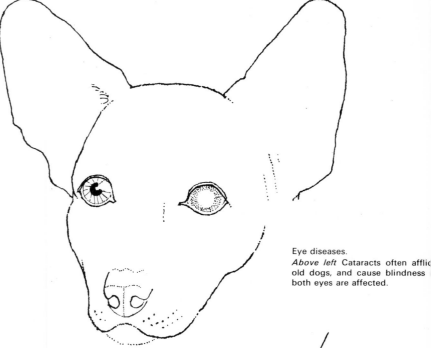

Eye diseases.
Above left Cataracts often afflic old dogs, and cause blindness both eyes are affected.

Conjunctivitis is an inflammation of the conjunctival membrane. It may be the result of local infection or irritation, or it may be the symptom of some general disease such as DISTEMPER.

Keratitis is an inflammation of the cornea, with which there usually appears an associated conjunctivitis. The cause of Keratitis may be a foreign body or an injury. The cornea becomes opaque, but as the condition resolves it will clear to some extent if not completely. Corneal ulceration is usually the result of some injury to the cornea. A keratitis may exist at the same time. Keratitis may lead to permanent opacity of the cornea and a corneal ulcer may perforate with subsequent scar formation. In view of these unfortunate developments it is unwise for the layman to attempt treatment without professional advice.

Cataract is an opacity of the lens and is a common cause of blindness in old dogs if both eyes are affected. Sometimes cataract occurs in young dogs; in these cases the surgical removal of the diseased lens will restore some degree of vision. The lens may become dislocated (luxated) and the effects on the surrounding structures in the eye are very serious, for the intraocular pressure will rise (glaucoma) and the loss of vision in the affected eye will be permanent. Some breeds, particularly the terrier breeds, are more subject to dislocation of the lens than others. Early surgical removal of the dislocated lens may prevent the development of glaucoma and restore some degree of vision.

Progressive retinal atrophy (P.R.A. or night blindness) is a degeneration of the retina leading to failing sight and eventually to blindness. The condition is inherited.

See BLINDNESS; HEREDITARY ABNORMALITIES.

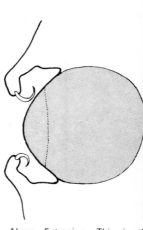

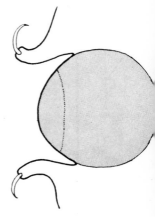

Above Entropion. This is t inturning of the eyelids so th the eyelashes brush irritatingly the cornea. With ectropion *(belov* the lower eyelid is turned out expose the conjunctiva.

Eyeteeth The upper canines.

F

Fading Puppies Deaths in puppies within the first week of life, usually referred to as neonatal deaths, can be a serious problem to the dog breeder. In many cases a whole litter may be lost. Originally all neonatal deaths were classed as 'fading puppies' but recent investigations have shown that these losses actually fall into one of three categories.

Approximately one-third of all neonatal deaths can be ascribed to miscellaneous causes such as exhaustion following a difficult WHELPING, suffocation, injury and similar individual tragedies which are difficult if not impossible to prevent, even in the best regulated kennels.

The remaining two-thirds of neonatal deaths can be avoided to a large extent. About half of these cases are due to infection. The majority are of bacterial origin; *Streptococci* and *Escherichia coli* being most commonly responsible. Occasionally Canine Virus HEPATITIS (Rubarth's Disease) is the cause. Veterinary assistance and attention to kennel hygiene can minimize losses from infection.

The other half of preventable neonatal deaths are due to hypothermia, commonly called chilling. An apparently healthy bitch whelps normally and has plenty of milk. All the puppies appear to be normal for the first twelve hours or so, then they stop feeding, gradually weaken and eventually die. This is the typical picture of the 'fading puppy' and most authorities now restrict the use of this term to cases of hypothermia.

During the first few days of life puppies are unable to shiver and are thus unable to maintain their body temperature without some external source of heat. Under reasonable conditions the nursing bitch provides the warmth necessary for the puppies' survival. If a puppy is rejected by the bitch and no other source of heat is available the puppy will rapidly cool, weaken and die.

It is easy to understand how chilling can occur in unheated kennels in the winter months. However, it is not generally appreciated that chilling can occur during the summer months, for the air temperature may fall dangerously low at night. Chilling may even occur when small breeds whelp and rear their puppies indoors, for room temperatures can fluctuate alarmingly and at night the fall can be considerable.

To prevent chilling, the temperature in the room, or whelping box, should be maintained at 70°F (21°C) day and night for the first week after whelping. If central heating is available it is only necessary to adjust the thermostat. An INFRA-RED LAMP over the whelping box may be used to maintain the desired temperature locally if it is impossible or uneconomic to raise the temperature of the whole room or kennel to 70°F. In the winter months an infra-red lamp alone cannot cope with the conditions and some background heating must be supplied. To ensure that an adequate temperature is maintained a maximum and minimum thermometer should be installed. The bitch and her puppies do not have to be 'cooked' and there is no need for the air temperature to exceed 75°F (24°C).

Faking Faking is the illegal alteration of dogs which are to be exhibited at shows or to be used for breeding. Most kennel governing bodies have rules against the practice which may bring disqualification of the dog and suspension of the exhibitor, and in the worst cases, denial of the right to register dogs. Common faking practices follow.

Colour: The colouring or dyeing of dogs, either to hide a disqualifying colour, or to enhance the beauty of the dog.

Surgery: Operations upon the ears of terriers to make them fold properly and to keep them from standing erect. Operations to straighten the tails of terriers to keep them from standing over the back and pointing towards the head, squirrel fashion. Surgery to bring down and anchor one or both testicles into the scrotum. Correction of ENTROPION or trichiasis in the eye which, although a humane act, disguises the hereditary fault carried by the dog. See EYE DISEASES.

Coat: The use of stiffeners to give the feel and appearance of a desired, hard coat to a dog with soft hair.

Tranquilizers: The use of sedatives or tranquilizers to disguise temperament faults in a highly nervous, hysterical, or shy dog during show hours.

Fall Hair falling over the eyes or face.

False Dogs The term 'false dogs' follows the nomenclature of the British naturalist and author, Ivan Sanderson. It covers those animals which, though doglike, are too far away from the main stream to be called true canids. Although they also sprang from *Miacis* (see ANCESTORS OF THE DOG) they split away very early in zoological history. Yet somehow they developed along parallel lines. This group includes the African Cape Hunting Dog, the South American Bush Dog, and the Dholes of Asia.

The African Cape Hunting Dog (Lycaon) is the oddest coloured of all the dogs, either true or false. It has the orange, black and white blotched colours of the tortoiseshell and white cat. But whereas those colours are sex-linked to sterility in the male cat, the Cape Hunting Dogs are fertile. If they were not, the race could not survive in that colour pattern.

Not less fantastic than its colour are the Cape Dog's ears. They are huge, round, bat-like and fully erect. No other animal, except perhaps some bats, can match those ears for relative size. The animal has long, slender legs which seem ridiculously fragile for the size of the body. Yet not even the wolf can match the Cape Dog in endurance. The animal has a short tail with a surprising tuft of hair at the end. It has only four toes, front and back, with no sign of dew claws.

Cape Dogs hunt in packs. They work in relays, with a lead dog to force the pace while others remain behind and cut corners. In this way, the fleetest antelope can be worn to exhaustion.

Cape Dogs inhabit much of the high plains and veldt areas of southern and central Africa. They are so feared that there are no game laws to protect them. They have been known to attack lions. One dog attacks the lion's throat, and if this dog is killed or is badly wounded, another takes its place. They are den dwellers; and their social organization is highly developed. One of their peculiar habits is to eat, then to vomit their food in front of a comrade. This dog, considering that he is being offered a present, eats the food. He may in turn make such a present to another dog. When eating, these animals often make peculiar cries.

The South American Bush Dog (Speothus) is a queer little animal which lives along the edges of the Amazonian jungles. When hunting for food, it often makes continuous whistling and mumbling sounds, as though talking to itself.

Bush Dogs have sparse, coarse hair, but the ears are well furred. These ears are small and rounded, and although set upon the edges of a massive skull, are erect. Their muzzles are short and also massive. Their bodies are long and fat, and are set upon short legs. They are very shy in captivity.

The Dhole (Cuon) is often called the Indian Dhole. However, one variety lives in Siberia, and another in Malaya and the South Sea Islands, such as Sumatra and Borneo. How these animals reached the islands is not known. The Indian Dhole, for example, has not spanned the water barrier from India to Ceylon.

Dholes are rufous red or brown in colour. They are larger than jackals, reaching three feet in length, but with short legs. This means that they are slower than either wolves or jackals. They have one less molar in each jaw than true dogs. And whereas dogs usually have ten nipples, Dholes have twelve to fourteen. They are savage and resist taming. They hunt in packs.

False Point In the field, an unproductive point, or one believed to have been made when no bird was present.

False Pregnancy The reproductive process in the bitch is governed by a cycle which follows a delicate and precise time schedule. The female germ cell, or egg, is called an ova, so long as it is in an early stage of development. Ovulation takes place when the matured eggs or ova escape from the ovarian follicle. In dogs, if the eggs are then fertilized, the cycle continues through GESTATION until the puppy is born.

But in many bitches, the cycle seems to be followed even when fertilization of eggs has not taken place. From the sixth to the ninth weeks, the abdomen swells and the mammary glands become enlarged. During the ninth week, milk may be developed, and the bitch may rush about frantically trying to make a 'nest'. Her appetite usually increases greatly, and there may be heavy deposits of body fat.

Of course, no puppies are born. The bitch loses her great appetite. Her hysteria of the ninth week subsides, and she may return gradually to normal weight. Her mammary glands will retract to normal, though in some cases, veterinary help may be necessary.

This unproductive cycle is called false pregnancy, or

False dogs share an early ancestor with true dogs but developed in a separate, if parallel, direction.
Top left The fierce African Cape Hunting Dog. Packs of these have been known to attack lions.
Middle left Bush Dog from South America with its rounded, furry, un-dog-like ears.
Bottom left The Indian Dhole, varieties of which are found in Malaya, the South Sea Islands, and even in Siberia.

Right Feathers.

sometimes pseudo-pregnancy, or phantom pregnancy. Some authorities consider that a false pregnancy is normal, and that failure to ovulate is more dangerous. In either case, the owner of the bitch should discuss the matter with a veterinarian. If the bitch is not to be used for breeding, he may recommend spaying as a means of avoiding this condition.

Fangs see Canines.

Farinaceous Foods Starchy foods containing flour are called farinaceous.
See DIGESTION; NUTRITION.

Feathers Longer hair on legs, ears, tail, and belly than on the rest of the body.

Federation Cynologique Internationale (F.C.I), (International Canine Federation) The federation was founded on 22 May 1911, the original participants being Germany (*Deutsche Kartell für das Deutsche Hundewesen*, and the *Delegierten Kommission*), Austria (*Österreichischer Kynologenverband*), Belgium (*La Société Royale Saint-Hubert*), France (*Société Centrale Canine de France*), and Holland (*Read van Beheer of Kynologisch Gebied in Nederland*).

Its purposes were and remain:

a The mutual acknowledgement of stud books.
b Mutual agreement on breed standards.
c Reciprocal agreements respecting prefixes and affixes.
d Reciprocal agreements respecting disciplinary measures applied to officials, judges, etc.
e The adoption of International Rules.
f Acceptance of the 'Certificate of Aptitude, Championship International, Beauty' (C.A.C.I.B.), and the 'Certificate of Aptitude, Championship International, Trials' (C.A.C.I.T.). See below.
g The recognition of International Judges.
h The control of the schedules of the Shows and Working Trials.

The F.C.I. Committee consists of a President, Vice President, General Secretary, Treasurer, three Technical Members and Sub-Committees concerned with Rules, Standards, Utility Dogs, Continental Gundogs, English Gundogs, Terriers, Greyhounds, Co-ordination of Show Regulation, Scientific and Warren Dogs.

The President, the Vice President, and the members of the Sub-Committees are elected every year. The General Secretary, the Treasurer and the three Technical Members every three years.

The General Assembly (or Annual General Meeting) is held annually in the country of the acting President. At this meeting, all problems presented by the representatives of each country and the reports of the Committee and Sub-Committees are examined.

C.A.C.I.T. – International Working Trial Championship. This Championship is for breeds for which Working Trials are applicable. In order to be a Working Trial International Champion, dogs of any age must have two C.A.C.I.T. certificates from two different countries and two field prizes in Working Trials in any International Championship approved by the F.C.I. Additionally, if under fifteen months old, whatever the number of dogs shown, they must have won a qualification of *very good* or a second prize in the open class.

C.A.C.I.B. – International Beauty Championship.

A. For breeds which are not required to compete at Working Trials. Four C.A.C.I.B. certificates given in three countries and by three different judges are needed, one at least of which is won in the owner's country or in the country from which the breed originated. Outside European countries, the four C.A.C.I.B. certificates must be won under four different judges, one of whom comes from another continent.

B. For breeds which are required to compete in Working Trials. Two C.A.C.I.B. Certificates won in two different countries and one first, second or third prize (at least five dogs competing) in a Working Trial in which Working Trial National Certificates are awarded, are necessary. In a *Test by points*, a 75 per cent pass replaces the qualifications above mentioned.

Federation Cynologique Internationale includes the following countries: France, Belgium, Holland, Spain, Italy, Switzerland, Monaco, Austria, Sweden, Finland, Norway, Jugoslavia, Portugal, Germany, Luxembourg, Czechoslovakia, Poland, Greece, Denmark, Hungary, Morocco, Mexico, Brazil, and Argentina.

Additionally, some other countries have reciprocal agreements concerned principally with the passing of information. They are: Indonesia, Venezuela, Colombia, Republic of South Africa, Japan, Peru, India, Israel, Chile, Uruguay, Paraguay, and the United Kingdom.

Feeding Dog feeding presents more problems to people than to dogs. Dogs are creatures of habit and thrive on monotony, including that of diet. Mixing flavours is an attempt to humanize the dog; it can make a finicky and unhappy eater of it. In ideal conditions, dogs tend to eat only to their caloric needs, and this is true regardless of the type of food given, except that moderate-to-low caloric diets are better in this respect than high energy diets.

There are many types of prepared dog foods. Canine dieticians list these as meal: pressed or cubed foods, extruded or expanded types, biscuits, canned foods, and the soft-moist, simulated ground meat foods.

Nutritionists seem agreed that the meal and pressed foods are adequate for growth and normal health. As a rule, they are cheaper than other types. Meal foods should be remixed, since nutrient siftings may have shaken to the bottom of the pack with handling. Both foods are lacking in taste appeal, as compared to the others, but dogs can be taught to eat them.

The expanded or extruded foods are cooked under less heat than are biscuits, and have high value. As a rule, they are sprayed with fat which increases taste appeal, acts as a preservative, and adds slightly to the energy production of the food.

The soft-moist, or simulated ground meat foods have high biological value, and are simple to feed. They are also very expensive, and they may lack sufficient roughage.

Biscuits are rich in starch and carbohydrates. But they may require vitamin and mineral supplements, particularly the former. They should be fed with meat. In a kennel, adding meat may raise feeding expense five to six times.

Canned dog foods may be considered as a normal maintenance diet, though insufficient for growing puppies or ill dogs. Canned foods are expensive because the buyer is purchasing approximately 70 per cent water; a twelve-ounce can may yield only three or four ounces of nutriment.

Cubes and expanded foods can be successfully fed from hoppers. Puppies grow well from weaning when fed in this way. The dogs do not over-eat. And they tend to drink only as much water as is needed for digestion. When the owner adds water he cannot know the dog's needs, and he may be doing it a disservice. For example, Boxers, Boston Terriers, and Mastiffs appear to have weaker stomach acids than other breeds. Adding water to the food further weakens these acids. The dog may regurgitate several times. When it then does keep the food down, it will be because it now has sufficient acid to digest the food.

Piggish dogs, which become very fat in the home, reduce weight slowly when food is always present in the dish. They quickly learn there is no need to gulp all possible food and reduce their intake to normal caloric needs.

Instructions sometimes call for feeding newly-weaned puppies five times a day. But experiments with Beagles have shown they will grow as well on one meal. An ideal compromise appears to be two or three meals per day for average size dogs until four months, then once or twice a day. Dogs of giant breeds can be fed three or four meals per day until fifteen months of age. Sick dogs should be fed more often but under veterinary supervision.

Kennel owners find the best time to feed is in the early morning. Many pet owners also feed in the morning, but their dogs will adapt to the convenient schedule of the owner, morning, noon, or night.

Hunting dogs work better if fed one fourth of their food very early in the morning and three-quarters at night. As a rule, they do not require more protein when working, but should receive more fat.

During GESTATION, some nutritionists feel the bitch should get an increase of about 20 per cent more food after the fourth or fifth week of PREGNANCY, and with an increase in high quality protein. However, adding too much meat to a balanced ration destroys its balance. It might then be necessary to supplement with vitamins and minerals. The bitch should get moderate exercise, and she should not be allowed to get fat. If a litter contains more than four puppies, then supplementary feeding can begin at 18 to 20 days. The puppies readily learn to lap.

Since the caloric yields in different dog foods vary, like the requirements of individual dogs, there are only two answers to the question: how much should I feed? If the puppy, or older dog, is allowed to eat as much as it wants from a constantly filled hopper or dish, and has free access to water, it will decide for itself. If the dog is fed individual meals, take up the food pan as soon as the dog lifts its head or walks away from it. It has indicated that it has had enough, even though it may return for a few more bites. Returning to nibble at the remains will spoil the dog's appetite and will make a finicky eater of it. At the next meal, proportionately less should be fed. In this way, one learns the needs of both the growing puppy and the adult dog.

Feeding aged dogs should be done under the direction of a veterinarian. Aged dogs need an increase in calcium and phosphorus. They also need a steady diet, since abrupt variation may cause stress. But because the physical conditions of aged dogs differ, practical diets should be worked out under veterinary supervision.

See DIGESTION; NUTRITION.

Felted Coat Matted hair, hanging in mats, as distinguished from cords.

Fetch The act of retrieving.

Fiddle Front Out at elbows, pasterns close, feet turning out. French front.

Field Dog Stud Book see The American Field – Field Dog Stud Book.

Field Spaniel To say that the Field Spaniel has had a 'bad press' over the years is almost to flatter it. Few, if any, breeds have been attacked as sharply. Admittedly these attacks have now ceased but this is probably because the dogs are so low in the popularity charts that they hardly rate at all. Whether these two facts are connected is a matter of conjecture.

The Field Spaniel's troubles really started when it split off from what we know today as the COCKER SPANIEL. The Cocker improved. It became shorter, more compact and robust. With Fields, however, the emphasis on low, long dogs became exaggerated. At the end of the last century exhibitors, inevitably blamed for ruining the breed, were certainly to be seen showing their dogs in stretched-out condition, and judges awarded bonus points for extra length.

Nineteenth century descriptions of the breed read as follows: 'Heavy-headed, crooked-fronted, sluggish and crocodile-like.' 'German sausage.' 'Caterpillars.' One writer went so far as to suggest that they should have been provided with an extra set of legs to keep their stomachs off the ground!

Much of this was justified. Pictures of some prize-winning spaniels at the turn of the century, for example, *Champion Solus*, *Ch. Matford Daisy*, *Ace of Trumps*, and *Barum King*, show that these animals were more like heavily-built DACHSHUNDS than working spaniels.

But these excesses have passed, and for the last 50 years a much more upstanding and robust type of dog has been the ideal breeders have aimed for. One can also say that they have succeeded in their object. But prejudice dies hard. Additionally, as mentioned earlier, the Cocker Spaniel has improved and therefore tended to take away the original work of the Field Spaniel.

The result has been the alarming slump in the popularity of the Field to the point that they are in danger of fading entirely from the scene. While this view may distress lovers of the breed, it is an undeniable fact that British registrations during the sixties averaged only ten

a year which is a mere couple of litters. In America it is unusual for even one to be registered.

Essentials of the breed: The skull should be well developed with a distinct occiput, the head long and lean with good length of muzzle. Eyes: small and either dark hazel, brown or nearly black. Ears: moderately long and wide and well feathered. Shoulders should slope well back and forelegs be of good length. The body must be of moderate length, well ribbed up and never slack. The hindquarters, strong and muscular. Feet: not too small, round and with strong pads. Tail: set on and carried low. Coat: flat or slightly waved, dense enough to resist wet weather and not too short; silky, glossy but without curliness. Abundant feather on chest, under belly and behind the legs. The Field Spaniel should always be self-coloured – that is black, liver, mahogany red, roan or any one of these colours with tan over the eyes, on cheeks, feet and pasterns. Weight from 35 to 50 lb. Height: about 18 inches at the shoulder.

Below A brace of Field Spaniels. Greatly overshadowed by Cocker Spaniels, they are now the rarest of the spaniel breeds.

Field Trials – American Field trials constitute the largest single activity in American dogdom. Although no exact breakdown can be given, at least 5,500 field trials are given annually. These range from unlicensed and unsanctioned 'coon dog chases' to championship trials under rigid rules. Sled dog races are not considered field trials, and are treated separately.

The following figures for major governing organizations will give some idea of the scope of field trial activity. In 1969, more than 3,000 sanctioned and licensed field trials were given under American KENNEL CLUB supervision. American field trials for pointers and setters totalled more than 700. United Kennel Club licensed 500 championship night trials for Coonhounds. The International Fox Hunters Stud Book reports some 300 American Foxhound trials. In addition to these, there are hundreds of UKC water races for Coonhounds; perhaps 500 'coon-chases' – daytime trials for both registered and mongrel stock; and probably 200 unrecognized Foxhound trials.

American Kennel Club annual events include 15 championship trials for Bassets; 412 for Beagles; two for Dachshunds; 255 for pointing breeds; 135 for retrievers; and 34 for spaniels. In addition, the AKC supervises about 2,400 sanctioned trials annually. Probably as many more unsanctioned, and so unrecorded, trials are given.

The International Fox Hunters Stud Book registered 4,393 American Foxhounds and 2,973 litters in 1969. Most of these dogs will grow up to chase fox, and about half of them will compete in trials. The Florida, Georgia, and Virginia state trials alone will average 500 starters each, and the national championship 300 to 450. Many of these trials last five full days.

Numbers are painted on the sides of all competing Foxhounds. They are lined up at daylight and cast off. The judges are mounted on horses, and must ride until the completion of the day's work. Dogs are judged on hunting, trailing, speed and drive, and endurance. They are faulted for 'babbling' – opening up, or giving tongue, when not on scent – for loafing, leaving the line, etc. Dogs giving poor performances are dropped at the end of each day.

Beagles, Bassets, and Dachshunds compete by starting and trailing cottontail rabbits. In Beagle and Basset trials, the sexes are divided, and Beagles are also divided by size – 13 inches and 15 inches. As many as 250 Beagles often compete at a single trial. The Beagles run in braces, except when the quarry is the hare, when the dogs compete in packs. Beagles are judged on speed, accuracy of trailing, endurance, and style. Demerits are given for babbling, running mute, pottering, leaving checks, racing, and running ghost trails. Bassets and Dachshunds are judged similarly.

Pointers and setters, which run under the minimum rules of the Amateur Field Trial Clubs of America and American Field supervision, compete in braces. Heats vary in length from 20 minutes for puppies, half an hour at most events, and up to three hours in championship stakes. Courses at non-championship events are usually circular. It may require 20 minutes for the judges to walk their horses around the 'back course'. The dogs

are then allowed 10 minutes in the 'bird field'. Here birds have been 'planted

The dogs must find, point, and remain steady to flush and pistol shot. Bracemates, if they come up, must honour the point. At championship events, continuous courses are used, and the dogs work on native game.

Brittany Spaniels normally follow the above procedure. But the German pointing breeds work on game, usually pheasants, which must be shot by official gunners. The dogs must mark the fall and then retrieve to hand.

Retrievers are tested upon ducks and pheasants, both on land and in the water. Competition is so great that nearly impossible tasks are set for the dogs. Each dog is often required to make three or four retrieves in one test. They may be asked to make a 'blind retrieve', that is, they will have to take directions to a dead bird which they have not seen, and which has been placed more than 100 yards away. In severe tests, only a single directional signal is given. If further directions have to be given, the dog is faulted.

At night Coonhound championship trials, the dogs are sent into unfamiliar woods and swamps to locate

Below Field trials. Under the rules of some authorities field trials are arranged and birds are 'planted' to test the dogs. Under others, trials are run as a day's shooting and are in no way artificial.

and 'tree' live wild raccoons. Probably no sport is so rugged for dogs, owners, and judges. Dogs are judged on a variety of points, and demerits are also given. Daytime water races are also licensed by the United Kennel Club. In these, a raccoon is caged upon a small raft. Dogs are lined up on the stream bank and, upon a signal, are released. The raft is drawn to the far bank. The raccoon is then walked ashore and is sent up a tree. The first dog to reach the tree and give tongue while leaping up the trunk is the winner. Sometimes, the winner is the first dog to enter a painted circle. Thousands of people attend such races, and betting upon them is heavy.

Coon *chases* are daytime events in which mongrels as well as purebreds and registered dogs compete. The scent is laid by dragging a bag containing raccoon faeces. The finish of the trail may be made by a raccoon on a leash, which is then sent up a tree. At Kenton, Ohio, as many as 1,300 dogs have competed and $40,000 in prize money has been awarded. These events are unlicensed and betting upon them is amazingly intense.

The American and English Cocker Spaniels have virtually disappeared from the American field trial scene. Welsh Springer Spaniels do not compete. So spaniel trials are almost exclusively for English Springer Spaniels. These dogs hunt on parallel courses at distances usually not greater than 35 to 40 yards from their handlers. Only pheasants, 'planted' on the course ahead of the dogs, are hunted.

When a pheasant is flushed, the dog must drop. Official gunners shoot the pheasant. The dog must remain steady to shot, and the dog on the other course must honour by dropping, or sitting. Upon command, the dog which flushed the pheasant must retrieve it to hand.

Field Trials (Gundogs) - British Field trials in Britain are competitions which take place in the field, on live wild game, fur and feather, under shooting conditions. They are recognized by the KENNEL CLUB, run on strict rules; the procedure, type of ground and game, time of year and working conditions being appropriate to the breed of gundog competing. The trial is run as a day's shooting and is in no way artificial. The birds are wild and free while the dogs are run under normal

working conditions. Tests are confined to situations likely to be encountered in a normal day's shooting. No bird is allowed to be handled, released or 'planted' in any way. They are 'walked up' or 'hunted up' by either dogs or beaters as is appropriate to the type of trial.

Field trials are divided into three main sections, one with a sub-section. (i) Pointers and Setters, with a sub-section for German Short-haired Pointers and other similar all-purpose breeds which have trials of their own, (ii) Retrievers, and (iii) Spaniels.

All these different sections perform separate functions. Their trials are run separately, each under Kennel Club rules, but in accordance with the appropriate procedure.

Pointers and Setters: The orthodox work of these dogs is to quarter the ground widely, to locate birds by their body scent, to lead the 'gun' up to the birds without flushing them, and to drop so that they are out of the way of the gun when the bird rises. When the shot is fired the dog's work is finished. It remains down until its handler picks it up, that is puts it on the lead. It is *NOT* its job to retrieve, a task left to retrievers and spaniels. The pointer or setter is then led away to start quartering its ground afresh.

Since retrieving is unnecessary, Pointer and Setter Trials are run on live birds outside the Shooting season. Blank shot is used and the birds unharmed. These trials take place from late March to late April on the paired partridges in the short spring wheat, and from late July to 12th August on the young grouse on the moors. In late August, grouse are actually shot over the dogs, which still do not retrieve, and in September partridges are shot on the stubbles, after the corn harvest. The trial season ends with Pointer and Setter Championship Stakes, run on either grouse or partridges. Pheasants are not used and 'fur' is an accidental interruption to the proceedings, dealt with as and when it occurs.

Trials are divided in Stakes of Puppy, Novice or Open. Other gradings such as Non-Winners or All-aged Stakes are run according to the regulations.

A 'draw' is made prior to the stake, pairing the dogs into braces of any breed eligible for entry in that stake, controlled by two handlers and belonging to different owners. There are two judges and one official 'gun', or sometimes two, if birds are actually shot.

These officials accompany the handlers who, upon a signal, slip their dogs, one to the right, the other to the left. The two dogs quarter the ground upwind – or, if very experienced, on a side wind – the former being preferable if the wind is right for the ground.

Heads up, they gallop in wide sweeps, out to each flank of the line; then each dog turns outwards and gallops to the opposite flank. Thus the whole beat is quartered by the dogs from flank to flank, passing always in front of the line of judges, guns and handlers, forward progress being made with each outward turn so that fresh ground is continually hunted.

When a dog scents live game ahead, it freezes into a point. Its handler claims the point by raising his hand.

Handler, gun and judge then go forward to take the point. Meanwhile the other dog has come galloping into sight of the pointing dog. This second dog must immediately 'back' the pointing dog, that is it 'points the dog on point'. It must not creep forward and try itself to steal the point. If it does not 'back' naturally, it is stopped by its handler and made to sit and watch the work of the first dog. The second judge stays with the 'backing' dog but watches the behaviour of both.

The first dog creeps up to the birds, accompanied by the handler and gun. When the birds lose their nerve and fly, the dog 'drops to wing' and the gun is fired. Both dogs are then started on a fresh beat, two chances at birds normally being given to each brace on the card in the first round.

After a judges' conference certain dogs are selected to go forward to the second round, the draw being made afresh. This procedure continues until the judges have reached their final decision, when the awards of prizes, usually 1st, 2nd, 3rd and Reserve are announced. Certificates of Merit are given to all deserving dogs which have not won a prize. This applies to trials for all breeds, as does the Kennel Club directive that judges must withhold any prizes or awards they do not think are deserved.

This arrangement permits good dogs who have been beaten by better or luckier dogs to receive some recognition, while denying inferior dogs major awards which might otherwise be won because they ran in a very poor field.

German Short-haired Pointers etc.: In trials for general-purpose pointer/retriever breeds the dogs have to retrieve, as well as point the game. Pheasants are used, as well as all other types of game, fur or feather. The dogs find the live, unshot game and point it, often in woodland, scrub or deep roots. The game is shot, and at the judge's discretion, the dog retrieves.

As this type of work is unusual in Britain, these continental type dogs have their own trials under Kennel Club rules, and are ineligible for competition in orthodox Pointer or Retriever Trials.

Retrievers: Retriever trials are always held in the shooting season, live wild game in its natural habitat being shot, as on an ordinary day's shooting. The Stakes are graded as in Pointer Trials into Novice, Open, and Puppy, the numbers competing varying according to the type of stake and the capacity of the ground.

Novice and One Day Open Stakes are for from 12 to 15 dogs, 24 dogs running in the two-day Open Stakes.

There are either three or four judges, procedures varying slightly according to the number of judges and dogs entered. For three judges, six dogs go into the line at once, two under each judge; if four judges, they judge in pairs taking four dogs only into the line. Under the three-judge system, every dog must be seen by two judges unless discarded for a cardinal fault. With four judges, each dog is seen by a pair of judges working together who may discard a poor performer forthwith. Cardinal sins earning immediate disqualification are

(i) running in, (ii) being out of control, (iii) whining or barking in the line, (iv) failing to enter water on command and (v) being hard-mouthed. (All three judges must agree that game is damaged and examination by the handler is allowed before a dog is disqualified for this.)

The retriever is required to walk quietly and freely to heel, that is without wearing a 'slip'. Alternatively it must sit quietly in a stand or butt until the birds are flushed by the beaters and shot. When one of 'his' two guns have downed a bird a judge may tell one of the two handlers to send his dog. The dog, who should already have marked the fall, goes out and either finds and picks up, or hunts the line where the bird has run. In either case, the bird should ultimately be picked up tenderly and retrieved at a gallop right into the handler's palm. The quicker a wounded bird is humanely despatched the better so retrievers are not required to 'sit' in front of the handler. Seconds count and frills are dispensed with. Style, speed and tender delivery to hand are essential. Whenever possible the dogs are tried in water. Dogs cannot be awarded the title of Field Trial Champion (F.T.Ch.) until they have proved they will sit quietly without whining in a 'drive'.

The card is worked through twice, so that every dog has been seen by two judges. When not working they have to watch other dogs retrieving without running in or interfering. After conferring, the judges select those dogs they wish to see again. At this stage, all the judges work together, comparing notes, ultimately reaching a final decision when the prizes and Certificates of Merit are awarded.

The whole Trial is always run on shot game and dogs never have to hunt up unshot game to the gun.

Spaniels: Spaniels are expected to hunt and quest through thick covert for all types of fur and feather, close to their handler. They search every tuft of grass or bramble bush until they locate game when they flush it to the gun. They then sit and wait until commanded to retrieve. If the gun misses they are set hunting again.

Two judges are used and two dogs at a time go into the line. One judge takes the odd numbers, the other the even until all dogs have been seen. The procedure is then reversed, each judge taking dogs he has not already seen. This completed, the judges confer and select those dogs they wish to see again.

Upon reaching a final decision, the awards are announced. If the judges cannot agree, a previously nominated referee has a casting vote.

As in Retriever Trials, game is always shot, dogs must not run in and game must be retrieved tenderly. Whether spaniels who whine or bark should be penalized as a retriever would be is a matter currently under review by the Kennel Club.

Field Trial Champion: in all trials, the title of Field Trial Champion (F.T.Ch.) is officially awarded to a dog who has won a given number of Open Stakes, the qualification varying for each section. A Championship Stake for winners is held annually for each section, the winner automatically becoming a F.T.Ch. The qualification for entry in this Stake varies according to the breed.

Fights see Dog Fights.

Fila Brasileiro The Fila Brasileiro is a breed native to Brazil. According to tradition, it is a descendant of dogs brought to the New World by the discoverers and conquerors. These dogs joined the soldiers in battle, and were trained to attack and kill the Indians. When in 1820 Brazil gained independence, history tells of these dogs used in the pursuit and capture of run-away slaves from farms in the states of Sao Paulo and Minas Gerais.

It is believed that the Portugese originally imported them to protect their homes in the new land. They were then (1500) known as 'dogs of Acores'. However the settlers also brought English MASTIFFS, BLOODHOUNDS and BULLDOGS; all were used for slave and cattle control. The crossing of these dogs developed a definite type and eventually a standard was devised.

From the Bulldog, the Fila has its temperament – gentle with members of the owner's family, but at times violent with strangers – the variety of colours permissible, and the back legs which are taller and less strong than the front legs. The Bloodhound influence shows especially in the loose skin, the marked occiput and the exceptional sense of smell.

Until about 1940, the breed was close to extinction. Since then, Brazilian breeders have joined to save and improve the remaining stock. In 1954, the Fila was recognized by the Brazilian Kennel Club. A club for the breed has formed which hopes to persuade all Brazilian Embassies to own a Fila Brasileiro. Used as a guard dog, this breed is, however, reputedly a dangerous adversary.

Below Fila Brasileiro.

Essentials of the breed: Due to its temperament, the Fila Brasileiro rarely permits a judge to touch it. This should not be considered a fault. The skin is thick and loose, especially on the neck and trunk, with short, thick coat. All colours and combinations of colours are permissible, but fawns and brindles seem to predominate. The head is of Mastiff type, and is large and heavy in relation to the body, with a square and massive aspect. Skull: big, narrowing at the beginning of muzzle. Eyes: of medium size, slightly slanted, set well apart. Ears: big in a V-form. Dropped ears are allowed but they must fall on each side of the cheek.

Body: strong. Ribs: well-arched and chest wide and deep. Tail: large at root, narrowing rapidly. Height: 28 to 30 inches on average.

Filariasis, Canine This is a disease caused by thread-like worms which invade the right ventricle and adjacent tissues of the heart. Two species are known in the United States, but one appears to cause the dog little inconvenience. The other, *Dirofilaria immitis,* causes the death of thousands of dogs annually. *D. immitis* is common on the Atlantic seaboard, in the deep South, and in the Caribbean Islands. It is less well known in the northern United States, but it takes a terrific toll of dogs in Japan, and other Asian countries.

The life cycle of the worm is complex. The female worm hatches eggs in her uterus. The offspring, called microfilariae, then invade the blood stream of the dog. They remain there for a year, and when the dog is bitten by a mosquito, they get ingested into the body of the mosquito. Here they grow for about two weeks, and migrate back to the proboscis of the mosquito host. They return to a dog when the mosquito feeds upon one. Two to four months later, they move to the heart, but it takes them another four months to mature completely.

Experienced veterinarians normally treat only carefully selected cases. Of these, two to five per cent die during treatment. Dogs which are not otherwise in good condition, and especially old dogs, are poor treatment risks. As a rule, they will live longer with the worms than if treated. Treatment consists of drugs to kill the adult worms, and others to kill the microfilariae. Some veterinarians feel that, if they live in infested areas, dogs should be given preventive treatment once or twice a year with the therapeutic drugs. Open heart surgery to remove the worms is successful in some cases. To prevent infestation, dogs should be kept in screened areas during the hours when mosquitoes are feeding, in late afternoon, at night, and in the early morning. Repellents can be used about the face of the dogs where the hair is short. After therapeutic drug treatment, dogs should be kept quiet for about three weeks. Hunting dogs should not be allowed to work for about four months.

Finnish Kennel Club see Kennel Club, Scandinavian Kennel Union.

Finnish Spitz In Britain the Finnish Spitz is relatively little known. Outside the United Kingdom (apart from Finland) it is even less known. And in Finland it is so well known that the practical Finns do not see any necessity to write about it.

The *Suomenpystykorva,* or Finnish Spitz in English, is far and away the most popular Finnish breed. Any walk in town or country reveals dozens of them. They play in the parks, peer from suburban windows and ride in smart cars.

More important, one sees them in farms and small holdings where they still work. Equally revealing is the fact that in the remote country districts one sees a cross-bred type of Finnish Spitz on every side. Most make no pretensions to purity. But their presence does suggest that the type is a natural product of the land in the same way that a short-legged cross-bred type of terrier is indigenous to Britain.

Legend says they have been around for thousands of years. Their ancestors lived in primeval forests helping the small clans of Finnish hunters, tracking any animals that moved, from bears down to squirrels. Even today they work with little training, although they have been weaned away from the four-footed beasts and towards birds, principally wood grouse.

They are regularly tested at field trials. They range well in front of the huntsmen and force the birds up to seek sanctuary in trees. Their ringing bark soon calls their master to the scene. And for good measure they freeze into a rigid point marking the bird's position.

Unfortunately, in the nineteenth century the breed was repeatedly crossed with other Scandinavian breeds until both type and working qualities faded. When at the beginning of this century the Finns appreciated the position, few pure specimens remained. So expeditions into the frozen north of Lapland were organized in search of original specimens. Subsequently the dog which came in from the cold has fared better. The Finnish Kennel Club instituted a breed register and maintained detailed pedigrees

In 1927 Sir Edward Chichester became interested. He spent months in search of a good brace and brought them to England. By 1935 the Kennel Club had also accepted them officially. They have made slow progress even in these boom days for pedigreed dogs; fewer than 100 are registered annually.

Why the Finnish Spitz misses popularity is a puzzle. It is small enough for modern houses, distinctive in appearance and both friendly and intelligent.

Essentials of the breed: In general appearance the body is almost square, and eyes, ears and tail indicate liveliness. The head is medium-sized and clean-cut, forehead slightly arched, stop pronounced. Muzzle: narrow and clean-cut. Nose: black. Eyes are medium-sized, lively and preferably dark. Ears: cocked, sharply pointed, fine in texture and mobile. Body – back: straight and strong; chest deep; belly slightly drawn up. Hindquarters: strong, hocks comparatively straight. The tail is curved forward, downward and backward, then pressing down against the thigh.

Coat on the head and legs short and close, on body longish, semi-erect or erect, and stiffer on the neck and back. On the shoulders particularly in males, the hair should be considerably longer and more coarse.

Above Finnish Spitz. Ch. Cullabine Glenda.

Colour: reddish-brown or yellowish-red, preferably bright but lighter on cheeks, under the muzzle, on the breast, inside the legs, at the back of thighs and under tail.

Size: Dog 17½ inches to 20 inches. Bitches: 15½ inches to 18 inches.

See colour plate p. 191.

Fire Precautions Fire precautions for the kennel should be no different than those for the home. However, kennels are often makeshift structures built by owners rather than by skilled builders, and may contain defective wiring for light and heat. Others have improperly vented gas stoves which represent a constant hazard. No year passes without reports of entire kennels of dogs being asphyxiated from gas fumes, or being destroyed in kennel fires. When these kennels have been attached to homes, the homes too have sometimes been destroyed.

Since dogs chew electrical fixtures, these must be adequately protected in the kennel. Heating units, electrical and otherwise, should be installed by professionals, and then should be inspected and passed by certified inspectors.

Most kennels have running water. It is therefore usually possible to install a hose which will have sufficient pressure to spray water in case of fire into every part of the kennel. Since kennels normally lack the inside finish of homes, the water spray offers the greatest protection while creating the smallest damage. A water connection to the outside will make it possible to spray the outside walls and roof. If a kennel is to be attached to the home, a fire wall and door give added protection to both home and kennel.

Plastic pails make possible added fire protection. Pails of water can be hung or placed in strategic areas of the kennel. It is only necessary to keep them filled with water. A handy pail of water doused instantly upon the start of a fire can be the difference between a scare and a disaster.

Fire extinguishers must be used carefully in a kennel. Because the dogs are low to the ground, the fumes pose a threat to them. If time permits, the dogs should be removed from the building. But this requires valuable time. And moreover, the opening of kennel exits may supply the smouldering fire with the oxygen it needs to burst out of control. Because the dogs are closer to the floor, smoke inhalation poses less danger to them than to the people fighting the fire.

First Aid see Accidents; Bandaging; Respiration; Tourniquets.

Fits When bodily balances are upset, fits or convulsions may occur. Severe vomiting or prolonged panting can produce a water imbalance which may result in convulsions. There is little tolerance in the salt balance of puppies and an imbalance may throw the puppy into a fit. Teething and severe worm infestations may cause running fits in puppies.

A careful examination by a veterinarian should be made to determine the cause. Meanwhile, it is essential to allow the dog to rest and to recuperate from the convulsion. The owner must remain calm, and he must also reassure his neighbours. Fits in dogs often cause an unreasoning fear in people. And in areas where RABIES is known to exist, or is suspected of existing, ignorant people are quite apt to claim that the unfortunate dog has rabies. Running fits, due to worms, are often mistaken for rabies. Convulsions caused by lead poisoning simulate rabies. LIVER is rich in lead, and the excessive feeding of liver to both cats and dogs has been blamed for such rabies-like convulsions. Frightened owners or neighbours may kill the dog, or may call police who will do so. A veterinarian should always be consulted. See EPILEPSY.

Flag Tail carried high and gaily. A term used in bird dog field trials.

Flank Muscle area between the ribs and hips.

Flare A blaze which is wider at the top of the skull than between the eyes.

Flat Bone Leg bone which is flattened rather than rounded.

Flat-Coated Retriever It is useless to shoot game unless you can find it after it has been killed, or even more important, after it has been wounded, and there-

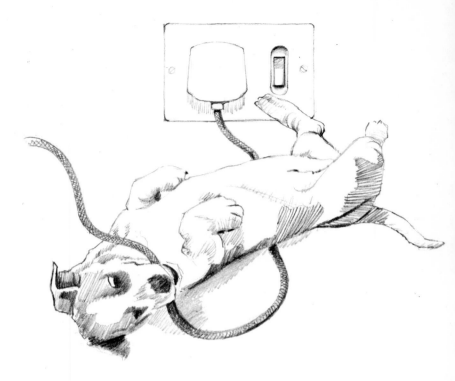

fore facing a possibly lingering death. When this fact had been appreciated by the sportsmen of more than a century ago they were no longer quite as satisfied with their 'springing' type dogs, whose principal interest was to 'spring' or flush the birds into the air so that they could be shot. Few, if any, of the setters and Pointers of that day were interested in retrieving the game for their master.

Clearly a specialist (a dog who would concentrate on retrieving) was called for. One of the early ones to present itself was the Flat-coated Retriever, or more correctly the Wavy-coated Retriever, as it was originally known.

The expression 'presented itself' is used advisedly. The point is that nobody knows how the first recorded specimens were evolved. There appeared at Birmingham (England) Dog Show in 1860, the dog *Wyndham* and the owner Mr. R. Braisford.

Naturally a representative of an unknown breed excited interest, particularly among shooting men. They questioned the owner on the dog's background but appear to have elicited very little precise information. They were left to form their own conclusions. Those conclusions, which they recorded, are still accepted as the most likely and probable to this day. They were that the foundation stock of this specimen was principally the Lesser Newfoundland dog and its offshoots which were the LABRADOR and CHESAPEAKE BAY RETRIEVERS.

They came in on the fishing boats which worked between St. Johns and the British ports. Perhaps they were originally accepted as mere guard dogs. But gamekeepers soon found a new use for them.

As an aside it should be noted that an essentially British breed, and one which even today is not in the first hundred most popular breeds in the United States,

Above Fire precautions. Accessible electrical fixtures are often irresistible to dogs who chew them with disastrous results.

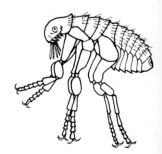

Above Fleas. The dog flea, *Ctenocephalides canis*.

is founded on stock from the North American continent! Of course, England added something. Probably it was a generous dose of setter with a dash of Pointer.

Then long after the breed was completely established came a near disastrous adventure. Some breeders decided the Flat Coat's jaws were too short to carry a hare. Almost unbelievably they introduced BORZOI blood. Admittedly they got long heads. But they also got a totally foreign type. Many years of careful breeding were necessary to eliminate the effects of this unwarranted experiment.

Even before this however the writing was on the wall. The Labrador and Golden Retrievers had arrived and had swept all before them. Despite this the Flat Coats staged a recovery in 1932 when over 100 of them were exhibited at CRUFT'S SHOW. This spurt was not sustained. Numbers dropped steadily until the nineteen sixties, when fortunately a greater interest was shown in the breed, at least in England. Currently, annual registrations in Britain are over 200.

Essentials of the breed: The head should be long, the skull flat and moderately broad with a slight stop between the eyes. Jaws should be long and strong. Eyes: of medium size, dark brown or hazel. Ears should be small and carried close to the side of the head.

The neck should be long, free from throatiness, and obliquely placed in shoulders. The chest should be deep and fairly broad, with a well-defined brisket. The forelegs: perfectly straight, with bone of good quality, legs should be well feathered.

The fore-ribs should be fairly flat, showing a gradual spring and well-arched in the centre of the body, but rather lighter towards the quarters. The back: short, square and well ribbed up.

Hindquarters should be muscular and the dog must neither be cow-hocked nor move too widely but must stand and move true all round. Legs should be well feathered. Feet: round and strong with toes close and well-arched. Tail: short, straight, carried gaily but not above the level of the back. Coat: dense, of fine quality and flat. Colours: black or liver. Weight: between 60 and 70 lb.
See colour plate p. 82.

Flat-Sided Said of dogs without adequate spring of ribs.

Fleas The dog flea is known scientifically as *Ctenocephalides canis*. It is one of the least specialized of fleas in that, if it cannot find a dog to feed upon, it will quite cheerfully jump upon a cat or a human being. Its order of preference for people is as follows: babies, youngsters, women, and finally, men.

The dog flea is ideally suited for life on dogs. It has a wedge-shaped head, a narrow but tall body, and it is higher in the rear than at the head end. This streamlining permits it to scurry rapidly between hairs. Moreover, there are no divisions between head and thorax, and thorax and abdomen as in most insects. Its hard shell is made up of overlapping segments, with backward projecting bristles. These help in the streamlining process. But they also help the flea to maintain position, as do the claws at the end of its six feet, a spiny head comb, and leg bristles. The mouth has three hypodermic needle-like parts for piercing and sucking blood. There

Below Flat-Coated Retrievers: Black Lion Rex of Ibaden, Ch. Flash of Ibaden, and Ch. Lili Marlene.

is no nose: the flea simply breathes through a pair of aerating vents in each of its ten body segments.

The male flea is smaller than the female. It is believed that, comparatively, it has the largest, and certainly the most remarkable, penis in the entire animal world. In fact, it is two. They are wrapped about each other like twining snakes. Blood is required by both sexes before mating. Copulation lasts from three to nine hours.

The female flea finds a suitable place to lay her eggs – in floor cracks, under the edges of rugs, under wall boards. Her selection of a spot is based upon privacy, and the presence of bits of food. But she – and her mate – deposit quantities of dried, undigested blood for the larvae which will hatch from the eggs. The eggs are about half a millimetre long and they hatch in two to twelve days, depending upon humidity and warmth, both of which speed up the process.

The tiny larval fleas are threadlike worms about a millimetre long. They are both blind and legless, but they grow to five millimetres in length in five to twelve days. They then double into a U-shape and spin a silky cocoon about themselves. This is the pupal form. It lasts seven to fourteen days, during which the adult flea is developed.

The flea does not hatch as soon as it reaches maturity within the cocoon – it may wait as long as a year before breaking out. What stimulates it to hatch is a vibration caused by an approaching animal, or by a human footstep. When it does break out, it is a fully adult, completely active flea which can jump as high as eighteen inches. And this it does immediately – if not upon a passing meal, then upon the wall, a chair leg, or a bush near which an animal is likely to pass.

Fleacides come in various forms. The most common is flea powder. But there are dips, aerosol sprays, and flea soaps. The powder form is the one used most commonly. Since fleas tend to migrate to the head, neck, and ears of the dog, powder dusted to the skin in these areas will usually kill all fleas.

Fleas appear to have some method of communication. A few fleas may live on each of a group of dogs. But if one dog becomes ill, the fleas on the other dogs are somehow notified. They then leave the healthy dogs and migrate to the sick one. Sick dogs, therefore, should be dusted over the entire body to prevent such attacks. This should not be done, however, unless the presence of fleas is detected upon the sick dog.

Under normal conditions, once or twice a week dusting during warm weather will completely control fleas, even in tropical and subtropical areas. If homes become infested, families tend to banish the dog. This is wrong, since many of the fleas would hop onto the dog instead of onto the baby.

Similarly, people who dispose of a dog – or cat – may face a severe infestation. For the adult fleas will have no animal upon which to hop, and the population which was kept low by occasional treatment of the dog, will have grown into a swarm.

The home can be treated as follows. The dog should be dusted over the entire body. Its bedding and any chairs in which it may have slept should be treated. An aerosol insecticide is excellent for this. Then, each room in the house should be treated separately. The spray can be directed along the edges of carpets, along wall boards, and not more than two feet up on walls. Chair and table legs should be sprayed. The room should be closed for at least an hour to allow the mist to settle. Since the spray mist may not kill the eggs or the pupae, treatments should be repeated at ten day intervals for a month to six weeks.

Dog fleas do not normally carry disease from dogs to people.

Flews Pendulous upper lips, especially at the corners.

Flies Stable and horse flies attack the ears of dogs, and sometimes body sores. Once blood has been drawn, these flies appear to communicate the good news to others. They come in droves and attack with savagery. These flies may appear in hordes in a particular area one year, then may not reappear for several years. Meanwhile, they will be attacking in other locations. When dogs are so attacked, they must be kept indoors or in screened areas, until the ears have healed and new hair has been grown. Or their ears must be heavily bandaged. See BANDAGING. Fly repellents are of no value once blood has been drawn. The blood odour appears to be stronger than that of the repellent. Flies will also attack open wounds, in which they lay eggs.

Control of flies depends first upon sanitation. Runs should be cleaned and feeding utensils should be kept washed.

Many of the pressurized insect sprays have considerable killing power. But they are expensive and their knockdown ability is temporary. Also they should be used with great caution, as they contain the danger of lung irritation for both dog and sprayer. Alternative methods of control are baited fly traps, and sticky fly-paper: both are effective.

Flush To spring birds from cover.

Flying ears Ears that stand erect when they should be folded or semi-prick.

Foot Early speed. Said of coursing or racing GREY-HOUNDS.

Foreface see Muzzle.

Foster Mother A bitch used to nurse puppies not her own can be helpful in rearing a large family or when a bitch is unable to feed and rear her own puppies. Breeders who know that a bitch is unlikely to rear a litter satisfactorily will make arrangements to mate another bitch, even a mongrel, at the same time so that she can help with the rearing of the puppies. This is particularly so when the breeder is anxious to preserve a bitch's bloodline. Valuable puppies are worth saving and bottle rearing is never as good as a foster mother. The work of bottle rearing is continuous. It seems endless and is often fruitless.

The puppies should be taken with a minimum of fuss

Colour plate Saluki. Ch. Alexandr of Daxlore.

(Continued on p. 193)

Left Afghan Hound.
Koolaba Matan.

Top right Deerhounds, Scottish.
Uplands Kyrrie and Uplands
Morag.

Bottom right Rhodesian
Ridgebacks. Ch. Fundu of
Footpath and Fungulwe of
Footpath.

Top left Greyhound.
Ch. Shalfleet Starlight.

Bottom left Harriers and
Foxhounds. The Southpool
Harriers, Devon, England.

Top right Foxhound, English.
Ch. Baymor Whitebluff Dan.

Bottom right Foxhound,
American. Ch. Kentucky Lake
Admiral.

Left Bloodhound. Ch. Barsheen Rosita.
Top left Basset Hound. Ch. Glenhavens Lord Jack.
Top right Beagle. Devenridge Snoopy.
Above Otterhound. Caliph of Skye Top.

Top left French Bulldog.
Ch. Ralanda Ami Pierre.

Middle left Bulldog.
Bill Buggins of Petworth.

Bottom left Boston Terrier.
Ch. Tops Again's Duke of Regards.

Top right Tibetan Terrier.
Luneville Princess Peory.

Bottom right Dalmatian.
Duxfordham White Hope.

Top left Tibetan Spaniel.
Ch. Sivas Mesa.

Bottom left Chow Chow.
Ch. Eastward Liontamer of Elster.

Top right Shih Tzu.
Ban's Joss Hotei.

Middle right Pekingese.
Ch. Copplestone Pu-Zin.

Bottom right Lhasa Apsos.
Ch. Verles Nying-Chem-Po,
Ch. Verles Tom Tru and
Ch. Brackenbury Gunga Din of
Verles.

Left Basenji.
Ch. Sir Oracle of Horsley.

Top right Norwegian Elkhound.
Ch. Vin-Melca's Vagabond.

Below, near right Keeshond.
Ch. Flakkee Jackpot.

Below, middle right Finnish Spitz.
Ch. Cullabine Toni.

Below, far right Schipperke.
Ch. The Raven of Shippland.

Top left Dachshund, Long-haired. Ch. Karlew's Triton.
Left Dachshund, Wire-haired. Ch. Westphal's Shillalah.
Below, left Dachshund, Smooth Miniature. Valentine's Cricket.
Below, right Dachshund, Long-haired Miniature. Ch. Raleigh of Bowerbank.

Left Dachshund, Smooth (dappled). Ch. Karlstadt's Mahareshi.

(Continued from p. 176)

from the dam and as unobtrusively as possible. They should be smeared with some milk from the foster mother and gently slipped into her bed. Once she licks them and nuzzles them against her it can be safely assumed that she will look after them. The foster's puppies should be withdrawn from her and taken quickly out of sight and hearing of their mother. If the original dam is distraught because of the loss of her puppies, one or two of the foster mother's puppies can be given to her. The remainder must be destroyed immediately. The earlier the transfer can be done after a foster's whelping the easier it will be.

See ORPHAN PUPPIES.

Foul Colour A colour not desired, but permitted in a breed standard.

Foxhound, American Few, if any, dog breeds in the world can match the American Foxhounds in general ability. They have the stamina to run a trail for eight to twelve hours, remarkable noses for trailing the fox, and a high order of intelligence. In addition, they have an unique ability to find their way home – the 'homing instinct' as Foxhound breeders call it.

Hunting with Foxhounds in the American South is done in the following manner. Hunters will gather at night, usually on a hilltop, and the hounds will be cast out. The first hound to strike the trail of a fox will 'give tongue'. The listening men will be able to identify the hound by its voice.

Shortly, another hound may be heard. To the hunters, this will indicate that the second hound is challenging for the lead, or has already taken it. The hunters are able to identify their hounds as they take the lead or lose the trail.

In the Northern States, fox hunters often kill the fox when they can. But to Southern hunters, this is a fault: the fox lives to run again and again. The hunters become acquainted with the individual running habits of each fox. This adds greatly to their interest in the chase, and the hunters know when the fox has outwitted the dogs.

American Foxhounds may be taken far from their home grounds for a night chase. The best of them find their way home from twenty to thirty miles away. But in many cases, during an all night hunt, the hunters will place their coats or blankets on the ground at the spot where the dogs were cast off, and will then go to a hotel or motel to sleep. When they return, their hounds will be sleeping on their clothing.

Field trials for American Foxhounds were first held in November 1889 by the Brunswick Foxhound Club of Albany Hills, Maine. See FIELD TRIALS, AMERICAN. The American Foxhound was developed from diverse sources, although chiefly from English, French, and Irish hounds. Robert Brooke brought the first pack of English hounds to Maryland in 1650. These were black and tan, and they worked well enough on the quarry of the day, the rather slow, grey fox. This fox 'goes to earth' much sooner than does the red. Brooke's stock was famous for more than 100 years, and it became the foundation line for the Black and Tan Coonhound.

ight Foster mother. Bitches are sometimes used to rear valuable puppies whose own mothers are unable or unwilling to raise them. This bitch has extended her mothering to a member of the cat family – an orphan tiger cub.

Fox hunting, American style, experienced a revolution with the introduction from England of the red fox. This probably began in Virginia as early as 1730. However, the first recorded release was in Maryland in 1738. To meet the challenge of this faster, wily, all night runner, breeders tried many experiments. The successful ones included crossing in French and Irish blood. The former gave greater size and a more musical voice, and the latter, greater speed. Lord Fairfax, Thomas Walker, and George Washington were importers. The French general, the Marquis de Lafayette, sent General Washington some French staghounds in 1785. Washington described them as having 'voices like the bells of Moscow'.

A number of great strains have been developed. Most popular is the *Walker*, whose origins began about 1840. The strain was developed by Gen. George Paupin and John W. Walker. They used an English import, *Rifler*, and a famous hound named *Tennessee Lead* upon bitches of Virginia and Maryland background.

Col. Haiden Trigg of Glasgow, Kentucky, developed his own strain by crossing *Birdsong* and Walker hounds, and by the use of a famous hound named *July*. At the time, the Birdsong hounds were already well known, and included Irish hounds, one of which was July. Trigg eventually bought July, but by that time, the dog had already founded its own strain. This was during the American Civil War period of 1860 to 1865.

Essentials of the breed: American Foxhounds average 22 to 25 inches in height at the shoulder. They can be any colour, and they have a close, hard coat. They are somewhat more 'leggy' than the English Foxhound, and are less heavy in body.

The rather long skull is slightly domed at the occiput, and is broad. The muzzle is long and square. The ears are set at eye level and reach nearly to the tip of the nose. The throat is clean and clear of throatiness. The

Top left Foxhound, America
Kentucky Lake Big Red.
Bottom left Foxhound, Englis
'Pembroke'. It is many years sinc
a Foxhound was entered in a re
cognized dog show in Britain be
the breed is still well known ar
widely publicized because of i
association with fox hunting.

shoulders slope and are not 'loaded'. The back is of moderate length. The chest is deep rather than broad, and a 28-inch girth in a 23 inches tall hound is considered good. Soundness of legs and feet are required, but bone so heavy as to make the dog CLODDY in movement is not desired. The tail has a slight curve, but should not be carried squirrel fashion over the back. See colour plate p. 183.

Foxhound, English In a book about pet or companion dogs the Foxhound, known in America as the English Foxhound, would find no place. In a book about show dogs, it would hardly warrant more than a line and this is because although an occasional specimen is shown in the United States, it is many years since one

In the years that followed improvement was somewhat irregular, each huntsman following his own whims. However by 1800 there had come into being a number of large and standardized packs, the best known amongst them being 'Brocklesby'. There was also available at this point a considerable amount of breeding data and the careful records kept by the packs and since incorporated in the stud books issued by the Master of Foxhounds Association, enable us to trace the ancestry of Foxhounds with greater certainty than that of any other breed of dog in the world. Years of selective breeding had the expected effect. Type became firmly established. The dogs were bred for a particular task and the result was a hard, efficient animal, capable of fulfilling its functions and of breeding true to type.

elow Foxhound, English. London's nearest Foxhound pack, e Enfield Chase, sets off on its pening meet of the season. ome of the hounds seem to have ready picked up a scent.

appeared at any recognized show in the British Isles.

Even so, the Foxhound is one of the best known, one of the most publicized, frequently painted and photographed, and one of the most readily recognized of any of the breeds of dog known to man.

All of this publicity comes from its work in the field. Its major task in life is assistance to the sport of fox hunting to which many have deep-rooted objections. It must be accepted that no dog, be it the fighting-pit dog of days gone by, the coursing Greyhound, the Bulldog or the Foxhound, is responsible for the uses to which man puts it. The Foxhound is a dog, an impressive and noble one at that, and this alone entitles it to a place in this Encyclopedia. Even the word 'dog' used in connection with this animal may arouse fury in the minds of some foxhunting purists. Frequently they insist that the Foxhound should always be referred to as a hound and never as a dog. But Foxhounds are perfectly normal members of the canine family and therefore the appellation 'dog' must sometimes be used.

The Foxhound's history is long and can be traced back without difficulty to the thirteenth century, when organized fox-hunting became established. Previous to that time it had merely been considered a way of keeping down vermin and the fashionable pastime had always been stag-hunting. One of the first tasks therefore was producing a rather more lightly boned and speedy animal than the Saint Hubert-type hounds then available which were descendants of the dogs brought over by the Norman invaders to England.

Foremost amongst the requirements were a robust constitution, a keen nose, good voice, drive and enthusiasm, and, when needed, a turn of speed.

The colour is so well known that it has come to be called 'hound markings' when used to describe similar breeds. One other curious feature is the particularly straight foreleg with the tightly knuckled feet, the whole resembling a clenched fist at the end of a forearm.

Inevitably a dog with such a striking appearance has attracted many who feel that it would make a good pet. Some have tried the experiment, but it has rarely been found completely satisfactory. The PUPPY WALKING scheme, currently operated in Great Britain, highlights the disadvantages. When very young, the pack Foxhounds are separated and put into the homes of hunt supporters. They live normal, reasonable, happy lives and behave in exactly the same way as other domestic pets. However, they are only trainable up to a point and with maturity there frequently develops a streak of defiance plus a perfectly natural wander-lust. The reason is that they are pack animals; they have been bred and have lived in packs for many generations past, and in their hearts they want and need the discipline both of kennel life and the pack. Experience shows that few who have kept these young, charming and engaging puppies are really sorry to lose them when they go back to the packs at approximately one year of age.

Finally, mention must be made of their incredible hardness. While some packs are taken to the 'meet' in motor transport, just as many go there on their own four feet. This may mean an 'approach march' of ten or fifteen miles before the day starts. Then follows a full day's hunting when distances of fifty miles hard running are by no means unusual. Finally when the day is over, the hounds jog back again to the kennel which they left anything up to twelve hours earlier.

From which it will be seen that the principal requirements of the breed are good legs and feet and the heart of a lion.

Essentials of the breed: Head of good length and breadth with low set ears lying close to cheek, the neck is long and clean, slightly crested and tapering from shoulder to head. The shoulders should be long, well sloped and muscular. Chest: powerful and back ribs very deep. The back and loin muscular with completely level topline and the tail (stern) well set on, carried gaily but not curved over the back. Hindquarters must be strong and stifles not over-bent. Legs: absolutely straight, strong with ample bone, especially at the ankle. Knuckling over not desirable but feet should be round and cat-like with well developed knuckles. Colours are black, tan and white or any combination of these as well as pied – usually white with yellow or tan fleckings. See colour plates pp. 182, 183.

Fox Terrier, Smooth The Smooth Fox Terrier has always been a popular but never a fashionable breed. This needs some explanation. The 'Smooth', as it is usually referred to, has always been popular in the true sense of the word because most people like it. Even today, although its heyday has passed, it is the ideal in many a middle-aged man's heart.

But fashionable it has never been: never the choice of film starlets, never a 'regular' in the pages of the glossy magazines. It was, is and will remain a down-to-earth, hard-bitten terrier, born to a task and anxious to do it.

The breed started life in or near stables. The dog's job was to keep the vermin down, which was no hardship to it because it delights in killing rats. If it had to dig for them so much the better. It follows naturally that in time it began to be used by the huntsmen who wanted escaping foxes dug from their holes.

It is uncertain when it first acquired its name. It is a logical name. The dog is called a terrier because it goes to earth. It goes there in pursuit of the fox. And the adjective 'smooth' exists to distinguish it from its cousin who has a rough or wire-haired coat.

Originally the two types were bred together regardless of coat. Indeed a Smooth Fox Terrier called *Jock* was also the ancestor of all the great 'Wires' as the result of a mating to *Trap*, a bitch of unknown antecedents but of undisputed rough coat.

In 1876, three years after the English Kennel Club came into being, the Smooths were given a separate register. The men who drafted this standard were hunting men. They must however have had some literary merit because the 'blueprint' of the characteristics reads well to this day.

'*The dog must present a general gay, lively and active appearance, bone and strength in a small compass are essentials. Speed and endurance should be looked for as well as power and the symmetry of the Foxhound taken as a model. The Terrier . . . should stand like a well made hunter, covering a lot of ground yet with a short back. . . If a dog can gallop and stay, and follow its fox up a drain, it matters little what its weight is to a pound or so.'*

Herein lies the rub however. There is, and always has been, a tendency for Smooths to become larger. In the pursuit of long heads and necks, breeders invariably also introduce long backs and legs. All goes well for a year or so because the dogs in question are undoubtedly stylish. Then however the reaction sets in. 'These dogs are too big to go to ground', becomes the cry. A rapid adjustment follows. The dogs revert to their original comparatively small size weighing around 16 to 17 lb. Then once again somebody sets off in pursuit of the longer head and neck!

Despite the fact that to some these dogs appear 'plain'

Top Fox Terrier, Smooth. Chelsto Passaford Piper.

Above Fox Terrier, Wire-Haire Ch. Falstaff Lady Fayre.

they have always been favourites with exhibitors and have produced some of the biggest winning dogs of all time, particularly in America. They have also produced some surprisingly high prices. Even fifty years ago sums of up to £500 ($1,200) were being paid to British fanciers by Americans for champion Smooths.

The breed is not now as sought after as it was. In an age of exaggeration the simple and uncomplicated must suffer. Even so, there is no risk to the continued existence of the breed. It has always had its faithful supporters and has held a place of affection in people's hearts.

Essentials of the breed: These are in all the main requirements the same as for the FOX TERRIER, WIRE-HAIRED except that the coat should be straight, flat, smooth, hard and dense.
See colour plate p. 371.

Fox Terrier, Toy American dog fanciers began to breed a miniature, or toy variety, of the Smooth Fox Terrier about 1900. By 1915, they had reasonably standardized a smooth-coated toy dog of general Fox Terrier type. Breeders applied for recognition of the breed to the American Kennel Club, but their application was refused.

The group then turned to the United Kennel Club, a privately owned all-breed registration office in Kalamazoo, Michigan. The United Kennel Club felt that the toy dogs were sufficiently different from the standard size Fox Terriers to be worthy of separate breed status and this was granted.

Progress of the breed was slow. American dog shows were chiefly under the control of the American Kennel Club. This meant that the Toy Fox Terrier could not be exhibited. The breed therefore lacked the sales promotion which dog shows give to breeds which are exhibited.

The United Kennel Club then helped to organize the National Toy Fox Terrier Association, and it began to license bench shows for the breed. Now some twenty-five championship shows a year are held for the breed in many parts of America. The United Kennel Club does not publish registration figures for any breed, but it is estimated that between 20,000 and 25,000 are registered annually.

Essentials of the breed: The Toy Fox Terrier weighs between 3½ and 7 lb. Dogs weighing over 7 lb. are disqualified from the shows. The dogs are usually white with black, or black and tan markings. The ears are carried erect. The muzzle is narrow, but relatively long. The tail is docked fairly short, and is carried erect.
See colour plate p. 370.

Fox Terrier, Wire-Haired This breed has a name which distinguishes it from many others in that it tells almost all you need to know about the dog's appearance and background. It is, and always has been, a little dog with a wire or rough coat, used to go to earth in pursuit of the fox. Like most true terriers it was 'Made in Britain' and this despite the continental origin of its name.

A hundred and twenty years ago the sole virtue of the Fox Terrier was its courage when facing a fox underground. Colour meant little except that huntsmen preferred a white dog so that it should not be mistaken for the fox when it broke cover. Shape was not all that important as long as a dog was built to gallop, and coat so little regarded that the broken-coated and the smooth-coated Fox Terriers were frequently crossed.

Its ancestry was also comparatively unimportant because huntsmen who used terriers as a part of their fox hunting activities developed the strain which suited their country and inclinations, and added such dashes of outside blood as they thought fit without bothering to record the details.

Almost certainly Old English Rough Terriers were used and they in their turn were mixtures of early types of DACHSHUND and BEAGLES. STAFFORDSHIRE BULL TERRIER types were probably also used and this in time brought about the division between the two coats. From 1876 onwards separate registers were kept in England for the different coated varieties, but cross-breeding between them was still permitted and practised.

The Fox Terrier Club was formed in England at this time and one of its first tasks was to draw up a breed standard. Those old terrier men knew what was wanted for work. Straight legs, compact feet, a strong jaw, a short back, well-curved stifles and sloping shoulders. Much is modelled on the horse which the dog had to follow and which was, after all, near to hunting men's hearts.

They reserved their best, if simple, prose however for the section dealing with the general characteristics. This read: '*The terrier should be alert, quick of movement, keen of expression and on the tip toe of expectation at the slightest provocation. Character is imparted by the expression of the eyes, and by the carriage of ears and tail.*'

The Wire had arrived. And it had come to stay! Once a man, and it must be admitted it is more often a man than a woman, has taken this breed to his heart, it stays there through thick and thin, even when circumstances, or maybe changing fashions, prevail upon him to keep a different dog.

The one black spot in the breed's otherwise honour-

able history was associated with a burst of extreme popularity just after the First World War. For nearly a decade it was the most popular dog in Great Britain and during this time, not only is it generally admitted that its temperament deteriorated slightly, but a number of people who follow fashions slavishly found themselves owning a breed they did not understand and did not really get along with.

The Wire is for people who are connoisseurs. For people who like a dog to look and behave as if he is the king of the earth; a dog who dances instead of walking, a dog with a permanent expression of injured innocence but with the mind of a man who kissed the Blarney Stone!

Essentials of the breed: The dog should be balanced throughout. His legs carried straight forward while travelling, propulsive power being furnished by the hind legs. The top line of the skull should be almost flat, sloping slightly and gradually decreasing in width towards the eyes, with skull and foreface of equal length. The foreface should taper from eye to muzzle. Eyes should be dark, moderately small and full of life. Ears: small, V-shaped with the flaps neatly folded over and drooping forward close to the cheeks, the top line of the folded ear above the level of the skull. The neck must be clean, muscular and gracefully curved. Shoulders: long, well laid back, and sloping obliquely backwards. The back should be short and level, the loins muscular and slightly arched. The brisket should be deep, the front ribs moderately arched and the back ribs deep and well sprung. Hindquarters should be free from droop or crouch; the thighs long and powerful; the stifles well curved, hock joints well bent and near the ground. Feet: round and compact. Tail set on rather high and carried gaily but not curled. Coat, dense, wiry – like coconut matting – white should predominate: brindle, red, liver or slaty blue are objectionable. Otherwise colour is not of prime importance. Size: a dog around 15½ inches high and about 18 lb. in show condition, with bitches slightly less, is the ideal.
See colour plate p. 370.

Fractures A fracture is a break in a bone. It can occur in any bone of the body and the damage can take many forms. The usual cause is some form of violence. If the fracture occurs at the site of the violence, the fracture is called 'direct', but if the break is some distance from the place where the blow occurred, the fracture is termed 'indirect'.

Occasionally fractures occur through the force applied to a bone by the muscles acting on it. This is seen particularly in the racing GREYHOUND. Abnormal bone structure may lead to spontaneous fractures.

There are several types of fracture including:
Simple fracture is one where the broken ends of the bone do not penetrate the skin. Although this name is used it does not imply that all simple fractures are simple to repair.
Compound fracture is one where the skin is damaged and the bone is exposed to the air.
Complicated fractures are those that involve gross damage to other tissues as well as to the bone. Nerves,

blood vessels or joints may be involved, or organs such as lung, liver or brain damaged.
Greenstick fractures usually occur in young dogs. The bone is bent rather than completely broken.

In most cases, signs of fractures are obvious. There will be indications of pain, a disinclination to move, a change in shape of the area involved, with swelling and, in the compound fracture, signs of damage to the skin, etc.

However, in some instances, a dog will give little indication that anything is wrong. There may be only a reluctance to move and some restriction of the use of part of the body.

Treatment must be carried out by a veterinarian. This consists of an examination of the injury to determine the type of fracture, its position, and any other injuries. X-ray examination is used for this. X-ray pictures properly taken will always show a fracture, and are advisable whenever a doubt exists regarding the possibility of injury to a bone.

The fractured bone or bones are placed in their correct position and immobilized to allow repair to take place. This usually involves an ANAESTHETIC. The immobilization of the bone may involve external support using splints, plaster casts, etc; or may be internal, where metal pins, screws, plates or wires are attached to the bone to give support. In the more complex injury, combinations of these may be used.

Broken bones will usually heal, although the time for this repair varies considerably depending on the type of fracture, the age of the dog and on other injuries that may be present that could delay the healing process.

French Breeds France has produced and sponsored a number of breeds well known to the outside world. Principal amongst these are the BRITTANY SPANIEL, BASSET HOUND, FRENCH BULLDOG, PYRENEAN MOUNTAIN DOG (or Great Pyrenees), BRIARD, and others dealt with elsewhere in this volume. Additionally, France has produced a number of breeds which, although popular in the country, have made little impact outside.

The breeds are divided into four main classes. They are:
1. Guard and Utility or working dogs.
2. Hunting dogs.
3. Pointing dogs.
4. Companion or 'pleasure' dogs.

In group 1, mention must be made of the Dogue de Bordeaux, an enormous Mastiff-type beast, weighing something over 80 lb., and although vaguely reminiscent

Fox Terrier, Wire-Haired.
Left The debonair, exuberant and energetic 'live Wire' needs an appreciative – and tireless – owner.
Right 'The Terrier', an eighteenth century wood engraving from the school of Thomas Bewick, shows a possible ancestor of the Wire-Haired Fox Terrier.

of a Bulldog, it is larger, standing up to 24 inches high at the shoulder. Within this group there is also the Berger des Ardennes, which could be described as a second cousin to the Pyrenean Mountain Dog.

In the second group came the Chien de Gascogne, a possible descendant of the St. Hubert Hound which also produced the BLOODHOUND, and the Griffon Vendeen, a wire-haired dog of the Basset type.

There are numerous examples of dogs in the third group. The main breeds are the Braques, the Barbets, the Epagneuls, and also the Griffon, which should not be confused with the toy Brussels Griffon.

Best known of the companion dogs is the Charnique, a comparatively small type of GREYHOUND. Some might include the PAPILLON in this list, but apart from its name meaning 'Butterfly' in French, there is little with which to identify it as a French breed as distinct from a continental one.

French Bulldog If a smile is detected on a French Bulldog's face it could be caused by the silly arguments which raged about the breed when it first arrived in Britain in the closing years of the nineteenth century.

The BULLDOG was and always had been essentially British. It was a part of the old John Bull image, like the Union Jack and Britannia's trident. Other countries used its noble blood to infuse into other breeds some of its stamina: America in developing Boston Terriers is an example. Taking the name of Bulldog without so much as a 'do you mind', was quite another matter. Yet that is exactly what the French did. The full horror of their 'crime' was realized when fanciers took some into Britain in 1898 and attempted to show them under the name of French Bulldogs.

The Kennel newspapers of the day sizzled with indignation. 'We English', said one correspondent, 'have a traditional affection for our old national dog, and object to a little nondescript creature imported from abroad being styled French or otherwise.'

The reference to 'nondescript' was less than fair. So probably, although much more restrained, was a booklet entitled *The History of the French Bulldog* written by W. J. Stubbs in 1903. This stated: 'There appears to be no doubt that the French Bulldog originated in England and is an offshoot of the English Bulldog.'

Some doubt still remained, however, supported by a fully documented treatise from Mr. George R. Krehl which had about it the ring of truth. Briefly his suggestion was that the breed had been in existence in Spain for three hundred years. It was fashioned, as was the British Bulldog, to attack and bait bulls. Mr. Krehl produced a copy of an ancient bronze plaque dated 1625 bearing an unmistakable likeness to the head of a bulldog. This dog had 'bat ears' as does the 'Frenchie'; the British Bulldog has always had 'rose' ears. The plaque bore the inscription 'Dogue de Burgos, Espana 1625'. Burgos is the historic home of bullfighting.

From Spain it was a short step to France. In Bordeaux the dog was used to fight not bulls but donkeys. On to Paris, where as soon as it had become fashionable, efforts were made to bantamize it.

It was at this period that the British influence was felt. For a long time past efforts had been made to establish miniature Bulldogs. Apart from reducing size, little had been achieved. These dogs, somewhat optimistically called 'Toy Bulldogs', despite weights of 20 lb. were useful to the fashion conscious French. Some were imported, and they were used as out-crosses. This, one suspects, is substantially the true background of the breed. The next step took place in the United States.

This was the standardization and improvement of the 'bat ear', a dominant feature of the breed. The bright appearance of the dog with this distinctive feature, the alert disposition, the relatively small size and the advantage of newness made it a big favourite in America. By 1913 it had made history in mustering a total of 100 exhibits at WESTMINSTER DOG SHOW held in New York.

The 'Frenchie' has many advantages. It is small enough to get out of the way but big enough to look after itself. It is normally peaceful but alert enough to warn of strangers. It is strong and robust, yet with a modest appetite. It is short-coated and therefore easily groomed.

Essentials of the breed: The general appearance is of a sound, active, compactly built dog, with good bone and a short, smooth coat. Head: massive, square and broad. Skull: nearly flat, with domed forehead. Muzzle: broad, deep and laid back, nose and lips black. Well defined stop. Lower jaw should be deep, square, broad, slightly undershot and well turned up. Nose: extremely short, black and wide. Eyes: dark, round, set wide apart and down in the skull. 'Bat ears' of medium size, wide at the base, rounded at the top, set high; carried upright and parallel are an essential. Mouth: teeth sound and

Left French breeds: Bonnard's impression of French dogs published in *L' Excarmouche* in 1893.

Right French Bulldog. Ch. Chaseholme Mr. Chips.

regular but like the tongue not visible when mouth is closed. Neck: powerful, well arched and thick, but not too short. Forequarters – legs: set wide apart, straight boned, strong, muscular and short; body: short, cobby, muscular and well rounded, with deep wide brisket, roach back, strong, wide at the shoulders and narrowing at the loins. Feet should be small and compact. Tail: short, set low, thick at the root and tapering towards the tip. Coat of fine texture, smooth, short, and close. Permitted colours are brindle, white, pied and fawn. In Britain, the ideal weight is 28 lb. for dogs, 24 lb. for bitches. The American Kennel Club has two classes, a lightweight class under 22 lb., and a heavyweight class, over 22 lb. but under 28 lb.
See colour plate p. 186.

French Front see Fiddle Front.

Frill see Apron.

Frog Face An overshot jaw and extended nose.

Front The parts of the body, excluding the head, when seen from the front of the dog.

Fungus Eczema Fungus eczema is called by many names, including flea-bite allergy, fungitch, summer eczema, and hot spots. Some authorities believe that

certain dogs are allergic to FLEA bites. Since fleas are more numerous in the summer than in the winter, the disappearance of the eczema during the winter seems to prove the point.

Fungus eczema tends to appear on the legs, about the rectal area, on top of the tail, and along the base of the spine. Fleas, on the other hand, tend to migrate to the neck and head. Moreover, Arctic dogs do not have fleas, yet suffer occasionally from the affliction.

Also, as the dogs grow older, the eczema comes earlier in the spring and lasts later in the autumn. In many dogs it remains the year round. Thus, while an allergic reaction to flea bites may be responsible for many cases, there must be other causes.

The eczema normally begins around the tail. It causes intense itching. The dog scratches and bites at the area until it becomes raw and bleeding. The diseased area spreads, and the itching continues even though the dog is carefully kept free of fleas.

Many veterinarians believe that the causative agent is a fungus, or a fungus spore. Such spores are in the air and on grass. Freezing weather reduces the numbers of both fungi and spores – this could account for the disappearance of the eczema during the fall and winter, except in the most severe cases.

Affected dogs should be kept in the house as much as possible, and they should not be allowed to lie or roll on grass. Since the eczema also tends to appear between the toes, it is best to keep the dogs off grass altogether if possible. DDT, although not normally considered a fungicide, has shown remarkable ability to cure, and keep cured, affected dogs. It is used in a ten per cent dusting powder. DDT is now being banned in many areas, but it can be dusted into open sores on dogs without toxic effects.

Other fungicides have been developed, and in addition, food supplements are now available which help in many cases. Since the fungi do not attack all dogs, it must be assumed that skin weaknesses permit some dogs to be afflicted. The food supplements are designed to strengthen the skin and hair by adding amino acids, unsaturated fatty acids, and various vitamins. Some also contain antihistamines which are useful in preventing allergic attacks.
See ECZEMA.

Furnishings The abundant coat required in selected places by certain breed standards. Examples are the profuse whiskers of KERRY BLUES, Wire-Haired FOX TERRIERS etc., the eyebrows of SCHNAUZERS and SCOTTISH TERRIERS, and the ear and leg fringes of AMERICAN COCKER SPANIELS. Without these adornments the breeds look 'unfurnished'. Hence when present, the dog is described as 'furnished'.

Furrow The median line down the centre of the skull to the stop.

Futurity Stake An event for young dogs which have been nominated before, or at birth. Additional payments, after nomination may be required at stated times before the event.

Above Frog face.

G

Gait see Movement.

Gastric Tympany see Bloat.

Gastritis Gastritis is an inflammation in the stomach wall which causes vomiting after the ingestion of food or water. It can be a low grade infection, as it often is in puppies which have eaten spoiled food, or indigestible materials, but it can be acute and chronic, as when it follows severe infectious diseases, such as DISTEMPER or infectious canine HEPATITIS. It may also be caused by ulcers or neoplasms (abnormal tissue growths). Finally, caustic poisons and certain drugs may cause gastritis. In large or repeated doses, ASPIRIN is an example of a stomach irritant.

In mild cases of gastritis, it is usually only necessary to withhold water and food for 24 hours. If the dog is very thirsty, it can be given ice cubes to lick. After 24 hours, the dog can be given a meat broth, and a bland diet which should be prescribed by a veterinarian.

In severe cases, the owner should waste no time in getting his dog to the veterinarian. Continued vomiting rapidly dehydrates the body, and the inability to take food greatly weakens the dog's recuperative powers. Drugs may be required to stop the vomiting, and intravenous feeding may be needed to sustain strength.

The owner should try to supply the veterinarian with all the information he can about the probable cause. For example, the dog may have eaten a large number of chop bones the sharp edges of which have irritated the stomach wall, while becoming impacted in an indigestible mass. The dog may have swallowed foreign objects which have caused the inflammation, or he may have ingested a caustic poison.

In some cases, X-ray pictures will be needed to determine whether TUMOURS, or foreign objects are present. In others, a stool sample will enable the veterinarian to determine whether internal parasites are the cause of the trouble.

Gastro-Enteritis This is an inflammation of the stomach and intestines. When it occurs there will be vomiting and diarrhoea, and, because of the loss of fluid from the body, an increased thirst. Water is drunk and usually immediately vomited. Immediate treatment consists of withdrawing all food and water and seeking veterinary advice.

Occasionally a dog will strain with this condition as though it is constipated, because of the swelling of the lining of the intestine. A laxative should not be given.

Gay Tail One carried high and forward, that is over and parallel to the top line.

Gene A gene is the material unit of heredity, the biochemical unit which corresponds to Mendel's factors carried from parent to offspring. Research in recent years has revealed in astonishing detail the chemical and physical structure of genes, which are now known to be composed of a double chain of substances called 'nucleotides', linked together in a very special way to form, in long chains, the substance deoxyribonucleic acid (DNA). Each gene is responsible, by its control of enzyme manufacture, for one particular chemical change during development of the embryo and of the life of the adult animal or plant. This development consists of an enormously complicated series of processes, following each other in an orderly fashion, and each initiated and controlled in minute detail at every stage by specific genes, each gene supervising one enzyme.

The wide range of variation between individuals is caused by the great *number* of gene pairs in every person which appear in an infinite number of different combinations of dominants and recessives. In addition, the expression of every gene can be modified by the environment, both internal and external. The alternative forms or *alleles* arise by mutation (see below), and if any mutant gene or new allele has too big an effect, the subsequent processes will be thrown into confusion, and the embryo will be abnormal, dying either before birth, or before breeding age. Such genes are called 'lethals'.

The action of genes affecting later processes in development depends on how earlier-acting genes have functioned. Thus genes controlling tail carriage cannot express themselves if, due to the action of other genes, no tail is developed. In reality the action of all genes is inter-connected, but these connections are not always obvious.

New genes arise by chemical changes or mutations. These occur naturally but only occasionally, one in many thousands of cell divisions. Great increases in the mutation rate can be caused by certain chemical and physical agents, of which radiation is the most notorious. It is therefore possible for a genetic abnormality to arise in a previously 'clear' strain of dog, and this is no disgrace, though failure to take action to eliminate the abnormal mutant by excluding the affected animal from a breeding programme, may be.

A gene controlling any character such as coat colour can have many forms, but each dog can only carry two of these alleles in its genetic make-up. The different alleles often show dominance in serial order, e.g. gene A is dominant to its two alleles a^s and a^t, while a^s is dominant to a^t. Thus, a dog that has

Aa^s is dark
Aa^t is dark
$a^s a^s$ has a dark saddle
$a^s a^t$ is probably intermediate
$a^t a^t$ has tan points.

As genes interact with each other, so they interact with the environment, which may alter the expression of genes. This is most obvious with genes affecting growth, since this must also depend partly on the diet, and with those appearing to affect the dog's 'character', e.g. placidity, where training and experience play a big part. In other cases the exact environmental influence is not obvious, but sophisticated statistical techniques used by geneticists show the extent to which the

Below Gene. All living things contain, in their chromosomes, long chains of DNA (Deoxyribonucleic Acid) in the form of a double helix. The sequence of the 'bases' stretching across the helix like the rungs of a ladder, is the genetic code, and controls the shape, colour, coat and other characteristics of the dog.

differences between individuals are under environmental control. The condition of COLLIE NOSE is mainly environmental in origin, although genetic factors can be involved. In such cases, selection in breeding stock will do little to reduce the number of affected puppies, because, as geneticists express it, heritability is low.

German Boarhound The GREAT DANE has sometimes been called erroneously the German Boarhound.

German Shepherd Dog The German Shepherd, or Alsatian as it is known in Britain and most of the Commonwealth countries, has, over the years, had more publicity good and bad than all the other breeds of dogs put together.

From nearly every country have come stories of its admirable work with the police, the armed forces and the blind; stories of it finding lost children, of doing nearly every task that man could possibly demand, and always doing it brilliantly.

On the other hand, there are often attacks on the breed: 'Alsatian runs amok.' It is accused of treachery and savagery, of sheep killing (Australia categorically

forbids imports of members of this breed). In view of this conflict, it is only right that the question of temperament should be dealt with first. Is it a super dog or a savage?

The German Shepherd has virtues which can be allowed to degenerate into vices: they are its active mind and body. Properly disciplined and given work to do, this dog is unbeatable. Left in bored idleness, shut in a suburban apartment or tied to a post in the garden, these very virtues make it potentially dangerous. It snatches at any chance of freedom and uses its brain and its brawn both to amuse and prove itself. Never having been taught either to work or obey, it amuses itself by sheep worrying, cat and car chasing, and intimidating lesser breeds; even on occasions by attacking human beings. These dogs' problems have been caused by inexperienced owners who have neglected training. Additionally, idle or elderly owners often fail to appreciate the amount of exercise this dog needs. It has been said that fifty per cent of the Alsatians in the world are owned by the wrong people and for the wrong reasons. The theory behind this is that many are bought by people for effect, overlooking the responsibilities of owning a strong and active dog.

Below right German Shepherd Dog. Ch. Lance of Fran-Jo.

It has to be accepted that some of the breed do have temperamental faults. This is by no means unique to German Shepherds. The difference is that when a German Shepherd bites, either from fear or from an over-developed aggressive sense, the results can be disastrous. In short, if a German Shepherd runs amok, it invariably makes newspaper headlines, whereas a Pekingese performing in the same way would not. This perhaps explains why on occasions there seems to be a newspaper vendetta against the breed. It seems to be the deliberate policy of certain security organizations to emphasize the guarding qualities of these dogs in order to enhance their deterrent effect. For every person who wants the dog thought of as a saint, there is another prepared to have it known as an unrepentant

sinner. All facets of the breed's temperament, and the differing viewpoints of those who own or work the German Shepherd must be appreciated before the breed can be understood.

The dog is German in origin and is also virtually a dog of this century, although its forebears are said to have been used for centuries for herding and other general farmwork. The first club for the breed was the *Verein für Deutsche Schaferhunde*, founded in 1899. Almost immediately the breed's working qualities were appreciated by the police. Additionally, the Germans realized before anybody else the value of dogs in war. Long before 1914, village training clubs had been established all over the country with Government subsidies so that when war broke out there were over 6,000 dogs ready for immediate service. The overwhelming majority of these were German Shepherds. They were trained as messengers to cross shell-torn fields, as medical dogs carrying drugs, as rescue dogs for wounded soldiers, as guards and sentinels.

The war over, soldiers from the occupying forces who had seen them fleetingly in the past, met them at close quarters in the cities of Germany. A number were taken to Britain, where somewhat foolishly and to avoid associating them with Germany, they were called Alsatian Wolf Dogs. Perhaps such a childish deception deserved to rebound. And rebound it did. The only word that stayed in many minds was 'wolf'. Those responsible had attempted to gild the lily; they succeeded in giving a dog a bad name.

The age-old question of whether there is in fact some wolf in the background of this breed must now be examined. Most people will admit that it is at least genetically possible that at some time in the past crosses were occasionally made with wolves (although normal wolves and dogs are mortal enemies). However, these would be so far back that they could not be of any interest at all today, and could have little, if any, bearing on the breed's temperament. The suggestion that crosses are still made is clearly without foundation. No breeder in his right mind would take his modern, highly developed, intelligent, biddable, streamlined German Shepherd and cross it with a wolf which is savage, badly conformed and often mangy and moth-eaten in appearance.

After the First World War, the history of the breed in Britain was startling. By 1926, it had reached the top of the popularity poll. Then came repeated adverse comment in the press. Serious accidents happened all too frequently and were reported. The change of name to German Shepherd Dog came too late. The breed slumped. In the space of six brief years, their annual registration had risen from 54 to 5,601, but then numbers again declined rapidly. The dog was out of favour for only a few years, its popularity steadily returning so that by 1967 it was once again Britain's favourite breed.

A somewhat similar drama was played out in the United States. Again the dogs went home with soldiers. Again they captured the imagination of the public. By 1926 more than one-third of all the pure-breds registered with the American Kennel Club were German

German Shepherd Dog.
Top left German Shepherds have highly active minds and bodies and resent idleness. A bored Alsatian is generally a bad one.
Lower left Jumping through a burning square is only one of many hazardous tasks a trained German Shepherd will tackle enthusiastically. This performer is a Royal Air Force police dog.

Right German Shepherd Dogs were used in both world wars not only as guard dogs but as messengers, rescue dogs, and medical pack-dogs. This is a post dog.

Shepherds. Then came their slump and also the long rehabilitating climb.

Now once again they are firmly established, not only in these countries but all over the world. There can be few, if any, lands in which the German Shepherd is not amongst the four most popular breeds. This even applies to Australia despite the ban on imports. Those taken there before 1926 have been guarded, bred from and have prospered, and all indications are that the breed will flourish there.

The dog's working qualities have been so well publicized that they hardly need mention. Apart from their trainability, they have the necessary qualities of ruggedness and determination. From the viewpoint of work with the armed forces another asset is that they can be posted to any country in the world as their dense, waterproof coats make them resistant to heat and cold.

To see them in the show ring is to realize immediately that great importance is attached to their movement. The gait must be elastic, reaching, seemingly without effort, smooth and rhythmic. It must also be tireless. In certain continental European countries it is the practice to gait them for very long periods, sometimes for an hour or more. Elsewhere they are moved for a length of time which would be quite unacceptable in other breeds. The dogs glide along without any evidence at all of stress. Frequently the handlers do not!

Essentials of the breed: The general appearance is a well-proportioned dog showing great suppleness of limb. The head is long, lean and clean cut, broad at the back of the skull, tapering to the nose with only a slight stop.

The cheeks must not be full or prominent. The muzzle is strong, long and tapering to the nose. It must not show weakness. The nose must be black. Eyes: almond-shaped, matching the surrounding coat but dark rather than light. Ears: of moderate size, but rather large than small, broad at the base and pointed at the tips. The teeth should be sound and strong, gripping with a scissor-like action.

The neck should be strong and fairly long. Shoulders should slope well back. The forelegs should be perfectly straight viewed from the front, but the pasterns should show a slight angle with the forearm when regarded from the side. The body is muscular, the back broadish and straight, strongly boned and well developed. The belly shows a waist without being tucked up. There should be a good depth of brisket or chest. The sides are comparatively flat. Hindquarters should show breadth and strength, the loins being broad and strong, the rump rather long and sloping and the legs, when viewed from behind, must be quite straight, without any tendency to cow-hocks or bow-hocks, which are serious faults. Feet should be round, the toes strong and slightly arched. At rest the tail should hang in a slight curve. The coat is smooth but double. Along the neck it is longer and thicker, and in winter approaches a form of ruff. As an average the hairs on the back should be from 1 to 2 inches in length. The colour is not important except that all white or near white unless possessing black points is undesirable in most countries, and disqualifying in some. Height: Dogs 24–26 inches. Bitches: 22–24 inches.

See colour plate p. 296.

Below German Short-Haired Pointer, Ch. Patrick of Malahide. This breed came into existence little over 100 years ago, but it is now one of the best-known sporting dogs in the world and one of the most popular in America.

German Short-Haired Pointer The German Short-haired Pointer has steadily improved its position until it is now one of the best known sporting dogs in the world. It is particularly popular in the United States. In 1969, for example, the German Shorthair ranked eighteenth among American Kennel Club registrations with 11,152 registrations. Another 1,985 were registered in the Field Dog Stud Book. Moreover, in championship trials in 1968 conducted under American Kennel Club rules, 1,489 German Shorthairs competed in nineteen trials for this breed only. And 5,978 took part in trials conducted for other pointing breeds.

Development of the German Short-haired Pointer began, as with so many breeds, in the period from 1860 to 1880. The Germans were searching for an all purpose hunting dog. Various breeds were used, including the German Pointer. But the major improvements appear to have been from crossing dogs of Spanish Pointer origin with ST. HUBERT HOUNDS; this cross was made to give the dog a trailing nose.

One great early breeder was Prince Albrecht zu Solms-Bauenfels of the House of Hanover. About 1870, he laid down the dictum that form should follow ability. Christian Bode of Altenau is said to have crossed in English Pointers to give a better wind scent nose and greater style.

Herr Julius Mehlich of Berlin caused great comment when his *Nero* performed creditably against Pointers and Setters at Buckow. In 1883, Nero tied for the German Derby with another German Shorthair, *Treff*. These two, Nero and Treff, are the great foundation dogs of the breed. In 1884, Nero's daughter, *Flora*, produced three great foundation dogs, *Waldin*, *Waldo*, and *Hertha*. And in 1892, Nero's grand-daughter, *Erra Hoppenrade*, was a great FIELD TRIAL winner.

About 1920, *Edelman Giftig* was a great German field trial winner. He became a great sire and served as a foundation sire for many of the dogs which appeared later in the United States.

Dr. Charles R. Thornton of Missoula, Montana, is credited with bringing the breed to the attention of American sportsmen. He imported *Senta von Hohenbruck* from Austria. She arrived in whelp, and her litter was born July 4, 1925. Dr. Thornton imported more bitches in whelp. He liked to hunt upland game, and the performances of his dogs gave the breed national attention.

The German Short-haired Pointer Club of America was organized, and the breed was admitted to the American Kennel Club stud book in March, 1930. The club's first national speciality show was held at the International Kennel Club of Chicago show in March, 1941, and the club's first field trial was held at Anoka, Minnesota, May 21, 1944.

It appears that German Short-haired Pointers were first exhibited in England at the Barn Elms show of 1887. It was at this same show, a year later, that Wire-haired Pointing GRIFFONS were first exhibited in England. The German Shorthairs exhibited at Barn Elms were apparently returned home, and it was not until the late 1940s that they were seen again in England.

Michael Brander, who wrote the *Roughshooter's Dog* and *Roughshooter's Sport,* was one of the first to try the German dogs. The breed gradually gained popularity with men who hunted on foot and needed a dog who could find game, point staunchly, remain steady to flush and shot, mark the fall, and make the retrieve. These sportsmen also liked the dog's willingness to face sleet and cold rain, heavy cover, and to enter cold, rough water to retrieve a duck.

The German Short-haired Pointer Club was founded in England in 1951. Since then, field trials for German breeds have been set up, as in the United States. In England, to become a bench champion, a German Short-haired Pointer must also win two prizes at different field trials in Open and All Age stakes. One prize must be won in a stake open to all breeds that point and retrieve.

Essentials of the breed: The nose projects slightly over a rather squared off muzzle which balances the skull in length, depth, and width. The ears are set above eye level, and the eye is dark. Light eyes and spotted or flesh-coloured noses are faults. Noses should be brown. The jaws form a scissors bite. The chest is deep, reaching to the elbows, with rounded ribs. The back is short, and slopes slightly from withers to the tail root. Long, sway, and roach backs are penalized. The hind legs are well angulated at the stifles and hock joints. The shoulders slope, pasterns are nearly vertical, and the feet are round to spoon-shaped, deep, thickly padded, and with heavy nails. The elbows turn neither in nor out. Colours are solid liver, liver and white spotted, liver and white spotted and ticked, liver and white ticked, and liver roan. Any colours other than liver and grey-white are not permitted.

Many of the early German Shorthairs which came to the United States had rather heavy, hound type bodies. But there is nothing ponderous about the modern dog. The standard calls for dogs weighing 55 to 70 lb. and of a height of 23 to 25 inches at the shoulder, with bitches somewhat smaller.
See colour plate p. 85.

German Wire-Haired Pointer This breed is known in its home land as the Deutsch Drahthaar; or German Wirehair. The breed was developed by crossing the offspring of a number of other breeds – the Wire-haired Pointing GRIFFON, the Stichelhaar, the Pudel-pointer, and the GERMAN SHORT-HAIRED POINTER. The modern dogs look very much like the Short-haired.

The German Wirehair was rather slow to gain recognition outside Germany, even though it has had an excellent record there since 1900. Unsuccessful attempts were made to interest American sportsmen in the breed about 1920, and again a decade later. It was not until after World War II that American outdoorsmen became interested.

By that time, the German Short-haired Pointer and the WEIMARANER had been spectacularly successful in the United States. German Wirehairs were then introduced to the American Midwest. There they proved to be excellent workers on pheasants, and even as waterfowl retrievers. The breed was officially recognized by the American Kennel Club in 1959. Only two years later, a German Wirehair won the National German Pointing Breeds field trial championship. Outside of Germany the breed is best known in the United States and Canada.

Essentials of the breed: The German Wire-haired Pointer resembles the German Short-haired Pointer in all ways except coat. The outer coat is harsh and wiry. In winter, the undercoat is soft, dense, and weather resistant. In summer, the undercoat virtually disappears.

The colours are liver and white, usually liver and white spotted, liver roan, liver and white spotted with ticking and roan, or solid liver. The nose is dark brown, and those with flesh coloured or spotted noses are penalized. The head is brown, and occasionally has a white blaze. The ears, too, are brown. Black in the coat is to be severely penalized. The dogs have bushy eyebrows, and beards and whiskers. The tail is docked to about two-fifths of its original length. Height: dogs 24 to 26 inches, bitches not less than 22 inches.
See colour plate p. 85.

Gestation The normal period of gestation in a bitch is sixty-three days. Healthy litters can be born at any time from the fifty-eighth day to the sixty-eighth day. Puppies born earlier rarely survive.
See HEAT OF BITCH; PREGNANCY and WHELPING.

Giardiasis see Protozoan Diseases.

Glaucoma see Blindness; Eye Diseases.

Glen of Imaal Terrier Outside Ireland, this short-legged little terrier is comparatively little known. As smaller and ever smaller breeds are constantly being sought, particularly those which are both unusual and natural, there is a strong possibility that they will become better known with the passage of time. Already some are making an appearance in the show rings on the mainland of the United Kingdom, and beginning to be noticed.

The terrier gets its name from the Glen of Imaal, a region in County Wicklow in Eire, where it appears to have been in existence for a very long time. Currently it is used to go to ground after such animals as badgers. However, in the past it was used to fight, one dog against the next, in the same way as were the STAFFORD-SHIRE BULL TERRIERS. One major difference is that these Glen of Imaal Terriers always fought in open fields as distinct from the cellar pits of the early Bull Terriers. As is well known the 'sport' of dog baiting has been illegal now for over a century and therefore the breed has to follow more peaceful pastimes. Even so, it is still not possible for one of this breed to attain the full rank of Champion until it has been tested for gameness in going to earth and attacking.

It has been recognized by the Irish Kennel Club since 1933 and the formation of a breed club at about the same time has helped to promote it further.

One of the most important points about the breed is that it is a 'natural' dog. By this is meant that even in the show ring it is not barbered or presented in artificial form. Like other working terriers, such as Cairns, Borders, and Norwich Terriers, any attempts at show presentation must be at least discreet. A modest tidying-up process is perhaps acceptable but not the immaculate, and many think unnatural, presentation of such breeds as SCOTTISH and SEALY-HAM TERRIERS.

Essentials of the breed: Head is fairly broad, moderately long, and with a fair stop. The eyes are round, of medium size, either brown or hazel. The ears are set high, fairly small and are dropped forwards; the muzzle is relatively short and tapering. Body: comparatively long with a firm straight back, roomy chest and powerful couplings. The legs: rather short, a slight bow being permissible in the fores, and with compact, well-padded feet. The tail is set and carried high and docked to medium length. Coat: moderately long and rather soft. Colours are wheaten, blue, brindle or blue-tan.

The height is approximately 14 inches at the shoulder with a weight of around 32 lb.

Top left German Wire-Haired Pointer. Ch. Mueller Mill's Valentino II. In the picture, left, is Judge Percy Richards.

Bottom left Glen of Imaal Terrier. This little working terrier is virtually unknown outside its native country, Ireland, but its plucky temperament, small size and 'natural' appearance forecast a more international future.

Golden Retriever The radiance of the Golden Retriever's burnished coat shines brightly in three separate fields.

Brilliant gundog, good natured pet, and conscientious GUIDE DOG FOR THE BLIND, its present popularity is based on solid virtues. Even so, it was a very tall story which gave this dog its day and set it on the road to popularity.

All of the books written prior to 1952, which mention even in passing the Golden Retriever, give the same story. Frequently this is repeated word for word.

Here is a typical example. 'In 1858 Sir Dudley Marjoribanks saw a performance at a travelling circus in Brighton, the English seaside resort. One act was a troop of trained Russian Trackers or Sheepdogs. Sir Dudley was so impressed with the cleverness and good looks of these dogs that he decided to acquire a pair of them. The trainer of the dogs was unwilling to sell, claiming that his act would be destroyed. Upon which Sir Dudley made an offer for the entire troop of eight dogs. These were taken to their new owner's estate, bred from and thereby laid the foundations of the breed.'

In the book referred to, the preface to the above says:

'The story of how the Golden Retriever came to be known reads more like fiction than fact.' This is hardly surprising because fiction it was. There is no foundation for the story in fact.

The general public loved the story though dog fanciers did not. They always appreciated that a real sportsman with considerable experience would be unlikely to buy dogs merely because they were good performers on the stage. This would of course indicate that they were obedient and trainable, but a good retrieving dog works as often without instruction as with it. Initiative is a vital factor. It could however be a distinct handicap with a dog required to perform in the circus.

Dog men also knew that the background of a herder or shepherd dog is by no means the best for a retriever. All sheepdogs hustle their charges along, if need be with little nips. A gundog is required to work in almost precisely the reverse fashion. It must get to the object of its attentions with as little fuss as possible, take it gently in its mouth and pay particular attention not to harm it further.

Finally, the knowledgeable were suspicious of the coat of the Golden Retriever which in texture, if not in

Below Golden Retriever. A nineteenth century forerunner of the breed, painted by Sir Edwin Landseer.

colour, bore a close resemblance to so many other gundogs.

In 1952, earlier doubters were vindicated when the kennel records of Marjoribanks' estate from 1835 to 1890 were published. As had always been expected, a routine practice of breeding from 'sports' – that is, animals who deviate slightly from the expected normal, had been followed.

The original dog was called *Nous*. He was a yellow dog bred from black FLAT-COATED RETRIEVER parents. He was mated to a small liver-coloured Tweed Spaniel which later was in effect a rather diminutive English Retriever. The union produced four puppies. Since these, and not the Russian acrobats, were the true foundation of the breed, it is fortunate that their names are on record. They were *Crocus, Primrose, Cowslip* and *Ada*.

The Golden Retriever, then, is pure gundog. Few who have seen it work would ever have doubted that fact. The drive and pace when searching for wounded game; the keen sense of smell; the systematic quartering of ground; the soft mouth and stylish retrieve, all denote generations of service in the field.

Less traditional is their present popular role all over the world of household pet. Large and strong, they fulfil the task of guards by acting as deterrents. As children's companions they are good-tempered and long suffering. They are also intelligent, loyal and kind.

Finally there is their increasing use as guide-dogs for the blind. The associations which train these dogs invariably demand animals which are clever, obedient, eager to serve and neither timid nor aggressive. In the Golden Retriever they found these qualities and all of the evidence is that the reject rate, the constant bugbear of guide dog trainers, is lower in this than in any other breed with the possible exception of the LABRADOR RETRIEVER.

Essentials of the breed: The skull should be broad, the muzzle powerful and good stop is essential. Eyes: dark, set well apart, kindly in expression, with dark rims. Ears: well proportioned, of moderate size and well set on. Mouth: neither under nor overshot. The neck should be clean and muscular. Forequarters: the forelegs should be straight with good bone. Body: well balanced and short coupled. Ribs: deep and well sprung. Hindquarters: the loins and legs should be strong and muscular with well bent stifles. Hocks well let down. Feet: round and cat-like. Tail: should not be too gay nor curled at the tip. Coat: should be flat or wavy with good feathering and dense, water-resisting undercoat. Any shade of gold or cream is acceptable but not red or mahogany. A few white hairs on chest permissible. White collar, feet, toes or blaze should be penalized. Weight: (England) dogs 65 to 70 lb., bitches 55 to 60 lb; (America) dogs 65 to 75 lb., bitches 60 to 70 lb. Height at shoulder: Dogs 22 to 24 inches; Bitches 20 to 22 inches. American regulations call for slightly taller dogs.
See colour plate p. 82.

Goose Rump Too steep or sloping a rump.

Gordon Setter When the Kennel Clubs of Britain first listed breeds they recognized forty-six different species. It would have been difficult then to imagine a time when the subdivision of breeds in Britain alone would have to be increased to more than 120.

Some of those original breeds, those 'basics', are now either nearly or completely extinct. The Gordon Setter has escaped this extreme, although for a time it was touch and go. This once popular breed was down to a mere twenty-eight registrations in England in 1962. Now it is at least approaching a hundred, the minimum annual figure at which the continuity of a breed is assured. In America figures are better at some 600 a year. But it is principally dog show fanciers who have kept Gordons in existence.

Top Golden Retriever. Ch. Cragmount's Hi-Lo.

Above Gordon Setter Ch. Legen of Gael.

The Gordon Setter is the only gundog produced by Scotland, despite that country's sporting background. Being hardy, Gordons are particularly valuable in early shooting. They can also withstand the August heat better than other dogs. Their legs and feet are strong enough to stand up to baked fields and brittle stubble.

More important, they are capable of working without water for longer than most breeds. This is a most useful attribute in dogs which must gallop in the summer sun: the season starts on the 'glorious' 12th of August.

The breed was developed and established by Alexander, Fourth Duke of Richmond and Gordon, who died at Gordon Castle in 1827. He had spent a lifetime perfecting these beautiful black and tan animals. He wanted dogs which were heavier and larger than other setters. He felt that his ideal dog would be nearer to hounds and further from spaniels. He also wanted dual-purpose dogs; handsome and capable of working.

Most breeds have one skeleton in the cupboard. The Gordons have two. First there are rumours of a BLOODHOUND cross. This could have influenced colour and may account for the habit of hunting with nose to ground.

The other skeleton may be a COLLIE. History relates that one of the Duke's shepherds owned a remarkable black 'Colley' – a 'natural' at finding game. She was often successful when setters had failed. Moreover, she froze in the direction of the game and 'pointed'. Inevitably she was frequently invited to ducal shoots. Some say she was ultimately invited to the ducal kennels and was mated with the Duke's dogs.

This could account for another Gordon idiosyncracy: a tendency, having found game, to circle it as though the dog would rather 'hold' than 'set'. Setters should work away from man and his gun. Then they are in a safe position. A dog inclined to circle game, that is behave as a sheepdog, could start his point on the wrong or far side. This would be dangerous, virtually prohibiting a shot. Fortunately, this tendency has now been eliminated.

Gordons participated in the world's first dog show, held in Newcastle Town Hall on 28 June 1859. It was confined to Pointers and Setters. The prize for the best Pointer was won by the Setter judge's dog. The Setter prize went to *Dandy*, a Gordon, owned by the Pointer judge! Accusations of 'back scratching' followed. But in the opinion of competent observers, both dogs were good and deserved to win.

Essentials of the breed: Head: deep rather than broad. Skull: slightly rounded and a clearly indicated stop. The muzzle: fairly long. The flews: not pendulous. Nose: big and broad, with open, black nostrils. Eyes: dark brown and bright. Ears: set low and lying close, of medium size and thin. Neck: long and arched without throatiness. Shoulders should slope well back. Forelegs: big, flat-boned and straight. Body: moderate in length, with deep, well-sprung ribs, and slightly arched loins. Hindquarters: hind legs from hip to hock should be long, broad and muscular. Feet: oval with well-arched toes. Tail: fairly short, straight or slightly scimitar-shaped, carried horizontal or below line of back.

Coat: on the head, front of legs and tips of ears, short and fine; elsewhere of moderate length, fairly flat and free from wave. All feathering to be as flat and straight as possible. Colour: shining black, with markings of rich chestnut. Black pencilling allowed on toes.

Weight and size (U.K.): dogs, 26 inches, about 65 lb; bitches, 24½ inches and about 56 lb.; (U.S.A.): dogs 24 to 27 inches, and 55 to 80 lb.; bitches 23 to 26 inches, 45 to 70 lb.
See colour plate p. 87.

Grass Eating Dog owners notice with astonishment that their dogs sometimes eat grass, and that the grass passes through them apparently completely undigested. The sections on DIGESTION and NUTRITION explain why the latter is so. But why then does the dog eat grass?

A reasonable supposition is that the dog is obeying an instinct. Undigested grass may supply the bulk necessary to expel TAPEWORMS with other food wastes. For the same reason, the dog may eat the hides and the undigestible hair of small animals which it kills.

Worms of any sort cause alimentary tract irritation. Perhaps it is irritation, whether caused by worms or not, or even an upset stomach, which stimulates the dog to eat grass. Another possibility is that the dogs may eat grass simply out of boredom.

Great Dane To be a lover of the Great Dane is easy and within the compass of all of us. To be a Great Dane owner we must first have space, which explains why the latter are far out-numbered by the former.

When Sydenham Edwards wrote *Cynographia Britannica* in 1800, things were different, and his suggestion that 'no equipage can have arrived at its acme of grandeur until a couple of Harlequin Danes precede the pomp' conjures up the vision of a way of life that can never return.

While the aristocratic mentality which would scorn the already sufficiently impressive DALMATIAN as outriders to a carriage in favour of black and white Danes is English enough, the dog itself is not. Neither does it appear to have any very close connection with Denmark, and a name which links it with that country is one of the many oddities with which the dogworld abounds. It is a translation of one of the many old French designations *grand Danois*, a misleading choice when one considers that it was also known as *Dogue Allemand* or German Mastiff, either of which would have been much more suitable.

While a somewhat similar dog has been known throughout recorded history – representations on Egyptian tombs of the Fourth Dynasty prove this point – it was in Germany that the breed reached its present standard of excellence. No German palace or castle was considered complete without one or more of these imposing animals, and they were special favourites of the Iron Chancellor, Bismarck, who made them his bodyguards and constant companions.

As was to be expected with a breed designed for the stern task of destroying wild boar, mere prettiness was deplored. The emphasis has always been on size and weight, nobility and courage, speed and endurance. Its work dictated that its ears should be cropped to lessen the risk of them being torn, and on the Continent and in the United States, this is still the general practice.

The breed had a stiff hurdle to cross in common with all big breeds. Modern wars, unlike those of old which provided work for the giants, threaten their very existence. However, the growing strength of the breed in America is heartening, and the United States now produces the best Great Danes in the world.

Great size and substance is, as always in the past, a number one priority. But despite their size, these dogs remain elegant. Few who have owned one would be satisfied with anything less regal. When they are friendly with strangers, and there is in them no hint of aggression, they convey the impression that they are bestowing favours. They meet on equal terms; each has confidence in its own unerring ability to pick a good companion.

Finally, there is their gentle behaviour, exemplified by the tender way they hold visitors' hands in their great jaws and escort them gravely to the master of the house. What more can one ask?

Essentials of the breed: The Great Dane should be remarkable in size and very muscular, strongly though elegantly built.

The head should give the idea of great length and strength. The length varies with the height of the dog; 13 inches from the tip of the nose to the back of the occiput is a good measurement for a dog of 32 inches at the shoulder. The bridge of the nose should be very wide, with a slight ridge where the cartilage joins the bone. Eyes: fairly deep set, of medium size and preferably dark. Ears should be small and set high.

The neck should be long, arched and well set in the shoulders. The shoulders should be muscular, with the elbows well set under body. The forelegs: perfectly straight with big bone. The body should be very deep,

Below Great Dane. Ch. Marjee Merrowlea.

with ribs well sprung. The hindquarters should be extremely muscular, demonstrating great strength and galloping power. Feet should be cat-like and nails dark except in Harlequins. The tail should be thick at the root and should taper towards the end.

Colour: Brindles must be striped with black. Eyes and nails: preferably dark. Fawns: golden yellow to deep golden yellow with a deep black mask. Eyes and nails: preferably dark. Blues: from light grey to deepest slate and pure steel blue. Black: Harlequins, pure white underground with preferably black patches (blue is not permitted in the U.S.A.). In Harlequins, wall eyes, pink noses or butterfly noses are permissible but are not desirable. Weight and size: The minimum height of an adult dog must be 30 inches, that of a bitch, 28 inches. The minimum weight: dogs 120 lb.; bitches 100 lb.
See colour plate p. 299.

Great Pyrenees see Pyrenean Mountain Dog.

Greyhound All too frequently the so-called history of a breed is little more than legend. Claims that particular dogs arrived in Britain with William the Conqueror or entered the Ark are myths.

There can however be no doubt about the antiquity of the Greyhound. Nor can it be disputed that over the centuries it has retained a greater purity of form than most of, if not all, other breeds. This is probably because it was fashioned for a purpose: that of covering a given distance in the shortest possible time. That means it was, and remains, a living running machine, built to the most elegant and stream lined design.

Evidence of its antiquity is not hard to find. It has been the subject of innumerable paintings, drawings, and etchings. Fourth Dynasty carvings and bas reliefs on the tombs of the Pharaohs show dogs that can only be Greyhounds. These animals also appear on many other ancient African and Asian monuments, and in the work of the old masters.

One reason for this wealth of pictorial history is that the Greyhound was for a long time associated with the upper classes, who had the means to commission representations of their favourite dogs. An old Welsh proverb made the point with: 'You may know a gentleman by his horse, his hawk and his greyhound.'

In 1016 a Canute Law stated that 'No meane person may keep any greyhounds'. As at that time the price of one of these animals was the same as that of a serf, the edict would appear to have been unnecessary.

Before the Magna Carta the punishment for the destruction of a Greyhound was the same as that for the murder of a man. Further proof of their favoured position is the fact that King John frequently accepted two or three Greyhounds from his subjects in lieu of tax.

In 1408 Juliana Berners wrote:
A greyhound should be headed lyke a snake
And neckyd lyke a drake
Footed lyke a cat
Tayled lyke a rat . . . .
Modern breed standards are more prosaic and precise. But they place particular emphasis on the generous proportions, symmetrical formation, clean

shoulders, deep chest, arched loin and suppleness of limb.

The origin of the name Greyhound is open to dispute. You may choose from 'Grais', meaning Grecian; 'Grech', an old British word for dog; 'grey', a reminder that this was at one time the most usual colour; or 'gaze', descriptive of a dog which hunts by sight. One suspects that the last is probably the most accurate because the Greyhound's task through the ages has been coursing deers, stags, gazelle, foxes and more recently hares.

Whilst almost everything is fully recorded about the sporting prowess of these animals, their merit as pets has been largely overlooked. This is rather curious because the breed has always had a gentle and affectionate nature. Their large size may have prevented many people from taking them into their houses. But 'large' does not necessarily mean cumbersome and certainly the Greyhound is normally unobtrusive and content to sleep in a surprisingly small space.

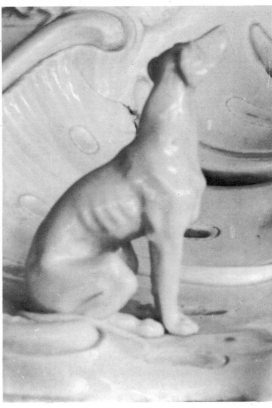

Greyhound.
Top right An early Greyhound type forms the decoration of a second- or third-century Roman hunt-pot found in England.
Bottom right A detail from an eighteenth-century porcelain ornament showing a Greyhound-like dog.

Other advantages are that they are short-coated and therefore easy to keep clean, and that their coats show a wide range of colours.

But perhaps the most remarkable thing about the breed is the ease with which they have always found new employment. In this modern, mechanical age they have taken up the sport of racing.

It seems they were always destined to receive homage. They were accepted as the only true God by the early Egyptians. Now they have become the recipients of honours from the thousands of worshippers who throng the world's Greyhound racing tracks.

Essentials of the Breed: Head: long flat skull, of moderate width, with slight stop. Jaws: powerful and well chiselled. Eyes: bright and intelligent, dark in colour. Ears: small, rose-shaped, of fine texture. Teeth: white and strong with scissors bite. Neck: long and muscular and elegantly arched. Forequarters: shoulders, oblique and muscular, forelegs: long and straight. Elbows well set under the shoulder. Pasterns: slightly sprung.

Body: chest deep and capacious; ribs deep and well sprung; back rather long, broad and square; loin powerful, slightly arched. Hindquarters: thighs and second thighs, wide and muscular; stifles well bent; hocks, well let down. Feet: of moderate length, with compact well-knuckled toes and strong pads. Tail: long, set on rather low, strong at the root, tapering to the point, carried low and slightly curved.

Coat: fine and close. Colour: black, white, red, blue, fallow, brindle or any of these colours broken with white. Height (U.K.): dogs 28 to 30 inches; bitches 27 to 28 inches. Weight (U.S.A.): dogs 65 to 70 lb.; bitches 60 to 65 lb.

See colour plate p. 182.

Greyhound Coursing Fast sight hounds have been used to hunt deer, antelope, wolves, and hares for at least 4,000 years. Ovid, the Roman poet who lived about the time of Christ, wrote an excellent description of such hare hunting. But it was left to the Celts, about 150 AD, to introduce true coursing to the Roman and Greek world. Coursing differs from hunting in a major respect. In hunting, the object is to catch and kill the quarry. In coursing, the major interest is in the matching of the speed and agility of one hound against the other. Arrian, the second century Roman writer who produced rules governing the sport in those days, indicated that the sportsmen were just as happy if the hare lived to run another day.

The Celts used a type of Greyhound known to the Greeks and Romans as the *Vertagri*. Scouts and beaters were sent out to flush the hares. Two dogs were then released. The hounds were judged on their ability to turn the hare, upon their speed, and, when it happened, upon the kill. Coursing in modern England, Ireland, Spain, and Australia differs little today.

The first coursing club, the Swaffham, was founded in Norfolk in 1776 by Lord Orford (who also attempted improvement of the Greyhound by crossing it with the BULLDOG to increase courage and stamina). In 1780, a coursing club gave a meet at Ashdown Park, and in 1781 another group gave a meet at Malton. Another famous club, the Altcar, was founded at the Waterloo Hotel, Liverpool, in 1825, and eleven years later the first Waterloo Cup meeting was held. It was then an eight dog (or bitch) stake; since the 1850s it has been a sixty-four dog (or bitch) stake, which means that the winner must have exceptional merit. Even so, some have won it two or three times.

In 1858, the National Coursing Club was founded and drew up a code of rules for British coursing. These are now recognized throughout the British Commonwealth. The Greyhound Stud Book was started in 1882 to register coursing Greyhounds, registered dogs only being accepted at official meetings. Currently many coursing clubs in Britain hold meetings under N.C.C. rules. The Irish Coursing Club controls the sport in Eire and dogs registered with the N.C.C. or I.C.C. can compete at each other's meetings.

The coursing season lasts from 15 September to 10 March. Eight and sixteen dog stakes are usually one day events, while national events of thirty-two and sixty-four dog stakes last two or three days.

At large meetings, betting takes place, but this is not the primary object of the sport which remains a competition of hounds' speed and skill. A 'kill' is of no particular importance and the majority of hares escape.

Two kinds of meeting are held in England and

Greyhound.
Top left Ch. Seagift Parcancad Bluebell.
Bottom left Ch. Barmaud Starbo Europa.

Ireland: the 'walked-up' and the 'driven'. At the walked-up meeting, competitors, hounds and the 'field' walk the ground in a line with the 'slipper' – holding two hounds in the slips – slightly ahead. Beyond them is a mounted judge. When a hare is disturbed and gets up from its 'form', those nearest shout 'Hare', to alert the slipper. If he is satisfied that the hare is strong and fit, he allows it some eighty yards 'lay' to collect its wits and have a fair start before he releases the dogs.

At a 'driven' meeting the competitors and on-lookers assemble at the side of a field while the slipper and hounds are concealed behind a canvas hide. Hares are walked up by a line of beaters, controlled by flag and whistle, who drive towards the slips. They attempt to drive hares through singly, as no more than two hounds are permitted to be loose at one time. Judges award points as follows:

is given a 30 yard start. Judges observe from towers or ride horses within the area.

The sport is strenuous for the dogs, as some of the following coursing terms indicate. *Lost back:* long back muscles torn loose during coursing. *Dropped muscle:* rupture of inner loin or shoulder muscles. *Sapling:* an inexperienced pup ten to eighteen months old. *Gyp:* a bitch. *Cute:* cleverness of one dog in forcing the other to do most of the work while it saves ground and strength and wins most of the points.

Greyhound, Eastern The Eastern Greyhound is not a breed. Rather is it a general term used to describe a whole group of loosely related dogs. Members of the Greyhound family are all rather similar in outline, variations being slight and principally a matter of head shape, tail carriage and coat.

Speed: 1, 2, or 3 points depending upon the superiority shown.
Go-by: 2 points for a dog which starts the course a full length behind his opponent, passes him and gets a full length in front; 3 points if he passes him on the outer side.
The Turn: 1 point where the hare is brought round at not less than a right angle from its previous line.
The Wrench: $\frac{1}{2}$ point where the hare is turned from its previous line at less than a right angle. (If the hare wrenches by itself no points are given.)
The Kill: 2 points or less, depending upon the skill displayed.
The Trip: 1 point where the hare is thrown off its legs but gets away from the dog.

Greyhound coursing in the United States is licensed and controlled by the National Coursing Association at Abilene, Kansas. It registers more than 40,000 Greyhounds annually. The American National Waterloo Cup has been run since 1895. There are spring and autumn coursing meets at Abilene in which 450 to 700 dogs compete during eight days. Four licensed events are held in Texas.

American coursing takes place in a fenced area, 450 yards long and 150 yards wide. Hares are fenced or boxed at one end. At the far end are escape hatches which mean safety and life for them. A hare – the American jack rabbit – is released for each brace, and

At the time when it became necessary to give permanent names to the breeds, the most popular was the smooth-coated variety. Since England was then responsible for allocating names and descriptions, this became the English Greyhound. All the other related types became Eastern Greyhounds.

Since then, many so-called Eastern Greyhounds have been given different and precise breed names and thus the term 'Eastern Greyhound' now has little significance, and will soon have even less.

The most outstanding of the Eastern Greyhounds were the Arab Greyhound, now known as the SALUKI, and the Persian and Afghan Greyhounds, which together (they differ little, if at all) have become AFGHAN HOUNDS.

Less well known was the Slughi, often confused with the Saluki, which is usually medium-coated and feathered. The Slughi was always smooth-coated, but the general description of it is remarkably similar to that of the Saluki, even down to colour which was 'biscuit, sand, a fawn with occasional black and brindle specimens'.

The Eastern group also included the Rampur Greyhound, found originally in the state of Rampur, India, and probably descended from the Slughi; the Banjara, another Indian breed similar to and probably descended from the Afghan; yet a further Indian

Above Greyhound coursing. Dogs have been used to hunt fleet-footed game for at least 4000 years. This fifteenth-century picture by Paolo Uccello shows a hunt in a forest.

Overleaf Greyhound racing. After one false start 100 years ago, this sport has drawn millions of enthusiasts to watch, applaud and lay bets on the fastest breed in the world.

variety, the Mahratta, another Saluki-type; and the Poligar, now extinct, but originally an undersized variety of the Rampur.

Greyhound, Italian see Italian Greyhound.

Greyhound Racing The first record of Greyhound racing appeared in the London *Times* on 11 September 1876. This was an account of a meeting held in a field behind the Welsh Harp at Hendon, outside London. A rail had been laid in the grass, some 400 yards in length, and carried in a groove a trolley on which was mounted an artificial hare. Despite the fact that the idea was successful and a considerable number of people watched the proceedings, there was no lasting enthusiasm for it.

In the late 1890s it appeared in America as an adjunct to a horse racing track at Miami. Again it failed to catch the public imagination. Then in 1909 at Tucson, Arizona the first track in modern form opened. This time it gripped and held the public fancy. Other promoters realized the commercial possibilities, and in quick succession a series of tracks opened in Houston, Tulsa (Oklahoma) and again Miami, between the years 1912 and 1922. An American, Charles Munn, a noted sportsman, brought the sport back to England, and soon the Greyhound Racing Association Ltd. came into being. The first track in England was built at Manchester, and the first meeting was held in 1926. By the time the first season closed it was estimated that close to half a million people had attended in less than three months. Following this success, other tracks opened in Liverpool and London. A controlling body, the National Greyhound Racing Club, was formed in January 1928.

In some areas, unrecognized tracks stage meetings, popularly known as 'flapping tracks', but an owner proved to have taken part in these unauthorized events runs the risk of being 'warned off'. Such tracks abound in devious methods and characters and show what can happen without careful control.

At the present time the Greyhound meeting is, in many cases, a social event. Many tracks have facilities which can rival a top-class hotel. Television covers many of the Classics, bringing an even bigger audience to this increasingly popular sport. The sport flourishes today principally in three countries: England, the U.S.A. and Australia.

The fastest dog in the history of Greyhound racing was *Pigalle Wonder* who set up a world record of 28·44 seconds for 525 yards in the Derby heats. To break 29 seconds dead is the mark of a very good dog. Pigalle Wonder broke this barrier nineteen times at the White City, outside London, and five times at Wembley. On top of this he broke seven track records. Another 'great' dog, *Endless Gossip*, won the Greyhound Derby in the fastest time ever recorded for a final. He was not only a great star on the track but a great coursing dog. He went to America where, as a stud force, he exerted a tremendous influence. *Trev's Perfection, Mile Bush Pride, Ballynennan Moon* are famous dogs which also spring to mind. But ask the man in the street who he thinks of when you mention Greyhound racing and the answer invariably comes back – *Mick the Miller*. This dog captured the public imagination as no other dog before or since. No doubt a lot of the credit for the popularity of the sport belongs to him. Whelped in 1926, bred in Ireland by Father Brophy who took him to England, he won a Derby heat and was then sold for £800 (almost $2,000).

Above Greyhound racing. A trial at London's White City Stadium between Fast Buffalo (6) and Aglish Gift (4). The picture shows two dogs in the two airborne positions: tucked and extended stride.

the end of the last century. There they had earned their keep around the stables and particularly those which housed the *fiacres* or hansom cabs. Originally they were mere ratters. However, their strong sense of self-importance and a determination to be with their owners at all times led to their travelling on the front seat of the hansoms when they were driven around the city of Brussels. Once established in this lofty and privileged position they soon appointed themselves as guards!

As is readily apparent from their appearance, Griffons are of mixed ancestry. Almost certainly they started off as a variation of the German AFFENPINSCHER, probably mixed with some small but presumably quite ordinary Belgian street dog. When through 'exposure' on the front seats of cabs they became fashionable pets, a smartening up process was undertaken. One can only guess what breeds were used. However, some which must have played a part in the transformation were Miniature BLACK AND TAN TERRIERS, YORKSHIRE TERRIERS, PUGS and even IRISH TERRIERS.

Each has left its mark. Enthusiasts will hardly need to be reminded that smooth black-and-tan Griffons are frequently encountered, as indeed are black-and-tan Griffons with a rough coat. All modern smooths show

Greyhound racing.
Above Mick the Miller, in the centre, who won the Derby in two consecutive years, is the best known of all racing Greyhounds in Britain.
Right The great American racer, Peach Comber.

Far right Griffon Bruxellois. The smooth variety of this breed is correctly called the Petit Brabançon.

He had changed hands again for £2,000 ($4,800) by the time he had qualified for the final. He won the Derby for his new owner, Mr R. H. Kempton, and he remained until his death at the age of thirteen with his trainer, the famous Sidney Orton. In 1930 he won the Derby for the second time, following this by winning nineteen consecutive races – a winning sequence which is still a record. In all he won forty-six out of sixty-one races. This great dog is preserved, stuffed, in the Natural History Museum, South Kensington, London.

Griffon Bruxellois (Brussels Griffon) The Brussels Griffon is a controversial dog. No two people see it alike. Some consider it wholly beautiful, others extremely ugly. Indeed the one point upon which there is complete agreement is that it is quaint, unusual and full of character.

The breed came to Britain from Belgium towards

a debt to the Pug and clearly the Irish Terrier has left its mark in the coat of rough red. It is also said that TOY SPANIELS were used perhaps to give the large, expressive eyes. Today are recognized two distinct varieties: the Rough, known correctly as the Brussels Griffon or Griffon Bruxellois, and the Smooth, frequently called by the same name, but correctly known as the Petit Brabançon. Both roughs and smooths are frequently born in the same litter.

The external differences between the two are confined to the coat. The roughs have a harsh, wiry, 'broken' coat while with the smooths it is short and straight. However, it is claimed that the real differences run somewhat deeper and that the two varieties have sharply differing characters. The Griffons' intelligence makes them sensitive. They can be quite self-conscious among strangers. Being determined dogs they are not the easiest of breeds to train. They hate to surrender any part of their independence. This can make them particularly difficult over lead training. It is wise to commence this at an early age – six to eight weeks being reasonable. If a start is not made until the dog is six months old complete success is unlikely. Such advice may be thought unnecessary, but it must be remembered that Griffon puppies stick so close to their owner's heels that the necessity for lead training can be easily overlooked.

Despite their size they become sturdy when mature and need no more attention than any other dog. Even so there are numerous hazards connected with breeding. First, bitches are somewhat irregular with their seasons. They do not always conceive when mated. The litters are inclined to be small and a single puppy is not unusual. Finally, the whelps' hold on life is slight and the hazards of the first three weeks after birth are considerable.

These facts explain why the breed has never become really numerous. Griffons have so many advantages, notably of size and behaviour, that it is possible that were a supply of puppies readily available they could become one of the more popular of all the small breeds.

Essentials of the breed: Small, terrier-like dogs with cobby bodies. Lively and alert. Head large and rounded, wide between ears. Nose black, short with large, open nostrils, set high. Wide muzzle with prominent, slightly undershot chin. Teeth should not show. Eyes: large, round and dark. Ears: semi-erect, high and small. Neck: of medium length. Chest: rather wide and deep. Back: short and level – neither dipped nor roached. Tail: two-thirds docked and set on high. Coats: *Roughs* harsh and wiry. *Smooths* short and smooth. Colours: clear red, black or black and rich tan.

Weight should be between 3 and 10 lb. with 6 to 9 lb. being most desirable.

See colour plate p. 384.

Griffon, Wire-Haired Pointing

The Wire-haired Pointing Griffon is a rather slow-working pointing dog with an excellent nose and a well developed retrieving aptitude. It works well as a pheasant dog but is also suitable for work on waterfowl. Because it is not a wide-ranging hunting dog, it is ideal for older sportsmen who hunt on foot, and in restricted areas.

Credit for developing the breed is given to Eduard Korthals. He lived near Haarlem, in Holland, and later moved to Germany. Because of his work, the dog was once called the Korthals Griffon and has also been called the Griffon d'Arret à Poil Dur.

The major period of the breed's development came between 1865 and 1885. The breed attracted great interest in France, partly because Korthals served as an agent for the Duke of Penthievre. Korthals made crosses to French dogs before standardizing his breed. Wire-haired Pointing Griffons were shown at English dogs shows from about 1885, and classes were made for them at the Barn Elms show in 1888. In 1901, the breed was introduced to the United States under its present name.

Essentials of the breed: The Wire-haired Pointing Griffon conforms to general pointing dog type. It is somewhat heavier in body, and has slightly shorter legs. Its coat is short and close – with bristles like those of a wild boar; it is never curly. There is a soft undercoat. The tail, which has no plume, is docked to one-third of its natural length. Colours are steel grey with chestnut splashes, grey-white with chestnut splashes, chestnut, and dirty white mixed with chestnut. Black should never be present.

Height is 21½ to 23½ inches, with bitches about two inches shorter.

Grizzle Bluish grey colour.

Groenendael see Belgian Sheepdog.

Top Griffon Bruxellois (or Brussels Griffon) is the name correctly applied to the rough haired variety of this breed.
Above Griffon, Wire-Haired Pointing. This breed is an efficient bird dog.

Grooming.
Top right All dogs need regular grooming to keep them and their surroundings clean. But while some short-haired dogs need only a quarter of an hour's attention per week, long-haired dogs may need hours of grooming, especially before shows.
Bottom right Brushes for grooming come in different shapes and sizes for varying purposes. Here are three examples.

Grooming The grooming of your dog serves many purposes. It contributes greatly to cleanliness, and it minimizes the nuisance of falling hair on carpets and chairs. Hair grooming stimulates the sebaceous glands to produce oil to condition the hair. It also contributes to skin health, it accustoms the dog to being handled, and it allows him to present his best appearance.

It is the amount of daylight which keys the shedding process as the seasons change. Since house dogs get about the same amount of light the year around, shedding is fairly constant, though with increases at normal shedding seasons. Consequently regular grooming is necessary. Long-coated dogs need daily coat care to prevent snarls and mats from forming. Grooming every three days may be sufficient for dogs with very fine, short coats. Yet all dogs appreciate the attention which daily grooming gives to them.

Dead hair can be loosened by massaging the skin gently with the fingers. It can be removed by stroking from head to tail with the palms of the hands. This method works for long-coated dogs as well as short-coated varieties. On long-coated dogs, the coat can be lifted, turned towards the head, and then rubbed with the thumb. Combing and brushing will then remove loose hair.

Grooming for appearance, or for dog shows, differs with each breed. So do the tools required (which include nail clippers and files, slant-toothed and straight rakes, mink or fox mitts, fine, medium and coarse combs, and many kinds of brushes). As a rule, there are excellent breed books which go into detail on show grooming. Pet shops often have relatively cheap sets of grooming instructions for most breeds.

A dog's feet should be groomed. Excess hair between the toes and spreading out under the foot pads gathers dirt which is then deposited in the home. This hair can be cut away. Toenails should be clipped short since, if allowed to grow too long, the foot is flattened and injured. Nails should be cut back almost to the end of the blood vessel which feeds the nails. It is best to get a veterinarian to do this.

Grooming should also include attention to the eyelids which can be cleaned with a piece of cotton wool, moistened with olive oil.

See BATHING A DOG.

Group System, Britain The British groups system, which is fairly closely followed in most Commonwealth countries, is substantially the same as that adopted by the majority of the countries in North, Central and South America.

Indeed the pattern is so similar that it is best described by outlining the differences. These are mainly (a) in nomenclature of the groups, and (b) in the British tendency, not always strictly adhered to, of including toy or miniature varieties in the same group as the standard variety which is normally the tap root.

The Toy, Terrier, Hound, and Working groups are similarly named in Britain and America. However, the Sporting group in the U.S.A. becomes the Gundog group in Britain, while the Non-Sporting is called Utility. Within the groups, the breeds are precisely

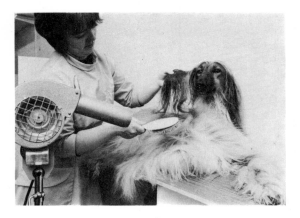

the same in the Sporting/Gundog group, the Hound group and the Terrier group.

In Britain, however, Schnauzers of all three varieties are classified under the Utility group instead of being split between Working and Terrier. Additionally, Toy Poodles are kept with the other varieties of Poodle in the Utility group instead of being placed with the Toys.

Finally, in Britain, Shih Tzus are also included in this group with their cousin the Tibetan or Lhasa Apso, rather than in the Toy Group as in the United States.

Group System, United States and Canada In the United States and Canada, the recognized breeds of dogs are divided into six groups. These are Sporting Dogs, Hounds, Working Dogs, Terriers, Toys, and Non-Sporting Dogs. The latter is a sort of catch-all group for those breeds which cannot be classified as belonging to the other groups.

Group I, Sporting Dogs, in the United States, includes Wire-haired Pointing Griffons, Pointers, German Short-haired Pointers, German Wire-haired Pointers, Chesapeake Bay Retrievers, Curly-Coated Retrievers, Flat Coated Retrievers, Golden Retrievers, Labrador Retrievers, English Setters, Gordon Setters, Irish Setters, American Water Spaniels, Brittany Spaniels, Clumber Spaniels, American Cocker Spaniels, English Cocker Spaniels, English Springer Spaniels, Field Spaniels, Irish Water Spaniels, Sussex Spaniels, Welsh Springer Spaniels, Vizslas, and Weimaraners.

Canada includes the Nova Scotia Duck Tolling Retriever, the German Long-haired Pointer, and the Pudelpointer in this group. None of the three is recognized by the American Kennel Club. All of the dogs in this group use wind-borne scents in hunting.

Group II, Hounds, is composed of those breeds which trail foot scents, or which hunt by sight. In the United States, the group includes the Afghan, Basenji, Basset, 13 inch and 15 inch Beagles, Bloodhound, Borzoi, Black and Tan Coonhound, Long-haired, Smooth, and Wire-haired Dachshunds, Scottish Deerhound, American and English Foxhounds, Greyhound, Harrier, Irish Wolfhound, Norwegian Elkhound, Otter Hound, Rhodesian Ridgeback, Saluki, and Whippet. To this group, Canada adds the Drever, a dog seldom seen in the United States.

Group III, Working Dogs, is made up of the guard dogs, sledge dogs, herding and cattle dogs, and breeds which at one time might have been used as draught dogs. In the United States the breeds are Alaskan Malamute, Belgian Malinois, Belgian Sheepdog, Belgian Tervuren, Bernese Mountain Dog, Bouvier des Flandres, Boxer, Briard, Bullmastiff, Rough and Smooth Coated Collies, Dobermann Pinscher, German Shepherd, Giant Schnauzer, Great Dane, Pyrenean Mountain Dog, Komondor, Kuvasz, Mastiff, Newfoundland, Old English Sheepdog, Puli, Rottweiler, Samoyed, Standard Schnauzer, Shetland Sheepdog, Siberian Husky, St. Bernard, and Cardigan and Pembroke Welsh Corgis. Canada, in addition, recognizes the Eskimo, and Canada considers the three Belgian breeds as one; the Belgian Sheepdog.

Group IV, Terriers, is made up of those breeds which normally would go to earth for prey such as the fox. The breeds in the United States are the Airedale, Australian, Bedlington, Border, and Bull Terriers, Cairn, Dandie Dinmont, Smooth and Wire Fox, Irish, Kerry Blue, Lakeland, Manchester and Norwich Terriers, Miniature Schnauzer, Scottish, Sealyham, Skye, Staffordshire, Welsh Terriers, and West Highland White. Canada includes the Lhasa Apso which, in America, is in the Non-Sporting group.

Group V, Toy Breeds in the U.S. is composed of Affenpinscher, Long-Coat and Smooth Chihuahuas, the English Toy Spaniels, Griffon Bruxellois, Italian Greyhound, Japanese Spaniel, Maltese, Toy Manchester, Papillon, Pekingese, Miniature Pinscher, Pomeranian, Toy Poodle, Pug, Shih Tzu, Silky Terrier, and Yorkshire Terrier. Canada also places the Cavalier King Charles Spaniel in this group, but places the Shih Tzu in Group VI.

Group VI, Non-Sporting Dogs, in the United States, has the following breeds: Boston Terrier, Bulldog, Chow Chow, Dalmatian, French Bulldog, Keeshond, Lhasa Apso, Miniature and Standard Poodles, and Schipperke. In Canada, the group is the same, except for the addition of the Shih Tzu.

Guard Dogs The world-wide rise in crime has brought an increase in the demand for guard dogs. For civilian use, guard dogs fall into two groups. The first is the home guardian, and the second is the professionally

trained dog which is used to accompany security guards or night watchmen as they make their rounds.

People who want guard dogs for their homes, tend to think in terms of those breeds which are notable for their property guarding instincts. And almost invariably they ask for large dogs. In this category belong the GERMAN SHEPHERD DOG, DOBERMANN PINSCHER, BOXER, COLLIE, ROTTWEILER, DALMATIAN, and others. Yet such dogs are not necessarily the only suitable guards.

A famous burglar once discussed the matter from prison. 'Burglars customarily "case" a neighbourhood and individual homes before they decide which ones to try to burglarize. All you need is a noise maker,' he said. 'Any dog which will bark furiously will drive away a burglar or a would-be attacker. For he must consider that the noise will wake up any sleeper in the home, and possibly will alert the entire neighbourhood. When I make preparations to rob a home, I always carry a chunk of fried liver. Then if the home has a dog, which I had not previously discovered, I offer it a bit of the liver. If I can get it to take the food, then I know it will not alert the neighbourhood.

'I do not recommend trained guard dogs which are likely to attack. They represent a danger to the neighbourhood, since most owners do not know how to keep them under control. But also, the burglar is likely to

Above Guard dogs. Any dog can be trained to guard; at this United States Air Force base the handlers work with a German Shepherd Dog and, unusually, with a Bloodhound.

Right Guide dogs for the blind are recruited from the larger intelligent breeds, and individually must have stable temperaments. Once trained, a guide dog becomes a blind person's constant companion and his 'eyes'.

be armed. The dog will undoubtedly drive off the burglar. But it will end up dead, for the burglar will shoot it to protect himself from injury.'

From this, it is obvious that a dog should be taught not to take food from strangers. This is simply taught by having strangers offer the dog food, while you prevent it from accepting it by stern voice commands, by slapping the dog on the nose, or by jerking it back. You then give the dog a food reward. Very shortly, the dog will accept food only from a member of the family, and will be suspicious of anyone who offers it food.

Dogs are now being trained for guard duty at night. Some will accompany guards as they patrol the area outside factories, equipment storage areas, etc. Others will go on patrol with watchmen inside buildings. Many department stores use such dogs which have proved invaluable. The dogs can search an entire floor while the watchman makes only a cursory check.

In some cases, professional training kennels supply the dogs which may be simply placed in a building alone. The kennel may also employ guards which are taught to use the dogs. Or the building or department store may train guards to use the dogs, or more usually, to partner a particular dog. The dogs are delivered in the evening and are picked up in the morning. Some major department stores have their own kennels, and their watchmen are trained not only to work with the dogs, but to feed and care for them as well.

Experience in department stores indicate that Dobermann Pinschers are best suited for this work. This is particularly true when the dogs are permanently quartered in the store. Most such stores are over-heated, at least during the day, and Dobermanns stand this heat very well. And they make less of a shedding problem than do some other breeds. For outdoor and factory patrol work, German Shepherd Dogs are most favoured.

See POLICE DOGS; WAR DOGS.

Guide Dogs for the Blind Association, Great Britain This Association has now been in operation for over forty years. It started in a very small way with one trainer at Wallasey, Cheshire, England, in 1931. The Association now has four training centres which are situated at Bolton, Exeter and Leamington Spa in England, and Forfar in Scotland. The headquarters are at Ealing, London.

The cost of training a guide dog in Britain is about £250 ($600), but no blind person is asked to make more than a token payment for his dog. It is the Association's policy that no applicant is ever refused a guide dog on financial grounds. The figure of £250 includes only the cost of training the dog and it does not include the training of the blind person in the use of it, nor does it include the very important matter of after-care.

There are approximately 1,500 guide dog owners in the United Kingdom. The Association trains guide dogs for new applicants and also provides replacements for dogs when they come to the end of their working life, usually when the dog is eight or nine years old. Guide dog owners needing a replacement are encouraged to come back to the training centre for retraining with a new dog as soon as possible.

The selection of the dog is of major importance, for on this foundation all else must be built up. They must have a high degree of intelligence and be willing to please. They must be free of vice and nervousness, of even temperament and have good concentration. LABRADOR RETRIEVERS are used mainly, but some GERMAN SHEPHERD DOGS (Alsatians), GOLDEN RETRIEVERS, BOXERS and a few cross breeds are also trained. Bitches are used in preference to male dogs which have certain disadvantages, but both are capable of efficient work.

When the blind applicant goes to one of the training centres he is allocated a guide dog that has been specially selected for 'compatibility'. About four weeks are spent in training the blind person with his dog.

When the blind handler leaves the training centre he is visited from time to time to see that both he and his dog are well and working together correctly. If there are any problems the trainer can normally correct these on the spot but if not the blind person is asked to return to the training centre for a few days.

Guide Dogs for the Blind, United States The training of dogs to guide the blind was pioneered in the United States. John Sinykin, a German Shepherd breeder, trained a dog for a blind U.S. Senator, which led to his setting up, in 1926, a school for guide dogs, The Master Eye Institute, known popularly as His Master's Eyes. Other schools followed in the next twenty-five years: The Seeing Eye (whose first trainer was Josef Weber) was founded in 1928, Leader Dogs for the Blind in 1939, Guide Dogs for the Blind in 1942, and Pilot Dogs in 1950. Since then many training centres have been established.

Gums The gums are formed by mucous membrane and the underlying tissues covering the bony sockets of the teeth, and the necks of erupted teeth. They are subject to several diseases, chiefly gingivitis and pyorrhoea, or alveolar pyorrhoea, as it is sometimes called. Foul smelling breath results from either disease.

In gingivitis, the gums become enlarged and spongy, and pus can usually be forced out from between the gum and the teeth. Receding gums often indicate alveolar pyorrhoea. A blue line along the gums is a major symptom of lead or mercury poisoning.

Malnutrition can cause a deficiency disease called 'black tongue' in the United States, and canine typhus or Stuttgart's disease in other countries. With this disease, the dog is so weakened that a dozen types of infective germs can often be found on or under the gums, and in the mouth tissues. Treatment for any of these diseases must be given under the direction of a veterinarian. Supportive treatment by feeding a balanced diet and the therapeutic administration of vitamins and minerals can be given by the owner. Under normal circumstances, dogs synthesize sufficient vitamin C for their needs, but in such diseases as those mentioned above, added vitamin C is believed to be helpful.

Gundog In some countries the term gundog is

applied to a hunting dog whose training or ability is not sufficient for entry into championship stakes. In Britain, it means the member of any breed in the Gundog group. See FIELD TRIALS (GUNDOGS)–BRITISH; GROUP SYSTEM, BRITAIN.

Gundogs, Preliminary Training Of The gundog enthusiast has available to him a wide variety of books which deal with the advanced training of specific breeds for the work they will be called upon to perform in the field. However, there is much basic education which can be given to the puppy long before any formal training is undertaken. Some of this is based upon very recent behavioural studies.

A widely held misconception is that the training of a field dog should not be begun until the puppy is eight months to a year old. It is held that early training will break the dog's spirit, and will slow it down until it becomes a potterer in the field. But this is true only if the dog is given severe formal training too early.

A puppy needs to be taken into the fields as young as possible because it must become 'field wise'. It can absorb this education while on walks with its owner. These walks should become longer as the puppy grows stronger. And they should involve tests which the puppy must solve on its own, or without knowing that it is being helped.

For example, there is the fence. Master climbs over. The puppy cannot do so. It may find a hole through which it can squeeze. If no such hole exists, then the master simply walks along his side of the fence until the puppy finds a hole under the fence. After a couple of such experiences, the puppy will learn to run back and forth until it finds such a hole. The fence may be low enough so that the master can jump over. He jumps back and forth a couple of times. The puppy quickly gets the idea, though the fence may have to be lowered.

Then there is the steep bank. The master scrambles up, but the small puppy cannot make it. Master then walks along the bank until he reaches a spot where the puppy will be able to climb up. The puppy quickly learns to hunt for such a spot.

When master and puppy approach a stream, the master selects a shallow place, removes his shoes and socks, and walks across. If the puppy is afraid to follow, master starts to walk away, while calling. The puppy then will follow. After a lesson or two, swimming will follow naturally. But in the meantime, the puppy will have learned to select a shallow place for crossing.

Some owners quite deliberately try to lose the puppy. When it finds it is lost, it is forced to work out the way to go home. If trained, young puppies never get lost.

Even at seven or eight weeks, the puppy should become acquainted with the type of game which it is later to hunt. A BEAGLE can be given the scent of a rabbit skin. Then while it watches from behind a fence, or while being held, the skin can be dragged along the ground, and out of sight. When the puppy is released, it will instinctively start to trail. Similarly, bird dog, retriever, and spaniel puppies can be given the scent of pheasant wings, perhaps nailed to a piece of wood. Though formal retrieving is not to be tried at this stage,

Gundogs.
Left A Labrador waits for praise after retrieving a bunch of turkey feathers during preliminary training.

Right A good gundog delivers the retrieved game to its master unmarked except by the shot.

play retrieving within the home or kennel can be done. Formal training later will be easy.

Simple obedience lessons – 'yard breaking' in the field training parlance – can be given to eight week old puppies within the home or kennel. The dog can be taught to walk at heel and to sit and stay, for example, while its meal is being prepared. These lessons should not be more than three minutes long. They can be given ten minutes apart, and three times morning and night.

A spaniel field trainer teaches eight-week-old puppies to come upon a whistle signal in the following manner. Someone diverts the attention of the puppies so that they go to the far end of the pen. He then blows his whistle and sets the food pans down. By this simple lesson, repeated two or three times daily, he establishes a conditioned reflex. The puppies then will come instantly when called, regardless of distracting circumstances.

Formal 'yard breaking', retrieving, and hunting experience can come much later. But the puppy will not have forgotten what he learned during those first weeks after weaning. The formal training will then come more easily.

Gundog Working Tests (British) Gundog Working Tests differ from FIELD TRIALS in that, while trials are run on live game in natural surroundings under normal shooting conditions, working tests are conducted with dummies or cold game, on a set course and under artificial conditions. The dummies are 'planted' or thrown by hand. The word 'trial' is reserved for the real thing while 'test' covers only artificially contrived contests.

There is usually one judge with fields of up to twenty-four dogs, although sixteen or twelve runners are considered ideal. Gundog tests, approved of by the Kennel Club as good practice for dog and handler alike. are not officially recognized. They are usually run by breed clubs and by adding sparkle and competitive interest to the non-shooting season, are becoming very popular. A good working test can extend the best of field trial dogs, if the course is planned by an experienced gundog man.

Each dog tries the test under identical conditions, unlike trials where luck plays a part. There are usually two separate tests in the morning, after which some dogs are discarded. The rest take part in three or four further tests in the afternoon when marks are added up and the winners announced.

Small prizes are usually given to the four placed dogs, but there are no titles and no official recognition.

A good course maker can really test dogs by, for example, setting an unseen dummy to be retrieved, with a seen dummy being thrown as a diversion. Alternatively, a long distance dummy may be hidden in cover, the dog required to find it by hand-signals. Tests may be given over or in water, using fences and woods, and artificial hares may be introduced to increase the difficulty.

Inevitably the stress and excitement of a real trial, where a live hare may suddenly jump into the dog's face, is missing. Even so, dogs can be thoroughly tried, the tests being graded according to whether it is a Novice or Open Test.

Working tests are invariably run for retrievers or spaniels. Tests of this kind with artificial dummies and cold game are unsuitable for pointers and setters.

Guns Expert shots who do the shooting over dogs at FIELD TRIALS.

Gun-Shy Dogs which fear gun-fire.

Left Gundog working tests, unlike field trials, are artificially set up and the dogs work with dummies or cold game.

H

Hackles Hair on the neck and along the spine which is raised in anger, fright, or uncertainty.

Hackney Gait A high stepping trot reminiscent of that of the hackney horse.

Hair A simple definition of a mammal is an animal which suckles its young by mammary glands, and whose body is covered with hair. This applies equally to man and dogs, and even to the so-called HAIRLESS DOGS which do have some hair.

Hair grows in recessed pits in the skin, called hair follicles. It develops in the foetal puppy so that, at birth, it is protected by a close blanket of insulation – hairless dogs excepted.

If cross-sectioned under a microscope, hair can be seen to be of different types. The straight, coarse, outer coat of many breeds consists of hairs which are round. Woolly hair tends to be elliptical in section. Wavy, or slightly curling hair is oval in section.

A small muscle, the arrector pili, is attached to each hair. In the dog these muscles are able to lift the hair to varying degrees in different areas of the body. Men say that their 'hair stood on end', but for the most part, it does not; men get goose-flesh or goose-pimples instead.

Dogs, and most mammals, other than man, have tactile and sensory hairs about the lips and cheeks – the 'whiskers'. They are believed to be controlled by the sympathetic nervous system. In the dog, they are only partially functional, if at all.

Hairless Dogs Hairless dogs have appeared in many parts of the world; in general, they have been named for the area from which they came. Among them have been the Abyssinian Hairless Dog, the African Sand Dog, Turkish Naked Dog, the Barbary Dog, and Chinese Crested Dog. As a rule, they have come from tropical or semi-tropical countries. However, a dog known seventy-five to a hundred years ago came from North China.

Sometimes the same dog has been known under several names. Thus, the Chinese Crested Dog has, at times, been called the Turkish Naked Dog, and the dog known in some countries as the Mexican Hairless has been called the Chinese Hairless, even in Mexico. This may indicate a Turkish origin for both breeds.

In the past, authorities have claimed that the hairless dog is not a breed but only a monstrosity within a breed. In 1900 it was contended that breeding hairless dogs to their kind would bring quick extinction to hairless animals. Yey the first Mexican Hairless Dog was shown in the United States as early as 1883, and it was recognized nearly 20 years before the CHIHUAHUA. Hairless dogs were common along the Mexican – United States border as early as 1840, and writers mention them as being popular in Mexican homes from Texas to Arizona. Mexicans called them 'Pelon Dogs' while Americans spoke of them simply as 'no hair dogs'. They were apparently much larger than the Mexican Hairless. One frustrating description says that the 'Pelon has a fat body as big as a watermelon', but watermelons vary greatly in size, so the comparison is not very telling. The writers said that the dog was descended from the Barbary Dog. However, there is no indication as to what the Barbary Dog was, nor how it reached the New World.

The Mexican Hairless does not have breed recognition in Mexico, and the American Kennel Club has withdrawn it from its list of pure breeds. In America this is because no dogs have been registered in recent years and it is assumed that the breed has died out. There are, however, kennels which breed what are purported to be Mexican Hairless Dogs.

Hairless dogs.
Top right Xoloitzcuintli, the only hairless breed recognized by Mexico.
Bottom right A Chinese Crested Dog, Ch. Winterlea Starba of Crest Haven.

Canada still grants recognition to the breed. The standard calls for a dog slightly smaller than the FOX TERRIER. The dog has erect, rounded ears, a smooth, entirely hairless body, except for a topknot between the ears. Broken or cut ears or tail, or 'fuzz' or any hair on the body, bring disqualification. The skin is hot to the touch.

The cause of hairlessness is not certainly known. It has been attributed to a blood factor deficiency, to a skin ailment involving pigmentation, and to an incompletely functioning gene. Whatever the cause, hairlessness is sex-linked to missing teeth. In some cases, all but the front teeth are missing, but in most, only the pre-molars are missing. Extreme examples have occurred in which the toe nails also are missing. In litters of both Mexican Hairless and Chinese Crested Dogs, an occasional puppy is born with normal hair and teeth. Such puppies are called 'powder puffs'.

Mexico recognizes one hairless breed, the *Xoloitzcuintli*. This dog cannot have been the Xoloitzcuintli of the Aztecs, which was a nearly hairless animal with a body four feet long, and one of three domesticated quadrupeds. This creature might have been the long extinct giant *quemi*, but it could hardly have been a dog.

The modern Xoloitzcuintli may be a descendant of the Pelon Dog. The preferred colours of the Xoloitzcuintli are a uniform dark bronze, elephant grey, greyish black, or black, pink and brown blotches being permitted.

Both the Mexican Kennel Club and the FEDERATION CYNOLOGIQUE INTERNATIONALE recognize the Xoloitzcuintli, and an official standard has been approved. This standard states that a peculiarity of the breed is that it has a temperature of 104 degrees F, or about three degrees higher than that of the normal dog. Norman Pelham Wright, the best known writer on the breed, also makes this statement. However, temperature checks on dogs made in Mexico and the United States have failed to show any variation from the normal – about 101 degrees F. Countess Lascelles de Premio Real, Mexico's best known breeder, also has stated that she doubts the dogs have other than normal temperatures. This misconception may have arisen because the skin feels hot to the touch. This skin warmth is apparently due to the lack of insulation furnished by the hair of a normal dog.

Essentials of the breed: The standard calls for a dog 12 to 20 inches at the shoulder. The muzzle tapers and is longer than the skull. The dogs are 'bat-eared'. The ears are about four inches in length. The nose is dark, or pink or brown according to skin colour. The neck is long. The body is well made, and the legs and feet have good bone. Disqualifications include hanging ears; clipped ears; cut or broken tails; albinism; and CRYPTORCHIDISM or monorchidism.

Handlers see Professional Handlers; Kennel Men and Maids.

Hard A term used to denote terriers which are determined fighters and diggers.

Harderian Gland see Eye Anatomy; Eye Diseases.

Hard-Mouthed Used to describe a dog which crunches or tears the game it is retrieving.

Hard Pad Disease Hard pad disease appeared first in England. Since it occurred in dogs which had been supposedly protected against DISTEMPER, it was considered to be a virus disease of similar type, but distinct from distemper. Today it is considered to be caused by the virus of distemper which has undergone a change that renders it unaffected by the antibodies produced by the original distemper vaccines.

Hyperkeratosis – enlargement and hardening of the foot pads – occurs. The external nose, that is, its tip, and the eyelids may also harden and enlarge. Dark speckles are often seen in the skin of the groin and in the inner surfaces of the ear flaps.

This form of distemper is now found throughout the world. Distemper vaccines have been developed which are strong enough to protect against all forms of the 'Distemper Complex' – this name being applied to all types of disease caused by the various distemper viruses.

Harefoot One in which the third digits are longer than the others.

Hare Lip see Cleft Palate.

Harlequin Patched or pied colouration, usually black on white, as in a Harlequin Great Dane.

Harness A double collar, with one band around the neck and one around the chest, fastened at the withers.

Above Harefoot.
Below Harlequin Great Dane.

Harrier The Harrier is perhaps the only dog which has been developed specifically to hunt the hare. Its name suggests that this was originally its purpose. However, the Norman-Saxon word for trailing hounds was *Harier,* and this term was often used for all hounds. As specific breeds began to emerge about 1850, the term 'harrier' came to mean the Harrier breed.

So far as can be determined, the earliest pack was established by Sir Elias de Midhope in 1260. The Cotley Pack of Somerset was organized by Thomas Deane of Broad Oak, Chard, in 1796 to hunt hares in front of sportsmen moving on foot. In more modern times, sportsmen have followed on horse.

The dogs were originally large, slow hounds in Southern England. They were badger, pied-lemon, or pure white in colour. Both BLOODHOUND and FOX-HOUND crosses were introduced. Eventually, black, tan, and white colours became so popular that the present tri-colours became predominant. The modern Harrier can best be described as a hound similar to the BEAGLE and the Foxhound, but intermediate in size.

Dogs which would eventually be called Harriers were introduced to the United States and Canada in colonial times, but in Eastern North America, there are no true hares, and the smaller hounds did not prove suitable for use in trailing the fast American fox.

Harriers used in hunting by packs has declined in England, and the Americans have failed to develop packs which might be used for trailing jack rabbits on the Western Plains. Harriers are used to some extent in the pack hunting of leopards in Ceylon, and in similar fashion, for trailing the large cats of Northern South America.

Essentials of the breed: The Harrier is between 19 and 21 inches tall at the withers. A peculiarity is that the standard permits a slight knuckling over at the pasterns, and cat feet whose toes turn slightly inwards. The breed is characteristically dish-faced. In other particulars, the Foxhound standard applies.
See colour plate p. 182.

Harvest Mite This is a minute mite, red in colour and too small to be seen by the naked eye. It is the larva of a species of Trombidium. It attacks dogs, cats, human beings, and occasionally other animals.

In dogs, the commonest sites of attack are the feet, between the toes. Small spots appear which, if left alone, develop into scabs which eventually fall away. However, the condition is extremely irritating and the dog affected with these mites will constantly lick the feet, producing more sores that prevent the original spots and scabs from showing.

Haw The nictitating membrane, or winking membrane, in the inside corner of the eye, exposed in some breeds.

Hearing The anatomy of the ear of the dog is basically the same as that of the human ear, though there are major differences in hearing ability. The ear of each consists of three parts, the external ear, the middle ear,

and those sensory nerves which carry impulses to the brain which translates them into sound.

The outer ear, or auricle, gathers sound waves and channels them down a tube to the ear drum. This tube is lightly covered with skin which contains modified sweat glands. Instead of perspiration, these glands produce cerumen, or wax.

On the internal side of the eardrum are three bones – commonly called the hammer, anvil, and stirrup because of their shape – which are connected to one another in sequence. These three bones rest in a small cavity connected to the eustachian tube. Air from the throat enters the eustachian tube to equalize pressure on both sides of the ear drum. The end of the stirrup fills a tube called the cochlea. The sensory area of the cochlea is called the organ of Corti, which picks up impulses and carries them to the brain.

Both low and very high sounds require greater volume if they are to be heard than do middle-range sound waves. In this respect, the hearing of man and dog varies only a little. The normal hearing range of man is from 20 to 20,000 cycles per second. The dog's range is from 20 to 30,000 or more.

The knowledge that the dog can hear high-pitched sounds far above man's hearing limit has brought about the so-called silent or Galton whistle. The dog hears the whistle, but its owner hears only the rush of air. Dog trainers have found that the 'sharpness' of the whistle is a factor in making a dog obey. The 'silent' whistles lack that 'command sharpness' which is characterized by other types of whistles – those audible to man as well as dog.

At birth, the puppy is both deaf and blind. The ears begin to open at ten to twelve days. Development of both sight and hearing then occurs. Some observers do not believe that puppies have an inborn sense of the meaning of sounds. For example, they must learn the meaning of their mother's growls and barks. They may learn this painfully, when the mother nips them at the same time as she growls. The puppies themselves experiment with growling and biting.

It is generally believed that dogs can hear sounds from a much greater distance than human beings. Experiments have been conducted both in the laboratory and in the field. Dogs and their owners were tested at varying distances when hunting horns were used. The dogs would alert to a blast from the horn when their owners could not hear it, even though the owner was deliberately listening for the sound and the dog was not.

The capacity of dogs varies both individually and by breed. Dogs with large erect ears can hear at greater distances than dogs with erect, but cropped ears. Again, erect, but cropped eared dogs can hear at a greater range than can those with dropped ears, and the smooth-haired Foxhound will be able to hear much further than will the Poodle or spaniel with heavily furred ears.

Dogs with erect ears can move them forward or to the side, the better to pick up sounds, and while drop-eared dogs try to erect their ears to hear better, they are only partially successful.

The ability of dogs to *locate* sound is superior to that of man. The dog cocks his ears, then may turn his head to face the origin of the sound. The man's ears are virtually stationary. When dogs are placed in the centre of a circle and then tested with sounds coming from various points in the perimeter, they can locate the source within five degrees. This may be because the sound waves reach the two ears at different times. Even though this difference may be of the order of ten-thousandths of a second, the ears are sensitive enough to pick up the difference, and the brain to interpret it.

Heart Diseases The dog's heart is a four-chambered pump. One half of the pump drives the blood to all parts of the body except the lungs, and in this way, oxygen, nourishment, antigens and antibodies are delivered to all the body's tissues. The other half drives blood to the lungs, to pick up more oxygen. The cycle is continuous throughout life.

There is no specific rate of heart beat for dogs, but small dogs have a higher rate per minute than large dogs. When healthy dogs are at rest, a small dog may have a heart beat of 100, while a large dog may have one under 80. The heart rate of human beings is 72.

If the heart is worked too hard in early life, it enlarges. But in doing so, it loses some of its ability to expand and contract. This condition is found in racing Greyhounds, field trial Pointers, setters, spaniels, and others which are put into severe training too early. There is no cure for an enlarged heart. The dog with such a heart must be kept quiet, and should be given only a minimum of exercise.

Endocarditis, a thickening of the heart valves, is one of the more frequent of the heart diseases. Chronic cough is often a symptom of valvular disease. Valvular diseases often follow severe or nearly fatal illnesses, such as DISTEMPER, 'black tongue' (Stuttgart's Disease or canine typhus) and tuberculosis. Pneumonia is a frequent cause. This disease blocks sections of the lungs so that they do not function with normal efficiency. The heart is overworked to supply blood and oxygen to the rest of the body. As the heart muscle begins to tire, valvular troubles start to develop.

Pericarditis is an infection of the area between the heart and the pericardium, or enclosing sack. An

infection of the heart muscle itself is called myocarditis. Endocarditis is an infection of the membrane lining the heart.

Fatty deposits sometimes build up about the heart, and interfere with its action. Sometimes the fats invade the fibres of the heart muscle or even the spaces between them, and the heart is then placed under great strain.

The dog owner can only follow the advice of his veterinarian when heart trouble has been discovered, but he can watch for the major symptoms of cardiac disease. These are chronic cough, breathlessness after slight exertion, an unwillingness to climb stairs and exhaustion after the climb, cyanosis (blue discoloration) of the gums and mouth tissues, and edema (swelling) of the limbs, or abdomen.

Heart Worm see Filariasis, Canine.

Heat of Bitch A bitch usually comes into season every six or seven months and the period usually lasts for about three weeks. Thus a normal bitch has two heats or seasons per year. Some bitches only come in heat once a year and some immature bitches may not come in season at all. If a bitch shows no sign of

Above Heart diseases afflict dogs as well as men. This mongrel is recovering from a hole-in-the-heart operation.

coming into season by the time she is fourteen or fifteen months old a veterinarian should be consulted. A bitch can, if necessary, be brought into season artificially by veterinary treatment and often mated successfully.

The first indication that a bitch is coming into season is usually a swelling of the vulva plus a discharge from the external genital parts. At first this discharge is almost colourless but in a few days it becomes a pinkish-red colour and later on bloodstained. This is caused by the breaking down of the walls of the uterus in preparation for the attachment of the fertilized egg from which will develop the foetus. The coloured discharge will usually last until the middle of the season, after which it diminishes leaving again a colourless mucous which lasts until the end of the heat.

The bitch is usually ready to be mated just when the colour begins to subside, that is from about the seventh day to the thirteenth or fourteenth day. This is the only time that most bitches will accept a stud dog although, of course, there are the exceptions. Some bitches seem to want to be mated on their fourth or fifth day and some not until much later at their sixteenth or seventeenth day. Such cases are infrequent but not abnormal.

At the beginning of the true OESTRUS – when the bitch accepts the dog – the ovaries discharge the ripe egg cells. These are held in the Fallopian tubes where they remain until fertilization. If the bitch is not mated the ova disintegrate and pass out of the body with other waste material.

A bitch in season must be carefully looked after and not allowed the opportunity to escape to find her own mate. House pets should be confined strictly to their own gardens or yards, and one of the proprietary mixtures of anti-mate rubbed or sprayed on her quarters and tail. This should help to keep unwanted male dogs away from the house.

The bitch in season must not be allowed to contract a chill by lying on cold wet concrete in a yard or kennel run. She should be sheltered from very cold winds and not left outside in such conditions. Neglect in this direction can lead to metritis, or inflammation of the uterus, which can be very serious requiring the removal of the uterus in severe cases to save the bitch.

If a bitch does unfortunately get caught by a dog during her oestrum the effects of this misalliance can be stopped by an injection given within 48 hours by a veterinarian. It will not affect any future litters that may be planned for the bitch, although the drug is dangerous if repeatedly given.

Heating of Kennels and Living Quarters

It is essential that dogs should be kept warm in cold conditions. There is no need to pamper them and it may be that a good bed of straw or wood wool in a draught-free kennel will be enough. Excessive heat is not good for a dog and this should be avoided.

Warmth is required by a bitch and her puppies particularly during WHELPING and in the first few weeks afterwards. Many whelps unfortunately die because of cold.

Invalid dogs need warmth to hasten their recovery and the temperature of their kennel or room should not be allowed to fall below 60° Fahrenheit or 15·5° Centigrade. No dog should be left to shiver in its quarters. See NURSING SICK DOGS.

Artificial heat can be supplied in various ways, INFRA-RED LAMPS being the safest method. It is essential to keep all electrical wiring out of reach of the dog, and the lamp should be installed with great care.

Underfloor heating has the advantage that heat rises and so the whole kennel will be warm. Unfortunately this method of heating has a disadvantage: fluid rapidly evaporates, and the floor becomes covered with dried urine which produces a strong smell that is difficult to remove.

Open fires of any sort should not be used because of the risk of accidents.

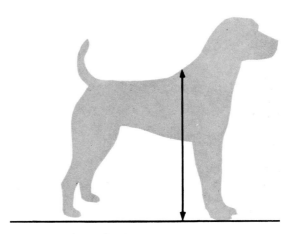

Height of Dogs The height of a dog is the vertical distance from the ground to the highest point of the dog's WITHERS.

The actual height of the giant breeds of dogs has been a subject of controversy for several centuries. There have been several reasons for this. One has been the tendency of owners to add one to three inches in making claims as to the height of their dogs. Another has been the failure to have accurate measurements taken by persons skilled in measuring dogs, and who lack bias. Finally, many measurements have been made by devices which are inaccurate.

The best study of IRISH WOLFHOUND height was made by the American breeder, Alfred W. DeQuoy. He made careful measurements of 75 Irish Wolfhounds. The tallest male was $36\frac{1}{4}$ inches at the shoulder; the shortest, $32\frac{3}{4}$ inches. The tallest bitch was 34 inches; the shortest, $30\frac{1}{2}$ inches. The average for males was $34\frac{1}{2}$ inches; for bitches, 32 inches.

From time to time, measurements of GREAT DANES, SCOTTISH DEERHOUNDS, and BORZOIS have been made using an oversized 'hound stick'. A hound stick consists of two posts connected at the top by a cross-bar. A hole in the centre of the cross-bar permits a rod to drop to the shoulder blades of the dog – this rod has a cross-piece which rests upon the shoulders.

Right Height of dogs. A dog is measured vertically from the ground to the highest point of the withers.

The distance from the ground to the cross-piece is the height of the dog.

At a representative show, 18 male Great Danes were measured. Two were 35½ inches; one was 35¼ inches; five were 35 inches. Two dogs were 33 inches, and none was under this height. One of those measured at 35 inches was actually being advertised as being 37 inches. On another occasion, a Great Dane was obviously taller than a yard stick placed beside it, but no accurate measurement was possible. An estimate of 37 inches was made.

Measurements of some 15 Borzois showed the tallest to be 33 inches at the shoulder, and the shortest 31⅞ inches. It should be pointed out that strongly roached Borzois will be considerably taller if measured at the highest point of the back.

The comparative rarity of Scottish Deerhounds makes it difficult to measure any large number of them. However, those males measured were between 30 and 32 inches at the shoulder, with one standing 33 inches.

Two conclusions can be made from this. There really is no world's tallest breed of dog although the Irish Wolfhound is generally accepted as such, and the giant breeds differ very little in average height.

Hematoma of the Ear see Ear Diseases.

Hemophilia This is a rare condition, seen occasionally in dogs, in which the animal bleeds very easily, and the natural blood clotting mechanism is retarded or non-existent. Unlike the condition in human beings, the disease can occur in either sex.

In the acute form, where the blood does not clot at all, the affected puppy usually dies at birth, or immediately afterwards, owing to blood loss. Where an animal suffers from the non-acute form, in which the clotting ability exists but is slow to function, the disease may not be discovered until injury occurs. This condition can present great complications if surgery has to be undertaken.
See CHROMOSOMES.

Hemorrhage This is the bleeding that results from damage to a blood vessel. It may be external or internal, and due to injury or illness.

External hemorrhage is the result of injury to the skin, allowing blood to escape. Internal hemorrhage results from damage to internal organs or blood vessels, causing bleeding into one of the body cavities. It also occurs when a blood vessel is ruptured, and blood passes into the body tissues. Thus a bruise is in fact a small hemorrhage where blood has escaped and lies between the cells of the affected area.
See DISEASES OF THE EAR; FIRST AID.

Hepatitis Hepatitis is an inflammation of the liver. As the liver is one of the most important organs in the body, cases of hepatitis are always serious. The initial signs of hepatitis include loss of appetite and tenderness of the abdomen. At a later stage JAUNDICE may develop. The disease takes two forms: infectious hepatitis and toxic hepatitis.

In dogs, the most important type of infectious hepatitis is caused by a virus producing the disease which is known by several names: Canine Virus Hepatitis (C.V.H.), Infectious Canine Hepatitis, or Rubarth's Disease. The first comprehensive account of the disease was given by Professor Rubarth of Stockholm in 1947 and since then its presence has been confirmed in Great Britain, Australia and the United States of America. In actual fact the disease was widespread long before this but it was confused with other diseases, particularly DISTEMPER.

All ages of dogs may be affected but it is usually a disease of puppies. The incubation period is from six to nine days. A typical case will show symptoms of fever for several days with abdominal pain. In mild cases the high temperature may be the only sign of illness and it may last only one or two days. In more severe cases there will be signs of CONJUNCTIVITIS and tonsilitis. Sometimes the disease process may be so rapid that no symptoms are noticed before the dog is found dead. Dogs which recover from the disease may develop a temporary corneal opacity a week or so later. The diagnosis of Canine Virus Hepatitis may not be easy, particularly as the animal may be suffering from distemper at the same time. As in distemper, 'prevention is better than cure'. Vaccination against the disease is most successful. Usually the vaccine is combined with the distemper vaccine and given at the same time.

The other type of infectious hepatitis occurring in dogs is sometimes found in LEPTOSPIROSIS. However it is rare for a case of leptospirosis to mimic a case of canine virus hepatitis and there is unlikely to be confusion between the two diseases.

In cases of poisoning, the liver may be damaged to such an extent that toxic hepatitis is produced. The POISONS which may cause this include carbon tetrachloride, chloroform, phosphorous and various arsenical compounds.

Toxic hepatitis is the end result of the poisoning: the initial symptoms depend upon the particular poison and the amount which was absorbed into the system. By the time damage to the liver is detected the prospects for recovery will be poor. If a case of poisoning is suspected professional advice should be sought as soon as possible.

Hereditary Abnormalities Man has changed the conformation of most breeds to suit his own purposes.

In show dogs, fashion demands special characteristics. A large proportion of the standards laid down for specific breeds are compatible with soundness, health and physiological normality. Unfortunately, there are some which are not. Any condition that prevents an animal from living a normal life must be classed as an abnormality.

Veterinary opinion all over the world considers some of these conditions to be of a hereditary nature. An increasing number of dogs suffering from such conditions are seen. This is due to (1) injudicious breeding; (2) lack of culling; (3) over-exaggeration of breed standards; (4) in some instances, a fault in the actual standards; (5) rapid miniaturization, with its attendant evils.

Factors (1), (2), (3) and (5) may be the result of the altered pattern of dog breeding, which has changed from the hobby of people who could afford to cull extensively, to a commercial proposition undertaken by some with little knowledge of genetics.

Excessively abnormal temperament is a great problem today. This covers a wide field, and is manifested chiefly as extreme nervousness, leading in some cases to mental deficiency or insanity. Such animals cannot possibly be a pleasure to their owners and the dogs themselves can get little enjoyment out of life.

In show dogs it is natural for attention to be paid to beauty and appearance. But these should be considered in relation to complete mental and physical health. For instance, extravagantly large heads can cause complications at birth, and thus a number of bitches experience WHELPING troubles. The eyes in many breeds are required to be large or small. Large eyes increase vulnerability to injury. Eyes that are too small and sunken in the head can lead to ENTROPION.

Some breed standards require that the hind legs must be perfectly straight, resulting in a stilted gait. Some consider this to be carrying a characteristic to extremes. Another example is screwed or kinked tails which can lead to friction dermatitis, or skin trouble caused by rubbing.

Crooked forelegs are the result of abnormal angulation of the carpus, or 'wrist' joint, which is unecessary, and must handicap the animal's movements. Excessively long ears in some breeds certainly predispose to otitis externa (inflammation caused by wax, dirt, parasites and lack of air penetration). See EAR DISEASES. The flattening of the face in other breeds – particularly when allied with a shortening of the skull – leads to nasal fold dermatitis; also to corneal irritation (which is often due to the direct contact of facial hairs with the cornea of the eye), and elongated, soft palates.

Most of these conditions become a source of income to the veterinary profession, but one which it would willingly do without.

While many of these criticisms relate to physical features which can be recognized by any intelligent breeder, there are other conditions of equal if not greater importance which can be recognized, or diagnosed, only by a veterinarian. For example: Progressive Retinal Atrophy (PRA or Night Blindness). This can be accurately diagnosed only by a very careful examination of the interior of the eye with an ophthalmoscope. However, the early signs may be an increase in the size of the pupil, signs of poor sight and, eventually, BLINDNESS. It is a problem in many breeds; and with present knowledge, difficult to eradicate – particularly since it is not always possible to diagnose until late in the dog's life. It is one of those unfortunate conditions which can crop up in any breeding programme, and especially when LINE BREEDING is adopted. In the early stages, the animal is distressed if unable to adapt itself to a restricted vision. The end result is complete blindness. The first breed found to be affected by Progressive Retinal Atrophy was the Irish Setter. Thanks to the co-operation of the Kennel Club (England), the breeders and their veterinarians, the defect has now been eliminated in this breed. See also EYE DISEASES.

HIP DYSPLASIA. This can be definitely diagnosed only by an expert X-ray examination of both hips. Nevertheless, it may be suspected due to an inability to jump, and a swaying action of the hips; but these signs in moderately affected dogs are not always present. This is another serious condition which, while apparently painless in the early stages, interferes with a working dog's ability and staying powers. There is evidence of pain in the later stages.

ENTROPION. Turning in of the eyelids is seen in many breeds. It causes pain and distress, allied to extreme irritation of the whole surface of the eye.

PATELLA LUXATION. Is evidenced by a noticeably *bent* limb, the knee-joint being turned inwards, the hock out, and the paw pointing diagonally inwards. The dog moves in a crouched position with a tendency to skip. Usually there is considerable pain at this stage. It is found more often in the straight-stifled breeds, and is satisfactorily relieved only by surgery.

DEAFNESS is often associated with the colour of the coat. See COLOUR INHERITANCE.

UTERINE INERTIA is the inability to whelp within a reasonably normal time. The bitch will appear lazy and often sleep for long periods between the arrival of each puppy. It is a condition encountered in some breeds, and should the bitch fail to produce all the puppies naturally, Caesarean section may be needed.

DERMATITIS is associated with excessively deep skin folds, causing distress and irritation. This is difficult to control, and to overcome the irritation permanently often requires cosmetic surgery.

Other hereditary abnormalities are EPILEPSY, *Pannus*, prolonged soft palate, certain types of chronic diarrhoea, and a form of anaemia found only in Basenjis.

It must be pointed out that many of the troublesome conditions described can be seen also in mongrels; but since these animals are not generally bred from, it follows that the incidences are less pronounced.

Hermaphrodite This is the term used when a dog actually has some organs of both sexes, or is so developed that it is almost impossible to determine whether it is male or female.

Hernia is the protrusion of an organ, or part of an organ, through the wall of the cavity that contains that organ. The term is commonly used to refer to the misplacement of the abdominal contents through a weakened area of the abdominal wall. Where abdominal contents protrude through a tear in the abdominal muscles (perhaps due to accident or injury) the name 'rupture' may be applied.

Commonest hernias in the dog are umbilical, inguinal, and perineal hernia, all of which are associated with the weakened area mentioned above.

Umbilical hernia is found in puppies due to the incomplete closure of the umbilical ring after birth.

There is a small soft swelling at the navel. When gentle pressure is applied the swelling usually disappears as the contents slip back inside. Occasionally the swelling will disappear when the puppy rolls on its back. A small reducible umbilical hernia like this is of no consequence in a young puppy. Usually the hole in the abdominal wall closes as the puppy grows, sometimes a very small hole will persist but will give no trouble. A large umbilical hernia, however, will require surgical repair, and if there is any doubt about a swelling at a puppy's navel, veterinary advice should be sought.

Inguinal hernia may be found in young dogs but it is more common in adults. A swelling will appear in the groin. This swelling may be on the left side or on the right side: very rarely are both sides affected at the same time. Often the swelling is only apparent when the animal is standing; if it rolls on its back the contents of the hernia will often return to the abdominal cavity. In the male dog an inguinal hernia may develop into a swelling in the region of the scrotum, when it is usually referred to as a scrotal hernia. Again it may occur on one side or the other, or even on both sides at the same time. An inguinal hernia may cause very little discomfort but it is always a potential hazard to life, and should be corrected by a surgical operation.

Perineal hernia occurs chiefly in old male dogs. The defect shows as a soft swelling to one side of the anus. Perineal hernia is difficult to repair but it always wise to seek veterinary advice when it is suspected in an old dog.

The contents of a hernial swelling depend upon its situation. An umbilical hernia or a perineal hernia may contain a loop of bowel. An inguinal hernia can also contain a loop of bowel, but in the bitch there may also be part of the uterus. If a bitch with an inguinal hernia becomes pregnant or if a pregnant bitch develops an inguinal hernia the results may be serious. So long as a hernia is reducible, that is, so long as the contents of the swelling can be returned to the abdomen by gentle pressure, harm is unlikely to result. If the hernia cannot be reduced in this way complications may follow. The complication to be feared is strangulation. If a hernia becomes strangulated the symptoms are obvious and dramatic. The swelling becomes hot and tense and the dog is in great pain. The condition can be rapidly fatal unless it can be relieved by a surgical operation.

A rupture is similar in appearance to a hernia but in a rupture the opening in the abdominal wall is not natural but the result of damage in an accident. Car accidents are a frequent cause of rupture in the dog. The diaphragm (that is the sheet of muscle dividing the abdomen from the thorax) may be torn by the force of the blow. If some of the abdominal contents pass through into the chest this is known as a diaphragmatic rupture. The symptoms depend upon the severity of the condition. There is no external swelling but the dog has difficulty in breathing properly and may be unable to take or retain food. The only treatment for a rupture is surgical repair. In the case of a diaphragmatic rupture this may be very difficult and if the condition is suspected professional help should be sought at once.

Highland Greyhound see Deerhound, Scottish.

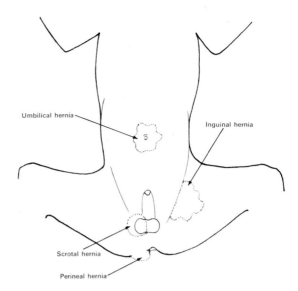

Left Hernias may appear at the navel, in the left or right groin, round the scrotum or to one side of the anus.

Hip Dysplasia Hip dysplasia is the name given to a number of abnormal conditions of the hip joint. Some of these conditions are hereditary. The normal hip joint is a ball and socket joint made up of a deep socket in the pelvis (hip bones) into which the rounded head of the femur (thigh bone) fits snugly. In hip dysplasia the socket is shallow and the head of the femur may be misshapen. A puppy affected with dysplasia may not show any outward signs at all, but as it grows and becomes heavier it may appear to be weak in the hindquarters. The condition may not be apparent to the casual observer until the dog is several years old. The only reliable means of diagnosis is by taking X-rays of dogs over one year of age. Any breed of dog may be affected but the condition is commonest in the larger breeds.

The Kennel Club (England) has a joint scheme with the British Veterinary Association to control hip dysplasia. The local veterinarian will take the X-rays. If the dog appears to be normal the radiographs are forwarded to a panel of specialists who report to the Kennel Club. A certificate is then issued. By making use of this scheme breeders can reduce the risk of their stock being affected. The problems of hip dysplasia are being studied by research institutes, breed clubs and breeders the world over.

Hock The dog's true heel. The bones forming the joint between the second thigh and the metatarsus.

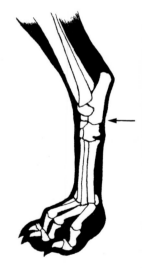

Above Hock.

Hodgkin's Disease This is the name used for a disease of human beings and sometimes for the condition in dogs where all the lymph glands swell within the body. These are most easily felt on each side of the throat, under the forelegs by the chest, in the groin, and at the back of the upper part of the hind legs. There is no known cure. The disease causes increasing weakness and loss of interest in life.

The name 'Pseudo-Hodgkin's disease' is also used for this condition.

Hookworms Hookworms are white or grey worms

about the size of a common pin. The head is turned, or hooked, and the mouth contains cutting plates. The worms hook themselves to the walls of the small intestine, and live by sucking blood. In heavy infestations, they may cover the entire intestinal tract, including the cecum, colon, and rectum. They tend to migrate from one feeding site to another. The wounds they leave do not heal for some time and bleeding continues.

Symptoms include diarrhoea, often with fecal material streaked with blood; anaemia; and sluggishness. In severe infections, stools may appear to be pure blood.

Hookworm larvae are swallowed in contaminated food and water, and may enter the mouth from contaminated toys. In some cases, they will enter through the skin, and even through the pads of the feet.

Those entering by mouth go directly to the intestines where they mature and begin to lay eggs within three to six weeks. Those which enter through the skin are carried by the blood to the lungs. They escape into the air sacs, are coughed into the throat, and then are swallowed. The worms are capable of entering foetal puppies. Eggs from infected puppies may appear in their faeces within eleven to fifteen days after birth.

The eggs are easily found in the stools. At the first indication of infection, stool samples should be taken to a veterinarian. He will recommend treatment and advise the owner on methods of preventing re-infection.

Among successful methods are these: lye (caustic soda), two pounds to ten quarts of cold water (see ANTISEPTICS); sodium borate, ten pounds to one hundred square feet, which can be used on earth runs, though not on grass. Applications should be made three to four times during the spring, summer, and autumn. Common bulk salt is also effective. It dehydrates both eggs and larvae, thus killing them.

Some kennels have broad salt pans, and require their dogs to stand in them while eating. The salt both kills larvae that might be trying to burrow through the pads, and toughens the pads themselves.

Hot Climates Dogs in tropical areas need slightly different care from those living in the temperate zones. Nutritionists have found that, as with Arctic climate dogs, they have higher caloric needs than dogs of temperate zones, Fleas, ticks, and lice are a greater hazard, both because they breed more rapidly in high heat and humidity, and because of constant breeding activities that do not depend on seasons.

FILIARIASIS, or Heart Worm, and RABIES are grave dangers. Dogs should be kept confined if possible in screened areas from an hour before sunset to an hour after sunrise to avoid mosquitoes. They should be vaccinated against rabies. Poisonous SNAKE BITES are a hazard in the tropics.

In general, snub-nosed dogs, such as Boston Terriers and Bulldogs, should not be taken to the tropics, and neither should the heavily-coated dogs. Yet Pekingese have prospered in Ceylon and Brazil; Bulldogs are popular in South Texas; Poodles have done well in Brazil and Venezuela, and the Arctic breeds – Samoyeds, Siberian Huskies, and Alaskan Malamutes – are popular in Southern California. Dogs with moderate

coats do well in the tropics, partly because they have better protection from mosquitoes than do very light-coated animals.

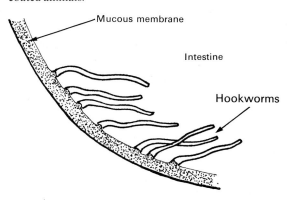

Temperate zone hunting dogs appear to lose their stamina in the tropics, though only after many generations. Heavily-coated Poodles have sometimes been shown in the tropics. Profuse coat is chiefly controlled by a genetic factor which is not altered by a change of environment, but environmental factors may cause heavy-coated dogs to be less successful in breeding, and this may be apparent after several generations.

Hound A dog used to hunt by trailing or by sight. See GROUP SYSTEM, UNITED STATES and CANADA.

Hound Markings Usually white, tan, and black. But the rule is: no good hound can be a bad colour.

Hound Shows Hound shows are events held in various countries under auspices other than the all-breed governing bodies. In Britain there is the Association of Masters of Foxhounds, the Association of Masters of Harriers and Beagles, and the Association of Masters of Basset Hounds. In America, Foxhounds are covered by American Kennel Club member associations, and the National Beagle Club of America caters for both Beagles and Basset Hounds. These authorities keep their own stud books recording pedigrees and organize events in their respective countries.

The major hound shows in Britain are at Peterborough, Aldershot and Honiton with other quite successful events held in other parts of the British Isles.

In Eire the shows are held in County Tipperary. In the United States of America hound shows are held in various parts, the major one being at Bryn Mawr, Penna., where American Foxhounds, Beagles and Bassets all share the same venue.

At hound shows either enclosed rings or roped-in areas are used. At some the hounds are shown on a leash but where the rings are enclosed hounds are taken off the leash and exhibited free. This is often referred to as showing 'on the flags'.

The classes cater for single hounds, couples and two couples – in America classes for four and eight couples are common. At most of the shows, the dogs have to be proven workers, but there are exceptions.

Hound Trails, Britain Hound trailing in Britain is a localized sport confined to the hill and lake areas of Yorkshire, Lancashire, Cumberland, Westmorland, and the Scottish border country. Recently however, some summer trails in Breconshire have been introduced. The sport is also very popular in Eire, particularly in County Cork and County Kerry.

Hounds run in these trails are of a distinct type: Foxhound in outline, eighteen to twenty-four inches at the shoulder, but somewhat lighter in substance, so as to be capable of great speeds. Trails are highly organized events governed by strict rules.

A trail is laid with a 'drag' or scent, and is some ten miles in length for adult hounds and five miles for puppies. The hounds, sometimes as many as ninety, are turned loose at the starting line, follow the line of the drag, and the first one to arrive at the finishing line is the winner. The ten miles is covered in 28 to 30 minutes unless the hounds have to negotiate high walls, in which case the course will take longer. Rules on the substance and method of laying the drag are specific, although they may vary slightly between one organizing body and another. Drags must be laid by two people, one leaving from the starting point and one from the finishing line, meeting in the middle. Woollen rags must be soaked in a mixture of aniseed, turpentine and paraffin. The trail rag may not be less than two feet in length and six inches in breadth and must be dragged by not less than six feet of cord. There must be four pints of the drag mixture for each Hound trail and one and a half pints for each Puppy trail, and the ingredients must be mixed in specific proportions, with heavy oil added if necessary.

Bookmakers and betting thrive. The activity is rigidly controlled in all its aspects by the various governing associations and rules are no less strict than those governing GREYHOUND racing or coursing meetings.

Each association keeps its own stud book and registration system but records are interchangeable in order to perpetuate both the sport and the breed. Regulations are similar to those concerning racing Greyhounds in that litters must be notified to the secretary of the association within three days of their birth. Within one month of birth each puppy in a litter is earmarked by an official appointed by the association. When earmarking is complete, each puppy is individually registered with the association.

The age of each hound is taken as being one year on 31st December of the year following its birth – thus, a hound born in June will not be considered to be one year old until is it, in fact, eighteen months of age. Consequently, a hound is eligible for entry into a Puppy Trail until it is, according to its birthdate, anything up to two years of age. As with racing Greyhounds, a bitch in season is not allowed to compete and must be given a rest period of 21 days.

Some owners and trainers are of the opinion that clipping out the coat of a trail hound will reduce the weight of the animal and also that this makes them run more freely. Consequently, though the more general colour is tri-colour or tri-colour mottled, the animals may appear to lack distinctive marking since the body coat has been removed.

It is customary for owners and trainers to shout, whistle and generally encourage the hounds over the last quarter mile of the trail in an effort to bring their hounds home ahead of the rest. Apart from the satisfaction of owning the winner, considerable money prizes are won. The trail hound season is from Easter until October.

Hound Trials, American see Field Trials, American.

House Training Dogs inherit what is known as the den dwellers' instinct. Animals which have this instinct can be house trained. Those which do not, such as the cow, bird, or monkey, cannot be. The instinct appears in puppies as soon as they begin to get upon their feet. They will stagger outside the nest to relieve themselves.

The purchaser of a six-week-old puppy can utilize the den dwellers' instinct by constructing a box, or indoor kennel, which will simulate a den. The box should have a lid or door, otherwise the puppy will try to get out, and will howl its loudest. The box should be only large enough for the puppy to lie down. If the box is too large, then the puppy may relieve itself in one end and sleep in the other; so if a large box has to be used, something should be put in it to make it smaller until the growing puppy needs the additional space.

Bedding should be flat newspaper. The puppy can be given an added feeling of security if some of the owner's old clothing is put into the box beside it; the odour will be reassuring in the new surroundings. It is said that a loud ticking alarm clock will also help to lull the puppy to sleep. The owner should not release the puppy from the box when it howls, but should allow it to cry itself to sleep as human babies are often required to do.

Puppies have to relieve themselves frequently during the day. They should be taken or carried out to a previously selected spot. This spot should be prepared by wiping up the puppy's first urinary mistake with a rag, then anchoring this rag at the spot. The odour will give the puppy the signal to use the spot.

The times when the puppy needs to be taken to this place are first thing in the morning, after meals, after naps, and at bedtime. Play stimulates urination.

The puppy should not simply be put out, but taken to its spot. If it is simply left outside, its interest in the

above House training. If the rag which has wiped up a puppy's first urinary mistake is fixed to a selected place outside, the odour will encourage the puppy to use only the chosen spot.

great world will distract it, and the owner will not know whether it has relieved itself or not. Bad weather should not deter the owner from taking the puppy out. It has a thick, insulating blanket of fur which will keep it from chilling. Bad weather will cause it to hurry, and so will actually aid in establishing the conditioned reflex which will cause the dog always to use that spot.

One should never teach a puppy to use newspapers in any part of the home. To do so is to establish a conditioned reflex always to use that spot. And this practice will corrupt the dog's instinct to keep its home clean. Often dogs cannot be retrained once they have been taught to use paper.

After the first few days in the new home, any mistakes by the puppy are likely to be caused by the owner's neglect. Spots where mistakes have been made should be cleaned up quickly. If the puppy is kept on hardwood or linoleum floors for the first week or two, the problem is simple. But every care should be taken to remove the odour, for the smell will always encourage the puppy to use that spot again.

The box, or a larger one, can be used throughout the dog's life. The dog will have been conditioned to regard it as its private, safe den. And it will have learned to be both quiet and content while in it. By continuing the use of the box, or indoor kennel, many later personality problems are avoided. These include howling or being destructive when left alone in the home.

Housing and Kennelling The housing and kennelling of dogs is a problem which requires intelligent planning. Dogs are happiest when they spend most of the time in the home. If an indoor kennel is provided, the dog will probably be happy and contented. A shipping crate, such as is used at dog shows, or a carrying case for toy dogs, can be used. See HOUSE TRAINING.

If the dog is to be kept outside, a draught-proof kennel should be provided. Such a kennel should be barely larger than the dog itself, since the dog will have to heat the area with its own body heat, and, the dog wants no more room than is required to lie stretched out in.

A flat roof slanting slightly to the rear, and with a front overlap to protect the door from rain, is best. If the roof is removable, or is hinged at the back, cleaning is made easy. A swinging door or flap will keep out the rain. In cold latitudes, the house should face away from the cold wind. The base of the door should be four to six inches above floor level so that bedding is held in and floor draughts are prevented.

A more elaborate kennel consists of two identical rooms separated by a partition which divides the kennel lengthwise. The 'front door' opens into one. To enter the second, the dog must jump through an opening at the back of the partition. This inner room is provided with bedding for cold weather. The dog can use the outer room in summer. Safe electric heating pads for kennels are now available in some countries. See HEATING OF KENNELS AND LIVING QUARTERS.

Serious breeders can now obtain detailed building plans for kennels of various sizes. Some commercial dog food manufacturers, for example, now supply them. These kennels are designed for low-cost construction, and for economic operation in terms of money and labour.

If a dog cannot be allowed to run free, a kennel run is always preferable to a chain. It is a mistake to build a very large run. Dogs seldom exercise just for the fun of it, so they do not use all the area. The larger the run, the more expensive it is to build, and the greater the maintenance and cleaning costs. Most professionals find six feet by fifteen feet, or eight by twenty satisfactory, depending on the size of the dogs. Dogs can be trained to use only the far end of the run for relief. If the run is slanted to the far end, and a gutter provided at that end, cleaning and disinfecting are made very easy.

Surfaces for kennel runs are, in the order of their merit: concrete, asphalt, driveway slag, limestone chips, gravel, and earth. Concrete is the most expensive. Concrete and asphalt are easily cleaned and disinfected. Snow melts away from asphalt quicker than from concrete, but asphalt is hotter in summer than concrete. Slag is excellent for keeping foot pads tough. Both slag and limestone chips are carried away with stools during cleaning, and grass and weeds tend to grow through them. Gravel and earth hold odours and are the most difficult to disinfect and deodorize.

To preserve local amenities, some areas will not permit a fence higher than three feet. This is sufficient for keeping in even very large dogs, if used in combination with an electric farm fence, set up temporarily. This should not be installed without veterinary advice. Properly set up, this will not harm the dog. After a few 'shocks', it will not approach the fence and the current can be shut off. A border of shrubbery outside the fence will often improve its appearance, and will shut off the dog's view and stop it from barking at every passing dog or person.

Hucklebones The top of the hipbones.

Humane Societies Under ancient common law, a man was considered the lord of his home and property. He could abuse his children or his animals as he pleased. The first attempts to prevent such cruelty dealt with the abuse of beasts of burden. Though a man

could still abuse them upon his own property, it was argued that cruelty to them upon a street constituted an offence against public morals.

The famed jurist and philosopher, Jeremy Bentham, argued that animals had rights. Using this argument, Richard Martin succeeded in getting the Ill-treatment of Cattle Bill passed by the English Parliament in 1822. Despite its name, the bill brought some protection to all beasts of burden, but not to pets.

Two years later, the English Society for the Protection of Animals (SPCA) was founded. It was successful in bringing prosecutions and protecting animals, and in 1840 Queen Victoria commanded that the prefix 'Royal' be placed in front of its name. An Act of Parliament of 1849 brought all domestic animals under protection. In 1876, an act was passed to regulate vivisection by protecting living animals from severe pain during medical research. Then in 1900 an act was passed to protect zoo and other captive animals from cruelty.

In 1866, Henry Berg organized the American SPCA. Two years later, George T. Angell of Boston organized the Massachusetts SPCA. The famed Angell Memorial animal hospital in Boston is named in his memory. Other societies in the United States were founded from coast to coast the same year.

In 1874, the American SPCA rescued a nine-year-old girl, Mary Ellen, who was being cruelly beaten by her foster mother. Since there were no laws to protect the child, prosecution was brought under the claim that Mary Ellen was an animal. The foster mother was convicted and was sent to prison. The case, still known as the 'Mary Ellen Case', brought world-wide attention to the plight of children, and soon there were laws to protect children in several countries.

Since the American SPCA is purely a New York humane society, many groups met in Cleveland in 1877, and as a result, the American Humane Society was formed in 1878. It function is to protect both children and animals. Humane societies still vary in the work they do. Some try merely to protect animals. Others also conduct work within the schools to educate children in humane concepts. Some function as antivivisection societies, and are interested solely in the abolition of medical research upon living animals. Still others try to reduce such research while working to improve laboratory conditions for the animals. At least one organization in the United States is campaigning for the substitution of living cellular research and testing for the use of living animals.

Hup The command given to a hunting spaniel to stop and sit.

Huskies In Arctic North America, the term 'husky' has usually meant a dog of impure breeding – a mongrel – but one of general Arctic type. Thus, one hears of Greenland Huskies, Alaskan Huskies, etc. Alaskan Huskies have been bred for sled dog racing, but are neither ALASKAN MALAMUTES nor SIBERIAN HUSKIES. The Siberian Husky is the only pure breed which is entitled to include 'Husky' as part of its name.

Hydatid This is an intermediate stage in the development of the tapeworm. It is cyst-like and can occur in many parts of the intermediate host.
See TAPEWORM.

Hydrophobia see Rabies.

Hygiene see Kennel Hygiene.

Hypothermia see Fading Puppies.

Hysteria Hysteria in dogs has been called by many names, including running fits, symptomatic epilepsy, psychomotor epilepsy, and furious rabies. Probably hundreds of thousands of dogs have been killed by frightened people who have mistaken hysteria for RABIES. A major difference in the two is that in furious rabies, dogs bite at anything which is placed before them. In hysteria, the dogs rarely make an attempt to bite.

Hysteria is a psychomotor, or psychoneurotic, disorder. It involves disturbances of the sensory, motor, vasomotor, psychic, and visceral systems. In major hysteria, there is such violent excitement that EPILEPSY is simulated. However, the dog seldom loses consciousness.

Hysteria may be occasional, or it may occur daily. The onset is sudden. The dog may begin to bark in a high-pitched, frenzied manner, although not in the odd pitch of the dog with furious rabies. It may begin to run. The pupils are dilated and vision is somehow distorted. The dog may run into trees. It may turn its head suddenly, as though to ward off an attack from behind.

If in the home, the dog may try to climb the walls and will run into furniture. Then it may stop, apparently to stare at a non-existent object. Convulsions, such as those of epilepsy, may occur, but the dog does not lose consciousness.

Many causes have been suggested. Worms are one cause. Mange mites gathered on the ear drum have been blamed. Diet, in which there is an insufficiency of vitamins A and B, and the lack of certain vital amino acids, has been shown to cause hysteria.

An odd feature of hysteria is that it may affect an entire kennel. There is no evidence that this is caused by a virus or bacteria. Instead, the other dogs, hearing the afflicted animal, begin to bark until they themselves are hysterical. There is evidence, too, that a dog which has suffered a severe traumatic experience in one location, may have a fit of hysteria when taken to the same spot again. In such cases, the dogs may never be afflicted at other times or in other places.

When hysteria occurs at frequent intervals, treatment is similar to that for epilepsy. Calming drugs are given daily by a veterinarian. These include phenobarbital, meprobamate, promazine, primidone, and diphenylhydantoin.

This condition is also seen in dogs which develop a low blood calcium level. This is seen in whelping and nursing bitches and occasionally in the non-pregnant animal. It appears to be most common in the Poodle. See FITS.

Ibizan Hound This is a country-lover's breed originating in the island of Ibiza (Balearic Islands) where the hound is found in large numbers. It is said that the best examples are found in Majorca. In these islands this hound is known by its original name or as 'Ca Eivissenc'. Three types exist: smooth-haired, wire-haired and long-haired.

The hound is strongly built, measuring between 23 and 26 inches at the withers with bitches proportionately less. Highly agile, very astute, intelligent and docile, they can jump to a great height without a take-off run. They hunt more by scent and hearing than by sight and will bark only when sensing a quarry. They all retrieve and point to the game. In the Balearic Isles they are used also to hunt hares, partridges and bigger game. They may hunt alone or in packs, and when a pack has caught several thousand rabbits, some of the hounds will no longer hunt until they have had a long rest. In their country of origin this is known as becoming 'over-rabbitized'.

Essentials of the breed: The head: long, lean and narrow rather like a cone truncated at the narrow end. The skull has a prominent occipital bone, and very lightly defined stop. The ears are always pricked, turned forwards, horizontally sideways or backwards. They are carried high when the dog is alert and they are very mobile. The eyes are slanting and small, and light amber in colour, with an intelligent look. The nose is slightly convex. The length from the eyes to the point of the muzzle is the same as from between the eyes to the occiput. The muscle is flesh-coloured to harmonize with the coat. The jaws are very strong and lean, and the nostrils open. Lips delicate and puckered and teeth well arranged with a level bite.

The body: the chest is deep, narrow and long with the breastbone forming a very sharp and prominent angle.

Ibizan Hound.
Below Sol, an Ibizan Houn[d] posing on a sarcophagus, loo[ks] remarkably like an ancient Egy[p]tian dog-god. *Below right* Anub[is] one of the Egyptian gods, made [of] wood and varnished black, [from] Tutankhamen's tomb.

The rib cage is flat. Back: straight and arched over the loins which are of medium width. Hindquarters are strong and lean with hocks bent and well let down. A good waistline is desirable. Feet are like those of a hare, paws long and tight with good feathering between the toes.

Tail: long and when passed between the legs, forward and up, should reach at least to the spine. In repose the tail hangs naturally. In action it can at times be shaped like a very stiff sickle and sometimes erect. It should never be curled.

Coat: smooth, wire or long, the latter being rough. Rather shorter on the head and ears, and longer on the back of the thighs and the underside of the tail.

Colours: white and red, white and tawny, or all one colour – white, red or tawny. Red is preferable to tawny and all other colours are barred.

Iceland Dog Nearly a thousand years after the migration of settlers to Iceland in the ninth century, Sir William Jardin and Col. Charles Hamilton Smith wrote: 'The Norwegian emigrants to Iceland seem to have carried a race of dogs to its shores, which at present, is not found in the parent country . . . It is not larger than that of Kamtschatka, and in fur like the Esquimaux. This race . . . may have been obtained from the Skrelings (Greenlanders) or Esquimaux, by the adventurers who first visited Greenland.'

Other early writers compared the Iceland Dog to the Lapland Dog, the Finn-Lapp Dog, Kamtschatka, Greenland Esquimaux, and Siberian sled dogs. That the Iceland Dog does belong to the great family of SPITZ dogs cannot be doubted. Some writers have called it the Iceland Spitz. Pistol, a character in Shakespeare's *Henry IV* (c. 1600) says 'Pish for thee, Iceland Dog. Thou prick-eared cur of Iceland.'

Sir Richard Burton wrote *Ultima Thule, or A Summer In Iceland*, in 1875. He wrote that good dogs were so valuable in Iceland that a horse might be exchanged for one. 'One of those which, they say, can search a sheep under nine ells (eleven yards) of snow. They are accused', Burton continued, 'of propagating amongst

their masters hydatid disease and intestinal worms.' Viggo Moeller, writing in 1887, also charged the dogs with spreading hydatid disease in people and 'staggers' in sheep. He quotes Dr. H. Krabbe as saying that every fortieth person had the disease. (The hydatid tapeworm lives as an adult parasite in dogs, and as a larva in man, sheep, and other animals. It is rarely found in man in Great Britain or the United States and Canada, but is common in Iceland, New Zealand, Australia, and Argentina.)

Great plagues nearly wiped out the Iceland Dogs during eleven epidemics, of which the first was in 1591. An epidemic in 1900 was said to have been 'akin to human measles'. Because of these recurring epidemics, and because of the great value of the dogs to the Icelanders, dog control acts were begun as early as 1869. By a decree in 1892, the importation of dogs was placed under a licensing system. A law was passed in 1928 banning the importation of mammals into Iceland.

Virtually all accounts credit the Iceland Dog with being of exceptional value to farmers. At first, the dogs kept pony caravans on the correct trail. They also kept

horses, cattle and sheep out of the home meadows, from which hay would be cut for winter use. Later, the dogs were taught to herd sheep. The sheep would be driven into the mountains during the summer. In the fall, the farmers would go up and drive home their sheep. The dogs were taught to range far away to discover sheep which would be hidden from the farmers' views. The dogs had to use great care and intelligence to bring the sheep down over especially difficult terrain without frightening them, and without driving them in such a way that they would be injured or killed by falls.

At the end of the last century, Iceland Dogs were taken to Denmark. The Danish Kennel Club recognized the breed, and dogs were exhibited between 1900 and 1914. Attempts at that time to train the dogs for war work, however, were unsuccessful. The first dog registered in England was *Chuck*, owned by E. Swain and registered as an Iceland Sheepdog, or Iceland Collie in 1905. In 1915 the English Kennel Club recognized the breed and dogs were then exhibited in the 'Any Other Variety' class. During the 1950s, carefully selected dogs were sent to England, where there are now some 50 to 60 of the breed.

Left Iceland Dog. Vaskur of Thor valdsstadir of Wensum, one o the carefully selected dogs sent t England in the 1950s in a attempt to establish the breed.

In recent years the Icelanders themselves have become interested in saving the breed from extinction, and in preserving its original type. Thus, during 1969 and 1970, a kennel club to sponsor the breed was organized in Iceland.

Essentials of the breed: The breed somewhat resembles the Norwegian Buhund. The present standard calls for a dog of general Spitz type, slightly under middle size, and lightly built. The head is light, rather broad between the ears, with the skull being broad and domed and the muzzle shorter than long. The stop is not deep; the nose black; the lips tight fitting. The ears are large at the base, triangular, pointed, and erect. The eyes are small, round, and dark.

The neck is short, strongly arched, and carries the head high. The shoulders are straight, not sloping. The back is short, the chest large and deep, with the belly tucked up. The stifle joints are not strongly angulated. The feet are oval, with well-developed pads. The tail: of moderate length, very bushy, and carried curled over the back. The coat is hard, of medium length, longer around the neck, and on the thighs, short on the face, and flat on the body. Colour is white with fawn markings, golden, light fawn with black tips to long hairs. Height is 15 to 18 inches, and weight about 30 lb.

Immunity Immunity is the ability of the body to resist specific infection, or attacks by certain poisons, and can be either inherited, acquired naturally, or acquired artificially.

Inherited immunity is a resistance that is inherent in an individual or a particular strain of dogs. *Naturally acquired immunity* results when a dog recovers from an infection, and as a result, is resistant to further attacks by the infective organism concerned. This resistance gradually wanes.

Artificially acquired immunity falls into two groups called *active* and *passive*. Active immunity is produced by injecting a vaccine or toxoid made specifically to produce resistance against a disease. Most of these are produced against a disease that is widespread, like DISTEMPER, viral HEPATITIS and LEPTOSPIROSIS. An autogenous vaccine is one that is made to protect a dog, or group of dogs, that is infected with a specific germ. This germ is isolated from the dog and the vaccine is produced from the actual germ so obtained. Actively immunized dogs are resistant to the disease against which they are protected for a long period but the resistance is gradually reduced as time passes. Protection develops after the injection so the resistance is not immediate. Passive immunity is a resistance to a specific disease that is produced by injecting into a dog serum taken from another dog that has been actively immunized. This serum is used either in its natural dilution or in a concentrated form (hyper-immune serum). The resistance so produced lasts for a short period only, but starts at once.

Acquired immunity gradually wanes and it is usual to 'boost' this at regular intervals to ensure that protection is complete.
See VACCINES.

Impotence see Infertility.

Inbreeding The mating of close relatives is called inbreeding, in contrast to outcrossing or outbreeding, which means mating distantly related, or so-called unrelated individuals. Inbreeding increases the chance of the offspring inheriting the same genetic pattern from both parents; in other words, it tends to increase homozygosity. If close inbreeding is continued for many generations there is nearly always a loss of general vigour: problems such as infertility, loss of size, weak 'unthrifty' offspring, and increased susceptibility to disease are reported from long-continued experimental inbreeding with various species of mammals. However, in the majority of these experiments, no selection against loss of vigour was practised.

Some inbreeding, often extensive, has been used in the creation or establishment of almost all breeds of domestic livestock, including dogs. However, wise breeders counteract inbreeding degeneration by selecting against loss of vigour, weakness and abnormality; and also by introducing an occasional outcross. Very close breeding, such as sire/daughter or brother/sister matings are used only occasionally and for special reasons. The form of inbreeding generally used in practice is LINE BREEDING, which is the mating of individuals tracing back to one or more specially good common ancestors or belonging to the same strain and closely related. Dogs with 'linebred' pedigrees are often less inbred than appears at first glance, because the contribution of an ancestor is halved at each generation. The chance of a particular GENE from a dog six generations back entering a puppy is thus $\frac{1}{2}^6$, or to put it another way, each puppy inherits, on the average, only one in sixty-four of the genes which were present in its g-g-g-g-g-sire. If the same dog occurs twice, six generations back, it will still contribute only a one-thirty-second part of the pup's inheritance, and this may not include any of the ancestor's notable genes.

It is therefore difficult to maintain, in descendants, a high proportion of genes from a chosen animal, unless intensive inbreeding to that animal was practised in its lifetime. Unfortunately, an outstanding individual's qualities can be the outcome of a heterozygous (mixed) genetic inheritance, or of the particular collection of polygenes (quantitative genes) which it happens to have. In these cases, inbreeding to it may not be successful in preserving its good qualities as the genetic contribution which it passes on may not be that which has helped to bring about its own success.

A fact some forget is that a single complete outcross nullifies all inbreeding, in the sense that the immediate offspring are not inbred at all. This is easier to grasp when considering two inbred animals belonging to quite different breeds, for example, a highly inbred Saluki dog and an equally inbred Samoyed bitch. Such a litter is obviously not inbred despite the inbreeding of both parents, for the genetic contribution of each contains no factors common to the other.

Incisors The upper and lower front teeth between the canines.

Infectious Canine Hepatitis see Hepatitis.

Infertility Reduced fertility is a common problem. It may be suspected when the number of pups in a litter is less than normal for the breed or when an apparently normal mating is not followed by a pregnancy. A few individuals are 'sterile', being completely unable to reproduce their kind. The sterile bitch is usually referred to as being 'barren'. Occasionally a male is found to be 'impotent', that is, he is unable to produce or to maintain an erection so that he is unable to impregnate the bitch.

There are degrees of infertility in both the dog and the bitch. In the case of the dog it is possible to examine the semen for quality (see ARTIFICIAL INSEMINATION) and thus obtain a clue to his probable fertility. However in the case of the bitch there is no way of assessing her fertility except by actually mating her, although her previous history may be a guide.

The investigation of the cause of infertility is difficult and the treatment is often unrewarding. If a positive approach is to be made to the problem, the factors influencing fertility must be considered. Both dog and bitch should be fit and well at the time of mating. To keep breeding stock fit an adequate diet is obviously essential (see NUTRITION). It is advisable to include a complete vitamin and mineral supplement. Neither dog nor bitch should be fat – in fact OBESITY is a common cause of infertility. Every dog and bitch should be exercised daily both on the road and running free in some open space. Daily GROOMING not only keeps the coat healthy but it also helps to keep the animal fit. The ideal is a dog or bitch in lean hard condition rather than a soft plump creature.

It is of the utmost importance that both dog and bitch should be free from both general and local disease. Bacterial infection is one of the commonest causes of infertility. Should there be any doubts on this score veterinary help should be sought at once.

The timing of mating is important. The bitch will usually accept the dog around about the tenth day of the HEAT period. The next few days are the most fertile. Most breeders mate the bitch about the eleventh day of the heat and again two days later.

In the male, fertility is reduced in old age. Too frequent use of a stud dog or, for that matter, too long intervals between use may also reduce fertility. Immature dogs may not be fully fertile.

In the female old age may reduce fertility, but in any case it is unwise to attempt to breed from very old bitches as the pups may be weak and the bitch may not be able to rear them.

Infertility may be the result of some hormonal disturbance. Veterinary science can explain some of these problems, even if the results of treatment are not very satisfactory.

Heredity plays an important part in fertility. Within a breed some families may be much more fertile than others. Breeders concentrate on these prolific lines because attempts to breed from less fertile strains, however attractive in other ways, are found to be unrewarding.

Infra-Red Lamps There are two types of infra-red lamps: the bright emitter and the dull emitter. They should be suspended at a height of not less than 16 to 18 inches above the dog's bed. They are used extensively in whelping quarters and provided they are used sensibly can be a most useful source of heat. Most makers supply necessary instructions for their use.

These electrical appliances should always be carefully checked before use and the cord should never be loose enough to be within easy access of the dog.
See HEATING OF KENNELS.

Inguinal Hernia see Hernia.

Inhalation see Respiration.

Insurance for Dogs Life insurance for dogs is difficult to obtain. Companies which are licensed to write it are rare: Lloyd's of London will do so, and other companies normally refer applicants to Lloyd's. The cost is very high, being normally 13 per cent or more per year of the total valuation placed upon the dog.

Lloyd's mortality policies may also include theft. Other companies either refuse to issue such insurance, or do so only as a favour to clients with large policies held by the company involved. Proof of theft must be shown before any company will honour a claim, and this is difficult to obtain.

Accident insurance is also difficult to obtain. When issued, the rate is usually higher than that for Life Insurance. Some companies may charge as much as 15 per cent for the first unit, and then lesser amounts for each additional unit.

Home owners' policies are usually comprehensive in

Below Infra-red lamps should be suspended not less than 16 inches above the dog's bed.

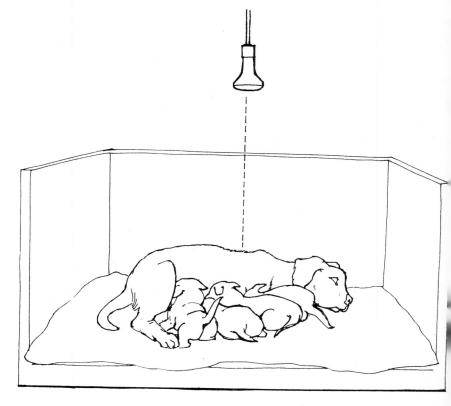

nature, but they do not cover dogs except for liability: most companies will pay if your dog bites someone, or even if it damages your neighbour's ornamental shrubbery. Normally, a home owners' policy will not cover dogs which are kept for breeding.

Home owners having comprehensive home policies can apply to have these strengthened. They can ask the insurers to explain in writing the extent to which they are covered and in cases such as cited, they can ask for written assurance that they will be covered in certain specific instances.

Attempts are sometimes made to establish health and surgical insurance policies for dogs. These usually fail because they do not meet the normal requirements for insurance: a person subscribes to health and surgical insurance plans because human medical and surgical costs are high; because the insured person may have a family to support; and because he, or she, may face total loss of income during the period of illness. A dog's medical and surgical bills may be high, but only comparatively so; they will not cause the owner to mortgage his home to pay the bills; nor will the owner face loss of income. In the rare cases in which the latter will occur, such as the illness of performing dogs, the owner can have special policies written to cover the particular situation.

The writing of insurance is governed by strict laws in most countries of the world. Companies do spring up which try to issue health and surgical insurance for dogs. But the rate of failure of such companies is very high. Insurance specialists therefore suggest that before buying such policies, dog owners should make a careful investigation with local, or national, insurance boards.

Dogs may be insured for shipment by rail, sea, or air. The rates are nominal. If, however, owners place what the shipper may feel is an unusually high valuation on the dog, the rates jump. In case of loss, payment at the insured valuation is not automatic. The owner will be required to prove the valuation. This may be difficult to do, and may require court action.

Interbreeding The breeding together of dogs of different breeds. Usually practised to bring desired traits into one or the other.

Interdigital Cysts Interdigital cysts are small inflammatory swellings which appear between the toes. Usually they are only found on the forefeet, but occasionally a hind foot may also be affected. At first the swelling is hot and it may be so painful that the dog is lame. Eventually the swelling, which is actually a little abscess, bursts and there is a discharge of pus. As soon as the abscess has burst the pain is relieved and the dog will improve. At this stage the condition may heal or it may become chronic, forming a considerable thickening which discharges pus from time to time.

Some breeds such as the PEKINGESE, the WEST HIGHLAND WHITE TERRIER and the SCOTTISH TERRIER are particularly prone to develop interdigital cysts. Other breeds such as the Border COLLIE, the GERMAN SHEPHERD DOG and the GREYHOUND rarely suffer from the condition. It has been suggested that the reason for

this is the shape of the dog's foot. All the breeds in the first group have broad flat feet. These 'flat-footed' dogs are more likely to suffer minor abrasions of the skin of the toes and to collect mud and grit in the hairs of the feet. The irritation to the skin of the foot is the initial cause of the resulting swelling.

The diagnosis of an interdigital cyst is usually obvious. The local treatment is hot fomentation. The affected foot should be placed in a bowl of warm water containing a little common salt or mild antiseptic and allowed to soak for ten minutes or even a quarter of an hour. The cyst should be encouraged to burst and to discharge pus by applying gentle pressure from time to time. After treatment the foot should be dried. There is no need to apply a bandage as progress will be faster if the foot is exposed to the air and no harm will result if the dog licks it. The hot fomentation should be repeated three or four times a day. In many cases this is all the treatment that is required. If the dog is unwell or very lame, or if no progress is made, a veterinarian should be consulted. Some interdigital cysts are infected with staphylococci or streptococci bacteria and in these cases antibiotic treatment is useful.

Prevention is usually better than cure. A dog is less likely to develop interdigital cysts if the hair on the feet is clipped short, paying particular attention to the hairs underneath, between the pads and between the toes. If the dog gets its feet dirty on a walk, rinse them with clean water on return home and dry them carefully. If simple rinsing with plain water is not sufficient to remove all the dirt the feet may be washed with any mild toilet soap. All traces of the soap should be rinsed away with plain water before the feet are dried. Should a dog develop any soreness of the feet it is wise to obtain veterinary advice.

Not all swellings between the toes are interdigital cysts. Occasionally a foreign body, such as a grass seed, will penetrate the interdigital web. The reaction to this is usually the formation of a large soft swelling between the toes. The first aid treatment is hot fomentation as described above, but the swelling needs to be lanced by a veterinarian so that the grass seed can be removed to allow healing to take place.

International Canine Federation see Federation Cynologique Internationale.

International Championships see Championships.

In Utero Used generally to mean the importation of, or purchase of, a bitch carrying puppies. Thus: 'Bought in utero.'

Irish Setter Some call him the Red Setter, or the Irish Red Setter. To the film maker he is just the 'Big Red'. It is all the same dog: the dog Britain and the U.S.A. know officially as the Irish Setter.

So well known is it that it hardly requires a description. Even so, few resist attempting one. It is big, handsome, red, with a silky coat. It has kindly eyes, a waving tail and remarkable speed.

Above Interdigital cysts are small abscesses which form between the toes. If they do not burst and heal by themselves, a hot fomentation should be applied regularly.

It should also be recorded that this dog came originally from Ireland. Possibly it was evolved by some cross with an IRISH WATER SPANIEL, and it is a reasonable assumption that ENGLISH SETTERS, GORDON SETTERS, SPRINGER SPANIELS and POINTERS must each have played some part in its evolution. In defence of this suggestion there is evidence that originally the majority were red and white. Even today this combination of colours is accepted in the show ring, although it is rarely encountered.

But if it was Ireland who gave this breed to the world, it was Victorian England which allowed it to flower to its present perfection. As a sporting dog, bred to work with the gun, what a Setter needs is space. And on the Yorkshire moors it found it. There was space to range well in front of the guns; space to gallop from right to left, left to right; to move steadily forward until every inch of the ground had been searched for crouching game like partridge.

When the Irish Setter 'finds' it freezes into a classic pose: head held high, nose pointing towards the birds, tail straight out, one paw lifted as though to take the next delicate step forward. In Britain (but not America) the sportsman approaches and urges it on. It inches towards the birds. As it nears them, they break cover. There is a flutter of wings as they soar. The dog has fulfilled its part of the bargain: it has presented the sportsman with the ideal target.

The breed, like many, has its detractors. There are those who claim this Irish red-head is too headstrong to accept the discipline of the shooting field, a taunt gleefully accepted by most Irishmen as being in keeping with their national character. They would also agree that on a boring day it is not above making a false point a quarter of a mile away from the place covey occupied days ago.

Even if true, this matters little now because it is as pets and companions that most Irish Setters earn their

Above Irish Setter Ch. Innisfail Flashback's Design.

living. It is the handsome good looks and boisterous good humour which ensure their popularity.

But even in this field they once encountered a serious setback. Soon after the war they developed a tendency to early blindness. To their credit, breeders made a determined attempt to correct the fault. First they publicized it and taught others how to recognize the early symptoms. Then with the help of the English Kennel Club they investigated the bloodlines concerned. In time the condition was controlled to such an extent that Irish Setters suffer far less from 'night blindness' than many other breeds. See HEREDITARY ABNORMALITIES.

Those days have passed and now the breed is firmly established. The dog's bright mind leads it on. A tearaway? Possibly. But a gentle one. Exhibitionist? Yes; but sensitive also. An extrovert? Certainly. But with a mood for every moment. In other words, a typical Irish gentleman.

Essentials of the breed: The head should be long and lean but not narrow, snipy or coarse. The skull should be oval with well defined occiput; brows raised, showing stop: the muzzle: moderately deep, and fairly square. Eyes should be dark hazel or dark brown; the ears of moderate size, fine in texture, set on low and well back, hanging close to head. Mouth: neither over nor undershot. Neck: moderately long, muscular and slightly arched, free from all tendency to throatiness. The ribs: well sprung. Loins: muscular, slightly arched. Hindquarters: wide and powerful. The hind legs from hip to hock: long and muscular; from hock to heel: short and strong. Feet: small, very firm, toes close together and arched. Tail: moderately long, set rather low, strong at root, tapering to a fine point and carried level with or below back. Coat and feathering: on the head, front of legs, and tips of the ears, short and fine. On other parts of the body and legs; of moderate length, flat and free from curl or wave. Feet: well

Left An engraving of Sir Edw
Landseer's portrait 'The Setter
Irish Setters are believed to hav
blood from both English an
Gordon Setters.

feathered between the toes. Tail should have a fringe of moderately long hair. All feathering to be straight and flat. The colour should be rich chestnut without black. White on chest, throat or toes, forehead or a blaze on the nose (in America a narrow, centred streak only on the skull), do not disqualify.

See colour plate p. 86.

Irish Terrier Many writers claim a long history for this breed, but its first official mention came as recently as 1875. Even Idstone's all-embracing *Book of Dogs* published in 1872 fails to record the breed.

There is certain evidence that dogs known as Irish Terriers have been around for a hundred years. Just three years after Idstone failed to notice the existence of the breed, a band of fanciers in Ireland planned to launch the Irish Terrier on the world. A show in Dublin was organized for their debut. And to everyone's surprise, around fifty 'Irish Terriers' were mustered for the event.

The competition rules were typically and engagingly Irish. No dog was allowed in unless it had a pedigree, but in fact written notes were attached to some dogs saying 'full details of breeding available at a certain address'. *Boxer*, the first prize winner, was boldly entered as 'bred by owner but pedigree unknown'!

Reports state that dogs of all shapes and sizes were entered. Many were virtually CAIRN TERRIERS. Others would have been glad to have had even this claim to purity. There was a class for under 9 lb., an unacceptably low weight today; the winner of the Open class weighed thirty pounds; and one specimen was pure white.

The resultant furore brought some attempt at order. In 1879 a breed club was formed which issued a standard not vastly different from that used today.

Soon after this the breed started to become popular. This was principally due to a Mr. Krehl, who was commissioned to write a brief article on the breed for a new and important work called *The Book of the Dog*.

Mr. Krehl was an enthusiast with little interest in impartiality, and oddly enough his contribution was accepted apparently without blue pencilling. He pulled out all the stops. Whatever could be done by any dog could be done better by a 'Mick', a 'Dare Devil', in short, an Irish Terrier. They were apparently brilliant at ratting, rabbiting, fox-hunting, badger-facing and otter-hunting. They excelled as gundogs and would work hedgerows like spaniels, retrieve like Labradors or quarter the ground like Pointers and setters. They were even-tempered, courageous, trainable, hardy . . . but why go on?

It would be more truthful to say that they are typical terriers, with all the qualities of terriers, and with an interest in all the things that all terriers like. They are inquisitive, venturesome and always prepared to trail their coat in front of an imagined or real adversary. In short, they make ideal companions for the young in heart but are somewhat doubtful assets for the aged and infirm. A growing lad could wish no finer friend to grow up with; mischief overlooked by the one will certainly be exploited by the other!

In size the Irish Terriers are midway between the WELSH or LAKELAND TERRIERS and the AIREDALE. They might also be said to be midway in general appearance. FOX TERRIERS may have been used in the general smartening up process over the years.

The Irish Terrier looks and behaves in a way which cannot be ignored. The strutting walk; the cocky self-assurance, the charm and blarney; the deliberately conveyed impression that he will take his coat off to you if you insist. And deep down underneath the very real good nature and warmth.

Essentials of the breed: The general appearance is of an active, lively dog, with substance, free of clumsiness and showing a graceful 'racing outline'. The head is long, narrow between ears, narrowing towards the eye. Jaw: strong and muscular, but not full in the cheek, and of good length. Eyes are dark, small and full of life.

Ears: small, V-shaped, set well on the head and dropping forward close to cheek, with the top fold well above the skull level. The teeth should be even and strong. Neck: of fair length and gradually widening towards sloping shoulders. Forequarters: the shoulders must be fine, long and sloping well into the back. The legs must be moderately long, well set from the shoulders, perfectly straight, with plenty of bone and muscle; the elbows working freely clear of the sides; the pasterns short and straight, hardly noticeable. The forelegs should be moved straight forward when travelling. The hair on the legs should be dense and crisp. Body: chest deep and muscular but not wide. Body: moderately long, with strong and straight back. Loins: muscular and slightly arched, ribs well sprung and deep. Hindquarters: muscular with powerful thighs. The hind legs, too, should be moved straight forward when travelling. Feet should be strong, moderately small, with arched toes. Tail: docked to about three quarters, free of fringe or feather, set on high, carried gaily. Coat: hard and wiry and broken; not long enough to hide the outline of the body. Dense and crisp on legs. Colour: always 'whole-coloured', preferably bright red, red wheaten or yellow red. The desirable weight is dogs 27 lb., bitches 25 lb. Height at shoulders: approximately 18 inches.
See colour plate p. 373.

Irish Water Spaniel The answer to the question 'When is a spaniel not a spaniel?' might well be: 'When it is of the Irish Water variety!'

The more you look at the dog the harder it is to believe that it is a true spaniel. It is so much larger than all of the other varieties, so different in shape, outline and general characteristics. Different, too, in that it alone is the possessor of a long tail, in that it sports not a flat and slightly waved coat but a mass of dense crisp ringlets.

But to doubt its spaniel connections is not to imply that it is not a gundog. It is a good gundog, particularly suited by virtue of its constitution and temperament to the rather specialized role that it performs.

We should like to start its history at the beginning. As so often however, that task is difficult because accurate records are comparatively recent. We are left therefore with theories.

Persian manuscripts of 4000 B.C. mention Water Dogs. References to Water Dogs, even Water Spaniels, also occur as far back as A.D. 17. Not surprisingly, these references, in common with another that appeared in the 4th century, are unaccompanied by illustrations and it is therefore difficult to be sure that the dogs referred to were in any way similar to those known today.

Hugh Dalziel, writing about eighty years ago, suggested that the Irish Water was the forerunner of all modern spaniels. Others have held contrary views, some having suggested that it is the result of comparatively recent crosses with POODLES from France. Yet others claim that it owes its ancestry to CURLY-COATED RETRIEVERS.

Right Irish Terrier. Ch. Brackenwood Carousel of Medris.

Clearly there is some close relationship between Irish Water Spaniels and Poodles. The only question is, which came first? The most likely answer to this is that it was the spaniel. It is known that dogs of this type existed in the Middle East some time before Christ. The probability is that they moved up through the Iberian Peninsula leaving behind species which still exist and are known today as Portuguese Water Dogs. In Europe they may well have sown the seeds of what later became the Poodle. And in Ireland, the limit of the penetration, the Irish Water Spaniels are amongst their descendants.

Apart from their general build and outline these three last-mentioned breeds have traits which lend support to the common ancestry thesis. There is a willingness to work, a keen desire to retrieve objects and carry them to their master, coupled with a particular aptitude for performing these tasks in water. All three breeds were used principally for duck shooting.

One of the best known gundogs in literature was an Irish Water Spaniel, called *Maria*. Here is one extract from the writings of the Misses Somerville and Ross dealing with this engaging personality:

'On shooting mornings Maria ceased to be a buccaneer, a glutton and a hypocrite. From the moment when I put my gun together her breakfast stood untouched until it suffered the final degradation of being eaten by the cats, and now in the trap she was shivering with excitement and agonizing in her soul lest she should even yet be left behind.'

One would have thought that a breed with such inspiring characteristics was assured of a permanent place in man's affections. Alas, this is by no means certain; indeed, after an unbroken history of centuries, there is now at least a risk that the breed may wither and fade. They do not feature in the first 100 breeds of either Britain or the U.S.A.

Whilst never widely popular they were at least seen frequently at the turn of the century. When breed statistics were first introduced after the First World War, English Kennel Club registrations ran at about 50 a year. This figure was maintained right up to the start of the Second World War.

Currently they are failing to keep up these figures. Sad but true, together with the FIELD and SUSSEX SPANIELS, the Irish Water Spaniel remains amongst the most neglected of this family of dogs.

Perhaps a turning point is near. Some traditionalist

Right Irish Water Spaniel. Comb Brownie Girl.

Overleaf Irish Wolfhounds. Left t right: Ballykelly Bawneen, Bally kelly Torram, Ballykelly N Rooney and Holmehill Torridan This breed, one of the world' tallest and oldest, is now well known, but was thought to b extinct 100 years ago.

Below Irish Water Spaniel C Trieven's Irish Angel.

with a taste for dogs of exceptional character may decide to save them before it is too late.

Essentials of the breed: The gait is a characteristic peculiar to the breed and differs from that of other spaniels. The head should be of good size with high dome and of good length and width. The muzzle is long, strong and somewhat square with a gradual stop. The face is smooth but the skull covered with long curls. Nose: large and well developed and dark liver-coloured. Eyes: comparatively small, brown, bright and alert. Ears: very long, low-set, hanging close to cheeks and covered with twisted curls. Neck: powerful and arching, covered with curls similar to those on the body. The throat should be smooth, forming a V-shaped patch from the back of the lower jaw to the breast bone. Forequarters: the shoulders should be powerful and sloping; the chest deep and of large girth; the forelegs well boned and straight. The back must be short, broad and level, with ribs carried well back. The loins: deep and wide. Powerful quarters with long, well-bent stifles, and hocks set low. Feet: large and somewhat round and spreading; well covered with hair over and between toes. The tail must be short and straight, thick at the root and tapering to a fine point. It should be low set, carried below the level of the back, and should nearly reach the hock joint. About three inches at the root should be covered by close curls, the remainder should be bare or covered by fine hair. Coat must be dense, tight, crisp ringlets with natural oiliness, the forelegs covered with ringlets to the feet. The AKC specifies a topknot of long, loose curls growing down into a peak between the eyes. Below the hocks the hindleg should be smooth in front, but feathered behind. Colour: a rich dark liver. Height: dogs about 21 to 24 inches, bitches one inch smaller. Weight (America): dogs 55 to 65 lb.; bitches 45 to 58 lb.
See colour plate p. 84.

Irish Wolfhound The Irish Wolfhound is usually regarded as the tallest dog in the world (see HEIGHT OF DOGS). The breed is also accepted as one of the oldest.

But are the current specimens genuine descendants of the original Irish Wolfhounds or are they a comparatively modern re-creation of those legendary dogs?

Around one hundred years ago, 'Stonehenge', an unusually reliable commentator, wrote: 'This grand variety is now extinct'. At about this same time a Captain Graham of Dursley, set himself the task of 'reviving' the breed. The question is, did his searches in Ireland reveal genuine descendants from which he could launch a revival, or was he forced to 'manufacture' a new line bearing some resemblance to the original but in fact composed almost exclusively of foreign breeds such as the GREAT DANE, DEERHOUND and MASTIFF? The question posed is unlikely to be answered.

In A.D. 393 Symmachus wrote from Rome to his brother Flavinius, then in Britain, thanking him for his gift of seven Irish hounds. He added: 'All Rome viewed them with wonder'. It is not surprising if they stood well over 3 feet at the shoulder and weighed 150 lb.

All through Irish history the legend of the great

Above Irish Wolfhound. Ch. Out
waite Clodagh of Boroughbury.

hounds persists. Cormac, the fourth century King, is reputed to have possessed several of them. In the twelfth century the King of Ulster offered six thousand cows for a Wolfhound called 'Aibe' and fought a battle when the offer was declined.

In the sixteenth century a presentation brace was sent to the King of Spain. In 1652 however, Oliver Cromwell forbade their export on the grounds that the hounds were scarce while wolves were far too plentiful.

Then come countless stories of the last wolf killed in Ireland by the traditional hounds. One of them is as late as 1780. Thereafter the work of the Wolfhounds had gone. The indications are that the dogs themselves had gone some fifty years later.

It was at this stage that Captain Graham began his life's work. It was a long and expensive business and perhaps it matters little whether he *revived* or *rebuilt* the breed. Sufficient that we have them today and that they are remarkably similar in form, outline, size and temperament to the original.

The mention of temperament prompts an explanation. Despite their background and their enormous strength, Wolfhounds are amongst the gentlest breeds known to man. Whilst their great size makes them unsuitable for small houses, as domestic pets they are quiet, well-mannered and extremely biddable.

The number of people who can house and feed them is limited. But they are in good demand in many lands, and particularly in America.

As with so many breeds, the eye is the key to the character. And underneath the shaggy brows of the world's biggest dog there lies an eye dark, soft and essentially peaceable. Indeed to look at one is to wonder how they were ever sufficiently warlike to take on such formidable enemies as fully grown wolves.

Essentials of the breed: The head and skull is long with little indentation between the eyes. Skull: not too broad. Muzzle: long and moderately pointed. Dark eyes and small ears, Greyhound-like in carriage. Neck: rather long, very strong and muscular, well arched. Shoulders should be muscular, giving breadth of chest. Elbows: well under, turned neither in nor out. Chest: very deep, long rather than short, well arched loins. Muscular thighs, long and strong as in the GREYHOUND. Hocks: well let down. Feet: moderately large and round. Toes: arched and close. Tail: long, slightly curved, of moderate thickness and well covered with hair. Coat:

rough and hardy on body, legs and head; especially wiry and long over eyes and under jaw. Colour can be grey, brindle, red, black, pure white, fawn, or any colour that appears in the Deerhound. The minimum height and weight of dogs should be 31 inches (America: 32 inches) and 120 lb.; bitches 28 inches and 90 lb. (America 30 inches and 105 lb.).

See colour plate p. 180.

Isabella Fawn colour, or greyish yellow.

Italian Greyhound The Italian Greyhound is the smallest of the true Greyhounds, but it belongs to the great GREYHOUND family which includes the IRISH WOLFHOUND, Scottish DEERHOUND, SALUKI, and AFGHAN. It is not known when, or by whom, Greyhounds were dwarfed in size to make the Italian Greyhound. There are, however, drawings of small Greyhounds dating from both Egyptian and Roman times.

The breed appears to have been well known during the sixteenth and seventeenth centuries. Veronese (1528–1588) included one in a painting, as did Van Dyck (1599–1641), Kneller (1648–1723) and Watteau (1684–1721).

In 1790, the great engraver, Bewick, compared the small Italian Greyhound to the larger Greyhounds, and wrote: 'The small Italian Greyhound is not above half the size, but perfectly similar in form. In shape it is exquisitely beautiful and delicate. It is not common in this country, the climate being too rigorous for the extreme delicacy of its constitution.'

Only thirteen years later, in the *Sportsmen's Cabinet*, Taplin wrote: 'There has not been even a plausible or satisfactory suggestion as to the origin of the variety. They are not able to officiate in the services of domestic alarm or protection; and in consequence, are dedicated over the comforts of the tea table, the fireside carpet, the luxurious indulgencies of the sofa, and the warm lap of the mistress.'

'Stonehenge' pictured the greatest Italian Greyhound of its time in 1859. The dog was *Gowan's Billy*, and he was intensely inbred to dogs from Italy. From this, it is evident that English stock of the period actually did come from Italy. W. Bruce Falkirk of Scotland was the foremost breeder of his time, and if the Italian Greyhound could survive in the Scottish climate and in homes without central heating, it would seem that tales of their delicacy were somewhat exaggerated.

The dogs of 1900 were hardly different from the modern dogs, either in type or in size. Two noted English dogs of the period were *Svelta*, 8½ lb., and *Saltarello*, 9¼ lb. A great American dog of the same period, *Tee Dee*, weighed under nine pounds. She was bred and was owned by Dr. F. H. Hoyt of Sharon, Pennsylvania, who is usually considered to be the founding father of the breed in the United States.

Until the last several decades, Italian Greyhounds have not been popular as show dogs in the United States. Dog shows were far apart and owners simply did not care to risk their dogs on railway journeys, and at two- and three-day shows.

ight Italian Greyhound. Ch. *Westwind's The Blue Max.*

The high stepping prance of the breed is characteristic. And it is said that the Matabele chief, King Lobengula, who ruled over this tribe in the nineteenth century, was so fascinated by this dog's prancing gait that he gave Luscombe Searelle of Johannesburg, South Africa, 200 head of cattle for one of his dogs.

Essentials of the breed: The standard calls for a miniature Greyhound, but one more slender in all proportions, and of ideal grace and elegance. The skull is long and narrow, the muzzle fine, the nose dark, the teeth level. The ears are rose-shaped, placed well back, and delicate. The eyes are large and bright. The neck is long, the chest deep and narrow. The back is curved and droops to the hindquarters.

The legs have fine bone, the front legs set well under the shoulders. The hind legs are well let down at the hocks with muscular thighs. The feet are long, but strongly arched. The tail is long, fine, and carried low. The skin is fine, the hair thin and glossy like satin. Two classes are provided, one of 8 lb. and under, and one for over 8 lb. A good small dog is preferable to a good big dog.

See colour plate p. 381.

Italian Greyhound.
Left Narrabo Giselle and Now
Alloro.
Above Classical carving in mar
indicates that the Italian Gr
hound, like the larger Greyhou
has changed its form very li
since ancient times. First cent
A.D.

J

Jack Russell Terrier 'When is a breed not a breed?' is a conundrum to which the answer is, 'When it's a Jack Russell'. To which must be added 'and when it is English'.

Even so, the Kennel Club in England does not recognize it. More convincing, not one kennel club in the world recognizes it, although between them these ruling bodies accept the existence of nearly 400 breeds.

Why then, this entry? Simply because the dogs that carry the name are enormously popular in Britain. Why this sinister plot against a breed which so many people know and have an affection for?

Again the answer is simple: the Kennel Club insists that it is not a breed but merely a type. To be recognized a breed must have a breed standard or 'blueprint' which lays down the physical requirements.

Every recognized breed has one; the Jack Russell has not. And this is because nobody has yet decided what it should look like. Perhaps, to be more precise, a number of people have decided, but always failed to agree amongst themselves.

Some feel they should have medium length legs, others insist on short ones. Some demand prick ears, while others favour the drop variety. Different factions insist that they should be black and white, brown and white, hound marked; that the coats should be smooth and soft, shaggy and wiry. Clearly without agreement

on these vital elements there can be neither progress nor recognition.

Additionally the name is to some degree suspect. The terriers that the Reverend Jack Russell owned and hunted were quite unlike those which currently trade under his name. The original sporting parson from Devon in England never bred a strain or type but bought any likely looking terrier he saw and which he thought would help his pack of hounds. There were, however, two sorts he would not tolerate: first, smooth-haired terriers because he suspected crosses with BULL TERRIERS and therefore a tendency to kill the precious foxes which were then in short supply; next, short-legged dogs for the simple reason that they could not gallop with hounds. He had no modern facilities for transporting terriers. He invariably used early and assorted types of Wire-Haired FOX TERRIER. He certainly never tried to get recognition for his 'own breed', although he was a founder member of the Kennel Club.

If the little dogs so popular today are not 'genuine Jack Russells', what are they? The answer is a likeable little cross-breed, a type that has existed round stables for as long as anybody can remember.

Where there are horses there is corn; and where there is corn, rats. To keep these down, farmers' grooms and hunt servants kept tough, hard-bitten little cross-bred terriers. The dogs some think of as being 'victimized' are descendants of these hard working dogs.

Their gayness, gameness and high spirits are irresistible, and their many attractions obvious. It should be said that they are also, being unrecognized, the under-dogs, the odd dogs out. This gives them an added

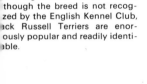

below right Jack Russell Terrier. though the breed is not recognized by the English Kennel Club, ack Russell Terriers are enormously popular and readily identifiable.

appeal. Small wonder they are popular and well loved. See colour plate p. 374.

Japanese See Japanese Spaniel.

Japanese Spaniel The Japanese Spaniel, the PEKINGESE, and the PUG appear to share a common oriental ancestry. The Japanese Spaniel, or *Chin*, may be a descendant of the Pekingese, or they may share a common parent. There are two theories as to the origin of the Japanese dog. One is that, in A.D. 732 a royal Korean mission sent a lap dog as a present to the Emperor of Japan, thus starting the breed there. The other is that Buddhist monks and teachers brought Pekingese dogs to Japan, along with Zen Buddhism, as early as A.D. 520.

The Japanese Chin developed solely in the homes of royalty and the court nobles. Lady Sei Shonagan gives some idea of the extent of this in a 'sketchbook', written between 991 and 1000 in which she tells of the troubles of the dog, *Okinamaru*.

Commodore Perry, the American naval commander, opened Japan to the West in 1853. He started home with seven Japanese Spaniels, or Chins. On board his own ship were five, of which three died en route. The other two were transferred to British Admiral Sterling's ship for presentation to Queen Victoria, but there is no evidence that they ever arrived. Two, on another ship, reached New York safely and were given to August Belmont. Though they apparently died without issue, they started a great wave of importations.

Hundreds of the dogs made the great voyage. The New York show of 1882 had nine entries; a tenth was entered in the Miscellaneous class as a Pekingese (China) Spaniel, but the three judges considered it to be a Japanese Spaniel, and the best of the ten. A Japanese Spaniel Club was organized in 1883, but it later became moribund; the present Japanese Spaniel Club of America was organized in 1912.

Robert Fortune, an Englishman, described the Japanese dogs in 1863: 'The lap-dogs of the country are highly prized both by natives and by foreigners. They are small – some of them not more than nine or ten inches in length. They are remarkable for snub noses and sunken eyes, and are certainly more curious than beautiful. They are carefully bred; they command high prices even amongst the Japanese; and are dwarfed, it is said, by the use of *sake*.'

Japanese Spaniels first appeared in England about 1880. Queen Alexandra had several. Sir Bernard and Lady Samuelson, and several members of the Rothschild family, became interested breeders. Sir Bernard became President of the Japanese and Pekingese Club, which was organized in 1895.

Essentials of the breed: The standard calls for a dog averaging about 7 lb. Classes may be divided into those 7 lb. and under, and those over 7 lb. The smaller dogs are preferred, if sound and of good type. Colour is black and white or red and white. But red includes all shades of sable, brindle, lemon, and orange. The white must be clear, and the colours evenly divided in patches.

The skull is large, broad, and rounded. The eyes are large, dark, rather prominent, and set wide apart. Ears are small, V-shaped, and set high, but carried forward. The dog is snub-nosed, and the nose should be the colour of the coat, that is a red or flesh nose in a red and white, and a black nose in a black and white. A nose other than black in the latter brings disqualification.

The neck is short and moderately thick, and the body square, compact and cobby, its length equal to shoulder

height. The tail is twisted to right or left from the root, and is carried over the back, but flowing to the opposite side. Ring tails are not desired. The feet are small, and the dog 'stand on its toes'. The coat is profuse, long, and straight, and free from wave or curl. It stands off at the neck to give a ruff, and there is profuse feathering on thighs and tail.

See colour plate p. 384.

Jaundice Jaundice is the symptom of any disease in which the skin, the mucous membranes, and the urine turn yellow. The yellowness is caused by bile pigments in the blood. Among other conditions jaundice may be a sign of arsenical HEPATITIS. Catarrhal jaundice is due to an inflammation of the bile ducts, in which dropsy may be present. Jaundice may be present in infectious canine hepatitis and in LEPTOSPIROSIS.

Canine Babesiasis is sometimes called malignant jaundice, as well as biliary fever and canine piroplas-mosis. It is a tick-borne disease in which the brown dog tick is the usual carrier. The disease is common in warm countries, including the American South, and the causative organism is often *Babesia canis*.

Infected dogs which recover, may harbour the parasites for a year. During that time, they are immune to the disease. Once they shed the parasites, however, they lose their immunity.

Treatment consists in the injection of chemicals directly into the blood stream. This must be done only be a veterinarian. Kennel owners can prevent infection by keeping their dogs free of TICKS.

See PROTOZOAN DISEASES.

Jaws In most breeds of dogs the jaws must meet equally, usually in a scissors bite. An overshot or under-shot jaw is considered a serious fault. However, in some breeds, a slightly over or undershot jaw is not penalized, and in others, like the BULLDOG, it is a desirable trait.

While most dogs use their jaws mainly for eating and chewing, some, like the GREYHOUND, use them in hunting – to disable the game – and in fighting – to slash with them and defend themselves.

Judging Dogs The methods by which dogs are judged differ very little in those areas of the world where dog shows are held. Each governing body or national kennel club will have a standard of perfection for each of the breeds which it recognizes. Often, this standard is the joint work of breed specialists and the governing body. Judges are required to know these standards, and to use them in evaluating the merits of the dogs which come under them.

The judges are therefore determining the quality of each dog against the standard of perfection which has been set up for the breed. But they are also comparing each dog against its competition.

If the judge believes that none of the dogs being exhibited in a given class approximates the standard of perfection, all awards can be withheld. Or, the judge might withhold first prize, but award a second, third, and where used, a fourth prize or 'reserve' as it is called in some countries.

Ring procedure is approximately the same at dog shows in all countries. As a rule, the judge will require the dogs to move around the ring, so that all dogs are studied together while in motion, and in profile. The dogs then may be placed in line, usually in profile position. The exhibitors then pose, or 'stack' their dogs so that their best points may be seen easily by the judge.

A physical examination of the dog is normally required. The judge approaches the dog from the front and examines the head, eyes, ears, and muzzle. The exhibitor may be asked to open the dog's mouth to display the teeth, or the judge may lift the lips to expose them.

The judge then examines the body, using both eyes and hands. The major points to be considered are the arch and length of the neck, the placement of the shoulders, whether the elbows turn in or out, whether the feet turn in or out, the depth of chest and spring of ribs, the strength and shortness of the loin, the muscular development of the thighs, the angulations made by the stifle and hock joints, and the set on of the tail. Since the toes may be covered with hair, the use of the hands is necessary to determine the arch of the toes and their depth, plus the toughness and thickness of the pads.

Following the examination of each dog, the judge requires them to be moved or 'gaited' individually. As a rule, the dogs start in front of the judge and move away in a straight line, then return along the same line. Sometimes, the judge may require the dog to be moved out, and then across the ring and back, so that the dog has been taken on a 'T' course.

In gaiting the dog, the judge discovers whether or not the dog moves in a straight forward thrust or whether it travels with a 'crabbing' or 'side-winding' gait; whether it is loose at elbows; whether its legs 'cross over' in front and behind; and in the case of the 'T', the amount of thrust provided by the hind legs. The judge also notes whether or not the tail carriage is as prescribed in the standard of perfection.

Having completed the gaiting of the dogs, the judge may then have them placed once more in profile, or have them placed side by side so that they may be compared in front and from behind. If unable to make a decision at this point, the judge may require that the dogs be moved around the ring once more.

In some countries, the judge is required to write a critique of each dog. In some cases, this may be dictated while the dogs are in the ring. Critiques are more or less detailed, according to the rules of the governing body and the desires and available time of the judges.

In Variety, Group and Best in Show judging, the Best of Breed winners compete. Again, the judge is considering each dog against the standard of perfection of its breed. The job of evaluation then is whether one dog comes closer to the standard for its breed than the other dogs come to their standards.

Junior Showmanship Junior Showmanship classes are a popular feature at American, Canadian, and Mexican dog shows. Those in Canada are still sometimes called 'Children's Handling Classes', but this term was abandoned in the United States because it was felt that boys and girls of fourteen to sixteen years of age would resent being called children.

Junior showmanship classes were at first held on a completely informal basis. Licensed judges or professional handlers were to officiate. But, as the classes became more popular, the American Kennel Club set up rules governing them.

These rules set up four classes, with two in each of two divisions. Division A is for boys and girls ten to twelve years old, inclusive. Novice A is for those who have not won in competition; Open A is for those who have won one or more times.

Division B is for boys and girls thirteen to sixteen inclusive. Novice B is for those who have not won in open competition; Open B is for those who have won before. First place winners in the Open divisions count toward eligibility to compete in national championships in the WESTMINSTER DOG SHOW at Madison Square Garden, New York, each February.

Under the revised rules, only professional handlers, licensed by the American Kennel Club, could judge. The quality of the dog is not counted, but only the junior's ability to handle it. Most shows permit the four winners to compete for Best Junior Showman. After trying out this system, it was decided that the revised rules had not been entirely successful, since the time, judge, and ring in which competitions were held were seldom announced until mid-afternoon. The competitions became very popular both with the juniors and with spectators. The American Kennel Club then decided to revise the rules to make the competitions more formal.

Revisions, effective from April 1971, were made. Licensed judges, rather than professional handlers, were to officiate.

Entries were to be made on official show entry forms, at the same time that dogs were entered. The time of judging, the ring number or numbers, and the entry totals were then to appear in the regular printed judging

Below Junior showmanship. T[?] young handler's ability to sho[?] his or her dog, and not the qual[?] of the dog, is on trial in this sort [?] competition.

schedule for the show. If the designated judge was also to officiate in breed classes, then the Junior Showmanship classes had to be included in his total assignment, which is a maximum of 175 dogs to be judged in any one day.

K

Kala-Azar (Leishmaniasis) see Protozoan Diseases.

Kangaroo Hound As early as 1855, Australians began to develop dogs capable of coursing kangaroos. These dogs were a mixture of GREYHOUND and IRISH WOLFHOUND, and were usually intermediate in size. The modern dogs are quite rare. They conform to Greyhound type, have short, harsh coats, stand 28 inches or more at the shoulder, and weigh 80 lb. or more. Their colours are brindle, pied, black, tan and white, and black and tan.

Above Kangaroo Hound.

Below right Karelian Bear Dog. An individualistic dog which hunts better alone. It has an excellent nose for bear and elk. This is Hostodalens Center.

Karelian Bear Dog This breed belongs to the great SPITZ family of dogs. It is a native of the area once known as Karelia in Northern Europe but which, since 1946, has been known as the Karelo-Finnish Soviet Socialist Republic. The dog appears to be a close relative of the Russo-Finnish Laika. The Karelian Bear Dog was recognized as a pure breed in 1935, and the FEDERATION CYNOLOGIQUE INTERNATIONALE (F.C.I.) gave official recognition to the breed in 1946.

The dog is used to hunt bear and elk. It has an excellent nose. The dogs are less than friendly with other dogs, and so are used alone. They are bold and intelligent, but are also intensely stubborn and individualistic.

Essentials of the breed: The Karelian Bear Dog conforms generally to Spitz type. It is 20 to 23½ inches at the shoulder, with bitches slightly smaller. The head is wedge-shaped with a domed skull, shallow stop and prick ears. The body is somewhat longer than the shoulder height. The outer coat is stiff, harsh, and lies flat, but the undercoat is soft wool. The colour is black and white, but the black may show a brownish sheen. The tail is bushy, and is carried over the back and slightly to one side.

Keeshond This breed, like a few others, has suffered from name troubles. Over the years and in various lands it has been called the Dutch Barge Dog (England), the 'Fik' (Southern Holland), the Foxdog, the Overweight Pomeranian (in Victorian Britain) and, of course, the Keeshond. They are listed as Keeshonden in the United States with the Dutch plural form of 'en' rather than the English 's'. This is perhaps unfortunate in that the correct name seems too difficult for most Anglo-Saxon tongues. Attempts to call it 'Cheese-hound' or 'Keeshond' are incorrect. It is pronounced 'Kays-hond'. 'Hond' means dog. 'Kees' (pronounced 'Kays') was the nickname of a celebrated Dutch patriot, of whom more later. The whole then meant simply 'Kees' dog'.

Clearly the dog is a member of the SPITZ group. Its ears, ruff, curled tail and comparatively straight hocks, all point to this. Its probable entry into Holland was via Germany, possibly in the form of a Wolf Spitz or a large Pomeranian.

In the Netherlands it quickly became very much a dog of the people. Nevertheless, some managed to get their portraits painted by celebrated artists. Examples are a drawing dated 1794 and many studies by Jan Steen and Gainsborough.

The French Revolution heralded political troubles for Holland. On the one side there were the established Orangists with a PUG as a mascot. Pushing hard for recognition was the Patriots Party, led by Cornelis (or Kees) de Gyselaer. His dog was one of these rather overgrown Poms. It was a dog of the people. And it became their symbol of resistance.

When the House of Orange finally triumphed, the breed received a setback. Few wanted even to appear to support a loser by flaunting a living symbol of allegiance. The towns neglected them, but the countryside did not, and they remained in fair numbers. In 1920, Baroness van Hardencroek became interested in the breed. When she looked around for suitable breeding stock it was found in abundance trotting restlessly up and down the decks of the countless barges on the Dutch canals. Riverboat captains had remained faithful to them over the years, as had some farmers. More surprisingly, some rough and ready attempts to keep stud books had been made.

Parallel with this, in England, Miss Hamilton Fletcher (later Mrs. Wingfield Digby) had been breeding from some specimens she bought during a yachting trip on the Dutch canals. The name 'Dutch Barge Dog', later changed, was almost inevitable.

A Keeshond Club was organized in 1925, and official

recognition came in England in that year, four years before the Dutch Kennel Club gave its own official blessing to the breed.

America took them up soon afterwards, in small numbers at first. Since the U.S.A. used British stock principally the two types are still very similar, and in the opinion of many, these are superior to the dogs found in continental Europe, including Holland.

In most countries they remain 'in between' dogs; never sensationally popular but certainly never neglected. They are also in between in size; neither massive nor diminutive. Around the house they take up even less space then might at first be envisaged. A hundred or so years on barges taught them to curl up and keep out of the way!

An additional good point is the fact that their coat, although full and long, needs very little attention. Apart from being water- and dirt-repellent, it does not mat. It should also be noted that Keeshonds are good-tempered, intelligent and very attached to children.

The most outstanding characteristic of their appearance is the 'spectacles'. These are composed of pencilled lines starting upwards from the eye corners to the ear with distinct markings on the eyebrow. The effect is undeniably quizzical and wholly engaging.

Strangely enough, they have never been used for work. They have no heritage of hunting, herding or pulling carts. They always have been, and still are, a pure and simple 'friend of man'.

Essentials of the breed: The general appearance is of a compact, alert dog with fox-like head and clean, brisk movement. The head viewed from above is wedge-shaped, with medium length muzzle and definite stop. The eyes should be dark with well-defined 'spectacles' as detailed above. Ears: small, triangular, erect and set high on head. Forelegs: feathered, cream in colour and with good bone. Hindlegs: similar but not feathered below hock. The tail must curl tightly and have white top plume and black tip. Coat: dense, off-standing, with thick ruff and a soft, light-coloured undercoat. Colour should be wolf, or ash grey. All-black or all-white is highly undesirable.

The breed standard calls for a dog 18 inches high, and a bitch 17 inches, but balance, conformation and type are more important than size.
See colour plate p. 191.

Kelpie (Australian Collie) In the mid-1960s, it was estimated that nearly 80,000 Kelpies were earning their living on the great sheep stations of Australia. Sheep men estimate that one well-trained Kelpie can do the work of six men, and that on some days, the dogs cover more than 40 miles of ground.

The Kelpie's job is to round up sheep which have strayed far from the flock. To do this, the dog must often work out of sight of its owner. When sheep are being moved, it usually stays at the rear, driving those which lag, or which tend to stray away from the moving herd. Sometimes, it must be sent to the front to restore order among the leaders.

After a long, hot drive, when sheep are thirsty, the Kelpie may be required to separate 50 to 100 sheep at a water hole, and to allow them to drink while holding back the others. He then may have to repeat this with another group.

Kelpies sometimes perform an amazing feat called 'tinning the chicken'. They must drive the chicken into a tin can without touching either the can or the chicken.

Kelpies descend from short-haired, prick-eared Scottish sheepdogs which were sent to Australia just prior to 1870. The mating of such a pair produced a bitch called *Gleeson's Kelpie*. A dog called *Caesar*, also a puppy from imported stock, was bred to Gleeson's Kelpie. A pup from this litter was named *King's Kelpie* after her dam.

The name Kelpie then appears to have been adopted as the name for the new breed. In Scottish folklore, Kelpie was a water spirit in the form of a horse. King's Kelpie won the first Australian sheepdog trials in 1872.

left Keeshond. Ch. Flakkee Sweepstakes.

Kelpie (Australian Collie).
right A Kelpie performs 'tinning the chicken' by nosing a chick gently and patiently into a tin can without touching either.
below right Kelpies are invaluable in Australian sheep stations where it is estimated that one dog, characteristically walking on the backs of the sheep, can do the work of six men.

Above Kelpie. The Kelpie's job is to round up sheep which have strayed too far from the flock. A good dog never nips but pushes a stray back to the mob.

Coil – known as the 'immortal Coil' – won the trials in 1898, making a perfect score in two heats. Between heats, Coil was run over by a carriage and had a front leg broken, but he made a perfect score the next day though one leg was dangling uselessly.

Essentials of the breed: The Kelpie standard calls for a dog from 18 to 20 inches tall, with bitches slightly smaller. Colours are black, black and tan, red, red and tan, fawn, chocolate, and smoke blue. The ears are prick, and are set upon a broad, slightly rounded skull. The moderately long muzzle tapers to refinement. The nose is body colour, and the eyes are brown, except in blues, which permits a lighter colour.

The legs and feet are refined in bone, but the feet have deep, well-knuckled toes and thick pads. The top line is level, and the body is slightly longer than tall, in the ratio of ten to nine. The tail hangs, has a slight curve, and is never carried over the back. It has a thick brush. Hind legs are well angulated. The chest is deep with well sprung but not barrel shaped ribs.
See colour plate p. 293.

Kennel Administration see Kennel Management.

Kennel Club, American The American Kennel Club is the largest registration organization for purebred dogs in the world. It now registers over one million dogs annually. But maintenance of the stud book is not its only function: it also licenses and supervises dog shows, obedience contests, and a variety of field trials. It is chartered under the laws of New York State.

The American Kennel Club was organized in 1884, when it took over the records of an earlier organization. Thus, the first dog registered in America was that of an English Setter, *Adonis*, recorded in 1878. Its five millionth registration was that of a Collie, *Lassie The Golden Glory*, recorded in 1956. Since then, registrations have risen rapidly each year. Thus, in 1958, 446,625 individual dogs and 207,520 litters were registered. By 1968, these figures had doubled with 909,300 individual dogs and 404,175 litters. In 1970, 1,056,225 dogs were registered.

In many countries, the national governing body is made up of individual people. But this is not true of the American Kennel Club. Instead, it is an organization of some 400 kennel clubs. Member clubs are elected to membership by those already members. Member clubs elect delegates to the parent organization. However, such delegates must be approved by the parent body.

Because of the vast distances within the United States, stretching from Hawaii to Alaska to Puerto Rico, most clubs find it too expensive to send their delegates to the quarterly meetings in New York City. They therefore elect delegates from among dog fanciers close to New York. It quite often happens that club members will never have met their own delegate to the American Kennel Club.

The American Kennel Club is known universally by its initials 'AKC'. It licenses about 1,000 championship shows annually. These are called licensed shows. Championship points can be won at such events. It also licenses more than 600 obedience trials each year. These are usually held with all-breed championship events, but about a hundred are held separately.

Not only does the AKC license these shows and trials, it also supervises them. It has set up elaborate and complex rules which clubs must follow; failure to do so results in fines being levied against the clubs. It maintains a staff of field representatives who attend the shows help to see that rules are obeyed, and report to the local office on the general conduct of the show.

The field representatives are also used to investigate reports of fraudulent registrations. The field representatives may visit their kennels to make certain that the facilities are adequate and the dog care up to standard.

There are some 750 PROFESSIONAL HANDLERS licensed by the American Kennel Club. Some are granted licences on a limited basis. They are permitted only to accept dogs at shows, and to prepare and exhibit them there. Others are licensed to conduct a full kennel operation. That is, they can board and train the dogs they are to show, and even conduct breeding operations for their clients.

Superintendents are similarly licensed. Some of these earn their entire living by superintending shows. They are licensed on an annual basis. Others, usually amateurs and club members, may be licensed for a single show only. Usually such a show will be a speciality, or single breed, event.

Judges, too, come under the rigid AKC supervision. There are some 2,250 men and women who are licensed to judge at championship shows. Some judge one breed only. A few more than 30 can judge all breeds. A severe code of ethics has been set up for these judges. AKC does not fine them for rules infractions, but it does suspend their judging privileges for varying periods of time.

Show-giving clubs are required to hold 'bench show committee' hearings when charges are brought against exhibitors, handlers, or judges during the show. AKC has printed detailed instructions for the conduct of such hearings. It will fine clubs which infringe the rules, and may deny them the right to hold future shows.

Such committees, acting as representatives of the American Kennel Club, can suspend the person or persons provided it finds the charges justified. Appeals can be made directly to the AKC which may uphold or reverse the original judgement. In addition, AKC has six regional trial boards which are convened to hear especially serious cases.

The American Kennel Club also recognizes another event – the sanctioned match. This is an informal show or obedience test, of which there are two types. They are often erroneously called puppy matches, though adult dog classes are given. They are required as training for clubs wishing to give licensed shows. Two of these must be held six months apart.

Nearly 1,000 field trials for individual breeds are held annually under AKC licence. Beagles, with more than 400 championship trials a year, lead. The pointing breeds follow with about 250. A majority of trials for English Setters and Pointers are held under the supervision of the AMERICAN FIELD, FIELD DOG STUD BOOK.

Brittany Spaniels, and the so-called German pointing breeds – German Short-haired Pointer, German Wire-haired Pointer, Weimaraner and Vizsla (Hungarian) – hold trials under AKC supervision, and also under American Field rules. Other breeds holding trials under AKC licence or sanction are Basset Hounds. Dachshunds, the retrievers, English Springer, and English and American Cocker Spaniels. By far the greatest single activity under AKC supervision is the sanctioned field trial. Roughly 3,000 are held annually.

Not the least of the American Kennel Club's work is that of its publications section. It constantly revises its *The Complete Dog Book* which contains the histories and official standards of all breeds eligible for registration in the stud book. It also publishes the stud book. Its official magazine is *Pure-Bred Dogs – American Kennel Gazette*. This magazine publishes lists of show and trial dates, the official results of all licensed events, lists of championships won, a list of member clubs with their addresses and delegates.

It publishes annually a booklet listing the names and addresses of all licensed judges, together with the breeds for which they hold licences, and revisions of this booklet every six months. Finally, it issues pamphlets listing rules for registration, show, obedience and field trial rules, rules for match shows, etc.

Kennel Club, The Australian National Kennel Council (ANKC)

The Australian National Kennel Council (ANKC) was formed in 1958 by the mutual agreement of the eight State canine administrative bodies. These organizations – one for each of the six States and two Territories – are autonomous in their methods of registration, exhibition and arrangements for championships, but reciprocal agreements exist between them. Selected or appointed delegates to the ANKC from each body meet three or four times a year for conference.

The ANKC is a purely advisory body which cannot compel the individual member states to follow its dicta and because of its limitations cannot be affiliated with overseas and international kennel clubs.

Kennel Club, Canadian

The Canadian Kennel Club is the governing body of pure-bred dogs in Canada. As such, it registers dogs, and supervises dog shows, obedience trials, and field trials. It was founded in September 1888, at London, Ontario. An

English Setter, *Forest Fern*, was the first dog registered.

Whereas the American Kennel Club is made up of member clubs, the Canadian Kennel Club is made up of individual members. These are elected after having served an 'apprentice' period during which they prove both their character and their enduring interest in dogs.

During the presidency of Col. G. F. MacFarland, and while the famed J. D. Strachan was secretary, the club signed a reciprocity agreement with the American Kennel Club. Each agreed to recognize the registrations of the other, and each made it easy for the other's dogs to compete across the border. This close relationship has continued ever since. The Canadian Kennel Club also publishes a book of standards for the breeds. In those breeds recognized by both clubs, the breed standards are for the most part identical. Bench show, obedience, and field trial procedures are also similar.

The Canadian Kennel Club also recognizes and licenses those judges which have been licensed by the American Kennel Club. The American Kennel Club has recently made it possible for Canadian judges to apply to judge at U.S. shows without following AKC licensing procedures.

Kennel Club, English The Kennel Club has been described as a benevolent autocracy, but it is not generally known that at its inception in 1873 the founders resolved that it should be a democratic institution with a properly elected committee. The electorate showed little enthusiasm and after the first year the committee was obliged to re-elect itself.

The Kennel Club produced a framework of rules and regulations within which dog shows and trials could be held successfully and dog owners could enjoy their hobby without undue restriction. Today, shows vary widely from village fêtes to CRUFT'S, the best known dog show in the world. Field trials vary from an informal day's shooting to the annual Championships for Retrievers, Pointers, Setters and Spaniels. Dogs themselves vary from minute Toys to huge Wolfhounds and Mastiffs. Owners vary from the one-dog, one-show-a-year exhibitors to the PROFESSIONAL HANDLERS – but the rules of the Kennel Club provides for all. The Club's position is unchallenged and the envy of many other institutions. Nearly thirty committees, subcommittees and councils work within the Club and more than 250 experts serve the canine community in Britain.

Each year more than 3,500 dog shows and matches and 300 field and working trials are held. The Kennel Club itself promotes Cruft's Show, the other shows being promoted by the 1,600 registered societies, within the jurisdiction of the Kennel Club.

At the headquarters in Clarges Street, London, there is a staff of seventy-five and there are few working days in the year when meetings are not held at the Club. The index of registered pedigrees contains 2,000,000 dogs' names but it takes only seconds to produce a dog's record. The present level of registrations is 180,000 dogs a year, and this number is increasing by nearly 10 per cent each year. The Kennel Club possesses far reaching powers in its disciplinary rules, invoked only on rare occasions. The majority of disciplinary cases are for cruelty or neglect of dogs, but occasionally the committee hears allegations of dishonesty in the compilation of pedigrees or in judging, or in the affairs of trials or shows, and all come within the description of 'discreditable conduct'. Conviction under Kennel Club rule 17 can mean a lifetime's suspension of the offender from the privileges of the Club. Wrong entries for shows and carelessness are dealt with by fines.

The Kennel Club has a working agreement with many overseas Kennel Clubs. British-bred dogs are still highly valued abroad, and one in every twelve pedigreed dogs bred in Britain is exported. The number increases each year. British judges travel far and wide, but as the cult of the pedigree dog spreads, more overseas judges officiate at British shows – visitors from overseas are now a feature of Cruft's Show.

The fees charged by the Kennel Club are small – 25 pence (60 cents) to register a dog – and that can mean keeping its records for fifty years. A dog show can be held for as little as 50 pence ($1.20) and these fees are in keeping with the traditionally amateur status of the British dog world – a world where dog breeding is looked on as a hobby, where show and field trials are run by voluntary committees, and where all accept the jurisdiction of the voluntary committees of the Kennel Club. During the first half of the Kennel Club's history there were a few attempts to form opposition Kennel Clubs but they died of lack of support, and in the past fifty years there has been no attempt to start a rival.

Kennel Club, New Zealand This club was founded in 1886, with the Governor of New Zealand, Sir William Jervois, as its first patron. It began by holding its own shows, but soon concentrated on formulating rules and regulations. A system for challenge certificates was inaugurated in 1905, and championship shows began to be held in New Zealand in the early 1920s.

The Club has many affiiliated societies and associated specialist clubs, and itself became affiliated to the Kennel Club in England in 1932. Field trials for Gun dogs are administered by the Club's Field Trial Executive, and the Club takes a particular interest in assisting and encouraging the sheepdog, New Zealand's national working dog. The New Zealand Kennel Club helps to arrange for visiting judges, especially from Britain and the United States, to officiate at shows.

Kennel Club, Portuguese (Clube Portuguese de Canicultura) Founded in 1931, re-organized in 1939 and 1959, and officially recognized by the Portuguese Government, the Portuguese Kennel Club owns and publishes the stud book *(Livro Português de Origens)*. It is a federated member of the FEDERATION CYNOLOGIQUE INTERNATIONALE and has a reciprocal agreement with the Kennel Club of England.

The objects of the Portuguese Kennel Club are the usual ones of development of breeds, keeping a stud book, representing Portugal at international organizations or cynological meetings, promoting shows and working trials, and authorizing judges.

The Kennel Club is composed of members elected by

the General Assembly. The committee of seven members is elected for a period of three years, and there are five sub-committees concerned with the stud book, shows, working trials, judges and scientific matters. The Portuguese Kennel Club currently has offices at Oporto, Evora and Luanda.

Kennel Club, Scandinavian Kennel Union The Scandinavian Kennel Union is an institution for co-operation between the Kennel Clubs in Denmark, Finland, Norway and Sweden. It was founded in 1953 and its purpose is to co-ordinate the canine activities in these countries. The aim is to bring about uniform rules for shows, field trials, championships, and the training and examination of judges.

A conference is arranged every second year in each of the four countries in turn. At this conference each Kennel Club has three representatives. They issue recommendations and appoint committees with different tasks having conformity in view. There is a special committee for co-ordinating the rules of shows, field trials, and championships; a standard committee and a scientific committee, which is divided into four sections representing genetics, veterinary medicine, nutrition and general cynologics. The Kennel Clubs have one representative in each of these four sub-committees.

The Finnish and the Swedish Kennel Clubs were founded in 1889, the Danish Kennel Club in 1897, and the Norwegian Kennel Club in 1898. Even if the four Clubs differ in certain respects concerning organization and structure, they have the same basic principles. All the Clubs have local sub-departments, and speciality clubs for certain breeds or groups of breeds. The Kennel Clubs take care of all registration, the arranging of shows, and to a certain extent of field trials. The speciality clubs also arrange shows for their breeds.

Each Kennel Club publishes a monthly magazine which is distributed free to all members. The speciality clubs also have their publications, usually in the form of annuals or periodicals.

In 1969, total membership of the combined Kennel Clubs was 84,500, and the total number of registrations was 102,500, the greatest numbers coming from Finland and Sweden.

Kennel Club, Spanish (Real Sociedad Central de Fomento de las Razas Caninas en España) The Spanish Kennel Club was officially recognized by a Royal Charter dated 30 October 1912, granted through the Ministry of Development. Its purpose is, the preservation, development and improvement of Spanish breeds; and the development of the various foreign utility and toy breeds.

The Spanish Kennel Club also promotes major dog shows in Madrid and encourages the formation of Specialist Societies and Clubs. It owns and publishes the official stud book, the *Libro de Origens Español*.

Members are selected individuals devoted to the improvement and development of pure dog breeds. There is a committee of eight members, and the headquarters are in Madrid, Calle de los Madrazo 20.

Kennel Club, United The United Kennel Club is a privately owned all-breed registration body which was organized in 1898 by Chauncey Z. Bennett. It is the second largest registration body in the United States.

While it registers all breeds, the UKC gets the bulk of its registrations in AMERICAN COONHOUNDS, Toy FOX TERRIERS, English Shepherds (a breed developed in the United States, which is similar to the Border Collie), American (Pit) Bull Terriers (which are registered by the American Kennel Club as STAFFORD-SHIRE TERRIERS) and the American Eskimo, which is a small dog of SAMOYED type, divided for show purposes into two classes – those weighing less than 17 lb. and those weighing 17 to 30 lb.

The UKC licenses field trials for American Coonhounds and English Beagles, and publishes *Bloodlines* every other month.

Kennel Hygiene The care of dogs within a kennel must at all times be aimed at maintaining the health of the dogs. This is termed kennel hygiene. Kennels must be cleaned regularly, disease controlled, and adequate food supplied. Sick dogs should not be in contact with other inmates, and dogs new to the kennel should be carefully examined before joining the other dogs to prevent the introduction of disease. If possible, new dogs should be isolated for three weeks to allow time for any incubating disease to develop.

The prevention of disease within the kennel is assisted by the regular disinfection of indoor quarters and outside runs, by fecal studies to detect the presence of worms, by treating for fleas, lice, and ticks, and by giving prophylactic shots to prevent such diseases as DISTEMPER, infectious canine HEPATITIS, and LEPTO-SPIROSIS. For methods of disinfection, see ANTISEPTICS.

Adequate ventilation is a necessity in kennel hygiene, and helps to eliminate viruses from the area. Humidity assists the spread of some diseases, and the hatching of worm eggs. In humid areas, therefore, a dehumidifier is an aid to hygiene. For breeds which suffer greatly from heat, air conditioning units are a benefit. But few, if any, such units reduce humidity.

Most kennel dogs are vaccinated against the major canine diseases – distemper, infectious canine hepatitis, and leptospirosis. However, vaccination does not confer lifetime immunity, and kennel hygiene should include regular booster vaccination against these diseases. Charts showing the last vaccination for each dog, and the time for the next one can usefully be kept.

A growing problem for kennels in some areas is the disposal of stools. A kennel septic tank is one solution. There are enzyme 'digesters' for such septic tanks, and many health departments will permit kennel sewers to drain into house septic tanks. Kennel manure also has some value as fertilizer for flower gardens and fields.

Flies always present hygiene problems. Insecticidal sprays used within kennels may not be toxic to dogs, but they can cause lung irritation. Screens are usually sufficient, especially if openings to the runs are covered by swinging doors or flaps, and sticky fly ribbons are effective when hung in kennels.
See BOARDING KENNELS; FEEDING.

Kennel Management The number of very large kennel operations has shrunk since 1930, chiefly because of high taxes, labour shortages, and increasingly higher wages required by kennel help. A large kennel of from 30 to 100 dogs requires a qualified kennel manager. It has been said of great kennel managers that they are able to see the signs of imminent illness before they become evident to anyone else.

Equipment is always a major factor in successful kennel management. Modern kennels have a deep freeze unit or a refrigerator, and a rat-proof food storage area. Special facilities for bathing and drying dogs are useful assets. Emergency equipment should be well placed for easy reach. This should include a well-stocked first aid kit, fire extinguishers, and some means of stopping kennel fights. See DOG FIGHTS. In some kennels, plastic pails kept filled with water are strategically located. They serve a double purpose – to douse a blaze and to stop a dog fight.

Each kennel should have a WHELPING and nursery room. Where possible, this should be shut off from the rest of the kennel, as a hygienic measure and to give the bitch a quiet environment. She should be introduced to this room, and placed there off and on, for some days before whelping. In this way she will get used to it. The nursery should be stocked well in advance. Preparations should be made to feed orphan puppies. See FOSTER MOTHER. Simulated bitch's milk and an INFRA-RED LAMP or other heat lamp should be included.

Record keeping is an essential part of good kennel management. In large kennels, the problem of remembering which dogs have been groomed, checked for worms, and examined for other health problems, is serious. Charts should be made up for each dog, and checks for each subject made as the dogs are handled. These records should show the dates when bitches have been in season, when bred, and when treated for pregnancy problems. Pedigree books are a necessity, as are records of whelping, of abnormalities appearing in litters, and of sales.

Good kennel management must also include a great deal of individual work, or socialization, with the dogs. Dogs which are to be taken to shows need more than grooming. They must be taught to walk properly on a leash, to pose, and to permit handling by the judge. Socialization should include car riding, walks along streets where noisy automobiles and trucks are passing, and the visiting of populous areas where many people will want to stop to pet the dogs.

The kennel management of field dogs must include adequate exercise to strengthen the dogs for field work, and careful examination of the dogs when they return from the field.

See KENNEL HYGIENE.

Kennels see Housing and Kennelling.

Kennel Work There are no duties connected with the running of a successful kennel that may be specifically designated as 'men's work' or 'women's work'. It can be argued that a female attendant at a WHELPING is to be preferred but this is not necessarily the case. It can also be argued that carrying sacks of dog biscuits is no task for women but in a modern establishment dog biscuits do not have to be lugged. Therefore, kennel work cannot be classed as an effeminate career for a male or an overly masculine job for a woman. In either case a sympathetic but not sentimental approach towards the dogs is required.

An outline of the normal range of kennel work may be useful. First in the morning is a general inspection as to health of the inmates and an immediate report if anything is amiss. Kennel cleaning, water bowl filling and feeding, washing the dishes, preparing the next meal, cleaning the dog kitchen and disinfecting, are all essential jobs for the kennel man or maid, and take their place alongside grooming, bathing, trimming, nail cutting and exercising.

There are many things which go to make a useful kennel assistant, and one of the most important is an unerring instinct for shutting doors or gates. An intelligent respect for the individual animal is essential – a completely fearless kennel employee dealing with an animal with a difficult temperament will certainly not prevent the animal from biting.

Kennel work is governed strictly by time, since dogs will respond in the mass to a rigid routine. There must be a time for release from kennel to run, a time for feeding, a time for exercise, and a time for grooming. Variations from the routine will confuse the animals and staff alike. Essential tasks are easily forgotten if definite times for their execution are not laid down. A kennel not properly cleaned will be twice as much work tomorrow; a dog not properly fed will quickly become too fat or too thin. A symptom which escapes notice will develop into a serious condition if not treated at once. Dogs in kennels depend solely on the care and attention they receive and quickly deteriorate if they are neglected.

Keratitis see Eye Diseases.

Kerry Blue Terrier 'Although there are no authentic records in existence to prove that the Kerry Blue Terrier was, as some aver, with Noah in the Ark, there are those living today who have undisputed proof of the breed being in existence over 100 years ago.' This comment on the breed was published at the turn of the last century.

Inevitably with a dog that has its background deep in the remoteness of South West Ireland there is an abundance of legends. However, the county of Kerry has never claimed this breed as its own and indeed one of the few early connections between the Kerry Blue and the county seems to be that Mrs. Casey Hewitt, who first exhibited one in England in 1922, lived in Tralee in the county of Kerry.

Kerry Blues have often been thought to have IRISH WOLFHOUND blood in them. The Irish peasantry was forbidden by the overlords to keep pure hunting dogs but terriers were permitted because they destroyed vermin. Surreptitious matings are however alleged to have been arranged between the farmers' terriers and the squires' Wolfhounds.

There are other stories. One says that the only survivor of a shipwreck off the coast of Kerry was a species of terrier, a fighter of such renown that it killed every dog it met. Thus it established the right to found its own strain.

Much more likely is the simple fact that dogs of Kerry Blue type are indigenous to Ireland. We have, for example, the IRISH TERRIER and the SOFT-COATED WHEATEN. Aside from colour and trimming styles, there are several similarities between these breeds.

Clearly the blue colour – possibly cloudy black originally – must have been intensified by selective breeding. It has also been suggested that colour and coat texture were added by the judicious introduction of BEDLINGTON TERRIERS. For many years most Irishmen called the breed the Irish Blue Terrier, and some still favour this name.

The Kerry Blue stands midway in size between the AIREDALE and the Bedlington. Puppies are born black but are expected to attain their true colour by the age of 18 months. With the exception of the POODLE they are the most barbered breed existing. The first seen in England was at CRUFT'S in February 1922. They were officially recognized by the Kennel Club in the same year. The first Champion in the breed was the Irish bred Champion Martells Sapphire Beauty, born 2nd June 1920 and gaining its title at the National Terrier Show on 23rd January 1923.

Kerry Blues were first shown in the United States in 1922 but had to wait until 1924 for official recognition

and until 1926 for the formation of the breed club.

Experienced observers believe the American Kerry Blues are now better than those of Great Britain. Additionally, good specimens are also to be found in Holland and Germany. Regrettably few, if any, of these good foreign specimens have been imported by Britain.

Essentials of the breed: Head: well balanced, long, proportionately lean, with slight stop, and flat over the skull. Foreface and jaw: very strong, deep and punishing; black nose. Eyes: dark and small. Ears: small to medium, V-shaped, carried forward but not high. Teeth: level with dark gums. Neck: strong and reachy. Shoulders: flat, with elbows close to sides. Powerful bone with front neither too wide nor too narrow. Body: short coupled with deep chest and level topline. Hindquarters: large and well developed. Feet: round and small with black nails. Tail: set high and carried erect. Coat: soft, silky, plentiful and wavy. Colour: any shade of blue, but dark colour until 18 months acceptable. Small white patch on chest permissible. Weight: dogs 33 to 37 lb. Height: 18 to 19 inches. Bitches: proportionately less.
See colour plate p. 373.

Kidney Diseases Dogs are afflicted with many complaints connected with the kidneys.

They are sometimes invaded by the kidney worm,

Below Kerry Blue Terrier. Ch. Melbee's Michaela.

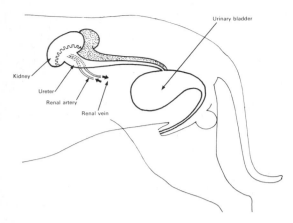
Urinary bladder
Kidney
Ureter
Renal artery
Renal vein

dioctophyma renale. It is a true round worm, being bilaterally symmetrical, and the largest of its kind. Males may reach eighteen inches in length and females forty inches. If the worm invades the kidney, it may not be discovered until after the death of the dog. Fortunately, it is not common among dogs.

Acute interstitial nephritis is caused by an infectious disease, of which LEPTOSPIROSIS is probably the most common. In turn the acute form may develop into the chronic type, also as a sequel to leptospirosis. *Polydipsia* (excessive thirst) and a consequent passage of abnormal amounts of urine are symptoms, and the dog's breath may smell of urine. Chronic interstitial nephritis is irreversible. Dogs suffering from such diseases should be under the care of a veterinarian. They should get plenty of rest, and should be protected from excitement. They also require very high quality protein – there are specially prepared diets for dogs suffering from kidney diseases, obtainable through a veterinarian.

King Charles Spaniel This breed would seem to have been devised especially to confuse students of canine history. The first possibility of misunderstanding arises because of the close similarity of name with that of the CAVALIER KING CHARLES SPANIEL. Next, both the King Charles Spaniel and the Cavalier King Charles are lumped together in some countries under the title of English Toy Spaniels. Thirdly, whereas we normally expect a spaniel to be a member of the Gundog or Sporting Group, this is in fact a Toy.

At the risk of complicating things further we must add that the two similarly-named breeds were originally one and the same. Toy spaniels have been in existence in England for many centuries. Slowly over the years the pattern changed. What were originally almost miniature SPRINGER SPANIEL types slowly became round headed, very diminutive characters, perhaps more akin to PEKINGESE than true spaniels. An American wishing to see a return to the type portrayed in various Old Masters offered special prizes for those nearest to that type. The newcomers received the additional title of Cavalier to distinguish them from what by then had become the normal King Charles Spaniel. Thus, for the last 45 years there have been two distinct breeds.

Disregarding from now onwards the Cavalier, we stay with the King Charles Spaniel from its early days

through the time of its change in shape until the present moment. Much of the story can be told in extracts from various books and writings. For example we know that Mary Queen of Scots kept a pack of small spaniels. At the time of her execution, 'one of the executioners espied her little dog which was crept under her clothes which could not be gotten forth but by force'.

King Charles II had such an affection for the breed that they ceased to be known as mere 'toy spaniels' and took his name. This closeness did not please Samuel Pepys, the diarist, who recorded that: 'They had access to all parts of Whitehall, even on State occasions.' Later he was even more critical with: 'All I observed there was the silliness of the King playing with his dog all the while and not minding his business.'

These acid comments however did not stop these toy spaniels from becoming increasingly popular with the aristocracy. Many paintings by Gainsborough, Rubens and Rembrandt of fashionable sitters and their pets exist to prove it. The portraits also provided evidence for the return to the original breed mentioned earlier.

Slowly the form of the King Charles changed. This was almost certainly achieved by interbreeding with Pekingese, PUGS and possibly JAPANESE SPANIELS.

Left Kidney diseases. The location of a dog's kidneys and urinary system.

King Charles Spaniel (English Toy Spaniel). Originally called simply toy or small spaniels, these dogs acquired their more distinctive name because of King Charles II's great liking for them.
Below and right Peregrina of Oakridges.
Bottom 'King Charles's Spaniels' or 'Cavalier's Pets' by Landseer.

Thus *The Field* in 1859 says in describing a King Charles that he had 'a fine but short muzzle of elegant form; quite a fairy amongst dogs'. Returning to the same subject later in the year that magazine said: 'Their noses are very delicate and their cry very musical, but they soon knock up. They are fit for better things than being lap dogs'.

Clearly the pure if diminutive spaniel was slowly departing. Youall spoke of the new short-nosed type as a 'recent innovation'. Stonehenge, in 1879, said: 'Nor is the shortness of the face of old standing when carried to the extent which now prevails'.

From the earliest time this breed was produced in four different colours and these became so divided as to be regarded almost as separate breeds. The colours were as follows:

Black and Tan. This is a rich, glossy black with bright mahogany tan markings on muzzle, legs, chest, lining of ears, under tail and spots over the eyes.

The Tri-colour (Prince Charles). A pearly white coat with well distributed black patches, brilliant tan markings in the same places as above but with a wide, white blaze running up the head between the eyes.

The Blenheim. The same pearly white background but with chestnut red patches and a red spot in the centre of the wide, clear blaze in the middle of the skull.

The Ruby. A whole-coloured rich chestnut red.

In recent years, the American inspired Cavalier has made considerable headway, doubtless largely due to the interest which Princess Margaret took in the breed, with much resultant publicity. Unfortunately the gains have been made at the expense of the old-time 'Charlie', as the King Charles is frequently called. Registrations are as low as they have ever been in the breed's history. Perhaps once again America will come to the aid of a threatened breed.

Essentials of the breed: The skull is massive, well domed and full over the eyes. Nose: black with large open nostrils. The stop is well defined, muzzle square, wide and deep and the lower jaw wide. Protruding tongues are objectionable. Eyes must be large and dark, set apart and with pleasing expression. Ears: set on low and flat to cheeks, long and well feathered. Coat: long, silky and straight, a slight wave being permissible. The legs, ears and tail must be profusely feathered. Colours: as described above. Weight: the most desirable weight is between 8 and 14 lb.
See colour plate p. 380.

Kink Tail A sharp twist or bend in the tail.

Kiss Marks Tan spots on the cheeks and eyebrows.

Knee The stifle joint.

Knuckling Over Abnormal structure of the carpus or wrist joint, permitting it to double forward when the dog is standing.

Komondor The Komondor is the largest of the Hungarian herdsman's dogs. It has been used by shep-

herds for hundreds of years, but usually as a guardian of flocks rather than as a herding dog, and as a guard dog it has been used to protect cattle as well as sheep. The dog is of Asian origin, and appears to be closely related to Russian herding dogs, such as the Aftscharka.

The dog has a long and profuse coat which tends to mat. Many breeders guide the long hairs into cords by wrapping short hairs around a central long hair. The cord then develops by itself. The cords and mats supply excellent protection against body injury during fights. In addition, the mass of corded or matted hair is excellent protection against weather, and requires little care.

The breed is doing well in the United States, chiefly due to the enthusiasm of the motion picture and television star, Oscar Beregi. Efforts are being made to keep the corded or matted coat, as it is a distinctive feature of the breed. The dogs can be bathed without disturbing the cords.

Essentials of the breed: The muzzle is shorter than the skull, but they are in parallel planes. The skull is covered with hair. The nose is preferably black, but may be slate-coloured. The eyes are brown. Blue-white eyes and any coat colour other than pure white are disqualifying. Major faults are light or flesh-coloured noses; highly set, small ears; smooth, short hair on the head and legs; and a strongly curled tail.

The body is slightly longer than high. The tail is set on as a continuation of the spine and reaches to the hock. It is profusely covered with hair, and tips up at the end, but should never curl.

The hair, while long, is shortest on the head and neck. It then grows progressively longer reaching maximum length on the thighs and tail. Curly hair is a fault.

Height: dogs from $25\frac{1}{2}$ to $31\frac{1}{2}$ inches, the greater height preferred.

Kuvasz The Kuvasz is said to have been brought into Hungary by the Kurds as early as the year A.D. 1100. Its name is a corruption of the Turkish *kawasz* which means a protector. Originally, the Kuvasz was a sheepdog, a guardian of the flocks, much like the KOMONDOR in function. It is recorded, however, that King Matthias the First, 1458–1490, used these dogs for hunting wild boar – their size and great strength made them ideal for such rugged hunting.

The similarity between the Kuvasz, the MAREMMA SHEEPDOG, and the PYRENEAN MOUNTAIN DOG, or Great Pyrennes, makes it obvious that they are closely related. The Kuvasz is slightly more suspicious of strangers than are the other two, which might indicate a longer history of guarding, both of livestock and isolated farm homes.

Essentials of the breed: The Kuvasz (the Hungarian plural is Kuvaszok) is a pure white dog, with a moderately long coat, which may be straight or only slightly wavy. The legs are strongly boned, yet the dog has remarkable agility. Cow hocks and splayed or turned out feet are serious faults. The tail reaches to below the hock and is covered with thick, fairly long hair. Height: dogs average 26 inches.

Overleaf Labrador Retriever Ch Candlemas Rookwood Silve Moonlight with pups. In Britai Labradors have become so popu lar in the last 20 years that they al jostling even German Shepherd for top position in the popularit polls.

Komondor.
Top near right A Komondor appea before Prince Rainier and Prince Grace of Monaco. The Komon dor's mass of matted hair not on gives it a unique appearance bu protects it against the cold whe it is herding sheep and cattle o the Hungarian plains.
Top far right Ch. Pannonia's Bat De Maria.

Right Kuvasz. Ch. Hamralvi De most Happy Fella.

L

Labour see Breeding.

Labrador Retriever Satin smooth and aristocratic, courageous yet peace-loving, powerfully built yet able to swim like a trout. See it after a 'runner' in a field of roots and it hunts with the drive and fling of a Foxhound. And when it comes to hand with your pheasant it carries it, even at the gallop, as discreetly as a butler bearing porcelain on a silver salver.

Who could doubt that this extravagant praise is reserved for the Labrador Retriever? And who could doubt that this magnificent animal has behind him centuries of assisting the shooting man in the field? The answer is anyone who knows a little of his history. The Labrador is not the member of an old breed. Moreover when first heard of in 1822 it had, so it would appear, never seen a gun.

It was working in Newfoundland for the fishermen. As it was too dangerous for the boats to approach close to the shore, the dogs' task was to go overboard and drag the ends of the nets through the water to men who took them over on shore and pulled them in full of fish. While the men on the shore attended to the catch the dogs swam back to the ship to repeat the process as another widespread net was thrown out. Additionally they had at all times to retrieve objects lost overboard by the fishermen. Thus they were ready-made 'retrievers', although not of birds!

A traveller wrote of them as 'small, but admirably trained water-dogs'. When one remembers that this report came from Newfoundland the word 'small' will be seen in its proper context as it was intended to differentiate between these fishermen's dogs and the giant NEWFOUNDLANDS, also found in those regions.

When the holds were full, many of the fishermen sailed for Britain to sell their fish there. Occasionally they sold the dogs as well. Thus the Earl of Malmesbury in a letter dated 1870 described buying his first dog of this breed from a fishing boat plying between Newfoundland and Poole. He said of the type he specialized in, 'We always call mine Labradors'. The name stuck and this was the first occasion on which the two different varieties of Newfoundlands had been divided.

Fairly soon after this the Labrador faded from the Newfoundland scene. In part this was caused by a heavy local dog tax, which few fishermen were prepared to pay. Next and more important, the English quarantine laws were introduced which stopped importations, thereby ending the fishermen's profitable sideline of breeding dogs for export. Fortunately by this time the breed was firmly established in Britain.

There is an amusing story told of the third Viscount Knutsford who at considerable expense went to Labrador and Newfoundland to see whether he could find any of the breed in their home country. Upon meeting a local dog breeder, he asked from where he could obtain Labradors. He was told: 'Go over to

England and try to get one from a man called Holland-Hibbert'. Holland-Hibbert was the family name of Lord Knutsford.

In Countess Howe's book on the breed published in 1957, she described Lord Knutsford as 'the Labrador's greatest benefactor'. This was more than generous, and anybody writing a book on Labradors today would surely give that palm to Lady Howe herself.

During her life Lady Howe owned scores, possibly hundreds of Labradors. She always insisted that a dog must be both good-looking and a worker. One of her best made history for ever. His name was *Champion Banchory Bolo* and he became a Field Trial Champion in 1919. In that same year he also became a Bench Champion and thus achieved the distinction of being the first dual champion the breed had ever seen. Only five dogs, three of them Lady Howe's, achieved this double distinction prior to World War II.

Perhaps even greater however, was Lady Howe's *Champion Bramshaw Bob.* This dog also became a Field Trial Champion. He then went on to win Best in Show at CRUFT's in 1933 and 1934. Never before or since has a Labrador achieved these heights. There is indeed a possibility that Bob might have won again were it not for the curious accident that Countess Howe was judging the breed in 1932 and 1935.

In those days the Labrador would most certainly not have featured in the 'top ten' in Britain or anywhere in the world. The story is different today. In England it is the second favourite, surpassed only by the GERMAN SHEPHERD DOG, which it is seriously challenging. In the United States it is in tenth position and still remains in front of all other sporting dogs. It is known and respected all over the world, particularly in Australia.

Essentials of the breed: The skull should be broad with appreciable stop. The head should be clean without fleshy cheeks. Jaws of medium length, powerful and not snipy. The nose should be wide and the nostrils well developed. The eyes: medium size, showing good temper, brown or hazel. Ears: not large or heavy but set well back and hanging close to head. Teeth: sound and strong, the lower teeth behind and touching the upper. Neck: clean, strong and powerful. Shoulders long and sloping. Forelegs: well boned and straight. The chest must be wide and deep with well-sprung ribs. The back: short coupled. The loins wide and strong. Well developed hindquarters: hocks slightly bent and neither cow-hocked nor too wide or close behind. Feet: round, compact with well-arched toes. Tail: thick at base, gradually tapering towards the tip, of medium length and clothed all round with thick, dense coat, giving that peculiar 'rounded' appearance described as the 'otter' tail. Carried gaily but not over the back. Coat: short, dense, without wave, with a weather-resisting undercoat. Colours: black, liver (chocolate in America) or yellow, free from any white markings, other than a permissible white spot on the chest. Height: (Britain) dogs 22 to $22\frac{1}{2}$ inches, bitches $21\frac{1}{2}$ to 22 inches; (America) dogs $22\frac{1}{2}$ to $24\frac{1}{2}$ inches, bitches $21\frac{1}{2}$ to $23\frac{1}{2}$ inches. Weight: dogs 60 to 75 lb., bitches 55 to 70 lb. See colour plate p. 83.

Ladies' Kennel Association This British association, usually referred to as the L.K.A., earns mention in this volume by virtue of the fact that it was the first to realize that women were destined to play a major role in the cult of the pedigree dog.

It was founded in 1895, at a point in history when the control and dominance of canine affairs was by men. Men had formed the English KENNEL CLUB twenty-two years earlier. Women were not admitted as members. There were comparatively few female exhibitors because dog showing was thought to be not quite respectable. A similar attitude was found in the few other countries then interested in dog shows.

Though it would be idle to pretend that this male dominance has been entirely eliminated, certainly the balance between the sexes is more even that it was. For

Labrador Retriever.
Above left Sh. Ch. Tadfield Kirb hall Sherpa.
Above Black Eagle of Mansergi

Above Labrador Retriever. Although Labradors began their career as Newfoundland fishermen's dogs, they have become very successful gundogs on both sides of the Atlantic and in Australia. In the picture are Nick, jumping, and Trigger.

Far right Lakeland Terrier. Ch. Jllscarf Spice of Lakeridge.

this, the L.K.A. deserves some credit. Its intention was to protect the interest of women at a time when suffragettes in England were still chaining themselves to lamp posts in an endeavour to secure equal voting rights. Its first show held in 1900 and described as The Ladies' Summer Show was confined to female exhibitors. It was a success.

Inevitably there was some conflict with the exclusively male and all-powerful Kennel Club. Right from the start the ruling body vetoed the Association's proposal to call itself the Ladies' Kennel Club and insisted that the word 'Association' be used in place of 'Club'. In 1897 the Kennel Club also vetoed a proposition that a Ladies' Branch should be formed.

In 1900 the L.K.A. again tested its strength. It inaugurated an off-shoot organization and announced publicly that it would be called The International Kennel Club. The Kennel Club ordered it to change the name forthwith to the International Kennel Association. The L.K.A. secretary sent back a cool reply saying that its committee 'can see no reason for changing a name that has been deliberately chosen!'

Three weeks later, perhaps by coincidence, the Kennel Club ruled 'that ladies should not be eligible to judge at the Kennel Club's own shows'. In fact, the International Kennel Club soon died of inaction.

However, in the meantime, consent had been given to the formation of a Ladies' Branch of the K.C. But in 1903 a formal request to be allowed to amalgamate the L.K.A. and the Ladies' Branch brought up male hackles again, and earned an icy 'No'.

By this time, perhaps both protagonists had learned to respect each other. Certainly there is no record of further open dissension. Whether the L.K.A. kept up its pressures behind the scenes is unrecorded; publicly they set about building up the importance and prestige of their own annual show. They dropped the 'female exhibitors only' ruling but retained an all-women committee and show executive, a rule which applies to this day.

Currently the L.K.A. show, held in early winter at Olympia, London, is one of the most important and prestigious shows in the world. A few figures prove the point. In 1970 it scheduled 102 breeds, received an entry of 11,702, made up of 7,469 dogs, and used almost 100 judges in 59 different rings. It forcefully re-stated its claim to the title of the 'Greatest one-day show in the World'.

Lakeland Terrier The English county of Cumberland, which adjoins Scotland, has mountains, dales, lakes . . . and foxes. It also has a lore which goes right back to John Peel, the celebrated huntsman.

Legend says that forerunners of the Lakeland Terrier accompanied the huntsman on his forays. But nobody has insisted that John Peel's hunt terriers were exactly like the modern Lakeland Terriers. These are modern developments or, if you prefer, 'refinements'.

In the Border country, hunting was not a fashionable and well dressed pastime. Nor was it normally conducted on horseback. Its purpose was the practical one of destroying foxes which preyed on the lambs.

Requests usually came from farmers who had lost stock. When the hunt moved in, complete with hounds and terriers, it stayed, if need be, for days until all the pests had been eliminated. Thus a dog's practical working ability was likely to be more important than its appearance.

Towards the end of the last century, mixed classes for local terriers were held at Lake District agricultural shows. Most common were blue and tans, grizzle red, wheaten and even whites. Later the whites were excluded, being considered more suitable for otter hunting. Otter hounds were occasionally over-keen with any animal faintly resembling an otter!

The terriers set against foxes were shaped appropriately for their job. When foxes went to ground the terriers went after them. Thus they had to be small but agile enough to crawl for long distances. Their legs could not be too short because foxes sometimes take refuge on rocky ledges, feet above the ground, so the dog had to be able to jump. Additionally these dogs had to walk or jog with the hunt from the kennels to the scene of operations.

Necessity also fashioned the shape of the head. In the south, few huntsmen wanted their precious foxes tackled and destroyed. They wanted them contained and alive for the next hunt. Killer terriers were unwelcome. In the Lake District the terriers were expected to destroy foxes. Delicately chiselled heads were therefore less desirable than strong punishing jaws.

As with most British terriers there was a fair amount of cross-breeding to improve the working qualities. Breeds almost certainly used were the nearby BEDLINGTON TERRIER, the equally close BORDER TERRIER and possibly the DANDIE DINMONT. Very much later, there is little doubt that FOX TERRIER crosses were made to smarten the breed's general appearance.

In 1913, attempts were made to organize a club for the breed, but the outbreak of war overtook the project. Another and more successful attempt was made in 1921 when a meeting decided officially to adopt the name of

Lakeland Terrier to describe dogs hitherto called by a variety of local names.

In 1928, Lakelands made their first appearance at a southern show organized by the Kennel Club. It would be wrong to suggest that they were a sensation. Few indeed suspected that they would ever make a mark in the show world. But the doubters were wrong: their success has been phenomenal.

These triumphs reached their climax in 1964 with a dog called *Champion Stingray of Derryabah*, bred by Mr. and Mrs. Postlewaite of Gloucester. Stingray made front page news in February 1967 as Supreme Champion of CRUFT'S. One year later his picture was on the front page of every New York newspaper. He had just won Best in Show at WESTMINSTER, America's greatest show. It was a unique double.

Despite its success, this breed remains a good working dog. A down-to-earth dog with an alert, lively mind. Even more important, despite its background, it is an essentially peaceful animal.

Essentials of the breed: The general appearance should be smart and workmanlike, with a gay, fearless demeanour.

Skull: flat and refined. The jaws powerful and the muzzle broad, but not too long. The length of head from stop to tip of the nose should not exceed that from the occiput to the stop. Nose: black. Eyes should be dark or hazel. Ears moderately small, V-shaped and carried alertly: not set too high or too low. Teeth: even, closing scissor fashion. The shoulders must be well laid back with straight, well-boned forelegs. The chest: reasonably narrow. Back: strong, moderately short, well coupled. Hindquarters strong and muscular, with long and powerful thighs. Feet: small, compact, round and well padded. Tail: well set on, carried gaily but not over back.

Coat: dense and weather-resisting, harsh with good undercoat. Colour: black and tan, blue and tan, red, wheaten, red grizzle, liver, blue or black. Small tips of white on feet and chest do not debar.

Average weight: dogs 17 lb., bitches 15 lb. Height should not exceed 14½ inches at the shoulder. See colour plate p. 373.

Lameness The word 'lame' chiefly means disabled in any limb; being not smooth in movement; or walking with a limp. Yet the term is often expanded to 'lame back' or 'lame jaw'.

If we restrict usage of the word to the feet, limbs, hips, and back, there are still thirty to fifty causes of lameness in the dog, including FRACTURES, shoulder and HIP DYSPLASIA, PATELLA LUXATION, INTER-DIGITAL CYSTS, ECZEMA between the toes, eczema of the soles, osteo-arthritis, osteo-myelitis, and fibrositis.

When a dog limps, the examination should be made of the feet: the dog may have cut pads which will require attention; burrs, hair balls, and even small stones and bits of slag may be caught between the toes. The nails should be examined to ensure that they are not too long. Eczema, either between the toes or in the pads themselves, is another cause of lameness.

When running, dogs may drive thorns or other foreign bodies into the pads. In one unusual case, a four-inch nail had been driven into the foot entirely to the nail head. At first, the dog showed only moderate lameness, and it was several days before the nail was discovered.

Dogs are subject to dislocation or fracture of the small phalangeal or foot bones. Routine examination by X-ray is now used to determine the cause and extent of the injury. Claws are often broken or split.

ARTHRITIS and myelitis are bone diseases as difficult to treat in dogs as in people. Many drugs are available to aid the treatment of arthritis. Warmth is also beneficial. Hot pads, and when possible, hot foot baths, can be used to relieve pain and stiffness caused by these diseases.

In most foot injuries, it is necessary to keep the dog from interfering with the injured area by licking and removing bandages. An Elizabethan collar can be used to prevent this (see BANDAGING). Fungicides are often helpful in foot eczema. The dog should be kept off grass or dead leaves until completely healed.

Some dogs suffer from lesions to spinal discs. The condition is more common in long-backed dogs. The condition can cause much pain as well as lameness, but surgery is successful in many cases.

Patella luxation is fairly common among toy dogs, some of the smaller terriers, and in the BOSTON TERRIER. The dog may trot along in perfect movement, then lift a hind leg and skip a step or two. Often, while standing, the stifle joint will be turned inwards, while the hock points outwards. In such cases the luxated patella, or kneecap, leaves its groove and lies medially to the internal condyle – the rounded eminence of the thigh bone.

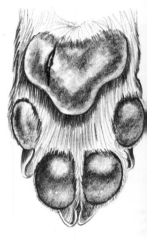

Above Lameness. Cut pads requir prompt attention.

Far left Lakeland Terrier. Ch Stingray Derryabah.

Although surgery is sometimes necessary, relief can be obtained through drugs. In some cases this condition can be a hereditary complaint.

Law, The Dog in see Legal status of the Dog.

Layback The angle at which the shoulder blade departs from the perpendicular.

Lead Training Lead training is not difficult if one begins in the proper manner and then follows through until the dog is thoroughly trained. Puppies of six to ten weeks of age require little training. They are so adaptable and alert that they quickly get the idea, and then become very responsive to the leash. They will, however, require additional training as they grow older if they are to walk steadily at one's side.

Older puppies, particularly those over four months of age, tend to fight the lead when it is first put on. The dog jerks back and may try to bolt in an effort to free itself. When not successful in doing this, it may lie down, and may even put its feet into the air. Efforts to coax it are usually unsuccessful. In such cases, the procedure which must be taken is drastic. The dog is coaxed by voice, and at the same time, the trainer pulls on the leash. Since the dog refuses to get to its feet, or to move, it must be dragged. The dragging must be done slowly and gently, but firmly. All the while, the dog is encouraged by voice. The dog will soon respond.

Many dogs which have been raised in a kennel have not been lead trained. For such a dog, the shock of training is considerably greater than it would be for a half-grown puppy.

If the dog is to be exhibited in the show ring, it must move gaily. A simple way to achieve this is to feed the dog once a day only, and then to give the training lessons just before feeding. The dog then looks forward to the training session because it comes just before it is to be fed. It comes to consider lead training as a pleasurable exercise before a desired meal.

An occasional dog seems to have a pathological fear of the restraint which the lead represents. This can normally be overcome by fasting the dog for 36 hours before a training session. The dog's hunger, and its expectation of a pleasant meal after training, helps to overcome the fear. Short lessons and gentleness are required.

The properly trained dog walks quietly beside its master. It neither strains ahead until it chokes, drags behind, nor strays out to one side. In obedience training, such a dog is said to walk at heel. There are various ways to teach this, and to correct dogs which have developed bad habits.

The dog should walk at the left side, or heel, so that the right hand is free. But during training, a long, light stick, or even an umbrella, can be carried in the right hand. If the dog strains forward, the owner simply taps the dog lightly on the nose, pulls back on the leash, and says 'heel'. The dog learns very quickly not to surge forward.

If the lead is held in the right hand, across the front of the trainer, the left hand will be free to encourage the dog by patting.

If the dog lags behind, light jerks on the lead and repeated commands to 'heel' are sufficient to bring the dog to the owner's side. A similar procedure can be

ead training.
Below right If the lead is held in the right hand, and the dog is on the left side, the trainer's left hand is free to correct or praise the dog. *Far right* Dogs should not be allowed to strain ahead. The correct walking position is at the left side, or to heel, but not too close to the master's legs. Note that the lead is hanging loose.

used if the dog goes too wide. In such cases, a simple trick will aid. The trainer can place the dog between himself and a curb or wall. The dog then learns to space itself at the distance required by its master. After a few lessons, the trainer can place the dog between the edge of a walk-way and himself. An occasional gentle tug will be all that is necessary.

Final training lessons should be given in the presence of strange dogs, and in neighbourhoods which are unknown to the dog. These lessons are necessary if one is to teach the dog that it must remain at its master's side regardless of strange dogs and the strange smells which the dog wants to investigate.

Sitting when the master stops walking is sometimes considered an integral part of lead training. If this is required, it can be taught at the same time, or along with, lead sessions. When the master stops, the dog is told to sit. At the same time, the master reaches down, presses on the rump of the dog with the left hand, and with the right hand grasps the collar and pulls backward. This forces the dog into a sitting position. The dog quickly learns to sit down as soon as its master stops.

Lean Head On without much flesh and a tight skin, such as that of a GREYHOUND.

Leather The ear flap.

Legal Status of the Dog The laws governing dogs in those countries with an Anglo-Saxon background are based upon English Common Law. Under this doctrine, the dog has the status of a brute creature – a living, sentient being which is inferior to man. Using the brute creature concept, the dog has been variously classified.

Some authorities divided the animals into two classes. In one group were placed the food and work animals. They were given property status. Their value as property was easily established, and they were given the protection of the laws concerning larceny and killing. Dogs, and other pets, were said to be owned for whim or pleasure. They were held to have no intrinsic value, were of a base nature, and they could not come under the protection of the larceny or illegal killing statutes.

English and American courts placed dogs in another classification: animals were divided into two groups, those of a generous nature (pigeons, doves, edible fish, oysters, swans, tame deer, etc.), and those of a base nature (dogs, cats, foxes, monkeys, parrots, cage birds, etc.).

Still other legal divisions were made. The animals were classified as dangerous, ferocious, mischievous, nuisance, or harmless. The dog was placed in the harmless group. But under certain circumstances, it could be placed in any of the other classes.

Under the Common Law concept of a dog being of a base nature, kept only at the whim or caprice of the owner, it is not normally considered to be property. Alternatively, the dog may be considered to be of an inferior type of property. He is therefore entitled to less protection under the law than is given to some other animals, such as cattle and sheep. The owner's rights might perhaps be upheld in a civil action but not one brought under the criminal code. This concept has some advantages for the owner. The dog is not ordinarily required to be listed for personal property taxation. It need not be listed as an asset in an estate, and it will be neither inventoried nor appraised.

However, the development of dog shows, obedience trials, and field trials, and the obvious willingness of owners to buy expensive equipment and veterinary care, has tended to raise the status of the dog. Many governments now permit the dog to be classed as a domestic animal to which a value may be attached. The dog is then considered to be a 'thing of value', a 'chattel' when that word is used to define personal property. Even so, most courts still tend to consider the dog to be property of an inferior, qualified, and imperfect nature.

One reason for this is the dog's propensity for getting into trouble. Another is the fact that many owners allow their dogs to roam, to be in effect, ownerless. The dog can easily move from the harmless class into the nuisance, mischievous, dangerous, or ferocious divisions. All governments of the world have therefore made the dog subject to drastic police control, although the courts have ruled that police action does not deprive the owner of his constitutional protection against the seizure of his property without due process of law.

Some governments permit sheep-killing dogs to be killed on sight. Some go even further and permit dogs to be killed when upon the property of anyone but the owner. In areas where wild game abounds, such laws may be modified to protect the dog while it is hunting such game. Others have modified the law to protect the dog while it is under the control of a responsible person.

Dog taxes, in the form of dog licences, may be levied by local or larger governmental groups, or districts. As a rule, such taxes are excise rather than personal property taxes. They are levied to pay for the damage done by marauding dogs, such as the killing of sheep. The tax is made high enough, not only to pay for damage claims, but also to pay for the costs of administering the law.

In some countries, states, or provinces, the courts have refused to recognize dogs as personal property unless listed for personal property taxation, and in cases in which the tax has not been paid, the courts have refused to sustain a civil action by the owner to recover the value of a dog which has been wrongfully killed.

Under the old Common Law, the owner of a dog was held to be liable for any damage done by the dog. Some courts have held this to be an absolute liability, and have refused to modify it. A badly bitten trespasser or burglar might, for example, win a damage suit against the owner or harbourer of the dog. The legal position would be that the initial wrong lay with the owner for maintaining a vicious dog. In cases of badly crippling bites, such courts have also held that the dog administered excessive, cruel, and 'inhuman' punishment.

This Common Law concept is so strong that some courts have upheld it even in the presence of laws to the contrary. An actual case may be cited as an example. In one American state an attempt had been made to modify the Common Law in this manner. A law was passed stating that the owner was responsible for any damage done by his dog unless the person bitten was trespassing, committing a tort or wrong doing, or was teasing or tormenting the dog. A 12-year-old boy was badly bitten by two guard dogs as he attempted to rob a junk yard, which was fenced. A lower court refused damages on the basis of the law quoted above. But the Supreme Court awarded damages to the boy's father. It ruled that the owners of the junk yard were at fault for maintaining vicious dogs; that punishment meted out by the dogs was too great for the crime being committed.

Some courts, however, have taken a more lenient attitude. A California court's decision serves as an example.

'The owner of an animal which is wild or known to be vicious, although obligated to use the highest degree of care, is not liable if the injured party imprudently or negligently places himself in a position to be injured, or by his own negligence contributes to the injury.'

The cruel and 'inhuman' punishment concept may be replaced by one of diminished danger when trained dogs are used for police work. Such decisions as have been rendered require that the dog be fully trained, and that it be under control of an equally trained officer.

If, in the performance of its duties, the dog bites someone, it can be considered that the person has suffered from a lesser injury than, for instance, being wounded by a gun. Finally, the liability which police officers and police departments must accept in the performance of their duties may be reduced when dogs, rather than guns, are used: there are numerous world-wide examples to show that in crowd control, the search of buildings, and in pursuit, persons are more likely to obey officers with dogs than those with guns.

Right Level back.

Leishmaniasis (Kala-Azar) see Protozoan Diseases.

Leptospirosis Leptospirosis has been known by many names – canine typhus, 'black tongue', Stuttgart's disease, and infectious jaundice. It is caused by a bacterium, the principal species being *Leptospira canicola* and *Leptospira icterohaemorrhagia*.

The disease is normally spread by oral or nasal contact with the infected urine of another dog. Genital contacts are sometimes blamed, and the bacterial agent is known also to be able to penetrate the tender skin between the toes. Or the dog may be infected by drinking contaminated water.

Dogs which have recovered may be carriers of the bacteria for months afterwards and although not ill, they continue to shed the infecting organism in their urine. Since it is essentially water-borne, the disease prospers in wet weather.

L. icterohaemorrhagia. The incubation period is five to fifteen days. The first signs of illness may be a slight lameness in the hindquarters, and soreness in the groin area. Vomiting may occur, the temperature may rise to to 103 or 105°F., and JAUNDICE may appear. After several days, the temperature may drop to subnormal. However, the clinical symptoms of leptospirosis are difficult to distinguish from those of infectious canine

HEPATITIS and DISTEMPER. Often, a proper diagnosis is not made until the dog has died.

The mortality rate is seldom higher than ten per cent. It is estimated that in some areas of the world as many as thirty per cent of the dogs have had mild cases and are either temporary or permanent carriers. More cases of the disease are reported among males than among bitches. There are excellent vaccines for immunizing dogs. Some of these are given by veterinarians in combination with distemper and hepatitis vaccines. Penicillin and streptomycin are used for treatment.

L. canicola. This is a disease of the kidneys which can be immediately fatal but which more often causes a chronic kidney weakness that leads to death in later life. One survey has indicated that as many as 50 per cent of all dogs living in towns show evidence of infection by this organism. The disease, in its active form, can be transmitted to human beings.

Level Back One which makes a straight line from withers to hucklebones, without roach or sway, but one which *is not necessarily parallel to the ground.*

Level Bite One in which the upper and lower incisors meet edge to edge.

Lhasa Apso In the United Kingdom, the Apso is often called the Tibetan Apso after the land of Tibet; in Canada and the United States, it is called the Lhasa Apso, after the capital city of Tibet. There has been confusion for forty years or more concerning the Apso and the SHIH TZU. The Apso appears to be a true Tibetan dog, whereas the Shih Tzu is said to have originated in Western China. Yet there was almost certainly a mixing of the two breeds at times.

The Dalai Lama gave palace-bred Apsos to high dignitaries, especially to those of foreign countries. So Apsos went to the imperial court of China, and to high government officials. But the Emperor of China, and officials under him, gave Shih Tzus to visiting officials. In this way, Shih Tzus were taken to Lhasa.

There are a number of theories as to the origin of the name. One is that the Tibetans called the dog Abso Seng Kye – barking sentinel lion dog. This theory holds that while the TIBETAN MASTIFFS (among the world's most

281

ferocious dogs), were the outside guardians of palaces and smaller mansions, the Apso was kept indoors to ward off intruders who might somehow have got by the Mastiffs.

A second theory says that Apso is a corruption of the Tibetan word for goat, or goat-like, *rapso*. In this theory, the Apso's coat is said to resemble that of the goats kept by Tibetan herders.

Whatever the answer, the breed was first seen in England about 1930. So were other Tibetan breeds, including the Shih Tzu. As a result, the Tibetan Breeds Association was formed in 1934 to try to settle 'boundary disputes'. For example, the Apso had been called by some a terrier; the breed was recognized in the United States in 1935 (as the Lhasa Apso) but confusion resulted when the American Kennel Club placed the breed in the non-sporting group, and the Canadian Kennel Club considered that it belonged to the terrier group.

Essentials of the breed: The Lhasa or Tibetan Apso is 10 to 11 inches at the shoulder. Its body is longer than its shoulder height. Since it is claimed that the breed is the true lion dog of Tibet, golden or lion-like colours are preferred. Other colours in the usual order of preference are sandy, honey, dark grizzle, slate, smoke, parti-colours, black, white, or brown. Dark ear and beard tips are desired. The coat is heavy, straight, hard, and dense, and is parted along the spine. It is of medium length.

The head is heavily furnished with a fall of hair over the eyes. The skull is narrow, and falls away behind the eyes. While not flat, it is neither domed nor apple-headed. The muzzle is of medium length, being about one-third the length of the skull, nose to stop and stop to occiput. It measures about one and a half inches in dogs of normal size. The nose is black, and the bite level or undershot. The eyes are dark; the ears, pendant and heavily feathered. The forelegs are straight and all four legs are heavily feathered. The well feathered feet are cat-like. The tail, also well feathered, is carried over the back, and may have an end kink. A low tail carriage is a serious fault.

See colour plate p. 189.

Liam A leash, or lead.

Above Lhasa Apsos originated in Tibet. They spread to other countries at first as presents from the Dalai Lama to diplomats. Tibet of Cornwallis.

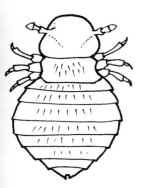

Above Lice spend their entire life cycle on their hosts. This is the dog louse, *Trichodectes canis*.

Lice Lice, unlike FLEAS, spend their entire life cycle upon their hosts. It is therefore something of a mystery how they manage to migrate from dog to dog. One extreme example is the Australian chewing louse, *heterodoxus longitarsus*, which has somehow managed to establish itself upon Australian dogs, though normally found only on kangaroos.

Dog lice, therefore, do not present a danger to human health, as they are specific to their host, and will not transfer to human beings.

Sucking lice have mouth parts for piercing, and they live on blood or lymph fluids; and chewing lice live on and are nourished by skin. There is some evidence that the sucking lice may spread infectious canine HEPATITIS from dog to dog, but this is not entirely proven.

Lice are not common in well kept kennels, but infestations of these parasites can often be found on farm dogs, and in farm kennels. Lice are also more common on European dogs than on those of North and South America. Straw, used for bedding, has sometimes been blamed for the spreading of these parasites. Close and prolonged contact by two dogs is considered to be the normal means of migration.

Adult lice lay eggs which they fasten to the dog's hair by a strongly adhesive substance. Inexperienced people often see these eggs and consider them to be only dust or scurf. Favourite egg attachment spots are on throat and neck hair, hair hidden by the ears of drop-eared dogs, the hair on the inner leather of such dogs, and even on hair within the ears. Hair in the rectal area is also favoured.

Adult lice and nymphs can be killed by insecticidal powders, although the blood suckers are much more difficult to kill than are the chewing lice. The eggs resist shampoo and continue to stick to the hair. The most effective way of destroying the pest is to clip off the egg-bearing hairs where this is possible. A stripping knife can be used to pull away those eggs which are left. The infested hair which has been cut away should be burned. Daily dusting with an insecticidal powder should continue for about four weeks, as the life cycle from egg to adult, is two to four weeks.

Tablets are available which, when given to the dog, kill lice and fleas.

Licences In most countries, dogs are required to be licensed. The terms, conditions and costs vary widely from one country to the next. Scandinavian countries levy high dog taxes, about £3 ($7·50) per annum. The cost in Britain is still surprisingly low at only 37 pence (90 cents) although this rate, constant for over eighty years, may soon be increased. In the United States the rates vary widely.

It is doubtful if any country makes much profit out of taxing dogs when one remembers the high cost of collection. To increase the fees to an economic level invariably increases the number of evasions; the law of diminishing returns also operates by reducing the number of dogs kept. The principal object of taxing dogs is to maintain at least some control over a country's dog population.

Dogs are the only domestic pet which are taxed, which gives them some legal rights but also saddles them, or rather their owners, with liabilities. If a person allows a dog to live on his premises, he is regarded as the owner of the dog unless he can prove to the contrary.

Dogs are not usually required to be licensed until they are six months old and many countries grant exemptions to dogs employed in selected occupations. Some countries insist on dogs wearing a tag on their collars to prove the tax has been paid.

See LEGAL STATUS OF THE DOG.

Lighting of Kennel Fluorescent lighting is the most economical method of illuminating a kennel. Some of the bulbs are 10 to 15 feet long, and are therefore capable of lighting several stalls or compartments. It is important that lighting be bright enough, and sufficiently diffused to illuminate all corners of pens. In poorly lighted kennels, owners may miss early signs of illness, or may fail to notice unsanitary conditions.

Cool white fluorescent bulbs appear to be the easiest on the dogs' eyes. Ultra-violet bulbs and reflectors should not be turned toward the dogs, nor should the rays be allowed to reflect back into the dogs' eyes, as serious eye damage can result. The purpose of ultra-violet lights is to kill airborne germs, but if improperly directed they can do more harm than good.

It should be possible to turn on lights in the grooming room and nursery area without turning on all the lights in the kennel. Light in these rooms should be sufficiently bright to permit careful grooming, and examination of the dogs for signs of ill-health.

Line Breeding Line breeding is the mating of two animals that are related but not as closely related as mother/son, father/daughter. It is a modification of INBREEDING, producing much the same results but not so quickly and perhaps less dangerously. One of the most debatable subjects with breeders has always been to what extent inbreeding can be practised with safety.

The object of line breeding is to have as close a relationship as possible to one or more animals of outstanding merit in the pedigree. It calls for the same high standards in the stock as is needed for inbreeding, but because genetically more diverse, faults in line-bred dogs are less likely to be fixed. Line breeding is probably the safest method for the novice breeder or a breeder who has only two or three bitches.

It is very important that the value of a particular dog or dogs should be recognized during their lifetime so that as many lines as possible can be secured amongst the descendants. If an animal appears on both sides of the pedigree and in more than one generation its influence will be appreciable. Line breeding will ensure that a good degree of relationship to an outstanding animal is preserved. After its death, breeding should continue to its best and nearest relative.

Relationship is halved with each generation and when an animal only appears once on a pedigree its influence is very slight, particularly if it appears four or five generations back.

See GENE and diagram p. 284.

Lining Mating, copulation.

Lion Dog Many breeds have been called lion dogs. With the exception of the RHODESIAN RIDGEBACK, these have all been small dogs with a real, or imagined lion-like aspect. The Rhodesian Ridgeback, originally came out of Africa as the Rhodesian Ridgeback Lion Dog. It is the only breed with any real right to the title. For the Rhodesians are big, strong dogs which come from lion country, and packs of which were sometimes used for lion hunting.

Other breeds using the name have been the PEKINGESE, the LHASA APSO (Tibetan Apso), and various members of the family of the Bichons. These have included the MALTESE, clipped in lion fashion, the Havanese, and the Manila. The Lhasa Apso has been called the Abso Seng Kye, or barking sentinel lion dog.

The most striking contestant for the name is the Löwchen, 'little lion', which appears to be closely related to the Bichon family. The dogs weigh about 12 lb. and are clipped in a fashion resembling the patterns placed on Poodles. They come in whole colours: white, cream, blue, and black.

The Havanese, now rarely seen, weighs two to four pounds, and is pure white. It may have been called the lion dog because of its fighting habits.

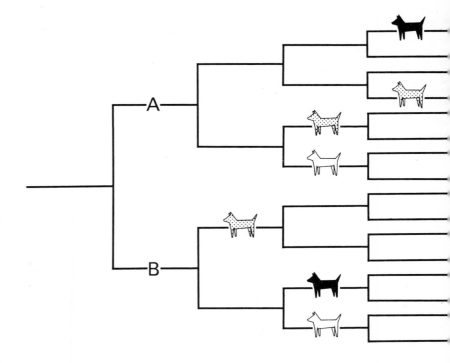

The Foo Dog, or Buddhist Lion Dog, is not a dog, but an imaginary animal. In countless porcelain and wooden figures, it is an animal with the mane of a lion, a shaggy tail, and the head of a Pekingese. Usually, a ball is held under one foot. The Foo Dog was the keeper of the jewel of the law.

Lippy Pendulous lips.

Litter A litter is a corporate description of the total of puppies produced by a bitch at one birth. A litter may

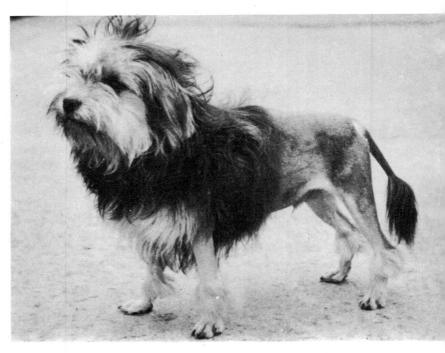

consist of anything from one to fifteen or even sixteen puppies, depending on the breed. Litters of one are quite common in the toy breeds but litters of fifteen and sixteen although recorded are rare.

A litter is due approximately sixty-three days after the bitch has been mated.

A study was made at the American Kennel Club of 506 litters evenly divided between those breeds in the American Sporting Group, and those in the American Non-Sporting groups. The 506 litters had a total of 2,490 pups. There were 1,301 males and 1,189 bitches.

Lion Dog.
Above left A sketch by Goya includes a little dog which closely resembles the Löwchen.
Above Cluneen Adam Adamant.

Among wide divergencies was a litter of eleven males and one bitch; one of six bitches and no males; and another of seven males and no bitches.

The American Kennel Club has been registering litters since 1932. It has therefore been possible to obtain exact data on litter sizes. On average, the larger the breed, the larger the litters, but almost all breeds have an occasional bitch which will produce a litter of startling numbers.

The American Kennel Club bases its records on the number of puppies alive at the time of registration. Thus, if a bitch gave birth to 20 puppies, 10 of which died shortly after, the litter would be recorded as containing 10 puppies.

An English Foxhound, *Lena*, was reported to have given birth to 23 puppies in June 1944. The litter was never registered, and there is a suspicion that the pups were from three litters born within a day or so of each other. A St. Bernard whelped a litter of 22, but while the litter application was being registered 11 died.

The largest litter registered by the American Kennel Club was one of 19 Great Danes. In 1912, a Bloodhound whelped a litter of 17, all of which lived. An Irish Setter whelped litters of 17, 16, and 15 in successive years.

64 breeds have recorded litters of 10 or more, and 21

have produced litters of 15 or more. Sporting breeds average the largest litters with 6·2 pups per litter. Working breeds follow with 5·6. The toy breeds are lowest with 3·2.

To prevent error, the American Kennel Club investigates any application to register a litter larger than the previous record litter for that breed. Current American records for 78 selected breeds follow.

Sporting dogs: Pointers, 14. German Short-haired Pointers, 16. German Wire-haired Pointers, 16. Chesapeake Bay Retrievers, 16. Golden Retrievers, 16. Labrador Retrievers, 15. English Setters, 16. Gordon Setters, 14. Irish Setters, 17. American Water Spaniels, 12. Brittany Spaniels, 15. American Cocker Spaniels, 14. English Cocker Spaniels, 14. English Springer Spaniels, 16. Irish Water Spaniels, 15. Vizslas, 12. Weimaraners, 16.

Hounds: Afghan Hounds, 14. Basenjis, 12. Basset Hounds, 14. Beagles, 14. Bloodhounds, 17. Borzois, 13. Black and Tan Coonhounds, 13. Dachshunds, 12. Greyhounds, 10. Irish Wolfhounds, 13. Norwegian Elkhounds, 14. Otter Hounds, 12. Rhodesian Ridgebacks, 12. Whippets, 8.

Working dogs: Alaskan Malamutes, 13. Belgian Sheepdogs, 11. Bouvier des Flandres, 15. Boxers, 15. Collies, 16. Dobermann Pinschers, 17. German Shepherds, 16. Great Danes, 19. Great Pyrenees, 14. Kuvasz, 11. Mastiffs, 10. Newfoundlands, 16. Old English Sheepdogs, 13. Pulis, 14. Samoyeds, 11. Standard Schnauzers, 12. Shetland Sheepdogs, 8. St. Bernards, 22. Pembroke Welsh Corgis, 9.

Terriers: Airedales, 15. Australians, 10. Bedlingtons, 12. Bull Terriers, 11. Fox Terriers, 10. Irish, 13. Kerry Blues, 11. Miniature Schnauzers, 9. Scottish Terriers, 11. Sealyhams, 7. Skyes, 10. Staffordshires, 14. Welsh, 14.

Toys: Chihuahuas, 11. Brussels Griffons, 8. Japanese Spaniels, 8. Pekingese, 9. Miniature Pinschers, 10. Pomeranians, 9. Pugs, 9. Toy Manchesters, 10. Yorkshires, 8.

Non-sporting Dogs: Boston Terriers, 11. Bulldogs, 13. Chow Chows, 10. Dalmatians, 15. French Bulldogs, 9. Keeshonds, 10. Poodles, 15.

The three varieties of Poodles are simply registered as Poodles. However, among litter applications, for Toy Poodles, the highest number of pups was seven.

See GESTATION; HEAT OF BITCH; PREGNANCY.

Liver as Food As far as dogs and dog shows go, liver is probably best known as a baiting material. It is boiled or fried and cut into chunks. It is then used to get the attention of the dog and to keep it alert. At times, the dog will be allowed to nibble at the chunk held in the owner's hand. Since dogs are usually passionately fond of liver, they can be easily taught, by this inducement, to pose, ears alert, eyes shining while the judge examines the dog.

But liver as food has important dietary functions. Those who have studied skin problems at length feel that feeding raw liver is one of the best ways to raise the level of the dog's health, and particularly that of the skin.

However, liver must be fed with care. It should not exceed one quarter of the daily diet. Liver can have a laxative effect. In addition, some researchers believe that the heavy feedings of glandular meats, including liver, can give rise to a propensity to cancer in some dogs.

Locomotion see Movement.

Loin Region on either side of the spine and between the last rib and the hips.

Longevity see Age.

Lost Back The result of the long back muscles being torn during racing or coursing by GREYHOUNDS.

Lost Dogs Experienced owners go on the assumption that, sooner or later, their dogs will get lost. They prepare for loss in several ways. One is to provide a collar with an identification tag. The tag should give the owner's name, address, and telephone number, but not necessarily the name of the dog. If the area requires that a dog be licensed, then the licence tag should also be fastened to the collar. The single word 'reward' should also appear.

There is an excellent reason why the dog's name should not appear on the collar. The dog has been taught to respond to its name. If the finder is dishonest, he then has the key to the dog's responses.

Since dog owners tend to look through their dogs rather than at them, it is often difficult for an owner to give a correct description of his own dog. An ear or flank tattoo makes identification easy. Many humane societies have tattoo sets, and some also keep records for a small fee.

Nose prints are used in registering dogs with the Canadian Kennel Club. These also provide positive identification. Some veterinary supply houses have the equipment for these methods.

A third and thorough method of identification is used by Greyhound racing associations, as well as by an occasional stud book. A chart of the dog, shaped like a flayed hide is made. Then all identifying marks are listed. The dog's weight and height are also given, together with the length of its hair, and even paw prints.

The concerned owner can do several things. Advertisements in the classified columns of local newspapers often bring results. Many 'lost' dogs have in fact been killed or injured in traffic accidents, and if the injured dog has the strength, it will often hide itself following the accident. The owner can get a Boy or Girl Scout troop to search the area thoroughly: this should include searching bushes and woods to a distance of 200 feet back from roads. Area humane societies should also be notified, and in many countries the police assist in finding dogs.

Löwchen see Lion Dog.

Lurcher The lurcher is a British dog type rather than a breed. Consequently it is not recognized officially and is unlikely to be in the foreseeable future.

The Oxford Dictionary defines a lurcher as a 'petty thief, swindler or spy; cross-bred dog . . . used especially by poachers'. The ideal required for its specialized, if illegal tasks as a poacher's dog, are often conflicting: it wants dash, patience and cunning; speed and fighting ability; intelligence and docility. And it must be able to hunt by both sight and scent.

Terrier/Greyhound crosses are the most commonly used to produce the type, but any sort of GREYHOUND cross of any shape is called a lurcher if it is effective and intelligent.

Lurcher is the general name given to intelligent cross-bred Greyhounds, which have the reputation of being poachers' dogs. *Left* 'Jason'.

M

Mad Dog see Rabies.

Mahratta see Greyhound, Eastern.

Maiden An unmated bitch. In some countries, a non-winner in show or field competition.

Malamute see Alaskan Malamute.

Malinois see Belgian Malinois.

Maltese The historian who would chronicle the background of the Maltese starts with a basic problem: did the breed take its name from the Island of Malta or from the Sicilian town of Melita? There is evidence in support of both contentions. Writing during the time of Elizabeth I, Dr. Johannes Caius wrote of Maltese: 'They are called Meliti, of the Island of Malta'. He went on, 'They are very small indeed and chiefly sought after for the pleasure and amusement of women who carried them in their arms, their bosoms and their beds'.

Fifteen hundred years earlier however, Strabo writing in A.D. 25 said, 'There is a town in Sicily called Melita whence are exported many beautiful dogs called *Canis Melitei*'.

You must choose which of these two stories to believe, but at least consider a third possibility which is that having lived for centuries in the general Mediterranean area, the breed had become separately established in both a number of the islands and on some mainland centres of civilization.

Even at the time Strabo was writing, a Maltese is known to have been in existence on Malta. It belonged to Publius, the Roman Governor and was named *Issa*. A poet of the time wrote as follows:

'Issa is more frolicsome than Catulla's sparrow. Issa is purer than a dove's kiss. Issa is gentler than a maiden. Issa is more precious than Indian gems. Lest the last days that she sees light should snatch him from her for ever, Publius has had her painted.'

More interesting than literary references, and also perhaps more precise, are portraits. And this is a breed whose fortune it has always been to attract, possibly on account of famous owners, the attention of famous artists. For example, Sir Joshua Reynolds' painting of Nellie O'Brien dated 1763 includes an unmistakable Maltese, and one which is in many respects typical of a modern specimen.

Sir Edwin Landseer also made a feature of a Maltese but proved himself a better artist than a prophet when he called the finished picture 'The Last of the Race'. Clearly he thought the breed was going to fade from the scene.

This 1840 prophecy seems to have been a shade premature because in fact today the 'race' is not only thriving well but on account of its small size, gaining adherents all over the world. Indeed when dog shows

first started some 20 years after Landseer had waved the breed goodbye, they were shown regularly and enjoyed considerable popularity. Not until World War I did they really fade and seriously become threatened with extinction. Fortunately that risk is now well past.

As with so many breeds, Queen Victoria's interest at one time earned them many friends. An unusual story concerns a Mr. Lukey who in 1841 found a pair of Maltese in Manila and paid a high price for them with the intention of presenting them to Her Majesty.

Regrettably they were totally neglected during the nine months sea voyage home and the condition of their coats on arrival made it inadvisable to press the gift! At least, however, the pair was bred from with success, and it may not be too fanciful to suggest that these two dogs were the forerunners of the majority of all Maltese at present living in Great Britain and the United States of America.

It is a breed with many friends. Its size, smart appearance, gay, volatile spirits and extremely good nature guarantee this. Indeed the only disadvantage to this glamorous imp is that if his full beauty is to be displayed, time must be set aside each day for grooming. This needs to be done with discretion if the coat is not to be broken and pulled out. Frequent grooming reduces the need for bathing.

In America their position is strong. Four thousand Maltese were registered in 1970, and the number is growing. In Britain over four hundred of them are registered with the Kennel Club each year and the number is slowly increasing.

Essentials of the breed: The dog should be smart, lively and alert, with free action. From stop to centre of skull and stop to tip of nose should be equally balanced. Nose should be pure black. Eyes should be dark brown and not bulging. Ears should be long, well feathered and hanging close to the side of the head. Mouth: level or scissors bite with teeth even. Neck: of medium length set on well sloped shoulders. Forequarters: legs should be short and straight. Body: well balanced, short and cobby with good spring of rib. Back should be straight from the tip of the shoulders to the tail. Hindquarters: legs should be short and nicely angulated. Feet should be round. Tail: well arched over the back and feathered. Coat should be good length, of silky texture and straight.

It should not be crimped and there should be no woolly undercoat. Colour: pure white. Light tan or yellow on the ears is permissible, but not desirable. Weight: under 7 lb., with 4 to 6 lb. preferred. Height: not over 10 inches.
See colour plate p. 383.

Mammary Glands and Diseases In the bitch, the mammary glands – the organs that secrete milk – are in two rows along the lower part of the abdomen. There are normally ten of them in two rows although in the smaller breeds the number may be reduced. Occasionally a bitch will have a different number of glands in each row.

The mammary glands function only when secreting milk for a litter, at which time they become enlarged and prone to mechanical injury, like cuts from sharp objects on the floor.

Inflammation of the mammary gland is frequently seen, often due to injury. The gland swells and hardens, becomes hot and painful, and may, in the acute form, develop an abscess which burst. Treatment must be begun immediately any of these symptoms are seen and is best undertaken by a veterinarian. Delay may cause a complete loss of milk with disastrous effects on the litter.

TUMOURS commonly occur within the mammary glands. These can be felt as hard lumps and may occur singly or in large numbers. It is important to treat these before they become too big. Treatment consists of surgical removal or, in certain cases, small doses of drugs given over a long period. Such drugs are usually given in the form of implants – a pellet of drug that is inserted under the skin using a local anaesthetic. The pellet is then gradually absorbed by the body over a period of several months. This form of treatment controls the tumours but does not remove them, so it is usually necessary to insert an implant periodically into the bitch to ensure that the growths remain quiescent. Unfortunately, implants do not work for all types of mammary tumour.

The mammary glands will become active if a FALSE PREGNANCY develops.
See TEATS.

Manchester Terrier It hardly needs to be said that this breed originated in Manchester, England. Just how it came into being is less certain. The most popular theory is that it was the result of a mating between a descendant of a much earlier breed known as an 'English Terrier' and a WHIPPET. The breeder is invariably named as a Mr. John Hulme of Crumpsall. However, one suspects that he was not alone in trying to produce a dog with a combination of virtues which included ability to kill rats in a pit and catch rabbits in the fields.

Mr. Hulme's dog was accepted as a cross-bred and described as being dark brown in colour. No details are available of the bitch. Certainly the produce was in no way as smart or as precise in the matter of markings as those of today. But since they were originally produced for work and not the show ring that was of little importance.

Left Maltese. Ch. Aennchen's Taja Dancer.

Colour plate Samoyed. Silver Sabre of Sword Dale.

(Continued on p. 305)

Top left Pyrenean Mountain Dog. Supreme Ch. Bergerie Knur.

Below, far left Bernese Mountain Dog. Oberga Achilles.

Below, near left Newfoundland. Ch. Lord Hercules of Fairwater.

Right Bouvier des Flandres. Ch. Konard du Rotiane.

pages 292–293

Left Collie, Rough.
Mystic Maid from Ugony.

Top right Old English Sheepdog.
Dambuster of Penylan.

Bottom right Collie, Bearded.
Ch. Benjie of Bothkennar.

Top left German Shepherd Dog (Alsatian). Alf Nibelung.

Bottom left Belgian Tervuren. Ch. Le Baron Rouge de Pacifigne.

Top right Shetland Sheepdog. Ch. Ceedees Squire.

Bottom right Belgian Sheepdog (Groenendael). Ch. Jet Mandara.

pages 296–297

Top left Rottweiler.
Ch. Chesara Dark Gossip.

Bottom left Dobermann Pir
Hotai Funny Girl.

Right Great Dane.
Kastor von Riedstern.

Above Saint Bernard.
Ch. Sanctuary Woods Going
My Way.

Right Mastiff.
Baron Winston of Buckhall.

Top right Boxer.
Summerdale Walk Tall.

Bottom right Bullmastiff.
Gabriam Samson of Oldwell.

Top left Siberian Husky.
Ch. Dichoda's Yokon Red.

Bottom left Briard.
Ch. Pa'chicks Rebel Deux.

Right Alaskan Malamute.
Indian Warlord of Seacourt.

(Continued from p. 288)

One early and well-known dog commonly accepted as a Manchester Terrier was *Billy*. In a contest he was matched to destroy a hundred large rats loosed in a wooden sided pit, in eight and a half minutes. He did it in 6 minutes 35 seconds. On a later occasion he skimmed this already phenomenal time to 6 minutes 13 seconds. Three and a half seconds per rat leaves little time for shaking. They had to be killed with one nip and dropped.

Like certain other breeds, the Manchester was threatened when blood sports themselves were attacked. This threat was intensified when the cropping of ears was forbidden in England. Owing to the fact that the ears had always been cut, the size of them had been totally disregarded in breeding programmes. Breeders had shocks when they discovered the size and untypical heaviness of the ears of the stock they had been hiding from themselves.

This problem was ultimately overcome and tipped ears as neat as those on any FOX TERRIER became normal. However, the Fox Terrier prospered at the Manchester Terrier's expense. Slowly, fanciers left the early breed as colour requirement became more exacting. Precise placing of the rich tan markings, the non-acceptance of any colour mingling plus the requirement of black pencilling on each tan toe broke the spirit of all but the hardiest fancier.

Fortunately the United States had by then taken an interest and now there is a modestly sized fancy on each side of the Atlantic dedicated to maintaining the breed.

Essentials of the breed: A long head is desirable, level and wedge-shaped and with tapering jaws. The eyes are dark, small and oblong. Ears: small, V-shaped, carried above the topline of the head. Shoulders should be clean and sloped with straight forelegs. Bodies: short, well sprung and slightly roached. The feet should be small with well arched toes. The tail tapers to a point and is carried level with the back. Coat: smooth, short and glossy. Background colour must be black with rich tan markings on muzzle, cheeks, above eyes, below knees, on each side of chest, and on the vent. There must be a black 'thumbmark' above the feet and pencilling on the toes. Weight: not more than 22 lb. Height: dogs, 16 inches; bitches, 15 inches.
See colour plate p. 372.

Manchester Terrier, Toy see English Toy Terrier (Black and Tan).

Mane Long and profuse hair on the top and sides of the neck.

Mange There are several forms of mange, each being caused by a particular type of mite. The most common are sarcoptic and otodectic. Adult mites pierce the skin, then burrow under to feed upon blood and newly formed skin. They are round or oval in shape, with spines and bristles. Eggs hatch in three to seven days and under optimum conditions, the entire cycle from egg to adult covers as few as eight days.

ight Manchester Terrier. Soris-ale Quarrel. Originally cross-red types and great ratters, these ogs were almost extinguished by ttempts to produce the right arkings rather than the right pirit. Timely interest in the United tates saved them.

olour plate:
op Welsh Cardigan Corgis. Ch. im of Critum and puppy.
ottom Welsh Pembroke Corgi. ormakin Busy.

Sarcoptic mange normally appears first on the lower surface of the abdomen, in the axillae or 'arm pits', and on the inner surface of the thighs. In many cases, the site of the infestation is the bridge of the nose, and the area about the eyes. Intense itching causes the dog to scratch and redden the skin. Crusts form and the dog may have a sweaty odour. One of the toxic effects of sarcoptic mange is to cause a disease known as eosinophilia.

Any infected animal can transfer the disease to man, and conversely, man can give the disease to his dog. Dogs can also become infested from contact with other animals such as cats, pigs, and horses. Those under stress, or in poor health more easily become victims of this infection.

Treatment of this form of sarcoptic mange must be left to the veterinarian. However, the dog's owner needs to build up the health of his pet: a high protein diet is recommended. The dog should be clipped, and the clippings burned. Clipping should go beyond the infected area, since the disease spreads out from the centre.

Otodectic, or ear mange, affects all dogs, but is more common in long-eared, long-haired dogs. Itching is intense at night because the temperature within the ear tends to increase then. This type of mange is easily treated. Debris and wax should be softened by a warm oil, then carefully cleaned out of the ear. The ear can then be treated by putting warm olive oil, containing one per cent rotenone, into the ear with a medicine dropper. However, since ear mange causes severe inflammation, this treatment must be given by a veterinarian. After the first treatment, the owner can be instructed to insert the oil twice a week. Three weeks should bring a complete cure.

A less common disease is Notoëdric mange. It is caused by *Notoëdris,* which is most commonly found on cats. It usually starts about the face, forms crusts, and the skin becomes thickened and creased like that of an elephant. Treatment is the same as for sarcoptic mange.

Psoroptic mange is another form, relatively rare in dogs. The mites live upon the skin, rather than in it, but they prefer hidden areas, such as the creases in the facial skin of a BULLDOG. Because the mites live on the skin, treatment is quickly effective, but should be directed by a veterinarian.

The most feared of all the manges, and the most difficult of all to cure is that caused by the worm-like *demodex canis.* This mite is present in the skin of many dogs which show no signs of trouble, and will often only become active when the dog becomes 'run down'. It occurs most frequently in puppies weakened by tooth changes, and after illness, such as distemper. As with sarcoptic mange, it can spread as an epidemic. First sign of infection is usually a bald spot, or spots upon the nose, lips, or skull. Hairs on the edges of the spots are easily pulled out. As a rule, there is little or no itching.

The first step in treatment is to try to build up the dog's general health to the highest possible level. The second is to clip away the hair in the areas surrounding the bald spots. A problem with demodectic mange is that a treatment which works well on one dog may be of no benefit on another. Veterinarians often vary the treatment every few days.

The recommended treatment should be administered by or upon instructions of a veterinarian and strict hygienic measures should be practised in the home, including the wearing of special clothing when treating the dog, and careful cleansing of the hands and face after treatment.

Manners in the House Manners maketh not only man but dogs, and bad manners make bad dogs. To meet a bad dog at a friend's house is an experience calculated to fray the bonds of friendship. To suffer in silence trouser-pulling, barking, snapping and white hairs on dark clothes is difficult. There is a temptation to criticize the animal, but one should really criticize the owner, because the fault is his.

Most irritating habits are deliberately taught to young puppies before their owners realize how annoying they can be. If you teach your dog to bark in the house you may regret it. You may think that unless he barks, he has no value as a house dog: experience will teach that it is the dog who barks at every noise who has no value.

Above Manchester Terrier. C
Sonnett of Chatham with C
Sundown of Chatham as a pupp

Jumping up to welcome master or mistress may well seem an engaging trait when the puppy is young and clean. But it can be an annoying trick when feet are muddy, and clothes spick and span. No dog can realize that you want him to jump up on some occasions but not on others.

The same applies to jumping on chairs and beds. It is a habit which should be firmly discouraged from the first performance.

A dog that is taught to pull at clothing, that is rewarded with food if it makes a nuisance of itself at the table, that is allowed to 'kill' slippers like rats, or to chase cats is annoying, not engaging.

Mantle Dark shaded portion of the hair on back and sides, similar to a 'blanket'. The term is used in connection with ST. BERNARDS.

Marbled Mottled colouring.

Maremma Sheepdog The Maremma is the best known of the Italian sheepdogs. It has been known under various names, such as the Maremmani, the Central Italy Sheepdog, and the Abruzzi Sheepdog. In Italy, it is a native of Tuscany and the Abruzzi region.

The Maremma appears to have a close relationship to the Hungarian KUVASZ, and the Great Pyrenees, or PYRENEAN MOUNTAIN DOG. It may therefore have originated in Central Asia. Whether it is related to the Russian Owtchar, and the Hungarian KOMONDOR is less certain.

The breed has been known in England since 1931, but few specimens have been taken across the Atlantic. There are therefore no classes for it at American and Canadian dog shows, and no provision for it even in the miscellaneous class. Progress of the breed was slowed down in England as well as in Italy because of the Second World War.

Essentials of the breed: The Maremma is normally pure white. Aged dogs sometimes show a tinge of biscuit or lemon in the ears. The skull is moderately broad with a medium stop, and with a fairly long, but tapered jaw. The eyes are dark brown, the nose black. The ears fold over to the sides of the head.

The body is slightly longer than the shoulder height and is without sway or roach. The chest is deep rather than broad, and there is moderate belly tuck-up. The

legs are well boned, but not so much as to cause clumsiness. The stifles are moderately bent, and the feet are oval, with strongly arched toes.

Except on the head, the coat is moderately long. The legs are well feathered, and the tail is heavily feathered to make a plume.

Males average 75 lb. in weight and are 25 inches at the shoulder. Bitches are slightly smaller.

Marie's Disease This is a condition in which new bone is deposited on existing bone. The cause is uncertain: TUMOURS, hormonal imbalance, and vascular changes have all been suggested, and the disease may have multiple causes. In Africa, ROUNDWORM has been reported as being connected with the condition.

Mask Dark facial shadings.

Mastiff In the centuries before the era of the pure-bred dog, it was common to call any large dog a Mastiff. Even breeds such as the ST. BERNARD and the NEWFOUNDLAND were sometimes called Mastiffs. Today only three breeds can properly be called a Mastiff. The best known is the Old English Mastiff which, in America and in many other parts of the world, is often called simply the Mastiff. The other two are the TIBETAN MASTIFF, and the Japanese Tosa.

The Tibetan Mastiff was very rarely seen outside Tibet even before the Chinese invasion of Tibet, and is now extremely rare.

The Japanese Tosa is of true Mastiff type. It is also a dog bred purely for fighting. Little effort has been

made to keep the Tosa purebred until quite recently. Yet the Mastiff characteristics (see article under MASTIFF, OLD ENGLISH) have always predominated. The Japanese claim that the Tosa dogs have been bred for 500 years, chiefly in Shikaku Province. Dog fighting has been thoroughly organized in Japan for about 90 years. The dogs are paraded on festive occasions trapped out in silk and gold blankets, with huge ropes covered with silk by which two people control them, one on each side.

The modern Tosa dogs are about 28 inches tall at the shoulder, and weigh well over 100 lb. They are black, tan, or brindle, with the two latter colours predominating. They resemble the Old English Mastiff, but are less ponderous, and have surprising agility for their size and weight.

See ALPINE MASTIFF; BULL MASTIFF; MASTIFF, OLD ENGLISH; TIBETAN MASTIFF.

Mastiff, Old English

That Island ... breeds very valiant creatures;
their Mastiffs are of unmatchable courage.

Shakespeare: King Henry V.

The Mastiff probably originated in Asia and was perhaps introduced to Britain by the Phoenician traders in the sixth century B.C. The dogs fought side by side with the ancient Britons when Caesar invaded in 55 B.C., and the Romans were impressed by their courage and ferocity. Soon many of these huge British dogs were sent back to Rome to fight in the arenas against bulls, bears, lions, tigers and even human gladiators. Ever since, the Mastiff's fighting qualities seem to have been its main claim to fame although the old names of 'bandog' and 'tie dog' indicate that they were also used as guards.

In the time of Henry VIII there was a Court officer with the title of The Master of the King's Bears, Bulls and Mastiffs. In Queen Elizabeth's day, plays were prohibited on Thursdays as the day reserved for bear baiting. Three trained Mastiffs were reckoned a fair match against a bear and four against a lion. Lord Buckhurst, Queen Elizabeth's Ambassador to France in 1572, owned a great Mastiff which, unassisted, successfully baited a bear, a leopard and a lion and pulled them all down.

The Puritans tried to prohibit bull baiting, but this was resisted, the Court holding it 'a sweet and comfortable recreation for the solace and comforts of a peaceable people'. Samuel Pepys evidently disagreed, because after a visit to the bear garden he wrote: 'It is a very rude and nasty pleasure'. In 1835 animal baiting was made illegal in England, and inevitably the Mastiff, in the front ranks as a fighting dog for over 2,000 years, lost popularity.

In 1908, only thirty-five were registered at the English Kennel Club. They then staged a partial recovery, only to be threatened again during the Second World War. Many British specimens were sent to America and only three litters were born in Britain during the six war years. When peace came, only twenty Mastiffs remained in Britain and most of these were too old for breeding. The Old English Mastiff Club took the unprecedented

step of buying from the USA descendants of their earlier dogs, and now the breed lives again in the British Isles.

Average annual registrations with the English Kennel Club run at about a hundred while in America they are approximately double that. There is therefore no immediate risk that the breed will die out. The liaison and exchange between the two countries both in stock and 'know how' is flourishing. Even so, a shortage of lines available as outcrosses limits expansion. Further, the sheer bulk of this breed reduces the numbers of people for whom they might be considered ideal pets.

For the moment however we can be thankful that this dog, historic and traditional, kind and gentle, noble and protective, of sombre face yet curiously light heart, still soldiers on.

Essentials of the breed: The general appearance is of a large, massive, powerful and symmetrical dog. The skull is broad, forehead flat, but wrinkled when excited. The muzzle is short, broad under the eyes, and nearly parallel in width to the end of the nose. The standard for length of muzzle to whole head is 1:3 in Britain, 1:2 in America. The circumference of the muzzle to that of the head should be in the ratio of 3:5. The stop should be well defined. Ears: small, thin, wide apart, set on high and lying close to the cheeks. Teeth: incisors level, or the lower projecting but not visible. The neck: slightly arched and muscular. Forequarters: shoulder and arm slightly sloping, heavy and muscular. Legs: straight, strong and set wide apart. Chest: wide and deep, ribs arched. Back and loins: wide and muscular. Hindquarters: broad, wide and muscular. Feet: large and round. Tail: should be set high, reaching to hocks or below, wide at root and tapering. Coat: short and close. Colour: apricot, silver (silver-fawn), fawn or dark fawn-brindle. Muzzle, ears and nose: black. Minimum heights: dogs 30 inches; bitches 27½ inches.
See colour plate p. 300.

Match Show A dog show held on an informal basis at which championship points are not awarded.

Mating a Bitch A bitch is usually ready to be mated around about her tenth to twelfth day of heat. See HEAT OF BITCH.

This should present few difficulties provided both animals are normal. If the STUD DOG is keen and the bitch is brought to him on the right day a mating will take place very quickly and conception should result.

Both animals should be exercised before mating and it is advisable not to feed the animals at least for a couple of hours before.

It is more sensible to mate an experienced stud dog with a maiden bitch and an inexperienced stud dog with an experienced BROOD BITCH that will stand very steadily and quietly for him.

If a bitch is shy and inclined to snap it is advisable to tape her as no breeder wants to risk upsetting a valuable stud dog. Once taped or muzzled the bitch is easier to control and apart from a little discomfort to herself there is no harm. The collar on the bitch should be held tightly at the back of the neck by the left hand whilst the right hand should support her hindquarters. It may be necessary to lubricate the vagina of a maiden bitch with a little vaseline. If after several efforts the bitch refuses to be mated it may mean that she has been presented to the dog too early. It is far better to leave her for another day than exhaust the stud dog.

Sometimes maiden bitches have strictures of the vagina and before mating it is wise to arrange for an examination by a veterinarian to make sure there is no obstruction. Usually these obstructions, if present, can be very quickly broken down with manipulation and thereafter a mating procured.

A bitch to be mated should never be allowed to run loose for any length of time with a stud dog. This can be most harmful to the dog and reduce his sexual drive.

When a bitch is ready to be mated she will draw her tail to one side and stand quietly for the dog while he mounts. Penetration by the dog is usually followed by a 'tie' which is considered to be a sign of a successful mating. Tying may last from ten minutes up to half an hour or even longer. During this time the bitch should be held firmly to prevent her becoming restless and perhaps injuring the dog. A tie is not essential for a successful mating and conception can result without it. To try to ensure that the bitch will conceive, breeders very often mate her twice in the hope that one or both services will coincide with ovulation. This is best done with about a 48-hour interval.

Measuring and Weighing, Britain The Kennel Club official standards of the breeds give, for many breeds, the ideal height or weight. In some cases both height and weight are quoted, but the Standards do not normally have the effect of regulations. For the majority of breeds, the heights and weights are only for the guidance of judges; the two exceptions are POODLES and DACHSHUNDS. In the case of Poodles (Toy) and Poodles (Miniature), the standards define the difference as under 11 inches and over 11 inches in height respectively, and before a dog of these breeds can win a prize the judge must measure it with a special measure. If the dog is under, or over, the regulation height it is ineligible for further competition at the show.

In the case of Dachshunds the regulations require Miniature Wire-haired, Miniature Long-haired and Miniature Short-haired Dachshunds to be under 11 lb. in weight, and before judging begins the judge or an official delegated by him must weigh each of the dogs on scales and reject any that are overweight.

For other breeds the standard is used only as a guide and if a dog does not comply with the standard it can be penalized by the judge but it cannot be disqualified.

Measuring and Weighing, United States Many breed standards provide for the disqualification from the show ring of dogs under or over certain heights or dogs weighing more than a certain amount. At the present time, the following system is used in the United States.

An exhibitor, feeling that the dog is a borderline case, may ask for a measurement or weighing at any time before the hour scheduled for judging that breed. For this purpose, clubs are required to have measuring devices and accurate scales, and each show must designate a committee to measure and weigh the dogs.

If the dog's measurements are above the standard limit, it cannot compete at that show. If found to be within the standard, the judge cannot require that it be measured in the ring. The judge may order a second *weighing* in the ring if he has doubts about weight.

The judge may require the measurement of any unmeasured dog when it enters the ring, as may competing exhibitors in the class.

Disqualification on grounds of height is permanent unless the exhibitor appeals to the American Kennel Club, which will appoint a special committee to remeasure the dog. If measured within the standard, the dog is reinstated. By contrast, if prior to the judging the dog was measured and found to be above the height limit, there is no disqualification; the dog is merely ineligible for that show.

In some countries, 'wickets' cut to exact height size are used. These are placed upon the dog's shoulders and if they do not touch the ground, then the dog is excused or disqualified. The American Kennel Club now prohibits the use of wickets.

It also prohibits the measuring or weighing of dogs in breeds where there is no disqualification on these points. For example, the Pug standard states that 14 to 18 lb. is the desired weight. The judge's decisions might be influenced by knowing the exact weight of the dog he is judging; the rules prohibit him from having the dogs weighed.

In classes divided by weight, dogs found overweight for one class cannot be transferred to another class at that show but may enter the higher or lower weight classes at future events.

Medicine The improvement in the general health of dogs over the last forty years is most striking. Modern research has revolutionized diagnosis, therapeutics and prophylaxis. Today the veterinarian aided by the most recently developed apparatus and laboratory tests is able to give a far more accurate diagnosis than in the past. Two very good examples of this are the use of the electrocardiograph (E.C.G.) and the electroencephalograph (E.E.G.) which are machines designed to record the electrical activity of the heart and of the brain respectively. Analysis of the recordings from the electrocardiograph help in the diagnosis of heart disease and in the assessment of treatment. Similarly the electroencephalograph can help in the diagnosis of diseases of the brain.

Another great advance is the introduction of antibiotics into animal medicine. Penicillin has been available for the treatment of dogs for a quarter of a century. Research is continually producing new antibiotics, thus today we have, for example, aureomycin, terramycin and penbritin and many others. Before the introduction of penicillin, streptococcal infection in dogs was a great problem. Now streptococcal infection is only a nuisance and all but the most stuborn cases can be cured. Thirty years ago pneumonia was often

Medicines, administration of.
Top right Administering a tablet: the dog's mouth is opened and the tablet placed on the back of the tongue.
Bottom right Administering a liquid: a pocket is made of one side of the dog's lower lip and the liquid cautiously poured in.

fatal, today thanks to modern antibiotics most respiratory infections rapidly yield to treatment.

Probably the most significant advance in canine medicine has been the control of DISTEMPER (including HARD PAD DISEASE). Distemper vaccination was introduced in the thirties, and since then the vaccine has been continually improved. Today most puppies are vaccinated at about three months of age and many are given a booster dose eighteen months to two years later. The widespread use of the distemper vaccine has been the major factor in the improvement in canine health. No longer do epidemics of distemper kill many dogs and leave behind numerous chronic invalids. There are still small outbreaks of distemper here and there but these will become even more rare as more puppies are vaccinated. Virus HEPATITIS used to be confused with distemper. In the last twenty years the disease has been identified and an excellent vaccine has been produced. Puppies are now usually vaccinated against hepatitis and distemper at the same time.

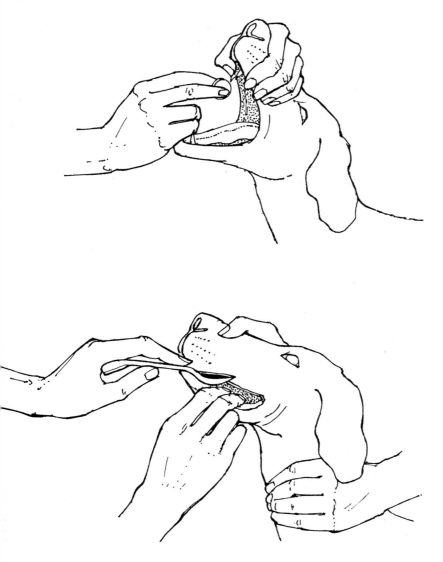

Medicines, Administration of The efficacy of any course of treatment depends upon the correct dose of the medicine being administered at the correct time. Very occasionally it is possible to mix the medicine in the dog's food or drinking water but this method is not suitable for drugs which have an unpleasant taste or smell. Usually the medicine is supplied or prescribed by the veterinarian in solid form as tablets, pills or capsules, or in liquid form as a mixture.

Administration of tablets: The dog is placed on a table and restrained by an assistant. The dog should stand or sit on the table and the assistant should grasp the dog's forelegs near the elbows from behind so that his or her arms also control the dog's body. The operator, if right-handed, stands in front and to the right of the dog. The left hand is placed over the top of the dog's muzzle so that gentle pressure can be brought to bear with the thumb and fingers on either side of the upper jaw just behind the upper canine teeth. Pressing the lips inwards in this way encourages the dog to open its mouth. Sometimes it may be necessary to use the right hand, already holding the tablet, to press downwards on the lower incisors to get the mouth open wide enough. As soon as the mouth is open wide enough the tablet is placed at the back of the tongue and the hand is rapidly removed. At the same time the pressure with the left hand is relaxed so that the dog can close its mouth. If the tablet has been correctly placed at the back of the tongue the dog will swallow. Some operators massage the throat and lower jaw to encourage swallowing. Speed and dexterity are the keys to success in the administration of tablets.

Administration of liquids: The dog is restrained by an assistant as for the administration of a tablet. The right-handed operator standing to the right of the dog, raises the dog's head just above the horizontal with the left hand and pulls out the lip on the left hand side to form a funnel. The right hand now administers the liquid from spoon or measure a little at a time. The liquid will trickle between the dog's back teeth and it will swallow. If too much is given at one time the dog may choke, so a little caution is necessary. The slow administration of liquids is thus the opposite of the rapid administration of tablets.

The veterinarian will often administer drugs by injection. The injections may be subcutaneous (under the skin) or intramuscular (into a muscle). If it is necessary for the owner to administer an injection the veterinarian will supply the necessary equipment and demonstrate the proper method. First, the syringe and needle must be sterilized. Usually this means that they have to be boiled. However it is now possible to purchase disposable syringes and needles already sterilized. This ready-to-use equipment is used once and then thrown away. Drugs for injection are usually supplied in rubber-capped bottles. The rubber cap should be swabbed with spirit (alcohol), the bottle inverted, and then the needle which is attached to the syringe thrust through the cap and the appropriate volume drawn into the syringe. The withdrawal is facilitated if an equal volume of air is first injected into the bottle. The dog should be restrained on a table by an assistant. To make a subcutaneous injection, the site is first swabbed with spirit and then a fold of skin is lifted between finger and thumb. The needle with filled syringe attached is thrust into this fold and the injection is made by pressing the plunger of the syringe gently. After the needle is removed from the skin the site is gently massaged.

Intramuscular injections are usually made into the thigh muscles. The needle is inserted through the skin into the muscle mass. Obviously the use of the correct size needle is important so that no damage is done to deeper structures. If it is necessary for the owner to give an intramuscular injection the veterinarian will give careful instructions on this point.

It is unwise to attempt to give an injection to a dog without direct instructions from the veterinarian.

Melena This is the condition in which the feces are black in colour and have a dark 'tarry' nature. It is caused by HEMORRHAGE into the first part of the intestine, where the blood collects and is partially digested producing substances that give the distinctive colour.

Membrana Nictitans see Eye Anatomy; Haw.

Mendelism Mendelism may be described as the basic theory of the science of genetics, and refers to certain facts or 'laws of biological inheritance' discovered more than a century ago by the monk Gregor Mendel, whose painstaking experiments and reasoning are basic to genetic theory, although study since has modified his conclusions to some extent.

Mendel, using garden peas, not dogs, deduced that inheritance depends on pairs of 'factors' (now called GENES) which remain separate from each other and are passed unchanged from one generation to another. Each plant or animal carries numerous pairs of factors, one of each pair being derived from each parent and carried on corresponding CHROMOSOMES. The genes of a pair may be alike (homozygous) or they may be different (heterozygous) in their effects on the development of the individual which contains them.

It is customary to indicate a dominant gene by a capital letter and its recessive alleles or alternatives by the same letter in lower case, the different alleles in a multiple series being distinguished by numbers or letters usually as superscripts. Other systems are used in more complex studies, but need not be described here.

For example, both in cattle and dogs there is a genetic factor which makes possible the development of a coloured (pigmented) coat, with an alternative form which prevents the pigmentation of hair, resulting in a white coat. If we call the gene necessary for a coloured coat W and its allele w, then an animal carrying the gene pair WW will be coloured (e.g. black or brown), while the ww animal will be white. If two such animals are mated, all the offspring will receive a W gene from one parent and a w gene from the other, giving them the formula Ww. In cattle they will be roan, i.e. their coats will be a mixture of white and pigmented hairs. In dogs,

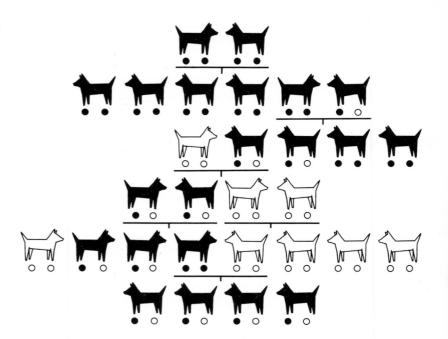

however, they will all be solid coloured like the WW parent (but often with a little white on the chest and paws). The gene W is 'dominant' over its allele w in dogs, but not in cattle.

There is another gene pair in dogs, of which the dominant member B enables black pigment to be made, while its recessive allele b alters the biochemical process of pigment formation in such a way that chocolate-brown pigment replaces black. The BB dog is black, the bb dog is chocolate-brown (liver) coloured, and the Bb dog is black because B is completely dominant. These colours are present not only in the coat but also in the skin and eyes.

Now to Mendel's second discovery: where two or more gene pairs are studied, they are found to be distributed among the offspring independently of each other (this is known to be true only if they are on different chromosomes). The resulting 'reassortment' may be illustrated by considering a mating between a white dog with a liver nose, showing it must have the formula wwbb, and a black mate having the formula WWBB. All their offspring must have the formula WwBb, so they will be black. If these are mated among themselves each resulting puppy can get only *one* gene of each pair from each parent, but all possible combinations are equally possible. The sex-cells of each parent will be of 4 types, WB, Wb, wB, wb, in equal numbers, and these combine at random with the sex-cells of the other parent. The permutations are best shown by a 'checkboard':

	WB	Wb	wB	wb
WB	WWBB	WWBb	WwBB	WwBb
Wb	WWbB	WWbb	WwbB	Wwbb
wB	wWBB	wWBb	wwBB	wwBb
wb	wWbB	wWbb	wwbB	wwbb*

Above Mendelism. Every dog contains two instructions or genes for coat colour, of which one may be dominant. Only one is passed from each parent to offspring. one or both of the parents have two instructions for dark colour (W – black dot), all the offspring must be dark, but if both parents carry recessive genes for 'colourless' (w – white dot), colourless offspring may appear, even when both parents are dark.

Left Those underlined solid will be black, those underlined with dashes, will be liver (chocolate) those dotted underneath will be white with black noses and dark eyes, and the one marked * will be white with a liver nose.

Thus, in the second generation, for every nine pups coloured like the black grandparent there will be, on average, only one coloured like the white grandparent; but two new colour patterns, solid liver, and white with black nose, have been formed by reassortment and appear in the proportion of three of each to every nine of the dominant grandparental type. Of course, these proportions, the famous 9:3:3:1 ratio, will only show up if some hundreds of puppies are bred; but if we are familiar with this expectation, when we make a mating of this sort, at least we know that two new colours may turn up, and that we shall probably have to breed quite a number of litters if we want to get several of the rarest class, the 'double recessive', wwbb.

Merle A genetic colour factor, as in BLUE MERLE.

Mexican Hairless Dog see Hairless Dog.

Milk, Bitch's The milk of all mammals contains three main proteins – casein, lactalbumin, and lacto-globulin. But the amounts of these proteins differ with the species which produces the milk. The milk of one species is therefore not always compatible with the young of another.

All mammal milk contains fat. But, as with the proteins, milks vary in both fat content and the digestibility of it. The puppy can tolerate a change in the fat-carbohydrate balance only within very narrow limits. For these reasons a hand-reared puppy gets a simulated bitch's milk.

The following table shows the average constituents of milk for three species in percentages.

	WATER	FAT	LACTOSE	PROTEIN
Cow	87·00	3·75	4·50	3·13
Dog	80·10	8·50	2·80	7·30
Reindeer	68·20	17·10	2·08	2·00

The bitch's *colostrum*, or first milk, contains antibodies which will immunize the puppy for eight to ten weeks against any disease for which its mother had built up an immunity. This immunity weakens and disappears gradually. The bitch's mammary glands may not be able to store enough to feed a large and hungry litter of puppies. Milk production depends on food. If the bitch's food intake is reduced as weaning time approaches, her milk production will be reduced accordingly. If at this time, the puppies are gradually introduced to other foods, WEANING and the ending of the bitch's milk supply occur together.

Miniature Pinscher Many people erroneously call the Miniature Pinscher a Miniature Dobermann, or conversely, call the DOBERMANN PINSCHER, a Standard Dobermann Pinscher. The Miniature Pinscher is a much older breed than the Dobermann. Dogs of its general type have been known for about 300 years. Although there is no evidence to support the idea that Louis Dobermann designed his dog to be a giant brother to the Miniature Pinscher, it is true that they do bear a startling resemblance to each other.

The Miniature Pinscher was developed in the German Rhineland, where it was sometimes called the *Reh Pinscher*. One reason for the name was that his stag-red colour often reminded people of the *Reh* or roe deer. The breed was first recognized by Pinscher Schnauzer Klub in Germany in 1895, and so the breed gained

Above Merle markings are as distinctive as the colour. Shetland Sheepdog, Loughrigg Blue Mantle.

Miniature Pinscher.
Below Ch. Bo Mar's Road Runner.
Below right Ch. Hayclose Bralstan Lemon.

Above Modelling: television and films. Susan Hampshire as Fleu with Mr. Perkins as Ting-a-Ling in a scene from the television serial *The Forsyte Saga*.

official recognition before the larger Dobermann Pinscher was granted full breed status.

Miniature Pinschers were exported to the United States in the 1920s, and the Miniature Pinscher Club of America was organized in 1929. The breed's popularity suffered during the Second World War, but the breed has since made an excellent come-back in Germany, and now enjoys excellent popularity throughout the United States and Canada, and is particularly favoured in Brazil.

Progress in the British Isles has been much slower. This is partly due to the strict quarantine laws, and partly because of the anti-cropping laws. However, English breeders are making excellent progress in breeding Miniature Pinschers with naturally erect ears.

Essentials of the breed: The head is wedge-shaped. The body is square with a deep chest, but without being barrel chested. The top line slopes from withers to the tail. The eyes are dark brown or black. The nose is black, except that it may be chocolate in chocolate coloured dogs. The hind legs are well angulated.

Colours are red, stag-red, or lustrous black with sharply defined tan, rust-red markings on the cheeks, lips, lower jaw, throat, twin spots above the eyes, on the chest, lower half of the forelegs, inside of the hind legs, and on the vent. There are black pencils stripes on the toes. A third colour is permitted; this is solid brown or chocolate with rust or yellow markings.

The ideal height of the Miniature Pinscher is 11 to 11½ inches. A dog measuring under 10 inches or more than 12½ must be disqualified. Other disqualifications include thumb marks, or any area of white on the feet or forechest exceeding half an inch in one dimension. See colour plate p. 381.

Miscellaneous Class A class for dogs of various breeds for which regular dog show classification is not provided.

Mis-Marked Mis-marked is a term used to describe a dog whose colour pattern does not conform to the standard for the breed. Often, mis-marking calls for disqualification. The term would not normally be used in the case of a solid coloured dog whose colour would disqualify – a pure white Cardigan WELSH CORGI, for example.

Examples of mis-marking are these: GREAT DANES which are a solid colour except for white legs, neck, and point of tail; MINIATURE PINSCHERS with thumb marks, or any area of white on the feet or forechest exceeding one half inch in its longest dimension; BOXERS with white or black ground colour, or white markings which exceed one third of the ground colour.

Modelling: Television and Films There is quite a demand, especially in big cities, for dogs as photographic models and as 'actors' in television and films. The same basic essentials apply to them all. First, the dog must have a good temperament. A dog with the

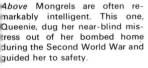

Above Mongrels are often re-markably intelligent. This one, Queenie, dug her near-blind mis-tress out of her bombed home during the Second World War and guided her to safety.

Above right Monuments and memorials. This memorial in Edinburgh, Scotland is to Grey-friars Bobby, the Skye Terrier, who followed his master to the grave and slept on the spot every night until his own death nearly ten years later.

slightest tendency to nervousness and the 'one man' dog which dislikes strangers are useless. Only extroverts succeed. Secondly, it must be trained sufficiently for the part, bearing in mind that what one dog enjoys doing another may not even attempt. Thirdly, it must be photogenic and if it is to be used regularly must be the sort of dog the public likes – or, more correctly, the sort of dog the advertising agencies believe the public likes. Eyes and expression are vital to a photogenic dog but colour and markings make a big difference too. Black dogs are very difficult to 'light', and photographers tend to avoid them. A dog with a big white blaze extending as far as the eyes can look rather peculiar in a photograph. The dog is usually only a small part of the whole picture and photographers try to avoid anything which will create problems.

For modelling, a dog must be trained to stay in any position: sitting, standing, lying down with its head up or on its paws, standing with its feet on a chair, and many other poses. And it must not mind flash bulbs going off behind it: some dogs that are perfectly happy in a film or television studio, are terrified of flash bulbs.

For film and television work, there are similar requirements, except that it is rarely possible to position the dog by hand. It has to come into camera and take up the desired position on command. Sometimes by verbal command but more often by hand signals only – this invariably applies to television work. It must also be very friendly and willing to react to anyone who speaks to it or pats it. Greed can be a great help here.

Even if the dog does not care for the artist, it may very well be interested in the biscuit in his pocket!

It is seldom necessary for a dog to obey commands from an actor, and indeed, it is seldom possible for the performer to give commands, for it is difficult to act with concentration and control a dog successfully at the same time. Professional dogs are always controlled by their handlers, with the co-operation of the artist and director.

Molera or mollera. Membranous space between the cranial bones in foetal life and infancy. The fontanel. The gap fails to close in the skulls of some CHIHUAHUAS.

Mongrel The term 'mongrel' applied to dogs, means a dog of mixed breed. The term is always applied to a dog one or both of whose parents were also of mixed breed. But it applies equally to one whose parents were purebreds, but of different breeds. In recent years, unscrupulous breeders have been crossing Cocker Spaniels and Poodles, or Pekingese and Poodles, and then selling the offspring as Cockapoos of Pekapoos. These puppies are simply mongrels. The term 'mongrel' should not be confused with 'hybrid'. The latter is a cross mating between two species, such as the lion and the tiger. Some countries permit the crossing of related breeds, as for instance English Cocker and English Springer Spaniels. The puppies are called 'inter-breds', but they are no less mongrels.

Monorchid see Cryptorchid.

Monuments and Memorials Considering how long dogs have been so close to man, there are surprisingly few monuments to them. Such few as there are have become well known.

Memorials are quite naturally more plentiful, but almost invariably unrecorded since they are frequently sited in owners' gardens or dogs' cemeteries rather than in prominent and public positions.

Greyfriars Bobby is perhaps the best known dog to earn a permanent memorial. Admittedly, the range of his fame springs more from Walt Disney's film than the little statue in Edinburgh, but possibly the film would never have been made had the statue not existed.

Bobby was a Skye Terrier and the inscription on the monument says he 'followed the remains of his master to this churchyard in 1858 and refused to be separated from the spot until he died' (nearly ten years later).

Fontainebleau is a memorial to a dog called *Bleau*, who was present when his master injured himself in what was then a forest. The dog, it is said, realized his master's need and located and scratched for water from an underground stream. The man later bought the forest, erected a fountain on the spring site and called it Fontainebleau.

In North Wales there is an inscription on stone to a possibly fictitious Deerhound, *Beth Gêlert*, accidentally slain by his master the Welsh Prince Llewellyn, who thought the dog had killed his child whereas in fact he had killed a wolf who was attacking the infant.

In Gujarat there is a stone tribute to *Carlos*, a retriever who followed his master, Sir W. Knott, all through the Afghan Campaign.

Igloo, a little mongrel, has a monument in Pine Ridge Cemetery, Boston. He accompanied Commander Byrd on his expedition to the South Pole in 1928. The inscription reads: 'He was more than a friend'.

Obo II, the forerunner of all American Cocker Spaniels, is remembered by a small plaque. *Jock of the Bushveld,* a Bull Terrier, has a road in the Transvaal named after him. A Foxhound buried in Euston Park, England, is remembered by:

'Foxes rejoice, here lies buried your foe.'

There is the monument erected by Lord Byron, in memory of *Boatswain*, a Newfoundland. The inscription is lengthy. One part reads:

Near this spot
Are deposited the remains of one
Who possessed beauty without insolence,
Courage without ferocity,
And all the virtues of man without his vices.

The most famous memorial to a dog in America is that to *Old Drum* in Warrensburg, Missouri. Below it is inscribed the following tribute by Senator George Vest.

'Gentlemen of the Jury: The best friend a man has in this world may turn against him and become his enemy. His son or daughter that he has reared with loving care may prove ungrateful. Those who are nearest and dearest to us, those whom we trust with our happiness and our good name, may become traitors to their faith. The money that a man has, he may lose. It flies away from him, perhaps when he needs it the most. A man's reputation may be sacrificed in a moment of ill-considered action. The people who are prone to fall on their knees to do us honor when success is with us may be the first to throw the stone of malice when failure settles its cloud upon our heads. The one absolutely unselfish friend that a man can have in this selfish world, the one that never deserts him and the one that never proves ungrateful or treacherous is his dog.

'Gentlemen of the Jury, a man's dog stands by him in prosperity and in poverty, in health and in sickness. He will sleep on the cold ground, where the wintry winds blow and the snow drives fiercely, if only he may be near his master's side. He will kiss the hand that has no food to offer, he will lick the wounds and sores that come in encounters with the roughness of the world. He guards the sleep of his pauper master as if he were a prince. When all other friends desert he remains. When riches take wings and reputation falls to pieces, he is as constant in his love as the sun in its journey through the heavens. If fortune drives the master forth an outcast in the world, friendless and homeless, the faithful dog asks no higher privilege than that of accompanying him to guard against danger, to fight against his enemies, and when the last scene of all comes, and death takes the master in its embrace and his body is laid away in the cold ground, no matter if all other friends pursue their way, there by his graveside will the noble dog be found, his head between his paws, his eyes sad but open in alert watchfulness, faithful and true even to death.'

Moulting Most Americans say that a dog 'sheds', but that a bird moults. In Britain the word 'shed' is never used. However, despite the different expressions, they are really speaking of the same thing. All living things moult. They shed skin, hair, and feathers.

Dogs normally shed their hair twice a year, in the autumn and in the late spring. It was once thought that changes in the seasons were the keys to the shedding process, as well as to the growth of winter coats.

Today it is believed that weather changes are less important than are changes in the amount of daylight and darkness. As the days grow shorter, the dog begins to grow a longer coat and a thicker undercoat. As spring brings longer days, moulting begins.

It is not known how light can control this process, but there is some evidence that the key to the control is in the eye, rather than in the hair. Dogs which are kept in the house get approximately the same amount of light the year round because we turn on lights as soon as darkness begins to come, so the house dog sheds hair fairly constantly the year round.

Some breeders claim that their dogs never shed, but this is only relatively true. As a rule, such claims are made for breeds which require constant plucking, scissoring, or other grooming to be kept in show condition, or it may be said of breeds with hair so short and fine that moulting is seldom noticed.

Alopecia, or baldness, occurs not as a disease but as a condition arising from ailments in other parts of the body rather than in the skin. Why this should be so is not known. Baldness may follow DISTEMPER and may

Right Monuments and memorials. The most famous dog monument in America, erected as a tribute to Old Drum by Senator George Vest and inspired by the dog's loyalty.

A TRIBUTE TO THE DOG
(BY SENATOR GEORGE GRAHAM VEST)

"GENTLEMEN OF THE JURY: THE BEST FRIEND A MAN HAS IN THIS WORLD MAY TURN AGAINST HIM AND BECOME HIS ENEMY. HIS SON OR DAUGHTER THAT HE HAS REARED WITH LOVING CARE MAY PROVE UNGRATEFUL. THOSE WHO ARE NEAREST AND DEAREST TO US, THOSE WHOM WE TRUST WITH OUR HAPPINESS AND OUR GOOD NAME, MAY BECOME TRAITORS TO THEIR FAITH. THE MONEY THAT A MAN HAS, HE MAY LOSE. IT FLIES AWAY FROM HIM PERHAPS WHEN HE NEEDS IT THE MOST. A MAN'S REPUTATION MAY BE SACRIFICED IN A MOMENT OF ILL-CONSIDERED ACTION. THE PEOPLE WHO ARE PRONE TO FALL ON THEIR KNEES TO DO US HONOR WHEN SUCCESS IS WITH US MAY BE THE FIRST TO THROW THE STONE OF MALICE WHEN FAILURE SETTLES ITS CLOUD UPON OUR HEADS. THE ONE ABSOLUTELY UNSELFISH FRIEND THAT A MAN CAN HAVE IN THIS SELFISH WORLD, THE ONE THAT NEVER DESERTS HIM AND THE ONE THAT NEVER PROVES UNGRATEFUL OR TREACHEROUS IS HIS DOG.

"GENTLEMEN OF THE JURY, A MAN'S DOG STANDS BY HIM IN PROSPERITY AND IN POVERTY, IN HEALTH AND IN SICKNESS. HE WILL SLEEP ON THE COLD GROUND, WHERE THE WINTRY WINDS BLOW AND THE SNOW DRIVES FIERCELY, IF ONLY HE MAY BE NEAR HIS MASTER'S SIDE. HE WILL KISS THE HAND THAT HAS NO FOOD TO OFFER, HE WILL LICK THE WOUNDS AND SORES THAT COME IN ENCOUNTERS WITH THE ROUGHNESS OF THE WORLD. HE GUARDS THE SLEEP OF HIS PAUPER MASTER AS IF HE WERE A PRINCE. WHEN ALL OTHER FRIENDS DESERT HE REMAINS. WHEN RICHES TAKE WINGS AND REPUTATION FALLS TO PIECES, HE IS AS CONSTANT IN HIS LOVE AS THE SUN IN ITS JOURNEY THROUGH THE HEAVENS. IF FORTUNE DRIVES THE MASTER FORTH AN OUTCAST IN THE WORLD, FRIENDLESS AND HOMELESS, THE FAITHFUL DOG ASKS NO HIGHER PRIVILEGE THAN THAT OF ACCOMPANYING HIM TO GUARD AGAINST DANGER, TO FIGHT AGAINST HIS ENEMIES. AND WHEN THE LAST SCENE OF ALL COMES, AND DEATH TAKES THE MASTER IN ITS EMBRACE AND HIS BODY IS LAID AWAY IN THE COLD GROUND, NO MATTER IF ALL OTHER FRIENDS PURSUE THEIR WAY, THERE BY THE GRAVESIDE WILL THE NOBLE DOG BE FOUND, HIS HEAD BETWEEN HIS PAWS, HIS EYES SAD BUT OPEN IN ALERT WATCHFULNESS, FAITHFUL AND TRUE EVEN TO DEATH."

OLD

DRUM

1870

occur in incipient DIABETES. Anomalies of the genital organs in both sexes can cause baldness. Degenerated or cancerous testicles are examples. Hypothyroidism is another cause. Thallium, often used as a rat poison, can cause total baldness if ingested. But, if the dog recovers, the hair slowly grows back.

Alopecia can be congenital, as it is in HAIRLESS DOGS. It is also believed that too extensive inbreeding, particularly in the small breeds, can cause baldness. Examples are Dachshunds and Toy Manchester Terriers which develop bald areas on the forehead, neck, and outside ear surfaces.

The castration of dogs with testicular problems often results in the return of a full coat of hair. Injections of female sex hormones have brought similar results in other dogs.

Mountain Rescue Where mountain accidents are likely, local enthusiasts have in many places, principally in Scandinavia, formed dog rescue teams. In the event of an alarm, volunteers go out and search until the injured or lost traveller is located.

The dogs most used today are GERMAN SHEPHERDS. The training and methods used are almost precisely the same as those employed by the police and army. The dogs use their sense of smell and of hearing to locate injured climbers, and will dig to find travellers buried in the snow.

The ST. BERNARDS, traditionally associated with mountain rescue in the Alps, are used less than they formerly were.

Movement (Locomotion) Unlike the horse, the dog is capable of considerable spinal flexion so that at fast paces and in jumping, the hinder part of the body acts freely as an extension of the hind limbs. Apart from the few examples arising from inherited or acquired defects, control of the nervous system is remarkably efficient in the normal dog. Unfortunately, many dogs are over-fed and under-exercised with the result that movement may become restricted at an unduly early age.

In normal dogs there are four varieties of movement with some intermediate types.
a A leisurely gait with frequent stops for inquiry into immediate surroundings.
b The fast walk or trot.
c The lope or canter.
d The gallop or run.

A balanced gait is one in which there is perfect synchronization between the two halves of the body, irrespective of whether the bisection be longitudinal or transverse.

During the slow walk three feet are usually on the ground at the same time (three-point suspension). During the fast walk only two feet are on the ground simultaneously. The order is then: Left hind and left front – LF and RH – RF and RH – RF and LH. The forefoot of one side lifts before the hind foot

Above Muzzle. A make-shift muzzle – necessary when treating injured dogs which may bite from pain or terror – can be simply made by knotting a necktie above and below the dog's mouth and then at the back of the neck.

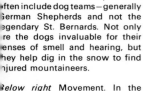

Left Mountain rescue operations often include dog teams – generally German Shepherds and not the legendary St. Bernards. Not only are the dogs invaluable for their senses of smell and hearing, but they help dig in the snow to find injured mountaineers.

Below right Movement. In the gallop, the hindfeet of breeds such as the Greyhound pass forward and land in front of the forefeet.

reaches the ground, so the body rolls towards the side momentarily left unsupported. The front end of the body, being the heavier, drops slightly forward and the head automatically jerks. At the trot the weight falls upon diagonal limbs, the order being LF and RH together, followed by RF and LH together. For a fraction of a second during the trot, all feet are clear of the ground.

In the canter the procedure is firstly all feet on the ground – LH alone – LF and both H – LF and RH – both F and RH – RF. In the gallop in such breeds as the Greyhound, the hind feet pass forward and land in front of the forefeet. This is made possible by extreme lumbar flexion enabling the lower back to act as a second thigh. The gallop is virtually a continuous succession of jumps through the air.

Jumping is operated on rather similar lines with the fore-end of the body lifted upwards. Propulsion via the rapidly extending hock carries the body over the obstacle.

Mumps This disease causes inflammation and enlargement of the parotid gland situated at the base of

the ears, near the angle of the jaw. It is primarily a disease of human beings, but can affect dogs. Antibodies against this disease have been detected in the blood of dogs.

Münchener Dog: another name for the Giant SCHNAUZER.

Mute Said of a hound which runs silently on a trail.

Muzzle, Muzzles Although this term can be applied to the face in front of the eyes, the word 'muzzle' is usually used for an instrument of restraint which is intended to keep a dog from biting, from tearing off bandages covering wounds, from barking, or from being destructive when left alone in the home.

The simplest form of muzzle can be made quickly. Bandage (or a necktie) is wrapped twice about the dog's mouth, is tied above and below the shin, and then behind the ears. This will prevent the dog from biting while it is being treated for wounds. It must not be used to prevent the dog from ripping off bandages covering wounds as this type of restraint can be used only for a short period at a time.

Most ready-made muzzles are made of leather, or are of open wire construction. Their chief purpose is to prevent the dog from biting or fighting. Aggressive dogs recognize that they are helpless, and so do not start a fight. However, it is not wise to allow such a dog to roam. Some of its enemies, or the occasional killer dog, may take advantage of its helplessness.

Certain muzzles, often called 'no-bark' muzzles, are designed to fit more tightly about the mouth. The dog can open its mouth slightly, can breathe fairly freely, and can even pant, but cannot open its mouth wide enough to bark.

This type of muzzle is made of leather, and must be specially made to fit the dog. Such a muzzle should be kept on the dog for long periods of time. Its usefulness comes when the dog is put out for relief, in particular in the early morning and late at night.

Muzzle Band White marking around the muzzle as on a BOSTON TERRIER.

N

Nails Puppies' nails grow at an astonishing rate and should be trimmed when puppies are about ten days old. Thereafter, they should be trimmed about once a week until the puppy is exercising on hard ground when frequent trimming becomes unnecessary.

When the puppy is still in the nest, it is quite easy to avoid cutting into the quick, as it is obvious at this stage and looks pink. The cutting of nails should not be attempted with scissors but the proper nail-clippers.

Dogs with faulty movement may wear their nails away to the quick, particularly those on the front feet and this causes LAMENESS. Lameness is also caused by brittle nails which crack and split. Dogs with such nails should be exercised on soft ground or grass only.

Dogs which do not get enough exercise can grow nails which turn over and get embedded in the pads. This causes a tremendous amount of pain to the dog and is usually accompanied by swelling and suppuration. Such nails must be cut right back to the quick (without making it bleed) and if there is any festering a poultice should be applied for a day or two and the foot kept in a padded bag until quite healed.

Neonatal Deaths see Fading Puppies.

Neoplasm see Tumours.

Nephritis see Kidney Diseases.

New Breeds It is estimated that there are 850 different breeds of dogs in the world but some of them are very obscure. Only 116 are recognized by the American Kennel Club and only 147 are listed in the Kennel Club (England) Regulations. Almost sixty of these latter are British native breeds and most have been registered for over a century. Occasionally a new breed is added to the list and its origins are usually authenticated by the Kennel Club of the country of origin.

It has been said that an invented breed has as little chance of being recognized by the Kennel Clubs as the proverbial camel has of passing through the eye of a needle. Occasionally a new breed is 'invented' but the inventor has little hope of seeing the breed stabilized and breeding true in his lifetime, and it is because of this that Kennel Clubs will not accept manufactured breeds. All the breeds recognized by the Kennel Club (England) were produced over a long period by breeding hundreds of generations and culling.

Newfoundland There are many theories as to the origin of the massive Newfoundland dog – one credits Lief Ericson with having brought a black 'bear dog' named *Oolum* to Newfoundland about the year A.D. 1000. Unless similar black dogs were brought also, Oolum would have had to mate with a large number of native dogs to establish a black race.

J. S. Skinner, an excellent American canine authority for his time, wrote in *The Dog and the Sportsman*, published in 1824, that Biscay fishermen brought PYRENEAN MOUNTAIN DOGS (Great Pyrenees) to Newfoundland in 1662 to protect their homes.

William Hickey, the English diarist, wrote that, about 1774, he went sailing with a Mr. Cane and his 'immense Newfoundland dog, *Tyger*'. Hickey gives no details of the dog. He later mentioned a sailing accident in which all were saved except a Newfoundland dog. It cannot be known whether these examples were true Newfoundlands.

James Watson, the greatest American dog authority of the 1900 period and earlier, described the Newfoundland as: 'A modern English development from a mixed lot of common dogs of various colours, coats, and sizes.'

Newfoundland.
Below A life-size sculpture of a Newfoundland in bronze and marble, made in 1831 by Matthew Cotes Wyatt. The black-and-white colouring marks this dog as a 'Landseer' Newfoundland, so named after a famous painting by Sir Edwin Landseer. Such dogs – an example is shown at bottom – are rare.

Final development and standardization of the breed did not come until dog shows began, and this standardization took place in England in the nineteenth century. Six Newfoundlands were shown at Birmingham in 1860. Kennel Club registrations began in 1878, and the Newfoundland breed club was established in 1886.

The prowess of the dogs in the water led to water trials being held in England at Maidstone and Portsmouth in 1876. Meanwhile, in the Canadian Arctic, some explorers were using Newfoundlands – and ST. BERNARDS – to haul their sledges. Newfoundlands were also used to re-establish the size and strength of the St. Bernard after disastrous epidemics had nearly wiped out the kennels at the great St. Bernard Hospice.

In 1922 G. Bland bred a dog called *Siki*. Siki was used as a stud dog in England and became a great sire.

Below Newfoundland. Ch. Pied n Crime of Esmeduna.

His sons and daughters were an even greater success in the United States and Canada. An early American breeder of this period was Miss Ada F. Coombes of Little Solon, New Jersey, and R. A. Gillespie of Abbotsford, Quebec, holds a similar position in Canadian Newfoundland history. Finally, the Hon. Harold Macpherson, developed the powerful and long enduring Westerland Kennel in Newfoundland itself.

Essentials of the breed: The head is massive, has a distinct stop, and is free of wrinkles. The muzzle is square and deep, and its length is less than the distance from stop to occiput. The eyes are small and brown. The small triangular ears lie close to the head.

The body length from withers to croup equals height, though bitches may be slightly longer than tall. The stifles are well bent. The large, cat-like feet are fully webbed from the centre pad to the base of each toe pad. Incomplete webbing disqualifies. The tail is broad, well furred, and reaches to below the hocks.

The coat is double, with the outer being water resistant, moderately long, but straight and flat. The colour is a dull black, but there may be a tinge of bronze or white on the toes or chest. Any other solid colour is permitted, though only black and bronze are encouraged. 'Landseer' Newfoundlands are white and black. Their name comes from Sir Edwin Landseer's famous painting: 'A Distinguished Member of the Royal Humane Society'. In this variety the head is black with a narrow white blaze, and an evenly marked saddle. Marking other than white on a black dog (the tinge of bronze excluded) disqualifies.

Male Newfoundlands average 28 inches at the shoulder and weigh about 150 pounds. Bitches are slightly smaller.
See colour plate p. 290.

Night Blindess see Hereditary Abnormalities.

Noisy Dogs As a rule, terriers are noisier than many other breeds. They are highly strung, enjoy romping and playing of which noise-making is a part, and enjoy insulting each other by barking through kennel fences. But there are highly nervous dogs in all breeds. Dogs often become noisy out of boredom. Noise-making, unless checked, may develop into a type of HYSTERIA.

Some suggestions have been made for keeping dogs quiet under KENNELS and MUZZLES; some other suggestions follow. A common complaint is that the dog jumps on chairs, looks out the windows, and barks at every passerby, man or beast. Such dogs often bark at persons who come to the door. They refuse to be quiet, and often must be shut in a room before guests can enter the home. Such barking may lead to biting.

When the dog begins its furious barking, it should be ordered to stop. At the same time, something should be thrown at the dog, and at least the first time, should be aimed to hit the body. The dog does not understand the extension of the arm which the thrown object represents. It is startled and becomes quiet, often retreating quickly; in this way the barking habit may be broken.

Above Newfoundland. Ch Edenglen's Falstaff. The adult Newfoundland can easily weigh 150 lb.

The problem of the barking dog outside is harder to solve. Some of the better-known remedies are often only partially successful. These include throwing tin cans at the dog – if it is close enough to be reached – and spraying it with water from a hose, but often, as soon as the owner returns indoors, the barking starts again.

If a wall is built around the outside of the kennel runs, the dogs cannot see out, and are less inclined to bark. In building his kennel, one man anticipated the problem, and prevented it in this manner. All the fence posts were of irrigation pipe. This pipe was connected to a water line. Each time the dogs barked, the water was turned on from inside the home, and the dogs got sprayed from all sides. This drove them into their kennels. After a few lessons, only a severe disturbance could excite them to become noisy.

Dog owners are often insensitive to the barking of their own dogs. Neighbours, however, may complain that the dogs bark more than they actually do. The kennel owner should be on the alert to stop barking when it starts.

Non-Slip Retriever One that stays at heel, marks the fall of game, and retrieves to command.

Non-Sporting Division This somewhat curious nomenclature for a major division of the recognized breeds of dogs has a historical background.

The Kennel Club was formed in England in 1873 and by the time it had organized its stud books, it found that it was acknowledging the existence of approximately forty different breeds. It was also realized that this number would soon have to be increased because some of these so-called breeds were in fact whole groups of breeds, such as 'Sheepdogs and Scotch Collies' and 'Broken-haired Scotch and Yorkshire Terriers'. Clearly more precise splits, increasing the total number of groups, were necessary.

With an immediate increase of another twenty or so breeds, the register became unwieldy.

The simple remedy was to split the total into two self-contained sections. This could have been done alphabetically, A–M, N–Z. However, it was decided to separate the sporting breeds from the others. This was a natural decision to make in a Victorian England passionately interested in the gentlemanly country pastimes. They grouped together the Greyhounds, Beagles and Harriers, all devoted to the pursuit of hares. With them they put all the dogs which helped the shooting men, such as setters, spaniels and retrievers. And then, for good measure, the dogs which helped Master of Hounds, that is principally Staghounds and Foxhounds but also those essential terriers which went underground when the hunt was up, such as Fox Terriers.

The name for this division clearly had to be the Sporting Division. This made it equally easy to name the remainder. They became the Non-Sporting Division, and nobody cared that the negative carried slightly derogatory overtones.

Inevitably a time came when further subdivisions became necessary. The Sporting Division was easy to subdivide. See SPORTING DIVISION. The toy breeds were separated as a 'Toy Group'. The remainder were kept banded together and retained their previous title, only modified slightly to the Non-Sporting *Group*.

The American Kennel Club originally followed both this grouping and nomenclature. However, it later made a very sensible further sub-division of the Non-Sporting Group and separated the traditional working breeds into a Working Group.

The rather mixed bag that remained, including Poodles, Dalmatians, and Chow Chows, retains the group name of Non-Sporting. When the Kennel Club of England decided that it also must put the working dogs into a separate group, the Non-Sporting Group title was finally abolished in England. Instead it became known as the Utility Group.

Norfolk Terrier CRUFT's Dog Show on 5 February 1965 was a red-letter day in the history of Norfolk Terriers. It was the day they made their bow to the public. Yet the Norfolk is not in the strict sense of the word a new breed.

As described under the heading NORWICH TERRIER, as long ago as 1880 there was a type of terrier in East Anglia which was fairly standardized and easily recognizable. Usually red, red wheaten, or black and tan, it was clearly a working terrier and since those days has been used by many packs of hounds both in England and in the United States.

Little is known of the precise background of the breed. It is, however, a reasonable assumption that some of the short-legged terriers were used – the CAIRN springs to mind – and possibly mixed with these was the blood of BORDER TERRIERS and much more probably IRISH TERRIERS. By the nineteen-thirties, they were standardized. In 1932 they were recognized by the English Kennel Club.

As with a number of other breeds, it was decided that ears could be either pricked (like a Cairn's) or dropped (like a Border's). Throughout the first thirty-three years of the breed's official existence, these two varieties existed side by side, were mated together and competed with each other in the same classes.

However, during this time they did not follow the

Right Norfolk Terrier. Ch. Timberfalling Red Spruce. An adult Norfolk Terrier usually weighs about 10 lb.

usual pattern whereby one variety dominates the other and drives it out. Perhaps even more unusual, the two types, far from merging, diverged on certain important characteristics until pressure in Britain began to mount within the breed for an official division into two varieties.

The Kennel Club therefore decided that as from January 1965 the prick-eared type should continue with their original name of Norwich Terrier, while the drop-eared type should henceforward be known as the Norfolk Terrier.

The 'new' breed then was already known; already established. A small, low dog, compact and robust, a good-natured animal and yet bred for work and still capable of doing it.

Its coat is harsh and wiry and it is not the custom to 'barber' or present them in over-trim fashion. They are 'natural' little dogs and breeders feel very strongly that they should be kept natural as distinct from artificial in appearance. Most certainly this unwritten rule has the merit both of preserving the weather-proof properties of their coat and of cutting down the work or expense for those who like a broken-coated terrier but dislike the regular trimming which is a feature of some other members of the terrier tribe.

Before the 'split' an average of 400 of the combined types were registered annually with the English Kennel Club. In the first five years after the split 1,389 of the 'new' Norfolks were registered (annual average 278) and 1,028 of the 'old' Norwich (annual average 206).

In this modern world the Norfolk has a lot of advantages. It is small, adaptable in its habits, at home in town or country, full of fun and never pugnacious. These qualities may well be sufficient to lift it further in popularity.

Essentials of the breed: Muzzle: 'foxy' and strong, length about one-third less than the wide and slightly rounded skull. Stop: pronounced. Eyes: dark, bright and keen. Ears: neatly dropped, carried close to cheeks

Below Norwegian Elkhound. Ch. Dauna of Eskamere.

and rounded at tips. Jaws: clean and strong. Teeth: strong with scissors bite. Neck: of medium length and strong. Shoulders: well laid back with short, powerful, straight legs. Body: short and compact, with well sprung ribs. Hindquarters: sound, well muscled, with good powers of propulsion. Feet: round with thick pads. Tail: medium docked. Coat: hard, wiry, straight and close; longer and rougher on the neck and shoulders forming almost a mane. Hair on the head, ears and muzzle should be short and smooth. Colour: all shades of red, wheaten, black and tan or grizzle. White marks undesirable but not disqualifying. Height: 10 inches at withers.

See colour plate p. 378.

Norwegian Elkhound To look at an Elkhound is to know that it is a working dog. It is also to know that it was a dog that worked originally within the Arctic Circle.

In outline, coat and in detailed construction it is a typical SPITZ breed. The sharp, erect ears, the comparatively straight hocks, the ruff round the neck and the tail curled over the back are all unmistakable signs of origin. In fact, its name tells quite clearly its task and therefore its home. It was, indeed still is, used to hunt the elk in Scandinavia in general and in Norway in particular.

The elk, a large, ungainly animal can be a formidable foe if cornered. Elkhounds are therefore trained carefully by sportsmen, first to locate their quarry and then bark quietly to alert the owner without alarming the elk. The next task of the dog is to circle the elk, thereby checking its natural inclination to run straight away from the approaching man. Finally the dog moves in, circling and barking to distract and enrage the elk who makes sweeping attacks on its tormentor. This enables the hunter to approach within shooting range.

In order to do its job properly the Elkhound must be hard, strong, active, forceful and imaginative. More surprising but even more marked is its extreme docility and devotion to man. Few dogs are more faithful; few more determined to share the family life.

The breed was first shown in Norway in 1879. Recognition by both the Norwegian and Swedish Kennel Clubs followed almost immediately. Exported from Sweden to Britain before the First World War, they had to wait until the formation of the British Elkhound Society in 1923 before making much impact on the general public. Concurrently they became known in the United States and were officially recognized by the American Kennel Club in 1935. While in Britain and most Commonwealth and European countries they are known simply as Elkhounds, in the Americas they are called Norwegian Elkhounds.

An authority on the breed once declared: 'An Elkhound which has not an outline has nothing'. There is much truth in this. The silhouette is all important. Regrettably a large number of the pet and even show dogs owned outside Scandinavia are somewhat over-fed which makes them lose their virile appearance. A rolling stomach does not suit either the appearance or the character of the breed. Kept in hard condition, when they hold themselves together, they look the Nordic warriors they are. Over-fed, they age prematurely and through over-concentration on their stomachs lose their sharp interest in life.

They are not of course the only breed to which this applies, but to a real Elkhound lover however, the results of overfeeding the breed are particularly depressing.

Somewhat surprisingly, in view of their background and coat, these dogs appear to thrive in tropical countries. With its long protective hair, the dog looks its best against a background of snow and forests. But then it is a Viking, and it looks it.

Essentials of the breed: In general appearance the Elkhound has a compact, short body, thick coat, prick ears and tail curled tightly over its back. The head is broad between the ears, muzzle broad at base, tapering gradually but not pointed. Stop is not large but clearly defined. Eyes brown, as dark as possible. Ears are set high, upstanding, pointed and with their height slightly greater than their width at base. Neck is of medium length, firm and muscular. Forelegs: firm and straight. Body is short-coupled with wide, straight back. Chest: wide and deep. The loins: muscular and stomach only slightly drawn up. Compact oval feet. Coat must be thick, abundant, coarse and weather resisting. It should be short on head and front of leg, longest on chest, neck, buttocks and underside of tail. Colour must be grey of various shades with black tips to long outer coat and lighter on chest, stomach, legs and underside of tail. Weight approximately 43 to 50 lb. with shoulder height 18 to 20½ inches.

See colour plate p. 191.

Norwegian Kennel Club see Kennel Club, Scandinavian Kennel Union.

Norwich Terrier In the United States the term Norwich Terrier covers both the drop-eared and prick-eared varieties, both of which compete against each other in the same classes. This was also the position in Great Britain until 1965 when the two varieties were split and given separate breed registers. This article deals with the prick-eared variety. The background, history and standards of the drop-eared dogs will be found under NORFOLK TERRIER.

Without documentary evidence of its background, we are left to guess what breeds and proportions produced the canine cocktail called the Norwich.

In 1870 a gentleman known locally as 'Doggy Lawrence' made a modest living selling small red terriers to Cambridge (England) undergraduates. They were probably small IRISH TERRIERS.

Amongst other people who acquired some dogs from him was a Mr. Fred Law, of Norfolk. He sent some to Mr. Jack Cooke, a celebrated Master of Staghounds, who in turn employed a man nicknamed 'Roughrider' Jones. When Jones later left Mr. Cooke's employ he took with him a few of the red terriers.

Rumour insists that he had already crossed them with BEDLINGTONS and with STAFFORDSHIRE BULL

TERRIERS. Later he is said to have used 'any hard-working terrier'. Oddly enough there is no mention at all of any crossing with CAIRNS or SCOTTISH TERRIERS, which must have been employed. The red dogs had, at this time, no official name, and were sometimes known locally as 'Trumpington Terriers'. In certain parts of England and in America they became Jones Terriers – 'Roughrider' had left his mark. In view of their early connection with Cambridge University, there was even a suggestion that 'Cantab Terrier' would be suitable. While used principally as working terriers, there was always a ready sale for these compact little dogs as pets. They were of very mixed type until a Mrs. Fagan took an interest in them in 1914, and bred them extensively. It is recorded that her stock was directly descended from dogs owned by Mr. Jones. By 1932 they appeared regularly at shows and were granted official recognition and a separate register in that year. Four years later they received the same recognition in the United States, having achieved modest popularity there.

Then came the split in types mentioned earlier. Until 1965 ears were permitted to be either erect or dropped. The difference sounds small. Breeders thought otherwise.

In truth, for no known reason the prick-eared and the drop-eared varieties had developed on significantly different lines. No longer was it simply a matter of dogs having ears of different shapes. The truth is, that the ears had *dogs* of different shapes!

In 1965, the Kennel Club agreed. The prick-eared retained their name of Norwich Terriers. The drop-eared variety became Norfolk Terriers. Thus a breed which had only officially existed for 30 years managed to split off another officially recognized breed. There is no parallel in the world of dogs, and lovers of the breed insist that the Norwich is without parallel in other respects.

Essentials of the breed: Muzzle: 'foxy' and strong; length about one-third less than the wide and slightly rounded skull. Stop: pronounced. Eyes: dark, bright and keen. Ears: erect. Jaws: clean and strong. Teeth: strong with scissors bite. Neck: of medium length and strong. Shoulders: well laid back with short powerful, straight legs. Body: short and compact, with well sprung ribs. Hindquarters: sound, well muscled, with good powers of propulsion. Feet: round with thick pads. Tail: medium docked. Coat: hard, wiry, straight and close, longer and rougher on the neck and shoulders forming almost a mane. Hair on the head, ears and

Above Norwich Terriers have prick ears, unlike the Norfolk Terrier. In the United States, the two still compete against each other in the same classes, but in Britain since 1965 the two breeds have separate registers. Ch. Jericho Gay Rascal.

Above Norwich Terrier., Ch. Jericho Gay Rascal, *left* with Ch. Jericho Whinlatter Hemp and Ch. Jericho Gingernut as a puppy (see colour plate on p. 378).

muzzle should be short and smooth. Colour: all shades of red, wheaten, black and tan or grizzle. White marks undesirable but not disqualifying. Height: 10 inches at withers.

See colour plate p. 378.

Nose (Scent) The term is used as an indication of ability in scenting: 'great nose', 'poor nose', 'no nose'. All canines use their noses for their everyday business much as a man uses his eyes. The ability to scent a quarry is much more pronounced in hounds.

The nose of a hound is really quite outstanding when one takes into account the scent memory necessary to ensure success. Apart from knowing which way the quarry is moving, it has to distinguish one particular scent from the various other smells that will cross the path. It may even be asked to hold a line along a road which has been fouled by petrol fumes, other animals, and human beings. It must stick faithfully to its line and not be induced in any way from it even when another of the same species that it is hunting crosses over it.

'Scent' consists of tiny particles of matter which are left by every living creature at all times of the day and night. It is unpredictable and can vary according to mood. It is believed that hounds can distinguish a

change in their quarry such as extreme fear, anger or even exhaustion. Variations of scent appear in individual hares or rabbits or whatever the quarry. Human beings have individual scents varying not only in aroma but also in intensity.

Atmospheric conditions can play havoc with scent. A breeze on a dry day will very quickly evaporate the particles of liquid which carry scent. A strong wind will dispel the line and carry the scent off. Scent is likely to be good when the air is colder than the ground. It is usually better on grass than on ploughed land. It is better on clay than on a sandy soil because clay retains the moisture longer.

Nova Scotia Duck Tolling Dog see Rare Breeds.

Nursing Bitch The nursing mother must be properly cared for and at all times protected from any undue disturbances. She must be kept warm and comfortable as heat is of great importance to her and her whelps. Many whelps die in the early stages because of the lack of it. The temperature should not fall below 70°F or 21°C for the first week. Thereafter it can be eased down very gently.

The nursing mother should be examined every day

for any sore spots, abrasions or swellings. See TEATS. Her diet is important. Four meals a day are generally advised with a good allowance of milk and meat. The addition of cod-liver oil and calcium is essential. Calcium helps produce good bone and prevents rickets and helps offset a very dangerous condition known as eclampsia. A strong BROOD BITCH in most breeds will rear five or six puppies without much trouble. This is a reasonable number. If she is left with nine or ten whelps it is advisable to help her by supplementary bottle feeding of the puppies. A toy bitch should not be expected to rear more than four healthy puppies without help. If large litters are reared several of the puppies may suffer if they do not get supplementary food and they will grow up to be weaklings, and the bitch herself will suffer.

Eclampsia can occur in the nursing mother at any time while she is nursing her litter but is more likely to happen during or just after WHELPING and in the later stage of nursing. This condition is caused by a lack of calcium in her bloodstream. Her own supply of calcium is passed, through her milk, to her puppies. A heavy demand is made at this time upon her own bodily resources. It is essential to replenish the calcium by giving her a supply in her own food.

The symptoms of eclampsia are excitability, weakness and difficulty in standing up. The bitch may even have convulsions when she will lie on her side and foam at the mouth. She has a far-away look in her eyes and rapidly loses interest in everything including her puppies. Help should be summoned immediately and

a large dose of calcium injected subcutaneously, or she will die quickly. The cure is certain if the nursing mother is caught in time but speed is essential.

See also: FEEDING PUPPIES; FOSTER MOTHER; MILK, BITCH'S.

Nursing Sick Dogs Gentle handling of sick dogs plus patience and devotion is essential. Good nurses are often born and not made. The natural instinct of a sick animal is to retreat to a hideout where it can let nature take its course. It wants little fuss and prefers to be left in peace. A kind word now and again, and a gentle pat will keep the animal as happy as possible, and reassure it.

Cleanliness and heat are important and the ADMINISTRATION OF MEDICINE or treatment must be carried out at regular intervals as instructed by the veterinarian. The canine nurse should be able to take a dog's temperature correctly. She should have experience in BANDAGING wounds. The nurse must observe any change in the patient's condition and be able to give a full yet concise progress report to the veterinarian.

The feeding of sick animals is always a great problem: they can feel so ill and depressed that food has no appeal. In the early stages of illness this does not matter much because they can rely on their own reserves stored in the body but this cannot go on for long. The strength of a sick animal must be maintained and often it will drink when it will not eat. Glucose and water or honey and water will help keep the invalid going until it can take something more substantial. It needs to be

Left Nursing bitch. Most bitches can feed five or six puppies without trouble but a bitch with a large litter should be helped by supplementary bottle feeding. A S Bernard, Fernebrandon Belinda of Pebblestreet, with pups.

tempted at this crucial stage and here considerate nursing can play an important part in the recovery.

On the other hand, the dog may be suffering from kidney trouble or some form of gastric condition when all it wants is to drink, but in this case all but a few drops of water must be denied. No matter how much it pleads with its eyes, withholding liquids will prevent the dog from upsetting itself further.

The nursing of infectious diseases such as HARD PAD or DISTEMPER requires those in charge of the patient to take stringent precautions to ensure that the infection has no opportunity to spread. Sick dogs should always be isolated if possible.

Nutrition The food requirements of the dog are water, proteins, fats, carbohydrates, vitamins, and minerals. Balancing these elements is the job of the canine nutritionist. According to his success, the dog grows normally, has a sound body, has the energy to perform work, and has the ability to reproduce successfully.

Water accounts for about 70 per cent of the dog's body weight. It is obtained by drinking; by the digestive process of oxydizing hydrogen; and from food. It is lost in urine and in feces, and by evaporation from panting, from the lungs, and to a lesser degree from the skin and foot pads.

Adult dogs and dogs of larger breeds can store more water than puppies and dogs of smaller breeds. Maintenance of a proper body level of water is always a delicate and critical process, but if water is always available the dog can manage without human help. This may not be so during illness; diarrhoea and vomiting can seriously upset the water balance; in KIDNEY DISEASES, the dog may drink four to five times its normal needs in an effort to restore the water equilibrium.

Proteins are high in meat and fish, low in cereals, and indigestible in most vegetables. Meat, soy beans and yeast are particularly valuable sources of protein because of their amino acid content. Milk and eggs contain valuable proteins, but should not be given in excess. Some nutritionists believe that, since the dog has evolved as a flesh eater, it will gain more benefit from meat than from other sources, yet dogs have been fed experimentally upon meatless diets with apparent success. In general, nutritionists attempt to balance a dog food with complementary proteins: for example, rice, bran and corn, tankage and corn, lactalbumin and corn, beef and wheat flour, or oatmeal and rice. Today one may find commercial dog foods which have been directly supplemented with amino acids, such as lysine and methionine. In addition, food supplements are marketed which contain these, and other, amino acids.

Fats are sources of energy and are required for normal cell health. The layers of fat under the skin serve as insulation against both heat and cold and act as a fat store. Some acids are utilized directly by the body, and particularly by the skin. Many amino acids are now used in food supplements designed to cure, or to aid in curing, skin ailments.

Carbohydrates contain starch and sugars. The dog does not have cellulose-splitting bacteria in its body, so that cellulose is usually considered indigestible, but it may be given as intestinal roughage. Thus, a dog food that could be digested totally, is not ideal for the dog.

Starch must be changed into sugar by the body, after which it is used to produce energy, and man helps the process by cooking the starch. The dog can then digest it more easily.

Minerals which are known to be required by the dog are: calcium, phosphorus, iron, zinc, copper, cobalt, potassium, iodine, sodium chloride, magnesium, and probably fluorine, and manganese. Most would be supplied sufficiently in any normal diet, but many dog foods are directly supplemented with them.

Calcium and phosphorus must be provided in a precise ratio, along with Vitamin D, or harm is done to the dog. Nutritionists, therefore, warn that there is grave danger in using vitamin and mineral supplements if added to dog foods which have been carefully balanced by competent manufacturers.

Vitamins are essential to the health of the body. They help in the absorption of minerals, and aid in fat utilization, while others are necessary in protein metabolism; all of them help to build resistance to disease; and some aid in bringing a cure of disease or help to keep the disease under control. Vitamins can be divided into those which are fat soluble – A, D, E, and K – and those which are water soluble – the B-complex, and C (ascorbic acid). The important B-complex of vitamins consists of thiamin, riboflavin, niacin, panthothenic acid, biotin, folic acid, choline, inositol, and B-6 and B-12. Vitamin C is normally not considered necessary for the dog since it is able to synthesize all it needs on a daily basis. But there is evidence that some sick dogs may need a vitamin C supplement.

There are a number of substances which are called 'anti-vitamins'. Raw egg white, for example, contains avidin which binds itself to biotin so that biotin cannot be utilized by the body. Avidin is destroyed if the egg is hard-boiled for five minutes or more. A thermolabile enzyme (one destroyed by heat) is found in raw fish and certain raw meats. Dogs fed continuously on raw fish, and to some extent on raw meats, could suffer a vitamin deficiency which causes paralysis. This would not arise if some of the food were cooked.

Estimates for the caloric needs of dogs have been worked out on a 'per pound of dog per day' basis. They are for average dogs. Those under stress, highly nervous dogs, and growing puppies need more. The latter will require about double the number for a mature dog of the same weight.

An adult five-pound dog will need 50 calories per lb., or 250 per day, while a five-pound puppy will need 100 per lb. or 500. Caloric needs, however, go down as body weight goes up. Thus, it is calculated that a 10 lb. dog needs only 42 calories per lb., a 15 lb. dog, only 35. A 30 lb. dog needs only 32 per lb. And a 50 lb. dog needs only 31 per lb. or 1,550 per day. However, these requirements are theoretical and each dog must be fed to its own requirements.

See DIGESTION, FEEDING.

Obedience Trials Obedience trials and training were a major development in the sport of purebred dogs after World War I. They are a result of several circumstances. Dog owners were impressed by the major contribution made by dogs during the war. Many owners became aware, for the first time, of the potentials of their dogs. Also, breeders and exhibitors of show dogs were under compulsion to prove that their dogs were intelligent as well as beautiful.

Obedience training, practised over most of the world, is not new. Much of it is the basic training given to field dogs, called 'yard breaking', by field trainers. This training is required especially for all pointing breeds, the spaniels, and the retrievers. Earlier, before 1914, when Europeans began to train dogs for police work, it became basic training for these dogs also.

During the First World War, the French alone were said to have had 10,000 dogs on the battle front, and another 8,000 sledge dogs in the Vosges Mountains. The Germans, who had pioneered early police training, had as many as 20,000 dogs on the battle front. Many of these dogs were simply police dogs re-trained for war purposes.

The work of these dogs fascinated English dog breeders, as did the talent of motion picture dog stars, such as *Strongheart* and *Rin Tin Tin*. The concept of obedience trials for purebred dogs of all breeds, to be held in conjunction with dog shows, then developed.

Competent trainers were available, not only to teach the dogs, but to work out the exercises. Following the war, war dog trainers trained dogs for police work and as guide dogs for the blind. Many of the early obedience trainers came from their ranks. Others studied under the war dog and guide dog trainers, then set up training schools of their own.

By the late 1920s, obedience trials were well established in Great Britain. In the meantime, many German trainers had emigrated to the United States. They set up training schools, taught some dogs to lead the blind, trained dogs in simple obedience, and a few dogs for guard or other police work. A group, made up chiefly of Dobermann Pinscher fanciers and trainers, organized the American Amateur Training Club in Chicago. Eventually, it franchised a regional club in Cleveland, Ohio.

A Poodle breeder, Mrs. Whitehouse Walker, visited England in the early 1930s, and witnessed obedience trials. She was particularly impressed by the work of the Piperscroft Poodles. She returned to America determined to have her dogs trained, and to have the sport licensed by the American Kennel Club. This was accomplished in 1934. The former German trainers were available to train dogs and trainers, and the American Amateur Training Club gave way to the training of all breeds, and to competition at the shows.

Today in England, there are approximately thirty-five obedience championship shows annually. Only ten of these are held with CONFORMATION championship dog shows. Conformation entries are so large that sufficient room for obedience trials cannot be found. Consequently, the other twenty-five are held separately. In addition, more than 400 trials are held annually, principally in the summer, at which dogs cannot qualify for titles. The trials are held simply for enjoyment and for the improvement of breeds. The title of Obedience Champion, usually abbreviated to Ob. Ch., is given to a dog which wins three certificates under three different judges.

There are also nineteen championship working trials at which other titles can be won. These include Police Dog (P.D.); Tracking Dog (T.D.); Working Dog (W.D.); Utility Dog (U.D.); and Companion Dog (C.D.). Dogs must score 70 per cent or more. If their scores are all above 80 per cent, the title Excellent (Ex.) is added. At the working dog trials, two certificates entitle the dog to the title Working Dog Champion.

Obedience trials in England are not limited to purebred and registered dogs. Cross-bred dogs, and purebreds among the miscellaneous breeds which cannot be registered for conformation, can be registered for obedience only. Border Collies, which belong in the latter class, have a remarkable record in this respect. The American Kennel Club does not permit crossbreds to compete in obedience, but dogs from the miscellaneous breeds can enter, and win titles.

In the United States, there were 678 licensed, or championship trials, held under American Kennel Club rules during 1969. Of these, 386 were given by show clubs in connection with their conformation classes. There were 54 tracking tests. These must be held separately, and are conducted in field areas. Sanctioned obedience trials – those which cannot qualify for titles – totalled 721. There were 52,237 entries in licensed trials competition, and 420 in the tracking tests.

American classes are advanced as follows: the Novice Classes, A and B, are for beginners. Such dogs can win a Companion Dog title by scoring 170 points or more out of a possible 200, at three trials under different judges. No dog can qualify if it fails to score at least 50 per cent of the points available for any exercise. The exercises are: heel on leash, stand for examination, heel free (off the leash), recall (come when called from the opposite end of the ring), sit for one minute with handlers away from their dogs, and lie down for three minutes. A handler or owner whose dog has won a C.D. title cannot, thereafter, enter any other dog in Novice A, but must compete in Novice B with a new dog which he has trained.

Open A and Open B are for advanced dogs which have won the C.D. title. They must score 170 points or more out of a possible 200 under three different judges. They must also score more than 50 per cent on any given exercises to qualify. In Novice and Open Classes, at least six dogs must compete in each. However, for this purpose, the competing dogs in the A and B classes may be added together. The exercises are: heel free, drop at command during the recall, retrieve on the flat, retrieve over a high jump, and long sit, and long down. The long sit is three minutes and the long down, five, with the handlers out of the ring and out of sight. The title won by successful competitors is Companion Dog Excellent (C.D.X.).

The Utility Class leads to the title Utility Dog (U.D.). The exercises are: scent discrimination, directed retrieve, signal exercise, directed jumping, and group examination. Scent discrimination consists in finding by scent alone, an article of leather, and one of metal, which have been handled by the owner. The article to be found and retrieved must be one of five which are identical, except that the handler has handled one of them. Directed jumping requires the dog to go away from the handler upon command, to stop and sit where told, then to jump. In directed retrieving, the dog must retrieve one of three identical gloves placed in different corners of the ring. The judge decides which glove is to be retrieved, and the handler must direct his dog to that glove, which must be retrieved without undue mouthing or playing with it. The signal exercise is done by using hand signals instead of voice command.

The tracking test is at least 440 yards long, but not more than 500. The track must be not less than one half hour old, nor older than two hours. The track is staked out by flags a day or two before the trial. The track layer follows the course of the flags. The start is indicated by two flags, and, 30 yards out, another indicates the direction of the course. As the track layer makes the trail, he collects all the flags, except one of the two at the start and the flag 30 yards out. He leaves a glove at the end of the trail. The dog is kept on leash, about 20 feet long, and the handler follows the dog at that distance.

Obedience trials are world wide. Most of the countries which hold dog shows also hold obedience trials. The rules differ in each country. Some, for example, do not have any equivalent to the Police Dog, and Working Dog titles given in England. But the rules are sufficiently similar in each country so the competitors understand each other. Thus, it is not unusual for a dog to hold titles in three or more countries. Licensed obedience judges in one country may also be licensed to judge in several of the others. Canada, despite its vast size, had 165 obedience trials and six tracking tests during 1969. Canada gives two tracking titles – T.D. and T.D.X.

American obedience training clubs organized Dogs for Defense at the start of World War II. They not only recruited the dogs, but in some instances gave them basic training before sending them to the services. Many obedience trainers were taken into the Armed Forces to aid in training the dogs for war. Since World War II, the use of dogs for police work has gradually increased in the United States. Some members of obedience

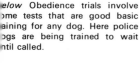

Below Obedience trials involve some tests that are good basic training for any dog. Here police dogs are being trained to wait until called.

training classes, or the class trainers, have joined police forces as trainers.

Obedience training is not limited to the training of pure-bred dogs whose goal is to compete at trials. Many clubs, as a public service, train mongrels to become better canine citizens. They teach the owners how to train their dogs. As a rule, one lesson is taught each week. The dogs 'go to college' for periods of ten to twelve weeks.

Obesity Dogs get overweight for a number of reasons. One might be a glandular problem. Another might be psychological, caused in puppyhood, perhaps even before birth. For example, the runt of a litter gets a poor start in life even before birth, and after birth, must fight its larger and stronger litter mates for food. This aggressiveness makes it bolt all the food available whether it needs it or not.

Bodily changes can cause the castrated male to tend to overweight, but it is not true that spaying the bitch will cause her to grow fat and sluggish. If she grows fat after having been spayed, it is for other reasons.

The major cause of obesity is the pampering of the dog. Its owners may give it regular meals of dog food. But then they give it between-meal snacks of cookies and cakes. They cause the dog to develop a taste for sugar. They make matters worse by giving the dog snacks of meat, and particularly fats, direct from the table.

In obesity, fat globules tend to replace muscles. A condition known as 'fatty heart' sometimes develops. The fat globules invade the spaces between the muscle fibres, and they line the pericardium (the membrane enveloping the heart). Fat also collects about the abdominal walls and the kidneys. In all these cases, the fat interferes with the normal functioning of the body.

That dogs should get extremely fat is usually due to boredom when a dog eats because it has nothing else to do. It has been demonstrated by many researchers that under ideal conditions dogs tend to eat only to their exact caloric needs. They will eat only as much food as their bodies need for growth and normal maintenance.

Because of this, a very simple way has been discovered to reduce the dog to normal weight without injuring its health. A pan of well balanced dry dog food is kept continually filled. The dog can eat as much as it wants as often as it desires to do so, but must not be allowed to become bored.

It is well known that the 'piecer' or the 'nibbler' never has much appetite. So, since the food is always before it, the dog never has any real hunger. The greedy dog, who has tended to bolt more food than it needs, may continue for a few days. But it gradually learns that it no longer needs to do so. There is always plenty of food for it. Such a dog gradually learns to eat only as much as it needs. The balanced food provides all necessary nutrients. Snacks and table scraps have been eliminated. Over a long period of time, the dog reduces to normal weight. Hard-baked dog biscuits should not be used in this programme.

Implicit in any method of reducing a dog's weight, as with the other, is that a nutritionally balanced food will

be used, and that the owner will be sufficiently strong willed to stop the feeding of snacks and table scraps, both during the reducing period and afterward.
See DOG BISCUITS; FEEDING; NUTRITION.

Occiput Upper back part of the skull. Prominent in some breeds, such as the IRISH SETTER.

Oedema This is a collection of fluid produced by the passage of liquid through the walls of blood or lymph vessels into the surrounding tissues. The fluid may collect in the connective tissue under the skin, the abdominal cavity, the chest cavity or any organ or tissue.

The cause may be violent bruising, damage to a blood vessel, circulatory disturbances or HEART DISEASE. It is sometimes seen in intestinal infections. Oedema of the lungs has been reported when an animal has been exposed to smoke in a burning building.

Oestrum see Heat of Bitch.

Old Dogs see Aged Dog, Care of.

Old English Sheepdog Until a system of registration of pedigrees was introduced in 1873, matings – particularly in working breeds – were less discriminating than they would be today. Those who wanted dogs for specific tasks thought more of the propagation of working qualities than the preservation of type. If need be, to achieve their ends, they were willing to introduce 'foreign' blood.

For the sheep farmers in the English West Country the chief requirements were intelligence, agility and hardiness. These qualities they fused together in the 'Bobtail', as the Old English Sheepdog is called.

Although described as 'old' there is no evidence that it has existed for much more than 200 years. Being a humble animal it would inevitably be neglected by fashionable artists and writers, but Mathew Dixon's (1640–1710) painting of 'The Duke of Grafton as a Boy' featured a dog not unlike the Old English, as did Gainsborough's 'Duke of Buccleuch'. However it was left to Philip Reinagle (1749–1833) to immortalize the breed in what some consider the best of his dog portraits.

At the beginning of the eighteenth century 'drovers' dogs' were largely used to drive sheep and cattle from the hills to the market centres. These dogs were exempt from taxes and to prove their occupation they were docked, a custom which originated both the present practice and their nickname of 'Bobtail'.

The popular belief that this has produced a breed of naturally tail-less dogs is false. While occasionally specimens are born without tails, the majority need docking. Since the dog has always been used for driving, as opposed to herding like its light-weight cousins, this lack of 'rudder' causes no inconvenience.

Like similar species of sheepdog to be found in Russia, Italy and the Pyrenees, its massive build was a virtue, for its secondary task was always to guard the flocks from attack. Indeed in its present role of

Old English Sheepdog.
Top right Ch. Fezziwig Ceiling
Zero and his litter sister, Ch.
Fezziwig Blackeyed Susan.
Bottom right Ch. Rollingsea Snow
Boots.

companion it could be said to be a shade too possessive in defence of what it believes to be its own.

Equally useful in its original role was its quite exceptional agility. Walking or trotting produces a somewhat lethargic amble, which, although characteristic, reveals no hint of the immensely powerful and elastic stride displayed in the gallop. Two youngsters playing together, twisting and turning like eels, accelerating, and clearing fences with effortless ease are a most revealing sight.

Like most dogs that have spent centuries in the service of man, Old English Sheepdogs are both faithful and trainable. Indeed, were it not for their long coats they might be even more popular today than they are. Profuse and weather resistant in summer and winter alike, both the soft woolly undercoat and the harsh outer coat will form into the most unattractive mats if not adequately groomed.

This has not checked their popularity. Their numbers have grown constantly in Britain, partly through the increasing tendency of advertisers to use them as

plenty of bone and well coated. The shoulders: sloping with the dog standing lower at the shoulders than at the loin. Body: short, compact, ribs well sprung, and brisket deep with loin gently arched. The hindquarters must be round and muscular, hocks well let down and the hams densely coated. Feet: small and round. Coat: profuse, of good hard texture, shaggy and free from curl.

Colour any shade of grey, grizzle, blue or blue merle, with or without white markings is permissible. Height: minimum 22 inches, slightly less for bitches.
See colour plate p. 295.

Old English Mastiff see Mastiff, Old English.

Old English Terrier While all admit that this breed, type or variety is no longer in existence, few agree on precisely what it was when it did exist.

In part this is due to imprecise naming because a variety of names were used for different dogs. Most commonly referred to under this heading was a breed

Left Old English Terrier. An engraving of Mr. Vero Shaw's 'Silvio' and 'Sylph', White English Terriers which could be the breed (now extinct) referred to as the Old English Terrier.

Right Otterhounds can follow the hours' old scent of an otter even when the otter has swum long distances under water. Few pure bred Otterhounds exist now although there are packs in which Otterhounds have been crossed with English Foxhounds. These two dogs belong to the Kendal and District Otterhounds, from Westmorland, England.

'models' for publicity purposes.

Additionally a number of prominent people in the United States have owned them which gives them even further publicity. Currently they are in the top 25 most popular breeds in Britain, the top 40 in the U.S.A. and in demand all over the world.

Essentials of the breed: Skull: huge and squarely formed, well-arched above the eyes, and covered with hair. Jaw: fairly long, strong, square and truncated with defined stop. Nose: black and large. Dark or wall eyes preferred. Ears: small, carried flat and moderately coated. Teeth: strong, large and level. The neck: fairly long, arched and coated. The forelegs: straight, with

more correctly thought of as the White English Terrier. This was an animal about the same size as a FOX TERRIER, with some indication of relation to the BULL TERRIER, and yet with the overall lines and raciness of a MANCHESTER or Black and Tan Terrier. The tail was long and fine, and carried in a prolongation of the topline. The ears were cropped until that was forbidden in England when neat folded ears similar to those of a Smooth Fox Terrier were produced. No specimens are believed to have existed for the last sixty years.

When dog shows first started, loose classifications were acceptable. Thus we now have AIREDALE, WELSH, LAKELAND and BORDER Terriers, the forerunners of which all competed in English Terrier classes.

Open Bitch A bitch ready for mating.

Open Class see Showing Dogs.

Orbit Bony cavity containing the eye.

Orphan Puppies Simulated bitch's milk is available in many countries today. Since it is the nearest substitute to the bitch's own milk it should be used when possible. A supply should be obtained before the litter is born. These products can be fed to orphan puppies from birth to weaning. And they can be used for the supplementary feeding of large litters.

The feeding tube is a new development for the care of orphan puppies. It is also remarkably successful in saving puppies which, at birth, are too weak to nurse, either from their dam, or from a nursing bottle. It consists of a length of fine plastic tubing which can be purchased at any medical or surgical supply house, and a 5 or 10cc hypodermic syringe. The puppy is fed directly to its stomach, and instructions must be obtained from a veterinarian before this method is attempted. This method of feeding may take a minute whereas bottle nursing might take 10 to 15 minutes.

The milk formula should be heated to body temperature – 101 to 102°F (38 to 39°C). Feeding cold liquid to very young puppies can cause constipation.

The dam stimulates elimination of wastes by licking the genital area of the puppy with her warm, moist tongue. This stimulation must be performed by the owner with, for example, a small piece of sponge rubber moistened with warm water.

If the dam has immunity against such a disease as distemper, she will confer a roughly eight to ten weeks' immunity to her puppies through the colostrum or first milk. Orphan puppies are denied this immunity. The owner must then consult a veterinarian who will immunize the puppies by vaccination.

Some nutritionists advocate feeding orphan puppies every two hours, but orphan puppies have occasionally been raised successfully on three feedings a day. Every four hours is usually accepted as ideal. Orphan puppies

of giant breeds should, however, be fed more often than those of smaller breeds.
See FOSTER MOTHER.

Otitis Externa see Ear Diseases.

Otitis Media see Ear Diseases.

Otorrhoea see Ear Diseases.

Otterhound Otters have been hunted by hound packs in England for centuries. Henry VIII and Queen Elizabeth were both Masters of Hounds, and as such attended the hunts. There are, however, no very good guesses as to the origin of the Otterhound. Among the better assumptions are that the Otterhound contains BLOODHOUND, spaniel, and possibly AIREDALE ancestors.

The average European otter weighs 18 to 24 pounds. But two weighing 35 pounds each have been killed by the hounds. Canadian and American otters grow to a slightly larger size.

Otters spend a great deal of time in the water; they live in holes dug under the banks of streams, with the

entrance to the hole – or 'holt' – under water. Upon land, the scent, or trail, left by the otter is called a 'drag'. Scent left on water is called a 'wash'.

The sensitivity of the Otterhound's nose is roughly equal to that of a Bloodhound, and it can follow a drag ten to twelve hours old. The otter may swim for long distances under water, surfacing just sufficiently to take in air. It then submerges and leaves a slight trail of bubbles to mark its course. Otterhounds are able to follow this wash. Following the otter, dogs have swum for as long as five hours following a wash, which indicates the sensitivity of the Otterhound's nose and the breed's great stamina.

In England, relatively few Otterhounds have been kept pure-bred. Many of the hunts have preferred packs in which Otterhounds have been crossed with English FOXHOUNDS. Purebred Otterhounds are seldom, if ever, seen at English dog shows.

Pure-bred Otterhounds were first brought to the United States in 1900, and two were exhibited at the Claremont, Oklahoma, show in 1907. H. W. Wardner of New York City is considered to have been the first American breeder, but major credit for the increasing popularity of the breed in the United States and Canada goes to Dr. Hugh R. Mouat of Amsterdam, N.Y., who has been breeding and exhibiting for more than thirty years. Though the characteristics of the breed have been preserved in America, the dogs are not used for sport, and otters are not hunted by dogs in the United States.

Essentials of the breed: The Otterhound has the general appearance of a rough-coated Bloodhound. It has the same rather loose gait with the tail carried gaily, but not over the back. The head is broader than that of the Bloodhound. The ears are of great length, and there is less tendency to exposed haws than in the Bloodhound. The neck appears short because of the ruff of hair at its base. The back is strong, with no tendency to sway or roach, and is comparatively broad. Thighs are heavily muscled, and the hocks well let down. Feet: large, and strongly knuckled up. The outer coat is harsh and oily; the undercoat is dense and also oily. As a result, the dogs are likely to have a strong odour unless bathed occasionally. Colours are grizzle or sandy, with black and tan more or less clearly defined.
See colour plate p. 185 and illustration p. 337.

Otter-Tail Very thick at the root, with hair parted on the underside. Seen in LABRADOR RETRIEVERS.

Out at Elbows Elbows turning out from body.

Outcrossing Mating of unrelated individuals of the same breed.

Overhang A prominent brow looming over a pushed-in face, as in some PEKINGESE.

Overshot A short lower jaw in which the incisors of the underjaw do not touch the inner surfaces of the upper incisors.

Top left Otterhound. Ch. Sky Top's Cedric Vikingsson.

Bottom left Otter-tail.

P

Pace A rolling gait in which the legs on the same side of the body move forward together.

Packs (Hounds), Britain Not all types of hounds used for hunting in a pack are 'ridden to'. Whether hounds are followed on horseback or on foot depends more on the terrain over which quarry is hunted than on the quarry itself.

FOXHOUNDS in Britain, of which there are about 230 recognized packs, hunt the wild fox. It is customary, as with recognized packs of any variety of hound, for the hunt servants and the master to wear livery when in action, and by far the most common colour for fox-hound pack livery is pink. (The shade is universal, so the packs are distinguished by a variety of coloured collars to the hunt coats, and also by the design on the hunt buttons.)

Foxhounds are usually followed on horseback but there are one or two exceptions, notably the packs hunting in the mountainous country of north Wales and the northern counties of England, that follow hounds on foot.

STAGHOUNDS in Britain and Ireland are slowly decreasing in number and there are now less than ten recognized packs. The hounds hunt the stag and are followed on horseback, and even, if roads are suitably placed, in motor cars. Here again, the more usual livery colour is pink.

Six packs of DRAGHOUNDS are maintained in Britain, some confining their activities to hunting the drag (a sack containing animal feces pulled over the terrain) and one or two combining this with the occasional fox hunt by permission of their neighbouring Foxhound packs. Draghounds are followed on horseback, or on foot in difficult country.

HARRIERS, about two inches shorter than the drag-hound at approximately eighteen inches high, hunt the hare and very occasionally the fox. They are usually followed on horseback, but again in mountainous areas it is safer to follow on foot.

BLOODHOUNDS hunting the 'clean boot' (the scent of a man) are capable of hunting in packs as well as singly. There are however, only two packs in existence today, and these hounds are 'ridden to'. The hunt is called a 'man-hunt' – an emotive word – but the quarry is never attacked.

Foot hounds – BEAGLES, BASSET HOUNDS and OTTERHOUNDS – are followed, as their name implies, by a walking field. Beagles, of which there are around 105 recognized packs in Britain and Ireland, hunt the hare. Again it is customary for hunt servants and the master to wear livery – the most usual colour in this case is dark green together with contrasting collar and appropriate hunt buttons. There are however some uniforms in blue, buff and wine. In addition to the usual Beagle which measures up to sixteen inches at the shoulder in Britain, there are packs in Eire of larger hounds, up to eighteen inches high. These are generally known as Kerry Beagles and hunt the extremely difficult rocky mountains. The quarry is the hare or occasionally the drag. The field in this case usually does not follow the hounds but takes up a stand on a suitably high point and watches the hounds working around the mountain sides.

Basset hounds also hunt the hare. There are ten packs in Britain. With one or two exceptions, the hounds are different from those described in the Kennel Club breed standard. They are usually longer in the leg with less crook to the forelegs and generally plainer in the head than the exhibition Basset. Members of the hunt staff have, where it is worn, livery of green, buff or brown.

The last breed of foot hound is the Otterhound, a much larger animal than its fellows. These hounds hunt during the summer season. Since the otter is hunted along river banks and water courses, it is not usually practical to follow on horseback. Otterhound packs which may consist of either the true rough-coated hounds, or of Foxhounds, are not very numerous:

below Packs. Louis XV with his pack stag-hunting at Fontaine-bleau, from an eighteenth century painting by Jean-Baptiste Oudry.

there are only eighteen packs in Britain. Livery colour is most frequently dark blue. The true Otterhound is now very scarce; Foxhounds introduced for the sport often overmatch the otter, since they are faster and more agile than the traditional hound. As the otter is considered a species of wildlife close to extinction, hunting may well be suspended at least until the population builds up again.

It is traditional for members of the field to pay what is termed a 'cap' and these sums of money are added to the hunt funds. Members of the hunt pay an annual subscription which varies enormously according to the type of hunting and whether the pack is a 'fashionable' one or not. Details of meets arranged by any of these packs are usually given in local newspapers. The hunt servants, in particular the secretary and the field master, are only too pleased to welcome visitors and give advice and instruction on how best to enjoy the sport without getting in the way.

The hunting season stretches broadly from mid-autumn until the early spring, apart from the Otterhounds which operate in the summer months, and the draghounds for whom there is no close season. Hunting dates for draghounds are largely governed by the state of agriculture in each pack's individual area since, obviously, one does not hunt the drag over growing crops, or through fields with young lambs.

Paddling Moving too wide in front, with feet usually turning out as they are raised at the end of the step.

Pads Cushions on the underside of the toes, covered with tough, horny skin.

Paisley Terrier see Clydesdale Terrier.

Paper Pads Thin, or shallow pads, usually associated with flat feet.

Papillon *Papillon* is French for 'butterfly', and it is the name given to these little dogs for an obvious reason. Their heads, with the thin white blaze running down the eyes, supported by the flared and fringed ears, remind one unmistakably of the fragile winged insects.

And at once, having established the background of the name, two points must be made. The first is that despite the breed standard's insistence upon a precisely-marked blaze, on many specimens shown today it is very irregular and in some cases entirely absent. It is much to be hoped that breeders will strive towards improvement in this feature. The second point is that although prick ears are essential to the butterfly illusion, drop ears are permissible. They are rarely seen

Above Paddling.

today and, when they are, are known rather charmingly in Britain as the *Phalene* (moth) type, and as the *Epagneul Nain* in America.

Neither name nor dog is new. It has in fact existed for several centuries past; has featured in more 'Old Masters' than perhaps any other breed. Those who have painted them include Rubens, Van Dyck, Rembrandt and Fragonard. Celebrated owners of the past include Madame de Pompadour and Marie Antoinette.

The country of origin is by no means certain. In Spain the breed was certainly well known in the sixteenth century. Equally, however, they were known in France, and in Italy particularly in Bologna. Perhaps the latter city established the most permanent niche in the history of the breed because there were a number of breeders there who dealt in them and established a thriving export trade.

Whatever their country of origin, it is certain that they travelled the continent widely. Perhaps being small they were more portable than some of the other fashionable dogs. We know that they were carried in the coaches of the aristocracy and perhaps also inevitably a number of them went to South America, presumably with the Spaniards, and became established in the colonies on that continent. This may have led to the theory advanced at one time that Papillons were Spanish-American in origin and therefore possibly related to the CHIHUAHUA. If there is in fact a relationship between the two, it is the Chihuahua who owes ancestry to the Papillon rather than the other way about.

Over the years it would appear that there has been a change in markings. Certainly many of the old ones depicted were of solid colours. Now the background is invariably white and indeed the modern breed standard demands this.

A puzzling thing about this breed is why, in view of its undoubted antiquity, it did not become popular when the dog shows of one hundred years ago increased the interest in all pedigreed dogs. In fact right up to the First World War they were virtually ignored even by Great Britain. Even as late as 1923 those which appeared at the Kennel Club Show in London were included in a miscellaneous class for 'foreign dogs'. However this seems to have been their turning point because during the following years they became recognized in England, which fact resulted in a number being imported from France.

At that same time they also crossed the Atlantic but in America they had to wait until 1935 for official recognition. Currently they are certainly well-known in both countries and annual registrations in Britain approximate 700, in the U.S.A. 300. It is reasonable to believe that their small size, attractive appearance, and high spirits will make them still more friends in the future.

Their fans make many claims for them. A large number are fully justified. However, one suspects that the suggestion that they are adept at killing rats is a flight of fancy in that many of them are clearly too small for this pastime.

Left Packs. A professional hunt servant exercises the Crawley and Horsham Foxhounds from Sussex, England.

Right Papillon. A portrait, painted in 1779, by Benjamin West, of Queen Charlotte of England with her Papillon. Artists have depicted this breed in their work for several centuries.

Essentials of the breed: The skull should be rounded between the ears, the muzzle one-third total length of head, pointed and thinner than skull, accentuating the stop. Eyes: medium size, rounded, dark, placed rather low. Ears should be large with rounded tips, heavily fringed, set towards the back of the head and completely erect or dropped. Scissors bite required with thin, tight lips. Medium length neck. Shoulders well developed and sloping back. Chest: rather deep. Forelegs: straight, slender and fine boned. The body should have level topline, well sprung ribs and slightly arched belly. Hind legs when viewed from behind should be parallel. Dew claws on the hind legs must be removed. Feet: fine and fairly long with tufts of hair between the toes. Tail: long, well fringed, set on high and arched over the back. Coat should be abundant, long, fine and silky on body with profuse frill on the chest; short and close on the skull, muzzle and front part of the legs. Colour: white with patches which may be any colour except liver. Head marking symmetrical about a white, narrow, clearly defined blaze. Size: the ideal height is 8 to 11 inches. See colour plate p. 384 and illustration p. 342.

Paralysis This term is applied when a nerve controlling a muscle, or group of muscles, does not function. It also applies to a loss of sensation.

Hemiplegia refers to paralysis affecting only one side

of the body. In *diplegia* both sides of the body are affected. In *paraplegia* all structures behind a certain section of the back are paralyzed. It is common with this form of paralysis for control of the bladder and rectum to be lost. Paraplegia is one of the commonest forms of paralysis in the dog and is seen especially in the long-backed breeds.

Spinal paralysis begins through injury or pressure on the spinal nerve. Paraplegia is normally caused by this and the two terms can be considered to have almost the same meaning. Cerebral paralysis is induced by damage or pressure on the brain.

Peripheral paralysis is a paralysis to an area or group of muscles due to injury to the nerve supplying that area or group. The usual form of this damage is radial paralysis where injury occurs to the radial nerve of the foreleg and the dog is unable to extend (or bring forward) the lower part of that leg. The elbow joint appears lower and the toes are pointed back. In many cases this type of injury will respond to treatment, although recovery is slow.

Parasites, External External parasites are discussed under their particular headings, such as FLEAS, FLIES,

LICE, and TICKS. Mosquitoes are treated under FILARIASIS.

Pariah Dog These traditional 'outcasts' are a group of families of dogs which have lived in a wild, or semi-wild state for hundreds, or even thousands of years. Their habitat is chiefly Asia Minor and Southern Asia. A few have been found on the northern shore of the Eastern Mediterranean.

Although earlier writers tended to dismiss the pariahs as simply mongrels, later students have placed them in as many as five families.

One family of pariahs resembles the coarse-skulled and heavy-bodied sheepdogs of Asia: the Russian Owtscharka, the KUVASZ, and similar shepherd dogs. A second group shows a resemblance to the DINGO of Australia. A third is, at least in skull and muzzle, of a short-haired COLLIE type. The fourth belongs to the Eastern GREYHOUND family, and some authorities have felt that a smaller breed of pariahs should be given separate classification. Pariahs of a BASENJI type appear in widely separated areas such as Liberia and Thailand.

It may be argued that both the Sinhala Hound of Ceylon and Thai Dog are purebreds which have been

eft Papillon. Ch. Baluch Little *ewel*.

ekingese.
op right Queen Alexandra of *ngland* and her Pekingese *ainted* by Luke Fildes in 1889. *Bottom right* A Pekingese puppy.

developed from pariah stock. The same may be said of the Canaan Dog, a breed which has been developed in Israel within the last thirty-five years.

Pariahs have a colour range as great as the range of their sizes. Many are whole colours with white legs. Black masks are sometimes seen on fawn dogs. Many are piebald. For example, the Canaan may be all black, but is usually white with large patches of brown, sandy to reddish brown, or black.

Pariah dogs live in burrows in uninhabited country. They may be solitary but they usually have some sort of pack relationship. They mark out territories for themselves, and quickly join human settlements when these are established, making dens under buildings if this is permitted.

The pariahs are true domestic dogs, being merely feral – domestic dogs gone wild. The tamed pariah makes an effective home guardian.

Parti-Coloured Having patches of two or more colours.

Pastern Part of the foot of the foreleg, between the carpus, or wrist, and the toes.

Patella Luxation Patella luxation is also known as 'slipped patella' or dislocation of the kneecap. The patella (kneecap) is a small bone which lies in a groove at the lower end of the femur or thigh bone. When the dog bends the stifle (knee joint), the patella slides along the groove. If the groove is too shallow the patella may slip out to one side or the other and the dog will go lame. Sometimes the dislocated patella can be returned to its proper position by manipulation and sometimes it will go back by itself, but the condition will recur from time to time. The defect may be so bad that the leg is useless and the dog can only walk on three legs. Should two legs be so affected the dog will be completely crippled. In some cases a surgical operation may improve matters.

Affected puppies usually show the defect by the time they have reached six months of age but it can develop at a much later age. Any breed can be affected but it is most common in the smaller breeds.

The tendency towards patella luxation is inherited. Affected animals should not be used for breeding and in addition it is wise not to breed from the normal litter-mates of affected animals.

Peak see Occiput.

Pedigree The record of a pure-bred dog's ancestry.

Pekingese It is customary for articles on this breed to start by insisting that Pekingese as we know them today had existed for one, two or even more thousands of years. There is in fact little or no evidence to support this statement.

A particularly detailed examination was made in V. W. E. Collier's excellent book *Dogs of China and Japan*, published in 1921. This writer had a surprising knowledge of the history and customs past and present

of China as well as a particular interest in dogs. Even earlier than this the Hon. Mrs. Neville Lytton had in her book *Toy Dogs and Their Ancestors* cast grave doubts on whether our modern Pekingese were in any way similar to the miniature dogs of ancient China. Indeed, in typically outspoken fashion, she said that our interpretation of their background was 'romantic nonsense' and then went on to say that in her opinion the only dogs that the British had ever succeeded in getting from China were the throw-outs.

To go back, we know that the Chinese had miniature dogs fifteen hundred years ago. In A.D. 565 the Emperor gave the name of *Ch'ih Hu* or *Red Tiger* to a Persian dog. When the Emperor was mounted the dog rode upon a mat placed in front of the saddle. In A.D. 620 it is recorded that a dog and a bitch whose height was about 6 inches were presented to the Emperor Kou Tzu. They were alleged to be highly intelligent and were said to be able to lead horses by the reins and light their master's path at night by carrying torches.

Similar references continue until the mid-fourteenth century when Kublai Khan was overthrown. Owing to the absence of Europeans in China for the next 300 years, documents currently available are scarce. When news of pets started to re-emerge, cats were mentioned more frequently, and it appears that they had virtually taken the place of dogs in high society.

Throughout all this history no mention had ever been made of dogs having excessively rounded front legs, long coats or, for that matter, short faces.

The cult of the lap dog in China reached its peak between 1820 and 1850. By that time, Peking housed many thousands of them. It also housed four thousand eunuchs in the 'Forty-Eight Places' whose special task was to produce what we now call Pekingese.

The Dowager Empress Tzu Hsi encouraged this activity. She also encouraged the breeding of a type which could be likened to the LION DOGS of old, thus linking both them (and herself) with the spirit lions of Buddha. One of her acts was to compose a special set of rules for the dogs, a brief extract of which reads as follows: 'Let it wear the swelling cape of dignity round its neck. Let its forelegs be bent so that it shall not desire to wander far or leave the Imperial precincts. Let it be taught to refrain from gadding about. Let its colour be that of the lion to be carried in the sleeve of a yellow robe . . .' Since the edict continued with a recommended diet of 'sharks' fins, curlews' livers and the breast of quails' it perhaps need not be taken too seriously. However, it does establish that the Pekes we know today existed then and refutes the Hon. Mrs. Lytton's contention that those which fell into British hands in 1860 were left deliberately because they were mis-shapen rejects.

At the time of the sacking of Peking in 1860, instructions had been given to everyone that, rather than allow the royal dogs to fall into alien hands, they should be destroyed. An Imperial Princess, too proud to flee, killed herself rather than be taken by the Dragoon Guards. However, she omitted to slay her dogs and four were captured. One of these was presented to Queen Victoria; the remainder were kept by the Duke of Richmond. Later, a few more specimens were obtained by less extreme methods and brought to Britain. This meant that a normal breeding programme could be followed. There was every reason why it should be: the romantic story and the royal association had made Pekingese immensely popular and demand for them was enormous.

Early critics often overlooked the fact that Pekes had more than this 'gimmick' to recommend them. They are the most remarkable little dogs with the most unusual character. They are an odd mixture of humourist and dignified traditionalists, and they are loyal companions. Mixed with this, however, is surprising stubbornness and sometimes almost a categorical refusal to obey orders. They love the silken cushion. But they also go rabbiting when, and only when, the mood takes them.

Their individuality was certainly enough to take them to the top, and it is certainly enough to keep them there. In Britain they have never been out of the top twenty breeds. They are just as firmly placed there today. In the

Pekingese.
Left It has been argued that only mis-shapen, throwout specimens reached the West from China. However, this silk scroll painting from the Ch'ien Lung period (1756–1800) shows Chinese Pekes looking quite like those we know today.
Right The Chinese have had miniature dogs for centuries but it is not clear when the Pekingese was developed. These small dogs were painted on silk by Shen Nan-Ping, a Chinese artist of the late eighteenth century.

United States of America to which they came at the beginning of this century, they have also been popular. There they are comfortably ensconced in the top ten.

Essentials of the breed: Head: massive; skull: broad, not domed; nose: very short and broad, with large nostrils. Muzzle: wide, well wrinkled with firm under-jaw. Profile should look flat with nose up between the eyes. Deep stop. Eyes: large, clear and dark. Ears: set level with the skull, carried close to head with profuse feathering. Level lips, must not show teeth or tongue. Short, thick, heavily-boned and bowed forelegs. Body: short with broad chest, falling away lighter behind, with distinct waist and level back. Hind legs: lighter but well shaped. Absolute soundness essential. Feet: large and flat. The dog should stand well up on them. Front feet turned slightly out. Tail: set high, slightly curved over back with long feathering.

Coat: long and straight with profuse mane; top coat rather coarse, with thick undercoat. Profuse feathering on ears, legs, thighs, tail and toes. Action: fearless, free and strong, with a slight roll.

Colour: all colours and markings except (in Britain) albino or liver.

Ideal weight: 7 to 11 lb. for dogs, 8 to 12 lb. for bitches. Extreme limit 14 lb.; medium size preferred. See colour plate p. 189.

Pencilling Black lines dividing the tan on the toes of certain breeds, such as the MANCHESTER TERRIER.

People's Dispensary for Sick Animals, The This organization was founded in 1917 in the East End of London by Mrs. M. E. Dickin, to provide free treatment for sick animals whose owners were unable to afford private veterinary fees. This principle is still maintained in the 80 permanent dispensaries and 24 mobile dispensaries which operate regularly in over 200 centres in the United Kingdom. There are also branches in France, Egypt, and South Africa.

Additionally, the organization maintains six regional hospitals for serious medical cases, runs daily ambulance services dealing with accidents and other emergencies, and has homes for stray cats and dogs.

A million animals are treated annually. More important, the P.D.S.A. officers teach as they treat by explaining the cause of the illness and giving general advice on pet care.

All projects are supported entirely by voluntary contributions.

Perineal Hernia see Hernia.

Peritonitis The peritoneum is the membrane lining the abdominal cavity and the organs within this cavity. When this lining becomes inflamed or irritated the name 'peritonitis' is used.

In acute peritonitis, infection is usually present, either being carried there through the blood stream or resulting from contamination by a wound which opens the abdominal cavity, or by rupture of one of the organs within the cavity.

The condition is serious and must have immediate attention. There is usually abdominal pain and distress. Fortunately, antibodies will usually control the infection as soon as the original injury is repaired.

Chronic peritonitis is caused by a slowly developing abscess or abscesses in the abdominal cavity and can be caused by foreign bodies that have become lodged in that area, or by tuberculosis.

Persian Greyhound see Afghan Hound; Saluki.

Perspiration In the dog, perspiration takes place mainly through the foot pads, through the mouth and tongue by panting, and only very slightly through the skin. The dog will pant until evaporation has sufficiently cooled its body.

Petit Brabançon see Griffon Bruxellois.

Pekingese.
Left Ch. St Audrey Debonaire of Elsdon.
Below left Ch. Goofus Bugatti who has won titles in America, Canada and England and is the only tri-international champion Peke ever in Great Britain.

Right The People's Dispensary for Sick Animals. A Golden Retriever, 'Sally', who panicked and jumped onto an electric rail, has been treated for burns at a P.D.S.A. clinic.

Below right Petit Brabançon, the smooth Griffon Bruxellois. Sanctuary Eliza.

Pet Shops The well-run pet shop can offer dog owners a great deal of help. Dogs and puppies are frequently sold straight from the shop, but it is well to remember that while a window-full of playful animals will attract attention, it will also encourage disease. A photographic display with a notice stating that the pet shop will undertake to arrange the purchase of any breed or variety is a safer and more hygienic method of selling.

'After sales services' should be available, and these include general advice on care of the animal, trimming, bathing and nail clipping. Advice and sale of suitable food, equipment and such medicines and remedies as are available without prescription should also be offered. It is not the place of the pet shop to infringe in any way upon the veterinary profession; but it can and should provide an extremely useful service in coat and nail clipping and in general coat care, if not in the diagnosis or treatment of illness.

Boarding facilities are not normally available at a pet shop, but many establishments have working arrangements with kennels whereby the pet store takes bookings, has a reception centre for acceptance and return of boarders, receiving commission on the fees. Such arrangements work extremely well, particularly for those shops set in large towns. If the site is unsuitable for a reception centre, a recommendation service for boarding can still be offered to clients.

Pharaoh Hound This hound belongs to the GREY-HOUND family and bears a very strong resemblance to the hounds with large erect ears seen in the ancient Egyptian drawings and depicted in the sculptured delineations in the Egyptian temples from before 4000 B.C. It is very like the modern IBIZAN HOUND in build.

A medium-sized dog, the Pharaoh Hound is extremely lithe and is noted for its great turn of speed and agility. It has a free, easy movement and looks almost square in outline. Its general appearance is one of grace with power and speed. It is very intelligent, friendly, affectionate and playful, and is ever alert and active. It requires a lot of exercise and has a marked keenness for hunting. The breed is not recognized in America.

Essentials of the breed: Head: the skull is long, lean and chiselled with the foreface just slightly longer than the skull. There should be only a slight stop, with sufficient width between the eyes. The top of the skull should be parallel with the foreface, giving the impression of a blunt wedge. The jaws should be powerful with a scissors bite and good strong teeth. The nose should be either flesh or light fawn coloured, blending with the coat. Eyes are oval in shape and deep amber in colour. They should be moderately deep set with a keen, intelligent expression. The ears are fairly high set and carried erect when the hound is alert. They should be broad at the base, fine and fairly large.

Body: the neck should be long, lean and well muscled with a clean throat line. It should be slightly arched. The shoulders should be well laid back and never heavy or loaded. The forelegs should have flat bone and must be straight and parallel to each other with elbows well tucked in. The pasterns should be upright and the feet tight and catlike. The topline should be almost straight with just a slight slope from croup to root of tail. The brisket should be deep almost down to point of elbow. The ribs should be well sprung. The hindquarters are strong and muscular with a slight bend of stifle. The second thigh should be well developed.

The tail: should be fairly high set, fine and rather whip-like reaching to the point of hock in repose. In excitement it can be carried high and circular but not touching the back.

Coat: very fine and glossy and short. There should be no feathering at all. Colour: chestnut or rich tan with white markings. A white tip to the tail is encouraged. White on chest preferably star-shaped and white on toes. A very thin white snip on centre line of face is permissible. No other white should be allowed. Height: dogs 23 to 25 inches, bitches slightly less.
See illustration p. 348.

Left Pharaoh Hound. Kilcrone Senjura.

Right Point. A dog freezes in position to indicate the whereabouts of a hunted bird.

Above Plaiting.

Pied or **Piebald** Parti-coloured.

Pigeon Breast A chest with a short, protruding breastbone.

Pig Jaw Grossly overshot jaw.

Pile Dense undercoat.

Pincer Bite see Level Bite.

Pinscher, Dobermann see Dobermann Pinscher.

Pinscher, Miniature see Miniature Pinscher.

Plaiting Placing one foot in front of another with a twisting motion. Crossing over.

Plume Long tail feathers, as on an IRISH SETTER.

Pneumonia This is the inflammation of the lung tissues. It may be caused by infection, circulatory disturbance, irritation or injury.

In the acute form, the blood vessels of the lungs become enlarged, and the air spaces smaller. Respiration is difficult. If this is allowed to continue, changes occur which eventually destroy the part of the lung involved, or even the entire lung.

In another form, the inflammation is distributed over the whole lung but does not affect all the tissue. Isolated areas are damaged. In the commonest form, the tissues slowly change to non-functional areas. The dog breathes with difficulty, especially after exercise or stress. There is usually a cough and the general condition of the dog gradually declines. Heart conditions and parasitic infection may be involved.

Point To 'freeze' into position both to hold game birds in their nests, and to indicate their presence and position to the hunter by the direction of the body.

Pointer The name of this breed is one of the few that needs no explanation. It is doubtful if it was originally a name. It may have been more a description of the dog's work and therefore did not originally have the distinction of a capital letter. At first it must have been called a 'pointing dog'. The 'pointing dog' in time became a 'Pointer'.

The dog points with its nose. Its work has always been that of finding game in open country, and it ranges over the ground in front of the guns. Like the setter, it searches for game with its extraordinarily sharp nose, and having found it, freezes into a classical point. It becomes a statue: the nose on the end of that finely-shaped face held high, often above the level of its brow, its foreleg lifted as though arrested in the act of taking a step; the tail carried straight out in a natural extension of the topline as though even allowing that to drop might disturb the game.

With such a beautiful and elegant worker it is very sad to realize that its area of usefulness is diminishing. Shrinking land areas available for sport must in time reduce the numbers of sportsmen who can find work for this breed.

Although the Pointer is always said to have come from Spain, this fact is by no means certain. We know these dogs existed in many countries in Europe and in many slightly differing forms. Clearly some of them were brought to England and it was in Great Britain that the development of the animal we know today took place.

they shot over. They had proved their dogs in the field but they were not satisfied. In addition to their dog being accepted as a proven worker, they also wished it to be appreciated by the world for its handsome looks.

This first show was not so much an exhibition as a competition. While there have since that day always been misgivings as to the organization of the show (for example, the judge of Pointers' dog won the setter classes and the judge of Setters' dog won the Pointers') the show did excite sufficient interest to ensure that others followed.

This meant that Pointer men, amongst others, aimed at a harmonious dog without exaggeration and certainly not made less elegant or attractive in appearance by the mixture of 'foreign' blood. Once again the aim became to produce a dog with purity of form. It remains so today. This is perhaps in itself a counter to those who argue that dog shows merely encourage beauty at the expense of brain. Without this encouragement, or check on quality, many of the breeds known to the world would by now be virtually unrecognizable.

Although the Pointer's role is decreasing owing to urbanization and the modern tendency to drive game, there is no reason to fear that the breed will ever fade from the scene. In Great Britain with approximately

At one time in an endeavour to make the Pointer more robust and also to give it more pace and drive, crosses were made with FOXHOUNDS. Clearly this practice was a serious mistake and this soon became evident. Indeed it nearly ended by destroying the character of the breed. The essence of a Pointer is that it should use disciplined and controlled intelligence. It should creep and virtually stalk its game. In contrast, the Foxhound is required to gallop right up to and preferably over its quarry.

Additionally, the Pointer must hunt with head held high searching for every whiff of air scent. The hound puts its nose to the ground and gallops. And this is precisely what the progeny of the cross did. These early improvers did not learn their lessons with this one near-disaster. They carried on and there is evidence that they thought at one time to improve the breed with crosses by BULLDOGS, GREYHOUNDS, BLOODHOUNDS and perhaps breeds even more unsuitable than these.

Dog shows came to the rescue, because in 1859 the first ever show took place in Newcastle-upon-Tyne in the north of England. For years shooting men had argued as to which was the most handsome of the dogs

450 registrations a year, these dogs are more numerous than they have ever been in the past, although they have not quite kept up with the general increase in pedigreed dogs.

In the United States most Pointers are registered with the Field Dog Stud Book. Nearly 25,000 Pointers started in field trials under Field Dog Stud Book Registration and American Field supervision during 1969. The American Kennel Club registers about 400 Pointers annually. Relatively few of these compete in AKC field trials. The majority are kept as pets or for show competition.

Essentials of the breed: The skull should be fairly broad, stop well defined. Nose and eye-rims: dark. The muzzle: the British standard (but not the AKC) calls for a concave muzzle giving a dish-faced appearance. The eyes should be equidistant between the occiput and nostrils, bright and kindly and either hazel or brown. Ears must be set on fairly high, should lie close to the head and be of medium length, pointed at tips. The shoulders should be long and sloping. The chest: wide with brisket well let down. The ribs should be well sprung and loins muscular and slightly arched. Hind-quarters: the hock should be well let down and thighs very muscular. The feet should be oval, well knit and with arched toes. Tail: of medium length, thick at the root, tapering to a point, carried level with the back. With movement, the tail should lash. The coat is fine, short, smooth and straight. Colours are lemon, orange, liver and black, all either with white or self-coloured. Height and weight (AKC): dogs, 25 to 28 inches and 55 to 75 lb.; bitches, 23 to 26 inches and 45 to 65 lb. See colour plate p. 81.

Pointer, German Wire-Haired see German Wire-haired pointer.

Points Used to indicate colour on the face, eyebrows, ears, legs, etc. Thus: 'with tan points'.

Points, Championship see Championships, American; Championships, British; Championships, Canadian; Championships, International.

Poisons Accidental poisoning takes the lives of more dogs than any other type of accident, except for traffic accidents. Pet owners are apt to claim that a human poisoner is in the neighbourhood, but almost always, the poisoning is not deliberate: death is caused by rat poisons, by insecticides, and even by poisons within the home.

Caution should be taken in selecting house plants for homes which have puppies or dogs which are gluttonous eaters and chewers. The bulbs of hyacinth, narcissus, and daffodil can cause death if eaten. A poinsettia leaf can kill a dog, and so can oleander leaves and branches. All parts of dieffenbachia and elephantsia can cause illness or death to dogs. Rosary peas and castor beans can be fatal, and so can mistletoe berries.

If the dog shows signs of poisoning, action must be immediate. First, the type of poison must be determined, and this information must be given immediately to a veterinarian.

In cases where the dog cannot be given immediate veterinary care it should be kept as warm as possible.

In most cases, the veterinarian will recommend inducing the dog to vomit. A very quick and effective method is to make a pocket of the dog's lips and then to pour in hydrogen peroxide which it will have to swallow. A tablespoon of dry mustard in half a cup of water works well. So does a cup of warm soapy water.

An antidote for most of the acid poisons is bicarbonate of soda, a tablespoon to a cup of water. Crushed egg shells, or even plaster torn from a wall and crushed, can be used by adding to warm water.

Alkali poisons require an opposite treatment. Three or four tablespoons of vinegar, or of a strong acid fruit juice, such as lemon or lime, will help.

Strychnine is a common rat poison. Symptoms of mild strychnine poisoning are twitching, nervousness, dilation of the eye pupils, and stiffening of the neck muscles. At this stage, an emetic can be given. This can then be followed by two to five ounces of strong tea. Some authorities advocate the use of phenobarbitals

after the tea has counteracted the poison. But this can only be given on a veterinarian's advice.

Dogs do occasionally get poisoned by sedatives, either those left about by their owners, or by an overdose of sedatives prescribed for their own use. In such cases, strong coffee is an excellent antidote. A teaspoon and a half of instant coffee to a cup of warm water is suggested for a 40 lb. dog.

'Warfarin' is perhaps the major rat poison used in the world today. Poisoned animals develop massive internal haemorrhages. The danger to the dog is that it may kill and eat a rat too ill to escape, or that it may eat a poisoned bait. Poison symptoms may then show up so slowly that the dog is past help before the owner knows it is sick. Occasionally, the symptoms are so vague that a diagnosis of Warfarin poisoning cannot be made in time to save the dog. If the owner sees his dog eat a dead rat or swallow what he suspects to be a poisoned bait, then he should try to induce vomiting immediately.

Arsenic poisoning causes watery or bloody diarrhoea, intense salivation, staggering, acute abdominal pain, convulsions, and vomiting. In cases of heavy poisoning, death may come suddenly and without pronounced symptoms. If there are symptoms, however, first aid treatment is often very helpful. One to two ounces of milk of magnesia should be prepared. If charcoal is available, crush at least a tablespoonful and mix it into the milk of magnesia. Administer the medicine, and follow with half a cup of strong tea.

Red squill, or squill, used as a rat poison is not supposed to be dangerous to dogs. It is supposed to cause the dog to vomit before poisoning can result. But it can and often does kill dogs. Convulsions, staggering, retching, diarrhoea, and body sensitivity to pressure are symptoms. Veterinary advice must be sought at once.

Occasionally dogs will lick agricultural insecticides from lawns or plants. But the usual method of insecticide poisoning is by absorption through the skin, or through the pads of the feet. In such cases, treatment by a veterinarian is necessary.

Police Dogs Dogs are used by police in many parts of the world. The breeds chiefly favoured are the GERMAN SHEPHERD DOG (Alsatian) and DOBERMANN PINSCHER. But various countries have used native breeds with which they are familiar, and which are readily available. The Nippon Police Dog Association in Japan considers the following breeds as being suitable for police work: German Shepherd, Dobermann Pinscher, COLLIE, AIREDALE, BOXER, and AKITA. BELGIAN SHEEPDOGS, BOUVIER DES FLANDRES, and PULIS have been used by some countries, and BLOODHOUNDS and LABRADOR RETRIEVERS have been used for specialized tasks.

The dogs are used for searching and patrolling buildings, parks and building sites, hospitals and other institutions. They are also used in the pursuit of fleeing suspects, in trailing suspects, in searching areas for objects which might serve as clues in the solving of crimes, and for scenting the presence of illegal drugs. Sometimes dogs are used in crowd and riot control.

Pointer.
Top left Sandylands Ernford Dido.
Middle left The Pointer's work has always been to find game in open country by its extraordinarily sharp nose.
Bottom left Crookrise Link, Ch. Crookrise Return and Crookrise Lynn.

Right Police dogs. A German Shepherd Dog scales an adjustable practice wall.

Bloodhounds have been used to locate lost children and elderly people who may have wandered and become lost. At least one police department has been able to train its dogs to detect hidden firearms through the scent of gun oil.

Dog patrol units are often summoned to buildings when a burglar alarm rings. The procedure is to guard exits while dogs are sent through the buildings. Police have reported that fear of the dogs is so great that, in some instances, just a threat broadcast over a loud-speaker, 'Come out with hands up or we'll send the dogs in' has been sufficient to bring quick surrender.

On street patrol, dogs are often sent down dark alleys to check at the back entrances of commercial establishments. They have been taught to alert the officer to opened doors or to persons hidden in doorways.

Dogs are able to chase and capture suspects who flee at night through back yards and over fences when an officer alone would be helpless. The dogs are taught to bark at a suspect who stops and remains still, but to attack and bring down one who resists. The dogs are also able to trail suspects through parks and wooded areas.

The use of dogs for police work began in Europe about 1910. Trailing dogs had been used for centuries, but modern police dog work was not known. After the Second World War, the London police dog units achieved world-wide attention because of their success.

The police department of St. Louis, Missouri, sent selected officers to London to be trained, and Baltimore, Maryland, hired a London trainer. After St. Louis had set up its own training grounds, it began to train units for other cities, including several in Canada. San Francisco, California, used a German trainer then living in the state.

In America, officers who volunteer for dog patrol work must have written permission from their wives since the dogs must live in the officers' homes. The training period for men and dogs is about fourteen weeks. In addition, both must take additional training. One department requires one day's training every twenty-one days, another department requires two hours a week.

Dogs, trained in wooded areas as well as in buildings, must scale walls, jump through windows and hoops of fire, climb ladders, go through sewer pipes, attack on command, etc. To keep the dogs interested in building searches, various types of factories and stores volunteer the use of their buildings. In this way, the dogs often have a different building to search.

Veterinary service is always available, and the officers take special training in the general care of their dogs. Some departments buy their dogs. In many cases, the dogs are donated by private citizens. The dogs must pass a rigid physical examination; they cannot be gun or storm shy; and they must have a stable temperament.

In San Francisco in 1969, the dogs were present or were involved in 65,907 incidents. They patrolled 49,045 times at schools and 33,579 times at hospitals. Parks and playgrounds were visited 42,409 times. The dogs participated in 1,302 felony arrests and were

Police dogs.
Top left 'Rusty', a trainee police dog and his handler anticipate a 'suspect'.
Bottom left A well-padded 'criminal' teaches a novice police dog to disarm a man with a gun.

Pomeranian.
The Pom is a diminutive member of the Spitz family of dogs and has the characteristic mane of hair round the neck (*top and middle right*).
Pomeranians originated in the Arctic Circle, but when they came to notice, they could be found only in northern Germany and especially in Pomerania which gave its name to the breed.
Bottom right Golden Star of Hadleigh.

credited with 1,581 assists. They were responsible for 2,188 arrests for misdemeanours and had 1,402 assists. And they made 10,285 building searches.

Poligar see Greyhound, Eastern.

Pomeranian The Pomeranian, despite its present diminutive size, is an unmistakable member of the SPITZ family of dogs; that is, those canines which came originally from the Arctic circle. They all have readily recognized characteristics such as pricked ears, a mane of hair round the neck, straight hocks and a tail set high and carried forward over the back. Other members of this group include HUSKIES, NORWEGIAN ELKHOUNDS, FINNISH SPITZ, SAMOYEDS and CHOW CHOWS.

By the time this particular variety was first noted it was to be found only in northern Germany and particularly Pomerania whence it got its name. These dogs were considerably larger than the Pomeranians we know today. Many were used as sheep dogs and some indeed were so large that they were used as beasts of burden. The average size dog would appear to have been perhaps as big as a KEESHOND.

Their arrival in England approximately one hundred years ago created little excitement. That country already had a sufficient supply of sheepdogs and did not use dogs to pull carts. Moreover, this newcomer had no sporting background and as far as is known has never been used in the field in any way. Indeed were it not for the curious fact that occasional small puppies were produced in otherwise normal litters, the probability is that they would never have achieved any degree of prominence.

These comparatively small puppies, normally weighing when mature between 15 and 20 lb. did however excite interest and controversy amongst breeders. Some disposed of them at birth considering them runts. Others, however, reared them and discovered that, although small, they were by no means stunted dwarfs and when fully grown appeared perfectly normal although miniature replicas of the originals.

As with so many breeds, public attention became focused on them when Queen Victoria took an interest. In 1888 she visited Florence, saw some Pomeranians, accepted one as a gift and made it her close companion. Soon after she founded a kennel of the breed and started to exhibit them regularly. The size she favoured was between 12 and 16 lb. which made the old style Pomeranian look monstrous, and soon the pattern set by the Queen became the norm.

In the course of time Her Majesty herself suffered at the hand of progress, which is certainly no respecter even of royalty. Without any loss of the traditionally robust constitution and character of Poms, breeders discovered that the bantamizing process could be continued until dogs of a mere 6 lb. were competing in the show ring. Queen Victoria's dogs began to look monstrous.

At this same time breeders also found that it was comparatively easy to produce dogs of much more interesting colour than the rather drab originals. For example, two blacks frequently produced brown

POMERANIAN

puppies; brown mated to black produced sable. Later came orange, blue, cream and indeed perhaps the widest range of pastel colours known to any breed.

Admittedly there were disappointments for those early breeders of coloured Poms before they realized that colour changes after birth are normal. Blues, for example, often become shaded sables and blacks turn into blues.

One dog who made a never-to-be-forgotten mark on the breed was a little sable who ultimately became *Champion Sable Mite.* Many commentators of the time described him as 'the finest dog I have ever seen'. An American breeder heard of him and offered the unprecedented sum of £500 for him. The offer was refused which not unnaturally created an even bigger sensation than the appearance of the dog!

At the present time Poms are smaller than they have ever been in the past. Although the breed standard seeks a weight of between 4 and 5½ lb. most of the top dogs are nearer the lower limit than the upper. And as size has gone down the cost has gone up until, dollar for ounce, this must be the most expensive breed the world has ever produced. This is principally due to their surprising success in the showring. These little dogs have hearts like lions and even at the end of a long, hard day stand four square on the floor demanding admiration and respect.

Essentials of the breed: The head and nose should be foxy in outline. Skull: slightly flat and large in proportion to the muzzle. Eyes: medium size, slightly oval, bright and dark. Ears: small and carried erect. Teeth: level, (but scissors bite in American breed standard).

Neck: rather short. Forequarters: the legs must be well feathered, straight and of medium length. The back must be short and level, the body compact, chest fairly deep. Feet: should be small and compact. The tail should be turned over the back and carried flat and straight.

Coat: there should be two coats, a soft, fluffy undercoat and a long, straight coat, harsh in texture, abundant round the neck. Colour: all whole colours are admissible, but they should be free from black or white shadings. Parti-colours allowed in America.

Weight: dogs 4½ to 5½ lb. Bitches: 4 to 4½ lb. In the United States, 3 to 7 lb.
See colour plate p. 382.

Pompom The ball of hair left on the end of the POODLE's tail when it has been put into a show clip.

Poodle, Miniature Alphabetically this middle-sized variety comes before the large Standard Poodle and the diminutive Toy Poodle. Chronologically, however, the Standard Poodle came first.

During the middle 1950s the Miniature Poodle became the top dog in the majority of countries in the world. Their rapid emergence was phenomenal and its rise so unsettled a number of canine statisticians that they mis-read the facts. They thought that this event signalled a whole change in our way of life. They presumed that the old sporting tradition had gone for ever and accepted that the majority of dog owners no longer lived in the country and therefore no longer wished to follow the country pursuits of hunting, shooting and fishing. They accepted it as a rather belated recognition of the fact that the ideal canine companion for any person is the one which best suits his way of life. With the knowledge of hindsight it can be stated that the popularity of the Miniature Poodle was in no way a rejection of either large dogs or sporting dogs.

The key to the success of the Miniature Poodle was its character: a dog full of fun, civilized, stately when the occasion demanded, but still of modest size. Additional points in its favour were that it was a non-moulting breed and therefore owners were not required to spend much time removing hair from furnishings and carpets. Overlooked for the moment was that these same owners would have to spend quite a lot of their spare time in removing unwanted hair from the dog!

All three varieties of Poodle have coats which need regular grooming if they are to avoid becoming both untidy and uncomfortable.

The Miniature Poodle is a natural and comparatively recent descendant of the variety known as the Standard Poodle. The majority of those existing today are the descendants of dogs bred down from Standard Poodles, and the Miniature Poodles in their turn were used to evolve the even more recent Toy Poodle. The Standard Poodle had been for centuries a gundog with a special aptitude for retrieving from the water. The Miniature Poodle inherited not only the make and shape of the original but also its characteristics. Additionally, since the Standard had always been trimmed in a special manner intended to help in its

Left Pomeranian. Gainsborough's portrait of Mrs. Robinson sitting with an early Pomeranian-type dog. These dogs were much larger than the Poms of today and were often used as shepherd dogs or even beasts of burden.

354

Poodle, Miniature.
Top right Ch. Frederick of Reucroft, once the top winning dog of all breeds in America.
Middle right Ch. Round Table Loramar Yeoman.

Bottom right Poodle, Standard. 'Mr. Walton's Performing Dogs', an engraving of Poodles and a Whippet. Poodles are reputed to have performed since the early days of the circus.

work, it became the custom to clip the Miniature Poodle in the same way, despite the fact that it was unlikely to be used for retrieving wildfowl from muddy streams.

With a breed which makes such rapid progress from comparative obscurity to near the 'top of the pops', there will inevitably be some criticism. Moreover, it is a fact that during the boom years many Miniature Poodles were bred from stock which was by no means suitable.

In part this was due not so much to the mercenary tendencies of some small breeders as to the lack of knowledge of pet owners. Having acquired a pet bitch for a reasonably high sum of money, they saw a rapid way of getting their money back by breeding to the dog next door. There was a ready sale for all of the offspring and the result was a flood of atypical specimens, many of which lacked the robust conformation and temperament of the originals.

However, Miniature Poodles are now as good as they have ever been. They retain the gaiety, strongness, good nature and intelligence which made them so popular. Additionally they have become remarkably standardized in appearance and the general quality of the breed is such that they have had great show successes all over the world.

Originally these, and indeed all Poodles, were recognized in three colours only, that is black, brown and white. Now they are accepted in a very much wider range, which includes creams, apricots, blues, silvers, cafe au lait and many more. This range of colours has uncovered a curious anomaly. It is that the black poodles, which are the least popular with the pet owning public, are the most popular with judges at shows. Let it be said that this is not prejudice. For reasons unknown the blacks consistently produce the highest quality, together with those special characteristics enumerated in the breed standard which is a judge's duty to search for and reward.

Essentials of the breed: The Miniature Poodle should be in every respect a replica in miniature of the Standard Poodle. Height at shoulder must be under 15 inches but not under 11 inches in Great Britain or 10 inches in America.
See colour plate p. 95.

Poodle, Standard Alexander Woolcott once wrote about Poodles. And when he liked something sufficiently to write affectionately, few writers in the world could do a better job. On this occasion he wrote about his own pet poodles 'Gamin' and 'Harpo' as follows: 'They clearly regarded themselves as having a special relationship to the human species. A bond traceable I suppose to the fact that for a thousand years their forebears travelled with the French circuses and in all that time had no fixed point in their lives except a person; no home at all save the foot of the boss's bed wherever it might be.'

This was true as far as it went. But it did not go far enough. The truth is that the Poodle was not bred as a circus dog. It was bred as a gundog. It was and remains a brilliant worker. It was an accidental bonus

355

that it happened to be intelligent, determined to please and to be a clown. With these attributes it was almost bound to be drafted into show business sooner or later.

Here we are talking of the Standard Poodle, the full-sized original, standing up to a couple of feet high at the shoulder. The Miniature Poodle, something less than 15 inches high is described under its own heading, as is the even more modern and diminutive Toy Poodle.

The precise starting point of the Standard Poodle is unknown. Maybe there is no precise location. Certainly there are early reports of it in France, Germany and Russia. Strange but true, each of these countries is said to have favoured, or at least produced, different colours. France produced white, Germany brown and Russia black.

This apparently clear cut line is however confused by the fact that both a painting by Franz Snyder (1595) and a lithograph by J. J. Chalon, show what are unmistakably parti-coloured Poodles: basically white but splashed with colour like a piebald horse. Today, what is called a 'mismarked' Poodle, is rarely if ever seen. What is seen, however, is a remarkably wide range of whole colours which apart from the three original colours now includes cream, apricot, silver, gray, blue, cafe au lait, champagne and quite a few other unusual hues.

Since the way the coat is cut is always distinctive, it deserves special mention. The traditional presentation is known as the Lion trim, a name which is both apt and descriptive. It is known in America as the Continental clip. There are historic reasons for its existence. When the poodle was used as a gundog he was particularly useful at retrieving duck from muddy lakes and ponds. To make swimming easier the dog's hindquarters were shaved. Later 'bobbles' were left on to protect the vulnerable joints from rheumatism. The hair was also tied back from its eyes, first with string, later with coloured ribbon so that it would be readily identifiable when swimming in muddy streams.

Despite this explanation, however, most of the general public, as distinct from show-goers, dislike the Lion trim. Most prefer the Dutch clip – that is a fairly close-cut body with baggy 'cowboy chaps' left on the legs. This style has the disadvantage of leaving the most hair in the place that collects the most dirt. Strange but true, the Dutch is harder to maintain than the Lion. In America it is not accepted in the show ring. Dogs under one year old can be shown in 'puppy clip', but all adults must be shown in either Continental or 'English saddle clip'.

Whatever the style, regular grooming is essential and it is no task for idle people. The coat does not moult, therefore no hair is left on the carpet, but it does mat. Several hours spent trying to tease the tangles out of a neglected coat make some wonder which is the lesser of the two evils.

Despite all their advantages, the big Poodles have never been wildly popular. Size, the one thing for which they are admired, is also against them. Fortunately, there has never been any risk of their dying out. They have always had a number of friends prepared to carry on breeding them. One suspects, and certainly hopes,

that they always will have; a world of dogs without large Poodles would not be the same.

Essentials of the breed: Head: long and fine with slight peak at the back. The skull not broad and with a moderate stop. Foreface: strong and well chiselled. The whole head must be in proportion to the dog's size. Eyes: almond-shaped or oval and dark. Ears: long and wide, low set on, hanging close to the face. Teeth: white, strong, even, with scissors bite; a full set of 42 teeth desirable.

Neck: well proportioned, of good length. Forequarters: shoulders strong, muscular and sloping. Chest: deep and moderately wide. Ribs: well sprung and rounded. Back: short, strong, slightly hollowed. Thighs: well developed and muscular, well bent stifles, hocks well let down. Tight feet proportionately small and oval, toes arched. Tail set on rather high, carried at a slight angle. Gait: straight forward trot with springy action, legs moving parallel.

Coat – profuse and dense, of harsh texture. Colour – all solid colours. Size: over 15 inches.
See colour plate p. 96.

Poodle, Toy When we look at the Toy Poodle's history we must consider the breed as a natural and comparatively recent descendant of the much older Standard Poodle, from which it has been bred down through the Miniature Poodle. The history of the Toy should be read in conjunction with those of the Standard Poodle and Miniature Poodle. Some breeders had been producing these Toys on a limited scale for many years when they found, in the 1950s, that there was a genuine and spontaneous demand by the public for them. Additionally, even those who normally bred Miniature Poodles found that the smaller specimens of this breed – say of twelve inches in height – sold more readily than those near the upper limit of fifteen inches.

By the middle of the 1950s the Toy variety existed in such large numbers in both the United States and Great Britain that the respective Kennel Clubs agreed to open a separate register for them. However, their regulations differed in one important matter. The American Kennel Club ruled that Toy Poodles should be under ten inches at the shoulder; the Kennel Club of England that these Toys should be under eleven inches. Only one inch difference, but in view of the fact that the dogs were already minute, the gulf was much wider than it might have appeared.

In any case it led to two entirely different thought processes on the part of breeders. In America speed was essential and some thought that they had to sacrifice some of the quality and type of the Toy Poodle by concentrating on mere diminutiveness. It has been said that originally far too many 'dwarfs' were used – that is, dogs which had comparatively short legs which got them under the measure but which carried undesirable traits such as fairly powerful bodies, coarse heads and pop eyes.

Great Britain was able to make haste more slowly. It bred down from Miniatures which were already of high quality. In a short time it had produced a large

Poodle, Toy.
Top left Warrenrise Maximilian.
Middle left Ch. Barsbrae Branslake Harriet.
Bottom left A nineteenth-century Poodle waits patiently for its mistress in Giuseppe de Nittis' picture of 'Races at the Bois de Boulogne'.
Top right A pair of Belgian faïence Poodles from the early eighteenth century.

Bottom right Portuguese breeds. The *Cão de Agua*, or Portuguese Water Dog, which is often used as a fisherman's dog in the Algarve.

number of Toys which were the equal of their larger cousins. In Britain, however, a fairly high proportion of these Toys grew over-size on reaching maturity.

Over the years the differences between the countries have been largely overcome, principally because of a generous exchange of stock. The two countries, however, still abide by their own height limitations and other countries in the world have followed either one or the other.

All of the features of the Toy Poodle are a direct inheritance of the larger ones. It is trimmed in the same way and for the same 'historical' reason – that it goes back to a gundog. It does not moult but needs the same amount of grooming although, mercifully, on a smaller scale. It has the same good nature and intelligence with perhaps even a shade more zest for life.

Certainly it is the smallest Poodle, the Toy, which is currently enjoying the greatest increase in popularity all over the world. This triumph was achieved originally in the face of considerable criticism and prejudice. It was considered wrong to breed a dog down in size. The fact that the Toys have suffered nothing in the process was unfortunately overlooked.

Criticism in no way depresses the large army of Toy Poodle owners. They seem to have their cake and eat it, to have all the pleasures of owning a big dog with all of the advantages of owning a small one. It should also perhaps be said that diminutiveness certainly does not depress the Toy Poodles either. For them size is unimportant. 'Am I not', their every movement demands, 'a pure and priceless Poodle?'

Essentials of the breed: The Standard of the Toy Poodle is the same as that of the Standard Poodle and Miniature Poodle, except that the height at shoulder must be under 11 inches in Great Britain and under 10 inches in the United States.
See colour plate p. 95.

Portuguese Breeds

Cão de Agua (Portuguese Water Dog)

The Portuguese Water Dog is believed to have come originally from the Middle East. The breed spread through Europe possibly producing both the POODLE and the IRISH WATER SPANIEL when crossed with local breeds. Today it is found principally in the Algarve district of Portugal.

Owing to their fondness of swimming and diving, they are often used by fishermen. Should a fish escape from hook or net the dog jumps into the sea to retrieve it, or swims for broken nets and loose rope. They are also employed as couriers between boat and land. They are intelligent and willing to learn.

Essentials of the breed: Head: strong, well proportioned and large. Skull: slightly longer than the muzzle, with defined occiput and with central furrow. Stop well pronounced, slightly further back than the inner corner of the eyes.

Nose: black in black, white or marked coats, and brown in brown coats. Eyes: roundish, black or brown. Ears: set above the line of the eyes and lying flat to the head. Neck: strongly muscled but without dewlap.

Brisket: wide and deep, reaching to the elbow. Back: straight, short and wide. Tail: thick at the base and tapering, not reaching down below the hock. When the dog is attentive the tail should form a ring. Feet: round and rather flat. Black nails preferred.

Coat: there are two varieties of coat. It can be long and wavy or short and curly. Colours: black, brown and white, or black and brown marked with white.

Height: dogs 20 to 22 inches. Bitches 17 to 20 inches.

Cão de Castro Laboreiro (Portuguese Watch Dog)

This is the smallest of the Portuguese Watch Dogs. Of MASTIFF type, it is an excellent guard which in the past defended herds from wolves. The dogs are strong and robust with agile, free movement.
Essentials of the breed: Head is of medium size, skull longer than the muzzle. Ears: set low and well apart,

pendant. Almond-shaped eyes from dark to light brown. Black nostrils. Tail: of sabre type, thick and pendant. Straight legs and cat feet. Short-haired, wolfish colour, dark fawn and brindle.

Height: dogs 22 to 24 inches. Bitches 20 to 23 inches.

Cão da Serra de Aires (Portuguese Sheepdog)

Portuguese Sheepdogs are intelligent, lively dogs devoted to their shepherd owners and to the herds of pigs, horses, cows, goats and sheep they guard.
Essentials of the breed: Strong head; stop well marked. Black or dark nose and eyes, drop ears. Strong legs with close toes. Long and smooth-haired, with moustaches and heavy brows. Coat texture similar to the goat. Colours: brown, yellow, grey, fawn, wolfish and black.

Height: dogs 16½ to 19 inches. Bitches 16 to 18 inches.

Cão da Serra da Estrela (Portuguese Mountain Dog)

Found mostly at Serra da Estrela, the Portuguese Mountain Dog is a MASTIFF-type sheepdog and guard.
Essentials of the breed: Strong head, long, slightly convex, with stop at an equal distance from the muzzle and occiput. Small ears. Oval, dark amber eyes. Black or dark nostrils. Tail thick at the base, ending in hook. Strong, straight legs and feet open. Coat: long or short-haired. Colour: fawn, wolfish, or yellow.

Height: dogs 25 to 28 inches. Bitches 24 to 27 inches.

Perdigueiro Portugues (Portuguese Pointer)

Together with the Spanish Pointer, this dog is possibly the ancestor of other pointer-type breeds. It has been known since the fourteenth century. A very good gundog, with excellent nose, and a good retriever, the Portuguese Pointer works happily in all climatic conditions.
Essentials of the breed: Head with well pronounced stop and flat forehead. Medium sized, rounded, pendant ears. Dark brown eyes. Brown or dark nostrils. Level back. Straight legs with cat feet. Tail docked at two-thirds. Coat: short and smooth-haired, Colour: yellow or brown, plain or with white marks.

Height: dogs 20½ to 24 inches. Bitches 19 to 22 inches.

Podengo Portugues (Portuguese Rabbit Dog)

This is a hound dog bred to 'set' and track rabbits. The breed is divided into three varieties; the large (*Grande*, 22 to 27 inches) is used for large game, the medium (*Medio*, 16 to 20 inches) and small (*Pequeño*, 12 to 16 inches) usually working in packs for rabbits.
Essentials of the breed: Flat skull, straight muzzle with pronounced stop. Small, oblique eyes from light honey to dark chestnut. Pricked, triangular ears. Level back. Legs straight with cat feet. Sickle tail, set high, of medium length. Short, hard coat, yellow, fawn and black or white marked.

Rafeiro do Alentejo (Portuguese Shepherd Dog)

The biggest of all Portuguese breeds, originally from Alentejo county where it is used to guard cattle and farms, the Portuguese Shepherd Dog is an excellent watch dog.

Essentials of the breed: The shape of the head reminds one of a bear, being well proportioned, muzzle shorter than the skull, with small, pendant ears, small, dark eyes and black nostrils. Thick, arched tail, without hook. Cat feet with strong toes. Coat: either short-haired or of medium length. Colour: black, fawn, wolfish or yellow, white or with white markings.

Height: dogs 26 to 29 inches. Bitches 25 to 28 inches.

Portuguese Kennel Club see Kennel Clubs, Portuguese.

Portuguese Mountain Dog, Portuguese Pointer, Portuguese Rabbit Dog, Portuguese Sheepdog, Portuguese Shepherd Dog, Portuguese Watch Dog, Portuguese Water Dog see Portuguese Breeds.

Left Portuguese breeds. *Cão da Serra de Aires,* or Portuguese Sheepdog.

Prefixes and Affixes (Kennel Names) These are used to identify a kennel, or to distinguish a dog's name sufficiently from others to make it acceptable to a registration body. For example, since over a million dogs are registered annually by the American Kennel Club, the search for a name not already in use in a given breed is often very difficult.

Serious breeders usually select a prefix, or kennel name, and then register it with the governing body. The registered name is granted for a five-year period, with a renewal option. The governing body then will prevent the use of the prefix by any other kennel or breeder.

Many individual owners would like to name their dog *King, Pete, Bess,* or some similar simple name. For registration purposes, this is obviously not possible. A more formal name must be selected, and for that purpose a prefix is used. The simple name can be the second half of the formal title, as well as the 'call name' of the dog.

Prefixes are worked out in various ways. A breeder living on Cranston Road might use *Cranston* as a prefix. John and Betty Jones could combine their first names to form *Jonbet Kennels.* A Beagle breeder might select *Rabbit Run,* while a retriever breeder might choose *Duck Blind.*

Serious breeders should register their kennel names since the name then serves to identify a strain of dogs. One breeder used the name *Marborn* for nearly 20 years, but failed to register it. He was then notified that another breeder had registered the name, so he could no longer use it.

Pregnancy For the first four or five weeks after MATING, the bitch requires no change in her routine. If she was not dosed for worms before mating she should be given a vermifuge about two weeks after the completion of her season. She should also be completely free from external parasites and can be given a bath if necessary. She must be given exercise even up to the last day or two before she is due to whelp. As she becomes heavier in whelp her exercising must be restricted and rather than galloping she will prefer a sedate amble by her owner's side. A bitch that does not take her exercise sensibly must be restricted. She must not be allowed to jump up or down from a height or to squeeze through a narrow door. During the last stages of pregnancy she should not be allowed to go up and down stairs. Normally the bitch will decide sensibly herself how much exercise she wants. The longer a bitch can be persuaded to adhere to her normal routine and take her exercise the better fitted she will be to whelp and the tougher and hardier her puppies are likely to be.

At the end of the fifth week or so there should be some indication of her condition. A slight thickening of the flanks can be looked for and her TEATS should show signs of enlarging. At the sixth week it is usually possible for the specialist to detect the presence of foetuses in the uterus. It is not advisable for the amateur to try to detect these foetuses as damage can be done to the bitch.

Sometimes a bitch lacks appetite during the early weeks of pregnancy but this soon rights itself. Normally bitches eat very well throughout their pregnancy but if a bitch goes off her food altogether about the sixth or seventh week, a veterinarian's advice should be sought.

After the fourth week the diet should be stepped up. If the bitch has been having one large meal a day, this should be increased to two. It is well to remember that the unborn puppies must be fed via the mother. If the dam is not fed well she cannot pass on extra nourishment. The addition of cod-liver oil, raw egg yolk and bone meal can be beneficial. Milk is a rich natural source of calcium which is essential for the puppies. The foetuses draw on the dam for bone formation and other developments, and if the dam has to supply it unaided from her own resources, it can cause eclampsia. See NURSING MOTHER. If the bitch is very heavy in whelp it is advisable to increase her meals to three or even four of equal bulk. If she is carrying a big litter there is pressure on the internal organs and she will find it uncomfortable to eat too much at any one time. This will unnecessarily tax her digestive system. Fresh water should always be at the bitch's disposal. The bitch should not become constipated and if necessary small doses of liquid paraffin or mineral oil should be given. Any more violent laxative should be avoided.

Never lift a pregnant bitch by the back of the neck or by the elbows alone. Place one hand under her chest and the other beneath the hind legs so that she is lifted in a horizontal position. Any movement should be done gently and sudden jerking movements must be avoided.

A bitch can show all the symptoms of being in whelp but when the due date arrives fail to produce any puppies. This is known as a FALSE PREGNANCY. No satisfactory answer to this problem has been found. The bitch increases in girth until about the sixth or seventh week and in many cases produces milk. This can be a very distressing time for the bitch and many have been known to make their beds in preparation for the imaginary young. False pregnancy can also occur in an unmated bitch particularly in a rather nervous and highly-strung one. In such cases the bitch should be freely exercised, fed rather scantily and given a laxative. Her water intake should be cut down to a minimum. It is advisable to mate these bitches on their next season.

Premature Birth Puppies that are born earlier than the fifty-eighth day of GESTATION stand little chance of survival. See WHELPING. Premature puppies need careful nursing and they must be kept in a warm temperature of 70°F (21°C). At first they may not be able to suck either because of weakness or because the bitch's teats are too big for their tiny mouths. In such cases they must be bottle fed until they are strong enough to feed from their dam. Simulated bitch's milk can be used. Premature labour is not very common in bitches and is usually the result of an accident, a shock, or some severe illness.

Prepotency An individual is said to be prepotent if the majority of its offspring resemble it more than they resemble their other parent. Similarly, a strain is prepotent if individuals of that strain conspicuously 'stamp their type' on their offspring from mates of other strains. The term is not an exact scientific one, and is used rather loosely in a general sense. Often it is a matter of opinion whether an individual or strain is prepotent and in what features. Prepotency appears to depend largely on the prepotent animal carrying DOMINANT or epistatic GENES, so that they suppress the action of the recessive or hypostatic genes contributed by the less prepotent mate.

Inbred strains are generally believed to be prepotent in 'type', which must depend on the interaction of very many genes. The existence of such prepotency is not easy to prove or disprove, since type cannot be measured and its assessment is subjective. Where type depends on simple dominant factors like black colour or short coat, its prepotency is to be expected.

Prick Ear Ear carried erect, often pointed at the tip.

Prince Charles Spaniel see Cavalier King Charles Spaniel; King Charles Spaniel.

Professional Handlers The American Kennel Club licenses professional handlers, a practice not followed in most other countries. It has developed in the United States because of the large number of dog shows, and because of the great distances which must be travelled to reach many of them.

Professional handlers often come from the ranks of amateur breeders who have an unusual ability to groom and show dogs. Others gain experience by working for

Above Prick ears on a German Shepherd Dog.

the licensed professionals. There are roughly as many women professionals as men.

Handlers' licences are of two types. One permits the handler to accept dogs at the shows, to groom them there, and then to exhibit them. Some of these handlers may be licensed for only one or two breeds. Some may specialize in only certain breeds, such as sporting dogs, or toys.

The second type of licence permits the handler to have a large boarding kennel. He will then be permitted to keep dogs there between shows, to groom and train them, and then to transport them to the shows. If such a handler 'goes on a circuit', he may be away from home for a month or more.

Such handlers must submit detailed plans and pictures of their kennels before they can be licensed. They may also be visited by a representative of the American Kennel Club. All handlers are carefully regulated by American Kennel Club representatives. They must dress respectably, must demonstrate good sportsmanship in the ring, and also upon the show grounds. A handler who accepts a dog with a disqualifying fault is in danger of losing his licence.

Judging schedules often pose a handler, who has a large number of dogs to show, with the problem of being wanted in two different rings at the same time. He is then permitted to designate another handler to show one of the dogs for him. If he finishes in one ring before judging of the class is completed in the other ring, he can ask the judge to take over the other dog. This permission is usually granted.

Exhibitors wishing to gain sufficient handling experience to obtain a licence, can show dogs for other owners. But they are not permitted to charge for doing so.

Professional handlers charge varying fees, by tradition keep all money prizes won, and often charge an additional fee for Group or Best in Show victories. They also charge a *per diem* rate for boarding dogs between shows. The handlers often select the shows at which they will show certain dogs, and generally make the entries. They then charge the owners for this service.

It is expensive to hire a professional handler. Yet the cost is usually less than the owner would pay were he to take the dog himself which would involve travel expense, hotel and meal bills, and probably some entertainment expense. Moreover, the handler can take the dog to a series of shows, many of them during midweek, which the owner might not be able to attend.

Professional handlers are not permitted to judge. However, many of them resign their handlers' licences and become professional judges.

Progressive Retinal Atrophy see Eye Diseases; Hereditary Abnormalities.

Prolapse This is the displacement of an organ or structure. The common prolapses include *rectal prolapse* – when the rectum 'telescopes' inside itself and protrudes through the anus; *uterine prolapse* – where the uterus inverts and slips out of the vagina; and *vaginal prolapse*, the same but not so advanced.

In *eye prolapse* the eyeball moves into a position so that the eyelids are behind the eye. This is most commonly seen in PEKINGESE.

Prolapse is usually seen in an animal after an accident or where the organ concerned is weakened for some reason. All prolapsed conditions require immediate attention by a veterinarian.

Protozoan Diseases Protozoans are one-celled animals, visible under the microscope, which are responsible for four major diseases in dogs. Coccidiosis and giardiasis infest the intestinal tract. Canine piroplasmosis and leishmaniasis chiefly inhabit the blood and, in the case of leishmaniasis, also the liver, bone marrow, and spleen.

Professional handlers.
Top left Professional handlers can take dogs to shows – often midweek – which the dog owner would be unable to attend. An American handler exhibits his protégé Golden Retriever, Ch. Seneca Riparians Chief.
Bottom left Here an English handler is showing a Wire-haired Fox Terrier, Ch. Mooremaides Mandytoo as a ten-month-old puppy.

Coccidiosis has spread rapidly from warmer climates into the high temperate zones.

As a rule, it is a disease of young puppies. It causes mild or bloody diarrhoea, loss of appetite, emaciation, and occasionally death. Adult dogs may retain a mild infection all their lives. While resistant to a serious attack, they are themselves life-long carriers. Infection in puppies usually lasts from three to ten days. Although the disease is considered to be self-limiting, it appears to be becoming rapidly more serious. Poor sanitation, stresses from worms, and inadequate diets combine to allow the disease to flourish.

Drugs which have shown some success in the treatment of coccidiosis include the sulfonamides, sulfamethazine, and sulfaquinoxaline. Nitrofurazone and the tetracyclines also have some success.

Giardiasis is caused by another protozoan, *Giardia canis*. The disease is also one of puppies and young dogs. In severe infections, bloody diarrhoea and stools with an offensive odour are common. The disease is steadily growing more common. Treatment is usually the same as for coccidiosis.

Canine piroplasmosis is sometimes called babesiasis because it is caused by a protozoan known as *Babesia canis*. It is a tick-borne disease. The protozoans are pear-shaped. They attack and destroy red blood cells. Acute cases may terminate in death. Symptoms include increased pulse rate, several degrees of fever, loss of appetite, but an increase in thirst. In mild cases, anemia, indifference to the surroundings, and intermittent fever are symptoms. Positive identification is made by finding the parasites in blood tests. Recovered dogs may harbour the parasites for as long as a year.

For this reason, it is important to keep the dog free of ticks, to keep it from getting the disease and from spreading it. The least toxic and most effective drugs appear to be the compounds of diamidino, such as phenamidine isethionate. Supportive aids, such as blood transfusions, are also used.

Leishmaniasis, or kala-azar, is a disease which is common in Southern Asia, the Mediterranean border, and South America.

The disease is caused by a non-motile protozoan parasite named *Leishmania donovani*. It attacks the liver, bone marrow, spleen, and lymph nodes. An inflammation of the skin occurs, which may be spotted or diffuse. There is loss of hair in these areas, and many lymph glands may be swollen. Drugs, such as those used in canine piroplasmosis, are employed in the treatment of leishmaniasis.

Pseudorabies This infection is also known as Aujeszky's disease, mad itch, and infectious bulbar paralysis. It is invariably fatal to dogs, usually within 36 hours. The virus causing the infection belongs to the herpes group. Because of intense itching, dogs tear their flesh, or scratch facial tissues. They show no tendency to attack people or other animals. Pseudorabies has been reported very rarely in human beings, usually veterinarians or laboratory workers, and it causes in them only a mild infection. Swine and rats are possible vectors. The disease is very rare in dogs.

Pug.
Top right Pugsville's Mighty Jim, a champion in America, Bermuda, Canada and Cuba in the early 1960s.
Bottom right The characteristic dark mask and wrinkled brow of the Pug.

Pug The Pug is said to take its name from the Latin *pugnus* (a fist), the suggestion being that the dog's profile resembles in some way a closed fist. Not all commentators accept this and certainly this name was never used until the late eighteenth century. The Latin countries prefer the name 'Carlin'. An alternative, and much more likely theory is that 'Pug' was taken from the old English word used to describe pets in general and pet monkeys in particular. This word was also used as a term of endearment.

Not only the origin of the name is in doubt. The background of the breed itself is by no means firmly established. It was generally accepted at one time that the breed came originally from Holland. In fact, we now know that the Netherlands was just the country from which Great Britain first imported the dogs. It is widely accepted that the dogs originally came from China, and that they were a smooth-coated cousin of the PEKINGESE. Over the years, the Peke became longer, lower and hairier, while the Pug became taller, heavier and smoother.

It reached England in the middle of the nineteenth century and became popular in an extremely short time. Alex Dalziel, a canine commentator said in 1870: 'The Pug market is over-stocked and everywhere in town and country these animals swarm.'

The slightly derogatory note evident here has always been reserved for whatever breed happens to be the most popular at any given time. A well-known maxim is 'the higher they go the harder they fall'. And Pugs certainly fell very hard indeed at the beginning of this century. By the time the first breed statistics were produced by the Kennel Club of England the terriers ruled the roost and the once all-conquering Pug had slipped to a position half-way down the list of breeds in the popularity stakes.

Another well known maxim is 'Champions never come back', but Pugs show every indication of regaining a lot of their former popularity. Twenty years ago annual registrations in Great Britain ran at a mere 250. Ten years ago the figure was 1,200. Admittedly the rate of rise has not been sustained since that time. In the United States, however, their popularity continues to

increase with current registrations totalling over 10,000 a year.

Originally, fawns were the most popular colour but, at the beginning of this century, some exceptionally good blacks were more favoured. This trend remained during the time the breed was in the doldrums but the return of popularity brought with it a revival of the fawns which now outnumber the blacks by about ten to one. Many feel that the lighter colour is more generally attractive by its contrast with the black mask and the dark, lustrous eyes.

Over the years there have been many notable owners. Recently the most celebrated have been the Duke and Duchess of Windsor who have taken their collection of some half dozen into more magazines than one can remember for any other breed of dog.

Finally some mention must be made of the rather distinctive noises this breed makes. Critics say they grunt, snort and snore. Fans reply that they talk with their enchanting snuffles and make comfortable noises when asleep. Perhaps beauty is in the eye, or rather the ear, of the beholder.

Essentials of the breed: Head: large, massive and round. Muzzle: short, blunt and square. Eyes: dark, large, bold and prominent. Ears: thin, small and soft. Legs: very strong and straight. Body: short and cobby, wide in chest, and well ribbed. Feet: neither long nor round, nails black. Tail: curled tightly over the hip, a double curl being perfection. Coat: fine, smooth, short and glossy. Colour: silver, apricot fawn or black. The muzzle, ears, moles on cheeks, thumbmark on forehead and trace (a line extending from occiput to tail) should always be black. Weight 14 to 18 lb.
See colour plate p. 384.

Puli There are four great breeds of shepherd dogs in Hungary, the KOMONDOR, KUVASZ, Pumi, and Puli. Outside Hungary, the Puli is the best known of the four. The Komondor and the Kuvasz are large dogs, capable of guarding against wolves or human thieves. The Pumi and the Puli are smaller.

In Hungary, the two small breeds have sometimes been joined together under the term, *Juhasz Kutya*, or Shepherds' Dogs. They come from the great Hungarian sheep grazing area known as the *Puszta*.

The actual origin of the breed is in doubt. A German writer, Heppe, wrote in 1751 of a dog believed to have been a Puli. He called it the Hungarian Water Dog, and said that it was used to hunt rabbits and ducks.

Perhaps the most logical theory is that it came out of Asia with the Magyar invasion. It may certainly have been used for hunting, particularly for duck shooting. Many, however, were taken into the cities as Hungary became more urbanized.

The breed was brought to the United States about 1930, where its corded coat created a sensation. The American Kennel Club officially recognized the breed in 1936. Pulis (the Hungarian plural is *Pulik*) have been successfully trained for police work in Germany. Few have reached England.

Essentials of the breed: The revised American standard was approved in 1960. The skull is slightly domed, the stop is clearly defined, and the muzzle is of medium length. The bite is level or scissors, and the eyes are large, deep-set, and brown. Some Pulis are born bob-tailed. Most have the tail curled over the back when alert, or hanging when at rest.

The coat is double, with a soft, dense undercoat and a longer, never silky, undercoat. The coat mats easily,

and is easily trained into cords. In the United States and Canada, until recently, the practice has been to keep the coat combed out. But more and more are now being shown with well corded coats.

Colours are solid black, rusty-black, shades of grey, and white. Nose, flews, and eyelids are black, with flesh colours being serious faults. Coats with areas of two or more colours at the skin, and white foot or chest markings are also serious faults. Height: dogs 17 to 19 inches. Bitches 16 to 18 inches.

Pulse The normal method of feeling the pulse of a dog is to hold the inner aspect of the upper part of the hind leg. The pulse can then be detected. The pulse rate of dogs varies from below 75 to 100 beats per minute. The lowest rates apply to dogs of giant breeds; the highest to the toy breeds. The pulse rate varies with exercise, health and age.

Pumi see Puli.

Puppy A show puppy is defined by various Kennel Clubs throughout the world as a dog of at least six months and not exceeding twelve calendar months of age on the first day of the show. In Australia, a Baby Puppy Class is scheduled and this includes puppies of between three and six months of age.

For general purposes a puppy is a puppy until it reaches its first birthday.

Many youngsters are puppies long after this, particularly in the bigger breeds where they do not reach maturity until they are at least two years of age. Understandably the larger dogs need much more time to mature, both mentally and physically, than the smaller breeds.
See BEHAVIOUR PATTERNS IN PUPPIES AND YOUNG DOGS, CLASSES AT SHOWS.

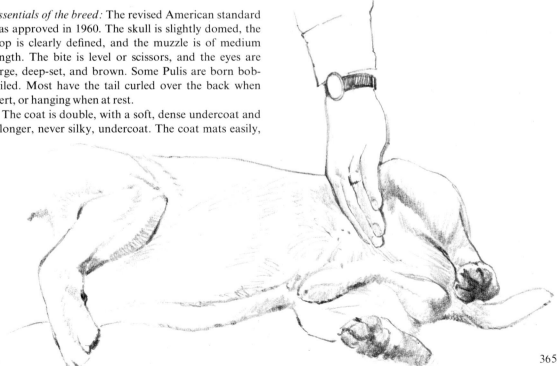

Top left Pug. Ch. Pugville's Kublai Khan.

Puli.
Far left Ch. Gyalpusztai Kocos Furkus, the only Puli ever to have held both American and Hungarian titles.
Bottom left Ch. Cinkotai Csibesz. Note the classical corded grooming.

Right Pulse: where and how to feel a dog's pulse.

Puppy Eating see Cannibalism.

Puppy Shots see Antiserum – Immune Serum.

Puppy Walk The name given to the system in which FOXHOUND pups are reared in private houses from the time of weaning until their return to the kennels at the age of about one year.

Pure-Bred A dog whose parents are of the same breed, and which are themselves descended from pure-bred dogs of the same breed.

Pyrenean Mountain Dog The Pyrenean Mountain Dog, or Great Pyrenees, belongs to the group of massive dogs which came out of Asia during various migrations into Europe. Its closest relative, in point of conformation, is the Hungarian KUVASZ, but it is claimed that it is one of the ancestors of the NEWFOUNDLAND.

The French name for the breed is *Chien de Montagne des Pyrénées*. Apparently the dog was not a herding dog but simply guarded the flocks of sheep and cattle from wolves, bears, and stock thieves. A smaller dog, the *Chien de Berger des Pyrénées*, was the herder.

The French historian, Bourdet, states that the Château of Lourdes was guarded by huge mountain dogs. Sentry boxes were made large enough to accommodate a sentry and his dog, and jailers were accompanied by one or more of these dogs. From this and

other references, it appears that many of the châteaux in southwest France were so guarded.

Madame de Maintenon accompanied the Dauphin of France to Barrèges, where they were impressed by the beauty of the dogs and took several back to Paris. About the same time, the Marquis de Louvois also bought Pyrenees dogs, and other noblemen helped to make the Pyrenees Mountain Dog a sort of official court dog.

Since dogs were used by the French, English, and other armies, it is possible that the Pyrenees dogs were also so used. Spiked collars of a size to fit them are still in existence.

French settlements were made on the Newfoundland coast in 1662. It is said that they brought the big mountain dogs with them to aid in the warfare against the British. For this reason some authorities believe the Pyrenean Mountain Dog to be an ancestor of the Newfoundland.

General Lafayette, the French general who had fought with the colonists in the American Revolution, sent a pair of the dogs to J. S. Skinner in 1824. In *The Dog and The Sportsman*, written by Skinner, he states that Lafayette recommended them as being 'of inestimable value to wool growers in all regions exposed to the depredations of wolves and sheepkilling dogs'. It was Skinner who had reported the importation of Pyrenean Mountain Dogs into Newfoundland.

Before World War I, the English pioneer of the breed

Above Puppy. Twelve St. Bernard puppies enjoy their dinner while the thirteenth enjoys some body else's. Puppies of the large breeds are not considered mature until they are at least two years old.

was Lady Sybil Grant. In more recent times, Madame Harper Troi-Fontaines worked to establish the breed in England. Mrs. Frances V. Crane founded her Basquaerie Kennels in the United States in 1933 when the American Kennel Club gave the breed official recognition. The present standard was approved in 1935.

Essentials of the breed: The head is wedge-shaped, and 10 to 11 inches from the dome to the end of the nose. The ears are a rounded 'V' carried close to the head. There is little stop, and the eyes are dark. The lips are tight and black tipped.

The chest is rather deep, but flat sided. The tail reaches to below the hock, and forms a wheel when at repose. The legs are heavily boned, the feet closely cupped. There are single dewclaws on the front feet, and double ones on the hind feet.

The coat is double, with a fine, dense undercoat and a long, flat, thick outer coat of coarser hair, either straight or slightly undulating.

The standard calls for a height of 27 to 32 inches at the shoulder for dogs, and 25 to 29 for bitches. Males weigh 100 to 125 lb., and bitches 90 to 115 lb. Colours are all white, or principally white with markings of badger, grey, or shades of tan. Shoulder height equals the distance from the shoulder baldes to the root of the tail.

See colour plate p. 290.

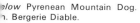

elow Pyrenean Mountain Dog.
า. Bergerie Diable.

Q

Quantitative Genetics The majority of genes probably have, individually, only very small effects; where the effect is one of increase or decrease of a quantity (such as height at shoulder, body weight, or milk yield) the GENES are called 'quantitative genes'. In most contexts this term is synonymous with 'polygenes', 'minor genes' and 'modifying genes', although these terms can include genes whose effects are not manifestly quantitative.

Probably most of the more elusive show points, as well as such working attributes as speed and 'natural obedience' are largely dependent on genes of this type. The effect of quantitative genes tends to be influenced by the environment (e.g. health and weight obviously depend on feeding during growth). Although the genes concerned must segregate and recombine like any other genes, calculations based directly on the Mendelian law are not helpful when hundreds of gene pairs are involved, and instead, calculations are based on statistical probabilities operating in large populations, that is among very large numbers of animals. Matings between individuals near one end of the range e.g. large × large (or small × small) tend to throw puppies whose average size is between that of their parents and the average of the population as a whole. Matings between opposite extremes tend to give offspring of intermediate size, and these, if interbred to produce a large number of puppies, will give offspring ranging in size from that of the largest parent to that of the smallest, or even beyond these extremes. The great majority will, however, almost certainly be in the middle part of the range, the numbers decreasing as the two extremes are approached. The same principle applies to all quantative characters, not only to size.

In the absence of genes having major effects, the usual way to try to increase the 'quantity' (e.g. height at shoulder) is to breed from individuals near the upper extreme. However, partly because of gene segregation and partly because of environmental effects, the puppies are most unlikely to include more than a small percentage as extreme (as tall, when fully grown) as their specially-selected parents. It is because so many 'show points' depend on this sort of genetic situation that matings between outstanding dogs and bitches often give disappointing results. However, the average of the offspring of such matings is likely to be above the average for the breed as a whole, and a few individuals may excel.

It sometimes happens that a desired feature or aptitude can be produced by various different 'collections' of polygenes; this can lead to a situation where two or more strains within a breed consistently produce winners, but when crossed together or to other strains, give disappointing results. This is because the complicated and delicate balance involving numerous gene pairs established within strains is upset when they are outcrossed.

Quarantine Quarantine is the period during which an animal (or person, ship, etc.) is kept in isolation when suspected of carrying contagious disease. Dogs are subjected to a period of quarantine upon entering most countries where RABIES is not endemic since they are suspected of carrying the virus which is present in most countries in the world. At the end of the quarantine period, if no symptoms have developed, the dogs are assumed not to be carrying that virus and are therefore released to their owners.

Quarantine Kennels There are now many quarantine kennels in countries that are rabies-free, all licensed and all having to comply with government rules and regulations. There are minimum requirements laid down as to the height of the fencing, and the law requires that fencing between kennels must be 'nose and paw proof'. In other words, dogs must not be kennelled so that they can touch each other, or find a way through the fencing to visit their neighbours.

One animal may not, of course, share a kennel with another and it may not be exercised other than in an enclosed space from which it cannot escape and into which other animals cannot penetrate. The regulations are sound, but one slip can undo all the good work of segregation. In addition, the rules are not always adhered to with sufficiently strict attention. It is advisable for every owner of an imported dog to visit a selection of quarantine kennels before the animal enters the country and begins its term. The kennel sizes vary tremendously, exercising space is frequently inadequate and badly fenced. Responsibility for the introduction of rabies must rest with the owner of the infected animal. It is therefore necessary to be assured that, if the disease appears, there has been no opportunity for its transmission to another animal.

Left Quarantine kennels. A German Shepherd Dog is weighed in isolation, at the quarantine kennels. It is essential that dogs do not come into contact with each other during quarantine.

Colour plate Bull Terrier. Ch Uglee Snowblossom of Lenste

(Continued on p. 385)

Top left Wire-Haired Fox Terrier. Ch. Gosmore Kirkmoor Craftsman.
Bottom left Toy Fox Terrier. Ch. 'PR' Rinebold's Laddie Boy.
Above Smooth Fox Terriers. Ch. Ellastone Gold Nugget and Ch. Ellastone Lucky Nugget.

Top left Manchester Terrier.
Ch. Eaglespur Lancehead.

Bottom left Airedale Terriers.
Trefin Slick Whiskers and
Trefin Samantha.

Top right Young Irish Terriers
from the Ballymakenny Kennels.

Below, near right Lakeland
Terrier. Ch. Brazen Blonde of Oz.

Below, far right Kerry Blue Terrier.
Torquil Joe's Pennywhistle.

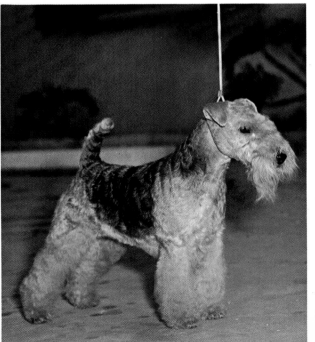

Top left Bedlington Terrier.
Ch. Pan Terra Torch O'Lochmist.

Bottom left Skye Terrier.
Happyhill Mini Major.

Top right West Highland White
Terrier. Ch. Alpine Gay Sonata.

Middle right Australian Terrier.
Faygate Flora.

Bottom right Cairn Terriers.
Brockis of Benliath, Blencathra
Mhairi and Grail Deeds of
Benliath.

Top left Yorkshire Terrier.
Ch. Raybrook's Rear Admiral.

Bottom, far left Norwich Terrier.
Ch. Jericho Gingernut.

Bottom, near left Norfolk Terrier.
Ch. Nanfan Heckle.

Top right Border Terrier.
Ch. Mansergh April Mist.

Bottom right Silky Terrier.
Ch. Koonoona Bo Bo.

Top left Cavalier King Charles Spaniel. Torset Rosen Kavalier.

Bottom left King Charles Spaniel (English Toy Spaniel). Ch. Holmehurat Merry Monarch.

Top right Italian Greyhound. Fleeting Farida.

Middle right Miniature Pinscher. Poco a Poco la Tigre de Danalec.

Bottom right English Toy Terrier. Ch. Harpers The Mikado.

(Continued from p. 368)

There are some points over which the dog owner has no control. For instance, he cannot be certain that the kennel staff will ensure that his dog never leaves 'toys' about in the exercising run for other inmates to sniff at and play with. Often rules concerning contact can be broken by the most well-meaning kennel staff – all with potentially disastrous results.

A good quarantine kennel will probably be isolated, with few, if any neighbours; it will have tough kennel buildings, strong fencing and foolproof locks.

Once in quarantine, the dog can be visited, and all such kennels have 'visiting hours'. The visiting of the pet dog in quarantine is of questionable value and some feel that it probably benefits the owner more than the animal. A pet cannot possibly understand that its owner will come again next week, and having just settled down and accepted its environment with reasonable grace, its life is disrupted by a visit from the owner. All quarantine kennels are happy to discuss a dog's progress on the telephone, or even to send a written report and they all, naturally, advise owners of any problems that arise concerning their dog.

Quarantine fees are normally paid one month in advance, and it is also the responsibility of the owner to pay any veterinary fees that may be incurred during the period. Once a dog is in quarantine kennels, the stay is assured for the whole period, excepting in the case of extreme dissatisfaction, when the owner may apply to the authorities for permission to move the animal.

For a pampered pet accustomed to constant attention, quarantine probably appears to its owner to be indescribable misery, but most animals will settle down given time and if they are left alone to adjust.

Quarantine Regulations In those countries where RABIES is not endemic, quarantine periods are enforced for both dogs and cats. Some countries, notably Australia and New Zealand, have a somewhat looser quarantine law than that which is in force in Great Britain. However, while the term of quarantine is much shorter than in Britain, these countries are also able to prohibit the importation of animals should an outbreak occur.

The law in countries which insist on quarantine is that a dog or cat must undergo a period of segregation in an approved establishment. The imported animal must, on arrival, be transported to the chosen kennel in such a way that it has no contact with any other animal. Once in quarantine, the animal may not be moved except with the permission of the authorities.

In those countries which do not insist upon quarantine but do wish to control the endemic disease, animals are required to be inoculated against the disease before entering. These inoculations must be boosted at varying intervals according to the age of the animal, the type of vaccine used and the virulence of the disease in the country concerned.

It must be appreciated and it cannot be overstressed, that rabies kills not only dogs and cats, it kills men. It is not widely realized that while cattle do not normally bite, and therefore do not transmit the disease in the usual manner, they can and do suffer from it. Rabies, particularly in South America, accounts for the death of an enormous number of cattle. Many animals are known to carry the disease and transmit it. It follows then, that a country really determined to prevent the introduction of the disease should enforce quarantine regulations for all animals which could possibly be carriers of the disease. No country is yet so strict.

In the light of a report by a Committee of Inquiry set up in Great Britain in 1970, it appears that for countries which impose a quarantine system, the best programme would be an inoculation against rabies before arrival in the new country, six months quarantine, and a second inoculation against rabies at the appropriate time prior to release.

Right Quarantine kennels. Although all dogs in quarantine kennels can be visited, this is often found to be unsettling for the dogs, if comforting for their owners.

Colour plate.
Top left Griffons Bruxellois Ch. Gaystock La Fable and Ch. Gaystock La Flambée, and Japanese Spaniel Gaystock Stepdancer of Rui Gu.
Middle left Pug. Ch. Cutmil Francis.
Bottom left Papillons. Ch. Picaroon Pan and Ch. Picaroon Parasol.

R

Rabies Rabies, also known as hydrophobia, is a virus disease of all mammals, including man. The virus affects the brain and once symptoms have developed, death is certain and horrible. The disease is most common in dogs and cats but other domestic animals may be affected as well as wild animals such as foxes. The infection is usually spread by the bite of the affected animal since the virus is found in the saliva.

The virus moves along nerves in the area of the bite until it reaches the brain. It proliferates until it invades the entire brain, moves into the salivary nerves and escapes into the saliva. Only then do symptoms appear.

In dogs, the first sign which is noticed is a change in temperament. Quiet dogs may become aggressive, while fierce dogs may become quieter. The second stage is the furious stage when the dog runs about wildly attacking anything in its path. This is the typical 'mad dog'. Finally the disease progresses to the paralytic or dumb stage. The dog loses control of its lower jaw and of its limbs, collapses and dies. Rabies in the dog runs its course quite rapidly, usually a matter of about a week from the first signs to the inevitable fatal termination.

There is no cure for rabies and unfortunately vaccination cannot be relied upon for prevention so that the control of the disease is difficult. In those parts of the world where rabies is endemic, such as the continents of Europe and North America, it is unlikely that the disease will ever be totally eliminated, as the wild life is infected. In such situations, vaccination of dogs may help control the spread of the infection, and re-vaccination is necessary, according to the type of vaccine used, annually or every three years.

Certain animals are known to be carriers of the virus. They do not themselves develop the disease, unless weakened by other ailments. Among these are the meerkats of South Africa, and the vampire bats of tropical Central and South America. Some North American bats also carry the virus. Skunks and foxes can harbour the virus for long periods before developing the disease.

A dog suspected of having rabies should not be killed. The dog should be quarantined until its condition is clear. If it dies, then laboratory studies of its brain are made. Other dogs which have been exposed to it should be kept under quarantine for six months. If known to have been bitten by a proven rabid animal, this period should be extended.

Great Britain has been free of rabies since 1922 apart from two isolated cases in 1969. This is principally due to the QUARANTINE REGULATIONS. Other countries which have remained immune include New Zealand, Australia, and many Caribbean countries such as Barbados. In each country, quarantine restrictions of various intensity are in force.

Racing A trailing hound which tries to outrun its brace-mate while depending upon it to hold to the trail.

Racy Tall dog, of slight build.

Radiography Simple X-rays are used to find fractures, bone abnormalities, osteomyelitis, calcified cartilage, and dislocations of the hip or shoulder. Radiography is commonly used today in diagnosing HIP DYSPLASIA, or in certifying that a dog is free from it. X-rays are also used to detect foreign bodies in the alimentary canal. Calculi, or stones in the bladder, can usually be seen on X-rays since they are made up of the phosphates of calcium and magnesium. Stones which have been driven under the pads of the feet and cannot be detected by other means can be located by radiography.

Complex techniques using contrast media (visualizing substances) injected into the body can be used to examine those parts of the body that do not normally show on direct X-ray examination. Thus, the chambers of the heart can be examined after contrast media are introduced into the blood in, or near, the heart.

A more simple technique is that of feeding a barium meal to the dog. Abnormalities in the digestive tract can be seen on a series of X-rays taken as the meal passes through the body.

Rampur Greyhound see Greyhound, Eastern.

Ranula This is the term applied to a swelling occurring under the tongue, produced by a collection of saliva in the ducts draining into the mouth when one or more of these ducts become blocked.

Rare Breeds It is important to make the distinction between breeds which are rare and dogs which are difficult to classify. Many breeds are numerically rare but well-known, such as the SUSSEX SPANIEL. Some breeds are very common locally, such as the Lapphund, but unknown in other lands. Dogs such as the Laika are occasionally included amongst rare breeds, when they are neither rare nor a breed, simply a type which is common, but rarely if ever seen at a dog show.

The breeds described or illustrated here include some of the more distinctive of the less widely known breeds.
Beauceron The Beauceron is sometimes called the Berger de Beauce, or the Pastor de Beauce. It resembles the DOBERMANN PINSCHER, being usually black and tan, red, grey, grey marked with black, or black. The head is wedge-shaped, and the ears are usually cropped. The tail is long, and reaches the hock, Although the hair is short it is usually about an inch long on the back. It is a French shepherd dog.
Bleu de Gascogne Two breeds of French origin use the name 'Blue Gascon'. One is a Basset which differs only slightly from the present popular type. The other is a larger dog which resembles the American Bluetick Coonhound. It is about 25 inches high, and usually has a blue-coloured head, long, pendant ears, and large patches of blue, plus blue ticks in a white background.
Bracco Italiano This is an Italian pointing dog. It is usually orange and white, has long, BLOODHOUND-like ears, and its tail is docked to six or eight inches. Height is about 25 inches at the shoulder.

Right Rare breeds. Drentse Partridge Dog.

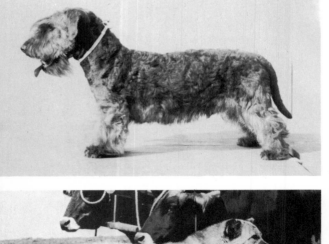

Rare breeds.
Far left, top Cěský Fousek.
Far left, upper middle Norwegian
Buhund.
Far left, lower middle Cěský Ter-
rier.
Far left, bottom Caucasian Sheep-
dog.
Top left Smooth-coated Dutch
Herd Dog.
Bottom left Steenbrak and puppies.
Top right Rough-coated Dutch
Herd Dog.
Bottom near right Portuguese
East African Hunting Dog.
Bottom far right Anatolian Kara-
bash, wearing spiked collar.

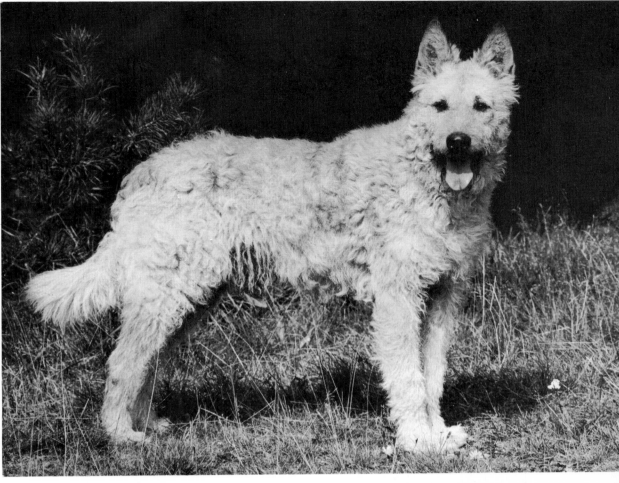

Rare breeds.
eft Puffinhound and pup.
Right An X-ray of a Puffinhound's
aw with its extra toe, on the left,
ompared with that of an ordinary
log's paw.

Drever The Swedish Drever or Dachsbracke resembles a rather slender BASSET. It is a rather slow trailing hound with an excellent nose and a good voice. Males are 12 to 16 inches at the shoulder. Drevers have long ears, but they are shorter than those of Bassets. Basic colour is white with patches of other colours.

Nova Scotia Duck Tolling Dog The breed is said to be derived from the CHESAPEAKE BAY RETRIEVER, though the conformation of the head is closer to that of the GOLDEN RETRIEVER. The colour is fox red. Males average $20\frac{1}{2}$ inches at the shoulder and weigh 50 lb. The dog's function is to create enough disturbance along shore to make ducks curious. The ducks then swim close enough to shore for the hunter to get a shot. The dogs are also excellent retrievers.

Sinhala Hound Ceylon has a native dog which very much resembles the BASENJI in size and type. Unlike the Basenji, it does bark. The dogs have a remarkable ability to live off the land as scavengers. Shades of brown, and dark brown brindle, are common.

Tosa Dog Public dog fights are still permitted in Japan, and the best of the fighting dogs are highly honoured. The dog used is the Tosa. It resembles the MASTIFF of England. A common colour is fawn with darker ears. The dog is somewhat smaller than the true Mastiff.

Other distinctive rare breeds include the Pudelpointer and the Vallhund.

See KENNEL CLUB, UNITED.

Rat Tail A tail of which the root is thick and covered with curls; the tip bare, as in the IRISH WATER SPANIEL.

Recessive A recessive gene is one which produces its full effect only in homozygous condition – when both genes of a pair are the same – because if an alternative or 'allele' is present its action will overshadow (DOMINATE) that of the recessive gene. In the simplest case, the heterozygous animal *Aa* is indistinguishable from the homozygous dominant *AA*, and the effect of the recessive alternative is manifested only in the homozygous recessive *aa*. In such cases, the only way of finding out whether an animal is homozygous or heterozygous is by a breeding test, usually by mating it to a homozygous recessive (*aa*) animal. If the animal is a carrier (*Aa*), half the offspring are expected to be homozygous recessives: *Aa* mated with *aa* gives equal numbers of *Aa* and *aa* offspring; but *AA* mated with *aa* gives all *Aa* offspring resembling the *AA* parent. This is the classical 'test-mating' used to discover carriers of recessive genes responsible for abnormalities like progressive retinal atrophy (PRA). In many instances, a recessive gene has some effect in a heterozygote, either through a slight expression of its main effect, or through some other associated effect. This allows carriers to be identified without test-mating.

Additionally, the term 'recessive' is often applied to features not manifested in the offspring of mates one of which shows the feature in question. For example, if a prick-eared breed is mated to a lop-eared breed, the ear-carriage of the puppies will vary, but none will be fully prick-eared. Breeding experiments indicate that

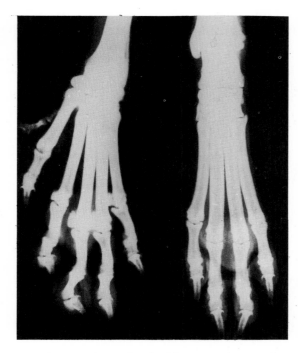

several gene pairs are involved in ear-carriage, so that prick-ears is not a simple recessive to lop-ears.

Sometimes the action of a gene, even in homozygous state, is obstructed by that of other genes, which gives a false impression that the gene is recessive. For example, an albino animal, which cannot make any coloured pigment at all, nevertheless carries genes at every point concerned with coat colour; none of these can be expressed in such an animal, although they are not themselves recessive to albinism.

Rectum This is the lower part of the large intestine leading to the anal canal. The walls of the rectum and anus are lined with longitudinal and circular muscle fibres, closely intermingled. Thick, ring-like external sphincter ani muscles surround the anal canal.

Many of the rectal muscles are connected by their nerves to the sympathetic nervous system. Control is therefore largely involuntary, and is governed by the rhythm of the entire digestive tract. There is some voluntary control over the external sphincter muscles. This control is probably greater in the dog than in most other animals.

The rectum is subject to various ailments. Dogs get rectal tumours, many of which appear to be malignant. Fissures, or cracks, in the rectal wall occur as a result of being damaged by the sharp edges of undigested bones. Abscesses sometimes form in the anal glands. These should be lanced and cleaned by a veterinarian.

Registration, Britain One of the first tasks of the KENNEL CLUB (England) on its foundation in 1873 was the compilation of a stud book, and the catalogues of shows from 1859–1873 were the basis for the first volume. In those days dogs were entered for shows by their pet names coupled with their owner's name, but in many cases entries simply read 'Mr. Brown's Dog'. Details such as pedigree and age were of no importance and therefore were not recorded. A newspaper report of an early show complained of 'Quantities of Shots, Bobs, Bangs, Jets, Nettles and Vicks, most of them insufficiently described and none of them being the well-known dog of the same name'.

The value of the first volume of the stud book was substantially reduced because of this and one of the first steps of the Committee was the provision of a registry of names in which dogs were entered by individual names, with details of age, colour, pedigree, etc. A distinctive name was given to each dog so that, on qualification for the stud book, there was no duplication and dogs, for the first time, were identified for pedigree purposes. From this register the present Kennel Club system of registration has been evolved, which records nearly 2,000,000 pedigrees.

Since January 1971 a dog has been ineligible for registration if it was not pure-bred or if its parents were not already registered. At the time of registration a name is allotted to a dog, and if after ten years the dog has not won a major prize or award the name may be used again, but if the dog has won a major prize its name is entered in the stud book, together with details of its pedigree and prizes, and the name cannot be used again for a dog of the same breed.

The following table shows the growth in the number of registrations in Britain each decade since 1900:

1900 – 11,650	*1940 – 13,968
1910 – 18,918	1950 – 100,433
*1920 – 16,189	1960 – 133,618
1930 – 48,784	1970 – 180,000

*These totals were affected by the First and Second World Wars.

Only the legal owner of a dog may register it at the Kennel Club and if the ownership changes a transfer must be recorded. A dog may be exhibited at a show or entered for a trial by the registered owner only. Before a dog qualifies for entry in the Kennel Club Stud Book, its registered name may be changed by the addition of the new owner's registered affix but the Kennel Club discourages such changes by charging a fee of £5 for the change.

A PREFIX or affix can be registered as an identifying name for a kennel for the lifetime of the owner on payment of a fee of £10. The chosen word must be used as a prefix when registering dogs bred by the owner and as an affix to identify dogs registered but not bred by the owner. So many words have been registered as prefixes at the Kennel Club that it is now difficult to find new words which the Kennel Club will accept. They ask for a selection of six words to choose from but a further selection is often required.

A dog without a pedigree, or with an unregistered parent or parents, or of no recognizable breed cannot be registered at the Kennel Club except in the Obedience Record and if it is entered in that record it can only compete in obedience tests and at working trials and the registration does not entitle its progeny to any recognition by the Kennel Club.

The fact that a dog is registered at the Kennel Club is no guarantee of its pure breeding, as in all animal breeding a great deal must be taken on trust. The signature on the pedigree should be accepted with the same reserve as the signature on a cheque, but the standard in the dog world is high and the majority of dog breeders are jealous of their reputations.

Registration, Canada The registration of dogs in Canada roughly parallels the rules governing those in the United States. (See: REGISTRATION – UNITED STATES). However, until 1970, Canadian registrations were handled by the Canadian National Livestock Records Co. They are now handled by the Canadian Kennel Club. Canada, as the United States, now requires the registration of litters. In addition to the U.S. rules, Canada requires a certification as to whether the litter resulted from a natural mating, or from ARTIFICIAL INSEMINATION.

Individual dogs must be identifiable by either a nose print, or a tattoo, before they can be registered. The Canadian Kennel Club provides nose print forms, or tattoo equipment at a nominal cost. The application to register the individual dog must give the number of the tattoo or nose print. If a tattoo is used, then the certification must include the three digits or numerals in the tattoo, the tattoo number and year-letter, and the place of the tattoo. For example, RE – right ear; RF – right flank, LE – left ear, or LF – left flank.

The Canadian Kennel Club also provides an agreement form for the disposal of a dog which is not to be used for breeding. The agreement covers not only the purchaser of the dog, but also any other person to whom he, or she, sells it. The second section of this agreement reads: 'The dog will not be used for breeding purposes by me, or any other person, partnership, or company, while this agreement remains in effect, and I hereby undertake to act as insurer and to pay to the seller the sum of $ . . . . . as liquidated damages if the dog is used for breeding purposes by any other person, partnership, or company.'

A third section reads: 'If, in violation of this agreement, this dog is used for breeding purposes, its progeny is not eligible for registration in the records of the Canadian Kennel Club nor may such progeny be represented as purebred.' The fourth section reads: 'Should I sell, or otherwise dispose of the dog, I will require the new owner to complete an agreement of this kind, a copy of which agreement I shall file with the Canadian Kennel Club.'

Sometimes a puppy, which appears to be unworthy at the time of sale, grows into an excellent adult of its breed. The Canadian Kennel Club has a 'consent to cancellation' form to cover such a contingency.

The Canadian rule concerning Artificial Insemination specifies: 'A litter born in Canada as a result of artificial insemination, the progeny of a sire and dam registered in the records of the Club, may be registered under the regulations approved by the Club and the Department of Agriculture of Canada.'

Registration, United States If a dog born in the United States is to be registered by the American KENNEL CLUB, it must come from a litter which has itself been registered. The American Kennel Club furnishes official litter registration application forms for this purpose. One section provides space for the owner or the sire to certify that the mating took place at a certain time and place. The sire and dam must also have been registered.

The owner of the bitch, or dam, must then certify that the litter was born upon a certain date, and the number of puppies in the litter, and the number of each sex. This does not mean the number born, but only those living at the time of filing the application to register the litter.

The American Kennel Club studies the application, and if it finds all details to be correct, it registers the litter, and then sends to the owner of the dam a 'litter kit'. The top half of a certification paper contains the litter registration. To the bottom half are attached individual registration forms, one – and one only – for each puppy in the litter.

The certification must later specify the person to whom the puppy was sold. If the breeder certifies the date of sale, but does not include the name of the buyer then it cannot be registered.

It often happens that the buyer of the puppy will re-sell it, or give it away, without first having registered it. For such cases, special transfer forms are supplied by the American Kennel Club. The original buyer must certify that he disposed of the puppy on a certain date, and name the new owner. Sometimes, a puppy will go through three or four owners before the application for individual ownership is made. For each of these owners, there would have to be a properly filled out and endorsed transfer form, or the puppy would not be registered. In this manner the American Kennel Club requires complete information on the chain of ownership. Only in this way can it be certain that the dog to be registered is the one which belongs to a particular set of registration papers.

Sometimes a registered bitch gets mated to two registered males of the same breed, and from the same kennel. The puppies would obviously be pure-bred, but because the owner of the bitch cannot certify which male is the sire, the litter cannot be registered.

The American Kennel Club recognizes the stud books of many other countries. To a certain extent, this means that it will register a dog from the particular foreign country, provided it is accompanied by a proper export pedigree.

However, it may happen that breeders in the foreign country wish to improve their breed by crossing in dogs of another breed. After several generations, the original breed will have the desired benefits derived from the other. The American Kennel Club will not recognize nor register these dogs. Though registered in their own country, they show 'interbred' two or three generations back, and this makes them ineligible under AKC rules.

Registration of a new breed is not easy in the United States. Those sponsoring the new breed, let us say the TIBETAN SPANIEL, must set up their own governing club. If sufficient numbers of the new breed are present in the United States, the American Kennel Club may then grant the breed status among the 'miscellaneous breeds'. Such dogs can be shown at dog shows, but they cannot win 'blue ribbons', nor championships. Ribbons awarded to miscellaneous breeds correspond in colour to those used at sanctioned match shows – rose for first, brown for second, light green for third, and grey for fourth. There are only two classes, one for dogs and one for bitches, which means that an AKITA, for example, would have to compete against the Tibetan Spaniel, IBIZAN HOUND, or other miscellaneous breeds.

A breed may get full recognition by the American Kennel Club when, in the Club's opinion, it is ready for it. As a rule, there must be at least 600 registered in the breed club's own stud book, and under certification procedures which the American Kennel Club finds acceptable. They must also be well distributed about the country.

Where breeds have originated in areas where stud books do not exist (the SIBERIAN HUSKY is an example) a foundation stock is approved in the United States, and the new stud book is then closed. A dog cannot then be registered unless it comes from a registered litter. Thus, one could not now go to either the Siberian or American Arctic, select perfect dogs, bring them to the United States, and have them registered.

The rules governing the importation and registration of dogs are extremely complex. For this reason, persons bringing dogs from other countries should obtain export pedigrees where possible, and should retain shipping and vaccination receipts, plus any other papers or pictures which would aid in proving that the registration papers actually belong to the dog in hand. Owners should make photo-copies of all records, and should mail them to the Foreign Registrations Dept., American Kennel Club, 51 Madison Ave., New York, N.Y., 10010. The Club will then send specific registration instructions.

A registered dog, or one eligible for registration, is entitled to registration papers, even if it has features which would disqualify it in the show ring. A breeder cannot 'sell' the dog's papers: he cannot say he will sell the dog for $100 without papers, and $150 with papers. In such cases, the American Kennel Club can order the breeder to supply the proper registration papers. However, a breeder can sell without papers a puppy which he believes to be unworthy for use in breeding or exhibiting and in such cases, the sale must be accompanied by a written agreement, signed by buyer and seller, that this is the reason for denial of papers.

Relatives of the Dog There are five families of animals, other than the dog, which have been described as true members of the Canidae. These are the maned wolf, the raccoon dog, the South American jackal, the fox, and the family of the wolf, coyote, and true jackal.

The maned wolf is certainly no ordinary wolf. Its colour is fox red. It has extraordinarily long legs and a relatively short body. These long legs give it great speed. Maned wolves have erect, rather large ears, triangular in shape, and their name comes from a sort of off-standing mane on the neck. They are great swimmers as well as runners, yet they do not use their

speed to run down their prey, but feed chiefly on small rodents and insects. They live along the southern edge of the Amazon Basin in South America.

The Raccoon Dog (Nyctereutes) gets its name from the raccoon to which it bears some resemblance. Its habitat is Japan and part of China. It has a rather heavy body and small, erect ears. The colours are brindle, grey, yellow, and black, and most have a black eye ring or 'spectacle'. Raccoon Dogs tend to migrate to the mountains in summer, and to return to the lowlands in winter. They hunt in packs and are nocturnal. Total body length is 32 inches.

There are several varieties of the South American jackal (Dusicyon carnivorus) which is also known as the crab-eating dog or crab-eating fox because it not only eats crabs but dives for them. True jackals inhabit south-eastern Europe, much of Africa except desert areas, and parts of Asia. They are small, many not being taller than 15 inches at the shoulder. They are nocturnal and hunt in packs. And though they often chase and pull down antelopes, they also feed upon carrion. Their habit of following lions to gorge themselves on the big cats' leavings is well known. They resemble wolves and dogs in DENTITION, the round eye pupil, and in a 63-day GESTATION period.

Foxes are more solitary than wolves; they hunt alone rather than in packs, and the sexes may remain apart until breeding time. A major difference between foxes and wolves and dogs is that the nasal passages of the former do not open into hollow spaces in the frontal bones. It is said, therefore, that foxes have no sinuses.

The wolf and coyote are closer to the true dog than are other members of the Canidae. Wolves vary greatly in size, from 50 lb. to 125 lb. Their colour is predominantly grey, though nearly white animals have been known in the Polar Arctic. The gestation period is 63 days, as for dog and fox. Litters of up to fourteen

pups have been reported. Puppies' eyes are completely open by fourteen days. Wolf bitches have their heat periods only once a year, in late winter; domestic dogs, the BASENJI excepted, usually have two heat periods a year. Male dogs become sexually mature at from eight months to a year, but male wolves do not reach sexual maturity until about two years old.

The coyote is usually described as a small wolf. Its height is about 20 inches, body length is 36 inches, and the tail 12 to 15 inches. Its range is from Alaska to Guatemala. It is normally a plains dweller, but it also survives well in desert areas. Coyotes live in dens during the day and hunt at night, alone or in pairs. Their yapping cry, which differs from the sound of the wolf, was once well known in the American West.

Research Dogs The use of the dog in research is a highly emotional subject. Facts indicate that where advances in curative and preventive medicine are made for man with the use of dogs, the dog population also benefits.

Through the years a wide variety of breeds and types of dog have been used and are still used, but the present trend is for the pedigreed BEAGLE of known source and origin to be used for long term studies. The reason for this is that in the early days of intensive drug testing, the United States had large numbers of Beagles available. The breed was then found to be eminently suitable because of its good temperament, convenient size, virility, early maturity, and freedom from breed exaggeration. When suitability became apparent, scientists looked further ahead and found that the purpose-bred animal, reared under as near as possible disease-free conditions and in a special environment, was better than the animal bought from an unknown source. As the use of the purpose-bred animal increases, less wastage of time and of animals will occur, and the risk

Relatives of the dog.
Above left Wolves are the closest relatives of the dog, and some, like the Timber Wolf, look very dog-like.
Above Jackals, like dogs, form one of the five families belonging to the genus Canidae.

of a much loved pet being stolen from the street will eventually be eliminated.

When a research study is done on a dog in one country and is repeated or elaborated upon in another, a dog of the same breed must be used, in order to compare results accurately. To use a different breed, crossbred animals, or a variety of breeds in one group would confuse the information gained, and make the results less valuable.

Research using dogs includes many simple tests. In experimental feeding trials, for instance, prepared dog-foods, tinned, dehydrated or complete, are tested before marketing is considered. Similarly, human food additives, prepared condiments, synthetic sausage skins – everything in fact that is not a 'natural' product, must be given exhaustive trials in order to ensure that there is no hidden source of danger to animal or man. Fertilizers, weedkillers, cosmetics, disinfectants, antibiotics, vaccines, serums – items both in daily and occasional use must be safe, and possible side effects must be known. For these purposes, dogs are providing information vital to man and to their own kind.

Respiration The rate of breathing or respiration varies according to the size of the dog. A Great Dane, when at rest, might breathe twenty times a minute or even less. But as size decreases, respiration increases. Thus, a Chihuahua might breathe from sixty-five to eighty times a minute.

Artificial respiration consists in aiding the dog to re-start respiration. An emergency which requires artificial respiration of a sort sometimes comes during the first few minutes of life for the puppy. An occasional puppy is whelped with fluid in the nasal passages. Unless this is expelled, the puppy will suffocate. The owner can place his lips around the muzzle of the puppy and give a sharp suck, or he may hold the puppy in the palm of his hand, head downward, and then, with a throwing motion, expel the fluid. The nasal passages will thus be cleared, but it may then be necessary to start respiration. This can normally be done by the mouth-to-mouth method, using only part of the air in the person's mouth to force the lungs to function, or by putting external pressure on the lungs.

It is, however, dangerous to use pressure on the newly whelped puppy, since the ribs may be severely damaged. The mouth-to-mouth method, therefore, is preferred.

With older dogs, rhythmic pressure against the chest is suitable. Moreover, it is often possible to apply this pressure with one hand while exerting equal pressure on the area of the diaphragm. This will bring a more complete expulsion of air, with a consequent increase in inspiration, when pressure is released. One must guess at the probable rate of respiration in the dog under normal conditions, and then should increase the rate by up to 50 per cent. Such artificial respiration is useful when the dog is near death from drowning, or from SHOCK.

Laboured and uneven breathing after a dog has been struck in a road accident may indicate a punctured diaphragm, and in such cases, veterinary help is required at once. No pressure upon the diaphragm area should be used until the injured dog has been examined by a veterinarian.

There are dozens of possible causes of difficult breathing, any of which may lead to lung collapse. Prolonged wheezing or coughing can indicate an obstruction of the air passages. Dogs sometimes suffer from the inhalation of chemicals, and they are subject to emphysema, pneumonia, and bronchitis. In pleurisy, fluid collects in the chest cavity so that the lungs can neither expand nor contract properly. In all such cases, treatment by a veterinarian is necessary.
See ASTHMA; HEART DISEASES.

Retriever see Chesapeake Bay Retriever; Curly-Coated Retriever; Flat-Coated Retriever; Golden Retriever; Labrador Retriever.

Reversion Return to an ancestral type. See THROW-BACK.

Rheumatism Rheumatism is a vague term used to refer to diseases of the tendons, muscles, nerves, bones, and joints where pain or disability occurs. Two forms, which may be separated from ARTHRITIS, are types of muscular rheumatism which affect dogs. One is called torticollis, or, sometimes, wry neck. It comes on so suddenly that it is often confused with a sprain. There is little or no swelling, and pain may be periodic. There are spasmodic contractions of the muscles of the neck which draw the head into an abnormal position. ASPIRIN, gentle muscular massage, and the use of a heating pad under the direction of a veterinarian normally bring relief.

The second form of muscular rheumatism is a lameness in one leg. This lameness may move from one leg to another as each leg in turn takes greater strain. The dog usually wants to lie quietly, without moving. It may suffer severe pain when it tries to get up. If lifted, it may howl in pain. When the lameness is in a hind limb, the dog may have great difficulty in accomplishing a bowel movement, resulting in constipation.

Bursitis and spondylitis are sometimes called rheumatism, though they are more closely related to arthritis. Bursitis is more common in the giant dogs, such as the ST. BERNARD and GREAT DANE. It is due to injury to the elbows or hocks.

Below Respiration. Artificial respiration consisting of rhythmic pressure on the rib cage should be used only on mature dogs, as a puppy's flexible ribs may be permanently and severely damaged.

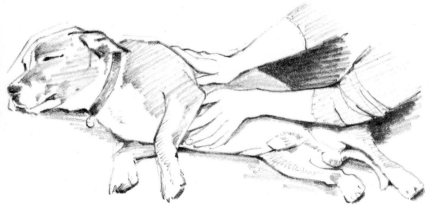

Spondylitis is a progressive disease of the spinal column. It occurs in older dogs. As a rule, it appears in the vertebrae near the end of the chest and in the lumbar region. Spondylitis may be treated as an intervertebral disc abnormality. It is most common in COCKER SPANIELS, DACHSHUNDS, GERMAN SHEPHERDS, and BOXERS. Treatment by a veterinarian is with cortisone drugs, and other drugs used in arthritic diseases.

Rhodesian Ridgeback Everyone seems to have two 'facts' at his command when discussing Rhodesian Ridgebacks. The first is that they came from Rhodesia. The second that they have a ridge on their backs. The knowledgeable know that while the latter is a fact, the former is a fallacy. This unusual breed came originally not from Rhodesia but from South Africa; it is the only breed of dog which South Africa has produced. The Ridgeback has existed in South Africa for several centuries. Nobody knows for precisely how long, but there is evidence that it was there before the first European settlers arrived in 1652.

It is tempting to presume that the tribes that inhabited the country before that had previously kept them as domesticated or even semi-domesticated pets. More probably, these dogs lived wild; ranging the open country in packs and keeping as far away from man as possible, in the manner of all untamed creatures. This aloofness broke down slowly as the settler sank his roots. The dogs gathered round the camps and farms, almost certainly attracted by the prospect of regular food. Thus it could have been a latter day replica of the early civilization of dogs.

The dogs would endear themselves even more to the newcomers when they gave warning of the approach of hostile tribesmen or wild animals. The final seal of approval would be granted when they joined the hunting forays, using their speed, endurance and tracking ability. Slowly but surely they became an accepted part of life in South Africa.

Later when the pioneers moved north to open up Rhodesia, the Ridgebacks went with them. Once again they went back to the beginning. They rediscovered the duties of camp guards. It was a task more essential than ever. Wild animals were abundant, but the dogs kept them back. Their fame grew as they tackled and pulled down lions which were particularly numerous in this

Below Rhodesian Ridgeback. Ch. Aldonnels Abo.

wild and unexplored territory, and stories spread out through a world now better supplied with means of communication. Since the stories emanated from Rhodesia, what more natural than that the dogs they referred to should become known as Rhodesian Ridgebacks?

But if the place name is misleading the name 'Ridgeback' is both accurate and descriptive. Alone of all the breeds in the world these dogs have a curious and distinctive ridge of hair on their backs. Short and dense, it grows in the opposite direction to the rest of the coat – that is, towards and not away from the head. Its form is that of a dagger. The hilt starts at the shoulders and has two 'crowns' or whorls where the 'handle' finishes. It tapers to a point at the hips. This feature is very dominant and in Africa it is by no means uncommon to see dogs which although apparently pure-bred Boxers, or Great Danes, have the tell-tale ridge on their backs.

Despite a promising start, the dogs have never really been popular although they are loyal and dependable, good natured and very trainable. Other advantages, particularly for those who like a fairly big and robust dog is that they are real family dogs which never tire of exercise but demand a minimum of time spent on grooming.

Essentials of the breed: The head should be fairly long with flat skull, rather broad between the ears, stop well defined and with nose in keeping with the colour of the dog. Eyes moderately well apart, round and bright with colour harmonizing with the coat. Ears should be set rather high, of medium size, rather wide at base, tapering to a rounded point. The muzzle should be long and powerful, jaws level and lips clean. Neck fairly long, strong and not throaty.

Forequarters: the shoulders should be sloping and muscular, the forelegs straight, strong and heavy in bone. The chest: not too wide but very deep and capacious with ribs moderately well sprung. The back: powerful, loins strong, muscular and slightly arched with a pronounced ridge as described above. Feet must be compact with well-arched toes. Tail: strong at the insertion and tapering towards the end. Not set too high or too low and carried with a slight curve upwards.

Coat: short and dense, sleek and glossy. Colour: light wheaten to red wheaten, a little white on chest permissible. White on toes permissible in the United States.

Weight: dogs, 80 lb. (America: 75 lb.). Bitches, 70 lb. (America: 65 lb.).

Height: dogs, 25 to 27 inches. Bitches, 24 to 26 inches. See colour plate p. 179.

Rickets This is a condition of puppies in which the ends of the long bones and ribs of the body are enlarged due to a deficiency of vitamin D. This vitamin promotes the absorption of calcium from the alimentary tract.

The bones are not only enlarged but structurally altered: they become soft and tend to distort when bearing the weight of the body. A bowing of the radius and ulna, and of the tibia is often seen. In severe cases, fractures can occur.

Ring Tail or **Ring Stern** Tail carried over the back in a near circle.

Ringworm Ringworm is caused by a fungus infection of the skin. The name is derived from the circular lesions that may appear on the skin. However, many cases do not show these and the condition can be detected only if skin and hair is examined under a special lamp or by the use of a microscope.

In dogs there are four main varieties of fungus that cause this condition. Ringworm can be transmitted to human beings.

Roach Back Convex curvature, or arch, of the back. Often over the loin, sometimes slightly forward of it.

Roan A mixture of coloured and white hairs, so finely mixed as not to be spots, or ticks: blue roan, liver-roan, etc.

Rose Ear An ear which folds, but is drawn back so as to expose the burr.

elow A Rhodesian Ridgeback howing off its ridge.

Rottweiler 'Nothing is known', wrote a German accepted as an authority on the subject some sixty years ago, 'of the earliest history of the Rottweiler.' This may have been true, but the statement suggests that most of the supposed background of the breed currently accepted as truth is pure fiction, and somehow this seems unlikely.

The reason for the lack of documentation is simple. Not until the comparatively recent cult of the pedigreed dog became widespread was it realized that the early details of breeds could ever prove of sufficient interest to warrant preservation. The 'story' of the Rottweiler is certainly an interesting one and may be largely true.

When the Roman legions were planning their assaults on other European countries, the supply of food was an ever-pressing problem. Today refrigeration and air lifts would solve it. Then, the only practical answer to the question of providing meat for soldiers was that it should follow them on the hoof.

These mass movements of cattle called for the assistance of working dogs. Fortunately, cattle dogs of various types were in existence. Clearly the most useful would be those strong and rugged enough to act as guards. A major supply route led over the Alps and through the St. Gothard Pass. From this high point the tracks led down in numerous directions, and at the foot of a number of them are to be found communes with dogs which could be descendants of the original travellers, usually with local distinguishing features and local names. Not all these Roman cattle dogs settled in the shade of the Alps however. Some wandered further afield: through southern Germany, driving north on the old military road through Württemberg and on to the small market town of Rottweil.

Centuries later this region became an important cattle area principally because of its central position. When it did, the still extant though somewhat altered 'Roman' dogs proved their value. Merchants had to visit the countryside to buy cattle. As an anti-bandit device they fastened their money bags around the necks of these powerful beasts. Robbers took the hint. The cattle purchased, the dogs – by now known as *Rottweiler Metzerhund* (Butcher's Dog of Rottweil) – herded them back to town. So was fashioned the distinctive build and temperament of the Rottweiler. It had to drive the cattle, guard them, control the bulls, and protect its master. It was in fact a ready-made twentieth-century police dog.

Then followed a period of waning. As the cattle markets declined, the breed became neglected until the latter part of the Victorian era, when interest grew in many distinctive but overlooked breeds.

In many cases this interest came too late. It was nearly so with the Rottweiler. For example, in 1900 the town of Rottweil itself could only produce one single female representative of the breed.

Then came the unexpected demand for police dogs, which in 1912 was merely a polite description of a war dog. In the company of AIREDALES, GERMAN SHEPHERD DOGS and DOBERMANNS, the 'Rotts' joined the colours. Like most other war dogs, they have been trying to live it down ever since.

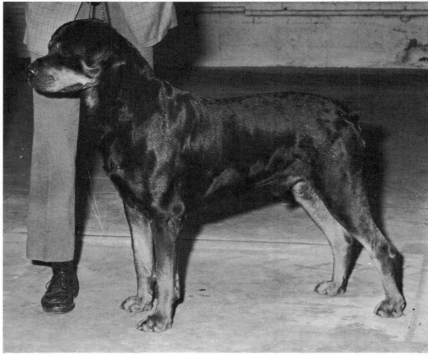

The enormous strength of these dogs, their robust constitution and their high degree of intelligence, coupled with trainability, soon made them many friends. In the early 1930's they crossed the Atlantic. In 1935 they were officially recognized by the American Kennel Club. In 1936 the first imports reached Britain and were exhibited at Cruft's. Thirty years later, in 1966, they were sufficiently numerous to warrant a separate register.

Now 400 a year are registered in the United States and nearly half that number in Britain. It is firmly established all over Continental Europe and Scandinavia. The Rottweiler, so often neglected in the past, is now here to stay.

Essentials of the breed: The head is of medium length, broad between the ears. The forehead line is moderately arched as seen from the side. Occipital bone is well developed. Cheeks: well muscled. Muzzle: fairly deep, and the same length as skull. The nose is black, well developed, with large nostrils. The eyes: medium size, almond shaped and dark brown. The ears are pendant, small, set high and lying close to cheek. The neck should be of fair length, strong, round and muscular. The chest should be broad and deep with well sprung ribs. The back should be straight, strong and not too long. The upper thighs strongly muscled, stifles well bent, hocks well angulated without exaggeration. The feet should be strong, round and compact with well arched toes. Toenails: short, dark and strong, rear dewclaws removed.

Gait should convey an impression of supple strength, endurance and purpose with powerful hind thrust and good stride. Tail: short, strong and not set too low, docked at the first joint and carried horizontally. Colour: black with clearly defined tan markings on the cheeks, muzzle, chest and legs, as well as over both eyes.

Height: (Britain) dogs between 25 and 27 inches; bitches 23 to 25 inches. In America, dogs between $23\frac{3}{4}$ and 27 inches; bitches $22\frac{3}{4}$ to $25\frac{3}{4}$ inches.
See colour plate p. 298.

Rounding Cutting the ear leather to round it. At one time this was done to FOXHOUNDS.

Roundworms There are three species of roundworms which infest dogs. They all belong to a group known as the ascarids.

The most common is *Toxocara canis. Toxocara leonina* is less common, except that it is the major roundworm in Alaskan dogs. *Toxocara cati* usually infests cats, and is only rarely found in dogs.

The eggs of *T. canis* pass from the dog in its stools. They have an adhesive quality and some may stick to the hair about the rectum. Others stick to any surface they may touch, and some will be swallowed. They hatch in the intestine into a larval form. The larvae burrow through the intestinal wall and are carried to the lungs or muscles. Those in the lungs enter the air sacs, are coughed into the throat, and then swallowed. Once back in the intestine, they mature and lay eggs. Those in the muscles remain there until a bitch is pregnant

when they become active and penetrate into the bodies of unborn puppies. Thus, although the bitch may be free of roundworms before she is mated, and is kept free from infection, her puppies may be infected. In unborn puppies, the larvae migrate to the intestine and become adult within a week after birth. Larvae may also be present in a puppy's stools; as she cleans the puppies, the dam will swallow them.

Adult roundworms are very seldom found in older dogs. It is now thought that older dogs have developed a resistance to them.

It is possible for the larvae of roundworms to invade the human body where they infect the liver, lungs, kidney, heart and eyes. The disease is almost always found in children under three, but is not common. For this reason, crawlers and toddlers should be kept away

from the bitch and her puppies. If these children do handle puppies, their hands and faces should be washed, and their clothes changed and cleaned.

In treating roundworms, piperazine salts, the common bactericide, hexylresorcinal, and butyl chloride are used. Two of the newer drugs are diethylcarbamazine and thiabendazole. The latter is added to the food on a continuous basis to prevent development of the eggs.

Puppies with roundworms usually have pot bellies and diarrhoea. They may also cough up worms which are active and tend to coil. Stools should be burned. Since the eggs are difficult to kill, living quarters should be cleaned with lye.
See ANTISEPTICS and KENNEL HYGIENE.

Royal Air Force Police Dogs

'Halt! Who goes there?'
An apprehensive silence follows.
'Halt! Who goes there?'
The traditional second challenge of the Services rings out. And again there is no response.
'Halt or I release my dog.'
Exchanges like the above have been a feature of Air Force airfields all over the world for the last thirty years. On the occasions when the suspected intruder has not answered the final challenge, the dogs have been

slipped. From then on neither darkness, speed or strength can save the victim. In seconds a GERMAN SHEPHERD DOG (Alsatian) has seized him and held on. In this way dogs have guarded remote airfields with huge perimeters which could otherwise only be effectively controlled by the use of hundreds of men.

The merits of war dogs have been appreciated for centuries. In 1799 Napoleon wrote: 'They ought to have at Alexandria a large number of dogs which you can easily make use of by fastening a short distance from your walls.' Even so, it was not until the First World War that Germany realized their possibilities, and not until 1940 did the Royal Air Force open its first dog training school in Britain.

Originally a variety of breeds was used, each to perform a separate task. Later came a switch to German Shepherds, each one being trained for every job.

This breed was chosen for three reasons. Firstly, German Shepherds are particularly trainable; next, their robust constitutions and weatherproof coats make it possible to draft them anywhere in the world at short notice; finally, they are the perfect deterrent. Many people have a respect bordering on fear for this breed, and thus a major part of their work consists of merely being seen. Air Forces are not interested in fancy arrests; they merely want all uninvited visitors to keep away.

An unusual aspect of Air Force dogs is that all of them were originally house pets, and came as free gifts from the general public. Admittedly, it was not always patriotism that inspired these gifts: many people find that Alsatian pups grow into big and boisterous dogs. The R.A.F. insists upon a pedigree, ignores looks, and rejects dogs which are temperamentally unsuitable.

New recruits, after medical checks and injections, are joined up with a volunteer, and equally inexperienced, dog handler for a joint course. The man learns to give orders, the dog to take them. This is often a shock for an ex-pet.

Ever since the school was founded by Colonel Baldwin in 1940 it has always been an invariable rule that no dog may ever be chastised. Training is based on the reward of praise. In the first two weeks the team is taught basic obedience – that is 'Sit', 'Down', 'Heel' and 'Stay'. Only after that is the big obstacle faced: that of teaching the dog that in certain circumstances it may bite. This sounds simple but generations of accepting that biting is the unforgivable canine sin has had its effect. Many dogs put up aggressive displays. Unless trained, most stop short of biting.

The principles of imparting this lesson are simple. Two weeks' discipline has made the handler a god in the eyes of his dog. A god who must be pleased. An experienced instructor adopts the role of 'teaser', flapping sacks at dog and man. The animal senses the handler's pleasure when it is aggressive. Finally the teaser simulates fear and runs away. The hitherto hesitant dog feels heroic and the stage is set for the next step.

When more confident it is allowed to grab the padded arm of the escaping teaser. More praise

follows. Later, never having known failure, but experienced abundant praise, it will attack with very little encouragement. From this point on a big thing in the dog's life is a satisfying bite! It becomes even more important than praise. This simplifies future training. To teach the dogs wind-scenting, a 'criminal' is hidden about 30 yards upwind. The dog knows it can taste again the forbidden pleasure if it reacts properly. Life has become very rewarding.

Progressively the training becomes more difficult. For example 'Leave', i.e. stop attacking immediately, must be applied, although the dog is rarely keen on absorbing this lesson. It is taught it must guard criminals but not attack unless escape is threatened, that fire can be faced without fear, that food must never be accepted from strangers, that obstacles exist to be negotiated, and that its handler's orders are law while those from others must be ignored.

Royal Air Force Police Dogs.
Top A specialist police dog retrieves a vital piece of evidence from a crash-landed aircraft.
Above Many Royal Air Force police dogs accompany their handlers overseas for guard duty.

All this is learned in seven short weeks. Then man and dog are posted to an airfield in Britain where life is earnest. From then on they can be sent abroad at any moment.

Currently over one thousand teams are in action in many lands. The number which might seem large is remarkably small when compared with the number of soldiers who would otherwise be required to police the R.A.F. airfields.

The Royal Air Force, by its system which enables it to take a raw dog and an equally raw man and turn them into a fighting team in less than two months, has been admired by many other services and the Royal Air Force has always been most helpful to other nations, not only teaching methods of instruction but, if need be, even training their dogs and their personnel.

Royal College of Veterinary Surgeons The Royal College of Veterinary Surgeons is the governing body of the profession in Britain. The Royal College was incorporated by Royal Charter in 1844 and its powers have been extended by subsequent Royal Charters. Parliament regulates the profession through the Royal College by the Veterinary Surgeons Acts; the first was in 1881 and the most recent in 1966.

Her Majesty Queen Elizabeth II is Patron of the Royal College. The Council is made up of appointed members and elected members.

A Register of Veterinary Surgeons is maintained and published annually. Only those persons who are registered may call themselves veterinary surgeons or practise in Britain. Registration is dependent upon academic qualification by examination either by the Royal College of Veterinary Surgeons or by a recognized university. See VETERINARIANS.

The Royal College is entrusted with supervising functions in veterinary education, and the Council appoints Visitors to universities to report on the courses of study, staffing, accommodation and equipment available for training in veterinary medicine and surgery, and also to attend and report on the examinations.

In addition to the Diploma of Membership, the Royal College awards a Diploma of Fellowship, a Diploma in Veterinary Radiology, and a Diploma in Veterinary Anaesthesia. It also grants scholarships and other awards, and administers the Animal Nursing Auxiliary scheme.

The Royal College of Veterinary Surgeons is responsible for professional conduct in both advisory and disciplinary capacities. This function is carried out by the Council committees.

The offices of the Royal College of Veterinary Surgeons are at 32 Belgrave Square, London, S.W.1. The Royal College of Veterinary Surgeons Wellcome Library is at the same address.

Royal Society for the Prevention of Cruelty to Animals The R.S.P.C.A. is the oldest animal protection society in the world. Its first meeting took place in the Old Slaughter's Coffee House in central London in June 1824.

oyal Society of Veterinary Surgeons.
op right A metal cage eases a
ock over the inner bandage with-
ut dislodging it.
ottom right A veterinarian clips
way the hair before giving the
oodle an injection.

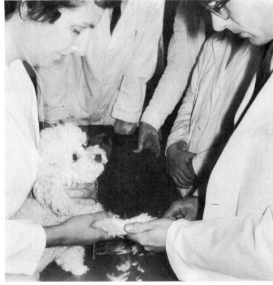

In 1822 Richard Martin, an Irish Member of the British Parliament, piloted through the House of Commons a Bill giving protection to domestic animals. This piece of legislation became known as Martin's Act.

It came to the notice of the Rev. Arthur Broome who decided to see that it was put into force, and he engaged inspectors whose sole work would be to see that Martin's Act was effective. To publicize his intentions, he put an announcement in a newspaper inviting sympathizers to meet him. The meeting he called at the Old Slaughter's Coffee House led to the formation of the Society for the Prevention of Cruelty to Animals. The word 'Royal' was added to the title when Queen Victoria, before her coronation, extended to the Society her royal patronage.

The Society has grown from employing one single inspector in 1824 to the present strength of 240 officers.

The R.S.P.C.A. has to investigate each year roughly 20,000 cases of cruelty to animals and arising from these investigations the Society takes nearly a thousand cases to court. In prosecuting people who have been cruel to animals, the R.S.P.C.A. is seeking to check cruelty and to advance education in the care of animals.

The relief of animal suffering by the provision of free veterinary treatment is another important service given by the R.S.P.C.A. This type of work began early in this century. The main part is undertaken in four fully equipped hospitals and in over seventy clinics established throughout England and Wales. In the more remote parts, mobile units are used to reach those requiring help.

First-aid and advice on animal welfare can be obtained from ninety R.S.P.C.A. animal welfare centres. The R.S.P.C.A. is also establishing homes where animals waiting for new owners may be housed. In one year the R.S.P.C.A. placed over 70,000 animals, mainly dogs and cats, in new homes.

The Society maintains an R.S.P.C.A. Air Hostel for Animals at London Airport where a million animals are handled each year. Work overseas has been extended recently by the Society's part in the founding of the International Society for the Protection of Animals.

The Society makes awards for bravery each year and in doing so acknowledges those who go to the help of animals in distress.

Rubarth's Disease see Hepatitis.

Ruby see Cavalier King Charles Spaniel; King Charles Spaniel.

Rudder The tail, especially that of a GREYHOUND.

Ruff Thick hair around the neck.

Runts see Whelping.

Rupture see Hernia.

Russian Wolfhound see Borzoi.

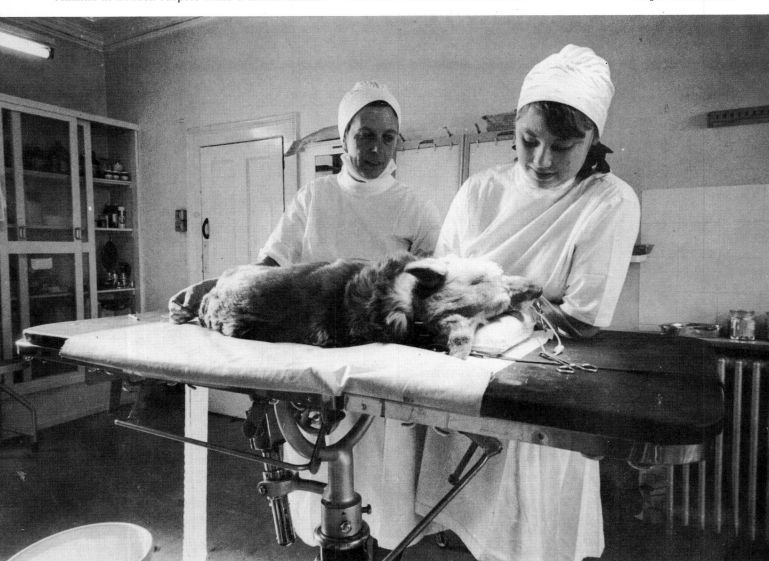

Below At the Royal Society for the Prevention of Cruelty to Animals hospital in London, a Corgi is given a cornea transplant.

Top right Sable colouring seen on a Shetland Sheepdog.

Bottom right Saint Bernard. Snow ranger Tello v. Sauliant.

S

Sable Black hairs over brown or golden base colour, as in COLLIES and SHETLAND SHEEPDOGS.

Saddle Solid colour on the back, resembling a saddle, and smaller than a 'BLANKET' in size.

Saint Bernard Many dog lovers might wish to turn back the clock and re-establish the St. Bernard as one of the most popular breeds in the 'Old World'.

Alas, it is only too certain that the really large breeds, with their attendant requirements of large pockets, large larders and large homes, have had their European heyday and from now on will only be kept there by connoisseurs. A few public-spirited persons are determined to preserve them for posterity. Fortunately in America things are different. So different, that against annual registrations in Britain of 300 a year, the figure in the United States is a magnificent 27,000, which takes the breed into the top ten.

The legendary St. Bernard shares with the NEW-FOUNDLAND the honour of being the only breed whose special task is rescue.

The Hospice du Grand Saint Bernard is not only one of the highest human habitations in Europe, it is also one of the oldest. A temple to Jupiter once stood on the site, a relic of the passage of the conquering Roman armies. After centuries of neglect, Bernard of Menthon (later canonized) rebuilt the refuge to offer hospitality to pilgrims, and devoted his existence to saving the lives of many of the poor and needy travellers who were forced to cross each year on foot.

Not until 1707 however, is there any mention in the records of dogs working in the Hospice, although it is possible to imagine they had been established there for thirty or forty years previously in the role of guards. Oliver Goldsmith (1728–74) writes: *'They have a breed of noble dogs, whose extraordinary sagacity often enables them to rescue the traveller. Though the perishing man lie ten or even twenty feet beneath the snow, the delicacy*

Saint Bernard.
Left Pebblestreet Amanda.
Top right Ch. Subira's Frederick, a smooth-coated St. Bernard.
Bottom right Dogs at the Hospice on the St. Bernard Pass in Switzerland.

of smell with which they can trace him offers a chance of escape.'

Napoleon was not so complimentary. According to Captain Coignet, during the crossing in 1800 he arrived at the worst part of the St. Bernard Pass when over 100 men had already been dragged over the precipice by the unwieldy guns, and shouted: 'Where are your men and your dogs while my soldiers perish may I ask?' The response was, 'They are out to rescue them, Sire'.

The St. Bernard's working role in the Alps is therefore centuries old. What are less certain are the many legends about it. Did it ever warm semi-frozen travellers with its body? Probably not, or at least this was never its intention. Did it carry a flask of brandy to save travellers' lives? Probably, once again, only in exceptional circumstances.

The truth is that it was not a sort of Alpine Bloodhound whose task was to find people, but rather a trained and trusted guide. Certainly this is how the monks used it, confident that such a heavy and discerning dog would never willingly desert the paths for the deep snowdrifts even when a human being could not distinguish between the two.

But to doubt some of the legend is not to lose respect for the breed. So much of their character and background is built into their appearance: the benevolent and kindly expressions; the broad back and deep chest point to an animal built to work; the dense coat designed for protection in extreme climatic conditions.

They have changed little since they were first introduced to the world of dog shows, and that was a surprisingly long time ago. The name of St. Bernard first came into use in England in 1865 replacing a number of loose descriptive names such as Alpine Mastiffs.

A breed club was formed in London in 1880 and it held its first show in 1882 with separate classes for the short-haired and the now more usual long-haired varieties.

In 1887 a Congress held in Zürich laid down a breed standard which became accepted internationally. And in 1888 the American Saint Bernard Club, one of the first breed societies ever formed in the United States, came into being and pointed the way towards a rosy future.

Essentials of the breed: Head: large and massive. Muzzle: short and square at end. Stop: abrupt and well defined. Eyes: small, deep-set and dark, showing HAW. Ears: close to cheeks. Neck: thick, muscular and slightly arched.

Shoulders: broad and sloping. Legs: strong in bone. Back: broad and straight. Wide and deep chest. Muscular thighs. Feet: large and compact, with well arched toes, dew claws removed. Tail: set on rather high and long.

Coat: in Long-haireds or Roughs, coat dense and flat, fuller round the neck; thighs well feathered. In Smooths or Short-haireds, coat close, slightly feathered on thighs and tail. Colour: white with orange, mahogany-brindle and red-brindle patches.

Overleaf Salukis. Left to right: Beth of Daxlore, Ch. Alexandra of Daxlore, Ch. Seamist of Daxlore and Ch. Alexis of Daxlore.

Height: dogs 27½ inches minimum. Bitches 25½ inches minimum. The taller the better, provided that symmetry is maintained.

See colour plate p. 300.

Saint Hubert's Hounds St. Hubert, who died in A.D. 727, is credited with developing the hounds from which all modern trailing hounds are said to descend. They have been described as black, black and tan, and white and black.

George Turberville, in his *Book of Venerie*, published in 1611, wrote that the black hounds came from Hubert's Abbey in Ardene. He added: 'These are the hounds which the Abbots of St. Hubert have always kept in honour and remembrances of the Sainte whereupon we may conceave that (by the grace of God) all good huntsmen shall follow them into paradise.' They were 'mighty of body with short legs, and slow'.

Saint Vitus Dance see Chorea.

Saluki The Saluki is a member of the GREYHOUND family. This family is one of the oldest, and the Saluki may be the oldest member of the family. In the tomb of Rekma-re, in Egypt, dated about 1400 B.C., there is a painting of dogs remarkably Saluki-like. The dogs show the slight ear and leg feathering, have similar hindquarters, and a similar tail. An even earlier painting at Hierakonapolis, 3600 B.C., includes a Saluki-like dog.

The Saluki has been called the Eastern Greyhound, Persian Greyhound, and Arabian Gazelle Hound. There are two theories as to the origin of the name. The first is that it comes from a southern Arabian town, now gone, named Saluk, reputed for its armour and its dogs. The second theory is that the name comes from Seleukia, a town in the Greek Empire in Syria. A smooth-coated version of this dog has been called Sleughi, or Slughi, in colloquial Arabic.

Another smooth-coated variety of the breed is called the Shami. Both varieties are believed to have originated in Syria, and thence spread to Egypt, to Persia, and to India and Afghanistan. The breed is clearly related to the AFGHAN HOUND.

The Arabs and the Persians have kept Saluki pedigrees pure for several thousand years, much as they have those of their horses. The dogs have been used chiefly to course gazelles. In many cases, the Salukis have joined forces with trained hawks or falcons. The falcons locate the quarry from the air. Horsemen get as close as possible, then release the dogs. On smaller game, the hawks dive and attack the game and the Salukis then hold the prey until the horsemen arrive.

Dogs from Persia and Arabia have been exported to the United States and England with partially cropped ears. Such dogs have been used in hunting jackals. As in dog pit fighting, cropping is designed to deny the adversary a hold on the ear, which tears easily, and bleeds copiously.

In 1895, a pair of Saluki puppies was given to Lady Florence Amherst. She fell in love with them, imported others, and tried to popularize the breed in Great

Britain. Though the dogs attracted great attention and were much admired, official recognition by the Kennel Club did not come until 1923.

In 1920, Brigadier General Lance imported *Ch. Sarona Kelb* and *Sarona-Sarona* from Mesopotamia. About the same time, Mr. Vereker-Cowley brought *Malik-el-Zobair* and *Zobeida-al-Zobair* from Egypt. These dogs became foundation stock in England.

A son of *Sarona Kelb* was among the first to be imported to the United States. *Ch. Marjan II*, owned by Mrs. Anna Marie Paterno, was the first great show winner for the breed in that country. Then in the late 1930s, Mrs. Esther Knapp of Valley City, Ohio, imported dogs from England, Arabia, Egypt, and Persia, and made her Pine Paddocks Kennels world-famous. The breed was given official recognition by the American Kennel Club in 1927.

Essentials of the breed: Except for feathering, there is no difference between the smooth and feathered variety.

The head is long and narrow, not domed, and with little stop. The skull and muzzle form parallel planes. The nose is black or liver, the eyes dark to hazel, and not prominent. The ears are long, hang close to the cheeks, and are covered with long, silky hair. The bite is level or scissors.

The chest is deep and narrow, with sloping shoulders. The back: wide and arched over the loins. The hip bones are set well apart. The stifles are moderately bent, and the hocks are low to the ground. The feet are of moderate length, strongly arched, and well-feathered between the toes. The tail is set on low, carried in a curve and feathered on the underside. Virtually all colours are permitted. Males average 23 to 28 inches at the shoulder.

See GREYHOUND, EASTERN.

See colour plate p. 177.

Samoyed The Samoyed is a SPITZ BREED named after a Siberian tribe called the Samoyedes.

One explorer-naturalist, Middendorf, found Samoyed dogs between the Ob and the Yenisei Rivers. He described them as long-haired white (and, rarely, black) dogs. The explorer Tooke (1779) said that the Samoyedes used their dogs to haul sledges, and that the people wore clothes made of shaggy dog skins. Nansen, the Arctic explorer, used white or white and black Samoyeds on his first polar expedition, from June 1893 to August 1896.

The first Samoyeds (then called Samoyedes) were brought to England about 1900 by fur traders who went north in Russia and Siberia to buy sables. Mrs. Kilburn Scott, the first great importer, got her first pair from north-east Russia. Mrs. Gray Landsberg got *Ayesha* from the islands of Novaya Zemlya. These islands lie off the north-eastern Russian coast, between the Barents and Kara Seas. It is noteworthy that, in 1870, Russia moved some of the Samoyedes families to these previously deserted islands. Mrs. Landsberg also imported dogs direct from the Samoyede peoples east of the Yenisei in Siberia. Still other Samoyeds came from Finland. Other foundation breeders in

England include Mr. Gordon Coleman, Mrs. D. L. Perry of Kobe Kennels, and Miss Keyte Perry of Arctic Kennels.

An odd fact is that Mrs. Kilburn Scott's great *Antarctic Buck* came from Sydney, Australia. It is for that reason that some of her greatest dogs were named *Southern Cross, South Pole,* and *Ch. Antarctic Bru.* Samoyeds were in Australia because Captain Robert Scott had taken some there when making his second attempt to reach the South Pole. On his earlier attempt, the dogs had weakened so badly that they had to be

Top Saluki. Ch. Srinagar Jen Araby Krisna.

Above Samoyed. Ch. Zarkoff of Kobe.

shot one by one. This time he took thirty dogs and nineteen ponies, and at the first advance station, the dogs were sent back to Australia.

Samoyeds are very popular in Australia, as they are in Canada and the United States. In 1914, Miss Ruth Nichols imported *Weimur* from England. Mrs. Frank Romer brought over *Tobolsk* and *Draga*, and later *Baren* and *Yukon Mit*. A son of Tobolsk died on Scott's trip. Mr. and Mrs. Harvey Reid imported *Ch. Toby of Yurak II*, another son of Tobolsk, and *Ch. Tiger Boy*. Other early breeders and importers to the United States were Mrs. Helen Harris, and Miss Martha Humphriss.

Essentials of the breed: Samoyeds are pure white, white and biscuit, or all biscuit. All other colours and blue eyes disqualify. The dog is slightly heavier in bone and in weight than a SIBERIAN HUSKY of equal height. This makes the dog notable for its endurance rather than for its speed. The outer coat is straight and harsh, and the undercoat is dense, soft wool.

The skull is wedge-shaped, broad, and only slightly crowned. The muzzle is of medium length and width. There is a pronounced stop. Lips and eye rims are black, though they may change to brown in winter. Scissors bite. The ears are thick, erect, triangular, and slightly rounded at the tips. They are well furred inside and out.

The body is strongly made with a straight top line and is about 5 per cent longer than tall. The chest reaches to the elbow. The feet are large, long, and slightly spread, with arched toes and thick, tough pads. The tail reaches to the hocks, has a profuse brush, and is carried over the back. It should not be carried tightly to the body, nor should it have a double hook. The stifle joints are well bent. The dog should trot, not pace.

Height: dogs $21\frac{1}{2}$ to $23\frac{1}{2}$ inches. Bitches 19 to 21 inches.

See colour plate p. 289.

Sappling An untested GREYHOUND pup, 10 to 18 months old. Sappling stakes are run at coursing meets.

Scaling Teeth Scaling the teeth consists of the removal of salivary calculus, commonly called tartar, from the teeth. The composition of tartar varies, but the chief ingredients are organic secretions containing food particles and salts, such as calcium phosphate, ferric phosphate, and calcium carbonate. Deposits of salivary calculus may begin when the dog is about two years old. It is brown in colour and very hard. It forms close to the gums, then spreads over the teeth and tends to push back and injure the gums. Foul breath and gum diseases result (see BAD BREATH; GUMS).

In scaling, instruments are used which tend to lift, or to split the tartar from the teeth. This must be done in the direction away from the gums, so that the latter will not be injured. To remove heavy tartar deposits from both the outside and inside edges of the teeth requires considerable skill. It is an operation which must be done by a veterinarian, since most dogs must

be put under severe restraint, including a gag, or even an anaesthetic.

It may be necessary to scale the teeth every three or four months. In some cases, veterinarians are willing to show owners how to scale the teeth at home. The owners can attend to this at regular intervals, and thus prevent severe tartar deposits from forming.

As an aid to clean teeth, dogs should be given knuckle bones upon which to gnaw, and large, hard dog biscuits to chew.

Scandinavian Kennel Union see Kennel Clubs.

Schipperke Various meanings have been given for the name Schipperke. These have included 'Little Boatman', 'Little Skipper', 'Little Captain', and less often, 'Little Corporal'. The name is Belgian. As with most breeds, the dog's origin is in doubt.

Schipperke historians believe that the two black dogs without tails, which are said to have rescued William of Orange from an assassin, were Schipperkes. If so, then the breed was well established during William's life, 1533–1584.

Top right Samoyed puppies.

Right Scaling teeth. When tartar forms on the teeth it tends to push back and injure the gums.

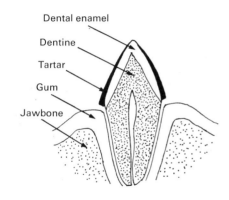

Dental enamel

Dentine

Tartar

Gum

Jawbone

Before 1700, shoemakers and some other craftsmen in the St. Géry area of Belgium, began the custom of parading their black, tail-less dogs on alternate Sundays, The dogs wore large, brass collars, many of which were of elaborate design. The craftsmen did not, however, call their dogs Schipperkes; the usual term for them was 'Spitz'.

This leads to one assumption as to the breed's origin: that it belongs to the large family of northern dogs called the Spitz group (see SPITZ BREEDS). Another theory is that the Schipperke is a small version of an extinct Belgian Sheepdog breed (not the modern Groenendael), or of another extinct small-sized breed, the Leuvanaar.

By the time of the Brussels dog show of 1880, the Schipperke was well established as the most popular of house dogs. It was also commonly seen on barges and boats moving along the canals of Belgium and Holland. Accordingly, prizes were offered for the 'short-coated terriers, all black, with erect ears, without a tail, a Flemish breed, schipperkes', but no dogs were entered.

In 1882, the Société St. Hubert was formed by hunting dog enthusiasts, and in 1885, the club was granted royal status as the Société Royale St. Hubert. The Société's stud book, *Livres des Origines St. Hubert*, granted immediate status to the Schipperke as a pure breed.

Tip, no. 146, was the first Schipperke to be registered. It was shown at the Spa Show in 1882, and it won first prize.

British sportsmen, who came to Belgium to hunt, took back dozens of Schipperkes. The crews of ships outward bound for the United States, stole dogs for sale in New York. As the dog became popular in England, formal importation of Belgian and French Schipperkes began. A Mrs. Berrie imported a registered dog named *Flo*, in 1887. George Krehl bought a dog of high quality, named *St. Hubert* from M. Reussens of Brussels, who had been a breeder for 65 years, and is considered the 'father' of the breed.

The Schipperke Club of England was founded in 1890, and the Northern Schipperke Club in 1905.

The first English-bred champion was *Ch. Uncle Pick*, bred by G. H. Killick, which won its title in 1899.

Walter Comstock of Providence, R.I., imported a pair of Schipperkes to the United States in 1899. Later, Frank Dole, a famed authority on dogs for many years, did pioneer work for the breed. The first American Kennel Club registrations came in 1904. The Schipperke Club of America was organized in 1929 to succeed an earlier club which had died. The greatest of the pioneer American breeders is generally considered to have been Miss F. Isabel Ormiston of Kelso Kennels.

Essentials of the breed: The Schipperke is a small, jet black dog. The head is fox-like with small, erect ears, a fairly wide skull, tapering muzzle, and with black nose and eyes. The teeth meet evenly or in a scissors bite.

The neck is slightly arched and rather short. The body is short, thick-set, and broad between the shoulders. The neck has a thick ruff. The hindquarters are lighter than the fore-parts. The stifles are well bent.

The coat is abundant, straight, and slightly harsh. It is longer around the neck and forms a ruff and cape. A jabot extends down between the front legs. The hair is also longer on the rear, where it forms a culotte. The tail is docked close to the body at birth.

Disqualifications include any colouring other than whole; drop or semi-erect ears; and badly undershot or overshot mouth. Light eyes and body coat longer than three inches are serious faults. Straight stifles, silky coat, cow hocks, straight shoulders, and weak elbows are also faults. Weight: up to 18 lb.
See colour plate p. 191.

Schnauzer, Giant The Giant Schnauzer is now known in Germany as the Riesenschnauzer, but for many years, it was known as the Münchener Dog. Its origin appears to have been in the highlands of south Bavaria, near Swabia. It was a cattle and drovers' dog, but as the need for such dogs declined, brewers and butchers replaced the farmers as their breeders.

Top Schipperke. Ch. Arbourlands Thruppence.

Above Schnauzer. The relative sizes of the Giant, Standard and Miniature Schnauzers.

Their first appearance in dog shows was at the October 1909 show at Munich. Thirty of them were shown as 'Russian Bear Schnauzers'. The dogs created such an impression that the Munich Schnauzer Club was formed within the next month.

The Giant Schnauzer bears a close resemblance to another drovers' dog, the BOUVIER DES FLANDRES. Yet there is no evidence that they are related. Nor is there any proof of Standard Schnauzer blood in the Giant Schnauzer. Other unproven theories are that the Standard Schnauzer was crossed in to get a wire coat and the pepper and salt colour; that the now extinct Thuringian Shepherd Dog was used to get erect ears; and that the GREAT DANE was used to get both erect ears and the black colour.

The Giant Schnauzer might have died out had it not been among the breeds selected for police and war training prior to 1914. After the war, the breed again declined. But after 1950, dedicated breeders in Germany restored the dog, both to great beauty and to greater popularity.

Essentials of the breed: The breed has the characteristic beard of the other Schnauzers. Its coat is hard, wiry, and dense. The colours are black, pepper and salt, and black and tan.

The head is rectangular. It differs from that of the Standard Schnauzer in that it is about one third the length of the back, whereas that of the smaller dog is one half the back length. The body is square, withers to ground and withers to set on of the tail. The tail is docked at the third joint. The chest is deep, with a visible breastbone, and a depth to the elbow. The ears are erect if cropped, and form a 'V' if uncropped.

Height: Giant Schnauzers normally range from 21½ to 25½ inches, but some dogs reach 27 inches.
See SCHNAUZER, MINIATURE; SCHNAUZER, STANDARD.
See colour plate p. 94.

Schnauzer, Miniature In Germany, the place of its origin, the Miniature Schnauzer is known as the Zwergschnauzer. The name Schnauzer comes from *Schnauze*, meaning snout or muzzle, but the meaning is somewhat wider than that, as *Schnauzbart* means a moustache, or a man with a conspicuous moustache. All three breeds of Schnauzers are conspicuous for their moustaches and beards.

The Standard and Miniature Schnauzers were also outstanding ratters. It is perhaps for this reason that the two smaller breeds were sponsored by the Pinscher Club, and later, the Pinscher-Schnauzer Club. *Pinscher* is the German word for 'terrier', and was coined for the dog because of its ratting abilities.

The Miniature Schnauzer appeared about 1900. It is not simply a diminutive Standard: it apparently derives from crosses of Standard Schnauzers with AFFENPINSCHERS. Crosses to other breeds may also have occurred, since the breeders wanted a miniature which looked exactly like the larger dog.

By the early 1920s, the Miniature Schnauzer had been fixed as to type. W. D. Goff is credited with taking the first one to the United States in 1923 and W. H.

Hancock began the importations of Miniatures to England in 1928. With the appearance of *Schnapp von Dornbusch of Hitofa*, and *Lenchen von Dornbusch*, the breed caught on in America. The latter became the first U.S. champion. Her son, *Don von Dornbusch*, won the first U.S. speciality show. The year was 1926, and in the same year the Wire-Haired Pinscher Club was formed to sponsor both the Standard and Miniature Schnauzers. In 1927, the club reorganized under the name Schnauzer Club of America. Then in 1933 came the split. The parent club became the Standard Schnauzer Club of America, and a new club, the American Miniature Schnauzer Club, was formed.

The Miniature Schnauzer has since become the most popular terrier in Canada and the United States. In Great Britain, it is not considered to be a terrier, and is placed in the utility group.

Essentials of the breed: Since its early history, the Miniature Schnauzer has undergone some standard changes. At first, it had to be limited in size to under 13 inches. The present standard for the U.S. and Canada calls for disqualification of dogs or bitches under 12 inches or over 14 inches at the shoulder. The European standard is a maximum of 14 inches for dogs and 13 inches for bitches.

Left Schnauzers of all three breeds are conspicuous for their moustaches and beards. The name Schnauzer comes from *Schnauze* meaning muzzle and *Schnauzbart* meaning moustache.

Schnauzer, Standard.
Top right Ch. Dondeau Wotan of Langwood.
Bottom right Ch. Pavo de la Steingasse.

There are slight colour variations between the three Schnauzer breeds. Miniatures can be pure black, black and silver, or pepper and salt. The latter is the most popular. Pepper and salt dogs are allowed to have light shadings of tan. A white smudge on the chest of black dogs is permitted. White dogs, or those with white body patches, are disqualified.

Miniature Schnauzers have slightly longer, more refined heads than the other two Schnauzers. They have strongly made, short bodies. When in stance, the stifles are bent so that the hocks are beyond the set on of the tail. If cropped, the ears are erect. If uncropped, they are set on high, and are folded over to a 'V' shape. The coat is hard and wiry, and on the body should be not less than three quarters of an inch long.

Faults include a level bite, a soft, slick coat, toyishness, light or prominent eyes, shyness and viciousness, sway or roached back, loose elbows, and bowed or cow-hocked hindquarters.

See SCHNAUZER, GIANT ; SCHNAUZER, STANDARD.
See colour plate p. 93.

Schnauzer, Standard

The Standard Schnauzer is the middle-sized member of the Schnauzer family, between the Giant and the Miniature. He would appear to be the oldest of the three breeds. There is an old statue in Stuttgart, Germany, of a watchman and his dog. The dog appears to have characteristics of the Standard Schnauzer. Albrecht Durer had a similar dog, and he painted its picture a number of times between 1490 and 1504. Lucas Cranach the Elder also incorporated a dog with Schnauzer characteristics in a tapestry.

As a type, the Standard Schnauzer is therefore very old, but as with most breeds, its actual origin is not known. Some researchers state that it results from a cross between two now extinct breeds, the Middle Ages Beaver Dog and a rough-coated dog which was used primarily for killing rats. Others believe that it evolved from crosses of the extinct Schafer Pudel and the Wirehaired German Pinscher.

Still others state flatly that the Standard Schnauzer was never a terrier; that it has little if any terrier blood in it; and that it descends entirely from shepherd dogs. These researchers cite its resemblance to the BOUVIER DES FLANDRES, the Giant Schnauzer, and to other shepherd and drovers' dogs.

It is likely that the Standard Schnauzer originated in the great cattle and sheep herding areas of Germany around Württemberg and Bavaria. Early accounts state that it was a good cattle dog, but it was also considered to be a ratter of extraordinary ability.

The breed was first shown at the third international dog show at Hanover, Germany, in 1879, and the winning dog was named *Schnauzer*. The following year German breeders set up a breed standard. During this period, the Plavia Kennels of Max Hartenstein were prominent. A speciality show in 1890 had 93 entries.

The first club to sponsor the breed was the Pinscher Club, formed at Cologne in 1895. The Bavarian Schnauzer Club was organized at Munich in 1907. In 1918, the two clubs merged under the name, Pinscher-Schnauzer Club.

The dog was inbred heavily to fix type. In doing so, two major lines of descent were formed. One came from *Schnauzer* and the other from *Seppel*. From them came three great pillars of the breed, *Ch. Rex van den Gunthersburg* and his sons, *Ch. Rigo Schnauzerlust*, and *Rex von Egelsee*.

After the First World War, dog lovers outside Germany became interested in the Standard Schnauzer. English breed pioneers were the Duchess of Montrose and Mrs. D. McM. Kavanagh. A breed club was formed toward the end of the 1920s. Major sire influences came from German imports, *Bruno von der Secretainerie de Chavalard*, *Bolz von der Brunnerberg*, and *Gaunir von Egelsee*.

In the United States, a Swiss import, *Resy Patricia*, became the first U.S. champion, and the great German champion, *Holm von Egelsee* was the first male champion in America. Mrs. Maurice Newton was the first to breed a champion in the United States: *Fracas Franconia*, a daughter of Resy Patricia.

The Schnauzer Club of America was founded in 1925, but as importations of Miniature Schnauzers began in great numbers, the name was changed to Standard Schnauzer Club of America in 1933, and the American Miniature Schnauzer Club was formed. The Standard Schnauzer was moved to the working group in 1945 and the Miniature Schnauzer remained among the terriers.

Canadian interest in Standard Schnauzers followed within a few years. The first of the breed to be imported and registered in Canada was *Cortlandt Curacco*, who came from the line of Ch. Rigo Schnauzerlust. Cortlandt Curacco was whelped in 1926.

Essentials of the breed: The Standard Schnauzer is a rough-coated dog measuring 18 to 20 inches at the shoulder; bitches 17 to 19 inches. Allowed colours are pepper and salt, from iron grey to silver grey, and pure black. In the former a grey undercoat is preferred, but a tan or fawn is not penalized. Fading to light grey or silver white on eyebrows, whiskers, cheeks, under the throat, across the chest, under the tail, leg furnishings, and under the body, are permitted. A smudge of chest white in blacks is permitted.

The head is rectangular. It narrows slightly from ears to eyes, and again from eyes to nose tip. Head length equals about half the body length from the withers to the root of the tail. There is a slight stop, with the top lines of the muzzle and the skull parallel.

The body is compact and short coupled with the height equalling the length from breast bone to the point of the rump. The thighs are broad and the stifles are well bent. The tail is set on moderately high, and is docked to not less than an inch, nor more than two inches. A squirrel tail is a fault. The coat is hard, wiry, and about an inch and a half long on the body. If cropped, the ears are erect; if uncropped they are small, V-shaped, and set on rather high.

See SCHNAUZER, GIANT; SCHNAUZER, MINIATURE.
See colour plate p. 94.

Scissors Bite A bite in which the edges of the lower incisors touch inner side of the upper incisors.

Scotch Collie see Collie, Rough.

Scotch Greyhound see Deerhound, Scottish.

Scottish Deerhound see Deerhound, Scottish.

Scottish Terrier To the question 'What colour is a Scottish Terrier?' most would answer 'Black'. In fact Scotties can also be of various shades of grey, wheaten, grizzle or brindle of any colour!

Indeed when the first standard of breed points was produced in the eighties, it insisted that the most desirable colour was red brindle with black muzzle and ear tips. No mention at all was made of black Scotties, which were virtually non-existent until around 1890 and not in any sense popular until forty years ago.

When, where, and how did the breed originate? These are questions unlikely to be answered with certainty. We know however that when Thomas Bell wrote his *History of British Quadrupeds* in 1837 there were only two distinct types of terrier in the British Isles. One was smooth, sharp muzzled, neat and symmetrical, usually black-and-tan. We can accept this as the prototype of the English varieties such as the MANCHESTER and FOX TERRIERS.

The other had rough, harsh hair, short and stout

limbs and was of variable colour although usually a dirty white. Here then is our typical terrier from Scotland. Over the years from this have been developed the CAIRN, DANDIE DINMONT, WEST HIGHLAND WHITE and of course the Scottish Terrier.

In those days the Highlands were remote and comparatively inaccessible. Therefore the terriers of Scotland varied considerably from one district to the next. This was partly because offspring resembled their parents which were local dogs. There were also the deliberate efforts of breeders to produce stock suitable for work in the local conditions. The Scottie, once called the ABERDEEN TERRIER, was evolved, bred and kept for work. Its particular task was the destruction of vermin such as foxes in the tangle of rocks and stones found in inhospitable countryside. Hence its essential toughness, the weatherproof qualities of its double textured coat, its indifference to punishment, its courage in attack, and its instinct to dig and burrow in the ground.

When first shown late in the nineteenth century, it competed in classes for 'Scotch Terriers', standing alongside Dandie Dinmonts, SKYES and even YORKSHIRE TERRIERS. Not until 1882 when a breed club was formed was it given a separate existence. In the years that followed it established itself as the most popular terrier in Britain, and held the position for a great many years.

It is not unusual to say that terriers have been ruined by dog shows. The reverse must be true of the Scottie. With the gradual disappearance of its original task might well have come the oblivion suffered by similar breeds. Instead, its smart appearance, structural soundness and devil-may-care air brought it recognition in the show ring. Best in Show awards secured popularity in many lands. Purists inevitably claim that excessive barbering has spoiled the breed. In fact, the essential character of the Scottie remains the same whatever its external appearance. It is a character which combines conceit and certainty. A character who clearly proclaims 'I am the cock of the North'.

Essentials of the breed: Head: long and narrow with distinct stop. Large nose. Eyes: almond-shaped, dark brown. Ears: neat, pointed and erect. The teeth must be large. Neck: of moderate length, muscular set into a sloping shoulder. The brisket in front of the forelegs. Chest: broad and hung between the forelegs. The back: proportionately short and muscular. Topline: straight. Hindquarters: very powerful, wide buttocks. Feet: well-padded, with arched toes. Tail: thick at the root and tapering with upright carriage. Coat: undercoat short, dense and soft; outer coat harsh, dense and wiry. Colour: black, wheaten or brindle. The American standard also includes steel or iron grey, grizzled or sandy. Weight: (Britain) from 19 lb. to 23 lb.; (America) dogs 19 to 22 lb., bitches 18 to 21 lb. Height: 10 to 11 inches.
See colour plate p. 375.

Screw Tail A naturally short tail, twisted into screw form.

Above Screw tail on a Pug.

Scrotal Hernia see Hernia.

Scurf see Dandruff.

Sealyham Terrier John Owen Tucker Edwardes, the undisputed 'father' of the Sealyham breed died in 1891 without ever seeing it established. More curious, he never tried to found a breed. Still less did he wish to found one destined to be a winning force on the show-bench and a terrier of fashion. That however, one of the many ironies in the world of dogs, is exactly what he achieved.

Captain Edwardes, an eccentric sportsman, lived at Sealyham, a country mansion between Haverfordwest and Fishguard, in Wales. His primary interest being otter hunting, he kept a pack of OTTERHOUNDS. Inevitably, he wanted terriers as well as hounds to hunt successfully. The local mongrel terriers were not ideal because they lacked both uniformity and courage. Captain Edwardes therefore bred a terrier which would suit his own purpose. The dog had to be small, game and active. It had to gallop with hounds and be small enough to go anywhere. And it had to have the courage to face animals regardless of disparity in size.

The Captain left no records of what 'breeds' were used to fashion the strain; probably most of the terriers used were not true breeds. He was not secretive; he never thought the subject could interest anybody.

He was a hard task master. He put his puppies out to work with local farmers, tenants and keepers. On rounds of inspection he took with him two bad-tempered, experienced terriers and a gun. If the pup gave ground in the face of these belligerent visitors, it was shot.

When the survivors reached one year of age, they faced an even more severe test. A live pole-cat was first dragged across a field and then confined in a small pit with a narrow entrance. The dogs, already experts at ratting, followed the trail without difficulty. The gallop warmed them up. If they went straight in and successfully attacked this formidable adversary, they lived to tell the tale. If they faltered, hung around outside,

Below Scottish Terrier. Ch. Gosmore Eilburn Admaration.

Sealyham Terrier.
Above left Polrose Plain Pleasure.
Above Ch. Polrose Pace Setter.
Right Young Sealyhams Phlame and Penny-halfpenny at home in a flower basket.

failed to attack instantly upon entering the pit, broke off the encounter or failed to score total victory, they also were shot.

Not surprisingly, with such a stiff 'survival of the fittest' test, the terriers of Sealyham were tough. Their modern descendants are astonishingly peaceful. They have also changed in other ways. Captain Edwardes would have disliked the smart, stylish animal with reasonable temperament. He was not trying to produce a show or family-circle type of dog. But what he wanted then and what the average dog owner wants today are very different, so it is fortunate that the Sealyham has proved adaptable.

Currently, most terriers are slightly out of fashion. Fox Terriers, Scotties and the like no longer rule the roost. But the world of dogs often turns full circle and one suspects that the day of the terrier may come again. When it does, this cheerful, short-legged terrier will surely be wagging its tail in the homes of rich and poor alike. It is that sort of dog, a dog with undoubted breeding and yet no trace of class.

Essentials of the breed: The skull should be slightly domed and wide. Jaws: powerful and long. The nose: black. Eyes: dark, round and of medium size. Ears: medium-sized, rounded at tip and carried at side of cheek. Neck: fairly long and muscular. Forelegs: short, strong and straight. Body: of medium length and level, chest broad, deep and well let down between forelegs. Hindquarters: powerful, thighs well bent at stifle. Feet: round and cat-like. Tail: carried erect. Coat: long, hard and wiry. Colour: mostly all white, or white with lemon, brown or badger markings on head and ears.

Weight: dogs up to 20 lb.; bitches 18 lb. Height: not to exceed 12 inches at the shoulder.
See colour plate p. 375.

Season see Heat of Bitch.

Second Thigh The lower thigh, from the stifle joint to the hock joint.

Sedge Dead grass colour, as in some CHESAPEAKE BAY RETRIEVERS.

Selection All controlled breeding implies selection. Some dogs and bitches are permitted to have offspring, while others, being considered unsuitable, are not. Breeders select dogs for breeding mainly on their appearance and behaviour, plus their relationship to outstanding individuals either ancestral or contemporary. Obviously the stringency of selection is limited by the total number to be bred from in proportion to the total number available. If from a hundred bitch puppies a breeder wants only five broods, he can be more selective than if he needs twenty. The five would be 'more highly selected' than the twenty.

Through selection, breeders 'push' the breed in the desired direction and maintain quality; the power thus exerted is called 'selection pressure'. This is the breeder's most valuable tool. If it is not used wisely, valuable qualities may be lost from the strain, and faults perpetuated and increased.

When a breed's popularity increases rapidly, selection pressure is relaxed because every puppy is saleable, and so animals which may be inferior are bred from. Conversely, when a breed's popularity wanes, culling becomes increasingly severe, often with a salutary effect on the breed. Breeds which are numerically small over a long period often attain a markedly high average quality because they are bred by a small circle of dedicated enthusiasts who keep only the best specimens, as they may have to destroy inferior puppies as unsaleable. This certainly helps to maintain high quality.

Unfortunately, culls, that is animals rejected for breeding purposes, are frequently sold as pets when they may be bred from. In theory this should be detri-

As a dog can serve numerous bitches, studs are more highly selected than bitches, although more stud dogs are normally available than the minimum number biologically necessary. Because of the number of puppies a dog can sire, studs carrying hereditary abnormalities are the greatest danger. Where the costly technique of test-mating for a recessive gene is applied, it can be applied to stud dogs in the first instances. If test-mated (non-carrier) *males* are then used, the harmful gene will only be passed on by one parent at each generation. The test-mating of bitches is more laborious and costly, and it can be postponed until the incidence of the gene in the breed has been so reduced by using only 'clear' stud dogs, that few bitches, when tested, will be found carriers. The appearance of the harmful gene will then be rare.
See RECESSIVE.

Self-Colour A single whole colour except for shadings.

Semi-Prick Ears Erect ears with the tips bent slightly forward, as in COLLIES and SHETLAND SHEEP-DOGS.

Senses, Special Dogs appear to have certain senses which are not shared by man. In some cases, both may have the same potentials, which have been more fully realized in the dog. The dog's ability to tell time is often observed. The dog seems to know when it is time for the child to come home from school. If free, it may go to meet the child, and if confined in the home, may position itself at a window to wait.

Some animal behaviour researchers have said that the dog has an internal clock which functions steadily and accurately. The dog keys the rhythm of its life to that of the household in which it lives, however, and it is a close observer of the home routine. The dog may react to clues which are unconsciously laid by its master.

The dog is supposed to be deficient in form perception. But if the owner puts on one jacket, the dog remains lying quietly on the rug, whereas if the man puts on the jacket he wears to walk the dog, the dog reacts with great excitement. This may not be form perception, but a variety of perceptions which might include movement, smell, time, and even unconscious clues from other members of the family.

The ability of some dogs to find their way home from long distances, over unfamiliar territory, has long been noted. The ability is more marked in dogs accustomed to wandering, which suggests that the dog has trained itself. But other factors may be involved: the dog may be able to navigate by the stars or by the infra-red rays from the sun, like the bee.

Such dogs may also be able to recognize odours which have little meaning for people. For example, dogs like to scratch and then snuffle up the odours of freshly turned soil. They may be able to scent their approach to home territory from the soil.

Dogs communicate with each other by sound, and human observers have catalogued as many as twenty

mental to progress. In some countries, such as Germany, breeding from pets is not permitted by breed clubs. Stud dogs and brood bitches have to be approved by a committee of breeders who decide what matings can be made. The fact that dogs from countries without this discipline are not inferior to those from controlled countries throws doubt on the system.

Linked with selection is the question of HEREDITARY ABNORMALITIES. These vary from clearly defined conditions whose mode of inheritance is known (such as progressive retinal atrophy or P.R.A.) to vague disabilities like low fertility, poor mothering instinct, unresponsiveness to training, which may appear to 'run in families' but are also much affected by environmental circumstances. In some cases abnormalities are actually the result of selecting for certain show points which are themselves abnormalities; prolonged soft palate in BULLDOGS is an example. Other abnormalities like HIP DYSPLASIA and P.R.A. have occurred and been perpetuated by chance, not by selective breeding.

Opinions differ as to how much selection pressure must be diverted from selecting for show points and used against the hereditary abnormalities. Some abnormalities do not prevent dogs from winning, even from becoming champions. They affect dogs in middle age or even after their show careers. Since the aim of most breeders is to produce winners, and few are interested in breeding pets, they may feel that such late-developing abnormalities are not important. Some, such as BLINDNESS, may be regarded by some as causing little inconvenience to the dog itself if it lives a restricted kennel life. In a pet or a working dog this would be a serious handicap. The hardship of withdrawing a top animal from breeding, thereby losing all its desirable GENES, to eliminate one abnormality is appreciable, but breeders do this readily enough when a show fault, possibly not detrimental to the dog's health or happiness, is involved.

different howls, barks, and whines which a single dog may make. These all have specific meanings for other dogs, as well as for observant owners. Dogs also communicate by an elaborate sign language. The puppy lies down and rolls onto its back, feet in the air when an adult dog approaches. The adult recognizes this as submission, and it seems bound by an unbreakable taboo not to attack or injure the puppy. Slinking, ears back, and tail between the legs is another pattern of submission, and so is bowing the neck to a dominant dog. The dog which crouches, holds its tail low, and wags it furiously, is not only making a gesture of submission but an overture of friendliness.

If two dogs approach stiff-legged, tails held high and stiff, but wagging slowly, there is likely to be a fight, unless their eyes are averted. If the dogs look at each other, the fight is almost a certainty.

Scientists argue that dogs do not have a sense of conscience; that conscience is simply taught morality, or a system of taboos. Dog behaviour sometimes *suggests* an inborn conscience, or subtle social instincts. Thus one dog was repeatedly observed to pull the burrs from the coats of other dogs and from its master's trousers after a hunting trip. An occasional dog has been known to lead about a blind canine friend. Perhaps while going blind the one dog learned to follow the other, but it cannot be denied that the sighted dog appeared to have accepted the responsibility.

There are many recorded cases in which dogs appeared to demonstrate extra sensory perception. Although the witnesses have often been reliable, proof is seldom possible. Yet the numbers of such cases would indicate that there is some substance in the stories. In discussing the '"mysterious" powers of animals' Prof. John Paul Scott, an authority on animal behaviour, wrote: '. . . we should not be too sceptical. Animal behaviour is not supernatural, but animals occasionally turn out to have powers which are definitely superhuman . . . In exploring new phenomena, we need to draw a line between explanations which are supernatural and those which are merely superhuman.'

Many dogs have seemed to know of the exact moment of death of a loved person, even when the death was some distance away, and before any other member of the household had been notified of the death.

There is a well-authenticated case in which a Standard Poodle, named *Pierre*, seemed to be able to take orders by thought transference. The dog had won an obedience title, and had been sent to an American professional handler to be groomed and shown in conformation classes. The handler, Thomas Crowe, was startled to discover that the dog seemed to anticipate his wishes. He communicated with the dog's owners, and they confirmed the dog's seeming ability.

Crowe began a series of experiments. He would command the dog to sit up, stand up, lie down, and roll over by thought only. The dog would obey faultlessly. Crowe would write out the order in which the dog was to obey the commands, seal the paper, and then get an observer to note the order in which the dog performed the commands. The dog is said to have obeyed even when Crowe was outside the building, which eliminates

the possibility that the dog could have got clues from unconscious movements by Crowe.

The most famous of the dogs which might be called 'mind-readers' was an English Setter owned by Sam Van Arsdale of Sedalia, Missouri. Sworn affidavits show that on seven consecutive years, *Jim* correctly picked the winner of the Kentucky Derby before it was run. The names of the horses were written on separate pieces of paper and sealed. The dog then would put his paw upon one slip. This was placed in a bank vault, and was not opened until after the race was run. Until then, no one knew the name of the horse which Jim had picked.

Septicemia This is a name given to the contamination of the blood by bacteria. The dog develops a high temperature and immediate treatment is essential.

Septum The partition between the nasal cavities.

Services see Petshops.

Setter see English Setter; Gordon Setter; Irish Setter.

Sex Play A dog that is over-sexed is not only a nuisance but an embarrassment. It will pretend to have sex play with things around the house, in the street and even with children's legs. If these habits become decidedly objectionable, a veterinarian can supply hormone preparations that may help to discourage the dog. The surest method of stopping it is to have the dog castrated. There should be no ill effects after CASTRATION and it is incorrect to think that the dog will become fat or lose its character. It should still be a lively dog and certainly much more pleasant to own than before its operation.

Shami see Saluki.

Shedding see Moulting.

Sheep and Cattle Dogs Herding breeds of dog are to be found in many shapes and sizes and in almost every country of the world. Some have been bred primarily to guard the flocks. For example, on the Maremma plain in Italy, the sheep are put into folds at night and MAREMMA SHEEPDOGS are left on guard, usually in pairs. They are left loose and instinctively stay with the flock all night. Woe betide any intruder, on two legs or four, who is bold or foolish enough to approach too near.

In Germany the GERMAN SHEPHERD DOG or Alsatian has been bred to herd and guard the flocks of sheep, but in other countries the Alsatian is better known as a police dog or guide dog for the blind.

In Britain there are several breeds and many types of sheep and cattle dogs, all bred primarily to herd. Although these types are frequently interbred, they are still pure-bred herding dogs and it is wrong to think of them as mongrels. During the past fifty years, there has been an increase in the numbers of Border COLLIES found on farms throughout Great Britain with a consequent decrease in other breeds and types. In Wales,

Corgis were used extensively by drovers to move large herds of cattle down from the mountains to market; and the Welsh sheepdogs did the same with sheep. Both cattle and sheep now travel in trucks, and the Corgi sits by the fire while the old Welsh Sheepdog has been so frequently crossed with the Border Collie that it is practically extinct.

In Scotland the Bearded Collie was a favourite with drovers and, although Beardies are still to be found working, most carry quite a lot of Border Collie blood. In southern England large numbers of sheep were folded on arable crops and it was the OLD ENGLISH SHEEPDOG, or Bobtail, which worked them. A modern version of this breed now adorns show benches and only remnants of the old type are still to be found in England on farms in Dorset (where they are known as Dorset Blue Shags) and Somerset. In East Anglia, Bobtails were crossed with Collies from Scotland to produce 'Smithfield Dogs' which drovers used to drive stock to Smithfield market in London. These in turn were crossed with GREYHOUNDS to produce a type known as the LURCHER.

The old-fashioned Scottish Collie, once common on all the lowland farms of its native country has, like the Welsh sheepdog been replaced by the Border Collie. The original has been turned into the modern show collie (the Rough Collie or 'Lassie' type) and has been 'improved' to such an extent that this now bears little resemblance in appearance or character to its ancestor.

The Border Collie has been exported all over the world and particularly to Australia and New Zealand. In Australia two national breeds have been produced from it: the KELPIE to work sheep, and the AUSTRALIAN CATTLE DOG or Heeler to work cattle. Some say they both carry DINGO blood and although there is no real evidence of this in the Kelpie, it may well be true of the Heeler.

In Europe there are many breeds of sheep and cattle dogs, some of which are still used as working dogs. A good sheep or cattle dog can do the work of several men – and do it better. Without sheepdogs the production of wool and mutton in such countries as Australia and New Zealand would be a more expensive operation.

Sheepdog Training Sheepdogs are not trained to herd or round up sheep. They are bred to do that instinctively, and trained how to do it properly. A

Below Sheep and cattle dogs. Three working sheepdogs 'fix' a flock with their eyes.

young sheepdog should be taught elementary obedience in the same way as any other dog. It must come when called and, even more important, lie down instantly at any time and in any place.

After that the trainer must wait until the puppy 'starts to run'. It usually does this (often quite suddenly and unexpectedly) when it is around six to ten months old. Some very carefully bred puppies will want to work at a much younger age than that but they should not be allowed to do so. They are not fast enough to pass the sheep and, if allowed to run, will merely learn to chase them.

A young dog may be encouraged to run by seeing a trained dog working which gives rise to the common belief that it is necessary to have an old sheepdog to teach a young one. Whilst it is very helpful to have a *well trained* dog around when training a young one, experienced trainers never allow the two to run together. This is because the pup will try to beat its 'opponent' and run close in to the sheep, very probably gripping the first one it comes to – a habit very difficult to erase.

The herding instinct of the sheepdog is a diversion of the hunting instinct of the wild dog and the vast majority of good young sheepdogs will attack a sheep if allowed to do so. That is why it is so important to teach a pup to drop instantly on command *before* it is allowed to run.

Sheepdog Trials in Britain The first sheepdog trial was held at Bala in Wales in 1873. This proved so popular that sheepdog trials soon spread to other parts of Wales. As the first trial was won by a Scotsman,

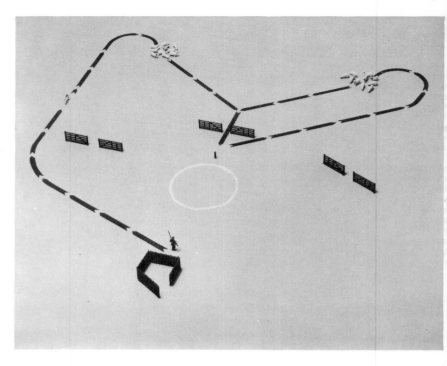

James Thompson, with *Tweed*, a Scottish-bred dog, sheepdog trials started quite a boom in importing dogs from Scotland to Wales.

In 1876 trials were held in England and Scotland and in 1906 the International Sheepdog Society was formed at Haddington in Scotland. Since 1922 national trials have been run each year (excepting war years) in Scotland, England and Wales with the twelve highest-

Below Sheepdog trials in Hyde Park, London. When the sheep are being 'penned', the handler must hold on to a rope attached to the gate, and leave all the work to the dog.

placed dogs from each country going forward to compete in the International held in each of the countries in turn. In 1967 Ireland took part in the competition for the first time.

Enthusiasm is not confined to the British Isles and sheepdog trials are also held in the United States, Australia, New Zealand and other countries.

Sheepdog trials are designed as far as possible to test a dog's ability to work sheep under natural conditions. As with most competitions, style counts for a great deal and many good all-round working sheepdogs would not stand a chance on the trial ground. On the other hand the great majority of trial-winning dogs can and do work sheep all the year round on farms.

The dogs used in British trials are Border COLLIES bred solely for work and therefore varying considerably in type. This breed is not recognized by most Kennel Clubs but has its own stud book in Britain kept by the International Sheepdog Society. Originally dogs could be entered in the stud book if they had qualified at trials, but now trial entries are confined to dogs entered in the stud book except under very exceptional circumstances. Conditions of registration into this stud book are far more exacting than those concerning dogs registered with most Kennel Clubs.

Shelly A shallow, narrow body, with too much tuck-up, and usually an insufficient amount of bone.

Shetland Sheepdog The Shetland Sheepdog has a descriptive name. We know at once that it is a dog from the Shetland Isles with a working background. When we look at the dog we realize that it is in effect a miniature

Scotch or Rough COLLIE. This fact leads some to believe that the Shetland Sheepdog has been deliberately bantamized by man to accord with the modern desire for miniature animals.

This is not the truth – at least it is not the whole truth. The Shetland Isles, apart from being small, are somewhat bare, rugged and hostile. Because of this, the Islands have always produced small animal, and doubtless this tendency has been intensified by selective breeding. The best known, of course, are the Shetland ponies; however, there are also comparatively small cattle, dwarf sheep and miniature sheepdogs which herd them.

To realize that they were originally working dogs is to appreciate that they were not always particularly elegant; indeed, books of seventy or eighty years ago frequently call them 'nondescript'. Since working ability rather than show points were required, this is not surprising. Most of the improvements in the breed's appearance have been made since the time that they were first recognized by the Kennel Club of England in 1909. There is no doubt that small Collies were used to make the improvement and this may account for the fact that even today the breed has a tendency to grow over-size.

The ideal height for 'Shelties' is 14 inches for bitches, $14\frac{1}{2}$ inches for dogs. Most show specimens come within this range but pets are usually larger. In America, as will be seen below, the breed standard allows for this.

Though it is doubtful if many Shetland Sheepdogs are actively working sheep at the moment, it is a fact that their background and heritage have produced a remarkably trainable animal. Their successes in the world of competitive obedience have been most marked, and it is perhaps unfortunate that they have to compete so often against their even sharper and more active cousins, the Border Collies. On the credit side, however, it must be stated that they make very much better pets than Border Collies which are apt to become troublesome unless given sufficient work for their active minds and bodies. The Shetland Sheepdog is never a troublesome pet, although care must be taken to avoid acquiring dogs of nervous or highly strung dispositions.

As with many other breeds, their coat is their glory, and fortunately it is not one that requires a great deal of attention. For show purposes, there is the disadvantage that frequent shedding leaves the dogs looking somewhat denuded for a part of the year, but simple combing to remove the dead hair is virtually all the attention that the dog needs from the pet owner to keep it looking smart.

Essentials of the breed: The head should be a long, blunt wedge tapering from ear to nose. Cheeks should be flat, skull and muzzle of equal length. Lips: tight. Teeth: sound and level. Eyes: of medium size, obliquely set and almond-shaped. Ears: semi-erect with tips dropping forward. The body is slightly longer from the withers to the root of the tail than the height at the withers. The chest should be deep and the ribs well sprung. Back: level. Tail: set on low with abundant hair and slight upward sweep. Feet: oval, with arched toes close together.

The coat must be double, the outer of harsh texture and straight, the undercoat short and close. Mane and frill should be abundant. Colour: tricolours, sables (clear or shaded) and blue merles, black and white, and tan.

Ideal height: (Britain) dogs 14½ inches. Bitches 14 inches. (America): between 13 and 16 inches.
See colour plate p. 297.

Shih Tzu Shih Tzu, pronounced Shid-Zoo, means 'Lion Dog' in Chinese. But even without this clear hint it would not be difficult to guess that this breed has been associated in some way with China. The similarity between the Shih Tzu and the PEKINGESE is too marked to be overlooked.

Even so they are Tibetan in origin, and are said to have lived there for centuries. From the time of the establishment of the Manchu dynasty in the sixteenth century, it became customary for distinguished Chinese visitors to Tibet to be presented with a pair of these little animals. In this way the Shih Tzu became established in China, and it is a reasonable assumption that over the years some were crossed with Pekingese.

The Peking Kennel Club issued a standard which must surely be the most flowery ever issued for any breed. Among other things, it says the 'Lhasa Lion Dog should have lion head, bear torso, camel hoof, feather-duster tail, palm-leaf ears, rice teeth, pearly petal tongue and movement like a goldfish'.

More descriptive of movement and certainly more modern was the remark of a ringsider that these dogs cover ground like a hovercraft, or the comment of a judge: 'They show me their pads when they go away'.

Despite their antiquity, their impact on the Western World is comparatively recent. General Sir Douglas Brownrigg brought the first pair from Peking to England in 1930. The Earl of Essex imported a few more in 1938. Even so they did not become sufficiently numerous in Britain to warrant a separate register until 1946. Since then progress has been steady and sustained rather than spectacular, and this despite astonishing success in the show ring.

The breed has also been recognized by the American Kennel Club. In 1969, classes were permitted for the first time and points became available for use towards the title of Champion. On the first day a few Shih Tzus were shown, and one of them had his name written on the scrolls forever by becoming Best in Show. This is the sort of news-stealing trick quite in keeping with the character of the dog.

Essentials of the breed: Head: broad and round with hair falling well over the eyes. Good beard and whiskers. Hair growing upwards on the nose gives a chrysanthe-mum-like effect. Nose: preferably black. Eyes: large, dark and round but not prominent. Ears: large with heavily-coated, long leathers; set below the crown of the skull. Mouth: level or slightly underhung. Legs: short and muscular with ample bone. Body between withers and root of tail should be longer than height at withers. Chest: broad and deep with level back. Feet: firm and well padded. Tail: heavily plumed and curled well over back, carried gaily, and set on high. Coat: long and dense, with good undercoat. Colour: all colours

Shih Tzu.
Left Ch. Ya Tung of Antarctica.
Right Aztec Ming Soo.

allowed, but with a white blaze on the forehead and a white tip to the tail preferred.

Weight: up to 18 lb., ideal 9 to 16 lb.

See colour plate p. 189.

Shock Shock has been defined as a complex of symptoms resulting from an injury, so that there is a derangement of many functions of the body. A frequent condition of shock is a reduction of venous return and a lowering of blood pressure. Shock can be serious, and if such conditions are not corrected quickly, they can progress until there is circulatory failure and death.

Among the causes of shock are extensive burns, traffic injuries, a blow to a vital area, poisoning, surgery, exhaustion, starvation, uncontrolled and long-standing diarrhoea, weakness resulting from wasting diseases, such as distemper, and anaphylaxis.

Anaphylaxis is most simply described as a serum or vaccine reaction, and the condition is often called anaphylactic shock. A hypersensitivity is sometimes induced in the body, following the subcutaneous or intravenous injection of an antigen into the dog, If, within ten to twelve days, the same antigen is injected, anaphylactic shock may result.

There is also a condition known as reverse anaphylaxis. It occurs occasionally when an antigen is injected, and followed by an injection of a specific antibody, which is the cause of the reaction. When reverse anaphylaxis occurs, there may be paralysis in a particular area, or a partial loss of muscle function. Many of the common symptoms of shock are present in anaphylaxis. In addition, there may be chills and high fever. Cyanosis, a bluish tinge in the colour of the mucous membranes, may also be present.

In all conditions of shock, veterinary aid should be sought immediately, although the owner can take certain actions until the veterinarian arrives.

The dog can be wrapped in a warm blanket, and given additional heat by such means as hot water bottles, placed at the back and not near the feet.

Shoulder In show parlance the term 'shoulders' embraces something more than the plain anatomical structure and is linked up with the disposition of the neck, the angle of inclination of the scapula (the shoulder bone) and with the way in which the base of the neck fits into the anterior portion of the trunk.

The basis of a 'good shoulder' lies mainly in the position of the scapula in relation to the dorsal vertebrae over which it lies. This includes the degree to which it slopes in respect to the level on which the dog stands. It is influenced also by the height of the scapular spine, the length of the scapula, and by the length of the humerus or upper foreleg.

On either side of the scapular spine there is a fossa or hollow which contains muscle. If the fossa is shallow owing to lack of height of the scapular spine, the contained muscle is likely to bulge outwards giving rise to an 'overloaded shoulder'. The shoulder should be almost flat with a visible outlining of the underlying muscles.

In average-sized dogs such as Springer Spaniels, one might draw a chalk line down the spine of the scapula commencing at the withers and ending at the shoulder joint. In a good shoulder the angle between this line and the humerus will be approximately 90°. A line drawn perpendicularly from the summit of the withers to the point of the elbow and then prolonged downwards would pass down the hinder border of the forelimb.

In a terrier with a very 'straight' front, the angle at the shoulder would still be (or could be) 90°, but the perpendicular line would descend about an inch behind the hinder border of the forelimb. The angle of the shoulder may be influenced by show standards and 'distorted' from the original 'perfect shoulder'.

In 'perfect shoulder' the neck slopes gradually from a head carried high. It merges into the withers, shoulders and breast in streamlined fashion without a definite break in the contour. In an undesirably 'straight' or upright shoulder, a line drawn from the upper end of the spine of the scapula to the shoulder joint will appear more upright and the angle between the scapula and the humerus at the shoulder joint will be greater than 90°, and the humerus may be relatively short.

A slight increase in the length of the humerus may increase the degree of inclination of the scapula since it carries the point of the shoulder forward. The advantage of a pronounced degree of scapula inclination is that the forelimb can be advanced further in a straight line with the length of the scapula than if the shoulder were upright. The knee can thus be lifted a little higher and the forefoot will be lifted well clear of the ground, giving an action unlike the 'daisy-cutting' which goes with the straight shoulder.

Show Classes see Classes at Shows.

Shows and Showing – Britain Dog shows were born when dog-fighting and bull-baiting became illegal in 1835, and they grew as transport became easier with the development of the railways. For the first time in history, large numbers of people could patronize such events and the railway companies encouraged excursions to shows of this kind.

In June 1859 in Newcastle-upon-Tyne, England, the first organized dog show was held with one class for Pointers and one class for Setters. Other dog shows followed and within ten years there was an annual calendar of shows. There were also many shows other

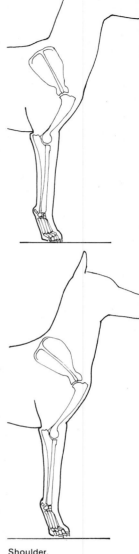

Shoulder.
Top 'Perfect shoulder'.
Above 'Straight shoulder'.
Below Shock. Until a veterinarian can arrive, the shocked dog should be covered with a warm blanket.

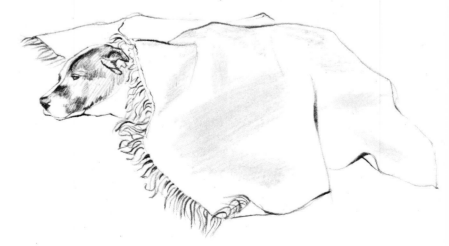

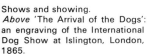

Shows and showing.
Above 'The Arrival of the Dogs': an engraving of the International Dog Show at Islington, London, 1865.
Above right English Setters being judged in the ring at Cruft's.

than dog shows, and halls were especially built in many parts of Britain to house them. When the Great Exhibition ended in 1852, the gigantic conservatory in which it had been held in Hyde Park, was moved to South London. The 'Crystal Palace' became a landmark for the next eighty years and the venue of many dog shows. The organizers of one of these, the National Dog Club, founded the KENNEL CLUB in 1873.

As the new sport grew, the demand for a variety of classes and a variety of shows grew; the Kennel Club provided for these demands with a graduated scale based on a dog's wins at previous shows. The same principle applies today in all shows including the big ones which each provide more than 1,000 classes for more than 8,000 exhibits.

There are approximately 150 different breeds of dogs registered at the Kennel Club and these are split into two main divisions, Sporting Dogs and Non-Sporting Dogs. Each division is further divided into three groups, Sporting Dogs into Hounds, Gundogs and Terriers and Non-Sporting Dogs into Utility, Working and Toy Dogs. Dog shows are divided basically into two groups, Open (to all exhibitors) and Members. The latter are almost without exception confined to dogs belonging to members of the show-promoting society but occasionally a show is held confined to dogs owned by exhibitors living within a specified area. Some shows provide classes for many breeds, some for a group of breeds and some for one breed only, the latter being known as specialist shows. Some Open shows offer Kennel Club Challenge Certificates: these are Championship shows and are the most important of all. At the lower end of the scale there are matches, often held in public houses in the evening, restricted to not more than 32 dogs and judged with two dogs only in the 'ring' at a time, on a knock-out basis. Exemption shows are held at village fetes usually for charity and 'exempt' from most of the Kennel Club Rules and Regulations.

The Kennel Club Show Regulations provide a basis of twenty classes (see CLASSES AT SHOWS, BRITISH) varying from Puppy to Open, in which eligible dogs can be entered. When a dog has won a Kennel Club Challenge Certificate, it cannot compete at a Members' show and, at Open and Championship shows, a dog is debarred from some classes as soon as it wins a first prize. It is eligible for fewer classes as it wins more prizes and thus, as it progresses, it must face the prospect of more serious competition.

The value of prizes in Britain is kept low as a matter of Kennel Club policy; at Members' shows the first prize money is rarely £1, at Open shows £1 is the usual first prize money, and at Championship shows, such as CRUFT'S, £2·50 is the top prize money. Entry fees are small, and even at Cruft's Show, £2 is all that is required to enter a dog in its first two classes.

Some of the larger dog shows are held in conjunction with agricultural and horticultural shows and the wide selection of shows provides plenty of opportunities for the dog owner to enjoy his hobby, and gives the dog breeder plenty of opportunities to show his 'product' to prospective buyers.

Shows and Showing – Canada Dog shows in Canada are quite similar to those in the United States. The differences are brought about, in part, by the smaller population, the great distances between cities, and the fewer opportunities to win championships. During 1969, the Canadian Kennel Club licensed and supervised 280 Championship dog shows, and 109 obedience trials. 74,000 dogs competed

The all-breed shows in the United States, and most of the speciality shows, are operated by licensed superintendents. In Canada, licensed superintendents are almost unknown.

Because Canadian shows are so much smaller than American shows, the judging system is different. Depending upon the size of the event, a judge may officiate over one to three groups. As he finishes one group, the Best of Breed winners are returned to the ring immediately. The judge then selects his group winners, that is, Best in Group, Best Canadian-bred in Group, and Best Canadian-bred Puppy in Group.

All eligible dogs are required to remain for group judging at Canadian shows. If they are absent without the excuse of a veterinarian or proper show officials, they lose any awards they have won at the show.

Canada also permits the same club to give two or three shows on consecutive days in the same building. This helps to overcome the great distances so many exhibitors must otherwise travel. A specialty show may also be given in conjunction with the all-breed event. For example, a Collie might be judged at the specialty show at 9 a.m. and then in the afternoon be judged by a different judge in the regular classes at an all-breed show.

The Canadian Kennel Club does not license PRO-FESSIONAL HANDLERS, but there are however excellent Canadian professionals who take strings of dogs to shows and some of these are licensed to handle in the United States.

Shows and Showing – United States The exhibiting of pure-bred dogs is widespread in the United States. Shows are held as far north as Fairbanks, Alaska, less than 150 miles from the Arctic Circle; at Brownsville, Texas, the southernmost city in the country; in Hawaii, 2,200 miles south-west of Los Angeles, California; and on the island of Puerto Rico in the Caribbean Sea. During 1969 there were 557 all-breed championship dog shows in the United States, and in addition, there were 546 separate specialty shows or championship events for single breeds. Some specialty clubs band together for a combined show, such as an all-setter or all-terrier show.

Many of the all-breed shows also offer classes for obedience competition. In the United States in 1969, there were 178 separate licensed trials. A licensed trial is one at which obedience titles can be won.

California is the leader in the size of its dog shows. An unofficial tally of 1970 shows gives California 11 of the nation's 20 largest shows. The Kennel Club of Beverly Hills has been a leader for several years, and has a winter and a summer show, both rating among the top twenty, as do the two shows of the Silver Bay Kennel Club of San Diego.

The winter shows in most areas of the United States must be held indoors. The International Kennel Club show at Chicago, Illinois, is the nation's largest indoor show, and also the largest indoor benched show.

The 20 leading shows for 1970 are given below. The figures represent the actual dogs in competition, and therefore do not count double entries or absentees.

1. Santa Barbara, Cal. (3278). 2. Chicago, Ill. (3102). 3. Trenton, N. J. (3083). 4. Detroit, Mich. (2885). 5. Philadelphia, Pa. (2879). 6. Harrisburg, Pa. (2601). 7. Ventura, Cal. (2585). 8. Beverly Hills, Cal. (June – 2530). 9. Beverly Hills, Cal. (Jan. – 2484). 10. Santa Clara, Cal. (2421). 11. Santa Ana Valley, Cal. (2369). 12. San Diego, Cal. (1st – 2227). 13. San Gabriel Valley, Cal. (2226). 14. Kern County, Cal. (2225). 15. Sun Maid (Fresno), Cal. (2212). 16. Westminster (New York City), N.Y. (2121). 17. Old Dominion, Va. (2106). 18. San Diego, Cal. (2nd – 2095). 19. Westchester, N.Y. (2044). 20. Chagrin Valley, Ohio (1968).

Because of the great number of shows, and the great distances to be travelled, many American shows are set up in circuits. Thus, there are winter circuits lasting one or two weeks in Florida and in Texas, and summer circuits in the North. Three shows may be held in three days in some areas. Other circuits may have shows every other day, with shows on Saturday and Sunday.

There are approximately as many women who show dogs as men. Many husband and wife teams work as PROFESSIONAL HANDLERS at shows. In other cases, the woman may be the professional handler who takes a string of ten to fifteen dogs to shows while her husband stays at home and runs the grooming and boarding business, and trains other dogs for future events.

The increasingly high cost of operating shows and the need for ever more space have caused most clubs to abandon the benched show. Attendance at shows has also decreased because of the increasing competition given by other sports. The remaining major winter benched shows are Kansas City, Boston, Cleveland, and San Francisco. Both the Westminster Show in New York and the Golden Gate in San Francisco have had to limit entries because of lack of space for benching. See WESTMINSTER DOG SHOW.

Of the specialty shows having more than 200 dogs competing, German Shepherds led with 20 in 1970. Poodles and Dachshunds had three each, Great Danes two, and Collies and St. Bernards, one each.

American dog shows normally begin judging at 9 a.m., and most shows are over by 7 p.m. The great winter shows in the North – Westminster, Boston, Chicago, Detroit, Kansas City, and San Francisco – have evening hours, with group judging in the evening.

Some of the larger shows, for space reasons, have had to divide their schedules into two sections. Three of the six group divisions will compete on one day, and the other three on the second. In such cases, the variety groups for the first three divisions will be judged on the first day, and only the three winners will be held over for the final judging on the second night.

Shyness Shyness can be hereditary, or the result of trauma, or severe shock. A third form is sometimes called 'kennel shyness'. Hereditary shyness is permanent and incurable. It is sometimes possible to cure, or at least to reduce, traumatic fear. Kennel shyness usually gives way to confidence, given time.

When a puppy is born in a kennel, and lives there for three or four months it conditions itself to the kennel world. If it is then placed in a private home, it may be filled with fear. The world to which it had adapted itself has disappeared, and the puppy has by now passed its most adaptive period – from six to twelve weeks. It will now adjust very slowly. During this period it will need sympathetic understanding and great patience from its owner. Many experts consider the commonest cause of shyness to be the owner's failure to handle the puppies before they are a week old. The very young animal is extremely sensitive to external stimuli and human contact in early life will often prevent fear of human beings. All forms of shyness are more common in dogs which have no human contact until they are three weeks old.

The symptoms of hereditary shyness are many. A normal litter of six-week-old puppies will scramble on the kennel fence trying to reach people on the other side, and will bark excitedly. Perhaps one puppy will sit by itself, or will go into the kennel room or nest. If the other puppies are let out, they will climb all over the visitor. The shy puppy may come out, but then will return to the safety of the pen.

A puppy in a litter of hunting dogs may refuse to range out to hunt like normal puppies. Puppies taken for walks at night may not leave their master's feet. The degree of shyness may tend to get worse as the dog grows older.

Shyness occurs in both mongrels and purebreds. It is not, therefore, a problem caused by inbreeding, or by breeding show dogs.

Many dogs are noise-, storm-, or gun-shy. In these cases, trauma may be involved. Although the storm-shy dog may not be gun-shy, trauma certainly does cause some dogs to be gun-shy, as experiences with dogs in war combat have shown.

An extreme form of shyness is called terror or fear biting. The fear biter may attack when its owner attempts to give it deserved punishment. The dog may bite savagely when frightened. It is quite usual to hear such stories as this: 'He was sleeping on my lap while I read. When I turned the page, he suddenly woke up and bit me. Afterwards he seemed sorry for what he had done'. Or: 'He was sleeping on the floor when my four-year-old walked by. He just woke up and attacked the child. Then he seemed ashamed of himself'. A veterinarian may advise that the fear biter be put to sleep.

Dogs showing signs of shyness should not be used for breeding.

Siberian Husky The origin of the name 'husky' is as puzzling as that of their Eskimo owners. Most authorities have tended towards the theory that the word derives from *Chukchi*, or *Chuchi*, the Eskimos of the Kolyma River in Siberia. A second theory is that the name derives from a *Tuski* or *Tchutski*, tribe. In 1853, Lieut. William Hulme Hooper of the English Royal Navy, published his book, *Ten Months Among The Tents of the Tuski*. The Tuski tribes had herds of tame reindeer. Some lived inland; some along the sea. Hooper's description of the dogs of the Tuskies, seems to fit the Siberian Husky.

'"The Tuski" travelling sledge is constructed principally for speed. The dogs vary from two to ten. As many as eight all run abreast, the single traces of their harness radiating from the main thong. The dogs are generally small, long-haired, and wiry, with pointed ears and bushy tails: they have many points resembling those of the wolf and the fox, the bark especially being a very melancholy whine.

'Reins there are none; the animals are to be guided almost entirely by the whip, particularly with strangers, their masters alone having the power of voice.'

Whatever the origin of the name 'Husky', the term has spread around the Arctic and has come to mean any sled dog. The Siberian variety is the only dog officially registered as a Husky.

Sled dog racing became popular in Alaska shortly before 1900. Racing drivers began to hear tales of fabulous racing dogs in Siberia, and Leonhard Seppala is credited with bringing in the first team of Siberians. Two teams appeared in races in 1909 and 1910, and thereafter, large numbers were brought in. At first, they were used chiefly for racing, but the American Eskimos themselves began to replace their larger, and slower, dogs with Siberian Huskies.

Mr. and Mrs. Milton Seeley of Wonalancet, New Hampshire were among the first to bring the dogs into the United States, and Mrs. Nicholas Demidoff of Fitzwilliam, New Hampshire, is another pioneer breeder. Mrs. Seeley and Mrs. Demidoff are still active as breeders and judges.

The breed has grown rapidly in popularity. Siberians adapt well to temperate zone climates. They are gentle with both adults and children, and are generally not quarrelsome with other dogs.

Siberian Husky.
Right Ch. Monadnock's Akela.
Bottom right Ch. Arctic's Storm Frost.

Essentials of the breed: The head: the distance from occiput to stop equals that from stop to muzzle. The skull is slightly rounded on top, and is medium in width. The ears are small and pricked, but moderately rounded at the tips. The eyes are usually brown, though one may be blue and the other brown which is undesirable. Rarely, both eyes are blue. The eyes are set slightly obliquely.

The body is moderately compact. The ribs are well sprung, the top line level, with neither roach nor sway. The front legs are parallel, viewed from either the front or side, with the pasterns only slightly sloping. The hindquarters are heavily muscled, with well bent stifle joints. The feet are oval, compact, strongly knuckled, well furred between the toes, and with thick pads.

The tail: well furred and bushy. In motion, the tail is carried sickle fashion over the back. It should not lie 'snap back' to the spine, nor to either side. When standing or working, the tail drops, or trails.

The undercoat is particularly dense. The thick outer coat is rather soft than hard and is of medium length. All colours and white are allowed, but various shades of wolf and silver grey, tan and black, with white points are common. Head markings are varied and striking in pattern.

Height is 21 to 23½ inches at the shoulder for dogs and 20 to 22 inches for bitches. Dogs over 23½ inches and bitches over 22 inches are disqualified. Weight: from 45 to 60 lb. for dogs, and from 35 to 50 lb. for bitches. The Canadian standard differs from the American in that there is no height disqualification, but in Canada dogs over 60 lb. and bitches over 50 lb. are disqualified.
See colour plate p. 302.

Sickle Hocks Hocks well let down, and with strong angulation of both stifles and hocks. Sickle hocks are essential to great speed, as in BORZOIS, WHIPPETS, and GREYHOUNDS.

Sickle Tail A tail carried in a semi-circle.

Sickness, Car Car sickness is caused by the inability to correct balance to the motion of the car. Most puppies quickly adjust, but some dogs are unable to do so.

There is some evidence that, in both people and dogs, car sickness may be caused by a build-up of static electricity as the car moves. In such cases, car sickness can sometimes be prevented by fastening a light chain to the automobile's rear axle, and allowing the chain to drag on the highway.

Puppies and older dogs which have a tendency to car sickness should not be fed for eight to twelve hours before the ride begins. Hungry puppies can be taught to look forward to such rides if the first rides are short, and the puppies are fed upon returning home.

Tranquillizers often fail to help dogs which get car sick, and a possible reason is that the tranquillizer is given just before the ride, instead of some hours in advance. Car and air sickness drugs can be given to dogs under veterinary supervision.

Side Winding see Crabbing.

Sight Sight for the dog begins when the eyes open. This may occur as early as one week after birth, or as late as sixteen to seventeen days. It is only rarely that a puppy's eyes are fully open at seven days, but most puppies have sight at two weeks. All the puppies in a large litter will not open their eyes at the same time.

What puppies see at first is not known as the sight centre of the brain is not fully developed at this stage. Naturalists, biologists, and human eye specialists, have learned a great deal about the eye of the dog, but not very much about what dogs see.

Sight is almost always connected with other sensations. The dog is said to have a 'nose brain', and smell may be a simpler identification and information-passing medium than are the complexities of sight. Yet the dog probably uses hearing, smell, and sight in combination to form a 'brain picture'. Thus, while the shotgun conveys a picture of death to some, it is a pleasing object to the hunting dog, which combines sight, smell, and remembered experiences and becomes excited. Without scent clues, form discrimination in dogs is impaired. A dog has no one to tell it that the image in the mirror is itself. Yet dogs sometimes seem to recognize members of their own species on television. Here movement aids the dog.

Movement is an important element in the sight of dogs. The dog is a predator. Its eyes, therefore, are adapted for movement, both its own and that of the hunted. If a rabbit sits quietly in a landscape, the dog will probably not see it; the rabbit may appear to be merely a mound of earth. If it moves, the dog's eye registers the movement instantly.

In experiments in form perception dogs seem to be baffled when neither themselves nor the object is moving. Form perception improves when the object moves, and is still better when the dog is also moving. In this connection it should be remembered that a basic instinct in all animals, including man, is to 'freeze' in order to avoid detection. According to our human eyes, many animals appear to wear camouflage, so that they blend into a landscape, but we cannot be sure that dogs' eyes record, or fail to record, this same camouflage.

Studies of the lens in the dog's eye indicate that the point of focus is at a point just in front of the retina. This would indicate that the picture conveyed to the brain will be out of focus, and therefore less sharp than would be the case in human vision. By comparison to man a dog has little capacity to focus its eyes. It may not need so sharp a picture; movement is a more important factor.

Like other mammals the dog's retina contains rods and cones. The rods are concerned with night vision, and nocturnal eyes (those of the nocturnal animals) are rod-rich. The canine eye is richer in rods than is the human eye, and this gives the dog better vision than man. The rods are concentrated on the outer parts of the retina and the cones in the centre. As darkness comes, the pupil expands to allow more light to enter. A substance known as rhodopsin, or visual purple, then begins to function to aid sight. This is made up of vitamin A and protein, and thus vitamin A deficiency, in people as well as dogs, can cause a condition known as night blindness.

The rods are not entirely useless in daytime vision. Since they are on the outer edges of the retina, they help in peripheral vision. The rods are aided in the dog, and in many other animals, by a 'reflection blanket' called the *tapetum lucidum*. Light rays which strike this blanket are reflected onto the rods and, in this way, the dog is able to use more of the available light during evening or night hours.

The cones of the retina are concerned with daylight vision. Dogs have cones, but not in the numbers possessed by man, and most researchers tend to believe that the dog is unable to see colour. A weak, hue-discriminating capacity may be present, but it may be so very weak that, within the limits of normal individual variation, it could be entirely lacking in certain individuals. Without colour discrimination, equal brightness for dogs cannot be the same as equal brightness for man.

Eye placement is important in canine sight. The GREYHOUND, a coursing dog, has frontally placed eyes. The range of one eye may be nearly 200 degrees, with a considerable overlap with the other eye at the front. Monocular vision in man is about 150 degrees and it is about the same for terriers, for the terrier's eyes are set deeply as a protection during fights. This protection is at the expense of vision. The COLLIE has eyes which, because of lack of stop, have poorer frontal vision; the range of each eye is lateral, and is useful to the shepherd dog. PEKINGESE and PUGS have large, protruding eyes. This should produce a greater range of vision, but it is at the expense of protection and health. Such an eye is easily dislodged and the dog has difficulty keeping the eyeball properly moist.

Dogs' eyes 'shine' at night. That is, when a flashlight, or car headlights strike the dog's eyes, this light is reflected back, and the colour of the 'shine' may range from orange to yellow, light green, blue or brown. In some cases the colour tends to match that of the dog's coat. In others, it may be one colour on one night and a different colour on another.

Silky Terrier (Sydney Terrier, Australian Silky Terrier). This breed bears the label 'Made in Australia', but its ancestry is British. Originally, the dog was called the Sydney Silky, since it was at Sydney, New South Wales, that the breed was first developed. Dog fanciers felt the need for a small terrier which might be suited to life in a small house, apartment or cottage.

Australia had already developed the AUSTRALIAN TERRIER, in the early 1900s and had also imported YORKSHIRE TERRIERS from England. The Silky is basically a cross between the Australian and the Yorkshire Terriers. There is a possibility that at some period NORWICH TERRIER blood was introduced. It is thought that the silken coat of the Silky comes from the influence of the early SKYE TERRIERS in the background of the Australian Terrier.

The breed was first exhibited as the Sydney Silky in Australia in 1907, during the period when so many of the modern dog breeds of the world were perfected. However, at that time, the Silky had not achieved its present standard. For example, the ears could be prick or folded. The Royal Agricultural Society Kennel Club at Sydney recognized the breed about thirty years ago, and was followed by the Australian Kennel Control Council. The first of the Sydney Silkies reached England about 1928. They were first exhibited in 1930, but they have failed to make much progress. The breed came to the attention of American military and civilian personnel in Australia during the Second World War. At about this time, the name was changed to Australian Silky Terrier, and it is now known to most of the world simply as the Silky Terrier.

Silkies began to appear in the United States and Canada in large numbers in the early 1950s, and in 1959, the American Kennel Club gave official recognition to the breed. Canada followed in the mid-1960s. Since then, the breed has grown remarkably in popularity. In the eleven years since its U.S. recognition, it has moved steadily upward until it is now one of the forty-five most popular breeds.

Essentials of the breed: The head is wedge-shaped, with the skull slightly longer than the muzzle. The skull is flat, the stop shallow, and the ears are erect and set high, with no tendency to flare to the sides. The eyes are small and dark, the nose is black, and the teeth form a scissors bite.

The body is about one-fifth longer than the shoulder height. The hind legs are moderately angulated at the stifle and hock joints. The top line is straight, though there may be a barely perceptible rounding off at the loins. The brisket reaches the elbows. The feet are cat-like, compact, and have dark-coloured nails. White or flesh-coloured nails are a fault. The feet turn neither in nor out. Dewclaws are removed. The tail is set high, docked, carried erect, and is devoid of plume.

The coat is flat, and is a fine, glossy silk. Mature dogs have a coat of 5 to 6 inches long from behind the ears

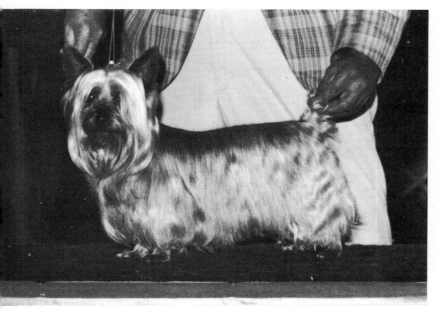
Below Silky Terrier. Ch. Koonoona Mr. Pip.

to the set-on of the tail. On the head it is sufficiently profuse to form a topknot, but long facial and ear hair is not desired. The legs from knee and hock joints are free of long hair. The hair is parted along the spine from the head to the set-on of the tail.

The colour is blue and tan, but the blue may be silver blue, pigeon, or slate blue. The tan should be deep and rich, and not 'washed out'.

The Silky Terrier weighs from 8 to 10 lb. and is 9 to 10 inches at the shoulder. A height of under 8 inches is considered a serious fault, since it accentuates toyishness at the expense of true terrier characteristics.
See colour plate p. 379.

Single Tracking Said of dogs which move their feet close together to achieve perfect balance, particularly at a fast trot. The feet then move forward almost in line.

Sinhala Hound see Rare Breeds.

Skirting Said of a trailing dog which runs beside its bracemate, not trying to pick up scent until the turn.

Skye Terrier Four hundred years ago, Dr. Johanne Caius, master of Gonville and Caius College, Cambridge University, and court physician to Edward VI, Queen Mary and Queen Elizabeth I, wrote as follows: 'A Cur brought out the barbarous borders fro' the uttermost countryes northward which by reason of the length of heare makes showe neither of face nor body'. The dog could have been a Skye Terrier.

If not flattering, this at least establishes the Skye as an old breed. A legend which has almost come to be accepted as fact, is that when the Spanish Armada was wrecked off the Islands of Skye some long-coated dogs swam ashore and established the breed we now call the Skye Terrier.

The weakness in this story is that the profuse abundance of coat now taken for granted is a comparatively modern phenomenon. Certainly it was not present in *Rona*, the best known of all Skyes. Rona's immortality is assured because she was owned by Queen Victoria who kept Skyes from 1842 onwards and who elevated them from obscurity to comparative popularity.

In Scotland in general, and the Islands in particular, the dog's job had been the destruction of vermin: foxes, badgers, martens, even wild cats. This meant burrowing and digging, often fighting in confined spaces. It also demanded powerful jaws which can still be found today beneath the abundant whiskers.

It might be unwise to sieze and examine the jaw of a Skye Terrier. They are not dogs to tamper with. While gentle and good natured with their owners and friends, they are frequently intolerant of strangers, and when a Skye disapproves he does not merely snap!

This tendency, while regrettable, should not earn them the reputation of being treacherous. They are the precise opposite. They are completely predictable. Perhaps this occasional intractability has affected their popularity. Perhaps also the beautiful flowing coat, while providing glory, presents grooming problems. Certainly this century has seen this distinctive terrier eclipsed by one after another of the newer breeds.

Serious Skye breeders are unconcerned. They make no changes in type to meet modern demands. Now, as ever, they stand by the motto of the original Skye Terrier Club of Scotland, 'Wha dour meddle wi me?'

No article on the Skye would be complete without mention of *Greyfriars Bobby*, one of the few dogs in Britain to merit a memorial. In 1858 Bobby belonged

Left Skye Terrier. Ch. Evening Star who has been 25 times Best in Show.

to an old Edinburgh shepherd, who died almost friendless. But Bobby remembered and remained loyal. He followed his master's body to the graveyard and slept on that grave for nearly ten years. Well-meaning people offered him comfort, took him home and fed him. Always he escaped and returned to his master's resting place. Finally the Lord Provost of Edinburgh gave him a permanent licence and an inscribed collar. Baroness Burdett-Coutts later erected a statue to him above a drinking fountain opposite the main gates of the cemetery where Bobby had kept vigil. See MONUMENTS AND MEMORIALS.

Essentials of the breed: Head: long with powerful jaws. Eyes: hazel, of medium size. Ears: when prick, feathered, not large, but erect; when drop, larger, lying flat and close. Teeth: level. Neck: long and slightly crested. Shoulders: broad. Chest: deep. Legs: short and muscular. Body: long and low, with level back. Feet: large and pointing forward. Tail: when hanging, upper part pendulous, lower half curved; when raised up, a continuation of topline. Undercoat short, soft and woolly. Overcoat long, hard and straight. Tail gracefully feathered. Any colour permissible, all with black nose and ears. Height: dogs 10 inches, length approximately 20 inches, but from tip of nose to tip of tail, up to 40 inches; bitches slightly smaller. Weight: 25 lb.
See colour plate p. 376.

Slab-Sided Description of dogs without adequate spring of ribs. See FLAT-SIDED.

Sled and Snow Dogs No one knows when the Eskimos reached the Arctic, nor even from where they came. But one thing is certain: they had to bring their sled dogs with them. They could not have survived alone.

Today we know four pure breeds of Arctic sled dogs – the SIBERIAN HUSKY, ALASKAN MALAMUTE, SAMOYED, and ESKIMO. But the Arctic is a vast area, and many isolated areas developed their own strains of Arctic dogs. Examples are the MacKenzie River Malamute, and the Greenland Husky. More recently, the Alaskan Husky, a dog intermediate between the Malamute and the Siberian, was developed for Alaskan sled racing.

When other men invaded the Arctic, they brought their own dogs, too. These interbred with the Arctic dogs, but so dominant is the type of the latter that all the characteristics of the dogs from the South quickly disappeared.

In the region below the Arctic Circle, and particularly in the forested areas, other breeds were tried as sled dogs. Thus, Edgerton R. Young, a famous missionary-author, used a ST. BERNARD as a lead dog.

Lieut. William H. Hooper of the English Royal Navy, reported in 1853 on some of the non-Arctic dogs. Lieut. Hooper spent ten months living with the Tuski Eskimos, in the Siberian Arctic.

'A favoured few of the Tuski were possessors of a tall and strong mongrel breed – probably by communication with the Russians – with short hair and something of a Pointer look. One train of dogs we saw resembled the staghound, and were capable of immense speed and endurance of fatigue but the native dogs will outlive cold and hunger, which the foreign breed would easily succumb to, the feet of the strangers being especially tender.'

In their book, *Discovery and Adventure in the Polar Seas*, written in 1832, Leslie, Jameson, and Murray, reported on the 'Esquimaux' dogs. 'Three dogs could draw a sledge weighing 100 lb. at a rate of a mile in six minutes, and one leader has drawn 196 lb. the same distance in eight minutes. A full team, however, comprises eight or ten dogs; though seven have drawn a full sledge at a rate of a mile in four minutes and a half; while nine, employed in conveying stores from the Hecla to the Fury, drew 1,611 lb. in nine minutes.

'Capt. Lyon reports most favourably of the team which he himself formed, who used to draw him from ship to ship, a mile distant, in the deepest darkness and amid clouds of snow, with the most perfect precision, when he himself could not have found his own way for a hundred steps.'

Capt. Sir Francis McClintock, writing in 1858 on the voyage of the *Fox*, said the following about the dogs when the temperature was −47°F. 'It is wonderful how the dogs stand it, and without apparent inconvenience unless their fur happen to be thin. They lie upon the snow under the lee of the ship, with no other protection from the weather.'

Dogs in other parts of the Arctic appear to have been less fierce than those of Greenland. Explorers and Eskimos reported examples of what would appear to be inborn 'conscience'. When an Arctic traveller is without food, it becomes necessary to kill and eat one of the dogs. Some dogs would seize and devour the dead dog immediately, so that the men had to fight to gain their own meal. Other dogs would not touch the dead dog until it had been frozen for 12 to 24 hours. But still other dogs would starve before becoming cannibals.

Snow dogs have a different purpose from that of sled dogs. St. Bernards have been used to guide travellers over difficult routes in the snow, and were also trained to smell persons buried in snow. Other breeds, including the GERMAN SHEPHERD, have been so trained.

See MOUNTAIN RESCUE; SLED DOG RACING.

Sled Dog Racing Sled dog racing is a great winter sport of the Northlands, but it has become so popular among Canadians and Americans that races are now held wherever there is sufficient snow. Racing takes place in all the states along the Canadian border, and in the mountains of Colorado, Utah, and even Southern California.

It is a family sport. Youngsters of no more than eight may start with one dog, graduate to two, and at sixteen be driving six to eight dogs. Women drive teams of six or more dogs. And men drive seven to fifteen. At one race meet, father, mother, and two teenage children, a boy and a girl, each drove teams.

The best-known sled dog race of the North was not against other teams but against death. This was the great race to carry diphtheria antitoxin from Nenana to Nome. Nome had a population of less than 1,450 people, and one doctor, Dr. Curtis Welch. Diphtheria struck, and Dr Welch had only a small quantity of five-year-old serum.

There was a railroad from Anchorage to Nenana, and air transport, but in January of 1925, airplanes could not fly in the Alaskan winter. By most overland routes, it was at least 680 miles from Nenana to Nome.

Anchorage sent antitoxin by train to Nenana. Twenty relays of dog teams and drivers took over. They travelled 675 miles in 127·5 hours.

In modern sled dog racing, some surprising breeds compete. Teams of IRISH SETTERS and COLLIES have raced. Border Collies have been used. Speed is the prime quality, and the dogs do not have to stand hard work during the long Arctic winters. The world championship is held annually at Anchorage, Alaska, and consists of three 25-mile dashes on consecutive days. A driver can start with any number of dogs, but he must finish each day with the same number. Thus, if a dog

Below Sled dog racing is very popular in Canada and the northern United States. This team is competing in Quebec.

bove Snipy.

goes lame, he must be brought in on the sledge, or even carried by the driver.

Dr. Roland Lombard, a veterinarian from Wayland, Mass., won for the sixth time in 1970. He used thirteen dogs the first day, then twelve, and on the last day, ten. His total elapsed time for the 75 miles was 324 minutes, 7 seconds. George Attla of Huslia, Alaska, a three-time winner, lost by 31 seconds, having lost in the previous year by only nine seconds.

Most of the dogs used in Alaskan racing are Alaskan Huskies. But other dogs have made records. In 1948, a team of SIBERIAN HUSKIES raced a measured ten-mile course in 35 minutes, and another team raced the same course three times in less than two hours. SAMO-YEDS seldom race in the far North, but because of their great beauty, they are used as dress teams. Racing Samoyed teams are used in the United States and lower Canada.

Snowbird, a MALAMUTE, is a legend in the Arctic. In 1910, he was lead dog in a team which hauled half a ton of freight 1,100 miles over a mountain range. Two weeks after completing that amazing trip, Snowbird led Iron Man Johnson's team to victory in the first All-Alaska Sweepstakes. The distance of the race was 408 miles, and the time, 72 hours and a few minutes.

Slipped Patella see Patella Luxation.

Sloping Shoulder One with the blade or scapula set obliquely.

Slughi see Greyhound, Eastern.

Smell, Sense of The dog depends upon its nose. Its sense of smell is very highly developed. The odours which interest the dog are basically those of urine, sweat, blood, decaying meat, oestral and anal gland secretions.

The urine of a female dog contains a repellent which keeps male dogs away. It is secreted by the luteal glands on the ovaries. As the bitch comes into oestrus, the luteal glands stop manufacturing the repellent. It is replaced by odours designed to stimulate male dogs. It is commonly supposed that the males can detect these oestral odours for miles, but it is in fact more likely that male dogs will be alerted by odour clues left by the female on her tracks (see OESTRUM).

A dog's nose is able to discover information both local and transitory. The wandering dog urinates on posts, tree stumps, and mounds of earth. Another dog reaches the spot, and by using its sense of smell, knows whether the first dog was male or female, healthy or sick, hungry or full fed, in oestrus or not. By the tracks, which have left sweat deposits, disturbed earth, and particles of soil brought from some other place, it will know where the first dog came from. It will be able to follow to find out where the dog has gone.

Dogs, like wolves, mark out home territories by urine splashes. A feral dog may make a kill, eat part of it, and then bury the remaining carcass. It will mark the spot with urine, and other dogs will recognize its ownership. An occasional kennel dog, having eaten a part or even all of its food, will then urinate upon the

food pan. It is obeying an ancient property marking instinct. Most dogs can detect one part of urine in 60,000,000 parts of water.

Owners, who are trying to house break puppies, often try to cover a urine stain with an odour. The new odour masks the urine odour for a short time. But the dog's nose screens out the masking odour, recognizes the one in which it is interested, and often urinates again on the same area. A given odour may be overpowering to both man and dog. But if subject to it long enough, the sensory apparatus of both becomes tired and no longer conveys the odour to the brain. Thereafter, dog or man will detect much weaker odours which had been masked by the stronger one.

New born puppies are blind and deaf. They are also unable to smell. Both the olfactory nerve and the smell centre of the brain are not fully developed, but the sense of smell develops more rapidly than the other two, for sight and hearing are less important to the dog.

Smooth Coat Short, close-lying hair.

Snake Bite Poisonous snakes are far less common than the non-poisonous and beneficial species. Poison-ous snakes are far more deadly to dogs than to human beings. As a rule, the larger the snake, the larger the amount of venom it will inject into a wound. But the larger the animal bitten, the less likely that it will die.

The snake-bitten dog should be kept quiet, and veterinary aid sought immediately. The bite should be covered with damp Epsom salts to delay the absorption of the venom.

In most countries, anti-venins are prepared for the venom of the snakes living there. People who take their dogs into areas where poisonous snakes are known to exist sometimes carry anti-venin kits, but unfortunately, anti-venin prepared for use against one snake's poison will seldom aid against that of another.

Snipy A pointed, weak muzzle.

Snow Dogs see Mountain Rescue; Sled and Snow Dogs.

Soap The washing and grooming of dogs is necessary in all breeds but needs vary from dog to dog. A dog can never be groomed too much, but too frequent washing can be injurious and should be avoided as it destroys the natural oils in the coat. It will also tend to soften a coat that should be hard.

A strong carbolic soap should never be used unless under the direction of a veterinarian. There are many special shampoos and soaps on the market today but for general purposes a green soft soap is both safe and effective. Any soap or shampoo used must always be very carefully rinsed out of the coat before the coat is dried.

See BATHING A DOG.

Soft-Coated Wheaten Terrier The Soft-Coated Wheaten Terrier is a native of Ireland where it has been an all-purpose dog. It has been used for cattle driving,

home and stable guarding, and as a rodent destroyer. The breed has been known for several centuries, but it is now relatively rare, even in Ireland.

The breed may be descended from the long extinct English Black and Tan Terrier. It is a relative of, and some say the ancestor of, both the IRISH and KERRY BLUE TERRIERS.

The breed was officially recognized by the Irish Kennel Club in 1937, and by the Kennel Club (England) in 1943. *Charlie Tim* became the first of his breed to win a championship. The breed is not recognized by the American and Canadian Kennel Clubs, though it may compete in the Miscellaneous Class in shows in those countries.

Essentials of the breed: Dogs are 18 to 19 inches at the shoulder and weigh 35 to 45 lb.; bitches are slightly smaller. The colour is a whole wheaten, and the coat is abundant, moderately long, and slightly wavy. The texture is soft and silky. Skull and muzzle are the same length, forming a moderately long head. The topskull is flat, and the stop well defined. The bite is either scissors or level. The body is compact and short. The tail is docked and is carried above horizontal. Trimming or dressing of any kind for the show ring is discouraged, and the dog should be presented naturally. See colour plate p. 374.

Soft Mouth A dog which retrieves without harming the prey by biting or tearing at it.

Soundness There is no exact definition of soundness; however a dog may be regarded as sound when it exhibits no visible defect likely to interfere with its usefulness. But soundness as viewed by a veterinarian may not correspond entirely with the soundness envisaged by a judge officiating at a dog show. The latter might regard a dog as unsound because it exhibited peculiarity of gait which would not prevent it performing a hard day's work and need not do so for some years to come.

A dog need not be any less active because it is technically unsound, nor need it be particularly active and useful simply because it is free from visible defect. Dogs kept as pets may be markedly unsound and yet such unsoundness may have little effect upon their behaviour or usefulness within their accustomed environment.

From a veterinary standpoint unsoundness may include eye defects, lameness, disease and any deformity inherited or acquired. For breeders and exhibitors

above Soft-Coated Wheaten Terrier. Binheath Mickle Miss (see 374) plays with Binheath Winston of Finchwood and two puppies.

unsoundness might include absence of some of the premolar teeth, detectable only by careful examination; too many or too few incisors; or jaws slightly undershot or overshot when the standard requires a level bite. Other reasons for penalizing otherwise fit show dogs might include slight bone curvature in the forelimbs; hocks which are not parallel; pasterns which are not sufficiently upright; feet which are splayed when the toes should be bunched and vice versa.

Additionally there could be too upright a scapula; too long or too short a back; obvious signs of lameness, or even a tendency to run the toes outwards or inwards and, of course, evidence of disease, hereditary or acquired. A judge might consider a dog unsound because it appeared straight in hock and stifle while a veterinarian might fault one which in accordance with its breed standard showed an extra long shin bone and what some would regard as excessive hind angulation.

Some judges regard a faulty temperament as an unsoundness while others pay greater attention to body than brain. One great difficulty is the fact that few judges are qualified to detect such HEREDITARY ABNORMALITIES as progressive retinal atrophy and HIP DYSPLASIA, although quite capable of detecting lameness, faulty movement or total blindness.

Spaniel see American Cocker Spaniel; Brittany Spaniel; Cavalier King Charles Spaniel; Clumber Spaniel; Cocker Spaniel; English Springer Spaniel; Field Spaniel; Irish Water Spaniel; King Charles Spaniel; Sussex Spaniel; Tibetan Spaniel; Welsh Springer Spaniel.

Spanish Kennel Club

Spaying This is the sterilization of the female dog by the surgical removal of her ovaries. Sterilization by other means, such as radiation, has been tried, but is not commonly used. Veterinarians do not agree about the proper time for spaying the bitch. Many maintain that the operation becomes more difficult as the dog grows older. They therefore argue for spaying as young as three to four months. Others believe that the bitch should be allowed to have her first heat period, because they believe that if a puppy is spayed at too young an age, it may later suffer from bladder incontinence, although evidence for this is not at all conclusive. The hormonal cycle which brings on oestrus also is important in the maturing of the dog, not only physically but mentally. When spayed very young, many dogs maintain puppyish ways all their lives. But, if the bitch is spayed two to three months after her first heat period, she is then mature physically and mentally. It is widely thought that a bitch which is not to be used for breeding, or whose breeding days are past, should be spayed.

Post-operative care of the spayed bitch has changed radically in recent years, just as it has in human surgery. Formerly, the spayed bitch might be kept at the veterinary hospital for a week. The time was then reduced to three days. Today, some surgeons send the dogs home the same day, and others keep them only overnight. The dog is happier and tends to recover more rapidly in the home environment. Moreover, it does not lose strength at home, as it would if kept in a hospital cage. Shorter hospitalization makes the operation cheaper for the owner of the dog.

The spayed bitch requires less food. It is not therefore the operation which makes bitches fat, as is commonly thought, but overfeeding.

Special Senses see Senses, Special.

Specialty Club (Breed Club) A club concerned with the improvement and promotion of a single breed, usually by means of club bulletins, newsletters, the organization of one or more Breed or Specialty shows, and where applicable, the running of obedience, working, tracking or field trials etc.

Spectacles Shadings or dark markings about the eyes.

Speed Of Dogs The GREYHOUND is the world's fastest dog for all distances up to half a mile. Louis Pegram has timed both Greyhounds and WHIPPETS, and he has set up exhibition races for AFGHANS and SALUKIS, as well as Whippets. Pegram rates the Greyhound as the fastest, and believes that the Saluki is slightly faster than the Afghan. His studies indicate, however, that the Whippet passes the Greyhound at distances greater than half a mile.

The *Guinness Book of World Records* credits the Saluki with reaching a speed of 43 miles per hour, although no authority is given for this statement. One Saluki is reported as having been paced by an automobile at 55 miles per hour, but automobile speedometers are notoriously inaccurate. Modern Greyhounds are timed by electronic clocks, so that accuracy is as close to perfection as is possible.

The great English Greyhound, *Trev's Perfection* won the English Greyhound Derby over a measured 1,575 feet course in 28.95 seconds. His average speed was 54.6 feet per second, or 37.1 miles per hour. The American Greyhounds, *Lucky Pilot* and *Feldcrest*, have run at a rate of 37 miles per hour. *Chief Pilot*, in Australia, raced 650 yards at a rate of 38 miles per hour, and during the first 440 yards, maintained a speed of 38.5 miles per hour.

In South Africa it has been claimed that BORZOIS are superior to Greyhounds in coursing jackals on the veldt. But coursing is not racing; it is not a test of speed alone, but includes rough country running,

quick turns, dodging trees, bushes, and other obstacles.

Until dozens of tests on dozens of dogs of these varying breeds have been made under equal training and running conditions, the Greyhound must be considered the fastest of all the dogs.

Spitz Breeds One of the dominant families of dogs is the Spitz, or Wolf Spitz, group. The dogs in this group are believed to have descended from the 'Peat Dog', or 'Swiss Lake Dwellers' Dog' of 6,000 years ago. Dogs of this type have been found preserved in peat bogs. These dogs are sometimes called the Northern Dogs.

Almost all the dogs of the Spitz group have prominent skulls, small pricked ears, straight and rather harsh outer coats, dense undercoats, and wedge-shaped heads with rather blunt, powerful jaws. Many carry their tails over the back, and some have quite tightly curled tails. The best known breeds are treated separately. These include the SIBERIAN HUSKY, ALASKAN MALAMUTE, SAMOYED, ESKIMO, KEESHOND, NORWEGIAN ELKHOUND, ICELAND DOG, POMERANIAN, CHOW CHOW, SCHIPPERKE, and AKITA.

The great German Spitz, or Wolf Spitz, was known as early as 1700. It is said that white dogs were kept in Pomerania, and black dogs in Württemberg. The German Spitz Club was organized in 1899. The larger Spitz averaged 17 inches at the shoulder at that time, while the smaller one was only about 11 inches tall.

Many of the lesser-known Spitz-type dogs remained unrecognized by official kennel clubs until about the time of World War II. Thus, the Swedish Kennel Club and the F.C.I. (Federation Cynologique Internationale) did not admit the Swedish Herder or Vastgolaspets to registration and official breed status until 1943. The Lapland Spitz was recognized in 1944.

The Swedish Herder conforms generally to Spitz type. It is 12 to 15 inches tall, and weighs 20 to 30 lb. The Lapland Spitz is about the same size. It may have a docked tail or may be born with a short, stump tail. The colours are black, black and brown, or white. The Italian Spitz, or Volpino Italiano, is a small white dog, 11 inches at the shoulder, 9 lb. in weight, and with long hair.

The Japanese Spitz is a white dog, about half as large as the Samoyed, and quite similar in type. As with most of the dogs in this group, the differences are minor as compared to the similarities. The breed is one of the best known in Japan, and is seen everywhere. A great companion for children, it is also a formidable watch dog.

The Nippon Inu is commonly known in Japan as the Japanese Middle-Sized Dog. It ranges from 17 to $21\frac{1}{2}$ inches at the shoulder, and conforms generally to Akita type. The Shiba Inu is another Japanese variety, 14 to 16 inches tall. It may have a bobbed tail, but is otherwise a diminutive of the Akita.

The Norwegian Buhund received breed recognition in 1943. It is 17 inches at the shoulder. Colours are usually black, a dark red, or wheaten. A white blaze and a narrow collar are permitted; so are a white spot on the chest and white on the feet, but whole colours are preferred.

Spitz breeds.
The Laika, *top*, is a member of the great Spitz family of dogs and is very common in Russia. A dog named *Laika* was the first traveller in space. The Samoyed, *centre*, is a show dog, Ch. Sleigh Monarch of Kobe, and the Lapphund, *bottom*, is another Spitz breed which is beginning to make an appearance at shows.

Some authorities have listed the Siberian Husky, Alaskan Malamute, Samoyed, and Eskimo as 'Nordic dogs', or hunting dogs, but in fact they are primarily sled dogs. If they have any passion for hunting, they never get a chance to indulge in it, for the Eskimos keep them closely chained when not using them as sled dogs.

Other Spitz breeds include the Dureghund; the Norwegian Elkhound; the Grahund, or Swedish Grey Dog; the Jamthund; the KARELIAN BEAR DOG, Norwegian Lundehund, and the Tahltan Bear Dog. The Swedish Grey Dog is about 20 inches at the shoulder and is grey with black-tipped hair, the outer guard coat being long and harsh. The Jamthund is larger, 23 to 24 inches at the shoulder, and is light to dark grey in colour.

The Tahltan Bear Dog is an American Indian dog of the far North. It once received Canadian Kennel Club recognition. Few have survived in the climate of lower Canada, and the dogs have been difficult to feed. They are among the oddest of dogs. Their height is 12 to 15 inches at the shoulder. Their tails are extraordinarily thick, five to eight inches long, and appear thicker at the end than at the root. The outer coat is thick, harsh, and long. The colours are all black, or blue-grey with white markings. The dogs are said to howl rather than to bark. The Canadian Kennel Club no longer registers the breed.

The American Eskimo is a small white Spitz which appears to be almost identical to the Japanese Spitz. It is not recognized by the American Kennel Club, but is acknowledged by the United Kennel Club. Since 'Spitz' is considered a generic term, neither club would accept the breed for registration simply as a Spitz. The United Kennel Club finally agreed to recognize and register the breed as the American Eskimo.

Splashes Patches of colour on white, or vice versa.

Splayfoot A flat foot with spreading toes and paper pads.

Spleen This organ lies on the left side of the dog, attached to the stomach, within the abdominal cavity. It is an extremely vascular structure and helps to form white blood cells, to destroy damaged red blood cells, and also to act as a 'store' for blood that is not required under normal conditions.

Sporting Division This division is not to be confused with the presently designated Sporting *Group* of the American Kennel Club which is a group of bird or gundogs such as Pointers, retrievers, setters and spaniels.

The Sporting *Division*, a term used by the British and some other Kennel Clubs, is wider in scope, embracing the other breeds which have some sporting role, that is, the hound and terrier groups.

As explained under the heading NON-SPORTING DIVISION the Kennel Club of England listed 43 different breeds when it was first formed. As this number grew, a division became necessary for administrative purposes. A decision was made to split it in two. Instead of doing this alphabetically or by breed sizes, it was done on the traditional roles of the breeds.

Thus gundogs, hounds and terriers became the Sporting Division. The toys, working dogs and remainder, which for want of a better name might be referred to as 'companions', became the Non-Sporting Division.

Oddly, when it became necessary both in Britain and America to subdivide each of these two divisions into three groups, the American Kennel Club retained the original names for one group in each.

Spread A term used to describe BULLDOGS when the front legs are spread to form an arch with the body.

Springer Spaniel see English Springer Spaniel; Welsh Springer Spaniel.

Squirrel Tail One curving forward over the back.

Staffordshire Bull Terrier This breed is not to be confused with the STAFFORDSHIRE TERRIER, met frequently in America, developed probably from similar stock but on quite different lines, and having a completely different breed standard.

The Staffordshire Bull Terrier was bred to fight other dogs in the pit. Man often seems less noble than the animals he considers his inferiors. The excesses of the Roman arenas, the bear-baiting of medieval England, bull-baiting of later days, cock-fighting, and dog-fighting show man's streak of cruelty.

Perhaps, however, the essence of all these 'sports' is not that man liked cruelty, but that he admired and respected courage. This may help to explain why the Staffordshire has for over a century past held an honourable place in the hearts of men who live hard lives in the mines and collieries of the Black Country in industrial England.

Around 1800 two most popular 'sports' were bull-baiting, in which dogs attacked bulls, and dog-fighting, in which two dogs were matched to fight in a wooden-sided 'pit'. The dogs used to bait bulls were an earlier version of today's BULLDOGS. They had comparatively short legs, wide, deep chests, and short, massive jaws. The fighting dogs, on the other hand, were of any shape. They were judged exclusively on performance.

It became accepted that a fighting dog must combine the strength and tenacity of the Bulldog with the terrier's agility and quick wits; hence the 'fusion' of Bulldog and OLD ENGLISH TERRIER. But there was still a wide variation in type, each district insisting that it had the ideal combination. From one of these varieties there later emerged the present-day sophisticated BULL TERRIER. The majority, however, remained rugged and nondescript.

In 1835, bull-baiting was outlawed in England which increased interest in dog-fighting. The dogs used, normally weighing between 25 and 40 lb. were called 'Bull and Terrier Dogs', 'Half and Halfs,' 'Pit Dogs' or 'Pit Bull Terriers'.

Ultimately dog-fighting became illegal, although doubtless it was carried on surreptitiously for many years after, and it is possible that we owe the survival of the breed to these illegal matches.

One view is that not until the police became particularly vigilant about dog-fighting in the early 1930s, did the fanciers turn their attention to the more peaceful and legal competitions afforded by dog shows.

In 1935 the Staffordshire Bull Terrier emerged from seclusion. A club was formed, standard of points drawn up, and respectability gained in the shape of a separate register given by the Kennel Club. Progress has been maintained ever since. Thus from 1939 until the time of writing, annual British registrations have increased from 340 to 2,000.

Despite its fighting background, like most animals which know their own strength, the Staffordshire Bull Terrier is docile and friendly. Unless deliberately 'set on', that is encouraged to fight or attack, it is a gentleman.

It is friendly to human beings, particularly children. Naturally it needs discipline and a firm hand when young, but with maturity it becomes easy-going, a good mixer and a 'character'. It also protects its master's property with purposeful determination. Not for this breed the snap and snarl: the quiet, workmanlike air conveys its own warning.

Essentials of the breed: Short, deep, broad skull, pronounced cheek muscles, distinct stop and short foreface. Eyes: preferably dark, round and medium-sized. Ears: rose or half-pricked, not large. The mouth should be level. Neck: muscular and rather short. Forelegs: straight and set rather wide apart. The body should be close-coupled, with level topline and deep brisket. The hindquarters: well-muscled, hocks let down with stifles well bent. Feet must be well padded and strong. Tail should be of medium length, low set, tapering to a point and carried low. Coat: smooth, short and close. Colour: brindle, red, fawn, black, blue, or white, or white with any of these colours.

Weight: dogs 28 lb. to 38 lb., bitches 24 lb. to 34 lb. Height: 14 to 16 inches.
See colour plate p. 374.

Left Staffordshire Bull Terrier. Ch. Rapparee Renegade.

Right Staffordshire Terrier. Pete's Chip of Devil.

Staffordshire Terrier The Staffordshire Terrier can be called an American breed with some justice. For it differs considerably from its cousin, the STAFFORDSHIRE BULL TERRIER. The two breeds had a common origin in BULLDOG and terrier crosses. They are alike in having extraordinary cheek muscles. But there are many points of difference.

The American Staffordshire is a dog 18 to 19 inches at the shoulder for males, and 17 to 18 inches for bitches. The Staffordshire Bull Terrier is 14 to 16 inches for either sex. Not only is the American dog taller, it is also much more likely to have a true terrier front than the Staffordshire Bull Terrier.

The Staffordshire in America has been mainly bred for fighting for about 150 years. Although 'game to the death' was the major factor, weight also became a consideration. Some American 'Staffs' have weighed as much as 50 lb., whereas 38 lb. would be heavy for the English dog.

As early as 1900, the American dog was called the 'American Pit Bull Terrier' or the 'Yankee Terrier'. The name was changed to American (Pit) Bull Terrier. The American Kennel Club refused recognition for the breed. But the United Kennel Club recognized the breed some 50 years ago.

Though most states had outlawed dog fighting by 1900, men continued to breed fighting dogs and conduct fights in secret. To mislead the general public, the meets were called 'conventions'. The fights were regularly reported in *Bloodlines*, the official journal of the United Kennel Club.

Dog fights are still held occasionally, though only in the Deep South of the United States. Because of the widespread antagonism to dog fights, the United Kennel Club now names the breed simply the American Bull Terrier.

The American Kennel Club recognized the breed as the Staffordshire Terrier in 1936. Some dogs thus have had dual registrations – as American Bull Terriers in the UKC stud book, and as Staffordshire Terriers in the AKC stud book.

The early pit dogs, though fabled as friends of men and children, were death to other dogs. *Bloodlines* once printed a letter from one of its readers which read like this:

'I bought a pup from Pete D—. When it arrived I was mighty disappointed in it. And I wrote and told him so. But he wrote back and said not to worry, but just to let that dog grow up. Well, I did. And one day it escaped, and before I could catch it, he had killed two dogs, and put three others in the hospital. It cost me $110 in veterinary bills, and made a lot of people sore at me. But I'm here to tell you that Pete D— has the greatest dogs in the world.'

The Staffordshire Terriers now being shown appear to have excellent, stable dispositions, and they seem less likely to fight than dogs of many other breeds. For the most part, they are gentle enough with adults and children.

Essentials of the breed: The Staffordshire Terrier has a powerful skull of medium length, which is broad between erect, cropped ears. The muzzle is moderate in length but deep and broad. The mighty cheek muscles are plainly evident. If uncropped, the ears should be rose, or prick, never dropped. The bite is scissors, the nose black.

The front legs are set wide apart to permit a powerful chest, but the legs are not 'out at elbow'. The back is short, the ribs are close together, carried well back, and the back ribs are unusually deep. The tail is rather short and is set on low. The hindquarters are powerfully muscled, and the feet are compact. All colours are permitted, but all white, more than 80% white, black and tan, and liver are not encouraged. Among faults to be penalized are Dudley nose, light or pink eyes, tail too long or badly carried, and over or undershot mouths. Height: 17 to 19 inches.

Stag Hound Stag hunting stands beside wild boar hunting in Greece, hare hunting in most of Europe, and gazelle hunting in Arabia and Asia, as the oldest of man's hunting sports using dogs. But the destruction of the forests to make room for expanding populations brought an end to most stag hunting. It is practised today in only a few places in England and Ireland.

Probably the only modern dog which can claim any stag hunting history is the Scottish DEERHOUND. The other great deer hound breeds are now extinct. However, it is claimed that the modern English FOXHOUND descends from the extinct stag hounds. Whether true or not, the dogs now used for stag hunting are over-sized English Foxhounds. Although not pure-bred, they resemble Foxhounds in most respects, and are noted for their endurance, soundness of foot, and excellent noses. The purists say they lack the beauty of the Foxhound 'music'. It is illegal to hunt deer with dogs in the United States.

Standoff Coat A long coat which stands out from the body, as in the CHOW CHOW.

Staring Coat A harsh, dry, ill-conditioned coat.

Station Comparative height, body to leg length; as high-stationed, low-stationed.

Sterility see Infertility.

Stern The tail.

Sternum The breast bone.

Stifle The joint between the upper and lower thighs.

Stilted A choppy gait caused by hocks which are too straight.

Sting A tail which tapers to a fine point, as in the BEDLINGTON TERRIER and IRISH WATER SPANIEL.

Stomach and Diseases of the Stomach The stomach is a dilated section of the digestive tract that lies between the oesophagus and the intestine. Diseases of this organ are usually indicated by discomfort. The dog may adopt a 'praying' attitude when it rests its chest on the ground, and raises its hindquarters.

Dogs frequently swallow objects that can rest in the stomach; if these are sharp they can penetrate its wall. This requires surgical treatment.
See GASTRITIS; GASTRO-ENTERITIS.

Stomach Tube This is used to empty the stomach of a sick dog, and to feed young puppies when they are hand-reared. There is the danger that the milk given via a stomach tube may be introduced too quickly and in too great a quantity. If this method is used, great care must be taken to ensure that the milk is at the correct temperature (101–2°F, 38·3–38·8°C). Instructions for administration can be obtained from a veterinarian.

Stones This name is applied to collections of crystals of various salts which may develop within the body. They can occur in many parts such as the kidney, bladder, gall-bladder, urethra, bile and pancreatic ducts. They usually contain the salts of potash, calcium, sodium or magnesium.

In the dog the commonest sites for these stones are the bladder, and the urethra of the male dog. The latter occur because small bladder stones that can be passed out of the body in the female are retained in the male due to the restricted size of the urethra.

Stop The indentation between the eyes where skull and nasal bone meet.

Straight-Hocked Insufficient angulation at the hock joints.

Straight Shoulders Insufficient slope or lay back.

Stray Dogs Most of the advanced countries of the world today make some provision for the care of stray dogs. Humane societies are organized and animal shelters are built. Dog wardens are hired to catch homeless and sick dogs, as well as to enforce leash and licensing laws. Efforts are then made to locate the owners of the dogs.

The costs of such operations are usually so great that the dogs can be kept only for a maximum period of a few days. Three days is normally an insufficient length of time for an owner to realize that the dog is truly lost. Many a male dog may be chasing a female in season, and be gone for a week.

Persons who locate their lost dogs at humane shelters should take them to a veterinarian for immediate treatment, as any dog community can be a breeding ground for disease.

If a person takes a stray dog into the home, he or she should make an effort to find the owner before turning the dog over to an animal shelter. Neighbourhood inquiries can be made. But the most successful method is to watch for a 'lost dog' advertisement in the local newspapers, or to place a 'found dog' advertisement in the same section of the paper.

Giving a home to a stray dog for periods of months to a year does not necessarily give legal ownership to the dog's rescuer. Nor does it when a licence tag is purchased, and a personal property tax is paid. Purchase of a dog from a shelter gives only a partial legal title. To avoid family to family battles, and court actions, humane shelters in America usually refuse to divulge the names of the persons who have bought dogs from them.

Straying Much has been made of the so-called 'wonder dogs' which find their way home from long distances away. Many of these dogs have been roamers most of their lives. They have learned to find their way about large districts. In so doing, they have learned the distinctive odours of neighbourhoods (see SENSES, SPECIAL). They have learned to know the points of the compass – East, North, South, and West. They may also have learned to estimate their locations by the position of the sun at a given time of day.

It is commonly said that certain breeds are more prone to straying or roaming than are others. Among breeds supposedly so inclined are the setters, spaniels, and Beagles. Such dogs are said to follow their noses because of superior hunting drives. There are, however, no figures to back up such suppositions. Greater sex drives in both males and bitches may be causes for compulsive straying. These drives are not limited to specific breeds.

Owners who keep dogs in their homes, and who do not have kennels or fenced properties should teach their dogs not to leave their home environment. This can be taught to puppies, regardless of breed, but it is difficult or impossible to teach an older dog, once it has developed the habit of wandering.

When puppies are first brought home at six to eight weeks a small collar is put on them. To this is attached one end of a light cord. The puppy is called, and then is pulled to the owner. It is complimented and praised even though it must be dragged. It will learn quite quickly to come when called.

The puppy is trained by allowing it to move to the edges of the property, then checking it by a jerk on a cord attached to a collar round its neck. People beyond the 'property line' can be asked to call the puppy, which is again checked with a jerk when it responds. This rather tedious training has its rewards for the owner when the puppy learns that it must not stray.

Stud Book Breeding records kept by Kennel Clubs.

Stud Dog In assessing the value of a stud dog it is essential to discriminate between what might be termed hereditary faults and faults brought on by poor rearing, circumstances and environment. Poor feet or coats, for instance, can easily be caused by neglect. Poor bone structure can be due to improper rearing rather than nature. Faults acquired in this way will not be transmitted but if these faults are hereditary, then they are likely to be passed on to at least some of the dog's progeny.

A good stud dog should have the power to stamp its image on its progeny irrespective of the bitches to which it is mated. In such cases the stud dog is considered to be PREPOTENT and can be most beneficial to its breed. This must not lead one to believe that if such a pre-potent dog is used that all the pups sired by it will be equal to its own quality. Really great sires are extremely rare in any breed and here it might be well to empha-size that any dog that has sired even one puppy showing some inbred fault must be suspected.

Before using a stud dog it is advisable to have a look at it as this is the only reliable guide when considering it as a mate for a bitch. The ideal stud dog should not only be DOMINANT for breed type but it should appear a strong, virile animal with a general air of masculinity and a bold temperament. A weak, bitchy-looking dog is rarely classed as a satisfactory stud.

Care of the stud dog is of the greatest importance. Stud dogs should be housed in draught-free kennels with good ventilation. Two stud dogs should never be kennelled together. A stud dog should not be fed for several hours before serving a bitch and it should be taken for a short run so that it may relieve itself before the bitch is put to it. It is unwise to kennel stud dogs in the vicinity of bitches in season as this can be very up-setting for them and make them fret and go off their food.

It is a bad policy to allow the stud dog to be used frequently at public stud before it is fully mature. On the other hand, if it is not used until it is about eighteen months old, it is often difficult to get the dog to under-stand what is wanted and sometimes impossible to get a union. If used carefully, the stud dog should remain fertile up to eight or nine years of age. Some stud dogs which have been well looked after throughout their lives will continue to sire litters long after nine years of age, but in most instances, a dog must be considered to be on the decline at this age.

The bitch should always be taken to the stud dog as the male will be more in command of the situation in familiar surroundings. If an experienced stud dog is always taken to the same room it will quickly learn to recognize it. The fewer people there are present when the service takes place the better. Sometimes a bitch placed in strange surroundings will show a temporary viciousness and become unmanageable. It is always a wise precaution to tape the mouth of such a bitch. This causes her no hardship or pain and will prevent her from biting both stud dog and handlers. A snappy bitch can upset a young stud dog and make it reluctant to mate.

After the service, the dog should be taken back to its own quarters, given food and water and allowed to rest quietly.

A dog of poor constitution or one that comes from a known strain of poor breeders can never be regarded as a good stud prospect no matter how well it may have been cared for throughout its life.

If the best stud dogs are available at a public stud, it is unwise for the novice or the small breeder to keep his own stud. If one houses a stud dog the temptation is to use it whether or not it really suits the bitch's blood-lines.

Stuttgart's Disease see GUMS and HEART DISEASES.

Superciliary Arches The frontal bones of the skull which form the eyebrows.

Sussex Spaniel In 1795, Mr. Fuller of Rosehill Park, near Hastings in the county of Sussex, England, started breeding dogs for a special purpose: that of aiding the rough-shooting sportsmen in districts where undergrowth was dense and impenetrable.

Thus one requirement was strength; another, bulk and stolidity. A fast-moving spaniel would lead at a speed that its master was unable to follow, so a third requirement was 'voice' – the habit of giving tongue, or barking – which is not acceptable in other spaniels. In Sussex, however, it was thought desirable, as otherwise the sportsmen had no way of finding the dog through the bracken and bramble. Stonehenge, writing about a hundred years ago made a special feature of this, saying 'He is gifted with a full, bell-like tongue which he varies according to the game before him, and by this means, an experienced shooter can tell whether to expect "fur" or "feather" and can distinguish a hot scent from a stale one.'

The breed was evolved by crossing various existing spaniels, including the now extinct liver and white Norfolk, the FIELD SPANIEL and possibly some early springing spaniels. The result was a dog of distinctive colour unknown in any other breed. It is a rich golden liver.

It first reached the show bench at Crystal Palace, London, in 1862. Then, a large number of kennels specialized in Sussex Spaniels and large sums of money were paid for well known winning dogs.

For the next 80 years they occupied a modest niche in the dog world. The First World War threatened them as it did so many other breeds, but by 1939 they had partially recovered. The Second World War admini-stered a serious set-back. In 1947 only ten were registered in Britain, and the current annual average is only about twenty. In other breeds similarly afflicted, such as the MASTIFF, dogs were imported from abroad.

In the case of the Sussex there were none to import. In 1970 only four Sussex Spaniels were registered in the U.S.A.

Inbreeding, beyond the bounds of normal prudence, was inevitable, and the result was that few puppies were born. Thus a serious position was intensified by the large number of matings which failed to produce progeny.

Then in 1964 the accidental mating of a litter brother and sister gave the breed a boost. Three of the best specimens for over twenty years were born. But these pups, bred in the way they were, and combining the entire existing bloodlines of their breed were hazardous as either sires or dams to any reasonably good Sussex Spaniels.

There the position rests. Enthusiasts say 'We must save this unusual breed from extinction'. But the question is 'How?'

Essentials of the breed: The skull should be wide with pronounced stop. Eyes: hazel, fairly large. Ears: thick, fairly large, set moderately low. Mouth: strong and level. Neck: long, strong and slightly arched. Chest: deep and well developed. Body: strong and level. Hind legs rather short and strong, moderately well-feathered. Feet: circular and well padded. Tail: set low, not carried above level of the back, docked from 5 to 7 inches. Coat: abundant and flat. Colour: rich golden liver, shading to gold at the tips.

Ideal weight: dogs 45 lb., bitches 40 lb. Height: 15 to 16 inches.

See colour plate p. 91.

Swayback Concave curvature of the spine between the shoulders and hucklebones.

Swedish Kennel Club see Kennel Club, Scandinavian Kennel Union.

Swimmers Puppies which are born with acute foetal rickets are called 'swimmers'. In the worst form, the rib cage is flattened, turtle fashion, and the puppy is unable to rise. The futile movements of the front legs resemble the arm movements of a human swimmer doing the breast stroke, or those of the swimming turtle.

The disease is called achondroplasis, or chondrodystrophia fetales. It results from imperfect development of cartilage into bone. Puppies only partially affected walk bow- or straddle-legged. Though swimmers occasionally appear in most breeds, they are commonest in the short-legged, heavy-bodied breeds. In these breeds, an hereditary factor may be involved. If swimmers can be got on to their feet, their rib cages tend to approach normality. Some breeders believe that swimmers should be destroyed, and although so very little is yet known about the disease, many feel that bitches which produce swimmers should not be mated again.

This term is used in America, and is not current among British dog breeders, although the condition is not confined to the United States.

Sydney Silky Terrier see Silky Terrier.

Synovitis see Arthritis.

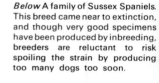

Below A family of Sussex Spaniels. This breed came near to extinction, and though very good specimens have been produced by inbreeding, breeders are reluctant to risk spoiling the strain by producing too many dogs too soon.

T

Tail-Waggers' Club The Tail-Waggers' Club, an essentially British institution, has proved an enduring one. Although not particularly ambitious in that it never advertises or openly invites donations and bequests, it is regarded with both respect and affection.

In part this is due to a fortunate choice of name. In part it is due to a rather curious and specialized approach to pets in general, and to dogs in particular.

It was formed in August 1928 by Captain H. E. Hobbs and fifteen members were enrolled at the opening meeting. In less than three months the club had 10,000 members which included the Prince of Wales and Princess Royal, the Duke and Duchess of York, the Duke of Gloucester and the Duke of Kent. Strictly speaking, the above were not members. They did however enrol their dogs: dogs only, as distinct from their owners, are eligible for membership.

The objects of the Club were, and remain, unusual. First, the aim was to counteract the ignorance of pets' requirements. It was assumed that deliberate ill-will was uncommon but that owners' lack of knowledge often caused suffering. To this end, press handouts were distributed on general care, and handbooks and a monthly magazine, still published, were issued.

Next came financial assistance to other institutions devoted to the welfare of dogs. Examples are contributions to a rebuilding fund of the Royal Veterinary College in London, the endowment of a Professorship of Canine Medicine, and the provision of a number of guide dogs for blind people.

Perhaps most important, the Club has always paid the dog licence fee for any old person unable to afford it. Currently it will help any member who is unable to meet veterinary fees and also assist where hardship is likely because of the expense of keeping dogs in quarantine.

The Tail-Waggers' Club is not an animal charity, but a self-help organization. It enrolled its millionth member in 1958 and now is heading for its two millionth. Its headquarters are in Barking, Essex, England.

Tapeworms There are probably twenty-five or more species of tapeworms, or cestodes, which infest dogs. Fifteen are found in North America alone. Some tapeworms are limited to Arctic regions, and some to small areas elsewhere. The best known species are world wide in distribution. Of these, *Dipylidium caninum*, the double-pored dog tapeworm, is the most common. It is also the most difficult to control since its intermediate hosts are the dog FLEA, and less commonly, the louse, Trichodectes.

The adult tapeworm has a head, called the scolex, which has suckers or hooks by which it anchors itself to the intestinal wall. It has no mouth, and no alimentary tract. It simply absorbs liquid food through the body wall.

Segments form in a chain behind the head, *D.*

caninum may have many segments and be 12 to 16 inches long. As new segments form at the head end, those moving back along the chain become increasingly big, and sexually more mature. When these break off, they are virtually nothing but cucumber-seed-shaped egg carriers.

Segments are carried from the dog on the faeces. They are pearly or reddish, in colour. They dessicate and free the eggs, which become infective. Adult fleas cannot swallow these eggs, but the larval forms do. Biting LICE can, however, swallow the eggs. The adult fleas are swallowed by dogs, and so the life cycle continues. The eggs hatch, reach the intestine, and there grow into adult worms.

Another species of tapeworm, *taenia pisiformis*, is often called the rabbit tapeworm by dog owners. Dogs become infected by eating the entrails of rabbits or hares which are the intermediate hosts. Another species uses rats and mice as hosts – as might be expected, this tapeworm is more common in cats than in dogs. Even certain fish serve as hosts for some cestodes.

Echinococcus granulosis, another tapeworm, uses farm animals as an intermediate host. The adult worm lives in the dog; the immature ones in the liver or lungs of the farm animals. This worm is dangerous to people, chiefly children, because it causes human disease. The problem is serious only in farming areas. Rigid hygienic measures should be used, both with dogs and their kennels, and with children. Children should not be allowed to handle puppies, or to put them to their faces, unless they wash carefully afterwards.

Arecoline hydrobromide was for decades the standard drug for the expulsion of all the cestodes. It requires a twelve hour fast, and may require a later enema. Niclosamide, also known as Yomesan, is the more recent, and probably the most effective drug. It appears literally to digest the worms, including the scolex, which other drugs sometimes miss.

Tartar on Teeth see Scaling Teeth.

Team At dog shows, usually four dogs of the same breed and ownership, shown together. Sled dog teams may include as many as 14 dogs.

Teats In a normal litter the whelps will find their own way to the milk supply and if they seem a little dilatory, a good mother will nudge them on to a teat. If a pup does not seem to manage to grasp a teat by itself, its mouth can be gently opened and the nipple inserted. This will usually give it the idea but if not, a little milk should be squeezed into its mouth very gently from the base of the nipple. The dam may be slightly upset at this interference but she will usually carry on and look after the puppies herself.

The bitch's milk glands must be watched carefully for an excess of milk which will cause her pain and discomfort if it is not drawn off. In such a case it is beneficial first to massage the breasts with a little warm oil. Inverted or indrawn teats can be drawn out by massaging with the fingers.

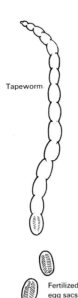

Tapeworm.

Fertilized egg sacs

Above Tapeworms. An adult tapeworm and two fertilized egg sacs. New segments form behind the head and become sexually mature as they move back. The end ones, which break off, carry the eggs.

It is essential that the teats of a nursing bitch should be kept clean, and watched for any signs of cracks or soreness. As the pups grow older and make more demands on the dam's teats, sore and cracked nipples often appear. Apart from the continual tugging at the teat by the healthy puppies whose milk teeth will be coming through, there is the problem of sharp nails. As the puppies go through the usual rhythmic motions with their feet on the dam's breasts, abrasions appear. These must be treated immediately to save the bitch any unnecessary suffering. They should be bathed gently, dried carefully and dusted with boracic powder. If necessary, a healing salve should be used. The nails of the puppies should be cut regularly.

If it is a small litter, some of the teats can easily be neglected as the whelps will always go to the teats offering the best supply of milk. This can cause milk to congeal in the unused mammae which will become hard and inflamed. This must be attended to immediately as it can cause the dam pain, and in extreme cases she will refuse to feed her puppies and go off her food. The affected parts should be washed in warm water, massaged with oil and when soft have the milk drained from them. From then on, all the teats should be watched to make sure that the puppies are not deserting some and only drawing milk from a few nipples.

Teeth see Dentition.

Telegony It is sometimes believed that a bitch having a litter by a mongrel or dog of another breed, becomes permanently 'spoilt' because future litters by a chosen sire would resemble the unwanted sire of her accidental litter. This, if it occurred, would be 'telegony', but it is, in fact, impossible.

There is no evidence that this has ever happened. Experiments designed to test the possibility have always failed to find any evidence that a previous mate can influence future offspring by another sire and current knowledge of heredity reveals no apparent way in which genetic material from a previous stud could be stored to enter future embryos. Thus, a bitch mismated is not spoilt for future breeding.

It is, however, possible for a bitch to produce puppies by more than one sire in the same litter, as the result of being served by more than one dog in the same heat period. This, of course, is not telegony.

Temperature see Body Temperature.

Terriers Dogs originally used to 'go to earth' (from Latin, *terra*) after foxes, badgers, or other animals.

Tervuren see Belgian Tervuren.

Testicles In addition to producing spermatazoa, the testicle also secretes male hormones, like testosterone. Testosterone produces the quality of maleness in the individual. Injections of testosterone, however, do not stimulate the formation of male characteristics, but may actually prevent such formation, and may injure the sexual potency of a stud dog.

The conditions known as monorchism, cryptorchism, and anorchism are discussed under CRYPTORCHID. An occasional dog will have three testicles, a condition known as triorchism. Sometimes one or more testicles are not only undescended, but are abnormally placed, often in the perineum. Such a condition is called ectopic.

Tetanus This is caused by infection entering the body through a contaminated wound. Affected animals stand stretched out in a fixed position with the jaws clamped shut. A common name for the condition is 'lockjaw'. Fortunately this disease is rare in dogs.

Below Thermometer: a Poodle has its temperature taken rectally.

Bottom Terrier: a dog used to 'go to earth', like the Jack Russell Terrier.

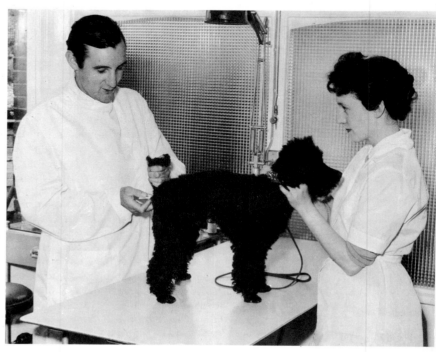

Thermometer The only satisfactory way to measure the temperature of the dog is to take it rectally. For this purpose, a heavy duty thermometer is made. Vaseline, or a similar non-irritating grease can be smeared on the thermometer which is then inserted to about three-quarters of its length into the dog's rectum. It should be kept there for three minutes before withdrawing. After the temperature has been read, the thermometer should be cleaned with cotton soaked in alcohol.
See BODY TEMPERATURE.

Thigh Hindquarter from hip to stifle joint.
See SECOND THIGH.

Throatiness Too much loose skin under the throat.

Throat Diseases The throat is composed of a number of organs and tissues. Inflammation of an area is usually referred to the actual organ or tissue involved: e.g. tonsilitis, laryngitis.

Infection of the throat is commonly associated with inflammation of that area, and is also a secondary site of infection in more serious diseases, like DISTEMPER.

Foreign bodies can cause obstruction within the throat.
See HEREDITARY ABNORMALITIES.

Throwback This term is applied to a puppy which unexpectedly resembles a distant ancestor or ancestral type. In breeds derived in whole or part from other breeds by crossing, animals which resemble the ancestral breeds are often called throwbacks.

The term often has a derogatory implication. It is interesting that many breeders are more incensed if their dog is said to resemble a known ancestral breed, than if it is likened to a breed of no known relationship. Thus to say a COLLIE has a head like a BORZOI, or a POINTER a FOXHOUND tail, is insult indeed!

Overleaf Tibetan Spaniels. Left to right: Ch. Braeduke Jhanki of Winaro, Braeduke Shan Hu of Northanger, Sivas Supi Yawlat, and Ch. Hunt Glen Braeduke.

Below Tibetan Mastiff. A noble dog, very rare. 'Tonya'.

Throwbacks however are prized if they resemble some famous ancestor in a valued quality currently rare in the breed. The genetic mechanism producing throwbacks is simply the segregation and reassortment of genes at sperm and egg production, and their recombination at the time of fertilization. The simplest form is when features dependent on simple Mendelian recessive factors turn up, after being concealed in 'carriers' (heterozygous DOMINANTS) for several generations. When, by chance, two such carriers are mated together, some of their puppies get the recessive allele from both parents and so show the recessive character.
See GENE; MENDELISM.

Thumbmarks Black spots on the PASTERNS.

Tibetan Apso see Lhasa Apso.

Tibetan Mastiff Before accepting the stories of Tibetan Mastiffs as wholly factual, certain points should be borne in mind. First, travellers in bygone days were prone to exaggerate. Next, giant dogs of a somewhat similar type have been a common feature of life in all countries. Thirdly, a hedgehog encountered in Tibet would probably be called a Tibetan Hedgehog by travellers, even if it had been imported from Iceland the day before. And finally, in bygone days the word 'Mastiff' or 'Mastie' was often used to describe a dog of mixed race.

A few attempts at a description of the dog follow. Aristotle: 'It is believed to be a cross between a dog and a tiger'. Chou King: 'The animal is four feet high and trained to attack men of a strange race'. Marco Polo: 'A large breed of dog so fierce and bold that two of them together will attack a lion'. And 'These people of Tibet have mastiff dogs as big as asses'. Vero Shaw, (*Book of Dogs*, 1879): 'The Tibetan Mastiff resembles a sour-faced, heavy-eared NEWFOUNDLAND. The coat is rough and hard, the tail carried well up over the back and the prevailing colour black and tan'

Robert Leighton, (*New Book of the Dog*, 1907), describing the journey home of *Bhotian*, a Tibetan Mastiff, exhibited by Major W. Dougall at Crystal Palace, London in 1906, wrote: 'Bhotian's journey through India was an expensive one as he had to have a carriage to himself. He effectively cleared the platform at all stations where he was given exercise'.

Brian Vesey Fitzgerald, in *Book of the Dog*, 1948, wrote: 'He has been imported into England and America but has never become popular'.

It is impossible to give a precise general description of a dog which is so rare, but the following gives some idea of the breed.

The Tibetan Mastiff stands about 28 inches at the shoulder, is ferocious, suspicious of all strangers, and a dog of remarkable fighting ability. It has a medium to long coat, black and tan, red and black, or black in colour. Its head structure is somewhat like that of a ST. BERNARD, with a short, broad, deep, and punishing jaw. The ears are set high, rather small, and folded over. The tail is plumed, and carried over the back when in motion.

Tibetan Spaniel Legend has it that at the time when the Indians had America to themselves and Ancient Britons roamed England wearing nothing but woad, Tibetan Spaniels were already an established breed. However, since there is no recorded history of Tibet until the Seventh Century, it would be hard to substantiate the claim. It is also difficult to prove the contention that the Tibetan Spaniel crossed with the PUG produced a new breed known as the PEKINGESE. As the early history of Tibet was linked with China, and as small dogs would have made suitable peace offerings between the noblemen of these countries, the Tibetan Spaniels were perhaps presented to the ruling classes of China. They may have crossed them with Pugs to produce Pekes.

The alternative argument is that the Chinese presented Pekes to Tibet where they lost their purity of form over the centuries, eventually developing into the markedly less distinctive breed now called Tibetan Spaniels.

The dog's early duties were varied: working a prayer wheel for religious owners who were long on piety but short on time; acting as sentinels; even, it is said, playing the role of hot water bottle for human companions.

The dog has a comparatively modern European name. Originally, all 'spaniells' were gundogs. Later the name was given to some toy breeds which, principally in ear-carriage, bore some resemblance to the originals. KING CHARLES SPANIELS are a good example. Some Japanese dogs were also called spaniels. It was but a short step to giving these Tibetans the name of spaniels. It at least distinguishes them from the Tibetan Terrier, and it is about as accurate a name, as neither dog is in any way related to spaniels or terriers.

The first known Tibetan Spaniel was brought to Britain by a Mr. F. Wormald in 1905. In the 1920s, Dr. Grieg, a medical missionary, brought several more home with her. But the establishment of the breed in Britain is a post-war phenomenon. In 1946, Sir Edward and Lady Wakefield brought a bitch named *Lama* into the country, and in 1947, they acquired another called *Dolma*. Lama and Dolma founded the breed as it is known today. With only a modest contribution from a descendent of one of the pre-war dogs, they initiated the enormous expansion which has taken place in the breed in Britain. Although there may be as many as 1,000 in the United Kingdom, the breed is still unknown in the United States.

While dog fashions can never be accurately forecast, it is unlikely that the Tibetan Spaniel will ever be a top dog. Despite its many charms, its appearance is not sufficiently distinctive to take it to the top. The uninitiated might think it a poor specimen of Pekingese, or, even worse, a cross-bred dog. Yet the breed gains adherents. Why? They will tell you: the breed has character.

Essentials of the breed: The head should be medium or small in proportion to the body with slightly domed skull and fairly short, blunt muzzle. Eyes should be dark brown, set fairly wide apart and not prominent.

Ears: pendant and well-feathered. They can have a slight 'lift' away from the side of the head. Mouth: slightly undershot preferred, but not showing teeth. Neck should be short and covered with a mane. The bones of the forelegs are slightly bowed. Body: longer from point of shoulder to root of tail than the height at shoulder. Hare-footed. Tail: set high, plumed and carried over the back. The coat should be double, silky in texture, and flat, with a mane on neck and shoulders. Colours: golden, cream, white, biscuit, fawn, brown, shaded sable, red sable, black, parti-colour or tricolour. Weight: dogs 10 to 16 lb., bitches 9 to 15 lb. Height: dogs up to 11 inches, bitches $9\frac{1}{2}$ inches.
See colour plate p. 188.

Tibetan Terrier The Tibetan Terrier, in spite of its name, is not a true terrier. That is, it was not bred to go to ground. For this reason, in Britain, it is not included in the Terrier group but put with the SHIH TZU and LHASO APSO in the Utility group.

In the United States it is virtually unknown and if shown at all must be in a Miscellaneous Class. If it is ever established and recognized there it will probably join its cousin, the Lhaso Apso, in the Non-Sporting group, the American equivalent of the British Utility group.

The Lhaso Apso is the breed the Tibetan Terrier most resembles. Indeed, pictures of some of the early imports are so similar as to be virtually impossible to tell apart. This is not to say the two breeds should be quite so similar. While the Apso is basically a long, low dog, the Terrier is square, that is, its longer legs make its shoulder height the same as the length of its back.

Another difference has been acquired over the years. The Apso has become 'presented', that is groomed and fashioned for shows in the same way as a Shih Tzu. The Terrier is presented much more naturally to give the impression of some resemblance to the OLD ENGLISH SHEEPDOG.

The breed is believed to be very old. Legend says that these dogs have been bred for centuries in the monasteries of Tibet. They were given to the nomadic tribes as 'luck bringers'.

They are used as mascots, watch dogs and guards, and can retrieve objects lost in places inaccessible to men. Also their heavy coat which is clipped in the hot weather for comfort can be mixed with yak hair and woven into soft but semi-waterproof cloth.

Although their head and body remind one of a miniature Old English Sheepdog, the tail does not. It is well-feathered, curled and carried over the back like a plume. This 'bang' of hair at either end has given the breed the nickname of the 'double chrysanthemum' dog.

Although established in Britain, they have never become popular, and annual registrations in recent years have averaged only about seventy.

Essentials of the breed: Skull: of medium length, narrowing slightly from ear to eye with a marked stop. The head should be well-furnished with long hair, falling over the eyes. Eyes: large, dark, fairly wide apart, with dark eyelids. Ears: pendant, V-shaped, heavily fea-

thered. Mouth: level, but a slightly undershot mouth is not penalized. Forelegs: straight and heavily furnished. Body: compact and powerful. Length from point of shoulder to root of tail should be equal to height at withers. Hindquarters: heavily furnished. The feet should be large, round and heavily furnished. Tail should be of medium length, set on fairly high, feathered and carried over the back. The undercoat: fine wool. The top coat: long, profuse, but not silky or woolly. Colour: white, golden, cream, grey or smoke, black, parti-colour and tricolour. Height: dogs 14 to 16 inches, bitches slightly smaller.
See colour plate p. 187.

Above Tibetan Spaniel. Ch. Braeduke Tam Cho.

Ticked Small, but distinct areas of black or coloured hair on a white ground colour.

Ticks The most widely spread of all the ticks which prefer the dog as host is the brown dog tick, *Rhipicephalus sanguineus*. It is the vector of *Babesia canis*, the malignant jaundice of France, Africa and the Southern United States.

In 1963, British war dogs in Singapore began to die from a mysterious disease which has been called tropical canine pancytopenia, tracker disease, idiopathic, hemorrhagic syndrome, and canine hemorrhagic fever. During 1969 and 1970, some 200 U.S war dogs in Vietnam died of the disease. Intensive study shows that a micro-organism causes the disease, and again ticks have been thought to be the vector.

The female brown dog tick engorges herself with blood and drops off of the dog. She lays up to 2,500 eggs, usually in a crevice in a kennel, or under a rug in the home. The eggs hatch in twenty to thirty days into

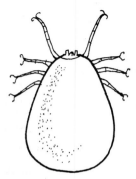

Above Tick.

seed-ticks or larvae. The larvae return to a dog-host more than once before emerging as adult ticks.

Ticks have an amazing ability to find spots where dogs will pass. If outside, they will climb upon posts or tree limbs along paths used by dogs. Or they may climb into bushes under which dogs will lie. In the home, they will climb as high as two feet on a chair or table leg, or on a wall. During heavy home infestations, they may climb up to pictures, or even onto the ceiling. They may have to wait six or eight months for a dog to pass, but they instantly sense the approach of the dog, and jump upon it as it passes.

To eradicate ticks, the infested home must be treated at ten-day intervals at least four times, then once a month for two or three months. Since ticks are immune to many insecticides, the spray to be used should clearly be described as a tickcide. In mild infestations, it is only necessary to spray as high as two feet from the floor, except for chairs in which the dog may have slept. Crevices, the edges of rugs, and floor or wall boards should be given a thorough treatment.

Kennels may require higher spraying than homes. Where it is practical, bushes about the home should be sprayed, and to be really thorough, lawns should be treated with an insecticidal dust. Outside areas should be treated three times at two week intervals during the spring, then once a month. The dogs themselves should be dusted with insecticide regularly as a precaution, and more intensively during an infestation.

Tablets are available which, when given to the dog, ensure that any tick that bites the dog will die. They are available from veterinarians.

Timber Bone, usually leg bone.

Toe, 'Knocked-Up' This is a condition of the dog in which the last joint of the toe is dislocated with a subsequent elevation of the last bone of that toe and of the nail attached to it.

Tongue The voice of trailing hounds.

Tongue The tongue is a mobile organ within the mouth, composed of muscular and fibrous tissue. The muscles of the tongue enable great movement in all directions. On the upper surface, which is a mucous membrane, are numerous papillae of various shapes, amongst which are the 'taste buds'. These buds enable the dog to determine the taste of objects, food and so on, touching them.

The function of the tongue is fourfold: to aid the movement of food into and within the mouth; to taste; to help to produce sound; to help to clean the coat. See BROWN MOUTH; RANULA.

Topknot Tuft of hair on the top of the head.

Torsion of Stomach see Bloat.

Tosa Dog see Mastiffs; Rare Breeds.

Tourniquet A tourniquet is a bandage or other device used to prevent loss of blood after major injuries, usually to the limbs. It is a dangerous instrument. If improperly used, it may cause serious, or even fatal, damage, so it should be used only when digital pressure above the wound fails to stop the spurting of the blood. It is used only for emergencies, and *must* be briefly loosened – the length of time depends on the amount of bleeding – at intervals of not more than ten minutes.

449

It should be removed as soon as possible by the veterinarian.

For minor injuries, a tourniquet is not required. If sterile gauze is placed over the wound, and then light pressure is applied for a few minutes, bleeding stops. This gauze should not be removed: to pull it away might renew the bleeding and such exposure might permit contamination of the wound. Instead, a second piece of gauze should be placed over the first. A light bandage can then be added (see BANDAGING).

The areas where pressure can be safely and effectively applied to stop bleeding are often called pressure points. The veterinarian can apply digital pressure to the appropriate point to slow down or to stop the haemorrhage but inexperienced dog owners cannot be expected to know the location of these pressure points, and so a tourniquet may be the only first aid measure available to the owner at the time of the injury.

The need for a tourniquet comes usually when a major artery has been cut or torn. If such an accident does not happen near a veterinary hospital, it is always an emergency. The dog owner, with neither the time nor the facilities for precise medical treatment, must use the materials available to make a tourniquet.

A lady's cloth belt, or a man's necktie or large handkerchief, can be used. This is tied about the limb, if possible at some distance *above* the wound. If the wound is just below a joint, then the tourniquet can be applied just above the joint. In no case, should the tourniquet touch the wound.

One method is to tie the tourniquet tightly about the limb so that arterial bleeding is stopped. But it should not be so tightly tied as to cut deeply into the skin. (Wire, rope, or rubber cord should never be used.)

A second method is to tie the make-shift tourniquet less tightly and then slip a pencil, a small stick or even a pebble under the bandage, and then rotate it, to tighten the tourniquet.

Toxic Hepatitis see Hepatitis.

Toy Manchester Terrier see English Toy Terrier (Black and Tan).

Toy Spaniels see Cavalier King Charles Spaniel; King Charles Spaniel.

Trace A dark stripe along the spine, as in some PUGS.

Tracking Trials see Working Trials.

Traffic Accidents – First Aid When a dog is hit by an automobile, the normal reaction of the owner is to rush into the street to rescue it. However, there is a danger that a following vehicle may then kill or injure the owner. If the traffic is heavy, three people may be needed to get the dog out of the street, one controlling traffic, the other two making the rescue.

This is not simple. The seriously injured dog may be killed or further injured if improperly carried off the street. And the rescuers may be bitten. The injured dog may feel pain when an attempt is made to move it, and

may then bite savagely. This can be prevented by tying the dog's mouth shut. A neck tie, a large handkerchief, a cloth belt or a head scarf will serve admirably.

An ideal way to remove the dog from the street would be to slide a large bath towel, or a blanket under the dog. It could then be lifted gently without creating a further injury. However, in most cases, neither would be available. A jacket, or a coat can serve. Whatever is used should be slipped under the dog as gently as possible.

Veterinarians report that a surprising number of dogs are knocked unconscious in traffic accidents, but suffer nothing more serious than a few bruises. Broken legs are the most common injury, and a broken pelvis the second most common. Cracked ribs and punctured diaphragms are less frequent injuries. Severe bleeding can occur in the case of badly mangled legs. In such cases, death from haemorrhage may result before the dog can reach a veterinary hospital.

BANDAGING, the application of TOURNIQUETS, and treatment of SHOCK are dealt with in separate articles. Dog owners can ask a veterinarian to show them the location of 'pressure points' – the areas where hemorrhaging can be stopped by pressing the thumb or finger against an artery. By this means the dog's life can be saved in cases of severe bleeding.

Trail To hunt by following ground scent. Also, the scent left by a moving animal.

Training a Dog Most dogs are easy to train because the dog by nature lives in a pack with a leader, several would-be leaders and a majority of followers. Dogs are not 'almost human' but, in many ways, it is easy for man to take on the role of pack leader.

The basic principles of training are simple. Dogs do not reason. They learn by the association of ideas. A five-year-old child can be told that if it touches a fire it will get burned. No so a baby. But if a baby gets its fingers burned, it is unlikely to go too near a fire in future. Likewise a five-year-old, told a box contains sweets, will open it to find them. A baby would not understand such an instruction but, should it accidentally open a box and find sweets, will re-open that particular box next time it sees it. A dog reacts like the baby rather than the five-year-old.

A dog learns to associate certain actions with pleasure and others with displeasure. Not unnaturally, it prefers the former. For training purposes the desired associations are built up by a process of correction and reward. In other words, the trainer has to correct the dog when it reacts wrongly (often behaves the way *it* wants) and reward it when it does as it is told. The minimum correction and the maximum reward should always be given. Correction can be a misleading term. It may simply refer to pushing a dog into a sitting position, without any chastisement.

The important thing to remember about correction and reward is not *how* to apply them but *when* to apply them. They must always be applied when the dog is actually reacting, rightly or wrongly, to a command. If a dog runs away and is punished on return, it will have been corrected for coming back, not for running away.

Tourniquets are used temporarily in emergencies, to staunch the flow of blood from a major injury to the limbs. They must not be left on for more than a few minutes.
Above The simplest tourniquet made from a cloth belt, necktie or handkerchief which is tied above the wound. A tourniquet should never touch the wound.
Below A second method is to tie the tourniquet less tightly and insert an instrument, such as a pencil, to adjust the grip.

It will then be just as likely to run away but much less likely to come back.

Dogs do not understand words. They simply understand sounds which they learn to associate with certain actions. To teach a dog to sit, say 'Sit!', push it into a sitting position (correction) and then reward it. Soon it should associate the sound 'Sit!' with the corrections and will sit in response to it. But it is just as easy to teach it to sit by saying 'Stand!', 'Lie down!' or anything else, coupled with the pushing action.

While it is unimportant *what* is said, it is very important *how* it is said. A young dog will instinctively obey a growl from an older dog. For this reason it is possible to correct a dog without touching it at all, but merely by scolding it in a harsh tone of voice. Likewise it can be rewarded by being praised in a friendly tone. And in both cases this can be strengthened by associating the sound with the action. If a gruff voice is used when correcting and a kind voice when rewarding, the dog should soon learn to associate the two different tones with doing right or wrong.

Training for Kennel Work

There are two schools of thought among employers of kennel staff: some prefer the inexperienced people who can be more readily taught; others prefer those who have had some previous experience in kennels and understand animals.

In those countries where dogs are business there are many establishments which undertake to train kennel maids and boys, offering experience of day to day routine, lectures on various aspects of the work and possibly a diploma or certificate of competence at the end of the course. The disadvantage of such courses appears to be the undeniable fact that an aptitude for kennel work is developed over many years, as is an understanding of the care and management of dogs in general. It is unlikely that during a course of perhaps six months or a year, every contingency will arise. Thus a diploma gained can only certify that in the opinion of the principal, its holder is suited to kennel work.

Since there are no short cuts to becoming a competent kennel maid or boy it is prudent to remember that this is a lifelong job with the opportunity and necessity of learning something new every day. Therefore to become a junior in a large establishment, working up slowly and steadily to a position of responsibility may be the best course. The large kennels, either boarding or breeding, will offer greater opportunities for learning since the more animals housed, the greater the number of contingencies that arise. A small, select one-breed kennel may seem appealing to the beginner and will offer the opportunity to learn a lot about a little; however, the time to specialize is when one knows the routine and requirements of the species as a whole.
In America, kennel workers often become PROFESSIONAL HANDLERS later in their careers.

Transmissible Diseases

A transmissible disease is one caused by a living organism. The organism may be in, or on, the body. In either case it disturbs the normal functioning of the body. A contagious disease is one which is transmitted from one individual to another by direct or indirect contact. All contagious diseases are infectious, but not all infectious diseases are contagious. For example, TETANUS is caused by a free living organism inhabiting the soil. So it is infectious but not contagious.

The transmissible diseases are caused mainly by bacteria, viruses and protozoa. As a rule, disease spreads from the escape of the infecting organism from one animal to another of the same species. Like tetanus, RABIES is inter-species-specific, since the rabid dog may infect a human being by biting. Conversely, a man suffering from tuberculosis, ringworm, or salmonella may infect his dog. Such cases are rare.

Because the host animal is always antagonistic to the invaders, the latter are usually destroyed. If, however, the organisms are able to survive, and to make slow progress, the resulting infection is called chronic. Sometimes the invaders quickly overwhelm the body's defences. The disease is then called acute or peracute – extremely acute.

Disease-causing organisms may be eliminated from the body through the urine or feces; by coughing or sneezing; by pus from abscesses; or through the saliva, as in the case of rabies. Normally such passage occurs during the chronic or acute stages of the disease.

But there are exceptions in which the host animals are called carriers. The war between the body and the invading organisms may reach a stalemate: the body is unable totally to destroy the invaders, yet these have lost their power to destroy the host. The disease-causing organisms are then excreted for weeks or months. Such is the case with the organism causing LEPTOSPIROSIS in the dog.

There are immune carriers – animals which do not get the disease themselves, but which are able to spread it to animals of a different species. This may be the case with the bat, which can spread rabies without itself developing the disease. In addition, there are contact carriers. These are animals which pick up dangerous germs from immune carriers, and then pass them on to other animals of the same species in the same way as the immune carrier.

There are many means by which infection is made. Contact by a healthy animal with a sick one is a major method. Some infections are air-borne. Dogs may snuff up the leptospirosis organism from the urine of infected rats or other dogs. Tetanus and gas gangrene result when infected soil gets into wounds. Blood-sucking insects, such as mosquitoes, LICE, and TICKS inject infecting organisms into the blood or body of their victims. When an organism, such as the heart worm (see FILARIASIS), must pass part of its life in an invertebrate host, that host is called a biological vector.

Some organisms may live peacefully in the body for years. They cause no harm until the host undergoes heavy stress. Then they are aroused to infective, and often fatal, activity. Streptococcus infections and pneumonia often occur in this way. MANGE mites sometimes show a similar history.

Disease-causing organisms affect the body in different ways. *Clostridium tetani*, the bacillus which causes tetanus, produces a neurotoxin which destroys

Traffic accidents. Temporary muzzles are needed for restraining injured dogs.
Top How to tie a muzzle on a long-nosed dog.
Above A muzzle for a short-faced dog, knotted below the chin, then at the back of the neck, then looped over the front, above the nose, and tied again at the back.

the nerve cells. The toxin has an affinity for the nerve cells of warm-blooded animals.

Viruses are nature's most highly developed parasites. They invade cells where they produce exact copies of themselves, and these new viruses invade other cells. As a rule, the invaded cells are either destroyed or are so altered that they cannot function. Because viruses invade the cells, they cannot be destroyed by chemotherapy – the antibiotics and the sulphonamides cannot reach them.

When a bitch nurses her puppies, the colostrum, or first milk, contains large amounts of antibodies which give the puppies a defence against those diseases for which the dam is immune. The puppies are then protected for the first few weeks of their lives. This immunity reduces, and other measures have to be taken to protect the young dog. In some diseases caused by bacteria, injections of the dead bacteria can fool the body into producing antibodies and consequent immunity. Virus diseases require living virus if the antigens are to stimulate antibody production. Since it is too dangerous to inject strong viruses into the body, they are weakened or attenuated, by heating to a point just below that which would cause death in the virus, or by other means to produce a safe vaccine.

Ironically, modern health measures have tended to shorten the vaccine's 'life', or the time during which it is effective. DISTEMPER vaccines make an excellent example. If a dog is vaccinated with live virus, and then is allowed to roam the streets, its immunity is likely to be life-long. The reason is that it is constantly meeting dogs which expose it to distemper. Such regular 'challenges' to its antibodies keep the immunity level at peak.

But, if vaccinated dogs are kept at home, so that they have no chance to be exposed to distemper, their immunity level drops rapidly. It is for this reason that annual vaccination is now recommended.

Many animal diseases occur in epidemics. In such periods, the general level of health is always a factor; and re-vaccination and quarantine are recommended.

Transportation of Dogs Transportation by land, sea or air is not the insurmountable hurdle that some believe. For overseas travel, bookings must be made through air or shipping lines of your choice. In many instances certificates of origin, health and export licences will take from several days to a few weeks to procure, so reservations must be made sufficiently in advance to allow for them. Once confirmed, details of reserved space, flight number or name of vessel, time of departure and estimated time of arrival must be despatched to the consignee.

Most of the states and provinces in the United States and Canada require health certificates and rabies vaccination certificates before they can be shipped. Shipping schedules should be arranged so that the dog does not reach its destination on weekends or holidays, since shipping offices are often closed on these days.

For exporting purposes travelling boxes have to be purchased. These should be non-returnable since it is expensive to have 'empties' returned from abroad. Many firms manufacture boxes specially for dogs, and

all appreciate that air freight containers must be light in weight. Sea freight crates can be of heavier construction. Air freight charges are based on weight or cubic capacity, whichever is the greater, but sea freight charges are based purely on the distance with weight and volume having no bearing on the cost.

The British Standards Institute recommendations on box size for dogs are simple. To arrive at the correct sized box, measure the dog from nose to tail root (A), and from ground to elbow (B). A plus B equals length of crate. The width across shoulders, multiplied by two, equals width of crate. Height from ground to top of skull in standing position, plus two inches, equals height of crate. Air boxes should not have handles or protruberances which increase the volume and therefore the freight charge. All boxes must have adequate ventilation in the form of holes, bars or wire mesh on at least two sides, preferably four, to permit free passage of air. Dogs travelling by air are not, of course, put in unpressurized compartments.

Dogs travelling by rail do not require the mass of paperwork but train times should be worked out before despatch. The best and safest time for a dog to travel is overnight when station staff are not so busy and dogs will travel during their normal sleeping time. The consignee should, again, be advised of time of despatch, route to be taken, station and estimated time of arrival.

Rail crates should be of heavier construction than air containers to withstand the inevitable banging about. Size of crate should be estimated in the same manner as for air or sea travel. Rail freight boxes should be painted outside in a bright colour to be seen easily, and the words 'LIVESTOCK – URGENT' painted on in large contrasting letters. Consignees are normally expected to return empty rail boxes to the sender.

Since it is against the law to use straw in export boxes, woodwool (excelsior), cedar shavings or newspaper should be used. Any of these commodities is cleaner

Above Transportation of dogs. All crates should have adequate ventilation (holes, bars or wire mesh) on at least two sides and as many relevant labels as possible.

Right Measurements for crates; the correct sized box for a dog should be: length – the distance along the dog from nose tip to tail root plus the distance from the ground to its elbow (A + B); breadth – twice the width of the shoulders (C); and height – the distance from the ground to the top of the dog's skull (D) plus two inches.

than straw and should be used for travel within one country as well as for overseas journeys.

Providing they are all relevant, one cannot put too many labels on a crate. Labels must be large, clearly printed and bear the consignee's name, address, telephone number, station or port of departure and destination and route. It is important to ensure that both sender and consignee can be contacted quickly in an emergency. Crates going overseas should also bear concise details of feeding, watering and exercising required, together with the pet name of the animal.

Before despatching an animal, it is wise to ensure that the crate conforms to the regulations of the transporting company: each freight line has its own rules. Every state and country has its own regulations regarding the importation of dogs. These should be studied before a dog is despatched.
See EXPORT OF DOGS.

Trials, Gundog – American see Field Trials, American.

Trials, Gundog – British see Field Trials, British.

Triangular Eye An eye set in tissue triangular in shape.

Tricolour White, black, and tan; or liver, white, and tan, etc.

Trumpet The dog's 'temple'. The hollow on either side of the skull, behind the eye socket.

Tuberculosis This infection is caused by a bacterium called *Mycobacterium tuberculosis*. The disease can occur in man and most animals and can be transmitted from one species to another. The incidence of tuberculosis in dogs is extremely rare.

Tuck-Up Lack of body depth at the loin.

Tulip Ears Ears curving slightly forward.

Tumours, Benign Dogs are subject to tumours more than most other animals, with the possible exception of man. Middle-aged and old dogs are more prone than puppies to them. Unfortunately for the dog, more of these tumours are cancerous than not. Tumours which are, or become cancerous are called malignant. (See TUMOURS, MALIGNANT.) Those which are normally harmless are called benign.

A tumour is an abnormal growth of cells or tissues. The growth is autonomous, that is, it grows independently of the laws of growth of its host. It is progressive; it grows slowly but does not invade the surrounding tissue or spread to other parts of the body. The cause of the tumour is unknown.

As a rule, these benign tumours cause no serious physical disturbance to the dog, other than inconvenience. There are literally dozens of types of benign tumours. A common one is a fatty tumour called a lipoma. It is rounded, and may be the size of a hickory

nut, or as large as a tennis ball. Usually it is under the skin, though some develop within the skin itself.

Anal sphincter tumours, the anal adenoma, and tumours in the anal area, develop in old dogs. They appear to be more common in FOX TERRIERS and COCKER SPANIELS than in most breeds. Also they occur about nine times as often in males as in females. The anal adenoma can be controlled by injections or removed surgically.

Sebaceous cysts, sometimes of considerable size, arise on the skin because of the blockage of the sebaceous glands, so that dead cells and other materials from the excretory ducts of the glands collect.

Fibroid tumours are of two types. One is hard and is called variously fibroma durum, desmoid, or dermoid tumour, and may be pea to table-tennis ball size. They occur on the head, chest, abdomen, and back side of the body. They are painless and move with the skin.

Soft fibromas appear about the mouth, neck, and abdomen. They often disappear without treatment, leaving as mysteriously as they arrived. If they do not disappear, they can be removed surgically, as can all the tumours so far described, and will not recur.

Another tumour is the angioma. As with so many others, the angiomas often appear about the tail and the face. One type is filled with blood vessels, and so is called hemangioma. The second is involved with the lymph system, and is called the lymphangioma. Both may be removed surgically.

The amyloid tumour is a non-malignant nodule which is usually on a vocal fold – one of the two membranous bands which control the pitch of the voice. The dog owner's first suspicion that such a tumour exists may come when he notices a change in the dog's bark. Oddly, amyloid tumours also sometimes appear in the bladder. The amyloid tumour may expand gradually, but it is encapsulated, and can be removed surgically.
See INTERDIGITAL CYSTS; WARTS.

Tumours, Malignant Malignant tumours or cancers grow rapidly and invade the surrounding tissues. They spread to other parts of the body, and if they are removed surgically they often recur. A malignant tumour is the cause of a general malaise in the animal. The most striking sign of ill health produced by the malignancy is the loss of flesh.

There are two types of malignant tumour, the carcinoma and the sarcoma. In the dog malignant tumours may occur almost anywhere, particularly in the abdomen or the chest. The symptoms produced vary depending on the organs affected. The treatment of a malignant tumour is difficult. In certain cases treatment with X-rays or radio-active material is helpful and drugs may slow down the malignant process.

In general the approach to tumours in dogs is the same as the approach to tumours in human beings. Any unexplained lump should be shown to the veterinarian, so that appropriate steps may be taken promptly.
See TUMOURS, BENIGN.

Turnup An uptilted foreface.

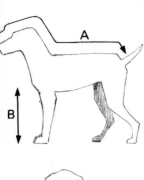

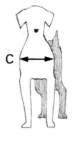

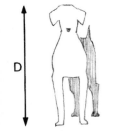

U

Umbilical Cord When the puppy is born, the umbilical cord is still intact and the puppy is enclosed in the foetal membrane. The bitch ruptures this bag and the puppy takes its first breath. The bitch then bites through the umbilical cord and starts to lick the puppy vigorously. If the bitch does not bite through the cord almost immediately it is wise to wait and see if she will do so once the AFTER-BIRTH is expelled. If she requires assistance with the cord (and this is often the case with the short-nosed breeds such as Pekingese and Bulldogs, etc.), then cut the cord as far away as possible from the puppy's stomach with sterilized scissors. The umbilical cord should need no further attention. It will dry off and disappear altogether in a few days.

Umbilical Hernia see Hernia.

Undershot A jaw in which the incisors of the under jaw project beyond those of the upper jaw.

United Kennel Club see Kennel Club, United.

Urinary Organs These organs constitute the excretory system which forms, collects and then expels urine. The system consists of kidneys (two), ureters (two), bladder and urethra.

The kidneys separate waste products from the bloodstream. The ureters carry the urine from the kidneys to the bladder, which stores the urine until it is carried from the bladder to the exterior by the urethra.

Uterine Inertia see Caesarean Operation.

V

Vaccines In modern usage, vaccination is inoculation to produce immunity against a given disease. Vaccines may be made from killed or live organisms, or those which have been attentuated (weakened).

While vaccines are normally used to prevent disease, some bacterial vaccines may be used to increase the immune response in an animal already suffering from the disease.

Vaccines commonly used in canine medicine include those to guard against DISTEMPER, infectious canine HEPATITIS, LEPTOSPIROSIS, and RABIES; a modified measles vaccine is also used.

Vallhund see Rare Breeds.

Varminty A keen, piercing expression, fox-like.

Vegetables Most vegetables are unsuitable for canine nutrition. They are too bulky for a digestive tract designed to nourish a carnivorous animal. Others must be processed in some way before the dog can utilize them. Dried tomato or other vegetable pomaces (the pulp left after extraction of the juice) are sometimes used. Dried kelp is used in some commercial foods. See NUTRITION; DIGESTION.

Venereal Disease The dog has few diseases that are transmitted during mating. *Venereal granulomata* are tumours that can be transmitted in this way. The condition is common in some parts of the world.

Vent The anal opening, or the area about it, often tan in colour.

Veterinarians (Veterinary Surgeons) In Britain a 'veterinary surgeon' is any person listed in the register maintained by the ROYAL COLLEGE OF VETERINARY SURGEONS. Registration is dependent upon academic qualification by examination. Prior to the Veterinary Surgeons Act of 1948, it was the examining body, the Royal College of Veterinary Surgeons, who awarded the Diploma of Membership of the Royal College of Veterinary Surgeons (MRCVS). After the passing of the Act, the following British universities were empowered to grant veterinary degrees: Edinburgh, Glasgow (B.V.M.S.); London (B.Vet. Med.); Bristol, Liverpool (B.V.Sc.); Cambridge (Vet. M.B.). Veterinary degrees are granted by universities in many other countries. Courses of study last about five years and are usually divided into two parts. The first part is devoted to pre-clinical studies, the basic sciences of anatomy, physiology and animal husbandry. The second part is made up of the clinical subjects, pathology, medicine and surgery.

It is essential that a veterinary student should acquire a varied experience of clinical practice. Thus vacations are spent with veterinarians in general practice.

Left Umbilical cord. Though still attached to the puppy at birth, the umbilical cord is usually removed promptly by the bitch. If not, the cord should be cut at the point marked with the arrow.

Veterinary education covers a very broad field. After qualification a veterinary surgeon may specialize in some particular aspect. There are various specialist diplomas such as the Diploma in Veterinary Radiology (D.V.R.), the Diploma in Veterinary Anaesthesia (D.V.A.), Diploma in Tropical Veterinary Medicine (D.T.V.M.), and the Diploma in Veterinary State Medicine (D.V.S.M.). To date there is no special diploma or degree in small animal medicine or surgery.

Veterinary surgeons are not allowed to advertise and the dog owner will not be able to identify a small animal specialist by his qualification. However, the veterinary profession is so organized in Britain that if the local practitioner requires assistance in the diagnosis or treatment of a particular case, he can obtain a second opinion from a veterinarian in a neighbouring practice or the nearest university veterinary school or the Animal Health Trust Small Animal Centre.

Veterinary Examinations at Shows In a number of countries in the past, all entries to any dog show had to pass a veterinary examination. Recently some, including Britain, the United States and Canada, have relaxed this rule and merely insist that a veterinarian is present at the show. The purpose of veterinary examination was primarily to detect cases of infectious and contagious disease, to ensure that male dogs were ENTIRE, and to exclude fraudulent preparation. The opponents of veterinary examination said, with some justification, that in the time available the examination could be expected to detect only obvious cases which should not be exhibited in any case. In many instances, the mere fact that there was a veterinary examination acted as a deterrent to unscrupulous exhibitors.

A case might be argued for a system of certification at dog shows. A certificate of vaccination against DISTEMPER and HEPATITIS could be produced for every exhibit and in addition, a certificate of health stating that the dog had been examined by a veterinarian within the last forty-eight hours. Many continental European countries already operate this system.

Veterinary Medical Association, American see American Veterinary Medical Association.

Viciousness A vicious dog is one which has the vice of biting, or which is known to be likely to bite. In English Common Law, a person who keeps a dog which has been known to bite, or which has given clear indications that it would, is guilty of harbouring a vicious animal.

The shepherd's dog may bite an intruder. In this case, the dog has a desire to protect the property of its owner. Under the law, the dog may be considered to be a vicious animal, yet it is doing its duty, according to its instincts and its training.

Poorly trained, spoiled dogs sometimes learn the vice. Dogs which are chained may also become biters. Excessive barkers may show the type of shyness which leads to viciousness. Examples are dogs which bark furiously while backing away, and those which, while barking, try to circle behind you.

Right Viciousness can be the result of poor training. A vicious dog is a biter.

In some countries, provinces, or states, the courts have applied an absolute liability against the owner of a biting dog. In such areas, the dog is not allowed a single bite, and no excuse for biting is allowed.

The owner of a dog showing a tendency to viciousness must therefore consider whether the risk keeping such a dog is not greater than the pleasure and protection the dog might give. He must consider, in particular, the risk of serious injury to children. Since one can neither sell nor give away a vicious dog, the only course is to have it put to sleep.
See SHYNESS.

Vitamins Vitamins – except possibly vitamin B_{12} – are present in variable amounts in all natural foods. They are required for the maintenance of life, and for normal growth. They are not themselves food, and they do not supply nourishment, but are catalytic agents which help transform food into energy.

Except for vitamin C, vitamins cannot be synthesized adequately by the body. The dog appears to be able to synthesize some vitamins to a greater degree than man, yet not in sufficient quantities to sustain life.

In exceptional periods of stress, the dog may require vitamin C supplementation, and this vitamin has been shown to aid dogs in certain cases of non-specific dermatitis. Vitamin deficiencies often appear in groups. This is because one vitamin may aid another or may be dependent upon it. If, for example, a dog is suffering from vitamin A deficiency, it will be unable to synthesize sufficient vitamin C for its daily needs. It is for reasons such as this that *a vitamin* deficiency may be treated by multiple vitamin therapy.

Adult dogs are normally able to store vitamins for use in emergencies, so a vitamin deficiency may not become evident through its symptoms for a long time. Puppies, however, either cannot store vitamins, or use all those available in natural foods during the process of growing. For this reason deficiency symptoms appear immediately in puppies.

Vitamins are divided into two classes – fat soluble and water soluble. They are listed below, together with their chief functions and their sources of supply. It will be noted that, however varied their roles may be, many vitamins are interrelated in action.

Fat Soluble Vitamins

Vitamin A is necessary for development of the visual pigments in the eye which permit night sight. Lack of the vitamin induces night blindness. The vitamin is also necessary for skin health, and for the growth of both bones and teeth. Chief sources of vitamin A are meats.

Vitamin D is called the antirachitic vitamin because adequate amounts of it prevent RICKETS. It is thus involved in the absorption of minerals. Over-use of this vitamin can cause serious structural faults. Sources are fish-liver-oils, eggs, and salmon.

There are three closely related compounds called tocopherols, which are lumped together as vitamin E. Vitamin E is called the anti-sterility vitamin. Lack of sufficient E causes testicular damage in the male. This vitamin has shown remarkable ability to aid in lactation and in the production of healthy puppies by the bitch. It is also remarkable for aiding in endocarditis and myocarditis in dogs. (See HEART DISEASES.) Recent evidence indicates that vitamin E may help in treatment of Muscular Dystrophy, and in therapy for burns. Major sources of vitamin E are wheat germ and LIVER.

Vitamin K acts upon the liver to produce prothrombin, a substance essential to the clotting of the blood. Dogs obtain this vitamin in sufficient amounts for normal life.

Water Soluble Vitamins

Thiamine or vitamin B_1 is called aneurin in some countries. This vitamin is involved in proper appetite maintenance, in growth, and in carbohydrate utilization. It is called the antineuritic factor because it aids in nerve health. A thiamine deficiency is a major factor in heart disease.

Riboflavin, called vitamin B_2, or vitamin G, concerns itself with the health of the skin and muscles, in which it aids vitamin E, and it also promotes proper growth. It is essential in cellulose oxidation. It must be balanced with both thiamine and pyridoxine. Lack of riboflavin causes skin, ear, and eye diseases. Sources are liver, yeast, kidney, heart, soya flour, and wheat germ.

Niacin, or nicotinic acid, is needed for the oxidation of carbohydrates. It aids in intestinal health and in the proper functioning of the nervous system. Sources include meats, yeast, and cereals.

Pyridoxine, or vitamin B_6, is an anti-dermatitis factor. It also aids in fat metabolism, in the prevention of anaemia, and in the production of blood. It must be balanced with thiamine and riboflavin. Sources are wheat germ, yeast, egg yolk, and some vegetables. A pyridoxine deficiency may develop in diets too rich in proteins.

Pantothenic Acid is important for growth, hair and skin health, and to the proper functioning of the nervous system. Puppies require more of the vitamin than older dogs. Deficiency symptoms include gastritis, enteritis, convulsions, and even collapse. It is normally found in most foods, and as a supplement is obtained as calcium pantothenate.

Biotin, or vitamin H, is found in yeast, liver, molasses, and in some meats. Deficiency causes paralysis and dermatitis.

Folic Acid, or pteroylglutamic acid, is essential to growth, in the prevention of anaemia, and in lactation. It is often called the anti-anaemia factor. Sources are liver, green leaves (in dog foods, often alfalfa meal), and the fermentation solids left from brewing beer. It is essential for the intestinal growth of *Lactobacillus casei* bacteria.

Inositol, or Bios I, occurs in muscles, and in the tissues of the brain and eyes. It is essential in the growth of certain micro-organisms in the intestines and to the growth of puppies. It may play a part in correcting alopecia, or hair loss, in dogs.

Citrin, or vitamin P, is a compound crystalline substance, normally isolated from lemon juice. It is a valuable aid in diseases which tend to weaken the capillary walls.

Vitamin B_{12} is an anti-anaemia factor, and is a valuable supplement in all cases of lowered resistance to disease. It also aids in the promotion of growth.

A number of other vitamins are known, and in addition there are substances known as provitamins. These include carotene which, in the liver, is changed into vitamin A.

Vizsla The Vizsla, or Magyar Vizsla, is Hungary's most famous native hunting dog. It was developed upon the central Hungarian Plain, known as the Puszta, which is an agricultural area with large sheep grazing territories. The plain is also famous for its game, including ducks, geese, partridge, and giant hares.

It is here that the Vizsla, the Hungarian 'Yellow Pointer', was developed. Attempts have been made to give the breed a history dating back to the Magyar and other invasions of a thousand years ago. However, it appears more likely that the breed was developed quite recently, probably within this century. Its background may include Transylvanian pointing dogs, and the WEIMARANER of Germany.

Because of the area in which it was developed, the Vizsla is not a specialist used to hunt one kind of game only. Instead, it is expected to be equally efficient at hunting and tracking the hare, in pointing and retrieving upland game, and retrieving ducks and geese from the water. In Hungary, the dog is trained to work reasonably close to a hunter on foot. It is neither so fast nor so wide-ranging as the POINTER. But it is trained to search very carefully and diligently, and to produce the game

Right Vizsla. Waidman Nagy.

in front of its nose. For this purpose, it has excellent scenting ability for tracking and for air-borne scents.

The breed suffered severely between the two World Wars, and was kept alive only by the dedication of a few breeders. After 1945 many sportsmen and breeders left the country and took their dogs with them. The dogs immediately caught the eye of other European sportsmen. In the United States the Weimaraner had been having a sensational success, and Hungarians living there remembered their own 'Yellow Pointers', so the Vizsla was brought to America.

The Vizsla was recognized by the American Kennel Club in 1960, and the present standard was approved in 1963. A national SPECIALITY CLUB has been formed for it. Field trials for Vizslas alone are given, but many of the dogs enter the German Pointing Breeds trials and appear in some of the Pointer and Setter trials which are so popular in the United States and Canada. They do well in their own and in the German Pointing Breeds trials, where pointing, marking the fall, and retrieving, are required. But they lack the wide range of the American Pointers and setters.

Essentials of the breed: The Vizsla is of general Pointer type, but rather lightly built. The head is lean, though the skull is moderately wide between the ears. There is a median line down the forehead, and a moderate stop. The muzzle is slightly longer than the skull, the bite is scissors, and the nose is brown. A black or slate-grey nose is objectionable. The ears are thin, silky, set on low, rather long, with rounded ends, and they hang close to the cheeks. The eyes are of medium size and brown; yellow is objectionable.

The back is short. The chest reaches to the elbow, and is moderately broad. There is only a slight abdominal tuck-up. The tail is docked, about one third being removed. The stifles are only moderately angulated. Soundness in front and rear legs is required. The feet are cat-like, compact, and well knuckled up.

The standard calls for a solid coloured dog, ranging from rusty gold through shades of dark, sandy-yellow, with the darker shades preferred. A small white chest spot, and white spots on the feet, are permitted. Males are 22 to 24 inches at the shoulder; bitches, 21 to 23 inches. A deviation of more than two inches either way brings disqualification from the show ring. The coat is short, smooth, and close lying.
See colour plate p. 92.

Vomiting Dogs vomit easily, and even at will. There is an excellent anatomical reason why the dog can vomit so easily: it has an elastic oesophagus, or gullet. It can therefore swallow very large chunks of food. This also necessitates a large opening into the stomach. Contraction of the stomach muscles and diaphragm forces food back through the cardia, and up the gullet.

Dogs vomit for dozens of reasons. It is quite common to see show dogs vomit in the ring when the leash is held so tightly that the oesophagus or the larynx is squeezed. Dogs often vomit after eating large amounts of grass. Certain blood conditions, such as urea in the blood, bile in the blood, or a sudden dropping in the volume of

blood being pumped through the body, can cause vomiting. When dogs suffer from diseases of the kidneys or other organs, emesis is caused by 'reflex irritation'.

Other causes of vomiting are obstructions of the bowel, foreign bodies lodged in the throat or oesophagus, obstruction at the pyloric valve, and such diseases as nephritis, metritis, peritonitis, and those of the ear and brain.

Prolonged vomiting destroys the delicate water balance in the body, and can be serious for the dog. In such cases, veterinary help should be sought.

Emetics are discussed under POISONS and their antidotes.

W

Walleye One with a whitish iris, also called a blue eye, fish eye, pearl eye, or glass eye.

War Dogs Almost since the beginning of recorded history, there are references to dogs as adjuncts to soldiers. War dogs do not necessarily fight but are valuable for other reasons. Homer mentions the use of dogs as messengers. Messages were tied to the collars of the dogs, and the dogs were then sent back to headquarters. Armies have used dogs as sentries, not only to guard camps, but to detect enemies approaching the front lines, as in the trench warfare of World War I.

A frieze from Pergamon, carved about 280 B.C., shows large Assyrian attack dogs with huge heads, short, strong muzzles and pricked ears. Herodotus, in writing of the battle between the Perenthi and the Paeoni, said: 'Man was matched against man, horse against horse, and dog against dog.' Many of these dogs wore collars ingeniously designed so that sharp knives or spikes stuck out at various angles. These severely injured both men and horses.

Huge dogs of ancient Britain, usually called MASTIFFS, were taken by the Romans to fight wild beasts in the arenas, but the Gauls used them as battle dogs, and put armour on them. Henry VIII of England sent 400 Mastiffs to Charles V of Spain for his war against France. The dogs were used in battle and also on reconnaissance.

Columbus, and later the Conquistadors, made use of dogs. Bartolome de las Casas wrote of the dogs which were taught to rip open the bellies of Indians. Las Casas said one dog could 'bite out the bellies' of a hundred Indians an hour. Las Casas wrote that on his second voyage, Columbus reached shore near Montego Bay, Jamaica, and added: '. . . and a dog which they let loose from the ship chased them (the Indians) and did them great hurt, for a dog is worth ten men against the Indians'. Las Casas also wrote: 'They feed their fierce dogs with human flesh or purpose to accustom them to tear men to pieces and devour them. They carry these dogs with them wherever they go, and barbarously murder the poor Indians to feed these savage curs.'

The fear with which the Indians regarded the dogs can best be shown in a story told by Colonel Joaquin Acosta, who wrote about the advance of the Spaniards against Bogota, in Colombia. 'Although the tribes of these valleys put up some resistance, they were soon broken down and routed by the horses [cavalry] for they held them in such terror that one night when the Spaniards were encamped close to a little village . . . two or three horses that had got loose and galloped through the valley neighing and jumping, were sufficient to disperse the Indians, who thought they were as ferocious as the bloodhounds, and argued that if the dogs made such havoc in their ranks, how much more terrible the larger animals must be.'

In World War I, French and Belgian draft dogs were used to haul machine guns and parts, and the French also used sledge dogs in the mountains. Both sides used dogs to search out the wounded and to bring them medical supplies. These dogs, called 'Red Cross dogs', also guided medical corps men to the wounded.

Towards the end of the war, the French captured a section of the German front line trenches. There they found a GERMAN SHEPHERD bitch with puppies. One of the litter became *Rin Tin Tin*, perhaps the most famous motion picture dog of all time.

All nations used dogs during World War II. Their chief use was as sentries. Dogs guarded all military installations, and they accompanied soldiers on beach

patrols. Some dogs were trained to lead reconnaissance patrols. They prevented ambush in jungle and mountainous territory. Other dogs carried machine gun parts, ammunition, and medical supplies.

Many breeds worked in the wars. German Shepherds and DOBERMANN PINSCHERS were the breeds chiefly used for sentry and patrol work. Arctic breeds hauled sledges and carried back-packs in the mountains. But the shortage of dogs of these breeds required the inclusion of dogs of other breeds and mongrels. In general, the dogs used weighed more than 40 lb. Small dogs, however, sometimes proved very valuable. A YORKSHIRE TERRIER, called *Smokey*, was found in a shell hole near Nadzab, New Guinea. Smokey came into the possession of an American soldier, William Wynne, who taught her tricks. At Lingayen, the U.S. Signal Corps had to run a telephone wire through an eight-inch pipe under an airstrip. Smokey hauled the wire 70 feet through the pipe.

Most armies now have their own breeding programmes. The German Shepherd is the most favoured breed. During peace, the dogs guard military installations along with human sentries, but reconnaissance, messenger and sledge dogs are still taught to work. See illustration p. 460.

Left Vizsla. Kisujfaldui Dani, winner of numerous awards in show and field in Hungary.

Right War Dogs. A detail showing armoured dogs from 'The Temptation of St. Anthony', painted around 1500 by Hieronymus Bosch. This is no flight of fancy: in medieval times dogs really did go into the field wearing suits of armour.

Above War Dogs. German Shepherd Dogs being trained for combat against guerillas in Vietnam.

Warmth see Heating of Kennels and Living Quarters.

Warts Warts, or verrucae, are benign TUMOURS of the skin. At least some forms of warts are infectious. Some are believed to be congenital – present at or before birth; others are acquired, and some dogs may inherit a predisposition to them.

In dogs, particularly in puppies, dozens of warts may appear simultaneously on the lips, tongue, palate, pharynx, cheeks, and epiglottis. Their sudden appearance is frightening. In some cases, they disappear almost as suddenly, and thereafter, the dog appears to be immune.

The viral origin of oral warts seems certain, but the means of transmission is not known. On the whole, warts are so species-specific (usually confined to one species) that transfer from one species of animal to another is rare.

A second type, called cutaneous, occurs in dogs of all ages, though chiefly in elderly animals. The warts may appear singly, or in small groups or colonies. They appear on the head, penis, prepuce, and often accompany chronic otitis on the inner ear.

An old remedy for cutaneous warts which is still used with some success is a daily application of castor oil. Vaccination has had varied success for many years. Some students of warts have reported successes; others have reported none. Recently, vaccines prepared from bovine wart tissues have shown some ability to protect dogs from warts. In some cases of surgical excision of a wart by a veterinarian, other warts have regressed slowly and finally disappeared. It is possible that some of the viruses escape into the bloodstream, which then builds antibodies to destroy the other warts. However, it is often noted that when warts are removed chemically, they tend to return, or to regenerate.

Wax in Ear see Ear Diseases.

Weaning This is an important stage in a puppy's life and must be completed very gradually and gently. Serious digestive troubles can be caused at this transitional period from the dam's milk to more solid food. The age at which weaning should begin depends much on the size of the litter and how well the bitch is feeding the puppies herself. With a small litter and a dam who has plenty of milk, three to four weeks is about the time to start getting the youngsters on to their new food. With a large litter weaning may start at three weeks or even earlier.

Normally the puppies are first introduced to a milk feed and this can be any baby milk food mixed to the correct consistency. A small quantity of warm milk should be poured into a small shallow dish and placed in front of the puppy. If the puppy shows no interest its nose should be gently forced into the milk. A little taste is usually sufficient to make it go back for more. It might be necessary to moisten a finger in the milk and let the drops fall into the puppy's mouth. The puppies will soon learn, and for the first few days just one meal a day should be given. From the start puppies should be fed separately as there are always the greedy ones in a litter ready to defeat the more gentle ones, which will obviously suffer. By the end of the first week of weaning, the puppies should be having two good milk meals thus relieving the strain on the bitch. By now they will have learned to lap well and at this stage the introduction of scraped raw meat sold for human consumption is advisable. A tiny amount should be given to each puppy twice a day, alternating with the two milk feeds. The meat meal is usually accepted with great relish but if there is any difficulty this can be overcome by rubbing the scraped meat on the puppy's gum when it very quickly realizes that meat is something good to eat.

At seven weeks the puppies should be weaned. The size of the meals should have been gradually increased over the period. By this time the bitch should be ready to leave her puppies and should certainly be away all day, returning only at night. She should be allowed to do this as long as she seems interested. This will not only keep her contented but it will ensure that her puppies are kept warm at night.

Right Weimaraner. Ch. Coninvale Paul of Acombdale.

A different method of weaning springs from recent work in large experimental kennels which has shown that puppies should be allowed to wean themselves. They can be weaned directly on to the food being fed to the dam. There is then no stress in the puppies, caused by a radical change in diet. The food is that which they will eat during their entire lives. However, some commercial foods are made especially for puppies. These chiefly differ in bite sizes.

The procedure is to leave a pan of food where four-week-old, and exploring, puppies will find it. They will start to nibble it. Often, the dam will show the puppies how to eat it. By the time they are six weeks old, the puppies will be entirely weaned.

As most puppies harbour roundworms they should be dosed for these when they reach about six weeks old. It is inadvisable to do this sooner unless it is obvious that the puppies' progress is being retarded. Professional advice should be sought if earlier worming seems necessary.

At eight weeks the puppies should be ready to go to new homes. This is a big step in a puppy's life and to help smooth this transition period it is advisable to give the new owner a diet sheet so that the puppy can continue with the same food it has already known. A change of environment for a puppy can be quite an ordeal. If its diet can be kept the same until it gets accustomed to its new surroundings this can help it settle down and avoid digestive upsets.

Weaving Crossing the forefeet or hind feet when in motion.

Weight of Dogs Men have always had the tendency to exaggerate the size of their dogs. For this reason, claims of unusually heavy weight for an individual, or a breed, must be doubted until accurate scales have proved the claim.

It is generally accepted that the ST. BERNARD is the heaviest of all dogs, on average. *The Guinness Book of World Records* lists two English St. Bernards as being the heaviest whose weight was ever recorded. The first, *Brandy*, owned by Miss Gwendoline L. White of Chinnor, Oxfordshire, weighed 259 lb. on 11 February, 1966. Another, *Westernisles Ross*, owned by Jean R. Rankin of Glasgow, Scotland, weighed 256 lb. on 28 April 1966.

At the St. Bernard Club of America national specialty show in 1963, eighty-eight St. Bernards were weighed upon a certified scales. The heaviest was *Ch. Powell's Tristan of Riga*, owned by Laurence Powell, which weighed 217 lb. Several others weighed about 200 lb. Most of the adult males ranged between 150 and 195 lb. Adult bitches ranged from 120 to 186 lb., though the average for bitches of good quality was 130 to 170 lb.

Few weights have been taken of MASTIFFS, but there is a record of one very large dog which weighed 208 lb.

Among the small breeds, adult CHIHUAHUAS may weigh as little as $2\frac{3}{4}$ lb. and POMERANIANS from $2\frac{7}{8}$ lb.

Weimaraner Some forty years ago, an authority on German sporting dogs wrote that the Weimaraner Vorstehund, or Weimar Pointer, was seldom seen at field trials, although it showed great intelligence at work. There were then less than 1,000 Weimaraners living, and all but a handful of these were in Germany. Yet the author bravely predicted that future prospects

Above Weimaraner. Ch. Ballinda of Merse-side.

for the breed were greater than they had been in the past.

The author could never have imagined the startling success the dog was to have in the United States and Canada. Nor could he guess that the breed would radiate out to many other parts of the world.

A grey dog, which looks similar to the Weimaraner, is shown in a painting by Van Dyck about 1631. There is no other evidence to indicate the breed's background. The best guesses are that it results from crosses of the ST. HUBERT, or other French hounds, BLOODHOUNDS, the rare German Schweisshunds, and possibly pointers.

It appears to have become a reasonably distinct grey hunting dog about 1810. Grand Duke Karl August of Weimar, the capital of Thuringia, is given credit for developing the breed, and for making it popular with his noblemen.

The breed was further developed by a private group of sportsmen. They bred for dogs which would enter the water to retrieve water fowl. They even attempted to blend the ability of trailing dogs with that of the pointing breeds. Thus, they were attempting to produce a true, all-purpose hunting dog.

The Weimaraner was recognized in Germany as a distinct breed in 1896. A year later, 20 June 1897, Weimaraner owners met at Erfort and organized the Weimaraner Club of Germany. The club was not formed to popularize the breed, but to save it from extinction – the club felt that the grey colour and all-round usefulness of the Weimaraner had to be saved.

Many German breed clubs have tried to supervise breeding. The Weimaraner Club did likewise. At first, no one could own a Weimaraner without joining the club. The new owner would then have to obey the club rules. Only approved dogs – approved or certified by a breed master or breed committee – could be mated. If the breeding was made without prior approval, the litter could not be registered. Puppies considered to be unfit had to be destroyed, and at one time puppies were only sold to members of the Weimaraner Club. A Major Herber, who died in 1939, enforced these rules, and is credited with producing the modern breed.

An American sportsman, Howard Knight of Providence, Rhode Island, hunted with Weimaraner owners in Germany. The all-round ability of the dogs impressed him. In 1929, he joined the Weimaraner Club of Germany, and then brought two dogs to the United States. German breeders of other breeds used to guard their stock so zealously that they often sterilized dogs sold for export and, Knight discovered that this had been done to his dogs. Nine years later, however, he

above Weimaraner. Ch. Wolfox Bittersweet.

imported some fertile dogs. These were a male, *Mars aus der Wolfsreide*, a bitch, *Dorle von Schwarzen Kamp*, and a bitch in whelp, *Aura Von Gaiberg*. With these dogs, Knight had broken the German ban, and other dogs were shortly imported. Knight did not sell dogs. He gave them to hunting friends. Later, he turned his entire kennel over to the Grafmar Kennels of Mr. and Mrs. A. F. Horn.

The Knight and Horn policy made it possible to control both ownership and breeding. The Weimaraner Club of America was founded in 1941, with Knight as president. In 1943, the American Kennel Club officially recognized the breed. Club members had to agree not to sell or give puppies to non-members, and to

obey breeding rules, to destroy unfit puppies, and so on. Club membership jumped phenomenally, and within five years, the Weimaraner Club of America had become one of the richest of all breed clubs. It hired famed publicist-author Jack Denton Scott, and from then on, the breed received a fantastic amount of publicity through newspapers, radio, magazines, and later, television. But North America is a vast area, and the parent club could not police its members. Puppies began to be sold to non-members, and at prices never before realized in any breed.

Though the breed had come to America advertized as a super field dog, it first made its mark in obedience competition. One dog won its Companion Dog degree in three straight shows even before the breed had been officially recognized. Another won the title in straight shows and only two days after reaching six months old – the earliest date upon which it could officially compete.

Today, the Weimaraner has settled down to steady registrations within the thirty most popular dogs in the United States. In 1970, 6,898 dogs were registered. Five licensed American Kennel Club field trials were held for the breed in 1969, but Weimaraners also competed in thirty-five trials which had stakes for other breeds as well. In addition, many Weimaraners compete in trials held under AMERICAN FIELD jurisdiction. Weimaraner history in Canada has followed, or paralleled, that in the United States. The breed is less well known in England.

Essentials of the breed: The muzzle from tip of the nose to the stop equals the distance from the stop to the prominent occipital crest. The ears are long, lobular, and are set high. The eyes are shades of amber, or grey or blue-grey. The teeth form a scissors bite, and there should be no missing teeth. The back is of moderate length and forms a straight, but sloping line, from the withers to the set-on of the tail. The chest reaches to the elbow and the abdomen is moderately tucked up. The tail is docked to be six inches long at maturity.

The forelegs are straight and strong, and the distance from the elbow to the ground should approximate to that from the elbow to the highest point of the withers. The hindquarters are well angulated. The toes are webbed and strongly arched. The nails are grey. Dewclaws should be removed.

The Weimaraner is a dog of medium height, 25 to 27 inches at the withers for males, and 23 to 25 inches for bitches. A deviation greater than one inch either way is a disqualification. So is a distinctly long coat. The colour varies from mouse-grey to silver-grey, with lighter shades on the head and ears. A small white spot on the chest is permitted, but white on any other part of the body is to be severely penalized. The nose is grey; the lips and gums pinkish.
See colour plate p. 92.

Welsh Corgi, Cardigan In the original Celtic tongue, *corgi* meant dog. Tradition in Britain states that, after the Norman Conquest in 1066, the Normans prohibited the native Britons from owning the 'blue blooded' Norman dogs – the dogs later to be known as the BLOODHOUND and the GREYHOUND. *Corgi* became corrupted to *curgi*, and finally to *cur*, and this word carried, as it does today, the meaning of mongrel.

Etymologists have a different view of the origin of the word, 'Corgi': *cor* means 'dwarf' and *gi* means 'dog'. According to them, the word does not appear until the time of Chaucer, perhaps about 1360.

In the beginning, if the Celtic legend be true, there was only one Welsh Corgi. The dog certainly was a dwarf dog. It was also a cattle driver. It could nip at the heels of cattle to keep them moving, and to keep them on the trail. It was small and agile enough to avoid the kicks of the cattle. The dog also served as a home guardian. Because of its isolated position in the south of Wales, it remained a relatively pure breed. It was also a DOMINANT type, so that occasional crosses quickly disappeared without altering the type of the breed. The dog resembles the Swedish Vallhund, a slightly taller farm dog, which also claims Celtic origin.

In 1925, Corgis began to appear at English dog shows. The Cardigan and the Pembroke (see WELSH CORGI, PEMBROKE) were then shown as one breed. In 1927, CRUFT'S gave separate classes for the two varieties, and in 1934, the English Kennel Club classified the breeds separately. Recognition as separate breeds followed in most of the world's Kennel Clubs. The Cardigan has never achieved the popularity of the Pembroke, though it grew in favour during the late 1960s.

Essentials of the breed: The head is moderately broad and flat between the ears, and the muzzle is in proportion to the skull in a ratio of three to five. The muzzle is neither pointed nor blunt, but is less blunt than in the Pembroke. The nose is black. The eyes are medium to large, and amber in colour. Blue eyes, or one blue and one black, are permitted in blue merles. A scissors bite is preferred, but a level bite is permitted.

The ears are large and prominent, slightly rounded at the tips, erect and sloping slightly forward when at attention. Flopping ears are a serious fault. The neck is muscular and well developed. The chest is broad, deep, and well let down. The forelegs are short, strong, slightly bowed around the chest, with a distinct but not exaggerated crook below the carpus or wrist. The elbows fit close to the body. A straight terrier front is a fault. The body is long, strong, with well sprung ribs and moderate tuck-up. The topline is level, except for a slight slope of spine above the tail. The hindquarters are muscular, with short, well-formed legs and round, well-padded feet.

The tail is long, or moderately long, and resembles a fox brush. It is set fairly low on the body line, and is carried low. At a run, the tail streams out behind, but is lifted during excitement or while tracking. It must never be carried over the back. A rat or whip tail is a serious fault.

The coat is of medium length, dense, slightly harsh, but not wiry. Very short or long, silky or curly coats are faulted. A distinctly long coat disqualifies.

The colours are red, sable, red-brindle, black-brindle,

Welsh Corgi, Cardigan.
Top Ch. Rozaval Blue Glint.
Above Ch. Echium of Hezelclos

black, tri-colour, and blue merle. Usually there are white flashings on the chest, neck, feet, face, or tip of the tail. Pure white disqualifies, and predominantly white is a serious fault.

The standard calls for a dog approximately 12 inches tall at the shoulders, and with a length of 36 to 44 inches from the tip of the nose to the tip of the tail. General balance is of the greatest importance.
See colour plate p. 304.

Welsh Corgi, Pembroke The Welsh Corgi from Pembrokeshire is said to have been a dwarf dog brought to England by Flemish weavers about the year 1100. The weavers, or some of them, eventually moved into the southwest corner of Wales. These dogs, much like those of Cardiganshire (see WELSH CORGI,

CARDIGAN), were essentially cattle drivers. Since the weavers were craftsmen, it is not explained how they happened to have drovers' dogs, except that the small size of the dogs made them ideal house dogs.

A different origin is therefore suggested for the Pembroke Corgi from that of the Cardigan. Since the Pembroke is believed to have originated among the Flemish, it is claimed that the dog descends from the great family of SPITZ dogs. It would then be related to the KEESHOND and SCHIPPERKE. Such a relationship might be given strength by the similarity of the fox-like heads of these breeds, but it would not explain the large ears, the long body, and the fact that some of the Pembrokes have been born tail-less, though Schipperke breeders have claimed that specimens of their breed have been born without tails.

The Pembroke and Cardigan dogs were inter-bred in the early years of this century. Apparently, this was done by the importation of Cardigan puppies into Pembrokeshire, rather than the other way round. After 1934, when the two types of dog were given separate

Above Welsh Corgi, Pembroke.
Ch. Lees Pennyfarthing of Treland.

breed status, the Pembroke began a remarkable rise in popularity. This was partly due to the ownership of several generations of Pembrokes by the British royal family. In 1936, King George VI bought *Rozavel Golden Eagle* for his daughters, now Queen Elizabeth and Princess Margaret, and this patronage assured the popularity of the Pembroke.

The breed is now known the world over, and is one of the most popular breeds in Australia. The Pembroke now far outnumbers its older relative, the Cardigan. The greater progenitor of the breed was *Rozavel Red Dragon*, who was born tail-less.

Essentials of the breed: The head is foxy, with a fairly broad skull, which is flat between the ears and has a moderate stop. The foreface is in the proportion of three

to five with the skull. The muzzle tapers. The nose is black. The eyes are well set, hazel, or blending with the coat colour. The ears are pricked, of medium size, with rounded tips. A line from the tip of the nose, through the eye, should pass through or close to the tip of the ear when erect. The bite is level or scissors.

The neck is fairly long. The forelegs are short, and as straight as possible. They curve slightly around the chest, which is both deep and broad. The elbows should be neither loose nor tied. The body is of medium length, and is not short-coupled. The top line is level. The hind legs are well angulated, and the hocks are straight when viewed from behind. The feet are oval, strong, and well arched. The tail is docked short, or the dog may be born tail-less.

The standard calls for a dog 10 to 12 inches at the shoulder and weighing 24 to 28 lb. There are self-colours in sable, red, fawn, and there are black and tans, and many with white markings on the legs, chest, and neck. Some white on the head and foreface is permitted. The coat is of medium length and dense, but not wiry.

See colour plate p. 304.

Welsh Springer Spaniel The Welsh dog breeds are the WELSH TERRIER, the WELSH CORGIS, and the Welsh Springer Spaniel.

Three dogs, but not these same breeds, are mentioned in the Laws of Howel Dda, a Welsh ruler of the tenth century. An extract reads, 'There are three higher species of dog; a tracker, a greyhound, and a spaniel'. It then explains that the spaniel was of equal value to a stallion or the King's buckhound.

Curiously enough, this reference to 'spaniels' precedes the introduction of Spanish dogs to Britain. More interesting, an old Welsh law of AD 300 mentions 'our native spaniel'. It is extremely doubtful if many people in Wales had heard of Spain at this time. The evidence suggests that both breeds and names are unconnected with the Iberian peninsula.

One theory is that these charming red and white Welsh Spaniels came with the Gauls in pre-Roman times. Certainly they are remarkably like the Breton Spaniels which have been centred in Brittany for centuries.

The colouring of both breeds is distinctive. It was first commented on by Dr. Caius in his book *English Dogges* of c. 1570. He wrote of 'the Spaniels whose skins are white and if they are marked with any spottes they are commonly red'. He failed to mention the brilliance of the white: it positively gleams. Moreover it stays that way because even the caked mud of a hard day's shooting brushes off with ease.

Other good points are that these dogs have a minimum of unnecessary hair on legs and ears, and are also easier to house and feed than the larger LABRADOR, but are more willing to do its job. They will also do the rough-shooting work of a COCKER SPANIEL. And being slightly larger, are even better fitted to explore dense undergrowth.

Welsh Springer Spaniels have never been fashionable dogs. Even today a mere 200 or so a year are registered

Welsh Springer Spaniel.
Above left Trigger of Tregwillym
Above Ch. Bruce of Brent.

in Britain, and, in 1970, only 16 in the United States. But in the farms and cottages of Wales there are hundreds more, unmistakably pure, despite homespun names like *Meg* and *Di*, and a total absence of documentary evidence. Most are kept for work. Apart from being tireless hunters, they are frequently used to drive cattle and herd sheep. The dog has clearly won its many friends, however, through its prowess in the hunting field.

Prints in old books frequently show the sportsman of bygone days accompanied by a type of spaniel, which may be recognized (without any difficulty) as a passable Welsh Springer. For centuries Welsh sportsmen have recognized the worth of this particular breed, and fostered them as sporting dogs. They used to be smaller than they are now, and seldom, if ever, were tails docked.

When they were first introduced into the show ring they were known as 'Welsh Cockers' and it was not until 1902 that the Kennel Club of England recognized their existence. They then became 'Welsh Springers'. A dog belonging to Mr. A. T. Williams, of Ynys-y-Gerwn, near Neath, Wales, was registered in 1901 as a Cocker and won many prizes. In 1902 it became a Springer; and went on winning.

A painting by Gainsborough hangs in Buckingham Palace showing Queen Charlotte, wife of King George III with a dog at her feet. The animal is always assumed to be a KING CHARLES SPANIEL. It might well be an early but typical Welsh Springer Spaniel.

Essentials of the breed: Skull: of moderate length, slightly domed with clearly defined stop. Muzzle: medium length, straight, and fairly square. Eyes: hazel or dark. Ears: set moderately low and hanging close to the cheeks, comparatively small and narrowing towards the tip. Jaw: strong and level. Neck: long, muscular and clean. Forelegs should be of medium length, and moderately feathered. Body: strong and muscular with deep brisket, and length in proportion to length of leg. Hindquarters should be strong, muscular, wide and fully developed. Feet: round, firm and cat-like with thick pads. Tail should be set on low, carried level with the back, and lively in action. Coat: straight or flat, and thick, of a silky texture, never wiry, wavy or curly. Colour: rich dark red and white. Weight: 35 to 45 lb.
See colour plate p. 88.

Welsh Terrier The Welsh Terrier could be said to be a miniature AIREDALE. It is vaguely like a black-and-tan FOX TERRIER, of which more later, and it is remarkably similar to a LAKELAND TERRIER. There are of course minor differences of size, colour and type, but these are more readily discernible by an expert than by a layman. Probably each was developed by fanciers unaware of the existence of the other.

Histories of the Welsh Terrier insist that it is an ancient breed. Even so, no reference to it can be found in writings of more than 100 years ago. This may well be because they had not then been named, or because Wales was relatively isolated until railways opened up Britain between 1825 and 1850.

North Wales appears to have favoured this type of dog but a similar black-and-tan terrier existed throughout the British Isles. Mountain foxes are difficult to hunt. The terriers used against them must be persistent. They must gallop with hounds and sometimes they must even *work* as hounds!

A family called Jones who lived for many generations at Ynysfor in the mountains adjoining Merionethshire and Caernarvonshire worked black- or blue-and-tan terriers from about 1750, mainly in OTTERHOUND packs.

They would not have considered them likely show-bench terriers. But early in the 1880's some specimens of the breed appeared at shows. Soon afterwards, local fanciers formed a Welsh Terrier Club. Descriptions of this first show held in Pwllheli in 1885 are amusing. There were three classes, each with thirty entries. The judges, two ageing Welsh squires, promptly sent to a nearby cottage for armchairs. Two heavy specimens of blackened oak were produced and the judges occupied them throughout the afternoon. They had each dog produced separately. They discussed it; agreed on good and bad points; made careful notes; and announced their awards and placings without bringing the dogs together for comparison.

At around this time a faction in the North of England tried to get a similar if slightly more refined terrier recognized as 'Old English Broken-Haired Terriers'. Exercising Solomon's wisdom, the Kennel Club agreed to classify both breeds together as 'Welsh Terriers or Old English Wire-Haired Terriers'.

The compromise satisfied no one. But whereas the English faction disagreed amongst themselves, the Welsh stood behind their Welsh Terrier Club and ultimately persuaded the Kennel Club to rule that 'whether of Welsh or English descent, all black-and-tan broken-haired terriers will be officially known as Welsh Terriers'.

Few would deny that the breed's appearance has since changed. Walter Glyn, an authority, hinted at the reason in 1932. He wrote: 'If you cross Welsh Terriers with even a white dog the issue will be black-and-tans; and if that issue is bred back to a Welsh Terrier it will breed black-and-tans'. He went on to say that a dishonest person could fake a pedigree to 'get a cross of Fox Terrier into the breed and exhibit impure specimens as pure bred Welsh'.

This must be true, and in fact the result has been a smartening-up of the breed. The secret was, of course, not to go too far. While still retaining its essential ruggedness, the Welsh has since achieved much in the show world. Despite the breed's numerical inferiority, a Welsh named *Ch. Twinstar Dyma Fi* was made Supreme Champion of CRUFT'S in 1951. Another 'Welshman', *Ch. Sandstorm Saracen* succeeded again in 1959.

Welsh Terrier.
Right Alert and active, the Welsh Terrier resembles in many ways the Airedale and Lakeland Terriers. *Below* Ch. Philtown Parader.

Essentials of the breed: The skull should be flat and wider between the ears than the Wire-Haired Fox Terrier. The jaw should be powerful, clean-cut, deep and punishing, the whole head being more masculine than that of a Fox Terrier. Eyes should be small, dark, expressive and keen. Ears: V-shaped, small, set on fairly high, carried forward and close to the cheek. Mouth: level. The neck should be of moderate length and thickness, slightly arched. The shoulders should be long, sloping and well set back. The legs straight and muscular. The back must be short and well ribbed-up, and the loin strong. Hindquarters: strong, with muscular thighs, hocks well let down, ample bone. The feet should be small, round and catlike. The tail should be well set on but not gay.

Coat must be wiry, hard and close. Colour: black-and-tan is preferred; alternatively black grizzle-and-tan, free from black pencilling on toes.

Height: should not exceed 15½ inches. Weight: 20–21 lb.

West Highland White Terrier Great Britain exports a large number of dogs, usually around twelve thousand per year, of which the majority go to the United States. Usually the world demands those breeds which are popular in Britain. Recently, however, foreign buyers have concentrated on the West Highland White. The 'Westie' has a charm easily overlooked, so it is often underestimated.

Originally the West Highland was merely a variety of CAIRN TERRIER. It had similar short legs, harsh coat, gaily carried tail, and foxy-faced head. It differed only in colour. And like all odd-men-out, it was disliked and mistrusted. These white 'sports' have always existed and over 300 years ago James I sent to Argyllshire for 'six little white earth-dogges' which he presented to the King of France.

But this had been forgotten by the latter part of the last century; and Cairn Terrier breeders were ashamed of the occasional white puppy. They regarded them as

West Highland White Terrier.
Left Two 'Westies' at a show wait their turn to go into the ring.
Right Ch. Highstile Priceless.

skeletons in the cupboard, and drowned them at birth.

Fortunately the Malcolms of Portalloch thought differently. They felt that a dog used to destroy vermin in the tangled rocks and crags of the Highlands was all the better for being white, because it was easier to see and less likely to merge with the drab background. So while most Cairn breeders were busy eliminating whites, the Malcolms deliberately worked the other way: eliminating all the coloured dogs from their strain. By the time Colonel Malcolm publicly introduced Westies at dog shows around 1900, they were firmly established. This keen fancier admitted that his father and grandfather had done all the groundwork in the previous century.

The Westie left its Highland home and went south to England before the Cairn. It met with a good reception. In 1907, it was recognized by the Kennel Club. The Cairn arrived in 1909 and found the white upstart already holding the floor. It held it for ten years until slowly the Cairn gained ground.

The Westie has always been a great favourite at dog shows, particularly with judges. Over the years it has won almost every honour on the show bench, and its run of success looks likely to endure.

As with all breeds, however, ultimate success revolves round its suitability for the home. Here it has many advantages. It is the perfect pet dog for the man who likes a terrier but feels that many are too volatile. The Westie has courage but seldom picks a fight. It is a hardy outdoor dog which willingly accepts suburban surroundings. It is a good companion for children yet content with modest exercise; smart, but not in need of constant 'barbering'.

There are some who think that white dogs collect more dirt. It is not true; they merely show the dirt. And when that happens to a Westie, five minutes with a chalk block and a stiff brush soon puts matters right.

Essentials of the breed: The skull should be slightly domed with a slight tapering from the ears to the eyes. The head should be thickly coated. The foreface tapering from eye to the muzzle. There is a distinct stop. Jaws should be strong and level; the nose must be black. Eyes should be set wide apart, medium-sized and dark. Ears should be small, erect and terminating in a sharp point. The teeth should be large and a scissors-bite is preferred. Neck: fairly long and muscular. The shoulders should be sloped backwards. Body: compact. Back: level. Loins: broad and strong. The chest should be deep and the ribs well arched, the hindquarters strong and muscular, wide across the top. Legs: short and muscular, the hocks bent. The forefeet are larger than the hind, round, thickly padded and covered with short hard hair. Tail: 5 to 6 inches long, covered with hard hair and carried jauntily. Coat: pure white, hard, about 2 inches long and free from any curl. Height: dogs about 11 inches, bitches about one inch less.
See colour plate p. 377.

Westminster Dog Show The first Westminster Kennel Club dog show was held in New York at Gilmore's Gardens 8–11 May 1877, with 1,177 dogs entered. A commentator of the day, 'Shirley Dare' wrote: 'We must be glad to hear that the show was a success. Possibly the Westminster Kennel Club may find it prudent to repeat the display often . . .' The

Westminster did find it prudent to do so. The show has been held annually since, and is the oldest annual event of its kind in the United States. Despite his hope that the dog show might be given again, 'Shirley Dare' was not especially complimentary: writing in *The Spirit of the Times* – The American Gentleman's Magazine – he had this to say:

'Speaking out of the depths of native ignorance, I assert that the extremely high-bred dogs of the bench show were the ugliest of their kind . . . the standard seems to be a select and formulated ugliness. The St. Bernards quite destroyed the romance attaching to their names by proving, one and all, uncompromising red or yellow dogs, with a savage cast of countenance. I should think that anyone lost in the snow, finding one of these monster St. Bernards pawing over him with its usual expression, would immediately expect to be saved from freezing by being eaten alive.'

And later: 'The great Siberians, for instance, brindled like tigers, with their ears cut short, images of cruel, despotic power, their enormous heads, thick as if hewn square, a cold savagery in their eyes as if they had eaten convicts till all the hate and despair of the lost had concentrated itself in that dreadful regard.'

The show had a large toy entry, and of them, Dare wrote: 'It is hard to understand the predilection of the ladies for the tiny, useless pet dogs that formed so large a class. The toy terriers and Greyhounds, thin, shivering, palpitating morsels, were an affliction to anyone used to healthy, natural dogs'. But Dare found the Mastiffs 'calm, full of dignity, and quiet friendliness', and he found that 'most of the dogs seemed eager for notice, and it was a sweet surprise to meet the entire trust and frank affection'.

The origin of Westminster is interesting. A group of sportsmen used to meet in the bar of the long vanished Westminster Hotel. They formed a club and built a boarding and training kennel for their hunting dogs. They hired a trainer, and imported some dogs from England to use with their locally bred dogs. They named their club Westminster after the hotel. And they made their club emblem with the head of *Sensation*, an imported POINTER. *Sensation* seems to have been less of a success than the celebrated race horse, born in 1877, which was named after him.

William Tileston was chairman of the first show, and Charles Lincoln was the superintendent for the first six years. James Mortimer was superintendent for the next thirty-one years and George W. Gall for the following twelve, George F. Foley for forty-three years after that. William Rauch held office as show chairman for 27 years, 1901 through 1927.

The 1880 show was held at the original Madison Square Garden, New York. Except for seven years, it has been held in the first, or the two succeeding Madison Square Gardens. For this reason, American and Canadian dog fanciers have long known the event as simply 'the Garden Show'.

The lowest show entry was in 1885 with 950 dogs. The highest came in 1937 with 3,146 dogs and 3,629 entries. But space limitations finally forced the show to limit entries to the 2,500th arrival through the mail. And as

a rule, entries closed early in December. Further restrictions included the banning of puppies and dogs which had not won a blue ribbon. The show was then limited to dogs winning a major point rating, to Open classes only, and to Champions.

The present Madison Square Garden Center is even smaller than either of the 'old Gardens'. For that reason, the 1970 show started a new system, limiting entries to 3,000 and benching the dogs of three groups on one day, and the other three on the second day. The 1970 show failed to meet its limited entry quota of 3,000 dogs, possibly because the new system was unfamiliar to all but California fanciers.

The Smooth FOX TERRIER, *Ch. Warren Remedy*, owned by Winthrop Rutherford, won Best in Show in 1907, 1908, and 1909. No other dog since then has been able to do this. However, Hermann Mellenthin's black AMERICAN COCKER SPANIEL, *Ch. My Own Brucie* came

Above Westminster Dog Show. The front page of a New York paper showing entries to the first Westminster Dog Show held at Gilmore's Gardens in 1877.

close to it. He was Best American-bred in 1939, and Best in Show in 1940 and 1941. Wire-haired Fox Terriers have been Best in Show 12 times since 1907, and terriers have captured the top honour 32 times since 1907. Four BOXERS have been Best in Show since 1947.

Wheaten Fawn, or pale yellow, tending towards red.

Wheel Back The strongly arched back of some GREYHOUNDS, WHIPPETS, and BORZOIS.

Whelping Bitches vary in their behaviour at this exciting time. Maiden bitches are more apt to become worried, upset and restless but normally after the first whelp arrives they settle down to their job. Other bitches show no sign of being worried and settle down to whelp as though it was an every day occurrence. These placid bitches usually go their full time and whelp quickly and easily.

A bitch should whelp about nine weeks from the date of mating. Healthy litters can be born at any time from the fifty-eighth to the sixty-eighth day. Puppies born earlier will need constant and very special attention if they are to survive (see PREMATURE BIRTH). If a bitch is overdue by four or five days it is essential that professional help should be called. If the bitch shows any signs of being distressed or discharging heavily from the vagina at any time after her due date then again the veterinarian should be consulted.

Sometimes it is difficult to know just how close to whelping a bitch may be. A fairly safe guide is to take her temperature daily from about five or six days before her due date. A normal dog's temperature is 101·5°F. (38·6°C.) and about 48 hours before whelping it should drop between 2 and 3°F. This is a reliable indication that whelping is imminent. A bitch should be introduced to her whelping quarters at least one week before she is due to whelp. Both the kennel and her whelping box must be scrupulously clean and the temperature in the kennel should be around 70°F. (21°C.). The whelping box must be large enough for the bitch to turn round in comfortably. A good precaution is to fit a rail round the inside of the box two or three inches from the side and a few inches from the floor, depending on the breed. This prevents puppies being crushed against the sides by the dam. Most breeders find that newspaper makes the best lining for the whelping box. This should be used plentifully, putting many thick layers down, and changing it regularly.

In the long-coated breeds it is wise to remove the abdominal hair two or three days before the bitch whelps. Otherwise, the hair collects dirt and worm ova can very easily be picked up especially by the short-legged breeds. The bitch should be clean and free from all internal and external parasites.

Imminent labour is usually preceded by the bitch preparing her bed, by tearing up the paper and trying to make it into a nest. Just prior to whelping certain changes take place in the pelvic canal and the hind-quarters take on rather a sunken appearance. Actual labour begins with the bitch straining. This becomes more and more frequent and increases in intensity until the water bag appears. (See BIRTH OF PUPPIES.)

If all goes normally, the less the bitch is handled the better. Most bitches will manage by themselves, completely unaided. It is sufficient for the owner to give the bitch some warm milk in between the arrival of one puppy and the next. This she will appreciate, but she will also appreciate being left unfussed. If her bed becomes wet, the paper should be changed gently and quietly. Instinct usually tells her what to do.

A bitch that has whelped easily is generally a good mother and takes care of all her puppies from the moment they are born. When the bitch has finished whelping, her bed should be made comfortable and clean. She should be persuaded to go out and relieve herself and thereafter be allowed to settle down with her new family. Drinks of milk or thin gruel should be offered to her but for the first 24 hours after whelping, bitches generally require little food.

For the first two days after whelping the bitch should not have solid food but plenty of liquid with perhaps an egg added to it and a spoonful of glucose. She will be disinclined to leave her kennel but she must be taken out, forcibly if necessary, to empty her bladder and bowels.

Some discharge from the vagina may occur after whelping. This should cause no concern unless it continues for more than a week. Diarrhoea often follows whelping but presents no problem if it lasts only two or three days.

Do not upset the bitch by handling her new family while she is present; it should be done only when the bitch is away from the nest. See SHYNESS.

Complications in whelping can be caused by a variety of reasons. The presence of a dead puppy may be indicated by a thick, nasty, dark green discharge although this colour is often seen during normal whelping; an abnormally large puppy causes the bitch endless straining with no result. This is indicated when the presentation is normal and the membrane can be seen at the vagina. A wrongly presented pup (see BREECH BIRTH) requires manipulation. Uterine inertia is the complete absence of labour pains or very weak straining which would never allow a delivery to be made. In all such cases it is wise to seek the help of a veterinarian promptly. If all else fails, it may be possible to deliver the whelps by a CAESAREAN OPERATION.

Whippet To describe a Whippet to somebody who had never seen one, you could not do better than say it was a GREYHOUND in miniature. It is smaller, if anything more refined, more gentle, and more symmetrical. It is perhaps the most perfect living racing machine ever fashioned by man.

Fashioned by man it certainly was, but this is not to say that it has always been fashionable. Indeed one hundred years ago it was hardly known and rarely seen outside the mining areas of Britain. Vero Shaw, writing in *The Book of the Dog* (1881) says it was, 'essentially a local dog and little valued beyond the limits of the [English] Northern Counties'.

The position has changed dramatically since then and this elegant and graceful dog with its suggestion of muscular power and strength is seen as often in the Ritz as in the pits. Fashion in dogs is not always based on commonsense by the Whippet's steady rise to popularity in so many lands suggests that on this occasion dog lovers are using wisdom. It is a breed born in the nineteenth century and yet apparently designed for the twentieth.

Almost inevitably there have been attempts to trace its ancestry further back than it can comfortably be stretched. The names 'whappet' and 'wappet' are picked from early writings as evidence that the breed existed. In fact these expressions were used to describe any small and noisy dog of no known breeding.

Returning to Vero Shaw (who appears to have been misinformed when writing of this breed), we read: 'it may scarcely be said to lay special claim to be considered a sporting dog'. Wrong again! The Whippet was only bred because the English Terriers used a hundred years ago were not sporting enough to excel at the 'snap' dog trials of the working man. These trials were a primitive pastime. Rabbits were released in an enclosed pit and the dogs despatched them against a stopwatch. Greyhound blood was infused with that of the terriers to improve their speed.

Anti-cruelty laws brought this sport to an end; and frustrated owners turned to straight racing. This demanded improved quality, and a handicapping system. Little dogs started on the front mark, big ones from the rear. And so another race was started: that of breeders anxious to produce small dogs with the same running power as the big ones. The already-existing ITALIAN GREYHOUND almost certainly helped this programme. Today a time of twelve seconds over a 200-yard course is not unusual. Set against this the trained athlete's pride when he beats ten seconds over 100 yards.

The secret is in the Whippet's remarkable powers of acceleration: many a jack hare has paid the final penalty for underestimating it. This immense power is the more remarkable when one considers that a first impression of the breed is of great fragility. The Whippet's habit of shivering readily does little to change that image. This false picture is, however, shattered as soon as one sees them working in their natural surroundings. Then their supreme disregard for adverse climatic conditions and major spills over unnoticed obstacles rouses wonder at their lion hearts.

But the major role of the breed is that of pet dog and companion. And here they have the advantage of reasonable size, short, easily-groomed coats, clean habits and gentle disposition. They can be kept together in numbers without their showing any of the aggressive instincts which might be expected of dogs with their background.

Essentials of the breed: Head: long and lean, tapering to the muzzle. Eyes: bright, expressive and alert. Ears: rose-shaped, small and fine. Mouth: level. Neck should be long, muscular and elegantly arched. Shoulders: oblique, the blades carried up to the spine and closely

Whippet.
Top Ch. Shalfleet Swordsman.
Above Ch. Leatty's Court Marshall.

Above Whippets – 'Wendy' (standing) and 'Toga' (sitting).

set together at the top. Front: not too wide. Chest: very deep, with brisket well defined. Back: broad, somewhat long and showing arch over the loin, but not humped. Hindquarters: strong and broad across thighs, the dog standing over a lot of ground and showing great driving power. Feet: very neat, split up between toes, knuckles arched, pads thick and strong. Tail: long, tapering, when in action carried upward in a delicate curve. Coat: fine, short and close. Any colour or mixture of colours. Ideal height (Britain) dogs $18\frac{1}{2}$ inches, bitches $17\frac{1}{2}$ inches. (USA) dogs 19 to 22 inches, bitches 18 to 21 inches.

See colour plate p. 181.

Whippet Racing Whippet racing began amongst the miners in the coalfields of Northumberland, Durham, Yorkshire and Lancashire in England, where the sport thrived at the turn of the century. Whippets were 'the poor man's racehorse'. Originally there were two types of racing, racing to the rag (a sprint over a set distance, normally from 150 to 200 yards) and racing after live rabbits. Dogs taking part in this latter form were known as 'snap dogs'. In 1911, a Parliamentary act stopped the racing to rabbits as it was cruel. There are tales of men travelling by train to these meetings with a crate of rabbits on the carriage rack and their dogs at their feet. This left racing to the rag, the dogs being trained to tear and hang on to the rag from as early as eight to ten weeks old. A handler or 'slipper' would hold the dog whilst the owner would back away, waving the rag and shouting encouragement. The Whippets soon learned what to do.

In the early part of the century good slippers were much in demand. The skill of holding a dog in mid-air by the collar and the root of the tail, of literally throwing the dog into the race as soon as the shot was fired, and of putting the dog straight into its stride as soon as it hit the ground, was the mark of a good handler: landing clumsily or in mid-stride could mean a lost race.

Training was necessary to ensure that the dog ran a straight race. The dog should not be a fighter or a chaser, one who ran after the dogs, or played around. By careful training and handling, the dog could be transformed into a near-perfect racing machine. The normal distance was 200 yards and a top dog could do this in less than twelve seconds – 16 yards 2 feet per second! The dogs were handicapped on size or weight, although in some areas they were handicapped on form, which brought obvious temptations.

The miners lavished care on their dogs, one of their few relaxations from a hard and often grim way of life. That their dogs loved racing there can be no doubt; the innate instinct to race is part of the Whippet's character. The sport flourished until the more commercial sport of GREYHOUND RACING appeared in the 1920s when lavish tracks were opened, and Whippet racing faded.

In the early Fifties it started again in the mining districts of Britain and gradually spread over most parts of the country, until now there are a great many racing clubs, the biggest still being found in the North and Midlands. It is common now in the north-east of England to see as many as 100 to 150 dogs at meetings, mainly held on Sunday mornings. See picture p. 48.

There are now no slippers. Starting boxes, similar to those used in Greyhound racing are in vogue and most clubs have their own sets; many owners, too, either buy or build their own to train their dogs. Betting too has gone, and though there will always be 'side bets', the malpractices associated with uncontrolled betting on dogs have disappeared.

Whippet racing attracts all social classes for it is no longer a poor man's sport, and Whippets are one of the few breeds which can distinguish themselves on both the bench and the track. They have not suffered the division in type which befell the exhibition and the racing Greyhounds.

The popularity of Whippet racing has spread to European countries, principally the Netherlands and Sweden. Here many of the tracks in major towns have facilities which can be likened to a miniature Greyhound stadium. The stock is usually descended from British dogs. Similarly in the U.S.A., great emphasis is set on the racing capabilities of the breed and the American Whippet Club's magazine contains details of the racing events held from the East to the West coast. Racing in America started when the mill workers from Lancashire emigrated to work in New England in the early nineteenth century. It followed the same pattern as in England, including a revival in the early 1950s.

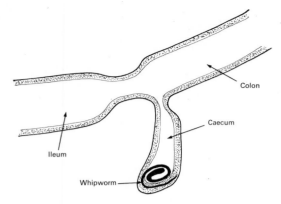

Left Whipworms usually inhabit the blind gut or caecum and cause disease when the dog is weak.

Whip Tail A tail carried stiffly at back level.

Whipworm Infection by whipworm is called canine Trichuriasis. It is caused by a white or grey, whip-shaped worm called *Trichuris vulpis*. It lives in the caecum, or blind gut, and in heavy infestations, is also found in the intestine. The worms appear to do little harm until the dog is put under stress by disease or hard work. Then the worms cause alternate constipation and diarrhoea, loss of weight, and diarrhoea with bloody stools.

The eggs are thick-shelled with a plug at each end. They pass with the faeces, become infective in two or three weeks, and are swallowed in contaminated water, food, or from contaminated toys. The worms mature in about three months. Since the eggs are quite fragile, they die quickly in kennels kept clean and dry, and in runs hygienically maintained.

Treatment for whipworm was once extremely difficult, and often involved surgical removal of the caecum. But a new drug, phthalofyne, has shown remarkable results. It is low in toxicity and can be given orally or intravenously by a veterinarian.

Wire-Hair Hard, wiry texture to the coat.

Wire-Haired Fox Terrier see Fox Terrier, Wire-haired.

Withers A dog's withers, although similarly situated, are not so prominent as in the horse. They represent

Below left Withers, indicated by the arrow.

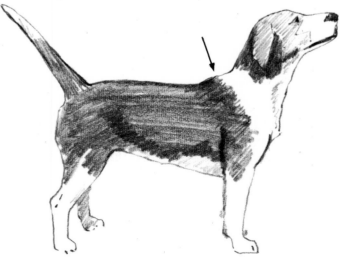

the upper portion of the third to the sixth dorsal spines, their highest level being over the fourth and fifth. The bodies of these vertebrae lie between the summits of the two scapulae which in the dog are devoid of cartilages as seen in the horse.

The upper edges of the scapulae, being bony, may be felt easily with the finger tips. The space between them varies in different breeds and within the same breed. In the coursing GREYHOUND, one can insert at least two fingers between the scapular edges, with the fingertips in contact with the intervening dorsal spines.

If when doing this the dog's head is depressed until the muzzle touches the floor, the fingers will be pinched, but in the exhibition dog the upper edges of the scapulae will meet before the head is halfway down. Such a dog can catch a hare but may be unable to pick it up and kill it, which shows that the standard of the exhibition Greyhound is designed only for beauty.

Working Trials (Hound) The BLOODHOUND is the only hound breed in Britain to which the term 'working trial' is truly applicable. Other hound breeds take part in organized events but they are not called 'trials', nor do they involve the same kind of activity.

Since Bloodhounds hunt the 'clean boot' (a man), their trials have nothing to do with hunting game, reaching the finishing post or killing the quarry. The aim is purely for each hound to follow the scent of man and find him. Having done so it is expected to identify its quarry – not attack it.

Trials are organized by the two clubs catering for the breed, the Association of Bloodhound Breeders and the Bloodhound Club, and are held under the rules laid down by the Kennel Club for such activities. Before being eligible for entry into any trial, a hound must have been awarded a working certificate. This will certify

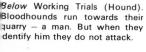

Below Working Trials (Hound). Bloodhounds run towards their quarry – a man. But when they identify him they do not attack.

that it is capable of following a line and that it is 'free from riot' or, in layman's terms, that it is able to use its nose to scent its quarry and that it will not chase sheep, fowl, cattle or motor cars. Having acquired the working certificate it may then be entered in the lowest stake for which it is eligible. Eligibility for various stakes (or classes) is dependent upon age and proven ability.

A hound may be hunted either free or on a tracking line and one person will go with it, usually the owner, to act as huntsman. He will be followed by mounted judges equipped with maps of the area showing the lines laid in order that they can decide whether the hound is working the complete line and not cutting corners or finding its quarry by chance.

Identification of the quarry is particularly important in Bloodhound working trials, and good 'identification' wins a comparatively large number of points. The runner or quarry should not be known to the animal. The hound is expected to use its nose right up to the point upon which the runner is standing. It is then expected to place both forefeet on his shoulders.

Hounds hunt both mute and 'giving tongue' and in the marking system at trials there is no preference for one or the other. However, a Bloodhound giving tongue on a line is a joy to hear. Marks are awarded for the style in which the hound hunts, the aforementioned identification and the speed at which it completes its line.

The Kennel Club (England) awards working trial certificates which are competed for, and one of the aims of hound trials is to provide the medium in which hounds can win sufficient honours to become working trial champions. Money prizes are only nominal. Bloodhound tracking trials are also held in America.

Wrench GREYHOUND COURSING term meaning to bend the hare from its line at less than a right angle.

X Y Z

Xoloitzcuintli see Hairless Dogs.

Yorkshire Terrier The Hon. Mrs. Neville Lytton wrote in 1911 'As for the unfortunate show Yorkshire Terrier with his unnatural existence as a "clothes peg", the less said the better'. Clearly she was then of the opinion that little would be said about this dog in the future. But she was wrong. This diminutive breed has forced its attentions for over one hundred years on people interested in dogs.

A dog show was held in Leeds in 1861. One of the classes was for 'Scotch Terriers', a loose description likely to produce any one of a dozen different varieties. But this proved to be a show with a difference. Instead of the usual collection of CAIRNS, SKYES, DANDIE DINMONTS, only one animal was on parade. That was a local product, a type of what we now call the Yorkshire Terrier. One uses the word 'type' advisedly, because those early dogs were very large and clumsy by modern standards.

One would like to be able to report exactly how the early Yorkshire Terriers were produced, and since their history covers little more than a century it might have been expected that this could be done. In fact little has been discovered about their ancestry from the Yorkshire working men who produced them. As these little dogs were in demand by the rich and influential families of the district, working fanciers with the chance of establishing a very lucrative sideline did not feel obliged to divulge their secrets to possible competitors.

But guesswork is not too hard. Quite clearly English Black and Tan Terriers must have been used in fairly large numbers. These would establish colour. Equally certain, a type of MALTESE would have been used to produce both quantity and texture of coat. And since a dog of basically terrier stock was desired, the use of Skyes as a means of fixing temperament was almost inevitable.

While the principles of breeding selectively from small stock were not then formally appreciated, dog fanciers then had an instinctive ability to do what is right without the help of textbooks. Repeated use of the smallest members of a litter clearly had its effect, but it did not introduce either lack of stamina or degeneracy.

The working-class background of this breed was certainly in the interest of the dogs. It was, and to a certain extent still is, customary to breed and rear them in the kitchens of modest houses, which gives the young dogs a good start in life. Here they get warmth and even more important, adaptation into the busy world where despite their small size, they will be expected to look after themselves.

Perhaps this accounts for the fact that although they are certainly very small and surprisingly glamorous, they remain spirited and possessed of a good deal of self-assurance.

Above Yorkshire Terrier. Chiano of Cartland.

Despite this, it would have been a brave man who in those early days would have forecast their present popularity. There is a theory that no dog is likely to succeed completely unless it is equally well regarded by both men and women. It has to be admitted that few men choose to own a Yorkshire Terrier and so the popularity of the Yorky shows the fallibility of the rule.

The breed was admitted to the Kennel Club registers in England in 1886. Even six years before that it had crossed the Atlantic and become established in the United States. Today the position in Britain is that the Yorkshire Terrier has not only become the most popular toy dog but is third in the list of popularity of all breeds, being beaten only by the GERMAN SHEPHERD DOG (Alsatian) and the LABRADOR RETRIEVER. In America it is not yet quite so successful, but its seventeenth place is an honourable position in a list consisting

Above Yorkshire Terrier. Ch. Luna Star of Yadnum.

of the hundred and sixteen breeds recognized in the United States.

The Yorky's coat is both its glory and its cross. In show condition, few dogs are more glamorous. But left to run free and live the unfettered life of a domestic pet, this coat breaks, shortens and loses the immaculate condition expected in the show ring.

Essentials of the breed: Head: rather small and flat, not too round in the skull or long in the muzzle. The fall on the head to be of rich golden tan. Eyes: medium, dark and sparkling, not prominent. Ears: small, V-shaped, erect or semi-erect, covered with short, rich tan hair. Mouth: even, teeth as sound as possible. Forequarters: legs straight, covered with tan hair. Body: very compact and level on top. Hindquarters: legs quite straight, well covered with tan hair. Feet: round, with black toe-nails.

Tail: medium length, carried a little higher than the level of the back. Coat: on the body, moderately long, straight, glossy and of a fine, silky texture.

Colour: a dark steel-blue, extending from the occiput to the root of the tail which is darker blue than the body. On the chest and legs a rich, bright tan. All tan hair should be darker at the roots than in the middle, shading lighter at the tips. Weight: up to 7 lb.
See colour plate p. 378.

Zygoma Zygoma is the arch formed by the union of the zygomatic process of the temporal bone and the malar muscle. To borrow a human term, one might say that the zygoma is the cheek bone. The zygoma muscles govern the masseter, used in mastication, and also much of the facial expressions, and are responsible for the grinning and teeth-baring actions of dogs.

Acknowledgments

The editors and publishers would like to acknowledge the help which has been received from many quarters in the preparation of this encyclopedia. Amongst those who have generously given advice and information are the following:

Miss Eileen Adams, Mrs Dana Alvi, Mr Forrest Andrews, Mrs Lisa Attwood, Mrs Betty Ballard, Mrs Margaret Beed, Mr and Mrs L. Benis, Mrs J. M. Bentley, Mrs M. Bertram, Mr and Mrs F. Brayton, Mrs Ann Brown, Mr C. Brown, Major C. Fordyce Burke, Mrs Barbara Burrows, Mr Carmen Cananzi, Mrs Donald Carter, Mrs Helen Case, Mr R. Catter (Librarian, Royal Veterinary College, London), Mrs Beverly Cohen, Mrs Felice Collesano, Mr L. K. Corbett, Mrs Betty Dangerfield, Miss M. Davidson, Mrs Ruth Gardiner, Miss Leslie Hay, Mrs Hugh Handwerk, Mr Robert Hetherington Jr., Dr K. Eileen Hite, Mrs Alden Keene, Members of the Staff of the Kennel Club (London), Michael Lyster (The Zoological Society of London), Miss Janet Mack, Mr Stewart Moat (Greyhound Racing Association, London), Mr Donald Mull, Mrs Elaine North (Australian News and Information Bureau), Mrs Ida Poore, Mrs Charles Rowland, Mrs Frances Sefton, Mr Richard Souza, Mr Harold Spira, Mrs Charman Steele, Mrs Irma Thomas, Mr John Thompson, Mrs Antoinette Vojvoda, Mr Charles Zimmer.

Sources of colour illustrations:

Alphabet and Image, 182b, 374c; Australian News and Information Bureau, 293b; Frank S. Brayton, 302a; Mrs B. R. Cohen, 297b; Anne Cumbers, 82c, 84a, 86, 87b, 89a, 89b, 91b, 179a, 186b, 191c, 295a, 301b, 372b, 373a, 373c, 374a, 374b, 377b, 380a; Dogs Magazine, 90; Earl Graham, 183a, 188b; Carl and Marjorie H. Lewis, 192a; Joan Ludwig, 93, 185a, 191a, 191b, 296a, 300a, 373b, 381b; Raybrook Kennels, 378a; Maxwell Riddle, 87a, 192d; J. Ritter, 85a, 85b, 92a, 92b, 92c, 94a, 94b, 95b, 183b, 185b, 185c, 186a, 189a, 192b, 192c, 298b, 302b, 376a, 379b; Anne Roslin-Williams, 377c, 379a; G. H. Santee, 296b; Sally Anne Thompson, 81, 82a, 82b, 83, 84b, 88, 91a, 95a, 96, 177, 178, 179b, 180, 181a, 181b, 182a, 184, 187a, 187b, 188a, 189b, 189c, 190, 191d, 192e, 289, 290a, 290b, 290c, 291, 292a, 292b, 293a, 294, 295b, 298a, 299, 300b, 301a, 303, 304a, 304b, 369, 370a, 370b, 371, 372a, 374d, 375a, 375b, 376b, 377a, 378b, 378c, 380b, 381a, 381c, 382a, 382b, 383, 384a, 384b, 384c; J. R. Trelease, 186c; Morry Twomey, 297a;

Sources of black and white illustrations, line drawings and diagrams:

Abingerwood Kennels, 61b; Robin Adler, 74d; Albert E. Allen, 364b; Alphabet and Image, 425b; Dr and Mrs Z. M. Alvi, 273b; American Kennel Club, 105; G. John Anderson, 315b; Mr and Mrs J. P. Antonelli, 288; Archives Photographiques, 155; Arctic Kennels, 427b; Ashmolean Museum, University of Oxford, 215, 241; Edward Ashpole, 144; Mrs K. Auchterlonie, 458; Austenwood Photos, 389c; Australian News and Information Bureau, 263a, 263b, 264; Miss F. Bagshawe,